By Harold Weisberg

Whitewash: The Report on the Warren Report
Whitewash II: The FBI-Secret Service Cover-Up
Photographic Whitewash: Suppressed Kennedy Assassination Pictures
Oswald in New Orleans: Case for Conspiracy with the CIA
Post-Mortem: Suppressed Kennedy Autopsy
Post-Mortem III: Secrets of the Kennedy Autopsy
Frame-Up

Second Printing, April 1971

Library of Congress number 70-149057
First published in the United States
of America in 1971
Design: Victoria Dudley
Outerbridge & Dienstfrey
200 West 72 Street, New York 10023

Contents

Introduction

Since November 22, 1963, I have devoted myself, with an intensity that has made at least two working days of every one on the calendar, to a close examination and investigation of the political assassinations and what is called the investigation of them. I have published the results of my studies myself—not for want of trying to interest regular commercial publishers, but because what I had to say was not what, for reasons that varied from publisher to publisher, they wanted to hear or perhaps wanted to have heard.

This book on the case of James Earl Ray and the assassination of Dr. Martin Luther King, Jr., was begun toward the end of June 1968, the month Robert Kennedy was assassinated. The last few days of that month and the first of July, I continued investigation in New Orleans and adjacent communities. On returning home, I completed the draft of the then-planned book. It contained what I could learn prior to the anticipated trial.

But there was no trial. There was, instead, a "deal" by which a full and public trial was avoided. On March 10, 1969, there was a "minitrial," a dubious proceeding not in any sense a trial, convoked to rubber-stamp that deal. There, instead of evidence, the promise of evidence was substituted, providing only enough for superficial and technical satisfaction of the law as interpreted by those party to that deal.

I then wrote a longer, second book, reporting and assessing this minitrial and the evidence there promised and there suppressed, including involvements and performances of the parties to the deal and many of the questions deliberately avoided.

The book that now appears is based upon the two earlier ones, updated to September 1970. Authors working in current non-fiction deal with developing information. The problem is not new. Nor, when it is in mind during the writing, does it ease the pains of birthing such a book.

The publishers did not tell me what to say or what not to say. They have reduced the long two volumes to a more acceptable size, one that can be of greater use to a larger number of readers, one that can be priced in the popular range. (For scholars and institutions, special arrangements can be made with the author for access to the longer original work.)

In the analysis that follows I shall refer often to the writings of two other men. One is Clay Blair, Jr.'s *The Strange Case of James Earl Ray,* which appeared in March 1969, several days after Ray's minitrial in Memphis. In his forward, Blair records that he was aided by the FBI, in itself enough to cast doubt on the book, for the FBI will not even give press releases to those they do not know to support them. In many ways, then, Blair's book is the "official" story. As to its merits, at this point perhaps it is enough to quote the review by Christopher Lehmann-Haupt in the *New York Times* of March 17. The book, he wrote, "bears all the earmarks of an 'instant book'" to be "read by an audience painfully confused. . . .Its literary merits are zero." The review ends: "Clay Blair's altogether inconclusive summary of the known record adds practically nothing."

But there is one thing of value in the book, and that Blair does not begin to understand. Tossed in at the end and in no meaningful way included in the content of the book is a transcript of the minitrial. Because in the official typescript it costs about $44.00, it is a considerable saving to be able to buy it for 95 cents. Also, it thus becomes available, now and in the future, to those who might not be able to spend $44.00 for it or who might not know it can be bought from Clerk of the Criminal Court in Memphis, J. A. Blackwell, at 90 cents a page. (The book does *not* contain the *official* transcript of the official defense reporting of the proceeding by Martest Otwell, the court reporter. In places it is not consistent with the official stenographic record, but it is faithful to the sense.)

The other writings are those of William Bradford Huie, and we shall have the opportunity to examine in detail both the writings and Huie's relations with Ray.

Huie bought Ray.

This is his standard operating procedure. Huie is a tough and tough-minded guy who is and boasts that he is without illusion. He is also a commercial success and commercial-minded, a master of simplified writing in simple, direct sentences comprehensible to those not really comfortable when reading. None of this need be interpreted as adverse criticism. It is not so intended. He *is* skilled in his craft, this bald, 58-year-old, hard-looking Alabamian, who poses for pictures with a slight smile that sneers a jaundiced view of life and fellow man. He is successful in his calling, and he has earned success. He was established and respected as a writer before turning to the awful racial crimes, the author of six works he calls "documentaries" and of five novels. Four of the eleven works were made into movies. Success for him means $150,000 a year and living under floodlights, with courage, still in his native (eighth-generation) Alabama, at Hartselle.

In a story by Mel Ziegler in the *Miami Herald's* Sunday magazine *Tropic* of November 17, 1968 (because Huie, like almost every other major figure in the case refused to respond when I wrote him, I must depend on secondary sources), the didactic Huie—asked about the South, he responds, thoughtfully, "We first have to define the South"— says, quite accurately, "There is a great advantage I have over other people in this business. When I go to Mississippi, I carry at least $5,000 in cash. No other reporter is in that position. . .I don't have any competition."

Huie's first foray into buy-and-sell journalism appeared in the January 24, 1956 issue of *Look*. James Earl Ray, Huie says, read it in Leavenworth Prison, where he was serving three years for forging postal money orders. He was impressed. After release, he read others of Huie's works.

Ray was picked up at London's Heathrow Airport June 8, 1968. He wrote Birmingham lawyer Arthur Hanes, whom Huie knew (they are on opposite sides of the same business). Huie told Hanes he would buy the literary rights to Ray. Huie's $30,000 check to Ray pictured on the *Tropic* cover is dated July 18. (It is, as we shall see, a cheap fake.) It is not inappropriate that the *Miami Herald's* artist drew a full-page picture of Ray with the dollar-mark for a mouth.

Or that Huie *never gave Ray a cent,* gave nothing to anyone on July 18, and issued no single check for $30,000.

"The truth is more important than the trial," Huie says.

We shall see how spectacularly he proved this and provided his "truth," as we shall see how easy the "trial" made it for "the truth" to be "more important."

He was not permitted to interview Ray in the Shelby County jail in Memphis, so Huie sent him a diary in which Ray detailed his account of his movements beginning with his April 23, 1967 prison-break from the Missouri State Penitentiary, the day after his brother John visited him. Ray also scribbled and printed other notes, a total of 20,000 words, on ruled yellow pads.

Much of what follows about Huie's analyses of the Ray case is based on three articles that Huie wrote for *Look* magazine.

Prior to the appearance of the first of Huie's *Look* articles in the November 12, 1968 issue he told the *Miami Herald* reporter "I know Ray will try to deceive me. . .it is natural for him to be deceitful. We assume that there are going to be a certain amount of lies. Then you go and you find out that you got the truth here and truth here. . .constant effort of trial and error, a constant effort to get the man to tell you the truth."

After Huie, knowing Ray to be a liar, established his "truth" and satisfied *Look,* it was white-titled on an all-black cover, "THE STORY OF JAMES EARL RAY AND THE CONSPIRACY TO KILL MARTIN LUTHER KING." *Look* described this as "William Bradford Huie's exclusive report on the accused assassin's escape from prison and his journey on the lam that led to a fateful trip south."

Inside there was a headline, "The Story of James Earl Ray and the Plot to Assassinate Martin Luther King."

Fourteen days later, still stark white on black, entitled "I GOT INVOLVED GRADUALLY AND DIDN'T KNOW ANYBODY WAS TO BE MURDERED," the description was "The Story of James Earl Ray and the Plot to Kill Martin Luther King—Part II."

The emphasis is on conspiracy, a plot to kill King, of which Ray was part.

At the end of the second piece, outlined in black and in large type, *Look* promised, "In a future issue, William Bradford Huie plans to tell in detail the personal story that may not be developed at the trial—the activities of James Earl Ray between March 23 [1968] and the day he was arrested in London [June 8, 1968]."

There is no doubting *Look's* good faith here. This is what Huie bought from Ray and *Look* bought from Huie. Nor is there doubt that much of what Ray could and did say could not be admitted into evidence in court. (However, the minitrial did "detail" some of "the personal story . . .the activities. . .between March 23 and the day" Ray was arrested.) In seeming deprecation of the FBI, for which, again, he cannot be faulted, Huie, who had spent not less than $40,000 buying his own information on the Schwerner-Goodman-Chaney Philadelphia, Mississippi, murders, had said of the FBI's purchased testimony, ". . .hell, they spent $100,000 of the taxpayers' money on this stuff. There is a difference between information and evidence, and all information is not admissible evidence."

Precisely correct. Huie was to prove this very personally. We shall understand what he bought.

Unless he published prior to the trial, however, all Huie could buy from Ray was the "inadmissible evidence," or what could not and would not be used in court. Ziegler said Huie "reserves for himself the right to make the distinction between information and evidence. 'Ray understands this. . .I will publish the truth only and inform constituted authorities if it is necessary.'"

Great guy, Huie. All heart, big, generous soul, and a little ego and condescension. Still, his intent is what we should be able to assume is the purpose of all who write non-fiction:

"I will publish the truth only."

In his unique way, Huie kept this promise: He published *both* sides, *each* with the promise *it* is the truth!

In *Look* of April 15, 1969, in his third piece on Ray, he retracted the earlier writing. He said there was no real conspiracy, that Ray was a loner, the murderer—the *only* murderer.

Look tried to cushion it. The appropriately cerise cover (the largest thing on it is a cerise Raquel Welch, *all* of her visible being naked and also cerise) carries the headline, much more modest in size than those of the first articles and shared with two others, "CONSPIRACY OR NOT? WHY RAY KILLED KING." Huie shares billing with two others, Ray's former lawyers, Arthur Hanes, Sr., and Percy Foreman. What *Look* says is that Ray was the killer and that there was no conspiracy.

In writing first that there *was* a conspiracy and Ray was *not* the killer and then that there was *no* conspiracy and Ray *was* the killer, Huie certainly kept his promise, "I will publish the truth." He slipped a wee bit, on the "only" part.

Huie also gave more than he promised. The headline on his part of the trilogy of the Ray "defenders" (all of whom proclaimed his guilt, as novel a defense as is Huie's bought-and-paid for variant of journalism), reads, "WHY JAMES EARL RAY MURDERED DR. KING."

This is not what Huie bought from Ray, not what Ray told him. This Huie got for free. It is his opinion: "I now believe he killed Dr. King to achieve . . . status."

Huie's book finally appeared, much after its originally scheduled publication date, early in the Summer of 1970, to the accompaniment of poor reviews and like sales. James Barkham's review in the *San Francisco Chronicle* of May 27 is titled "The Non-Story of James Earl Ray." It concludes, "What Huie's book boils down to is a reporter's account of a big story he went after but failed to get." A Southern newspaper editor, Edwin M. Yoder, Jr., writing in *Book World* of May 17, found Huie's account of Ray's flight after the assassination "entirely persuasive." But, Yoder complained, Huie "constantly intrudes on the narrative to boast his deductive powers or to deprecate (usually after the fact) his invasion of the privacy of those who haplessly crossed Ray's path." Of Huie's dollar journalism, the editor Yoder said, "it makes me uncomfortable to find that a man accused of heinous crime must sell his story to pay his lawyers."

Here Yoder errs. It was not necessary for Ray to sell his story to have legal representation. Only, he fell into mercenary hands. Huie and Hanes, we will see, cooked up this deal and sold Ray on the need for it.

Huie's book is an enlargement of his magazine articles. It contains nothing new about the crime and amounts to little more than self-justification and to the self-glorification of a fallen ego, one pretending it is still erect. In what follows, there has been no need to change the analysis and argument based on Huie's *Look* articles.

If, as I hope, this book is attractive to the reader as a non-fiction detective story, still he must remember that it is *not* fiction. Therefore, I eschew the hackneyed but successful devices of fiction and make explicit at the beginning what this long work has led me to believe.

Our law requires that, for conviction on a criminal offense, the jury must be satisfied beyond reasonable doubt. If there is reasonable doubt, then the jury must find the accused not guilty. There is a difference between "not guilty" and "innocent." A man may, in reality, be guilty of the crime with which he is charged and the prosecutor may fail to establish guilt beyond this requisite reasonable doubt. Such a man, while not innocent, is also not guilty.

With James Earl Ray the issue is more complex. As always the question in court, had there been a bona fide trial, would not have been of innocence but of the establishment of guilt beyond reasonable doubt. In addition, Ray never said he did the killing and protested the attempt to extend the admission he did make in the substitute for a trial and in the reporting thereof.

I believe Ray did not do the shooting. More, I am convinced that the so-called "evidence" said to prove his guilt, on this, the first analysis it has ever had, proves exactly the opposite—more than that he did not do the shooting, but that he could not have done it.

xii

The official evidence may be wrong. Some of it cannot be, but whether right or wrong, it is the official evidence that controls in court.

Beyond reasonable doubt, this evidence establishes, as I believe the reader will come to agree, that someone other than James Earl Ray was the shooter.

Does this mean he is entirely innocent?

No. The official evidence alone shows there had to have been a conspiracy. So does the ignored, the "unofficial" evidence.

Was Ray part of this conspiracy? I believe he was, as decoy.

If this is true, as I am convinced it is and as I believe the reader will be too, the terrible crime is unsolved and assassins roam the land, their liberty an official blessing.

The evidence in and gathered for this book has become the basis for the new legal actions that may yet move the assassination of Martin Luther King, Jr., into court, where there can be a judicial determination of fact. It may yet be determined whether or not there was a conspiracy and who the conspirators are; whether or not Ray was a conscious part of it and, if he was, his role.

This book is my own work. Without hesitation, I accept full responsibility for it. Aside from the haste with which it had to be written, I also make no apologies for it.

But no book is the exclusive work of any one author. In many ways, sometimes in ways of which he is unaware, every author is indebted to others, for small and large favors. Many have helped me. They range from the young woman someone must have had in mind in coining the phrase "sweet young thing" to world-famous journalists. They include friends who read and clipped newspapers and the dedicated lawyer who, from sincerest principle, handled and handled very well the precedent-establishing case under which I ultimately won access to some of the suppressed evidence—after the book was written. They cannot all be named, so I name none. They all have, as I believe they understand, my deepest gratitude.

Harold Weisberg
Route 8
Frederick, Maryland
September 1970

xiii

"Though the heavens fall,

let justice be done."

1. Will the Real James Earl Ray/Ramon George Sneyd Please Stand Up?

Of these two high-priced writers who commercialized the King assassination, one without disguise, the other with lofty pretensions, Clay Blair, Jr., abandons his *bête noir* at the moment of capture, June 8 at Heathrow Airport, and then jumps to Ray's minitrial in Memphis nine months later.

I mean abandons him the very *moment* of capture. He doesn't even take the reader to jail with the accused. He has written the "complete story" in the "complete book" without a word on the extradition proceedings in London's Bow Street Court or the legal manipulations following it. Blair had ample time to include the proceedings in England —to digest and understand them—*and* to compare them with the Memphis farce. His reason for not doing it can be conjectured. It is consistent with commercialism and with contempt for his task and his craft, and for the reader. Omitting a discussion of the extradition proceedings also facilitated the basic dishonesty of the work, as will become clear immediately and on subsequent occasions.

The minitrial, for its part, is neatly tucked in, uncomprehendingly but authoritatively, both at the end, to lend an air of completeness and reliability, and hastily, inadequately, and with scholarly misrepresentation, is also slipped in, out of place, in the form of a scanty condensation, at the beginning, to con the reader into crediting the work.

Blair treats Ray in London in a brief eight pages. He is able to achieve even this minichapter semi-nakedness only by prejudicial padding. He uses the alleged opinions of those who saw Ray—and here it is not unwise to add "or the alleged Ray"—and disliked him, with that fine and precise instant dislike that is so often facilitated by hindsight.

Blair has Ray in London continuously from June 4 on. On page 201, in his brief eight pages on this, he (like the FBI in a "leak" to Drew Pearson) has Ray engaging in petty crime in England. Blair is unequivocal: "On the same fateful June 4 [that is, of "the assassination of Robert Kennedy"—which was June 5], Ray, who now was apparently very low on cash, entered the Trustee Savings Bank in the Fulham District" and robbed it of "60 pounds, or about $144 U.S. currency."

On the same page: "On the afternoon of Wednesday June 5 . . . Ray abruptly departed the New Earl's Court Hotel" (where he had been staying). On the same day (and the next page), "Ray appeared at the YWCA Hostel on Warwick Way in Pimlico. It had rooms for men but they were all filled." Same paragraph: "Ray appeared at the Pax [a hotel three doors down the street] during a violent thunderstorm." He "looked very tired." No doubt from this exhausting physical effort, walking three doors down the street.

Foregoing other minor delights, which do not remove Ray from London or the Pax, we learn (page 204), "That Saturday morning— June 8—Ray checked out of the Pax Hotel early." As we shall see, it certainly had to be *very* early for the rest of his hegira to have been possible.

On the next—and next to the last—page, Blair has Ray arrested at Heathrow Airport by the very polite Detective Sergeant Philip F. Burch, with the gentleness so typically British, "Would you please step into our office, Mr. Sneyd [Ray's alias]?"

All the detail is there. "At 11:30 on the morning of Saturday, June 8, Birch was at his post, standing by the immigration counter at building #2 . . . checking passports." Ray was "wearing a light-colored raincoat, a burgundy sports jacket, gray trousers and horn-rimmed glasses" as he "approached the desk," when "he took out his wallet and displayed his two Canadian passports." He had about $168 and a snubnosed .38-caliber "Liberty Chief" revolver loaded with five bullets when searched.

The detail is there, but the necessary explanation is not. What was Ray doing at the airport immigration desk—which is for those *entering* the country only—at 11:30 A.M. (which we shall see may even be the wrong time) when he had left his London room so "early" apparently no one saw him?

Don't ask Blair. He doesn't say. In fact, he in no way indicates anything unusual about a man on the lam going to an airport immigration desk and up to a policeman, for no apparent reason. He could not and still have written his book.

All of this information Blair could have had from a selective reading of the newspapers. But he could not have read them, as without doubt

2

he did, and not known the rest of the story all of whose perplexities are missing from the book.

The arrest was put at 11:15 A.M. London-time by the newspapers and was in plenty of time for the evening papers in the United States. The Associated Press story begins with the terse reporting of Ray's arrest, then says, "The announcement was issued under the names of Attorney General Ramsey Clark and FBI Director J. Edgar Hoover, but neither was present when it was given to newsmen at the Justice Department. Other FBI officials declined to elaborate on it or answer any questions. The announcement said Ray, using the name Ramon George Sneyd, was passing through England, on two Canadian passports, en route to Brussels"—and so presumably had not been in England from June 4 on.

Later in the story this is repeated, "Ray was reported to have been arrested at Heathrow Airport as he was going through immigration procedures on arrival from Lisbon, Portugal."

Blair's use of the 11:30 hour may be a misinterpretation of a too hastily read story appearing the next day in a paper to his liking, the *Washington Post* [1]. There the lead says, "The Justice Department announced the arrest at 11:30 A.M., Washington time [that is, the announcement was made at 11:30]. Ray, who was carrying a fully loaded pistol when apprehended, was taken into custody at 6:15 A.M. (EDT), 11:15 A.M. London time." (A point that may confuse readers is that Ray had been held by the police for five hours before being placed under arrest. He had been *picked up* at 6:15 London time, which should not be confused with the 6:15 Washington time equivalent to the London time of his *arrest*, 11:15.) Again, the same information on Ray's itinerary: "Ray . . . was passing through immigration control at the airport, on his way to take a flight to Brussels . . . Scotland Yard said that Ray arrived back in London on a flight from Lisbon yesterday and was going to travel on to Brussels."

The Associated Press story for June 9 morning papers, under a Washington date line, repeats this still another time in the first paragraph, ". . . arrested in London Saturday as he was about to fly to Belgium, the FBI announced." Several paragraphs later, "FBI Director J. Edgar Hoover said Ray . . . was seized before he could reboard a plane bound from Lisbon, Portugal, to Brussels." Still later, this added detail, "He had checked his luggage through to Brussels when he boarded the plane in Lisbon but got off when the aircraft made a refueling stop in London."

We never hear of that checked-through luggage again.

All the early stories say, "Hoover praised the cooperation of the Canadian police and Scotland Yard." In the United States, Hoover's turf, this was taken to mean the FBI did the job, with slight help from its Canadian and British counterparts. Considering that, between them, they did *all* of it, the Mounties identifying and fingering Ray as Sneyd and Scotland Yard, unassisted, except by Ray, arresting him, could Hoover have done *less* than "praise their *cooperation*"?

By the next day's papers, questions were being asked. Assistant Attorney General Fred Vinson, Jr., had arrived in London to take charge of getting Ray back. As soon as AP reported this, it got to one of the already perplexing questions:

> Airport sources said that Ray, seized Saturday while trying to board a flight for Brussels, could have gone from the Lisbon plane that brought him to London directly to the transit lounge, and thus avoided immigration officers. His capture indicated he left the transit lounge—either to meet someone or possibly to kill time—and consequently got caught.

The perplexities mount. A Reuters dispatch from Lisbon, dated June 9, beginning, "James Earl Ray spent nine days at a third class hotel here last month," also quotes Portuguese police as saying that the nine days had been May 8–17. (The police were told to look for Ray under the name "Sneyd" by the FBI "after May 17"; in short, too late. Is it not a good thing the fabled FBI has "cooperators"?) Further, the Portuguese police "had no information Ray was here Saturday, and airlines officials said the flight to Brussels carried no mention of the name Sneyd on its passenger list." We shall see even this is understated.

For morning papers of Monday, June 10, AP had what might then have been thought clarification. Its correspondent, Michael R. Codel, wrote from London,

> Ray was seized by immigration officials at Heathrow Airport after he stopped over at 6:10 A.M. Saturday on a British European Airways jet from Lisbon. He was headed for Brussels . . . Police made their formal arrest at 11:15 A.M. five hours after Ray's arrival. But they kept a close security check on him and repeatedly denied they were holding him even after the announcement of his arrest came from Washington.

4

Then this paragraph:

The Daily Express said Monday Ray had been living in London since mid-May, contrary to the official reports that he arrived in London from Lisbon Saturday.

The *Express* also said, "Scotland Yard detectives believe Ray flew here from Lisbon between May 16 and May 20." But,

Scotland Yard refused to confirm or deny the Express report . . . declined to go beyond a reconfirmation that Ray was arrested here Saturday as he was about to board a plane for Brussels.

And the *Daily Telegraph* rather authoritatively placed Ray in London from May 17 until at least June 6. They were then in touch with him.

By now it should be apparent that Ray could not have flown to London from Lisbon on June 8 without a ticket and a passport. If there is no record of "Sneyd" booking and using such passage on this date, it must be obvious that he either used other means, had another passport under still another name, or wasn't in Lisbon to begin with.

Or: there *is* a record—and official silence about it.

For at least another day, Scotland Yard was badgered and held to to its story. This paragraph is from the June 10 story of the *New York Times'* London bureau, published the morning of the 11th:

Scotland Yard officials continued today to maintain that Ray was arrested here on Saturday morning following his arrival from Portugal, when he attempted to pass through immigration while in transit to Brussels. However, there were reports indicating that Ray may have been in London for some time before his arrest on Saturday.

On that same day, June 10, Karl Meyer wrote an account that could hardly have been more explicit. It appeared in the next morning's *Washington Post:*

Contrary to previous reports, James Earl Ray, the fugitive wanted in the death of Dr. Martin Luther King, had not just arrived from Lisbon when he was picked up at London airport last Saturday.

Instead, Ray had been in this city for at least 11 days, moving from one nondescript tourist hotel to another and making telephone calls to a London newspaperman in an effort to find out how to join white mercenaries in Africa.

Why Scotland Yard and airport officials allowed the initial false impression to stand must be counted as a further minor mystery in the greatest manhunt of modern times.

Telephone Calls

Ray's presence in London under the alias of Ramon George Sneyd might have gone unreported, for a while at least, but for two telephone calls that Ray made last week to Ian Colvin of The London Daily Telegraph.

On Tuesday, the 40-year-old fugitive called the Telegraph foreign desk and said that he wanted to talk with someone who knew about foreign mercenaries. The desk referred Ray to Colvin, author of a recent book on Moise Tshombe and the Congo, and of several articles last month dealing with Maj. Alistair Wicks, a British mercenary officer.

As Colvin reported in Monday's Telegraph, "When we first spoke, a Canadian or perhaps American voice said to me: 'This is Ramon Sneyd. I want to join my brother who has been in Angola.'"

Toward the end of this dispatch:

> Mrs. Thomas [owner-manager of the Pax Hotel] said she passed on messages to him about postponed reservations on flights from London on Thursday and Friday. But finally he booked a seat on a Saturday flight to Brussels and when he turned up at the departure lounge he was stopped and arrested.

There it is, explicit and undenied. Ray had *not* been on the Lisbon plane, had been in London "for at least 11 days."

If this was a "minor mystery" then, what is it now with Ray sentenced to lifetime incarceration and denied access to the outside world (even a lawyer required a court order to see him)? Despite all the marvels attributed to him, no one has yet seriously suggested he could have been in both London and Lisbon at the same time.

In the July 5 story by Karl Meyer, which Blair has followed so closely in his book, Meyer reported that fingerprints found on a bag at the Trustee Savings Bank robbery of June 4 matched Ray's. If the language is imprecise, the import is not. Ray was then in England.

Going along with this are consistently different descriptions of what cannot be a single James Earl Ray.

Eyewitnesses often confabulate. That is, their minds later fill in gaps, resolve contradictions and anomalies, and in time what was not seen is fixed in the mind as having been seen. Also, observations that later have significance seem innocent at the time they are made and there is no reason for them to be fixed in mind. Oft-times, the most sincere eyewitnesses are the least dependable sources of information. However, sometimes they are the only sources, as in attempting to determine the appearance of someone at a certain time and place. It is not unusual, then, for there to be different descriptions of one man, in this case, of the man said to have been James Earl Ray.

Still, what tends to put the inconsistent descriptions of the London James Earl Ray into a different category is the consistency in the descriptions by the persons who report seeing him at different places. Descriptions of the Ray at the New Earl's Court Hotel from different people who saw him there, for example, are in general agreement. And these witnesses say he looked like the published pictures of Ray. This man, however, does not fit the description of the man at the Pax Hotel. And neither description of this or these men is really consistent with descriptions of the man observed in Toronto.

The differences noted by various people are in height, size, and other physical characteristics and features.

If this is considered alone, it is, I think, of some significance. But when combined with the other deeply vexing questions, as it is here, I think it can be granted more significance. Particularly when authorities ignore them, leave them entirely unexplained. If these discrepancies could be easily explained, it would seem that officials, already beset with more than an adequate set of troubles, would have done so, if not to ease their own burden, then at least to ease public disquiet.

With the absolute certainty that a single "Ray" could not simultaneously have been on the British European Airways plane arriving from Lisbon at about 6:10 A.M. and in London all the while, reported leaving the Pax Hotel at 9:30 A.M. (it was not "very early," as Blair says)—the one "Ray" in custody by 6:15 A.M. and the other still at the hotel—and with authorities not only failing to resolve this impossibility but, more, refusing to address it in any way, the credibility of all official accounts is in question.

More doubt is cast upon officials and their accounts by independent investigations. Peter Dawnay in England tried to resolve the extant questions and found instead ample cause for less trust in both officials and their stories. Mrs. Anna Thomas, of the Pax, told him she was first approached by the press, which "swarmed around her like flies round a honey pot." The police did not approach her "until four days after the story had broken in the papers that Ray had stayed at" the Pax. Then they asked her "only routine questions."

She had no listing for the hotel telephone. It was explained that she didn't need a listing, all her rooms being full, and avoiding the listing eliminated late-night telephoned inquiries. Her explanation to Dawnay is that she had, in the past, been leaned on rather heavily by the police, the inference being blackmail, that they had framed her with a minor offense when she didn't accede, and that thereafter she had trouble with "obscene telephone calls and things like that." When "Sneyd" walked in, her rooms were not all engaged. There was one for him.

That the police took her register was confirmed by a former employee who found it convenient to leave after all this excitement. When Dawnay inquired four months later, it had not been returned.

Her recollection of her telephone calls for "Sneyd" and those from airlines—part of the information that led Karl Meyer to call the official story about Ray's presence in Lisbon until June 8 a "minor mystery"—is not convenient for the official accounts. How could the airlines be discussing reservations with Sneyd in her hotel in London when he was in Lisbon?

There are other questions. She was subpoenaed by the prosecution in Memphis, certainly not because Ray/Sneyd was *not* at her hotel. She showed Dawnay the subpoena. She was in this connection visited by an FBI agent reinforced by *four* Scotland Yard officers. It is as though the post-Dallas script had not been rewritten, as though only the names were crossed out and new ones written in. They told her that when in Memphis and on the witness stand she was to answer only those questions asked. When she volunteered to them what they found uncongenial, like finding a hypodermic syringe in the room Ray had occupied after he left, she was "virtually told" she was lying. They "made her swear not to tell anyone" of their visit. In this connection, one of the British officers repeatedly used such warnings as "if you know what's good for you, you won't tell anyone."

Of the many parallels with the investigation of the Presidential murder, I cite merely two: When schoolteacher Jean Lollis Hill immediately reported having heard five shots, she was told by the Secret Service that, with three wounds and three empty shells, the official story would be three shots. When officials of Klein's Sporting Goods in Chicago, which sold the so-called Oswald rifle, were seen by the FBI, as virtually every witness was, and gave to the FBI their records, they were so impressed with the FBI injunction to total silence that they wouldn't even tell the Secret Service until powerfully pressured. At that time, the Secret Service did have jurisdiction in the crime and the FBI did not.

It is like the TV show. "Will the real James Earl Ray/Ramon George Sneyd please stand up?"

Who would?

The man at the New Earl's Court Hotel or the one at the Pax?

The man in Lisbon or the man who robbed the bank on June 4?

The man who got off the plane from Lisbon and needlessly went through immigration inspection, not required for passengers in transit, or the man who left the Pax more than three hours after the pick-up to go to the airport?

Two London papers do establish there was Ray/Sneyd in London at the time the man arrested was placed in Lisbon. Not until after publication of the *Express* and *Telegraph* stories was this apparent. One thing is certain: If Ray/Sneyd was not then in London, as all evidence seems to prove he was, there nonetheless was someone using his name, presenting himself as Sneyd and using the proper address for the "London Sneyd." At the very least, if this is a different person, he was part of a conspiracy. Ray/Sneyd was not alone.

The reluctance of the police to pursue the other existing proofs that Ray was not alone does not encourage faith in their determination to uncover all the evidence. For example, there remains the young blond man seen with "London Ray" at the YWCA, an abandoned mystery. This finds perfect parallel with Lee Harvey Oswald and men seen with him and never sought or found, especially the young Mexican in New Orleans.

One of the major mysteries is the continued insistence by Scotland Yard on their original story *after* all the proof of existence of a "London Ray" *continuously* in London until hours after the interception of the man on the plane from Lisbon was public: They arrested a man on the Lisbon flight.

The determined Dawnay, whose interest in the assassinations caused his bankruptcy, persisted. Five and a half months after the arrest, he heard from Scotland Yard. It still insisted, "The man was in transit through Immigration on arrival from Lisbon on his way to another country."

9

NEW SCOTLAND YARD,
BROADWAY, LONDON, S.W.1
01-230 1212, Extn.2422

21st November, 1968

5/68/530 (P.2)

Dear Mr. Dawnay,

Further to my letter of the 18th November and in confirmation of my telephone conversation with you this afternoon, the following is a Press Release issued by this office at 5.5. p.m. on the 8th June, 1968:-

Raymond George Sneyd born 8.10.32 Toronto, Canada, no fixed abode and no occupation was arrested at 11.15 a.m. on 8.6.68 at London Airport and later charged at Cannon Row with possessing a forged passport and possessing a firearm. He will appear at Bow Street Magistrates Court at 10.30 a.m. on 10.6.68. Detective Chief Superintendent Butler and Detective Chief Inspector Thompson are in charge of the enquiry. The arrest was the result of liaison with the F.B.I., the Royal Canadian Mounted Police and New Scotland Yard. The man was in transit through Immigration on arrival from Lisbon on his way to another country.

I do hope this will help.

Yours sincerely,

M. G. Dove

Public Relations Officer

Peter Dawnay, Esq.,
Peter Dawnay Ltd.,
1 Westmoreland Place,
London, S.W.1.

Four days before Scotland Yard wrote Dawnay the November 18 letter, which he never got, British European Airways responded to inquiries Richard Bernabei, another independent investigator, had made about Sneyd's travel arrangements with BEA (presumably the airline which he used). Their reply confirms the seeming impossibility of the Scotland Yard version, for BEA issued no such ticket and has no other record of Ray's "having travelled" on their plane on June 8.

BRITISH EUROPEAN AIRWAYS

P.O. Box No. 7

Bealine House, Ruislip, Middlesex.   Telephone VIKing 1234   Telegrams BEALINE LONDON

DS/P4/1

14th November 1968

Mr. Richard Bernabei,
Department of Classics,
Queen's University,
Kingston, Ontario,
CANADA.

Dear Sir,

        Thank you for your letter of the 30th October about the movements of James Earl Ray. Mr. Ray travelled under the name of Mr. R. Sneyd from London to Lisbon on the 7th May by BEA on the last flight coupon of a ticket originally issued by BOAC. He was arrested at London Airport (Heathrow) while attempting to travel from London to Brussels on BE.466 on the 8th June. We assume that he had travelled earlier that day from Lisbon to London but if he did so there is no record of him having travelled on a BEA service and indeed no ticket was issued for that purpose. It is possible that he travelled from Lisbon to London on a one-way ticket issued by TAP in Lisbon but we have been unable to confirm this.

        It is, therefore, something of a speculation as to how he got to Heathrow on the 8th June in time to be arrested.

                        Yours faithfully,

                        M. J. Lester
                        Secretary & Solicitor

(The FBI, naturally, had it both ways: Ray arrested in transit and not in transit. Anxious to get credit not his due, J. Edgar Hoover, joined by Attorney General Clark, immediately issued a formal statement saying what Scotland Yard later said. Then, for all the world as though it had never issued this statement, the FBI told reporters Ray had been in London when apprehended.)

This, then, leaves at least one "Sneyd" who, at the moment the "Lisbon Sneyd" was apprehended, was and had been in London. The evidence reinforces the belief, consistently supported by the later evidence that we shall examine, that there were at least two men, only one of whom was arrested and charged. It is consistent with the suspicion, if not the belief, that the right man got away, that the man caught was, by the other or others, intended to be caught—was a decoy.

In any kind of police work, this kind of induced and perpetuated confusion sponsors the most serious doubts about its competence and integrity. When the crime is of the magnitude of this one, when the consequences are as serious or, what usually motivates the police, as exceedingly costly as they were in this case, this is not usual police public relations or practice. More particularly is this so with the history of open dissatisfaction over all official behavior and actions in the Presidential murder and the remarkable coincidence of the Ray capture and its announcement with the murder of Robert Kennedy. Here, when British and Canadian officials—who did the real work—were properly silent, Hoover's, Clark's, and possibly other officials' concern for their own public image was such that they made the announcement of the capture during the murdered Senator's funeral.

If all of this could have been resolved, simply or not, if the police of the countries involved could have made a credible case for a single suspect, a one and only Sneyd/Ray, they should—and would—have done it. This would in no way have jeopardized the rights of the accused or the prosecution.

Quite the contrary.

Silence, then and since, is subject to but one interpretation: The police cannot resolve this conflict.

Which means there may have been two men. And that, in turn, means conspiracy, a conspiracy to murder King.

There was a court proceeding in London. Ray was extradited. Both governments were involved, that of the United States and that of Great

12

Britain. Here was an excellent and immediate forum for eliminating confusion and establishing truth and fact.

But on this—and on too many other things—silence or deceit, as we now see.

2. An "Ordinary Visitor"

Ray enjoyed all the formalities of defense provided by law,
British and American. Yet it cannot be said he had his day in court..
This is not because he was not offered the formalities, the minimum
requirements of the law. It is because those defending him did *not
defend* him. If this is less true in England that in the United States, it
is true in both countries. He had the trappings, not the reality, of the
protection of the law. It was made to look as though he were defended.
He was not.

Even for a formality, his first London hearing was brief—less than
two minutes—just under a minute and a half—88 seconds, by the
timing of Karl Meyer, who was there and reported what happened
June 10. It was in Bow Street Magistrate's Court in the Covent Garden
market area, at about 10:30 A.M., Case 24. Present were about thirty
spectators and the functionaries. These included Assistant Attorney
General Fred M. Vinson, Jr., who watched but did not openly
participate. Chief Magistrate Frank Milton asked if Ray had anything
to say. Ray murmured an almost inaudible "No." Trial was set for
June 18 on the two alleged violations of British law, carrying a
concealed weapon and using a false passport. Bang! went the gavel
and that was it. Off went the well-guarded prisoner, not permitted bail,
this time to Brixton Prison (which just happens to be in the heart of
one of London's larger black ghettos) for later transfer to Wandsworth
Prison, where he could be watched more carefully and held more
securely.

Ray was represented by the firm Michael Dresden and Company, to
which the case had been assigned. The key issue was not Ray's alleged
violations of British law but the basis on which he could be extradited,
legally speaking, not a simple matter.

The charge that Ray conspired to murder King was the only one that gave the U.S. federal government a legal basis for entering the case, but this charge did not meet the definitions of the extradition treaty between the U.S. and Britain. Further, had extradition been granted and had he also been tried and convicted of the alleged offenses against British law (for which the maximum combined penalty would have been 42 months), he could not have been extradited until after he served his time. (Another unique provision of British law — and one I wish had applied in Memphis—once the extradition proceeding began, he could not waive or be persuaded to waive his rights [1]. The law required the completion of the trial.)

The next day, Tuesday the 11th, the State Department let it be known it had the documents for the extradition proceeding required from the states of Tennessee (King murder) and Missouri (jail break) and "will be transmitting them to London shortly." Meanwhile, Scotland Yard let it be known that they were investigating Ray on the murder-conspiracy charge, scouting his movements, but using the passport charge as their legal basis for holding and investigating him. They also let it be known that, in the words of the Associated Press dispatch,

Although he had been traced to two London hotels between May 28 and his arrest, there was an unexplained gap of about 10 days starting on May 17, when he left Lisbon for London.

In short, at the very beginning, detectives knew he had been at the Pax and when he left there, or that he had been at another and undisclosed hostel. FBI agents, who have no legal authority in England, were disclosed to be working with Scotland Yard.

Wednesday, June 12, the necessary documents arrived and were processed through the Foreign Office to the Home Office (counterpart of the Department of Justice) for the magistrate. The various accounts of the documents are identical, obviously from the same official source. The Associated Press described them as "at least an inch thick when handed in to the Foreign Office by U.S. Consul General Jack Herfurt." The *Los Angeles Times* syndicate said "a folder of documents at least an inch thick."

There is this paragraph in the *Times'* account to which I direct special attention for reasons that will soon assume significance:

None of this evidence becomes part of the public record, and therefore publishable *until the formal hearing* [emphasis added].

15

On Tuesday, June 18, the extradition hearing was set for the 27th, a Thursday. Roger Frisby, representing Ray/Sneyd, asked as much time as possible to prepare the defense. The British elected to forget the crimes for which they allegedly arrested Ray.

By the 18th, it had become apparent that extradition was not an open-and-shut matter. These two paragraphs from the end of the Associated Press report of that day present several of the legal problems involved:

> Under the 1931 extradition treaty between Britain and the United States, British courts can grant extradition only if U.S. authorities present evidence sufficient to send Ray to trial under British law.
>
> Extradition of Ray was also asked because he is wanted by Missouri to complete a prison term for armed robbery. While extradition on this charge would be almost automatic, the U.S.-British treaty specifies that a suspect can only be tried on the charges for which he has been specifically extradited. Therefore, unless he is extradited for the murder of the Negro civil rights leader, he cannot be prosecuted on that charge in the United States.

In other words, if Ray were to be tried for the King murder in the United States, to extradite him from England, the United States had to present, in open court, evidence sufficient to warrant his trial on that charge in England, for a similar offense in England. And once returned to the United States, Ray could not be tried on any other charge.

Also at this time, Arthur Hanes emerged as the lawyer of Ray's choice. He announced in Birmingham that he had been phoned by Ray's British court-appointed lawyers, after which he had received a handwritten letter, signed "R. G. Sneyd," asking him to represent "Sneyd." As soon as he could make the arrangements, he flew to London and was promptly denied permission to see his client. He had arrived in London on Thursday the 13th, causing what is described with delicacy in press accounts as "a certain amount of embarrassment in legal circles" in London. Hanes, again in the words of the same source, "was left in no doubt that Ray's court-appointed British attorney would not welcome American aid or an interview with the suspect." After several fruitless days, he flew back to the United States.

The question that here arises is not whether Ray was denied competent counsel, but was he denied access to counsel of his choice. By this time, his defense in England was in the hands of Michael Eugene (also of Michael Dresden and Company). For reasons that will

16

evolve, I think it pertinent to ask if the requirement of American law, counsel of his own choice, was fully met in England. Perhaps it need not have been as a matter of law, for in England only British law and British interpretation of British law obtain. However, with such decisions as *Esposito, Miranda,* and others in the United States, granting of immediate and unrestricted access to counsel of choice is the requirement in the United States. Eugene and the others are of undoubted competence. But, so are the FBI, and look at their record! So were the members and staff of the Warren Commission. How can one, from these illustrations alone, be satisfied that competence of counsel is the core? This does illustrate the wisdom of the United States decisions.

The point I make, I reemphasize, is not of legality. It is of propriety and ethics. The fact is that, for almost a month after his arrest, Ray did not have access to the attorney of his own choice and the attorney he did want was denied permission to see him, which was, apparently, the desire of his court-appointed attorney. Nor is this to say that the pleadings had to be handled by the American lawyer in the British court. But, Ray should have been able to take counsel with the man he felt he had reason to trust, the man obviously selected because of his background and record (defending accused Klansmen), the man whose independent appraisal of his British lawyers and their strategy Ray should properly have had.

How often the same United States government had rent the welkin with its strident protests when other Americans, especially those accused of being its spies, were fully protected by court-appointed lawyers in other countries but were, by those governments, denied permission to see, not lawyers of *their* choice, but those selected by the United States government. And how much more important it is for the accused in *any* country to have as counsel those *he* chooses rather than those his government chooses for him.

When it, more than its accused spies, was on trial in other lands, the United States government was loud, bitter, and pointed, screaming bloody murder. But when it is the accuser, it is party to precisely that which it declares immoral and wrong when others do it.

Nor did it complain when, too late to have meaning, after the June 27 extradition hearing which Ray lost, the British government granted permission for Ray to see him. It then ruled Hanes could not see Ray as his attorney but could as an "ordinary visitor." (At that, this was better treatment than he was later accorded in the United

States, where Ray was denied visitors and his own lawyer had to get a court order to see him.)

So it was not until July 5 that Hanes got to see Ray, with Eugene, for about 35 to 40 minutes—after flying all the way back to England. In the interim, it was disclosed (with remarkably little attention in the press) that Ray had made written request for permission to see Hanes. There was a "mix-up." Home Office permission was not granted until after Hanes had emplaned for Birmingham. Two days before Hanes landed in London the second time he had been phoned by Eugéne. He left the next day.

Further the short 40 minutes that client and lawyer-visitor-but-not-lawyer had together they shared with prison officials, who were in the cell with them. The accused, normally, is entitled to privacy when he takes counsel.

It is little wonder that Hanes did not have much to say on leaving Wandsworth Prison. He did report "Sneyd," the name signed to the three letters he had gotten, seemed in good health, that no group, "leftwing or rightwing," had offered to pay or help pay his costs and fees, that he was not worried about being paid, that he did not plan to run for governor, and that he took the case "because it's a big case, a challenge." As we shall see, he had also gotten Ray's signature on several papers that pertained to the merchandizing of Ray's story.

When Hanes visited "Sneyd" the next day, they had a few minutes more than an hour and only the prison guards for company. Those things they did not want overheard he and Ray passed to each other in notes, through the glass panel and thick metal grillwork that separated them. This time Hanes got "names and other leads" for his pretrial investigation and returned to the United States.

Meanwhile, preparations were set for appeal of the adverse decision. Speculation indicated its basis would be that the crime charged was a political crime and not extraditable. Every week, as required by British law for those denied bail, Ray was produced in court for the magistrate's inspection. But then, with many avenues, including appeal to the House of Lords, still to be explored, Ray, before the appeal could be heard, told his English lawyers to abandon it and not to fight extradition.

Little was made of it, but the fact is that Ray had no choice. In Lawrence Malkin's story from London for morning-paper subscribers of the Associated Press, in which he reported, "Michael Eugene, his British attorney, said Ray signed a statement accepting extradition

18

rather than pursue an appeal in the British High Court," there is this intelligence, ". . . the British had refused to continue legal aid for his appeal."

A kind of repayment for American aid?

In the United States, the indigent accused and convicted are provided free legal services. Such a wealthy and influential attorney as Abe Fortas handled one of the landmark decisions on legal rights (Gideon vs. Wainright) in the Supreme Court for a man in jail. This was costly to Fortas, in the time it required and more so for the Southern enmity it earned him. But he did it. That is the concept of American justice.

The nature of the case against Ray is such that appeal should have been made, for his rights and those of others. More often than not, the rights of the more respectable members of society are established in defense of those of law-breakers.

Once again, Hanes was not in England, but he rushed back, getting there the next day, the 16th, midst top-secret preparations for Ray's top-secret flight to the United States. Hanes had recommended to Ray that he return to the United States for speedy trial and so "he can confer with me and others," often and in private.

Hanes appeared less than cool and collected after again seeing Ray. Ray's request that Hanes accompany him on the flight had been denied. Hanes charged an "unprecedented, vicious press and television campaign" in the United States to picture Ray as "a convicted murderer, a monster . . . ." He alleged Ray's rights had been and were about to be denied, that denying Ray's request that he accompany the prisoner on the flight was a violation of United States law because it could subject Ray to questioning outside the presence of his counsel. He was hot. But it did not good. He said, "Ray fears being in the company of the Justice Department alone" and appealed to Attorney General Clark, without success. But he made enough fuss to assure that, even if the government had had the intention, they would hardly risk questioning Ray while they had him alone. Hanes had instructed him, "Keep your mouth shut." He charged the arrangements were being "overplayed" to achieve the "melodramatic," that this was "without justification" and "I am convinced he will be taken out secretly and spirited away."

He was right.

At about 10 P.M. the night of the 18th, Ray was taken from Wandsworth Prison. The two charges under British law were dropped. When the rumor spread that Ray had departed about midnight, the

19

Embassy confirmed that he had. It was 4,500 miles to Memphis where, after a ten-and-a-half-hour flight in an Air Force jet, he was in jail at 4:34 A.M. July 19. Again, there was publicity, a dramatic picture of the accused weighted down in bullet-proof covering and handcuffed to a very large leather belt that was too big for him.

As with Oswald, all of whose rights were systematically denied him so so thoroughly that even the empaneling of a jury might have been impossible and most of the alleged evidence could not have been used, one wonders at the behavior of the government. If any necessary purpose was served by refusing the accused's request for his lawyer to be with him, it was not revealed by the government and is not apparent to the layman. Not only might this have been the basis for appeal of a conviction but, conversely, honoring the request was a sign of good faith by the federal government and eliminated one possible ground for reversal of conviction.

So, when Ray set foot in the United States, he had never had confidential consultation with his lawyer of choice, had been questioned at the airport in Britain without counsel (a violation of the *Miranda* decision in the United States), and had been in American custody for a long, uninterrupted stretch—to, on, and from the plane—after questioning outside the presence of his lawyer, and was denied access to his lawyer when he wanted him and felt he needed him.

It would seem that none of these things was necessary and that they can be interpreted as abridgment of his rights. If they need not be done, why were they? What purpose was served by even the semblance of denial of all rights to the accused in so sensational a case, where it could be anticipated there would be endless appeals over the years and any one technicality could result in a reversal and an acquittal?

Can one attribute the errors to ignorance? I would offer another hypothesis. Had it ever come to pass that Ray had been convicted and then released for legal error, the government would have had the conviction it needed for the case to be "solved" and the convicted man, not guilty of the crime, from the available evidence, would not have been punished for it.

Had Jack Ruby not shot Oswald, this is what would have happened in that case, for the government's own evidence is overwhelming proof that Oswald killed no one and the error in that case, immediate and permeating, would have precluded a sustained conviction.

If this was a "precaution," as with Oswald, what subsequently happened ended the need for it.

The patterns are so close it seems they were cut from the same model.

In recounting this sequence of events, in order to record at one point the essentials of the story of the accused in the hands of public authority, I have omitted the actual presentation of evidence at the formal hearing.

To that we now return.

3. Dry Run for the Minitrial:
The Automatic Decision

All governments use propaganda, ours more than most, if not all, others. It is doubtful if ever in history, anywhere, there have been in any single employ as many engaged in public relations, the euphemism (not always appropriate) for which is "public information."

Thus, the government let it be known it would send a "fingerprint expert" to the formal extradition proceeding at Bow Street Magistrate's Court June 27, 1968.

Mostly everyone immediately assumed that there was air-tight fingerprint evidence proving Ray the murderer. Why else send a fingerprint expert? In general, everyone assumes there are always fingerprints that are always clear and an expert can establish guilt by them in a murder. The latter perhaps was the intended effect of the release. In any case, it was the effect achieved.

If the government felt it necessary to announce in advance that it was sending witnesses or a witness (and there can be no trial without a witness, for evidence can be adduced in no other way), if it felt that the obvious had to be made more obvious, it did not so subtly have to prejudice the rights of the accused and poison the minds of all prospective jurors.

Any conceived need of "public information" could and would have been served adequately with the announcement that it would produce evidence. Even this was not needed, but it was enough, much more than the government says when it does not want publicity. Then it merely refuses any comment.

Behind the pretense of strict adherence to the proprieties, by what it did and said and what it leaked and inspired, the government was successful in capturing the public mind with endless news stories the other side could neither answer nor refute. This did amount to propagands. Hanes's quoted objections are not without foundation. Public opinion had been formed by the government in its favor by the time the hearing opened in Judge Frank Milton's Bow Street Court, in which the shades had been drawn against the sun that hot and humid Thursday, June 27.

It was a sticky, sleepy day. Ray sat with his white collar open at the

neck but with the vest of his blue suit buttoned. (This "blue suit" does suggest that his baggage did get to him, but this is nowhere reported, so we do not know whether it was from the Lisbon plane or from the checked-in baggage at Heathrow Airport.) He looked "hot and limp." Fortunately for the lawyers, the formalities of other British courts did not hold here, so they were in business suits only, without the heavy gowns and the sweaty wigs customary in more formal British courts.

The United States government was represented by Barrister David Calcutt, tall, dignified-looking, with hair receding steeply from the middle of a high forehead over his thin, long face. Ray's courtroom work was again by Barrister Frisby, assisted by Solicitor Eugene.

If the advance publicity led to the belief that the government would produce many Memphis witnesses, there was disappointment. But one witness from the United States was used. He is Jacob Bonebrake, experienced FBI fingerprint expert, who testified to having made "more than a million" comparisons in his career as an agent. Peter Hopkirk, writer for the *Times of London,* was called to testify to the attitudes he had observed while covering the Presidential primaries in the United States, including several days spent in Memphis after the King murder. The rest of the evidence was by affidavits, there being no live witness produced. Calcutt read the affidavits. This was a prelude to what happened in Memphis.

By means of the fingerprint testimony, the man in the dock was identified as the man who escaped Missouri State Prison and was wanted to complete the remaining twelve years of his twenty-year sentence (for which he was not being extradited, hence not germane), as well as the man whose fingerprints were found on the rifle said to have been used in the murder, on its telescopic sight, and on a pair of Bushnell binoculars recovered near the scene of the crime in Memphis.

Calcutt read from an affidavit by Dr. Jerry T. Francisco, a forensic pathologist who, as Shelby County's Medical Officer (King's murder took place in this county), had done the autopsy. The doctor had sworn to removing "a battered lead slug" from King's corpse. Rather than produce a ballistics expert, a category of experts with which the government is adequately supplied, it presented Calcutt's word, "The bullet which killed Dr. King was examined when removed and there is a strong likelihood that the bullet came from the rifle found by the police." It thus avoided presenting a witness who could—and would— have been cross-examined.

This rifle and its purchaser were the subject of two more affidavits

23

read by Calcutt. Donald Wood, son of the owner of the Birmingham Aeromarine Supply Company, and John De Shazo, a customer, identified Ray as the "Harvey Lohmeyer" who had bought a Winchester rifle there on March 29 and exchanged it for a Remington Model 760 the next day, which was five days before the murder. Nine cartridges for it were found and the empty casing from which the bullet was allegedly fired was in the weapon.

Ray was placed at the scene of the crime through the affidavit of Charles Quitman Stephens. (Published accounts also spell this name "Stevens." The two transcripts spell it both ways.) He had a room near 5B, said to have been Ray's. Stephens said he had seen this man with the manager, Mrs. Bessie Brewer, when he engaged the room. Calcutt represented the Stephens affidavit as a positive identification and Judge Milton so accepted it. This is the way, according to newspaper reports, Calcutt put it:

> At 6 o'clock Mr. Stevens says he heard a shot fired from the bathroom. He came out of his room and saw a man leaving below. He says it was the man who he had seen booking in earlier.

This is *not* what Stephens said, which is one of the reasons Anglo-Saxon concepts of justice require the presence of live witnesses who may be cross-examined so that, if they speak falsely, it can be established, and, if they are imprecise, doubt can be eliminated. The words of Stephens' affidavit, an *ex parte* statement that could not be cross-examined, prepared for and by the government to present that which it wanted presented only, fall far short of Calcutt's representation. They are:

> Although I did not get a good look at him, I think it was the same man I saw earlier with Mrs. Brewer.

The strongest statement Stephens made is *not* positive identification. He only "thinks" it was the same man and specifies, "I did not get a good look at him." That man was going down the stairs and Stephens was above him. When the FBI showed Stephens pictures of Ray, all he would then say is that the profile looked like the man he saw.

This is the essence of the "evidence" presented by the United States. Most of it was not subject to cross-examination. Indeed, it was presented in a manner that precluded any possibility of cross-examination when, in the United States, this right is mandatory. It was not represented in court with complete fidelity, but it did the job. We shall analyze it later as it should have been but was not and could not have been analyzed in Bow Street Magistrate's Court.

In presenting his argument to the court, Calcutt employed language remarkable for the lawyer representing the government that had charged Ray with conspiring to commit the murder for which it sought his extradition:

> There is not a shred of evidence to show that the murder took place to further the ends of a higher enterprise. No other man or other body was involved . . . evidence before this court points to a lone assassin for private purpose.

So, while the government, in its effort to retrieve Ray for trial, charged him with conspiracy, its lawyer says this charge was a fabrication. When Calcutt said "the evidence before this court," what he was really saying is "the evidence *I presented to this court*," for he did present *all* the evidence offered. What evidence existed and was not presented, *he* did not present. That he did not present evidence tending to show there had been a conspiracy does not mean it did not exist. It means merely that he did not offer it. This, in turn, could mean he did not have it, did not understand it, or was directed not to by his client, the U.S. government. In fairness to Calcutt, all he did have is what the government gave him. It is not unfair to him to say he could have better understood or represented some of what *was* given to him, for it, like the cited case of Stephens, does not say what he said it does. We shall delve further into this in analyzing the minitrial, where supposedly the identical evidence was used.

Even more incredibly, while this was going on in Bow Street, back on the ranch in Washington, Calcutt's client, the Department of Justice, once again was saying exactly the opposite. These are the words of the Associated Press:

> In Washington, a Justice Department spokesman said the case is still under investigation. In answer to a reporter's question, he said the government has not eliminated the possibility of a conspiracy.

From the foregoing, we have three different and contradictory accountings of the same set of facts about the same vital element, the question of conspiracy, all existing simultaneously, and all from the same, single Department of Justice which is the pillar of the law and the prosecutor of perjury by ordinary mortals:

There definitely was a conspiracy of which Ray was part.

There definitely was no conspiracy of any kind—Ray was alone.

A conspiracy is a possibility; the government does not know.

This is impermissible. If the Department of Justice could honestly charge Ray was part of a conspiracy, it could not honestly have fostered Calcutt's contrary courtroom assurances. If it could honestly stand behind what Calcutt said on its behalf and without doubt based upon its representations to him, it could not honestly have charged Ray with conspiracy. And the only possible explanation for the statement in Washington that the government did not know whether of not there had been a conspiracy, aside from future use in face-saving, is its knowledge that *both* other statements are false and were known to be false—that Ray was *not* the murderer.

This is beyond excuse or explanation, anywhere in any government, most of all in that part of the government charged with enforcement of the law and defense of the rights of citizens under the law.

Bear in mind, also, that simultaneously the same Department of Justice was preventing the normal functioning of Anglo-Saxon law and legal precepts by preventing the cross-examination of all but a single one of the witnesses whose completely untested words were used and accepted as the equivalent of open, cross-examined testimony, of established probity. Along with this, it was then, at the least, considerably extending what these untested witnesses and affidavits actually do say.

The federal government is not without funds or means. It would have been no great burden to send the key witnesses to England. Aside from compliance with the law as it relates to government, which should not improvise on the law for individual situations, a more dependable record would have resulted. Or was this the government's fear? Then, too, it would have been a courteous gesture to a friendly government. That the government did not send a few of the witnesses made important by its use of their affidavits, like Stephens, is subject to the interpretation that it preferred not to hazard a competent cross-examination. In short, it appears that the government lacked faith in its own witnesses and evidence, lacked confidence in their survival in open court.

What this really adds up to is that the government played dirty tricks with the law and its procedures.

And what it requires is that every statement made or used by the government in this case be regarded with skepticism.

Judge Milton had his bench piled high with law books. During the proceedings, he peered across them over the top of his half-spectacles. At lunchtime, after this material had been laid before him, he rose from behind his stacked books to announce, with what the press described as brusqueness, that he would disclose his decision at 2 P.M., after lunch. However, not all had been said. Ray wanted to say something. Frisby had to call Milton back. Then Ray rose to make personal complaint about what he regarded as the denial of his rights, to protest politely that he should have had "more freedom to write and visit people" (he meant be visited by others).

The decision by Milton was that there was a prima facie case "based on this verbal and affidavit evidence before me" and extradition was ordered. I have quoted Milton's exact words because on the facts of the case, as opposed to the opinion elicited from Hopkirk, the *Times* reporter who testified on attitudes in the United States, there was but a *single* source of *verbal* evidence, the single FBI agent sent, Jacob Bonebrake. His specialty is precise. There was little leeway for cross-examination. Aside from Bonebrake's testimony (and that, too, was buttressed by an affidavit he had executed earlier), all of the evidence was non-verbal, was not subject to cross-examination. In short, most of the evidence presented was in such form it was impossible for Ray's lawyer to contest it. It was beyond the capacity of any mortal to show if it was in any way defective, false, exaggerated, or distorted. With the best of intentions, humans do err as witnesses. Those events that later come up in court are often of no significance at the time they are observed, may happen so fast they cannot be observed accurately, frequently are not clearly recalled, and sometimes are influenced by what the witnesses later hear and see.

For all practical purposes, once again in a political murder, there was a court proceeding in which the normal course of justice was denied. Our courts and our law were not permitted to work as they must for meaningful, traditional justice to be the end product.

Lest the reader misunderstand, I emphasize these things:

What was at issue is not whether the man arrested in England under the name of Sneyd had used a forged passport and had a gun on his person, whether he is the man who escaped from prison with a dozen years to serve, or whether he was in any way involved in the murder of Martin Luther King, Jr., *except as the lone assassin.*

His fingerprints could have been over everything without its proving he was the lone assassin or an assassin at all. His fingerprints on the alleged weapon and other items proved that he had handled them. They may have been his property. They may even have been used in the crime. But they did not establish that he *alone* had committed it—or that he had committed it at all. Assuming the accuracy of Bonebrake's testimony, it did not and could not prove Ray *the* murderer or *a* murderer. This was the central issue in the extradition proceeding. Any other charge made it impossible to try him for the murder in the United States because, under British law, he had to be tried for the offense for which extradition was granted.

Of course, he did not have to be proved guilty beyond reasonable doubt, the standard of the ultimate trial, in order to warrant extradition. There had to be only a *prima facie* case. Loosely, this means a solid reason to believe he was guilty, not absolute proof that he was.

To help understanding of this, I repeat the exact words of the magistrate's decision, with added emphasis:

> *On this, on the verbal and affidavit evidence before me,* there can be no doubt.

What Magistrate Milton did was, properly and openly, qualify what seems like an absolute statement.

"On this" means on what was presented in his court, no more.

The affidavit evidence was not subject to testing to establish whether or not it was correct or even credible at all. It could not be without cross-examination, and lawyers cannot cross-examine a sheet of paper.

The evidence before him was mostly of this mute character. The nature of the evidence of the one live witness who could be questioned was not central, could not, by itself, prove guilt, and was not readily subject to cross-examination. This, no doubt, is why a fingerprint expert only was sent.

So the reader can better understand and evaluate this, can see what his government contrived in sending but one witness who could be cross-examined (and I interject that he was one long experienced in such procedures and skilled in the avoidance of the purposes of cross-examination by this long experience), I here list others whose affidavit "evidence" was presented. These are those identified in news dispatches only:

Bonebrake himself, the one live witness
Charles Stephens

Donald Wood
John De Shazo
Henrietta Hagemeister
Corda York
N. E. Zachary
Dr. Jerry Thomas Francisco

There were others not named.

One of the more important is Robert A. Frazier, "Chief of Firearms Identification unit of the FBI with 27 years of experience." It is Frazier whose testimony before the Warren Commission was so indispensable in framing Oswald and falsifying history. Despite (or should I suggest because of?) his long experience, he carefully avoided the essence of the evidence in that case. He freely testified of the bullet alleged to have inflicted seven non-fatal injuries on President John F. Kennedy and Texas Governor John Connally that it had been cleaned before it reached him (this in no way troubling him). Residues that could have been examined and tested remained—and he at no time examined or tested them. His Warren Commission testimony can better be evaluated when it is understood that those human traces that had to have remained on any bullet with this imputed history were almost indestructible. *But,* had he made this required study, if it did not prove there *were* human residues and those consistent with what would remain from the bodies of the President and the Governor, Frazier would have established Oswald's innocence.

Here several important things become obvious:

Before the Warren Commission, Frazier admitted not making the scientific tests any complete and honest examination of the evidence required. Yet he had long, professional experience in this field and knew exactly what he failed to do—and that it was the very essence.

Before the Warren Commission, there never was any cross-examination, so he knew he would not be exposed there. He had every reason to believe he would never be exposed, for it was then planned that only the Commission's conclusions, its Report, would be made public.

He was not produced before Magistrate Milton, so his ballistics evidence, once again, could not be subject to scrutiny.

Thus, the urgency of cross-examination can be seen—and the reason the United States government precluded the possibility of it. In making it impossible for its most important witness to be cross-examined—for all but one of its witnesses of any character to be questioned in any way—what the government was doing and knew it was doing—and intended doing—was framing Ray. It is that simple. It made the decision of the British court almost automatic, for it prevented the presentation of *any* evidence other than the *ex parte* representation of only that evidence it permitted.

Thus, Magistrate Milton, quite properly, ruled on "the affidavit evidence before me," for there was nothing else he could do.

He could not rule on any evidence not before him. He had no way of knowing whether the evidence before him was tainted or wrong. He could not know whether there was any evidence withheld from him, what it would or could mean, or whether there was contrary meaning to that affidavit evidence produced before him and interpreted by the United States government.

This whole situation disturbed me deeply. Once again the federal government was preventing the workings of our own law, frustrating the concepts of our own kind of justice—contriving evidence and shaping it to fit a predetermined political need.

This is what it did in the Warren Report. Here it was accomplishing exactly the same ends.

4. Orwell, 1969

When it seemed possible there would be a real trial in Memphis, I bided my time. Once that unparalleled rape of history and justice was an accomplished fact, with precisely the pat formula of Magistrate Milton's court duplicated in the United States, I decided to examine for myself and for the reader this affidavit evidence never, anywhere, tested in any way.

I do not resort to devices and ask rhetorical questions. There was ample reason to doubt this evidence. Only the gross misrepresentation of what Stephens signed is noted above. This is hardly the full story of the deliberate deception by the federal government there perpetrated. The newspapers contain much more. We examine the evidence with the examination of the minitrial.

So, on the assumption that public evidence *is* public evidence; that what is used and adduced in open court is open, not secret, evidence; that what American and, presumably, British law calls and identifies as "public domain" is no less than that, I undertook to obtain this public evidence. "Public domain" means belonging to the people, to everyone.

I wrote Phil Canale, the District Attorney General of the Fifteenth Judicial Court of Tennessee. As the Shelby County prosecutor who agreed to the minitrial, he is responsible for what was presented in court there against Ray and for what was not. There was much he decided not to use. For example, he did not use a single one of the affidavits used in the Bow Street hearing. In fact, he was careful to keep them out of evidence. His assistant merely told Judge W. Preston Battle, who presided over the minitrial in Memphis, what, in his opinion, the witnesses who signed the affidavits would have said if they were witnesses.

These affidavits were the basis of his case. About 25 per cent of the transcript, in pages, consists of the paraphrasing of the contents of the affidavits by Robert Dwyer, Canale's executive assistant, who droned through the material so monotonously that it appears as a single supercolossal paragraph in Blair's transcript. It contains most of the words spoken in that minitrial. This material, very much, *was* used in the minitrial. There could not have been any proceeding without it. And there is little doubt that, prior to the minitrial, prior to the extradition hearing, there was an even greater volume of material collected by Canale's office on its own or presented to it by the FBI. This was touted as the largest criminal investigation in the FBI's very large history.

Immediately after the minitrial, when it became clear to me that the essence of the evidence would not be in the papers, that only those interpretations of those selections made by the prosecutor with the connivance of the man who then represented Ray had been printed, I asked Canale for access to the unpublished but publicly used evidence. There is nothing unusual about this. Court evidence is almost always available[1].

"Especially because of the existing and new questions," I wrote Canale, "do I believe that those few of us who may have some knowledge of the case should have access to the official records. Otherwise, we are forced to depend upon the press, which cannot be complete and, with the best of intentions, may still be inaccurate."

Response, dated March 24, 1969, by Lloyd A. Rhodes, his administrative assistant, was curt and to the point:

> None of the evidence not in the transcript will be available to anyone.

This means that the prosecution had the eaten cake. It had interpreted that selection of the affidavits it chose to present in that formality and denied anyone, under any circumstances—forever—a chance to see if it fairly and honestly presented what the affidavits say and do not say; if there is error, deliberate or accidental, in them; or even if Dwyer, by accident if not by design, made any slips of speech, misinterpretations, or misrepresentations.

This is a wholeheartedly subversive kind of American "justice."

The only other content of Rhodes' letter, which told me how to buy the transcript, served no purpose, for by the time I got his letter I had obtained and read the transcript—and been even more disturbed by what it disclosed. After explaining this in a second letter, dated March 30, I wrote:

> There are several aspects of this I would like you to consider.
> The tangible evidence, for example, the ballistics evidence, cannot be in the transcript. Why cannot at the very least pictures be available to writers and through them to the people of the country?
> You and Mr. Foreman got together on a deal that, clearly, was not

understood by the defendant or is not in accord with his beliefs and wishes—and statements. With the best intentions in the world, this is a mechanism conducive to error. It would seem to me that if you did err, you would be anxious to learn about it. Have you stopped to consider the alternative? Do you want, throughout history, to be considered the prosecutor who made a deal to frame a man with a heinous crime he did not commit? Do you want your children and theirs through the generations to be so stigmatized? All of us who have or may have knowledge and who have looked into this should be able to examine the evidence as closely as possible precisely to assure that, to the degree humanly possible, any error might be detected. It seems to me the interest of justice and yours personally require this.

On the other hand, how can your refusal to let those of us writers who are qualified study the evidence be regarded as other than an effort to cover-up? This implication, I would hope, you would also be anxious to eliminate.

I tell you frankly that regardless of Mr. Foreman's satisfaction with the evidence presented, it has remarkable deficiencies. It is for this reason that I want to examine the evidence, for it may well be more convincing than what was presented in court. If it is not, that, too, should be reported. To date, what has been published amounts to little more than handouts. This serves no impartial, no genuine national interest, and I suggest it also does not serve yours.

If lawyers did not provide the other side, did not test the evidence as is done under our adversary system of justice, then writers must. I hope you will reconsider and make this possible.

When more than three weeks passed and neither he nor any assistant responded, I again wrote him, on April 23. This is that letter, in full:

Although you have told me the evidence in the Ray case will "not be available to anyone" and you have not replied to my letter of March 30, I write you with specific questions that should involve no question of secrecy, the rights of the accused or anything like that.

Does the evidence establish the manner in which the telescopic sight was mounted and adjusted to have been by an expert gunsmith, not by an average handyman-mechanic?

Does the evidence establish the exact make and type of bullet used in the murder, and if so, what? The press indicates soft-nosed Peters only but a number of kinds of bullet with varying charges are available. If it does not and there were other bullets in the weapon, what kind and make were they, with what charges? Does the evidence prove or do the experts believe the bullet used was a hollow-point or similar bullet?

Was the mark of the rifle on the window-sill used to prove that the rifle was rested there for the shooting? If not, for what other purpose was this evidence introduced?

These are questions I as a writer must ask myself and must report the answers. I hope you will agree with me that in a case like this one, with all the unusual aspects and special interests involved, nothing that can properly be made available to the people should be suppressed.

One other question: was there spectrographic or similar testing to establish manufacture, etc., or origin similar or identical to any bullets found in the weapon or elsewhere?

Thank you for any information you may provide. In fairness to you, I tell you that if you refuse to answer I will feel it incumbent upon me to report that in my book. Without it I would not be able to record or report why the essential information is not in it, why I might have to conjecture. I will also offer the opinion that this is the kind of evidence that would have been offered and tested had there been a trial and that only the deal that eliminated the trial makes it possible to suppress it.

Since then, silence. The facts require no amplification, nor does the attitude of the prosecutor.

In this letter, I had carefully restricted myself to the most obvious aspects of the tangible evidence. The prosecution claimed Ray had used the rifle it produced in court, the rifle found at the scene of the crime. It had the missile taken from the body of the victim. What I sought was proof that the very precise science available proved this to be the case, that the bullet *had* been fired from that rifle to the exclusion of all others, the proper requirement of evidence and the law. Certainly, there could be no secrecy about this, the very heart of the case.

But there was.

Narrowly as I had restricted this simple request, I had read the transcript and had been persuaded that, guilty or innocent, Ray was framed. I did not anticipate Canale would permit examination of what he deliberately suppressed. Therefore, the day after my second letter to Canale, I wrote Carl W. Belcher, Chief of the General Crimes Section of the Criminal Division of the Department of Justice, regarding, among other things, the transcript of the court proceeding in England. He had replied to a letter I had written Attorney General John Mitchell about the Presidential assassination. In it he had said, without really responding to my letter, that "we do appreciate the sincerity of your offer of assistance to us," that "we would welcome receipt of your views from time to time," that my "views will receive due consideration." (The official attitude is politely but with brutal frankness stated this way, "There is no reason to believe that further investigation would serve to eliminate the doubts you and others have voiced." And, "further exchanges of correspondence between yourself and the Department of Justice on this matter will serve no useful purpose." In plain English, despite the contrary public statements of the Department of Justice, there is no continuing investigation of the Presidential assassination and the government will not seriously consider the possibility the Warren Report is in any respect in error. And, it will not respond to proper inquiry.)

Also, after writing Mitchell, I had gotten unconfirmed reports that FBI agents in New Orleans had been spreading slander about me, and I had asked in my letter if this were true (for I found it difficult to believe) and, if not, for written denial of it. Further, there were a number of other outstanding questions left by earlier correspondence with the Department of Justice. His silence, his failure to make available to me what is required to be, his refusal even to give me copies of press releases, impelled me to recount some of the unanswered open questions. Here I quote only portions of my response:

If you were a judge rather than an attorney, would you say the record is consistent with the content and tone of your letter of March 26 to me or inconsistent, that you have been open with me, that through you the government has been responsive?

I asked of you certain material to which I believe I am entitled. I asked questions the answers to which had been promised in the previous administration. I believe, without benefit of a law degree, that the material I seek is guaranteed me by the law you are supposed to be upholding.

And there has not been even the *pro forma* denial that might have been expected to the report that agents of the FBI had defamed me. . . .

On March 31 I asked for the evidence presented in court in England in the case of James Earl Ray. Now it would seem that what was presented in open court is public, that you have copies of it, having presented it, and that there should be no problem in providing copies to me. I asked for permission to read the transcripts of the court proceeding. Are you classifying this as "secret"?. . .

After waiting a month and a half, I again wrote the new Attorney General, referring to my requests concerning both the Presidential assassination and the Ray case:

After I twice wrote you beginning three months ago, I got a non-responsive reply, for you, in the name of your Assistant Attorney General in charge of the Criminal Division, from his Chief of the General Crimes Section. Without my ever having gotten any kind of honest or meaningful answer to any inquiry of your Department, under any administration, this one began with the bald statement "that further exchange of correspondence between yourself and the Department of Justice on this matter will serve no useful purpose."

At this point, after five unanswered letters subsequent to my receipt of this accurate forecast that you would never respond, letters in which I asked for access to what I am entitled under the law it is your obligation to enforce, it looks very much as if the Department of Justice is more afraid that correspondence *would* serve a useful purpose, a purpose it fears.

As I wrote earlier, I do understand that busy executives must delegate to those under them what they cannot attend personally, as they must also depend upon others for the information they have. This in no way diminishes the responsibility of those in charge. The Attorney General still runs the Department of Justice. It is, I believe, your responsibility to see that the laws are observed, by you and by your Department, as it is to see that citizens making proper inquiries get proper response within a reasonable time.

When a citizen asks his Department of Justice for access to court records and cannot get an answer, things have passed a deplorable state in a country such as ours. I have made this request; you have not responded. Practically, this means you have refused me. I believe you cannot.

After you or your office referred my first two letters to Mr. Belcher, I thereafter wrote him. Because he has not once responded, in any way, I again address you. I have two purposes. To the degree I can, I want to be certain that you know the situation, for the responsibility is yours, and, if necessary, I want to invoke the laws that entitle me to that which I seek. I prefer not to have to resort to this, as I would hope you would, too.

I made specific requests for specific information in letters to your Department between March 30 and April 23. If I am refused this information, I respectfully request citation of the authority under which you refuse it. In each case I also ask that you provide me with the forms and instructions I will need to seek to obtain this information under the "Freedom of Information" law. It is my intention to invoke the provisions of this law, if necessary. May I call to your attention that I have, in the past, asked the Government for the means of utilizing this law without ever having been so equipped? I do not think this was the intent of Congress in enacting the law.

I itemized those things I had requested and been improperly denied. The letter concluded:

Among those unanswered requests referred to above is the evidence presented in court in England. I would now like to broaden that to include that used in Memphis, directly and indirectly, in the case of James Earl Ray.

When I make requests of the National Archives, there now is a delay of not less than two months before there is any kind of response, when there is one. I believe this, in itself, clouds the purposes and integrity of the government. Your own Department does not respond at all. I do hope you will correct this, that you will agree that when a citizen and more, a writer, makes proper inquiry of the Government, response should be as prompt as possible.

The Attorney General, too, considers himself above the law. No forms. No response.

With this long and incredible history of government suppressions, there was no mistaking the intent to continue suppressions, for they had been deliberate and there was no reason to believe that the government that did the suppressing would, without compulsion, end them. Here, however, as required by the "Freedom of Information" law, I asked to be put in a position to invoke this law.

If I try to sue without complying with the law, without filling in these forms, the government has automatic response, a means of getting my suit thrown out of court. They need only allege I failed to "exhaust" my "administrative remedies," the legal phraseology. And it would be true, for the government prevents it! They cannot lose—and the law has no meaning.

In blatant violation of this law, every agency of government of which I had asked the requisite information and the requisite forms had failed to respond, refused to send them—which means tried to keep me from using the law Congress enacted to insure "Freedom of Information." The Attorney General, the nation's foremost upholder of the law, by failing to respond, eliminated any doubt the other and numerous cases could be accidental. He made it clear this is formal government policy.

Hoping the respected traditions of England might still be followed in the era of political assassinations, that its political vassaldom to whatever administration holds power in the United States might not overcome the well-known British love of the law, I made a number of efforts there.

Several friends among British reporters made unsuccessful efforts to get the public evidence for me to study. I was surprised not to hear of any protest in their papers.

When the Chief Magistrate was asked for a copy of the trial transcript, he directed his chief clerk to answer. This is what he said:

> There is not available any complete transcript of the proceedings and the arguments at the time of Ray's appearance. Certain oral evidence was given including the making of a statement by Ray, but all copies of that were sent to the Secretary of State at the Home Office in London for transmission to the State Department at Washington, together with the papers which had been sent to this Court from Washington. As far as I know the Home Office has not retained copies of those papers.

If this is not in the tradition of Runnymede, it is consistent with courts and justice in the era of American political murders. A court that doesn't have any complete record of its own proceeding!

I asked a young woman in England (whose identity I disguise to prevent the reprisal that is possible) to make a number of requests for me, including at the United States Embassy. Here, predictably, there was a brush-off. Ditto for the British government. After consultation with a British lawyer, she phoned the Michael Dresden firm, was told Michael Eugene was "in charge of the case," and spoke to him.

"It turns out he has all the papers," she reported to me, "but he said he can't open his files as the case is not closed yet. . . . He said you were about fifth on the list [so it would seem my reporter friends *had* asked for the evidence] . . . . Also, he wasn't familiar with your name so he said he would check with the FBI."

"Check with the FBI"? *Ray's* lawyer check with the FBI? This is the philosophy and the practice of the police state. I could hardly believe it. I asked my friend if it were possible she had misunderstood or had made a mistake. She, too, had been considerably shaken by it and had consulted someone she trusted, immediately fearing there might be retaliation against her. In response to my inquiry, she assured me "there was no mistake," she had it straight.

To eliminate any possibility of error and still hoping to be able to study the *public* evidence, not any secrets, on May 24 I wrote Eugene:

> Miss _____ spoke to you on my behalf at my request. She asked for copies of the papers filed by the United States Government against your then client, James Earl Ray. She reports you declined to make this information available because "the case is not closed yet" and because a hearing is scheduled on his behalf. She also reports that because you are not familiar with my name you said you "would check with the F.B.I."
>
> This combination fills me with the deepest misgivings. Of course it is possible that bright as she is, Miss _____ might have misunderstood or misinterpreted what you said. Therefore, I write you directly to eliminate any possibility of error.
>
> The United States papers report you represented Ray's interest when the request for extradition was filed (I imagine a thankless, unpleasant task). They also report the data I seek is part of the court record, part of the public record, what in the United States is termed "public domain."
>
> Now, the F.B.I. represents the side opposed to your client. It also is the side opposed to me and my work and writing. It is the federal police. Is it customary for English lawyers to consult the federal police when known writers who have established credentials in the field of their work (and if mine were previously unknown to you, they were, I am confident, reported) make proper inquiry, especially for access to the *public* record? Would you regard it as proper for the F.B.I. to make any response to your inquiry at all? Do you believe the federal police in your country or mine should maintain files on or spread any information, favorable or unfavorable, about any citizens, particularly, in our societies, writers? Further, do you expect the F.B.I., which I have accused in the subtitle of one of my books of engaging in a "cover-up" and whose dubious record in the

assassinations and their investigations I have exhaustively exposed to public scrutiny, would be dispassionate? When you consider you need dependable information, do you customarily consult the enemy of those about whom you seek fact?

Under the circumstances, I presume you will extend me the courtesy of copies of your inquiry and any responses.

What I seek is the alleged evidence *against* your client, by those *prosecuting* him, not what is secret from the prosecution because it is his defense. What I seek in particular is the "evidence" presented *by* the F.B.I. When I have doubts about the integrity of this "evidence" and for that reason seek it, not to be dependent upon the press accounts of it, do you think it was the proper course to check with the F.B.I. about me, the customary police-state method? And how does denying those who write that Ray killed no one the evidence that, properly analyzed and understood, might establish this, help either justice or him? I fail to see why you deny me the public record, particularly because I have written that your client is not guilty of that with which he is charged, was "framed." (I believe and have from the first believed and repeatedly said on radio and TV here that he was a decoy.)

Perhaps you did not ask yourself why a writer in the United States seeks from England that evidence made public in England by the United States Government. The answer is simple. Despite the clear law, such as the "Freedom of Information Act," which requires that the government make this information available, it refuses to make any response at all to the request. Of course, I can sue. But such a suit, if I could afford it, which I cannot, could also be indefinitely postponed and for all practical purposes, my situation would be unchanged. I would not have this information to which I am entitled. The record on this and on this subject is entirely one way on this, whether or not you had any way of knowing it. And were I to win, as another plaintiff did several months ago, the government would appeal. And that it would also continue through all the available channels so the result would be the same.

I hope the foregoing is sufficient for you to understand the apprehensions what Miss _____ reported cause me. I would welcome your assurance that there is a misunderstanding. Because of the present situation, I think it would be helpful to the record and to you if you would also give me the assurance that neither you nor your firm have or have had or anticipate any connection of any kind with the United States Government or any of its agents or agencies. I do not assume this. But because of the foregoing, I do think this assurance, in writing, would help eliminate any suspicions that might develop.

My purpose in asking for those approximately 200 pages of "evidence" presented by the side opposed to you was to be able to quote it directly. I have written most of the book. The new hearing is scheduled for before you can receive this letter. When it is completed, I expect to complete the book as expeditiously as possible, as I believe you can understand. If I have not had access to the documents used against Ray, I will, as I think incumbent, specify in the book exactly why. I will say who I asked, what response, if any, was made, and then quote the papers, the only course left. And the papers will leave no doubt that I have been denied the *public* record, what in this country, under our law, cannot be denied anyone, especially not writers.

I sincerely hope you will see your way clear to providing copies of the "evidence" and to answering this letter at your earliest convenience.

Again, it seems unnecessary to make further comment. I merely report that the mold manufactured for the Presidential murder, the shape into which everyone and everything is forced by the federal government, is neither broken nor avoided. The silence is permeating. It has become an awful crime, this silence.

Michael Eugene, too, is silent.

The one exception was Canale. His brief, brusque slit in the shroud of silent suppression, perhaps attributable to the separation of Memphis from the seat of federal power, is affirmation of the obvious.

It has been ordained that, as long as it can be compelled, law or no law, any possibility of examining the evidence will be eliminated.

This is to ordain truth, justice.

This is the reality, not the trapping, of the police state.

This is Orwell, 1969.

5. Arthur Hanes Loves the Gatlinburg Ski Slope and Defends Communist Dupes

These are not the only letters I wrote, but the single statement for Canale by his administrative assistant — "None of the evidence not in the transcript will be available to anyone"—is the only response. It is also a prediction, for all those with custody of the evidence have imposed *total* suppression on it. None not used in the show minitrial is ever to be seen by anyone. I have written to just about all the silent principals of the case — not just the officials but all the other concerned parties (all those whose addresses were readily available). I think it important to record the unofficial silence that parallels the official, the steadfast and complete refusal of all those in any way involved to say anything, answer any questions, do anything—save, on some occasions by a few, to make propaganda — or money — out of the crime and the accused. In due course and proper context, we shall come to them.

Now we return to Ray. His "first visit with his lawyer since being returned from a London jail," in the words of the Associated Press, was while "tucked behind the most elaborate security screen ever seen here."

June 16, United Press International carried a story from Birmingham telling about and quoting Hanes. As of then, he had "tentatively accepted this case." He was identified as "mayor of Birmingham in the early 1960's when the city was the center of civil rights demonstrations led by Dr. King. He later defended two Ku Klux Klansmen charged with murdering Mrs. Viola Liuzzo, a white woman . . . . [when] Klansmen Collie Leroy Wilkins, Jr., and Eugene Thomas [were tried] on State charges of murdering Mrs. Liuzzo," the Wilkins jury hung and Thomas was acquitted. "He later represented both men against federal charges that they conspired to violate Mrs. Liuzzo's civil rights. The two men were convicted and sentenced to 10 years in prison."

Further, "Hanes is a former agent for the Federal Bureau of

Investigation. He said he resigned from the FBI 'because I felt I couldn't express myself about the growing Communist influence in our country as an agent."

With these credentials so uniquely identical with extremist belief, "Hanes said he had 'no idea whatsoever' why Ray asked him to represent him."

UPI might have had a few more words on Hanes's record. AP did two days later, reporting that, when he was Birmingham's mayor, "international attention was focused on Public Safety Commissioner Eugene 'Bull' Connor and the use of police dogs and fire hoses" against human beings. It says he defended the men in the Liuzzo case (the story refers to three of them) and, "When he way mayor, Hanes accused King of being one of the instigators of Birmingham's troubles.... Hanes, 51, comes from an old Alabama family. His grandfather was a Confederate officer . . . father was a Methodist minister. . . ."

The wire services, particularly in such a case, could have been more definite in their reporting on Ray's lawyer (two days later, on June 20, Hanes stated that he was taking the case: "As of now, I will be his lawyer"), but they did give the proper tone to the inadequate portrait.

Hanes offered different and contradictory accounts of his being paid or how he would be paid. The June 20 AP story from London carried each of these: "he 'would not discuss fees and the source of any funds' "; "Asked who paid for the trip, he replied, 'No comment.' " Later, he said of his fee, "Somebody will provide, the neighbors or some way" (Ray's neighbors? In Missouri State Penitentiary, perhaps?). "I have faith I'll get by." "Hanes had been quoted as saying he 'understands that this man has funds.' When asked whether sufficient money was available for a long legal battle, he replied, "I'll start it off, like the kickoff of a game. If any group were behind it, I'd of course carry it on.' "

We will see why he had "no comment," "would not discuss fees," whether he ever depended on "the neighbors" to "provide," and if he had no more than the pious hope, "I'll get by."

The same day, in a *New York Times* interview, he was quoted thus:

I work for money, but I will not tell you who will pay. I can not discuss the fees. I have the faith I'll get by and I'll meet expenses.

He regarded the case as "a challenge." He said his well-known anti-civil rights views were "far afield."

Time magazine for June 28 added this little note:

> In 1963, though just out of office as a bitterly anti-integration
> mayor, he continued to fight against Martin Luther King's
> Birmingham campaign . . . .

Soon the AP had dug up his statement that the black efforts to get better treatment than having police dogs and high-pressure water hoses turned on them "were not spontaneous but had been carefully plotted at a Communist-inspired workshop . . . ."

The docile blacks, content at being battered and bitten, in the Hanes view of life and people, would never, left to themselves, have a word to say. Nothing pleases them more than such abuse (for which Hanes was responsible). To protest, they have to be "inspired." This protest has to be "plotted." It could not be natural or "spontaneous." And where "plotted"? In a "workshop" that was "Communist inspired" — the phrase used to escape retribution for false use of the libelous slur "Communist." It is a standard propaganda term of the most extreme, the fascist-minded. It is used to say the person or persons they do not like are "Communist" when they dare not use this word because if they do they can be sued.

In short, any black protest is Communist, King was a Communist, and — here we take a small jump — anyone who did anything to or against King thus became a true patriot.

On his return from his third trip to England, interviewed by the AP at New York's Kennedy Airport, Hanes alluded to "powerful forces at work" to divide Americans against themselves. "It has been shown that there is such a thing as an international Communist conspiracy and you must admit they are working in this country," he said.

Presumably, not his racist enemies but "the Communists" were responsible for King's murder. No wonder Hanes found the FBI too restricting for his views! Hanes's "defense" is not of Ray but of racists, of whom he is one of the smoother.

Hanes set the stage for the trial, his adventure, the "challenge."

Security precautions were stringent. Reportedly when he saw his client, Hanes had to frustrate such devices as closed-circuit television, which certainly would intrude on the secrecy with which client and lawyer should be able to confer.

On July 22, at the hearing to determine the date of his trial, Ray was silent in the courtroom. In response to the two indictments — the first for shooting and killing King, the second for "carrying a dangerous weapon" — Hanes said, "The defendant wishes to enter a plea of not guilty." Trial was set for November 12.

A week later, AP reported Hanes "confirmed" that he had carried a pistol on one of his trips to see his client at the Shelby County jail, crossing the state line between Alabama and Tennessee. But he said he surrendered it voluntarily before seeing Ray.

"I had a gun on me," Arthur J. Hanes said in Birmingham, Alabama. "As soon as I walked into the building I displayed it and my briefcase, just as anyone would."

Naturally. What is more natural than lawyers carrying guns, with all those "Communist plots" fermenting? And, of course, "anyone would" carry a pistol across state lines and into a jail!

It made no difference that his Alabama permit was invalid in Tennessee.

By this time, July 29, it was not only King who was the "red" victim:

Hanes, in an airport news conference, declared that Ray was a victim of a "Communist left-wing conspiracy."

There was relative silence in the press in the next few months. The first indication of trouble appeared in reports about Ray's contacts with the lawyer, J. B. Stoner, a would-be American Hitler, lawyer for and head of the National States Rights Party, a tiny, racist political party that, like its members, finds the Klan too moderate. On this basis, it recruits from the Klan. Stoner and the NSRP are even more anti-Semitic than the Klan is anti-black.

On September 27, 1968, in court and about the time it leaked out that Ray was in touch with Stoner, Hanes said: "Serious difficulties have arisen between me and my client on the best way to handle the defense. At some future day I may have to withdraw as counsel for James Earl Ray." He said this statement had been agreed to by Ray the day before.

On October 2, Martin Waldron wrote in the *New York Times:*

J. B. Stoner . . . National States Rights Party . . . Ku Klux Klan . . . apostle of anti-Negro violence, visited James Earl Ray in his Memphis jail cell last Saturday . . . discussed with Ray the possibility of his joining Ray's defense . . . Ray's attorney, Arthur J. Hanes, of Birmingham, refused to accept Mr. Stoner as an associate in the defense.

We shall see more of Stoner as the story progresses.

Then, on the eve of the trial, Ray fired Hanes.

Friday, November 15, 1968, five days after it happened, the *New York Times* interviewed Hanes at "The Club," a plush dining and drinking place high above Birmingham's south side, on Red Mountain. Hanes was a little philosophical, a little more specific, and disclosed a little more about himself, Ray, and the Ray family.

In addition to his career as an FBI agent, Hanes is also "a one-time contract employee of the Central Intelligence Agency." (Part of the CIA's Bay of Pigs preparations were in Birmingham.)

It was "entirely possible" that he had been picked as Ray's attorney to underscore the racial aspect of the assassination of the Rev. Dr. Martin Luther King, Jr., and that he had never been expected to be the actual trial lawyer.

Hanes also said it is "possible that Ray had been told, even before Dr. King was murdered, that 'he should contact me' if he was arrested."

But he is a little put out at "the brusque manner in which he and his son, Arthur Hanes, Jr., were dismissed from the Ray case last Sunday night" —when they arrived at the jail to give Ray a new gray suit to wear during his trial. He was handed a note saying he had been fired.

For some months he had been aware of many indications that Ray might be preparing to switch attorneys and about a month ago he became virtually certain that this was Ray's plan.

He had discussed this with Judge W. Preston Battle and Shelby County District Attorney General Phil Canale.

"But Ray didn't say anything and Art and I had to proceed on the assumption that we were going to trial and so we put together just a great defense for Ray, including a few bombshells."

"Put together" are exactly the right words. Whether it was "for Ray" may be questioned. We return to that. But, when "he became virtually certain" that Ray was going to dump him, was this derring-do lawyer, this former big-city mayor who had been willing to face international public indignation to turn vicious dogs on people, this man who had qualified for both the FBI and the CIA, too timid to ask his client? If he had any reluctance about being spurned, so to speak, at the very altar, could he not have asked Ray? And what about his statement in September?

Hanes also disclosed that he was not Ray's only choice and that he had received advance assurances of the availability of an enormous fund for his fee. Ray had also asked famous Boston trial lawyer F. Lee Bailey to handle his defense. Bailey immediately telephoned Michael Eugene, Ray's English lawyer, to report he could not. Eugene then phoned Hanes from England June 13, saying Ray "told me that $100,000 was available." This should have been enough to satisfy Hanes's expenses and fees. He had no reason to believe Ray had this kind of money. This should have suggested the existence of a conspiracy. It could explain his statement, "of course I'd carry on" if "any group were behind it." He had said, recall, "I work for money." One hundred thousand dollars *is* "money," a powerful concomitant of principle.

The very first thing he and his son did was to go away for three days and mull it over—as soon as they got "the Eugene telephone call and the letter from Ray."

They surely did "put together" quite a package, a line of reasoning it is no exaggeration to describe as "a few bombshells." In their three-day retreat at their summer home, he and his son

concluded that for an assassin to murder Dr. King and to elude capture for more than two months while more than 3,000 Federal Bureau of Investigation agents were searching for him would require elaborate planning.

So far, his reasoning is sound.

Mr. Hanes said they could think of only two groups that they considered capable of carrying out this type of plan—the C.I.A. and black militants, with Red Chinese or Cuban backing.

He quickly eliminated his former employer, the C.I.A.

Mr. Hanes decided that he and his son should undertake Ray's defense, notwithstanding their conclusion and that they should proceed on the assumption that the murder had been plotted and financed by what he called "black militants with foreign ties."

The *New York Times*, apparently, found it not at all unusual that this soaring spirit, so restrained in its anti-Communism by FBI employment, was willing to defend a member of a "Communist" conspiracy. This is a mite stronger than the "Communist-inspired" demonstrations he found so reprehensible. There he used dogs. This is a conspiracy to kill a great public figure, by "black militants, with Red Chinese or Cuban backing," a conspiracy to tear the country asunder. With that $100,000 to buttress his principle, Hanes was willing to defend the man he presumed a Communist dupe—and defend them through him.

Mr. Hanes said that the attitude of Ray's brothers, John Ray and Jerry Ray, had helped him form the conclusion that he was never to be the defense attorney at Ray's trial. "You would expect the family to flock around the attorney to offer help and advice, but I couldn't even get close to them. I offered to meet them in St. Louis, Memphis, Birmingham or anyplace else. But I never did see either one of them."

The Rays have their own explanation of their relations with Hanes, as we shall see.

Not until after Hanes was dismissed did he learn that "the two brothers had ordered a copy of the British hearings." "That certainly indicated they had tried to find another attorney," he said.

If it does, it is not immediately apparent why and how it does. Having the court record in their brother's trial more likely means they had great interest in knowing what happened there, *exactly* what happened and was adduced. In turn, this could mean they were curious about their brother and his predicament. But it could also betoken other interests. It certainly meant that they were not the impoverished men portrayed in the newspapers, for transcripts are expensive, or that they had sources of funds for such purposes.

But it did not require this *ex post facto* revelation to tell Hanes the brothers wanted another lawyer. The newspapers had earlier quoted Jerry Ray's desire that Percy Foreman handle the defense. It was not at all secret or late in becoming known.

We have not exhausted Hanes's logic, inconsistencies, and theories, nor have we really plumbed his "defense." To that we return. We leave him with his devotion to principle, befitting a lawyer, a former FBI and CIA man, the former mayor of a major city—not with remorse over never having gotten that $100,000 or his consuming concern over the "Communist plot" that was about to take over the country, but with his philosophic resignation over the contempt-of-court citation based on his allegations of the non-existing "red" plot. (The charge had been brought against him by Judge Battle, on the grounds that such pretrial comments would prejudice potential jurors.) Hanes had:

. . . . posted a $1,000 cash bond with the court in Memphis Tuesday as a guarantee for his return later to be sentenced for the contempt of court.

"They can keep the $1,000," Mr. Hanes said. "But I guess I'll have to find a new ski resort. I don't suppose I can ever go to Gatlinburg again." Gatlinburg, Tennessee, is a ski resort town frequented by many residents of Alabama. Mr. Hanes said that under Tennessee law he cannot be extradited for contempt of court.

Rather than leave the reader tormented by the great personal tragedy that befell this noble man of principle in the undaunted pursuit of his strong and ennobling beliefs, I risk anticipating what is to follow to note that, when the judge who sat on the case died (of one of the numerous convenient heart attacks that are so frequent in the stories of these assassinations), one of the first acts of his successor was to nullify the contempt citations.

So, the Arthur Haneses, junior and senior, can safely ski in Gatlinburg.

I wrote Hanes, Ray's defender (whose faith in his client's innocence is not reported in any of the numerous news stories I have quoted), as I wrote all the principals in this case. He did not respond.

If the Haneses never latched onto that reported $100,000, they did get adequate recompense from what Huie paid Ray for his story. As we shall see, they admit getting $31,000.

His next good offer in this case was from *Look*. He tried to deal with *Life* but didn't make it. So he signed with *Look* and, in the issue that carried Huie's third installment of his version of the Ray case, proclaimed his client's guilt. He was in good company in that April 15 issue. With him were Ray's other "defenders."

6. William Bradford Huie:
"I Cannot Reveal All That
I Have Found To Be True . . .
I Know . . . I Have Learned . . .
the Features of the Plot"

If Hanes presents himself as befits a lawyer, as a man of the loftiest principle, Huie makes no such pretense. He frames himself in dollar bills and for them claims not purity but effectiveness. He presupposes the guilt of those he buys and assumes he gets what he buys and pays for, information. This simple formula has worked well, made him rich and famous, a writer whose books make movies and millions.

Until James Earl Ray.

Ray made a fool of him.

It may be that Huie needed little help—that his conceit made a fool of him, with only a little help from Ray.

Whichever way it is, it happened.

He is the man about whom Mel Ziegler wrote, he "likes to say he is in the 'writing business,' and he thinks of himself as something of a William Bradford Huie Corp., his typewriter mass-producing words at a rate of 500 a day for $150,000 annual income. Researchers, lawyers, accountants, agents, producers, editors and publishers—Huie is fond of saying—depend on his productivity."

"The great advantage that I have over other people in this business," this inventor of "dollar journalism" said, is money. "No matter what it costs me, I'm willing to pay it . . . . If I have to give some rascal a couple of thousand dollars to find out what happened, well, for godsake, I give it to him and find out . . . . I don't have any competition."

He paid rascal Ray's beneficiaries more than twice as much as he paid all of those from whom he bought the stories of their participation in the Emmett Till case.

Perhaps the problem faced by this man who "pries . . . lips apart with dollar signs" was dual: the large stake he had in this case and his failure to heed those warning signs he did see. His investment began with a sum larger than the $30,000 he acknowledged. He spent a fortune traveling and ostensibly checking out what Ray told him. As he must have realized early in his own investigations, he also invested his reputation and the future of the William Bradford Huie Corp.

He says of those he buys and sells, they "are not criminals in the ordinary sense. These are men who commit murders and think they are doing right." They have the approval of their white supremacist society. "If you lined them up, they would all have something in common. But if you put Ray in that group he doesn't fit. Sure, he has certain inherited racial attitudes, but he doesn't fit."

The cynic knew Ray didn't fit, but the dollar sign pried back.

He knew Ray was a liar and said so. He knew the others he bought also lied.

He also knew Ray was lying to his own lawyer:

> I know Ray will try to deceive me. When he starts with his own lawyer, it is natural for him to be deceitful. We assume that there are going to be a certain amount of lies. Then you go and you find out that you have got truth here and truth here and truth here and then, maybe you run up against something that is obviously not truth. So, you circle around and come back with something else. It's a constant effort of trial and error, a constant effort to get the man to tell you the truth . . . . Hell, he's a moody sort of individual.

After poking fun at the FBI for spending more than twice as much as he had for their Neshoba County information in the killing of the three civil-rights workers so brutally murdered before being buried under the dam being built ("hell, they spent $100,000 of the taxpayers' money on this stuff"), he pontificated, "There's a difference between information and evidence." He then proclaimed, as I quoted earlier, "I will publish the truth only."

In a way, to recall for the reader, Huie kept this promise. He and *Look* published *both* sides. He first implied Ray's innocence of the crime of murder—and was well paid for it—and said there had been a conspiracy. He later called Ray the lone killer.

His first *Look* story, in the issue dated November 12, 1968—the date scheduled for Ray's Memphis trial—is explicit in title and doctrine: "The Story of James Earl Ray and the Conspiracy To Kill Martin Luther King." It says that of which there can be, in my view, no doubt:

51

There was a conspiracy. It does not say Ray was the murderer.

Well in advance of publication, helped by leaks and releases, the article was widely and accurately reflected in the stories and headlines that sell magazines. For example, the *New Orleans-Item* of October 29, in a three-column-wide story, carried this head, "Ray To Claim 'Decoy' Role In Murder, Author Says."

Saying he was disturbed by all the pretrial publicity, from both Hanes and the government (publicity dominated by what he didn't pinpoint, deliberate "leaks" from the FBI), Judge Battle appointed a committee of seven local lawyers to study the situation and whether or not it could influence the fairness of any trial. On November 4 they "advised" him "to institute contempt of court proceedings" against Huie and *Look*. This was but a week before the trial was scheduled. Huie said, "Everything we have published about the Ray case has been carefully screened by expert legal counsel." *Look* later announced its "fullest confidence in Huie and stands ready to help him in any way possible." So, in addition to that great and unique Huie talent, these stories had the full benefit of *Look's* and Cowles Publications' enormous facilities and "expert legal counsel." (It was on the basis of this committee's assessment that Judge Battle also charged Hanes.)

I was in New Orleans on my continuing investigations of the Presidential assassination when the first story appeared. Naturally, having written a book dealing in part with him, I read Ray's story with great interest. Much of what Huie said was impressive. In essence, it made sense and was in accord with what was, from the beginning, obvious to me. (When asked about the King assassination in radio and TV appearances prior to Ray's capture, I had described the then-unnamed assassin of the news accounts, later Eric Starvo Galt, as a decoy.)

Still, Huie had devoted much of it to the easy stuff, to what was not related to the murder. With the expenditure of much time and money, he had retraced much of Ray's traveling after his jailbreak. This, it seems, is the kind of stuff Ray could safely disclose without worry about the retribution of fellow conspirators who might easily reach into jail or have long memories. That Ray told the truth about his easily checked travels did not mean he told the truth about either his part in the conspiracy or about those he served.

There was very little on the conspiracy or conspirators. This worried me, but *Look* promised more on that in the next issue, in two weeks.

In this first article, Huie's account of the man who recruited Ray into the conspiracy, in Canada in August 1967, is as follows:

> A man whom Ray calls Raoul and describes to me as a blond Latin about 35, and whom Ray took to be a seaman, showed interest in him.

Precisely at the point where he goes into the conspiracy and Raoul, just a few paragraphs before it but on the same page, Huie palms off Ray's adoption of the "Eric Starvo Galt" name and identity he assumed in Canada while living there after his jail break, and with it all the other false identities and identifications as accomplished by Ray working alone, with no help, no fellow conspirators:

> He chose Eric S. Galt, and since there is a real Eric S. Galt in Toronto, the assumption has been that Ray saw his name in print. But he says no. Between Windsor and Toronto, he passed the city of Galt, and he says he chose Galt when he saw it on an exit marker. He says he chose Eric only in the process of seeking something different from the more common first names.

There is a lemming in this writing. Ray took the name Eric *Starvo* Galt. Huie says Eric *S.* Galt. Thus, he avoids the need to explain the odd middle name, which cannot fit this scheme. (From the newspapers alone, Huie should have known the truth about "Starvo," as we will see in our assessment of the evidence bearing on conspiracy.) Aside from the astounding Ray resemblance to the real Eric Galt and two other Canadians, Paul Bridgeman and Sneyd, whose identities he had assumed, complete with identical scars, it is asking too much to believe Ray could have made up so unusual a name and, with the right middle initial, caught a live one he also resembles.

Here Huie casually omits reference to Bridgeman and Sneyd, thus hiding either the ease with which Ray conned him, or his own dishonesty, or both. This little incident about the Galt name characterizes Ray as a brazen rather than an accomplished liar and Huie as much less of a cynic and skeptic than he pretends to be. He should never have fallen for this story.

Huie depends on a remarkable, entirely isolated, coincidence to get Ray into the conspiracy:

> He frequented Neptune Tavern, 121 West Commissioners Street. I visited it. The ceiling lights are suspended from pilot wheels. There is a pilot wheel up over the bottles back of the bar. The furniture is massive oak, in its natural color, and signs welcome all seamen,

promise highest prices for English money and inform you that "Nous Servons les Repas." The menu is chalked on a blackboard furnished by Molson's Biere.

On his third or fourth night in the Neptune, Ray says he "sort of let the word get around that he had had a little trouble down in the States, that he was looking for ID and capital, and just might be available for activities that didn't involve too much risk." This resulted in a contact. A man whom Ray calls Raoul and describes to me as being a blond Latin about 35, and whom Ray took to be a seaman, showed interest in him. They began cautious verbal explorations, with Raoul hinting that if Ray was willing to assist in certain projects, Raoul might be able to provide Ray ID and capital. Ray says this exploration continued during "at least eight meetings" over a period of three weeks.

This is the novelist in Huie, not the reporter. All of that color and detail lend credibility and are calculated to lend credibility to a weak tale, one that should have inspired his suspicion as it should ours. That the menu is chalked on an ad for beer in an oak-furnished bar with pilot wheels is immaterial. What *is* material is what is missing in all this first-person stuff—anything connecting an obscure Canadian bar with a conspiracy to murder King in Memphis the next year.

Again using novelists' techniques, Huie switches to Ray's brief affair with a sensitive woman. He devotes the balance of this page, the next two, and the beginning of the third to the sex and schmalz, then returns to Raoul briefly, only to return to the woman with whom Ray bedded. This relates to nothing but an innate contempt for the reader. It is a disguise for Huie's failure. The woman serves two purposes: to establish that Ray could have sex with a woman, if he waited not less than eight years for it (so what?); and to make the rest of Ray's very thin version of the conspiracy seem credible. What is needed and is totally lacking here are two things: any confirmation of Ray's "Raoul" story and any indication, no matter how slight, that Huie even looked for it. It would seem a safe assumption, given his experience and the value of all the money he paid and expected, that he looked and did not find.

Ray reports at least *five more* meetings at the Neptune with Raoul. Huie cites no person he found who saw either man or even thinks he might have. Here is Huie's version:

From August 8 to the 18th, Ray says he talked at least five more times with Raoul in the Neptune Tavern. And Raoul made him this proposition:

1. That Ray would meet Raoul in the railroad station at Windsor at 3 P.M. on Monday, August 21.

2. That Ray would make several trips across the border from Windsor to Detroit for Raoul, using both the bridge and the tunnel border crossings, carrying packages concealed in the old red Plymouth.

3. That Ray would then sell the Plymouth and go by train or bus to Birmingham, Ala. There, Ray would lie low, take no risks, pull no holdups, accumulate a little ID, and wait for instructions by general delivery mail.

4. That Raoul would pay "living expenses" and also come to Birmingham and buy Ray a "suitable car."

5. That after a few weeks or months, after a little joint activity, Raoul would pay Ray $12,000 and give him a passport and "other ID" and help him go "anywhere in the world."

6. That Ray would ask no questions. (Ray told me: "Every time I tried to ask Raoul a question, he told me straight to remember that he wasn't paying me to ask questions.") Raoul did, however, reveal to Ray that he (Raoul) had spent some of his time in New Orleans, and he gave Ray a New Orleans telephone number.

Ray wrote to me: "Well, I didn't know what to do. If I took Raoul's proposition, I had to go back to the States and risk the Missouri Pen again. I didn't want to do that. I had sworn I'd never go back. But I was running out of capital again, and I didn't want to risk another hold-up in Canada. I couldn't get on a ship. I couldn't get I.D. So I told Raoul okay I'd meet him in Windsor. But I didn't know then whether I'd meet him or not. The woman in Ottawa seemed to like me. She was my last chance. I hadn't had time to talk to her in Montreal about the passport. So now I was going to Ottawa and tell her something about myself, and if she'd help me get the passport, I wasn't going to meet Raoul."

About the New Orleans number Raoul gave Ray, we hear nothing else from Huie. Either Huie didn't ask for it or Ray wouldn't give it—or Huie got it and found it a fake. Here was the chance to check out the story, a real, solid, tangible lead, and Huie, that stalwart friend of the murdered King, flubs it. He had other sources available, as again we see when we examine the conspiracy evidence, and these, too, he avoided.

Now Huie switches back to the woman for confirmation of what he cannot, through her, get confirmed, in an effort to establish that Raoul is a real person of that name and Ray was truthful:

"Yes, he came to see me," she said. "He had kept in touch by telephone, and he arrived here on August 19. He stayed in a motel on Montreal Road. But he was without a car. We used my car, and I rode him around and showed him the sights."

"He still had the old car," I said. "He told me that he hid it from you, and told you he was without a car, trying to play on your sympathy."

"That sounds strange," she said. "But he did seem worried. For long periods as we rode around, or while we were together at the motel, he said nothing. He just looked at me, like he was trying to get up the nerve to say something.

"I showed him where I work, and all the government buildings and the headquarters of Royal Canadian Mounted Police."

"That's what worried him," I said. "You see, he came here to decide whether to risk telling you some of the truth and asking you to help him get a passport by swearing that you had known him for two years. He told me that he had about decided to risk you, but when you showed him where you worked, and all the government buildings, and the Mountie headquarters—well, he said he just had to conclude that if he told you the truth, you'd just naturally have to turn him down and probably deliver him to the Mounties."

She shook her head. "That's sad," she said. "I never suspected that. And maybe the saddest part is that if he had told me, I guess I would have turned him down. I don't think I would have delivered him to the Mounties, but I couldn't have sworn a lie and helped him get the passport . . . ."

Hearts and flowers. The novelist and his devices, not non-fiction. A careful construction to obscure the fact that nothing in it offers any support of Ray's version of how he got into the conspiracy. This is where Huie's first installment ends.

Huie begins his second piece with his conclusions:

After communicating in writing for two months with James Earl Ray through his attorney, and after traveling to Chicago, Montreal, Ottawa, Los Angeles, and Birmingham and Selma, Ala., to verify what Ray has told me, and to investigate further, I have reached these conclusions:

That the plot to murder Martin Luther King, Jr., existed as early as

56

August 15, 1967, eight months prior to the murder on April 4, 1968. That Ray was drawn unknowingly into this plot in Montreal on August 18, 1967, and thereafter moved as directed by the plotters.

That as late as March 23, 1968, less than two weeks before the murder with which he is charged, Ray did not know that the plot included murder or that it was aimed in any way at Dr. King.

It may all be true. At least, the essence is. There was a conspiracy to kill King and Ray was part of it. This seems without substantial doubt.

Huie then recounts Ray's Raoul-inspired and directed life of petty crime, following which, on Raoul's orders, he goes to Birmingham, ending up in a "boarding house managed by Peter Cherpes at 2608 Highland Avenue." Ray told Huie: "Raoul said he would find a meeting place in Birmingham and mail me the address and time. (I also had the New Orleans phone number he gave me.) I received the letter from him about my second or third day in Birmingham"—"Monday August 28, 1967" Huie adds in brackets.

Here it is necessary to point out that this is the second reference to the mysterious alleged boss of the conspiracy in New Orleans and to his telephone number which Ray had and Huie apparently did not have. That phone number can be the most important single clue to the solution of the crime.

We may also wonder how, with Ray unable to fix the date exactly, Huie did establish the one day on which Ray got Raoul's letter. He does not print or quote the letter. If Ray had had it with him, the authorities would have gotten it. (If they did, what a monster cover-up of a conspiracy!) If Ray had it hidden somewhere, Huie still does not use it. In any event, postmarks indicate the date of sending, not of receiving mail. Another minor mystery of the Ray case.

Now, there is separate confirmation of Ray's contact with a mysterious, wealthy racist in New Orleans. It had been published well before Huie began his work. Louis Lomax, the black writer, wrote a series of sensational stories for the North American Newspaper Alliance within three weeks of the assassination. In Hollywood, Lomax found a former resident of New Orleans, a songwriter, Charles Stein, who had driven from California to New Orleans with Ray in an automobile that seems exactly like the one we will soon describe. Together in a rented car, Lomax and Stein duplicated Stein's trip with Ray. Quite naturally, this was major news in New Orleans. The morning *Times-Picayune* for April 25 carried information "uncovered" by Lomax "about Ray's New Orleans contacts":

On Dec. 16, 1967, Ray was in telephone contact with a major New Orleans industrialist, a man who is considered the economic and political "killer" of the community.

On Dec. 17, 1967, Ray met in person with this New Orleans industrialist. On the day of the meeting, Ray was registered in a motel in New Orleans. The contact between Ray and the industrialist was made from this motel and the meeting with held [sic] in "downtown" New Orleans.

Stein had told Lomax of Ray's phone calls to this New Orleans industrialist before they left the Los Angeles area. He gave a precise description of the Texas gas station from which the calls were made, near a town after they passed El Paso. After some searching in the area that seemed familiar to Stein, he slammed on the brakes of the car and shouted, "This is it! Thank you, Jesus."

Lomax wrote, "And as I sat in the car, as Stein had done with Ray in December, and watched Stein race around the left side of the station to the hidden phone booth, I became convinced that this was indeed the place. The location of the booth is so uncommon and an abutment, which makes it all but invisible even from the front of the gas station, are so unique, even in Texas, the odds are a million to one against the existence of two such phone booths."

With this precise identification of the phone and the time of the call, authorities are in a position to learn to whom Ray made the call and all about him or to prove Lomax and Stein are entirely wrong. On this matter, I find no evidence of anything but official silence, predictable once there was the official decision to ordain that there once again had been no conspiracy.

There is ample confirmation of Stein's story about Ray's presence in New Orleans. His relatives met Ray. Ray's motel registration was found. He stayed at the Provincial Motel, at 1024 Chartres Street, a block from the Mississippi and the New Orleans waterfront. He was there for the days Stein said, December 17–19. And he registered a car of precisely the correct manufacture and state registration.

Returning to Huie's italicized quotation of what Ray wrote him:

At this time [in August in Birmingham] I didn't have very good I.D. (identification) under the Galt name, but all the postal clerk asked me when I asked for my mail at the general delivery window was my middle initial. In the letter Raoul told me to meet him that night in the Starlite Cafe, on Fifth Avenue North, right across the street from the U.S. post office. I met him and he told me to get a good car, around $2,000. Next day I found such a car and described it to him that nite at the Starlite. He said it sounded okay, and next morning on the street he gave me $2,000 in 100 and 50 and 20-dollar bills. The car was a white 1966 Mustang, with red interior and about 18,000 miles on it. The only thing I didn't like about it was the color. Raoul didn't like that either, but he said go ahead and get it. At his request I gave Raoul a set of keys to the car, and he took my home address and telephone number and said he'd either write or call me in maybe six weeks. He also gave me $500 for living expenses and another $500 to buy some camera equipment he described to me. (Ray still does not know why he was asked to buy the photographic equipment.) He said for me to just lie low and stay out of trouble.

This is the kind of data that can be verified. Huie did some checking. Had he not been too important to read newspapers, there might have been less complete mystery about the potential use of the photographic equipment. We'll examine that in a different context.

That camera equipment was on Ray's mind. There is a suggestion it also was on Huie's, although he attempts no interpretation of the reason for purchasing it. There are several other references to the equipment—none given significance by Huie. The next one is for the period about six weeks after Ray reached Birmingham. Here it is related to nothing, not what precedes, not what follows. Ray just threw it in, which may be the way he thinks and writes. But Huie neither edited it out when he was making a selection nor gave it meaning:

I bought the camera equipment for Raoul, but had to ship some of it back.

In the middle of Ray's account of his comings, goings, and doings in Mexico (where he went after Birmingham), right in the middle of an account of apparent smuggling into Mexico with Raoul, "He also told me to keep the photographic equipment for the time being."

Withal, Huie does not use this meaningful and confirmed data, which is good solid evidence of conspiracy. As we shall see, there is solid confirmation of this part of Ray's story, and so partial corroboration of a conspiracy.

Most of the remainder of the article is a rehash of what had appeared in the papers, the difference being Huie could and did put much of it in the first person. All of the unimportant details of the inconsequential things Ray did in Mexico, his languid vacation allegedly awaiting instructions, his later easy living in Los Angeles, going to barkeeper's school, taking dancing lessons, and other boringly mundane things, were well known and could have been written by Joe Ordinary.

One point, though, should be noted. Especially because of what he was to write after he and Ray's other "defenders" sold him out, I think it significant that Huie places Ray in Los Angeles from "late in November 1967" until after an unspecified time beginning March 15 when

> he received by mail . . . the directive he had been expecting. He was wanted in Selma and Birmingham, Ala. He drove his white Mustang from California through New Orleans, and on Friday, March 22, 1968, registered at the Flamingo Motel in Selma.

With King then leading demonstrations in Selma and Birmingham and getting extensive nationwide coverage, including prime TV, Ray—instead of killing him on camera—the next day left for Atlanta. Only to the Huies is this logical or reasonable—if, as they maintain, Ray did the job alone.

Huie's conclusions do merit serious thought, even if some of them may be no more than the shrewd afterthoughts of a canny professional:

> The outline of the plot to murder Dr. King now begins to become visible to me. It may not be visible to my readers because, until Ray has been tried, I cannot reveal all that I have found to be true. But from what I know, from what I have learned from Ray, and from my investigative research, some of the features of the plot were:
>
> *Dr. King was to be murdered for effect. His murder was planned, not by impulsive men who hated him personally, though they probably did hate him, but by calculating men who wanted to use his murder to trigger violent conflict between white and Negro citizens.
>
> *He was to be murdered during the election year of 1968.
>
> *Since he was to be murdered for maximum bloody effect, he was to be murdered, not while he was living quietly at his home in Atlanta, but at some dramatic moment, at some dramatic place where controversy was raging. By March 15, 1968, the plotters clearly had begun aiming at murdering him at some point where he was forming or leading the Poor People's March.
>
> *He was to be murdered by a white man, or white men, who would

be described as "Southerners" and "racists."

*Preferably, he was to be murdered in Birmingham or Montgomery or Selma, since these cities were milestones in his career as an advocate of racial change.

*There was no necessity, after the murder, for the murderer or murderers to be murdered to prevent a trial or trials—because a trial or trials could yield extra dividends of hatred and violence.

Therefore, in this plot, Dr. King was the secondary, not the primary, target. The primary target was the United States of America.

It is quite possible that Huie did learn what he felt he could not publish until after the trial. However, when later he did publish (in his April 15, 1969 article), he did not disclose anything warranting this choice of words. He said the opposite.

King *was* "murdered for maximum bloody effect" and "the primary target was the United States of America." How much this should have been a beginning, not the end, of Huie's writing! His exposure of what "I have learned from Ray" and, through him, "what I know . . . from my investigative research" can be *so* important—if it is valid!

And the "trial or trials could yield extra dividends of hatred and violence." This may yet come to pass. But is this why there was none?

On the other hand, how safe it is to write *after* the fact, *after* King *was* murdered "during the election year 1968," that this had been the plan.

In any event, in November, Ray's case took a radical change. Hanes, as we have seen, says he anticipated it. Huie and *Look* also should have. All plans and schedules were dramatically altered when Ray, at the most exciting last minute, the eve of his trial, fired Hanes. Regardless of Ray's real purpose—and he cannot now tell us and did not when he could have —the effect was to play for time.

It gave Ray time, for jail is jail, and if you have to be there, one is no better and no worse than another.

It also gave Huie and *Look* time. They did not use it. In the ensuing four months before the minitrial, they published nothing.

Meanwhile, Ray's newest—his fourth—"defender" and his third lawyer (counting all the members of the first two firms as one) took over, very firmly.

He changed everything.

7. Percy Foreman:
"I've Given Away $300,000 This Year"

Percy Foreman is the kind of lawyer about whom novels are written.
The wonder is he hasn't written them himself—about himself. He looks
as though cast for his role by a stroke of Central Castings genius. He
dresses and talks as though playing a part. In the Ray case, he played a
part probably no other lawyer could have. Certainly no other could have
gotten away with it. Few would have tried.

For the only time in a long, unusually successful and remunerative
career, he was almost at a loss for words when that curtain fell. Great
wealth and fame, both well earned, having flowed from the marvelously
regulated flow of exactly the right words at the right time (with silence
when it is golden), in itself is remarkable.

Percy Foreman is blessed with a friendly face that wants to smile and
seems to when it doesn't, that can smile with seeming genuineness when
inwardly he is teeming with violently different emotions. At 66 he looks
younger, despite rich gray hair slicked straight back in coarse furrows, as
though the greasy kid stuff had been unevenly anointed. He is six feet
four inches tall, weighs about 250 pounds, yet when he walks he seems
shaped like a thin spinning top, thinnest at the bottom and fullback-
broad at the shoulders. He looks like a man who was a professional
wrestler in his youth, as he was, and who has never abandoned the
physical conditioning it requires.

Throughout his 41 years of law practice, he has been well reported in
the press. He sees to it. Because he, too, never answered my letter, what
follows comes from the press.

Had he opted for a political career (in which he could not have
honestly amassed the fortune his special practice of the law yielded), he
would have fitted into the Lincolnesque tradition: He was one of eight
children of a country sheriff, born in a log cabin in the piney woods of
southeast Texas near the town of Livingston. He began working at eight,
without false pride, each of his menial occupations in its way serving to
prepare him for the many facets of his coming career. These ran the

gamut from shining shoes to oratory on the Chautauqua trail. *Time* (March 21, 1969) cites topics betokening an early contempt for the yokels, "The High Mission of Women in the 20th Century" and "How to Get the Most out of Life." Regardless of what or how much he knew when his natural bent for that kind of oratory was earning University of Texas Law School tuition fees, in his maturity, he is an authentic expert. He has gotten more from his life than most people can dream of.

"I don't need money," he says, with high accuracy. Therefore, he demands and gets astronomically large fees. He has been accused of taking wedding rings; sometimes the women, too. Among the charges he has faced and beaten is adultery.

Other charges on which he was also acquitted include operating a policy racket and using abusive language (which certainly has been lavished upon him, the more publishable epithets being "a cad and a louse"). But he has paid fines for letting weeds grow too high on his property and, on a single occasion, paid fines for 122 parking tickets. He then got almost that many dismissed.

He takes property in lieu of fees to collect what he regards as his due. He is merciless about his fees. He is as tough, for all the charming smiles and smooth talk, as they are high. Yet he also takes cases without fee if they "interest" him.

Two weeks after Ray dismissed him, which was a few days too late to get out of the plea that Foreman had arranged for him, but not for Foreman to have signed a lucrative contract getting 60 per cent of Ray (more of this later), Mrs. Geneva Ann Singleton filed a two-million-dollar "professional misconduct" suit against him in Tampa, Florida. She charged he got her to sign up for an excessive fee by taking advantage of her in a divorce case, when she was "distraught, confused, apprehensive and was not fully aware of the contents" of the agreement. The fees began with a $25,000 retainer. When it is understood that she engaged him on February 10, 1969, and fired him February 28, exactly when he was supposedly exhausting himself preparing to save Ray's life, conducting the most thorough investigation and preparing for the ordeal in court (could he have been?), when it is also understood that he is alone in his firm, having only a secretary—he even does his own investigating—it is possible to understand just how hard he works for his money and his clients. And how mightily he labored for Ray.

Time calls him a "man of bewildering contradictions," but he is not when money—other people's and how he makes it his—is involved. In this area he is consistent. Although "his personal charm, when he cares to exercise it, is overwhelming," he "has been known to snarl at a dilatory witness: 'I get $200 an hour and you have taken up $60 worth.' " One wonders how he can afford to move his bowels.

A Texas editor tells me Foreman has a warehouse to hold his legal loot until such time as he can make favorable disposition of it. However, in one of his more celebrated cases, that of beautiful young Candace Mossler, married to old multi-millionaire Jacques Mossler, with whose murder she and her young lover-nephew Melvin Powers were charged, he didn't await his final and even for him reportedly very high fee. The law prohibits a criminal's profiting from his crime. If Candy were found guilty, all those beautiful millions would not have been hers for Foreman to tap. He took assorted jewels from her in advance, as security for his fee. After the sensational trial, one of the sexiest, in which he got her acquitted, they had a bitter falling out. She brought suit to recover her jewels.

On the other hand, he took without fee and won the case of four policemen accused of brutality. For this, 200 Texas officers kittied up to buy him a diamond-studded watch. (What do you give the man who has everything?) Yet a month later, two other policemen beat him up when he won an acquittal in a murder case.

Foreman represented Mrs. Singleton for only eighteen days, but that is more than four times as long as the four days he had the case of Jack Ruby, the man who shot Lee Harvey Oswald. In resigning from Ruby's defense, he wrote, "You know, I don't let people tell me what to do in a case." That is his version. It is subject to a different interpretation that should be borne in mind when we analyze his handling of the Ray case. He could have been saying that his clients do what he tells them; he does not do what they desire.

If in court he seems and looks like a backwoodsman uncomfortable in his baggy trousers, "a shambling hulk," as *Time* described him, it is part of his act, not because he is not possessed of "a superbly-skilled legal mind." He combines this with "a brilliant sense of showmanship."

Ray had a high opinion of Foreman when he sought F. Lee Bailey and Arthur Hanes. His brothers, John and Jerry, from the moment of his arrest, pressed James Earl to seek Foreman. Jerry even wanted to arrange for a Foreman defense before asking James. In an undated letter written before he gave up his appeal from the decision to grant extradition—that is, sometime between June 27, and July 16, 1968— James Earl told John

64

You mention Percy Foreman. He is a good attorney, but I will wait until I get back as I want some attorneys who can work together, so I will let Hanes decide on someone he thinks could be best.

With his word, which we do not have, we still would not be certain of James Earl's reason for not selecting Foreman to begin with or what impelled the last-minute switch to Foreman. It is possible he had it all planned out, switching to the best one for the courtroom work and effecting a delay by the shift. It is also possible it had been figured out for him in advance. However, Jerry gave me credible explanations. They will hold our attention later.

Whatever the reason, it did happen. Hanes said he was not surprised. He also said the opposite. His ambivalence is as understandable as his embarrassment. There he was, former mayor, former CIA-man, former FBI agent who had quit a rewarding career, with early retirement and all sorts of other fine fringe benefits, in order to fight what he regards as the "red" danger, the man who had the courage to take one of the nastier Ku Klux Klan-type cases, and when he had the very biggest race case of all—with a sweetheart contract—he was dumped more spectacularly and unceremoniously than the bride jilted at the altar.

"The first I knew of this was 8:20 this evening," he told a brief news conference he called Sunday night, November 10, 1968.

On November 11, Henry P. Leifermann, reporting for UPI from Memphis, wrote that Ray had planned the move to fire Hanes "for as long as a month." He gave no source for his information. But elsewhere in the same story he said, "sources close to Ray said the defendant maneuvered the lawyer change to delay the trial in the vague hope that something might change the picture and the case against him might be dropped."

"Sources close to Ray," unless this is a disguise for improper official contact, seems to limit this to his lawyers, his brothers, or Huie, the former most likely.

Leifermann also wrote,

Hanes had suspected for some time that he might be fired. The suspicion apparently was strengthened last Wednesday, his final meeting with Ray. It was reported that Ray and Hanes argued whether Ray would testify . . . Hanes advised against it.

Without espionage, this had to have come from Hanes and no one else [1].

65

What he told Foreman by phone is distilled gall. Until he was paid off, he said, "Don't call me; I'll call you." This appears to have been in reference to turning over his files on the case, the results of his investigation, his research on the law, correspondence, the works. But the way Foreman handled the case, these files had no value even if they were the world's best. Foreman didn't need them.

Money was always a big issue, with everyone. Somehow, only those who cannot agree with official fiction, who criticize the government for its mishandling of the assassination investigations, are criticized about money and they are, with a few notable exceptions, the only ones not to have gotten any profit. They are "scavengers," but not Huie, Hanes, Foreman, or even William Manchester, who manufactured further and needless scandals to become a millionaire through them. Foreman immediately pretended to be the exception he was not.

AP's Bill Johnson wrote from Memphis on Monday, November 11, in time to make the morning papers of the day the trial was postponed:

> Percy Foreman, the Texas lawyer who has taken over the James Earl Ray defense, said Monday the question of money for his fee wasn't bothering him. And he made it plain he had not been hired by the Ku Klux Klan "or any other right-wing organization" . . . . The arrangement . . . was strictly Ray, Ray's family and himself, Foreman said. And while he declined to discuss the financial arrangements, he said they are not of primary importance. "I've given away $300,000 this year," he said.

If that was in cash, he wasn't hurting.

More than by the possible money, Foreman gave the press to understand, he was "intrigued by what he termed a number of unanswered questions in the case. 'I take cases partly because of the fact that they are interesting and partly because the client wants me,' he said."

With Ray, he had both interests, the one he talked about, whether or not sincerely we may better evaluate later, and the one he pretended was in this instance beneath him, money. But not for long. AP reported January 30:

> Author William Bradford Huie on Wednesday gave Houston attorney Percy Foreman $5,000 as the final payment for a handwritten manuscript from Foreman's client James Earl Ray.
>
> Huie said it was the last in a series of payments—"more than

$30,000"—which were made earlier to Ray's former counsel, Arthur Hanes, Sr., of Birmingham.

The manuscript Ray wrote is reported to be 20,000 words long.

Now, if this is accurate, Huie had really paid through his own nose rather than prying others' lips open. It says that *more* than the earlier-reported $30,000 is what he paid. It says that, prior to this $5,000 to Foreman, he had already paid "more than $30,000" to Hanes. And "more than $30,000" plus $5,000 is a considerable sum. As we learn, he also gave Foreman more.

The full story on Klan interest, however, is not quite as the lead of Johnson's story puts it, for Foreman also acknowledged, "the Klan several times had asked him to take the case." Sort of like Hanes not shying away from "any group."

And it would be more accurate to describe the arrangement for him to "defend" Ray as initiated by Ray's brothers and reluctantly agreed to by the prisoner.

Unless Sheriff William N. Morris, Jr., lied, the decision was *not* made *before* Foreman saw Ray. He said that on the 10th, Ray's brothers and Foreman had visited Ray. *"During the course of this visit certain decisions were made* [emphasis added] and a letter was written to Mr. Arthur Hanes, Sr., attorney for James Earl Ray," Morris announced. "This letter was presented to me for reading by Mr. Foreman and it declared an intent by James Earl Ray to dispense with the legal services of Mr. Hanes and his son and of an intention to obtain new counsel and a Tennessee lawyer."

How delicate can you get? The "new counsel" was not even named. Hardly the personal light touch of James Earl Ray![2]

Sheriff Morris's statement makes unavoidable the suggestion that the long campaign of the Ray brothers to get Foreman in as James's lawyer finally succeeded, that it was on their initiative and not James's. And it makes more provocative several other minor things little noticed. James broke jail in Missouri the very day after John visited him. And in the undated letter quoted above, from the British jail, he asked his brothers to advance funds to Hanes. He promised, "I will straighten it up with you when I get back," but he was captured virtually penniless, as they knew. The inference is that they *knew* he had money available in the United States, in his own secreted horde or from others, and that he had to go through them to get it. From this, it seems possible that the brothers were able and intended to influence the course of events, whether or not independently or without external inspiration. In this connection, it is interesting to note that the publicly available information indicates that while James may have had no racist history, they do.

And if James Earl, as seems highly improbable, decided upon firing Hanes and pulled the switch on him entirely alone, the best public-relations counsel in a country where hundreds might vie for this rank, could not have improved on his timing—for the Monday morning papers of the day before the trial was scheduled, with a full press corps present for that trial.

As Foreman had told Sheriff Morris he would, he appeared in Judge Battle's court Tuesday morning to request a continuance, a delay in the trial. Instead of the trial, a new date, March 3, was agreed upon. Assistant Prosecutor Dwyer, in his "piece of business" comment quoted earlier, complained that Ray had been "here four months or better and it appears to me he is trifling with the court . . . . The state of Tennessee is ready for the trial. We have something like 90 witnesses alerted nationally and in various parts of the world to come here." The number of witnesses Dwyer gave is about a fourth of those the prosecution had told Hanes about, but it is still impressively large. It must have had an intimidating effect upon Ray.

Several parts of Foreman's motion are worth noting. He claimed Ray had not been able to "adjust his thinking" to Hanes, that "a serious disagreement with reference to his defense has arisen between him and his said attorneys, both as to strategy and policy . . . says he cannot cooperate with his said attorneys and desires to engage and employ other counsel. . . ." From this, it would seem that, before taking the case, Foreman had satisfied himself the same strategic and policy differences would not separate him and Ray. As it turned out, when a new one did, Foreman's powers of persuasion were able to overcome it. He averred, "This application is not made for delay but that justice be done."

He then filed a pauper's plea, saying that Hanes had been paid "approximately $30,000 to date and an additional $12,000 is required before they will release their statements, interviews, depositions and the results of their investigation." Ray's "family and friends hope to be able to raise this money," he added, without indicating who the "friends" were. Not one exists in the public record. But he held forth no prospect of their success.

At a breakfast interview with reporters, Hanes said the disagreement with Ray was over a delay, Ray wanting it, hoping he would "do better" under the incoming Nixon administration, and Hanes opposing it. He directly denied remarks attributed to John and Jerry Ray about a disagreement over money. He said that there had been no such disagreement and charged "this is some scheme by the brothers. What for I don't know." He reiterated the accusation that they had "refused to cooperate or even talk" with him from the first. Then he alleged, "They have been working against us," the plural apparently referring to him and his son. "We've had to fight them."

His reason does not explain it: "They could not run the case [as presumably they intended to do] with me as the lawyer." This they could not have known without speaking to Hanes, which he says they never did, and if somehow they divined it of him, they had to have known then they could not "run the case" with the famous Foreman.

The brothers' version of the dispute with Hanes appears in a later chapter.

Regardless of Foreman's assurance that "this application is not for delay," it had that precise effect. Dwyer's objection was vigorous. Judge Battle, after Dwyer's plaint, himself complained, "Well, you gentlemen have dumped this right in my lap." But he had no alternative. He had to give the new lawyer time for familiarize himself with the case. Dwyer's specification of "90 witnesses" recorded the extent and complexity of the prosecution evidence. Battle set a December hearing for assurances the case would proceed on the new schedule and on the 18th was quoted as "insisting" the trial commence March 3.

All of Foreman's moves, whether one assumes they are justified at face value or one suspects an ulterior motive, could not have been better designed for intimidating his client and laying the basis for further delays, should he desire them.

Four days after the November hearing, the Memphis *Commercial-Appeal* quoted Foreman as saying, "it is his client's desire that a Tennessee attorney also be hired to assist in the defense" (which is exactly what he would have said were it his idea alone because he represents and speaks for his client). To this, he added, "About 20 Memphis attorneys have been considered but none has been available." This may be interpreted as excessively polite language. It also is imprecise language. In itself, it does not say even a single Memphis attorney had been *asked* to join the defense and had refused.

Then, in the December hearing, Foreman presented Judge Battle with Ray's pauper's oath, saying he had neither "money nor property." As we have seen, this was false, for Huie—from the public record alone—gave Foreman $5,000. These two things, Foreman's seeming claim that no Memphis attorney would join the defense, as Ray wanted, and Ray's total lack of resources of any kind, forced Battle to take an "unprecedented" step. He "ordered" the public defender's office to "assign as many persons as necessary" to help Foreman. When Foreman's other activities and obligations are considered, this may, in practical terms, mean the taxpayers of Tennessee paid for just about all the work done on the case.

In charge of the people assigned to Foreman was Hugh M. Stanton, Sr., Shelby County public defender. He was appointed as Foreman's co-counsel. Stanton's assistance will be examined later.

The wily Foreman, again, had left the judge little option. He declared, on the record, that he "works alone" and could not possibly duplicate the FBI's investigation which, he said, had cost $1,400,000. This would have been enough, but further to box in the judge, whether or not to frighten his client, he added that all of the results of this enormous investigation had been turned over to the prosecution but had been denied him. In view of what he was later to say of how he persuaded Ray to plead guilty under conditions that assured he would never leave jail alive, this complaint should not be forgotten.

Even here he did not stop. He "told the court," in the words of the brief AP dispatch for the morning papers of December 19, which got little attention, "it would be a 'miracle' if the case is ready for trial by the March date."

In saying "he understood from FBI sources" that the King file "reportedly says for two years before April 4 [the date of the murder] there was a squad of FBI agents assigned to prevent the assassination of Martin Luther King," he gave the FBI a chance to make a Foreman-type, legalistic response that was no response. Its spokesman said, "The FBI does not offer protection for individuals."

Foreman did not do a disservice to the FBI. He certified they had made an enormous investigation of the murder and gave them the chance to seem to say they had done everything to prevent it that the law permitted, which is both irrelevant and false. The magnitude of the investigation is not important. Its efficiency and direction, integrity and success are; and the FBI could have been protecting King even if not directly doing so through cooperation with the local police.

With directness and simplicity that amounts to sheer brilliance, and with little public attention, Foreman thus accomplished these things:

He laid the foundation for seeking and getting another delay in the actual trial;

He got the State of Tennessee to pay expenses that properly were his by claiming Ray was a pauper, when Foreman got—through Ray—at least $5,000 and when Foreman had every reason to expect a fee, as we shall see, well into six figures;

He indebted the FBI to him while seeming to criticize it;

He terrified his client with the magnitude of the FBI investigation of the murder and the claim that later was made to seem false, that he had no way of learning anything about it.

If Ray, as the available evidence indicates, did not commit the murder, what Foreman did *publicly,* in court, in front of Ray had to persuade Ray that the FBI had framed him with it beyond any possibility of acquittal. Foreman later let it be known, in less straightforward language, that this is what he did in private.

For those who can afford him, Percy Foreman earns his fees, whether or not he works hard and long. In this case, there is no available proof that he did *any* work, except *on* his client.

8. The Deal

While Foreman was separating the lady who sued him in Tampa from a large amount of the money she had and expected, as she says, by taking advantage of her, there was an almost complete blackout of news on the Ray case. At the end of January there was a small story, the quoted account of Huie's delivery of $5,000 to Foreman, after false claim of pauperdom and after the State of Tennessee had picked up the major part of the cost of the defense.

Hidden by the silence, Foreman was working on his client. If he was also doing anything about preparing to counter the prosecution case, I have not seen a word from him or from any other source indicating this.

I examined the papers and magazines and listened to radio and TV attentively for precisely this. If the free services rendered him by the State of Tennessee, through the assignment of all necessary personnel by the public defender's office, yielded anything useful to this end, again there is no indication, no matter how slight, that it did or that Foreman was interested in it.

Here the reader should understand the requirements of the trial and of the defense, for they are quite simple. The defense did *not* have to prove that Ray did *not* commit the crime. It did not have to prove that Ray was not involved in it. It did not even have to prove his innocence of anything—of the murder with which he was charged or of any other possible involvement, for example, as a decoy (which I believe is confirmed by my study of the available evidence). Actually, it did not have to *disprove* anything if nothing was proven. Ray was innocent until proven guilty "beyond reasonable doubt."

On the other hand, to get a conviction, the prosecution had to prove that Ray, and he alone, again beyond reasonable doubt, *did* commit the murder. Not that he could have or might have, not that he was in a position to or was or might have been involved in any other way. Unless the State was able to convince the jury—and a predominantly white southern jury at a time of inflamed public opinion and racial tension to boot—that, without any reasonable question, Ray was the murderer, the jury was bound, under our law, to find him not guilty, to free him on this charge.

All the defense had to do was to satisfy the jury that reasonable doubt existed. There is no question in my mind, particularly after close study of the evidence not still suppressed by the State and federal governments, that any competent lawyer, certainly many not possessed of Foreman's touted and earned reputation, would have succeeded in this. Nor is there any reason to suppose the still-suppressed evidence is the prosecution's strongest.There is every reason to believe exactly the opposite, that what it withheld and is withholding, even more than what it disclosed, proves the opposite of its allegation.

Besides fleecing the State of Tennessee and Ray, even if he was not shearing a distraught woman (and Foreman, too, is innocent until proven guilty beyond reasonable doubt), he was cooking up a deal. It ended in what was promptly and properly dubbed a "minitrial."

This was at the time miniskirts had become accepted. This new, couthie, female style, the most abbreviated couturiers had dared, exposed the until-then maximum extent of the lower part of the female anatomy. It is the briefest non-sports female garb ever—at least, since "Penguin Island."

Once the press seized upon this apt phrase to characterize Foreman's ultimate Memphis proceeding, everyone involved expressed strong objection. Their complaints are invalid. Considering the extreme brevity of the trial, there can be no objection to the comparison, for . that substitution for the law and its majestic working is more comparable to the micro-miniskirt. If objection to the term is based on the argument that some regarded the miniskirt as indecent, again, any bastardization, corruption, or avoidance of the law, in a society with the pretenses of ours, is no less than indecent.

In a case like this one, calling the March 10 trial in Memphis an indecency is a kindness.

It was carefully arranged and staged, the arranging taking some doing.

When it could not be pulled off by the date set for trial, March 3, Foreman asked for and got a further extension, until April 7, on the grounds that he had not been able to study the case completely and prepare a defense. This, it will soon be apparent, was tantamount to fraud. That was not the reason he required and was given the extension. I repeat—I *emphasize*—there is no available reason to believe Foreman intended to take this case to open trial, none that he made any preparation to, none that he even really tried to analyze and assess the evidence available to him. In his own way, without so intending, he has come close to confirming this.

This is not to say his intent was evil. The great and the near-great tend

73

to arrogate godly powers, rights, and insights to themselves. He may have sincerely believed what I believe he could not, that he was doing what was best for his client. Perhaps he thought it was best for the country, too.

His intent could not have been what he said it was, to serve the ends of justice. He frustrated justice.

What he contrived, a very daring and almost impossible thing, did not require him to prepare the case, to do any work. If he could not pull it off, he need only have gone back into court and told the judge he could not proceed, that he and his client could not agree on tactics and strategy. Hanes had already laid the foundation for this. Ray's legal history would have tended to confirm it. At worst, there would have been a further delay. This would not have hurt Ray. It might have served his purpose, if Hanes's opinion, that he wanted delays, is correct.

By virtue of the extraordinary agreement he had with Ray (the details come later), had Foreman resigned from the case, it would not have hurt his financial interest—unless the next lawyer took the case to trial.

First glimmer of the Foreman coup was in a deliberate "leak" to the Huntsville, Alabama *Times* [1].

On Friday, March 7, a month to the day before the rescheduled trial, the Huntsville *Times* was told by what it and the wire services described as "a source close to the case" that Ray "will enter a guilty plea Monday and receive a 99-year sentence."

Monday was the 10th, the first day of court after the leak that in this case also had to be a plant, to prepare public opinion for the unacceptable (exactly as in the so-called investigation of the Presidential murder). What the *Times* printed was exact and accurate in the finest detail. There had been a deal and it had the particulars, even the timing and the required trappings.

The judge and prosecution had agreed in advance. Because this could not be accomplished without sentence by a jury, a jury's agreement was required. Meaning, also, *in advance* —without having heard or seen *any* of the evidence!

The *Times* and all other media proclaimed "the guilty plea would be 'the only way Ray can escape the death sentence.'"

In time for the afternoon papers of Friday, March 7, "A spokesman for Judge Preston Battle . . . said Ray's lawyer had sought and been granted the hearing." But he "would give no indication what the hearing would cover."

74

When Foreman was asked about the leak, he attracted more, not less, attention to it by his characteristic answer, "It's none of your business."

The *Times* provided this intimate and precisely accurate forecast:

> After a prima facie case involving a few witnesses, the court would accept a guilty plea, recommend the 99-year sentence and allow the jury to retire to confirm the sentence, the source said. Ray is expected to be behind bars at the Tennessee state prison in Nashville by Monday night, the source added.

Even the movements of the about-to-be-convicted accused had been plotted in advance.

Right away, "Newsmen accredited to cover Ray's April 7 trial were notified at midmorning that Foreman had been granted the Monday hearing by Judge Battle," AP reported. "There was no elaboration." There need have been none, for it was all out, all planted in advance to prepare a climate of acceptability.

Aside from the magnitude and sensational character of the crime, it is neither the concept nor the function of juries to "affirm" deals. It is their function to determine guilt or innocence. The rubber stamp is not in the Constitution.

One of the strange aspects is the silence of Judge Battle. Under the guidelines he himself had imposed and under which he had charged Hanes, Huie, and others with contempt—that any pre-trial publicity would influence potential jurors—he was bound to move against the *Times* and its "source." He never did.

The timing of the leak was professionally perfect. It was to a small, out-of-state paper located where, if there were the unlikely investigation, suspicion would be focused on Hanes, a prominent man in that state. It was arranged for the last day of business before the hearing and facilitated arranging for that hearing. The attention it received alerted the entire press, for it alerted the entire world. Thus, especially with the unique character and dramatic nature of the deal, a maximum press coverage was assured. This was essential. It was required, not only for public acceptability—this was a pretty bad-tasting dose to get and keep down—but even more, for the largest possible attention to the one side that was to be presented in court. There was no defense. Whatever the prosecution alleged to be evidence, Foreman, in advance, rubber stamped as true and uncontradictable.

With the courts closed and personnel scattered Saturday and Sunday, there was least chance an enterprising local reporter—the national and foreign press were not yet there—would find and question anyone or get something embarrassing from them. The next thing in the press was the finalization of the deal.

In the entire package Foreman says he arranged (his comments are given later), he had only one problem: Ray was opposed to it. This is what took the time and required the haste. Ray could change his mind. He could fire Foreman and get another lawyer. This is what he did, but not until it was too late. (Incredibly, in the interim, he was his own lawyer and he did meet the minimum necessities.) Had not Ray's acceptance been the stumbling block, this would all have been consummated earlier. In getting Ray's agreement, Foreman missed the scheduled trial date by less than a week. The Huntsville *Times* had the story of the agreement and printed it the end of the week in which the trial had been scheduled.

Like the *Times,* I cannot reveal my source. Nor can I confirm it. For whatever it may be worth, I report what I have, from a source in a position to know. In the last minute, just before the hastily scheduled March 10 hearing, Ray backed out on the deal. A jailer learned of it. Foreman was phoned. He hurried from Houston, going right to the jail, leaned on Ray all over again, told him he would be electrocuted if he did not go through with it, and in other ways kept him in line until after the deal was signed and sealed. (Confirmation of this report is treated later, in the next chapter.)

Collateral corroboration of this appeared the morning of the minitrial. Jim Squires reported in the *Nashville Tennesseean* "there had been increasing speculation earlier yesterday that Ray was balking 'and might still renege.' But following a series of secretive courthouse meetings between Ray and his attorney, Percy Foreman, and between Foreman and Dist. Atty. Gen. Phillip M. Canale, reliable sources said the agreement 'is still on' . . . Foreman . . . returned from Houston shortly after noon yesterday. Reporters attempting to ask him about reports that Ray was 'very upset' were told in an angry tone: 'I'm trying to save a man's life . . . I don't have time to help you make a living.'

"The famed Houston trial lawyer went directly to the jail, where he conferred with Ray more than an hour and with Canale about 45 minutes . . . a source close to the defense reported 'things are a little up in the air but the deal is still on' . . . ."

In arranging the initial leak of the deal, necessary to cushion the shock such an incredible end to the sensational case inevitably had to cause, even with a complaisant, servile press, it was necessary to await the last possible minute. There was always the chance Ray would back out. This is why Foreman had to ask—and got—an immediate hearing instead of awaiting the April 7 date. The case was stamped and officially closed before Ray could do anything, before any questions could reach him. One of the consequences is that the entire press could not be prepared, that individual reporters were shocked, and the principals were not really prepared to fend off all inquiries.

At the minitrial, the only departure from the script was by Ray. Had the judge not been part of this American variant of Nazi "vote ja" justice, what Ray said would have been enough to ruin the neat arrangement. It happened outside the presence of the jury, before the jury was in the courtroom—before it was empaneled. Ray denied Foreman's denial that there had been a conspiracy. We shall assess Foreman's statement in detail in our analysis of the proceedings. Here it is enough to say that the first seed of doubt was planted and repeated by Ray and only Ray—not Foreman, his lawyer—and that Foreman instead smoothed it over, with the collaboration of the judge.

The proceeding was micro-mini. In all, it took but three and a half hours, including the selection, indoctrination, and seating of the jury, the formalities by which Battle, the prosecution, and Foreman all covered themselves, and the offering of what, for lack of a suitable word in the dictionary, was called "evidence." The "decision" was handed down at 12:12 P.M.

It was all wrapped up in plenty of time for the afternoon newspapers. It was a lead story. The New Orleans *States-Item* had a three-inch-high, very black banner across the top of its front page. It read, "RAY GIVEN 99 YEARS ON GUILTY PLEA."

It was properly sanctified, made to appear legal as even technically it may not have been—exactly this kind of deal was then under legal attack—and everybody was holy and righteous.

Foreman was his sanctimonious best. "I've never had any hopes of anything except . . . to save this man's life," the great one let mere mortals know. "It took me months to prove to myself . . . that it was not a conspiracy."

What was not reported was that he had convinced himself, beyond a shadow of doubt, that Ray was the murderer and the prosecution could prove that beyond reasonable doubt. Presumably, he had.

In the Tuesday morning papers, the story remained the lead, the major attraction and the major focus of attention. The *Washington Post*, which preferred to carry less than most major papers about the assassinations once they were the subject of official investigation, played the story in the main three columns of its front page, the subheading reading "No Evidence of Any Plot, Jury Is Told." This has been the *Post's* predetermination from the first about both the King and the Presidential assassination.*

Not all papers were satisfied, but all soon forgot their misgivings.

In that morning's Chicago *Daily News,* where there was also a front page, three-column display, its reporter in Memphis, Jerry Lipson, raised questions reflected in the headlines: "Mystery Remains— Was Ray a Part of Plot on King." Alas, that is not the only question remaining. The still-existing question is, "Did Ray kill King?"

On its front page, the *New York Times* offered the fine irony of another Monday decision, the Supreme Court's posthumous "clearing" of the murdered black leader on charges growing out of his confrontation with Birmingham (meaning Hanes) and its (his) dog-sicking Bull Connor in the 1963 civil-rights struggles.

In all, the *Times* devoted more than a full page to the case. In addition to the page-one lead story by Martin Waldron and the story on the Supreme Court decision, it printed almost 30 column inches headed "A Few Puzzles Remain To Be Solved in Ray Case," and countered this reporting of what no uncontaminated jury would have swallowed with almost a column calling Ray's forced plea "Realistic and Essential." There was just under two columns of placebo assuring the country "U.S. Will Continue Its Inquiry on Ray," undiluted Department of Justice propaganda emphasizing the claim that there was no evidence of conspiracy—which is refuted in the "Few Puzzles" story, had anyone in authority been at all interested. Buried at the end were brief statements by the widow and the successor as leader of the Southern Christian Leadership Conference. They believe there was a conspiracy.

The *Times'* lead editorial, while carefully ignoring any consideration of the evidence, is an excellent statement of the widespread indignation and the reasons for it. It is the best expression of the outrage and the ensuing discontent.

---

*I know that its book reviewer was ordered not to review *Whitewash* after he had read it and decided on a favorable review.

TONGUE-TIED JUSTICE

The aborted trial of James Earl Ray for the assassination of Dr. Martin Luther King, Jr. is a shocking breach of faith with the American people, black and white, and of people the world over still numbed and puzzled by the gunfire that struck down this international leader.

Ray is entitled by all legal means to avail himself of the defenses open to him under the law. But by no means, legal or pragmatic, should the doors of the courtroom and the jail be slammed shut on the facts, the motives and the doubts of this horrible murder.

And yet that is just what has occurred with stunning suddenness in a Memphis courthouse. By pleading guilty, Ray has been sentenced to 99 years in prison. The jury had to go along with this prearranged deal between the prosecution and the admitted killer's attorney. Circuit Judge W. Preston Battle went along with this deal, treating the whole matter as if it were a routine murder case.

Nothing but outrage and suspicion can follow the handling of this long-delayed and instantly snuffed-out trial. Percy Foreman, the defense lawyer, tells the public that it took him months "to prove to myself" that Ray was not part of a murder conspiracy. Ray himself acquiesces in the deal made on the guilty plea—then says publicly that he refuses to go along with the statement that there was no conspiracy.

Why should this assassination case be tried by statements instead of formal legal procedures, subject to examination and cross-examination, the presentation of all the evidence by the prosecution, the appearance of the accused in open court? What in either sense or jurisprudence does it mean that the defense attorney convinced *himself*? In the ghetto and in the world outside the ghetto, the question still cries for answer: Was there a conspiracy to kill Dr. King and who was in it?

The state's case has been read to the jury. But that is hardly enough in a case of this magnitude. This was not a street crime but, on the surface, a racist or quasi-political assassination. It is not enough to say that the state accepted the guilty plea and agreed to end the case because the death penalty has not been used since 1961 in Tennessee.

No one was demanding blood; everyone is demanding facts. Are we going to get the facts from Ray's lawyers, past or present, one of whom is trying to peddle the story to magazines? Are we going to get the facts from William Bradford Huie, the author who has "bought" the "rights" to Ray's story? What a mockery of justice for the facts to emerge in marketed justice!

Unless proceedings are convened in court—Federal, if not state—we shall never know the adjudicated truth. There should be no Warren Commissions necessary—a month or a year from now—to still our doubts and do what a Tennessee court has failed to do.

Had the *Times* used its not inconsiderable facilities for looking into the case, it might less readily have assuaged its editorial suspicions.

Even the Associated Press's Bernard Gavzer, an unabashed apologist for the official fictions in the Presidential murder and blind to what he saw in six months allegedly spent examining the files on it, suddenly became half a reporter. Assuming Ray's guilt, he nonetheless sent a perceptive story from Memphis. He said the plea "put the lid on a court trial which may have aired puzzling questions . . . ." Gavzer then asked some of these questions. Thereafter, his reporting on the aspects he addressed (those enabling him not to rock the AP boat too much) is a fine job and a belated, journalistic atavism, a throwback to the earlier days of inquisitive and penetrating American journalism.

If it is argued that the case had to be raw to nauseate the Gavzers, it is that raw and he is not alone in the nausea set in type and aired. In almost any other country, in this one in the pre-assassination era, the doubts so well-founded and widely expressed would have caused an official action, an investigation. Here the silence smothered, and the press did not sustain its indignation. In so abdicating its function, the American press has much to answer for.

For a week the journalistic turmoil continued, in response to popular incredulity and indignation. The minitrial succeeded in its intent, to frustrate the workings of American law and justice, which requires an adversary proceeding that is entirely public, a vigorous presentation of opposing sides. No journalistic voice, no matter how meekly, asked if it were possible perhaps Ray had not, really, fired the shot. Many asked if it were not possible he had not been alone.

While the controversy was raging around the periphery (with the papers not asking if Ray had been the murderer but half-heartedly asking if he had been entirely alone), the *Washington Post*, which has excellent connections with the Department of Justice, was the beneficiary of a special leak. The story, written the day after the minitrial, got a three-column, front-page treatment, rather prominent. It was written under a Memphis dateline by Staff Writer Paul W. Valentine, who would author a Sunday piece about Ray himself saying there had been a conspiracy. Under the headline, "Mrs. King, SCLC Cleared Disposition of Ray Case," the first story began:

Court officials in Memphis said today the controversial disposition of the James Earl Ray case was cleared in advance with the Southern Christian Leadership Conference and with Coretta King, widow of Dr. Martin Luther King, Jr.

The third paragraph says, "Justice Department officials in Washington were notified of the plan in advance and raised no objection."

I suggest the Justice Department was more than "notified." And I also suggest that, although, without doubt, the effect was to "dispose" of James Earl Ray and "his" case, the intent and the hope was to dispose of the case of the murder of King.

The final sentence of the story, uncritical in the best *Post* Pollyanna tradition of incisive assassination investigative reporting, quotes Canale, the prosecutor who saw to it there was neither prosecution nor testing of his evidence, as saying, "if any evidence of a conspiracy comes to light 'the conspirators will be promptly and vigorously prosecuted.'" Can one imagine the spontaneity with which evidence of a conspiracy would "come to light," how avidly the escaped conspirators would seize on every opportunity to facilitate it?

This leak was carefully fed the uncritical influential paper, the only local morning paper available to Washington's opinion-makers and national leaders.

It was a fraud and a deception, an absolute falsehood, to say the family and closest friends and associates of the victim had given their assent, concurred in the deal, were really satisfied with this end to the case—or even that it was ended. Their own statements are contrary. Canale sought to give the impression the whole thing was normal, including the consent of close relatives, and that such cases are common. If this is the usual Southern white courtesy extended all the widows of all the murdered black men—who can believe that?—its prominent, inspired use served but a single purpose when the monstrous deal was under attack, to invoke the names of those closest to the victim in a context that, with skilled dishonesty, said they were entirely satisfied with Memphis mimicry of justice.

This was no kindness to the bereaved. It was an obscenity. It served to emphasize the great care with which the coke that fueled the fabricating oven was prepared before the fire was lit.

It is the rottenest kind of deliberate lie. It could have been of official concoction only, whether the actual origin was in Memphis or in Washington. Denial was immediate. It received but minor, inconspicuous treatment. Where it was mentioned at all, it was usually at the tail of a longer story. Because the survivors could not and did not anticipate it, they were neither immediately available nor had they prepared statements.

The understatement distributed by the Associated Press read, "The SCLC denied reports quoting court officials in Memphis that arrangements for Ray's guilty plea had been cleared beforehand with the SCLC." Its executive director, the Reverend Andy Young, in Atlanta, thought if the representation had *any* basis in fact, that was "our statement a month ago that we didn't believe in capital punishment for anyone."

Young's hunch was a good one, for it later became known that, when the government had approached Mrs. King's New York attorney, Harry Wachtel, he had replied that she "wanted it made clear that such a deal did not mean she and others in the family thought there was no conspiracy" and that they "were 'opposed in fact and in principle to capital punishment and would not wish to see Ray electrocuted . . . .'" This is anything but collaboration in the arrangement, anything but prior endorsement of the deal. In any event, it was not for them to replace the jury or authorize avoidance of a trial.

In Chicago, where he headed the SCLC's "Operation Breadbasket," King's close personal friend and associate, the Reverend Jesse L. Jackson, in a statement widely ignored, showed just how much this deal was endorsed by the victim's associates, how wholeheartedly they concurred in the mimicry:

> We were told justice was done by giving a puny, sick white man a 99-year sentence in exchange for the assassination of our black prophet. But far from justice, the American judicial system would not allow even insensitive and unconcerned inquiry into the murder of a world leader.

Because its position was so radically contrary to the traditional posture of a free press, which should never be an arm or an instrument of free government, I believe the stance, really the campaign, of the *Washington Post* warrants special consideration.

While busily engaged in its news and editorial columns defending everybody involved in the deal and confusing its own departments of fact and opinion, it reluctantly conceded in its lead editorial of March 12, "But it is also possible that there was a conspiracy and that the evidence of it has not been uncovered." How could it have been "uncovered," for the *Post,* when in fact it had been published (those things that had been in the papers saying that more than one person was involved, Ray's own published, public claim in the minitrial, the Lomax series, etc.)? This paper, always listed as one of the "top ten," certainly one of the country's most influential, took comfort from the latest of the unending switched positions of the Department of Justice (the prevailing situation determining whether it said there could or could not have been a conspiracy): "Fortunately, the Department of Justice has given assurances that its investigation will continue." From that moment forward, there was not the single indication of any investigation, but the *Post* had taken its saintly stand and performed its traditional ritual of sanctifying whatever the government at any time did about the assassinations.

About the trial, it advised, "there is not much point in jumping to the conclusion that the mystery would have been cleared up if Ray had been tried on a plea of innocent." Ray might not have taken the stand, but if he had, "he might not have thrown any light on the conspiracy charge." With the addenda irrelevant, for the point was not what Ray might or might not say or do, but the correct working of American law and justice, the establishment of truth and fact beyond reasonable doubt, the acceptable solution of a major crime, the *Post* could not have understood its thoroughgoing condemnation of the entire concept and system of American jurisprudence.

It wound up that week with a lengthy, signed article presenting the following opinion as fact:

> A full trial of the case, contrary to what some critics feel, would not have revealed much more than what prosecutors presented at the guilty plea hearing last Monday. Neither prosecution nor defense appeared ready to develop a conspiracy theory.

It is not accidental that the *Post* misleads here. What other evidence might or might not have been presented is not the issue. On this, it had no way of knowing, either way. The central question was and remains the integrity of what had been presented. That was unchallenged, entirely untested. But, on the basis of what had appeared in the papers, it was at best dubious, as we shall see.

With no less a person than the accused proclaiming in court that there *had* been a conspiracy, how much less justification could there be for the *Post's* last sentence? Unless the defendant was not part of the defense! The *Post* skirted around this with a deprecating, four-column headline, "Ray Alone Still Talks of a Plot." Aside from the utter falsehood of it, for there was Senator James Eastland on one end of the spectrum and all of King's family and former associates on the other still talking of a conspiracy, who else did the *Post* expect to "talk" of it? The other escaped conspirators, perhaps?

Immediately before the *Post* falsely said Ray was "alone" in saying there had been a conspiracy (in other words, since one conspirator says it, do not believe it), it had published similar statements by other legislators, including the moderate New York Republican Congressman, Ogden Reid, Jr., a number of black Congressmen, and King's former associates. That very week, Hanes's former Memphis associate, Russell Thompson (who saw the same "red" plot that Hanes saw) had publicly asked the Legal and Educational Fund of the National Association for the Advancement of Colored People to assist his continuing investigation of conspiracy. (Predictably, the NAACP did not consider it was constituted and financed to defend those conspiring to murder black leaders.) Earlier, on January 19, a former close associate of the victim, Reverend James Bevel, had announced existence of proof of a conspiracy. We shall consider this at length. In its January 20 issue, the *Post* accurately reported Bevel's claim, "I have evidence that would free" Ray.

How little difference, indeed, a real trial would have made. How entirely "alone" Ray was in declaring he had been part of a conspiracy.

My intent here is not to single out the *Post* for abdicating its nigh-to-sacred obligations, for electing itself part of government. It is not alone. It was most abject in swallowing what should have nauseated it. It was intent on not reading its own news columns. So was the major part of the monolithic press, which supported what could not be supported by honest papers, honestly accepting and pursuing their obligations in a country like ours. All the papers failed us. It is merely that this old lady was most immodest [2].

Right after the minitrial, the Chicago *Daily News'* Jerry Lipson interviewed Foreman. Here is his account:

Foreman said that "within 30 minutes" after Shelby County public defender Hugh M. Stanton, Sr. was appointed co-counsel in December [through the assistance Judge Battle felt compelled to give Foreman], Stanton started talking about a guilty plea.

"I authorized him to explore it, and he told me two or three weeks later that he thought it could be done and I started to explore it," Foreman said.

Foreman said he'd also discussed the situation with Ray, pointing out the likelihood of a death sentence if he were convicted.

Finally, Ray, in a letter, authorized him to seek a deal, Foreman said, and he set the wheels in motion. Canale said he was first approached on Feb. 21.

Though Ray apparently had agreed to forgo a full-scale trial, Foreman conceded there were "difficulties" right to the end. He was concerned that one of the parties might back out.

Throughout his tenure as Ray's lawyer, the bear-sized Texan said, he never discussed the slaying directly. "I never asked Ray that question," he said when asked if Ray had told him he had pulled the trigger.

A day later Foreman acknowledged more. The Associated Press report for Wednesday's morning papers said:

Defense Attorney Percy Foreman said he never asked Ray pointblank if he was part of a conspiracy, but added that he did ask enough questions to convince himself that Ray "was not a hired gun."

Foreman had a thing about that "hired gun" bit, maybe from TV. It goes well there.

So he assumed the "defense" without asking the defendant if he was the murderer and he never asked, assuming the guilt of his client, whether he was alone or part of a conspiracy. Foreman is a gracious, thoughtful man, no less courteous than government. So he "extends" his clients "the courtesy of assuming their guilt," as he later put it. This was a "courtesy" to Ray akin to the government's to the widow, family, and friends. (Actually, it would seem that on conspiracy, Foreman not only did not ask "pointblank"—he did not ask at all. Pressed by reporters on leaving the courtroom, he blurted out, "I don't give a damn if there was a conspiracy.")

Foreman has said much, if not enough, about his handling/ mishandling of the case. It requires close study, as does his role.

85

Pending that inquiry, let us examine how the deal came about.

Almost if not exactly his first act, as he told Lipson, was to authorize his unhired hired hand, so providentially provided by Tennessee taxpayers to save the unneedy Foreman cash, to "explore" the possibilities of a deal. It is not as foreshortened as his account to Lipson.

Nor was it as Lipson wrote, that "Canale said he was first approached on Feb. 21."

Gavzer also looked into this. His report was on the AP wire for March 15, with versions for both morning and afternoon use. He said the deal "was the result of lengthy and closely-guarded negotiations" in which the widow, Tennessee Governor Buford Ellington, and Attorney General Clark "concurred" in the afternoon and "approved" in the morning papers. But both versions make clear the widow did neither, never doubting there was a conspiracy.

The agreement, according to Gavzer, was first proposed in mid-December. He gives two versions of who acted first.

> . . . Canale . . . spoke by telephone with the Civil Rights Division of the U.S. Justice Department Dec. 19.
>
> "In this call, I outlined the procedures that would be involved under Tennessee law. The key points to the agreement were a plea of guilty and a sentence of 99 years. I wanted the Department's views."
>
> Canale said he acted on his own and that "from the standpoint of a prosecutor seeking a compromise, plea and punishment is the custom instead of the exception."
>
> But Hugh Stanton, the public defender, said that on the basis of the defense investigation there was a solid feeling that Ray would risk getting the death penalty in a trial and that Stanton thought a deal could be made for a guilty plea and 99 years.
>
> "I talked to Canale about this at least a week before Christmas, and as I remember, he said he wanted to check it out with his associates," Stanton said.

From either of these contradictory versions of what there should never have been any doubt about, one wonders what happened during the "less than a half hour" after the state assigned Stanton to "help" Foreman and December 19 or thereabouts, when whichever—if either— of the Canale–Stanton accounts of what transpired actually began.

It is less clear than it could be that the initiative in conversations with the Justice Department ("his associates") was taken by Canale. It is by no means clear that there was initial insistence on the 99-year penalty, which is the most severe possible short of the death sentence and, in reality, was more severe than that would have been. (We shall see why later.) Such a penalty is hardly the "compromise" Canale described. If he had been in touch with Stanton (if not Foreman), as it would certainly appear he had been, Canale had not, really, "acted on his own."

Whatever that "defense investigation" to which Stanton refers was— if it *ever* was (and from the available indication it was no more than the official case as presented to them)—there is nothing to show any basis for the "solid feeling," whatever that might refer to or be, that there was any serious prospect of electrocution. In any event, the "compromise" has as Stanton's beginning point what was at best a very bad ending, the most severe possible penalty. *That* at least was set *before* Canale's admitted December 19 conversation with the Justice Department. Pretty fast man, that Stanton.

Those of Canale's notes on his phone conversation to which Gavzer alludes show that on January 3 he spoke to both Wachtel, the King family's New York lawyer, and Justice, where he "was informed that the plan had been discussed with Atty. Gen. Clark and that such a procedure had his approval." (Clark had an added personal stake. He was the first to proclaim "no conspiracy," before he or anyone else had the remotest idea of what had happened.)

If, as the Stanton–Canale versions seem to show, a deal had been worked out before January 3 (when Charles Edmundson's story reporting it in the *Commercial-Appeal* was denied "by a source close to the defense"), if not before December 19, there can be but bewilderment about what Gavzer next wrote (or the deepest question about the integrity of those who provided his information):

> Sometime in February, . . . Battle . . . had a discussion with Percy Foreman . . .
>
> "He asked me then, informally, for information regarding a guilty plea," the judge said. "He also asked whether a guilty plea could be settled with a life sentence. I said, 'Whoa, that's only 13 years in this state and the very least I'd consider is 99 years.' I told him that before anything could be done there would have to be a full agreement between the defense and prosecution, that there would have to be a waiver of the defense motion and that examination of

Ray would have to take place in open court at which time Ray would would have to make clear that he understood what the plea meant."

Lest the reader hastily assume that the good judge was concerned for Ray and the preservation of his rights, it might be worth considering whether this was not, in fact, a mechanism for covering the judge.

If the judge's account is accurate, than it would seem that it is he, not Canale, who refused to settle for less than the 99-year sentence. Or we have an untruthful judge—a liar—who just hid his participation in the deal and by coincidence only, two months later, arrived at exactly the same conditions for the plea-copping that Canale had stipulated two months earlier and to which Canale had already gotten federal assent.

In all of this, it should be apparent that there is, besides unpardonable contradictions in conflicting accounts of what there should never have been any doubt about, on an issue that required each participant to keep an accurate and precise record, a deliberate vagueness that is no less inexcusable. Why did Canale have to choose language that permits any interpretation he might later want to make, for example, on who initiated his phone conversations with the federal government? Or the nature and extent of federal involvement in the initiation or making of the deal?

Gavzer concluded by saying that, after the conversation between Canale and the judge, "The defense and prosecution began careful negotiations." If these did not begin until after "sometime in February," what in the world was going on earlier, in all those months?

They wanted to avoid a leak which would prematurely bring the agreement into the headlines and perhaps disrupt it. Also, according to Stanton, there were dealings regarding Ray.

What the last sentence means may only be guessed. All the "dealings" were "regarding Ray." Who else?

And who would "disrupt" the deal and why? Certainly, anticipation of public approval did not inspire this fear. Clearly, the wheeler-dealers trifling with justice did not anticipate approbation or, with public knowledge, that Ray would not wise up.

The afternoon of the "decision" in the minitrial, Lawrence Van Gelder, of the *New York Times,* interviewed Judge Warren E. Burger, then of the U.S. Court of Appeals, in Washington, and chairman of an American Bar Association committee that had made a study and issued a report on such deals. Van Gelder described "copping a plea" as popularly regarded with mistrust, "as an act with sinister overtones."

Burger (soon, of course, to become Chief Justice) told him:

This is the essence of propriety so long as everything is on top of the table and so long as the judge has not committed himself in any final sense in advance. The significant thing is that everybody clearly understands what is going on and we particularly emphasize that the judge should not be party to a definite agreement prior to the time of his imposing the sentence.

Can a judge be "less committed" than by being, as was Battle, *part* of the negotiations and insisting on the sentence in a "very final sense in advance"?

One of the cases to be considered by Burger's court, accepted April 7, is to the point here. If it did not directly relate to the Ray case and would not influence it, it did raise the question posed by the *New York Times'* headline, "Supreme Court to Review Laws to Let Defendant Negotiate Plea." The account begins:

The constitutionality of "plea bargaining" by defendants who plead guilty to escape the threat of death sentence will be reviewed by the Supreme Court next fall . . . the Court agreed to consider a ruling by the United States Court of Appeals for the Fourth Circuit, which declared unconstitutional all of North Carolina's capital punishment laws.

That case involved the often-charged criminal, Henry C. Alford, of Winston-Salem, "whose attorney advised him that the jury would sentence him to death if he did not plead guilty."

Before returning to Judge Battle, I note the Supreme Court's action reported five days earlier by the *Washington Post* in the case against William J. McCarthy, vacated after his guilty plea because "he was confused." The court insisted that judges personally question "defendants who offer to plead guilty." Presumably, this insistence on close judicial questioning was for a purpose, not a formality to pacify the Supreme Court, and that purpose was to be certain "that the plea has a 'factual basis,'" that the accused is deprived of none of his rights, and "that he understands its consequences."

The reader will be able to decide for himself whether the Ray deal met these requirements. The immediate question is whether Judge Battle did.

Gavzer interviewed Battle again. His story for Monday, March 17, morning papers begins:

Judge W. Preston Battle said Sunday he believes the full truth still is not known about James Earl Ray and the assassination . . . [he] remains puzzled about several unanswered questions. But he is convinced that a trial would not have produced the answers . . . "I would truly like to know how Ray actually found the spot from which to fire. How did Ray know where Rev. King would be? How did he determine the type of weapon to be used? What are the details of the actual purchase and selection of the weapon? Was he alone in surveillance of the Lorraine Motel? Most puzzling of all is his escape from Memphis. To me, it seems miraculous that he was able to flee to Atlanta despite the all-points bulletins without his white Mustang being spotted on a highway."

The reader will learn what the judge never did.

These are the questions the judge publicly acknowledged bothered him *after* the minitrial! (He hated that term, admitted his irritation over its use, and told Gavzer "it was not a trial.") These also are the very items of so-called evidence supposedly addressed by the prosecution in front of him! He continued:

I was convinced then and am convinced now that the trial would have muddied our understanding of the substantial evidence which established Ray as the killer. It is an error to assume the prosecution would have had a chance to cross-examine Ray . . . . Suppose he had taken the stand, the public should understand that this would not guarantee that this would have cast light upon these puzzling questions. In an adversary proceeding, each side tries to make the best case, and so some things might be exaggerated, some minimized or obscured.

This is a remarkable commentary, a remarkable epitaph.

It is a judge's plea of no confidence in himself, his court, and courts and the law in general; a denunciation of the entire judicial process and of the American concept of justice like none ever recorded. To say "the trial would have muddied our understanding" is to beg that there be no trials, and to say "the substantial evidence" could not withstand examination in a trial is to say it was spurious.

This is the "justice" of the Nazi courts. It is the Nazi "legal" concept.

Battle acknowledged he "could have refused to accept" the defense-prosecution agreement:

> It was entirely in my power to do so. But my conscience told me that it better served the ends of justice to accept the agreement. Had there been a trial, there could always have been the possibility, in such an emotionally charged case, of a hung jury. Or, though it may appear far-fetched now, he could have perhaps been acquitted by a jury.

That a presiding judge would voluntarily make such statements is exceeded in incredibility only by the silence with which they were greeted in this land of laws and respect for the laws and their spirit. This is *not* because it was little noted. The *New York Times* carried a column-long account under the headline, "Ray Judge Holds Truth Unknown." The *Washington Post*'s three-column-wide story was headed, "Questions Remain, He Says; Ray Case Puzzles Trial Judge." Its carry-over was four columns wide. It also emphasized the judge's bewilderment. Other papers accorded like treatment, one in my possession going so far as to print a four-column headline reading "Ray Judge Doubts Truth Told." Imagine that! With only the prosecution presenting *any* "evidence," "Ray Judge Doubts Truth Told"!

There were no editorial denunciations of this judicial condemnation of every American tenet and belief of fair play and protection of the innocent, of this open confession of the railroading of justice, for that is what Battle's self-justification really amounts to. The editorial ire is reserved for the real enemies of security and justice, those female guitar-strummers, long-haired boys opting for peace, and the nefarious baby-doctor. These, not such eminences as Battle, are the real enemies —from the editorial pages.

In his statement, Battle pretended what is entirely false and, in the pretense, subconsciously reflected his concept of his function and aim, to close the whole mess up and seal it before Ray could find his Pandora. Battle assumed, contrary to law and fact, that the only way any fact could be deduced was from the defendant, under cross-examination. This is quite contrary to our entire concept of law. The way in which fact is presented in an American criminal court is *without* access to the defendant and as a result of the independent work of the prosecution. It is wrong to seek or expect it from the defendant. Yet, Battle anticipated no other possible source. He talked only of Ray's taking the stand, and he said that would not "have cast light upon these puzzling questions." In saying this, he as much as said the prosecution

91

had no case, certainly no answers. He acknowledged the existence of a conspiracy while pretending there was no evidence of one!

Most shocking of all is his reason for not refusing to agree to the deal in which, Chief Justice Burger's and the Bar Association's injunction to the contrary notwithstanding, he had been an integral part: Without it, there was the possibility *Ray would not have been found guilty!* Battle could not have been more explicit in his fear of the "emotionally charged case" ending in a "hung jury" (which is the same as acquittal, as the long history of racist murders and trials in the South so overwhelmingly show). His second concern was Ray "could perhaps have been acquitted."

Yet this is the judge who was party to the frustration of justice, that indecent deal; the man charged with the upholding of the law and the preservation of all the rights of the accused, without which the law is prostituted and all citizens lose their rights.

Did any judge ever better self-portray himself as a "hanging judge"?

Battle said there *was* a conspiracy; that the most fundamental questions remain *after* presentation of the *unquestioned* prosecution case—questions about even the most basic fact; and that, if he had not agreed to the deal to which he had improperly been party, there was great danger *the accused would not have been convicted!*

This is *justice?*

Oh, the awful crime of silence.

Three weeks to the day after the minitrial, James W. Beasley, one of the three prosecutors, walked into Judge Battle's office and found him slumped over his desk. He was pronounced dead at the hospital. The coroner's verdict: Heart attack—one of the so very many abrupt deaths in the assassination stories. Ray already had addressed an appeal to him. It is this appeal he was considering at the moment of death. It was on his desk, under his body. In some quarters, the combination of circumstances prompted suspicions that seem without warrant.

9. The Minitrial

While it received little attention at the time, the papers did report Ray had made an appeal to Battle *before* the judge made these statements but that it had not reached him before the statements were published. Even later, in its April 1 obituary on the judge, the *New York Times* was still reporting: "On March 18, Judge Battle received a letter from Ray stating his plans to seek a review of his plea . . . ." This sequence is, at best, deception created by the state. Battle's statements were made Sunday, March 16. They appeared on the 17th. If those confining Ray delayed his appeal—and there is neither propriety in it if they did nor proof that they did it deliberately—he, in any case, wrote it Thursday, March 13, *five days earlier.* (I have a copy and reprint it in the next chapter.) All prison mail is censored. The state knew of Ray's appeal *immediately, before* Battle granted Gavzer the interview, even though the appeal did not in literal fact reach Battle's desk until the 18th.

In turn, we can only wonder whether there is hidden significance in Battle's words, and also in this obituary:

It would be presumptuous of us to discuss this case too much. It may well come back before me on a post-conviction motion. I understand this man's a pretty good jailhouse lawyer. If I discuss the case I might have to excuse myself and make some other judge go through what I have for the past year.

Concern over the "jailhouse lawyer's" possible motions is passing strange when the deal included a waiver of just such motions!

The obvious import is that the judge did know of Ray's intent to appeal, that he had fired Foreman, that the fat, indeed, was on the fire. It, therefore, becomes appropriate, with this possible understanding of the judge, his motives, aims, and functions, to consider the record and performance of the man who should have been no less concerned about exactly those things that perplexed the judge, no less concerned about justice and the rights of the accused: counsel for the defense.

Percy Foreman's first act on Stanton's joining the "defense" was to "authorize" his deal-seeking. This was before Foreman could have conducted an investigation of any, even the most rudimentary, kind. We do have his solicitude for his clients, as he expressed it, the "courtesy" bestowed of assuming their guilt, which is not at all what the law does and requires but is exactly the opposite.

Moreover, nothing is or could possibly be more inconsistent with Foreman's long, spectacularly successful, and enriching career.

"During a career covering more than 40 years," *Time* said of Foreman in the issue dated March 21, "he has served as defense counsel in at least 1,500 capital cases. By his own count, a mere 64 of his clients were sentenced to prison and only one was executed."

To Foreman, Steve Mitchell, the one convicted killer he lost to the chair, was "as sweet and kind a person as ever lived." On one occasion, when only favorably compared to Clarence Darrow, Foreman demurred, "I've tried more murder cases in a year than Darrow did in a lifetime."

Time's and other accounts of this man the superior of Darrow make the most fascinating reading. He once defended a woman named Mahotah Muldrow. She and her husband had had an argument.

He belted her around a bit. Thereupon she shot him five times and then left him for dead in the front yard. She drove herself to the police station to turn herself in, but for some reason, changed her mind and went back home. There, in the presence of several neighbors, who by now had gathered around Mr. Muldrow's body, Mahotah fired a sixth shot. (*Time.*)

In the case of Mahotah Muldrow, Foreman did not cop a plea, did not enter into negotiations with the prosecution before familiarizing himself with the case—as his first order of business. This was not an impossible case for Percy the Great. Again from *Time:*

Foreman won an acquittal by convincing the jury that the first five shots had been fired in self-defense.

How about that long interval *after* the five shots, when Muldrow was prone, if not dead (and who knows which shot really killed)? He made the jury believe "that the sixth shot was 1) the result of some sort of nervous reaction, and 2) had missed."

Here is the real-life Perry Mason if ever there was one.

Foreman, after the minitrial, celebrated his performance as Ray's "defender" with an appearance on ABC's "Dick Cavett Show." Breathlessly introduced as the man who had defended 400 clients in murder cases and lost but one to the executioner, the great one corrected the comedy-show impresario to say his clients have totaled more than 1,200, of whom 400 went to trial. To Cavett, as it should be to anyone, this is an "incredible string of successes."

Foreman says, and apparently believes, that the murder victim often is a rascal badly in need of killing. On the Cavett show he went so far as to say most hired killers perform a "service to society." This was his approach in the Candy Mossler case, where the beautiful young woman was accused of killing (and was universally believed to have killed) her old and very wealthy husband, Jacques Mossler. Foreman belabored the jury with the alleged depravity of the victim, calling him a deviate a rather large number of people may have wanted to kill. He won.

In the case of two Texas policemen, successfully defended without fee against charges of brutality, his approach was "Forgive them, Lord, they know not what they do."

On another occasion, the showman in him convinced the jury. His client, the widow of a cattleman, claimed her husband had whipped her. As he addressed the jury, Foreman put all 250 pounds into repeated vicious cracking of a whip on the counsel table. *Time*'s comment: "By the time he was through, the jury seemed willing to award the lady a Medal of Honor."

In his cynicism, Foreman quotes Aaron Burr, saying the law is "whatever is boldly asserted and plausibly maintained." In his career, he has been ever willing to assail the impossible. No one ever has achieved his record in the legal accomplishment of the seemingly impossible.

His function, as he expressed it to Cavett, is, "I enforce the law against the state." Defense counsel, he said, with precise accuracy, is also the agent of the law. Foreman says he holds the state to strict observance of the law.

For some reason not immediately apparent and not in any way explained by his own attempts at justification, Foreman made an exception in the Ray case. Here he turned chicken before he heard the fox howl.

His own claim, which we will assess, is, "I saved his life." Foreman is never modest. Perhaps without this vaunting ego, he could not have done what he has.

After Jack Ruby shot Oswald, Ruby claimed that all he had wanted to do was spare Jackie Kennedy a trip back to Dallas for the trial. Ruby and Foreman have a single accomplishment in common: Each prevented a trial that could not have resulted in a fair conviction.

Foreman, in mock humility, told the court, "I never expected or had any idea when I entered this case that I would be able to accomplish anything except, perhaps, save the defendant's life." On leaving the court, as he did immediately thereafter, he faced the TV cameras. He began by taking credit for saving Ray's life. The next issue was the conspiracy. Oddly, or perhaps not oddly (depending on whether one believes him to be a serious man of honest intent, genuinely dedicated to his calling and to principle, and to serving the country), he professed complete disinterest in any conspiracy or evidence of it. This surely made his client bear the burden of the co-conspirators. The words he blurted out are, "I don't give a damn if there was a conspiracy!" Can a better face be put upon those words?

Foreman insists here that the function of defense counsel is not justice but the defense of his client as he (Foreman) sees that defense. Later, on the Cavett show, he was to say the opposite, declaring that defense counsel is the agent of the law, that it is his function to seek justice, etc.

So, there is no point in expecting consistency from Foreman. Several inconsistencies, of varying degrees of importance, are to be noted in his comments on the Ray case.

Foreman wrote in *Look* dated April 15, 1969, "I then, over several weeks, spent 40 hours in conversation with him [Ray], endeavoring to bring him to believe that I knew more about the law than he did . . . ." In court he said, "I talked with my client more than 50 hours, I would estimate." Whereas in *Look,* after the fact and for pay, Foreman said he spent the time "endeavoring to bring him to believe I knew more about the law than he did," he gave an entirely different account to the judge (Trial transcript, p. 16; further references to pages in the transcript are identified by "T"), in seeking to justify the so exceptional thing he was doing in guaranteeing that his client would never get out of jail:

> "I talked with my client more than 50 hours, I would estimate, and cross-examination [sic] most of that time, checking each hour, minute, each expenditure of money down to even 50 and 75 cents for shaves and haircuts . . . ."

Now, the big question here is not the discrepancy between the 50 hours for the judge and 40 hours for *Look,* and how he spent them— vital as that discrepancy is when the integrity of the lawyer is involved —but his simple truthfulness with simple fact. The truth here is that Percy Foreman is as great a liar as he is a lawyer—and he is a very great lawyer. In *Look,* Foreman wrote he spent all 40 hours trying to persuade Ray he knew the law, whereas Ray did not. In court, where he had his action to defend and justify, he said he spent "most of that time" in "cross-examination," and that he had actually accounted for "each hour and each minute," for "each expenditure of money down to 50 cents."

But when? Certainly not in the 10 hours he allowed himself for this not inconsiderable task, if he did not deliberately lie in *Look;* and not in all 50 hours, if he did not deliberately lie in court.

Remember how early he "authorized" Stanton to try to make a deal? Before he had any chance to learn the facts of the case. In court that came out entirely differently:

"... Took me a month [meaning at most a 40-hour month or a 50-hour month!] to convince myself of that fact which the Attorney General of the United States and J. Edgar Hoover of the Federal Bureau of Investigation announced last July; that is, just what [District Attorney] Gen. Canale has told you, that there was not a conspiracy."

It would be more precise to say "no evidence of a conspiracy." (Clark had proclaimed "no conspiracy" immediately, not waiting three months.) Still, might one not have expected defense counsel, especially one such as Percy Foreman, to exploit the fact that the government charged his client with conspiracy while maintaining there was none? This, certainly, cast a shadow over everything the government said. Instead, Foreman was on Clark's side.

One glaring lack here is Foreman's certification that his own independent investigation confirmed every entirely untested allegation by the prosecution. That you will *not* find in the record, court or journalistic. And how could Hoover ever make a mistake, especially when a police record is opposed to the client of the lawyer who successfully defended so many hundreds against precisely such police records?

Foreman used his brief court statement well. He had only the best to say about everyone opposed to his client. He left no enemies in Memphis officialdom.

To understand what Foreman did and did not do, could and could not have done in the brief 40 or 50 hours he claimed to have invested, "convincing" himself (and we may well believe he can and did do with either 40 or 50 hours what no one else could or would), we have to consult his out-of-court statements.

On TV, where he reached millions of gullibles, he told Cavett and his audience *not* that he learned what he learned from his client, cross-examined or not; *not* from his own investigation, if any at all he had made; but from what he described as a close study of the allegations *against* his client—precisely what it was his function to examine critically and destroy. It was precisely these allegations that Hanes, the former government agent, claimed, when he was Ray's lawyer, that he could not get to see. Fascinating that former FBI (and CIA) man Hanes, who insisted on a trial, could not see this stuff, but Foreman—who began trying to cop a plea almost immediately—did.

There were 420 FBI agents, he said, involved in the largest man-hunt in history, etc., etc., in a multimillion dollar inquiry.

This great man of the law, who cracks whips at some juries; convinces others that men interested in sex with their wives deserve murder; the master of the Mahotah Muldrow delayed-non-premeditation-of-shooting before scads of witnesses who know her defense; the undaunted Percy Foreman, suddenly became self-daunted and believed every word of the untested FBI material before it was even in court—and denied it the cross-examination his client's and the nation's interest demanded.

If the FBI, the other side, said it, that was enough for Foreman—and enough to cook Ray.

How he could have conducted an investigation—if he did—must remain a mystery when we recall the traveling he *did* do in this same time, the speeches he made, what he did and did not do to, with, and for women clients and others, and his in-court and out-of-court activities and their requirements. The modest representation of the evidence (and for *420* of the FBI's best and *millions* of the taxpayers' dollars, it *is* modest) made in court by Canale (T. 14) is "over 5,000 printed pages of investigative work" (they *print* it now?) and "over 300 physical bits of evidence, physical exhibits." To make a close study of all this in the time Foreman had is no mean accomplishment.

If he did.

What he did and did not do and say, in this and other cases, could be carried further, in itself to book length. Let us leave him with his dead horse and consider whether he did, nonetheless, serve his client's interest (he did *not* serve the nation's!) by making a good deal, by actually saving Ray's life, and how he was able to pull it off.

From the first, Ray opposed *any* deal. There is not now and never was any doubt about this. He was Foreman's *only* real obstacle. What Foreman spent at least a large portion of his time (if not all of it) doing was trying to persuade Ray. We have his words to the this effect. If we understand his *Look* comment about his efforts to convince Ray that he, Foreman, knew the law to mean to convince Ray of the consequences of not following his advice, Foreman's claim makes sense and might be the truth.

We have as well the strange report by Gavzer, "Also, according to Stanton, there were dealings regarding Ray." Gavzer quotes Stanton:

"At first he kept saying he wanted to take his chances and go to trial," Stanton said. "But when we pointed out the evidence that was against him, and what our investigation produced, which was very little, he agreed to change his plea and take the 99 years."

(Parenthetically, it should not pass unnoticed that Stanton's own, and perhaps the only, description of the so-called defense "investigation" is that "it produced very little." Again, he is without comment on the essence—investigation of the case *against* Ray. The defense did *not* have to prove Ray innocent.)

Master of words that he is, Foreman was cuter on the Cavett show where he was asked how he got Ray to change his plea. "I didn't get him to change his plea," he purred, all smiles. "I merely told him I thought he'd be executed if he didn't." Everybody laughed. This is really the kind of thing to break people up, isn't it?

As he successfully persuaded juries, Foreman finally persuaded Ray. He worked on everyone who had access to him. Brother John Ray was interviewed by the St. Louis *Post-Dispatch,* whose March 13 story quoted him thus: "Foreman warned us that if a trial were to take place, Jimmie would possibly go to the chair to be made an example of . . . ." Two days earlier, the Chicago *Daily News'* Jerry Lipson quoted Jerry Ray in this manner: "Asked why his brother had agreed to plead guilty, Jerry Ray replied, 'They were gonna burn him.'"

Jerry tells me that at first Foreman held out the prospect of acquittal "until the Government and Huie got to him"—more about the Huie proposal later—then changed. "Once the government and Huie worked out a deal with Foreman," Jerry said, "then he really went to work on my brother, among other things he told him he was making it rough on his relations, that his relations wish he would plead guilty. He told him that he couldn't win the case as the government had spent around two million dollars to catch and convict him." On the guilty plea: "If I was under the strain that my brother was, I couldn't have held out that long." (In his view, the security precautions contributed to the terrorization: ". . . they kept the lights on 24 hours . . . two policemen in the same cell with him at all times . . . kept him on television (closed circuit) 24 hours per day, he couldn't even use the wash room in private . . . .")

Jerry also says Foreman went to St. Louis and put the heat on all the family so they would pressure James Earl, convince him electrocution was the alternative to following Foreman's advice.

Even James Earl Ray, who had been kept almost completely out of contact with any non-officials and had not had a single private moment from the time he was returned to the United States, told Nashville prison officials (to whose jail he was spirited after the trial) exactly the same thing, "When I went to court Monday I was convinced if I didn't plead guilty I was going to the electric chair." During the move, he told his guards: "My attorney and my brother told me about six weeks ago the best thing for me to do was plead guilty if we could work out a deal to keep me out of the chair. They told me they thought this could be done. I was thinking about it and every day they thought I would plead guilty. Last week I just told them if they thought this was best and what I ought to, then I would plead guilty . . . I couldn't say exactly what I wanted to in court."

He made his unexpected comment in the courtroom, even if he "couldn't say exactly what I wanted" under threat of burning, as he told his guards, because he thought "this had better be in the record."

So, there is universal agreement among all who could know. It was difficult to get Ray to agree to plead guilty. Foreman says this was the only way to save Ray's life, and his was a purely humanitarian motive, to save this life, the only hope he had held from the very first. It was also the only way a public trial, with the presentation and examination of evidence, could be avoided.

There was also the question of conspiracy. Here again, complete accord.

It should be understood that Ray's insistence (which we will see) that he was part of a conspiracy does not in any way enhance his image. It also destroys the alleged motive attributed to him. There is nothing heroic about the role in which he thus cast himself. If his concern was selfish, he served no selfish purpose by this insistence. To kill King as a loner, believing he thereby served a useful or worthwhile purpose by the murder, could present Ray to some as heroic or patriotic. But to have been part of a conspiracy, especially a minor part, diminished the alleged glory of the crime, at least, diluted it and for most demeaned it.

More, were he the killer insisting he was not alone, he was, in effect, pleading a worse offense, eliminating any possibility of emotional motivation, making it a willful, conscious, premeditated crime, certainly less romantic and less likely to receive sympathetic consideration.

Yet, he insisted in court that there had been a conspiracy. Foreman, who, as we shall see, glossed over this in court, switching the subject, getting the judge away as quickly as possible, tried to ridicule it out of court.

Here is Jerry Lipson's account of Foreman's analysis of why Ray did this:

> Foreman later told The Daily News that Ray had said that only to keep the conspiracy notion alive in order to make money selling stories.
>
> "He's got a gold mine in stories. He didn't want to kill the golden goose," the gravel-voiced attorney said . . . .
>
> "Like everyone else, he (Ray) at first believed all this talk (about conspiracy) was true," but soon found out he could verify none of it, the attorney said.

Lipson, too, allowed himself to be diverted. First, there was no reason for Ray, in his own defense, to "verify" a conspiracy. But for that matter, Foreman did not lack verification. Enough of it was public knowledge. The judge himself specified several evidences. As for Ray, if he wants to stay alive, the last thing he would do would be to finger living co-conspirators, whose living depends on his silence.

Second, as to that alleged gold mine: if it exists, it cannot be mined by a man permanently jailed. In agreeing to Foreman's pressures and the guilty plea, Ray simultaneously lost all need of or use for money. He thereupon became the financial responsibility of the state, in perpetuity.

More, Foreman's statement, "He's got a gold mine in stories. He didn't want to kill the golden goose," is and was to his knowledge so totally false he cannot be too strongly condemned for it—especially because it is Foreman, personally, who saw to it that there *could* be *no* return to *Ray* from any of the stories and *Foreman* who *is* their beneficiary, not Ray. In coming chapters we will expose the suppressed contracts into which Ray was pressured and inveigled. I have them. Foreman was all too well aware of the enormity of this lie when he uttered it.

The day of the minitrial, Jerry Ray told Lipson, "I still think there was a conspiracy." He has greatly amplified this to me, alleging the involvement of the FBI and others in covering it up.

According to John Ray, Foreman's explanation for refusing to have anything to do with any conspiracy angle was "because it would make Jimmie look like a hired killer rather than someone who may have killed King because he thought he was a Communist or different in his beliefs." John also told the St. Louis *Post-Dispatch* that James Earl had told him during a jail visit, "I am not the only one in on this." This was but "two days before he entered the guilty plea." At that time, James Earl "was still trying to figure out what to do—whether to take a plea or insist on going to trial. He wanted to testify . . . . My brother said there was someone else in on this 'deal' [the murder], but it had been hushed up by the Federal Bureau of Investigation."

(Privately, without citation of the proof he claims to have, Jerry made the same charge to me, that the FBI was engaged in a cover-up.)

At the trial, before the jury was brought in, Judge Battle went through the formalities of getting Ray's agreement to the deal on record (in the stenographic transcript, T. 4–8). Ray said he had agreed to the deal. When Battle asked, "Has any pressure of any kind been used on you to get you to plead guilty?" (Blair transcript), he never got a direct response. The first time Ray asked, "Now, what did you say?" The judge then rephrased what he had said, using different words. This time he asked (T. 8), "Are you pleading guilty . . . because you killed Dr. Martin Luther King under such circumstances that it would make you legally guilty of murder in the first degree under the law as explained to you by your lawyers?"

Now, he did *not* ask Ray, "Did you kill Dr. King" or "Did you alone kill Dr. King." He hedged his question very carefully so that a response did not even mean Ray said he was, in fact, either *the* or *a* killer. First, Ray had to judge if his involvement was "under such circumstances that it would make you legally guilty of murder in the first degree." This could mean that Ray was guilty of the technical charge by his part in the conspiracy, not because he fired the shot. To emphasize the limits of the question, Battle added these two things, "under the law" and "as explained to you by your lawyers." Now, certainly, no judge would expect Ray to know the detail and complications of Tennessee law on murder first. So all he was asking Ray is not whether he had, in fact, been the killer, but had he been involved "under such circumstances" that "under the law as explained to you by your lawyers," it was legally the same as if he had been the killer.

To this question, then, Ray responded in the sense in which it was asked and in this sense only: "Yes, legally guilty, uh-huh."

Any dispassionate reading of the transcript makes it clear that, for whatever purpose, the judge was *not* asking Ray if he *was* the killer and Ray was careful not to say that he was. *At no point did he admit the killing. At no point was he ever asked!*

No less incredibly, no one ever alleged anything other than the very technical wording of the judge, that the plea was "of guilty to murder in the first degree," not to the actual killing! These quoted words are the prosecutor's, and all he added (T. 12-13) was that, under the law,

> We have put on proof of what we lawyers call the proof of the corpus delicti which is the body of the crime. We will also put on several lay witnesses or police officers to fill you in on certain important aspects of this case, and then we will introduce certain physical evidence through these witnesses . . . .

In short, all the prosecution claimed it would prove is that King was murdered and Ray had some connection with the murder. It never claimed it would prove he was the murderer. We shall see it did not. It merely placed him at the scene of the crime.

Foreman's entire plea in court is a brief 700 words (T. 15-9)—in Blair's transcript, but a single long paragraph. He began with praise for everyone opposed to his client. Then, as soon as Foreman spread the last of his unction, on the press, he reworded the official claims of not having proof of a conspiracy to make them positive and unequivocal, which they were not. He uttered the sentence quoted above, of how he had finally persuaded himself that his prosecution opponents, the Attorney General of the United States and Hoover, were right, concluding "there was not a conspiracy" (T. 16). But immediately before this rather odd kind of "defense," Canale had twice said something very different. He had said merely, "we have no proof" (T. 14). He did not even say he had no reason to believe there had been a conspiracy. He was technical, legalistic—and quite indefinite.

He never said there was no conspiracy! Only Foreman did.

Now, one way of having "no proof" was not to look for it, and no one did. Such evidence, of course, would have made the legal cooking of the bird-in-hand, Ray, more difficult, not easier. It would have had to be related to him as the murderer, to the exclusion of anyone else.

Foreman helped only his adversaries. He uttered no single word on behalf of his client, had nothing at all to say of him or on his behalf, was full of praise for everyone else (Canale "is a man as big as his office, if not bigger, a man who is not primarily concerned with the scalps on his belt" [T. 18]) and he defended only the deal he made (T. 16-17). This merged smoothly into his examination of the jury.

Satisfied that he had a hanging judge, Foreman saw to it he also had a hanging jury—a jury that would agree to the forever-more sentence *in advance of any evidence.* It was not the *prosecution* who sought to guarantee Ray's lifetime incarceration but his *defender,* the man who was "sure" the judge "would excuse" any juror unwilling to pledge, *in advance of presentation or consideration of any evidence whatsoever,* first, to find the accused guilty and, next, to agree to a life-plus sentence.

This is one of the most unusual "defenses" and jury-examinations in legal history. It deserves preservation in the proper context. It follows in full (T. 18-23). Foreman has just assured the prospective jurors "all that we have here is . . . equal justice being applied," not special punishment being meted out to James Earl Ray:

MR. FOREMAN: Now, with that, I want to ask each of you individually just one single question. It is polling the jury in advance.

Mr. Black, who is Mr. Black? Mr. Black, are you willing to assess the punishment that His Honor and Gen. Canale and the attorneys for the defense have agreed upon in this case, 99 years?

MR. BLACK: Yes.

MR. FOREMAN: You are. Thank you, sir. And Mr. Blackwell, are you likewise willing to—is there anything in your conscience that would rebel at writing this penalty agreed upon in this case?

And you, Mr. Abrams, is that your answer also, and if accepted as a juror in this case, you will underwrite the verdict and the judgment of the Court and prosecuting attorney and defense counsel?

MR. ABRAMS: Yes, sir.

MR. FOREMAN: Thank you, Mr. Abrams. And you are Mr. St. Pierre?

MR. ST. PIERRE: That is correct.

MR. FOREMAN: That is St. Pierre, isn't it? I bet they haven't pronounced it right here yet.

MR. ST. PIERRE: That is one —

MR. FOREMAN: Are you, Mr. St. Pierre, willing to subscribe to the verdict of 99-year sentence in this case if accepted as a juror?

MR. ST. PIERRE: Yes.

MR. FOREMAN: Thank you. And you are Mr. Williamson?

MR. WILLIAMSON: Yes, sir.

MR. FOREMAN: Is that your answer also?

MR. WILLIAMSON: Yes, sir.

MR. FOREMAN: And if you are sworn as a juror in this case, you will assess the penalty agreed upon and as recommended by your Attorney General and approved by His Honor, Judge Battle?

MR. WILLIAMSON: Yes, sir.

MR. FOREMAN: And you, Mr. Howard?

MR. HOWARD: Yes, sir.

MR. FOREMAN: Will you likewise assess the penalty of 99 years if you are accepted as a juror in this case?

MR. HOWARD: Yes, sir.

MR. FOREMAN: Thank you. And you are Mr. Counsellor?

MR. COUNSELLOR: Yes, sir.

MR. FOREMAN: Thank you, Mr. Counsellor. Is your answer the same as these gentlemen on the back seat?

MR. COUNSELLOR: Yes, sir.

MR. FOREMAN: You will underwrite the verdict—

MR. COUNSELLOR: Yes, sir.

MR. FOREMAN: —if accepted as a juror. And you, Mr. Stovall?

MR. STOVALL: That is my answer also.

MR. FOREMAN: Thank you, sir. We have a Judge Stovall in Houston. Mr. Pate?

MR. PATE: Yes, sir.

MR. FOREMAN: Would you underwrite the verdict of 99 years as agreed upon and recommended by your Attorney General?

MR. PATE: Yes, sir.

MR. FOREMAN: And agreed to by the defense in this case and by the Defendant? And Mr. Shaw, is that your answer also?

MR. SHAW: Yes, sir.

MR. FOREMAN: You would write the same verdict also? Your answer is the same?

MR. SHAW: Yes, sir.

MR. FOREMAN: Mr. Cariota, is that your answer, sir?

MR. CARIOTA: Yes, sir.

MR. FOREMAN: And you, Mr. Ballard?

MR. BALLARD: Yes, sir.

MR. FOREMAN: You would? Thank you. Thank you very much. Thank you, Your Honor.

THE COURT: Do both sides accept the jury?

MR. FOREMAN: We do, Your Honor.

GEN. CANALE: The State does, Your Honor.

When the country-boy pseudo-friendliness was taken seriously by Juror St. Pierre and he started to make response, Foreman cut him off immediately—so fast St. Pierre had time for but three very short words. When Counsellor was so anxious to agree before Foreman got the whole formula out, Foreman persisted in getting Counsellor's specific agreement to each clause. No shortcuts, no doubts. Every juror nailed and nailed firmly.

It is at this point (T. 23-25) that, timidly, Ray found voice. He not only made clear that he was not admitting he was the actual murderer, he disputed what his own lawyer had added gratuitously, claiming there was a conspiracy. He likely was frightened, but then so probably was everyone else. In the context of the courtroom, the whole deal was about to fall apart. Note that it is Foreman, not the judge or Canale, who saved the situation. Canale in fact remained silent throughout.

Ray feared being burned if he said too much. He was careful to begin with the assurance he did not want to run the risk of electrocution.

MR. RAY: Your Honor, I would like to say something too, if I may.

THE COURT: All right.

MR. RAY: I don't want to change anything that I have said. I don't want to add anything onto it either. The only thing I have to say is, I don't exactly accept the theories of Mr. Clark. In other words, I am not bound to accept these theories of Mr. Clark.

MR. FOREMAN: Who is Mr. Clark?

MR. RAY: Ramsey Clark.

MR. FOREMAN: Oh.

MR. RAY: And Mr. Hoover.

MR. FOREMAN: Mr. who?

MR. RAY: Mr. J. Edgar Hoover. The only thing, I say I am not—I agree to all these stipulations. I am not trying to change anything. I just want to add something onto it.

THE COURT: You don't agree with whose theories?

MR. RAY: I meant Mr. Canale, Mr. Foreman, Mr. Ramsey Clark. I mean on the conspiracy thing. I don't want to add something onto it which I haven't agreed to in the past.

MR. FOREMAN: I think that what he is saying is that he doesn't think that Ramsey Clark's right or J. Edgar Hoover is right. I didn't argue them as evidence in this case. I simply stated that underwriting and backing up the opinions of General Canale, that they had made the same statement. [Speaking apparently to Ray] You are not required to agree or withdraw or anything else.

THE COURT: You still—your answers to these questions that I asked you would still be the same?

MR. RAY: Yes, sir. The only thing is I just didn't want to add anything onto them. That was all.

There are minor differences between the official and the Blair transcripts. Blair's, for example, has the judge asking at the very beginning, "Mr. Who?" when Ray mentioned Clark. In all important respects, the transcripts are in accord, although they sometimes have different words expressing the same thoughts. On Ray's insistence there had been a conspiracy, they are in verbatim agreement. What Ray said here is that he had not agreed to say there was no conspiracy and he was not saying it, that "I don't want to add something onto it which I haven't agreed to in the past"—meaning to his lawyers and as part of the deal (what Jerry Ray told me James said he meant).

Everyone, naturally, was stunned. But that Chautauqua glibness saved Foreman and his repackaging of history. First, he took over for the speechless judge. Then he twisted what Ray was saying just enough not to antagonize Ray further, not enough to cause him to blow entirely, but enough to save the judge's face and the deal. Then he "persuaded" Ray, at the end, that he was not "required to agree or withdraw or anything else" (in Blair's transcript, the wording is even stronger: "you are not required to agree with it at all").

Quite a performance. Foreman *is* a brilliant trial lawyer. Here he was spectacular.

James Earl Ray is no fool. It required a sharp mind to pick up what the clever Foreman tried to pull on him. None of the many newsmen present did, nor has any analyst who has since commented on it. He had to be courageous to risk execution to record that he had not admitted and was not admitting committing the murder and to insist there had been a conspiracy.

Foreman grabbed the ball from Ray, who had said all he dared in any event. It seems what Foreman wanted to do was to get away from this subject as quickly as possible, to put it away, out of the judge's mind. His "explanation" (T. 24–5) is false, a deliberate misrepresentation:

> I think that what he is saying is that he doesn't think that Ramsey Clark's right or J. Edgar Hoover is right. I didn't argue them as evidence in this case.

This is entirely irrelevant.

> I simply stated that underwriting and backing up the opinions of General Canale, that they had made the same statement. [Apparently to Ray] You are not required to agree or withdraw or anything else.

(In the Blair transcript, the second sentence is "I didn't argue *that* as evidence in *the* case" and the explanation to Ray is "You are not required to agree with it all." The words "and backing up" are not in the Blair transcript.)

As we have seen, Foreman did *not* say what Canale said. He was neither "backing up" nor "underwriting" Canale. He was *extending* the deal and the plea to pin the actual murder on Ray, the man he was supposed to be defending. This gratuitous, unagreed, unrequired, and inaccurate falsehood served no other purpose.

Only Foreman said, in effect, that Ray was the murderer—if there was no conspiracy, there was only Ray—and for this Ray would not remain quiet!

The judge did not say it, the prosecutor did not, the accused did not, and Foreman did not have to. Clearly, this was not part of the package he had conned and terrified Ray into accepting. Ray agreed to plead guilty to a technical charge, and Foreman tried, entirely without need, to slip in his pleading guilty to the actual murder. Who Foreman served may be a question. It is not a question whether in this he served his client, for that he did not do, could not, under any possible extension or interpretation. The prosecution and court were satisfied with the plea to a technical charge rather than to the actual killing. With the deal all neatly agreed to wrapped up, there was no need to add what Ray had never accepted or agreed to—had not even been *asked,* as Foreman later acknowledged in *Look* for April 15, 1969.

If Foreman had gotten away with this subtle claim to the commission of the actual crime by his client, he would have given the government what it does not have, a solved crime. It is impossible to consider that the man who, in his own estimate, is so much the superior of the fabled Darrow, this successful defender of so many murderers, merely stumbled in court. He did not blunder. This was no accident. He did and said what he intended doing and saying. (The news accounts describe how he spent the time not talking to his client—saying they exchanged not a single word—while awaiting the arrival of the judge. They say he was going over his prepared statement.) But, accident or not, it gives point to his entirely unnecessary insistence that there was no conspiracy when his own client does plead guilty to being part of that conspiracy. More so when Ray had to do it in his own defense— had to be his own lawyer—to keep the actual murder from being attributed to him.

Foreman's real client was not James Earl Ray. It was the government. He served it well. Better, perhaps, than anyone else could—or would. In this way, the minitrial began.

10. Would Ray Have Been Executed?

Foreman's trying to put words in Ray's mouth, trying to make a record that Ray admitted being the lone killer, was not all the shaking up Ray got. Ray must have been really desperate when he heard the presentation of the "evidence." It requires no lawyer, no Foreman, to understand that this evidence did not convict him of murder. We will examine it carefully, point by major point. But, when it was all over, there was nothing, given his view of what might happen to him, that Ray could dare do. If he tried to break the agreement in court, after it was too late, he had to worry about execution, about then being steamrollered to the chair. So before we examine the evidence, to which we must give extended scrutiny, let us take up the issue of execution.

He seems to have thought of it after the trial, through the day and into the night.

The leak to the Huntsville *Times* about the entire deal was by a source privy to what most officials were not. Similarly, the Nashville jail did not know Ray was to be rushed there that night. He was, about 1 A.M. Accounts differ, but they may not be contradictory. As he left Memphis, Ray is said to have been dressed as a deputy sheriff, carefully surrounded in one State Police car by seven others, in an 80-mile-an-hour motorcade which was probably the only real danger he faced from the moment of capture.

On arrival at the jail, he was wearing ordinary clothing. He was photographed in a sport coat, head and face down, in manacles and chains, with his wrists and ankles both cuffed, surrounded by a very large, heavily armed guard. This photograph was staged. He could have been driven into the jail. He did not have to climb its steps before the camera.

News of Ray's conversations with his captors soon reached the *Nashville Tennessean.* It attributed this statement to "prison sources":

> "When I was in court Monday I was convinced that if I didn't plead guilty I was going to the electric chair. I wish the hell I hadn't now because with what they had on me I believe the worst I'd gotten would have been life."

"Life" sentencing could have meant as little as thirteen years. What Foreman arranged for him is at best, forty years more, or until he is about ninety.

Ray at this time also "made inquiries about an attorney." He asked Highway Patrol Captain Richard Dawson on the trip from Memphis. Another "source" heard him comment, "To get to federal court you've got to come up with a mistake before your trial."

The papers carrying this news—usually not prominently, in those cases of which I know—added Huie's self-justification of his changed view about Ray: "Ray is just smart enough, in his criminal mind, to be putting everybody on."

Somebody, it can be agreed, surely did "put everybody on." The best evidence is that Ray is not the one [1].

James Earl Ray may not be the most impartial authority to invoke on the matter of who is putting on whom. No one is more involved than he; at the same time, no one knows more. It seems appropriate to examine two letters he wrote Judge Battle after the trial. The reader can decide for himself whether his bitterness over his legal representation is warranted, his words justified. This is his first letter, dated March 13, three days after the trial. It is Ray's view of Foreman's handling of the case—and notice that Ray had fired "Percy Fourflusher" and intended "to file for a post-conviction hearing."

3-13-69

Dear Sir;

I wish to inform the honorable court that that Attorney Houston atty. Percy Dauflusher is no longer representing me in any complicity. My reason for writing this letter is that I intend to file for a post conviction hearing in the very near future and don't want him making any legal moves unless their in my conole behalf.

Sincerely,
James Earl Ray

FILED 4-1-69 2:55 P.M.
J. A. BLACKWELL, CLERK
BY J. A. Blackwell D. C.

Still, one can ask: had Foreman *really* served his client and his obligations? Did he *really* save Ray's life? If he had not worked out this deal, would Ray have been electrocuted? Interwoven with this question is another: Had Foreman, as he carefully lead everyone to believe, taken the case without fee?

We have quoted Bill Johnson's story discussing Foreman's interests when he first entered the case. "Percy Foreman, the Texas lawyer who has taken over the James Earl Ray defense, said Monday the question of money wasn't bothering him." This is the story in which Foreman claimed"I've given away $300,000 this year." The financial arrangements were not of "primary importance." His real interest was in those "one or two questions" remaining unanswered that "fascinated" him. (No doubt, this makes sense of his first move after getting free legal assistants from the state—within a half hour—that of starting work on his big deal.)

Two weeks after the minitrial information of another sort became public. I first heard it on the March 24, CBS radio 8 A.M. news. CBS asked, "How much is it worth to defend a man accused of murder?" Its answer, "If it is James Earl Ray, it may be as much as $175,000." It mentioned magazine and movie rights among others. CBS quoted Foreman as adding, "And I'll get 60 percent of it." (The specifics of these arrangements will come.)

All of this information on that early morning excited me, for it meant a shocking truth the papers should have noted, raised a question CBS should have asked.

What did Ray have that was worth all this money *before* there was any kind of legal proceeding? Foreman's question, a calculated deception, designed to mislead, is how was Ray going to "earn" anything. The issue was not how he could "earn" anything, but if he had anything to sell, and what?

Ray had one thing to sell, his story.

Now, unless Ray's story was sold *before* the trial, what came out in the trial was not worth anything to Foreman *et al.* At that moment it became what the law calls "public domain." It is anybody's and everybody's. No one need pay anyone anything for it and, more, it is "privileged," as is any court proceeding. Every experienced writer knows this, as Huie certainly does, and the least competent attorney, which Foreman is not, also knows it.

In short, unless Ray was capitalized *before* trial, they had nothing to capitalize!

If Ray said anything in court, the exclusive right to it would be lost. Whatever evidence was produced became the property of every writer. Thus, *after* the proceeding, what Ray had to sell (not how he could "earn" anything) is what remained untold of that story, plus authorization for the use of his name on it. Nothing else.

While Foreman bragged of giving away $300,000, he was also greedy enough to demand and get 60 per cent of the gross to be milked from Ray and his crimes. What a conflict confronted him! A trial was tantamount to guaranteeing he would get no money. It was to Foreman's personal interest, and a very large interest—as much as a half-million dollars—that there be none.

That Foreman saw to. It was not easy. But he did it.

With an ordinary lawyer, this would—and *should*—be of barassociation interest.

Foreman "said Look magazine had guaranteed another $85,000 for Huie's series of articles on Ray's life, and that he was entitled to 60 percent of that also. The attorney said that his 60 percent share of the movie, book and magazine rights might total $400,000 or so, but that he would take only the $150,000 agreed upon with Ray."

That afternoon, in an AP story by Hal Cooper, it became known that the magazine rights were Huie's, to go to *Look,* and the movie interest was to go to Carlo Ponti, husband of Sophia Loren.

Reporting was less consistent and more confusing than it need have been. Nowhere did the papers give this aspect of the case much attention. (Only when those disagreeing with official fictions are alleged to be making money—when most have not—does the press use the term "scavengers" and play the stories prominently, with indignation.) The Associated Press, for example, quoted Foreman from both Houston and New York on the same day. The *New York Times* found part of the AP's story not the news that is fit to print. And the omniscient *Washington Post* rewrote and abbreviated what it carried.

Jerry Ray told the *Nashville Tennessean,* which wrote a copyrighted story, that "Foreman said he would take $150,000 [of the various rights] if my brother pleaded guilty but he wanted everything he would earn if he didn't."

AP's lead was a response to this statement—Foreman's denial "that he had used financial pressure to obtain a guilty plea from James Earl Ray." The story went on: " 'How is any man doing 99 years in the penitentiary going to earn anything?' Foreman asked.

'That's ridiculous.' " It seems reasonable, but Foreman knew better, knew the dirty pool he was playing was real dirty.

As the AP story was published in several papers, it then reads,

> Foreman said he asked Ray to specify a reasonable fee three weeks after he received a letter from Ray asking for a guilty plea and Ray said $150,000. "I didn't fix the fee, he fixed it," Foreman said.

Obviously, Ray could not be consulted and was not quoted. But it is also obvious this is entirely inconsistent with what Foreman earlier had led everyone to believe—especially the court—and, more significantly for what follows, inconsistent with what is known about Ray and his relation to Foreman. Simply put, it is not the whole truth.

At this point, the same AP story is different as it appears in different papers. In the New Orleans *Times-Picayune,* this then follows:

> Foreman said he originally was to get 60% of a contract for picture, book and magazine rights. The 60% will probably be more than $400,000, he said.
>
> "When it appeared the plea was going through," Foreman said, "in view of the fact that I would be relieved of the responsibility of appeal, I thought there should be an adjustment of the fee in his [Ray's] favor."
>
> Foreman said he plans to place his 60% over the $150,000 fee in a trust fund for Ray's family, and is waiting until they decide on a bank.
>
> Picture rights have already been sold for $175,000 plus 13% of the receipts, he said.
>
> Foreman said he advised Ray to plead guilty "because I believed he would be electrocuted if he didn't."

Given the sums of money involved, is there any wonder Foreman had said he was not concerned about his fee?

The *New York Times,* without indicating it was rewriting the AP's dispatch, abbreviated the details, apparently deeming the converting of the accused and then convicted murderer into big business not fit to print. It made Foreman look like Texas Big Heart No. 1 in this fashion:

> Foreman said he plans to place his 60% [that is, 100 per cent of his fee!] of the picture, book and magazine rights in a trust fund for Ray's family. He said he had told the family, and was waiting until they decided on a bank.

By no means did Foreman give up his promising cut of the commercialization.

The *Washington Post,* which also uses other wire services, printed a story that was a rewrite of stories from various services. Where Foreman is quoted by AP as saying "that's ridiculous," the *Post* story began by saying Foreman called the report "a bunch of bull," which is probably closer to what he actually said.

The *Tennessean* quoted Foreman as saying he had taken over the arrangement that existed between Ray and Hanes. This, we shall see, also seems like undue generosity to the man who in any case began with the pretense he was getting no fee at all.

Foreman's great generosity—keeping what he claimed was his, "only the $150,000 agreed upon with Ray"—did not come out, however, until Jerry Ray smoked it out. But perhaps, in the course of educating so many prosecutors and juries, country-boy Foreman may not have taken time to learn about the counting of unhatched chicks.

Cooper also had quoted to Foreman a comment by Jerry that Foreman "would take $150,000 if my brother pleaded guilty, but he wanted everything he would ever earn if he didn't," writing of the response that "Foreman described this as 'a bunch of ———.' " As the comment might refer to Jerry's use of word "earn," Foreman may have been on firm ground. Wages in southern jails are low. But contracts with commercially minded publishers need not be.

On the 25th, the *Washington Post's* rewriting of wire-service stories quoted Foreman as saying "he understood that Arthur J. Hanes of Birmingham, Ala., Ray's original lawyer, had been paid $35,000." If so, no tears for him. And if so, this means that Huie had shelled out not less than $40,000 plus his own considerable expenses—only to wind up with a minority share of his own property—if any. (As late as his June 9 appearance with Cavett, Foreman was saying he had gotten no "bread." It was a lie.)

That same day the *New York Times* had bitter news for the crime commercializers posing as public benefactors. Ponti's New York attorney told it there had been discussions with Foreman and Huie "but that Mr. Ponti had not bought any rights. The lawyer questioned the need to buy Ray's story. He said there was enough information in the newspapers to make a film." Is not this book—most of which was, in one form or another, in the papers—proof of Ponti's wisdom?

During all this time, the name of Hugh Stanton, Memphis Public Defender, had been absent from the papers, save for a single vignette.

His son and assistant, Hugh, Jr., had a miraculous escape from death in New Orleans in the crash of an ancient chartered, pre-World-War-II-vintage DC-III. It tried to land at New Orleans when the fog was so thick its actual fiery crash at the airport itself was undetected. Sixteen were killed. All in the back of the plane, including Stanton, survived.

Phil Canale brought Stanton's name back to the papers during this brouhaha over the money Foreman would get, saying that, with all this loot, "He [Foreman] should consider repaying the State of Tennessee for the work done by the public defender's office."

This does not mean that Canale, the prosecutor, and the "public defender," who began working on the deal as soon as the judge assigned him to help Foreman, are in any way connected, much as the record justifies the suspicion.

"I assume he will now want to carry out a proper reimbursement for the services from the public defender," Canale said of Foreman.

From the ensuing silence, he assumed too much.

Ray's second letter, dated March 26 (the hole punch eliminated the "2" when it was officially filed), goes into all these business matters. (It also is the actual document accepted as his appeal. Those legal papers subsequently filed are but amendments to it.) Here is that letter:

3-.6-69

Hon. Judge W. preston Battle
Judge of the criminal court
Memphis, Tennessee.

I would respectfully request this court to treat this letter as a legal notice, of an intent to ask for a reversal of the 99 year sentence petition received in aforementioned court. I understand on one avenue of appeal, I have only 30 days in which to file review notice, to have previous sentence set aside. That is the appeal route, to which I address the court.

I also would like to bring to the attention of the higher court, That Mr. percy Foreman, The attorney who was suppose to be representing me on this charge, stated in open court.

one, That since he "Mr. Foreman" was receiving no funds to help prepare case for trial, and he did not think he should be required to use his own funds, he requested court to appoint consul to keep defrey costs. The court appointed public defender to investigate case and assist Mr. Foreman.

Two, Mr. Foreman said in open court he did not want, or expect to receive, a cent for his efforts.

I think from Mr. percy Foreman statement to the press that he had a contract from me and Mr. William B. Huie, "upon entering" this case for $4 00,000, and that he was now to receive $150,000, should lay to rest the above two lies Mr. Foreman told the court.

Three; I, James E. Ray in turn, have not presently received, a cent from Mr. William B. Huie.

My only reason for bringing the aforementioned facts to the attention of the court is that I would respectfully move that the court appoint an attorney, or the public defender to assist me in the proceedings I have no study books, nor have I received any funds from any source to engage consul.

petitioner uses the word "assist", as I hively request the court, that I be personly present at the hearing, and to assist court appointed consul so that their be no repetition of Mr. percy Foreman actions.

Respectfully

FILED 4-1-69   56 2 c.M
J. A. BLACKWELL, CLERK
BY J.L. Blackwell D. C.

James Earl Ray
Station A-West
777 S B H or 3
Nashville, Tenn. 37303.

Apparently, Ray really burned over Foreman's poor mouthing, in and out of court.

If by now the reader is uneasy in the stomach and sees with jaundiced eyes as he regards Foreman, there still remains the possibility that he really saved Ray's life, did him a great service nonetheless, by making a good deal. While encouraging the reader to withhold final judgment, I present the available facts without deceptive literary devices.

Before Ray was returned to Memphis, in a June 10 story reporting security preparations, UPI carried these concluding paragraphs.

> Although Tennessee law requires the death penalty in a conviction of first degree murder without extenuating circumstances, it appeared unlikely that any convicted killer would be put to death.
>
> Since the last execution in 1960, the nine cells on death row at State Prison have remained virtually full. But there have been no executions, at first because of questions raised about the law and civil rights and later by the personal convictions of two governors.

Two days later, the American Civil Liberties Union urged Canale not to seek the death penalty.

After the minitrial, Jean White made a study of capital punishment for the *Washington Post* of March 25. In all the United States, she reported, it had been almost two years since the last execution, although 500 men were then in the death rows of penitentiaries, one 14 years after being sentenced to death. She found "a death-sentence moratorium after a dramatic decline in executions." From 1935 there had been a steady decline in executions. Where this penalty had been meted out, it was "stayed because courts have been examining legal challenges." She also found "a growing reluctance of judges and juries to hand out death sentences." In addition, "there has been a reluctance on the part of most governors to sign death warrants," an "awesome responsibility" when "death is irreversible."

The fact is that, throughout the world, there has been a steady downward trend in capital punishment—with a single exception. Ironically, in our context, the single exception is South Africa. In 1968, the rate of public hangings there was one every three days at the Praetoria Central Prison. This accounts for half of all the executions outside the Communist bloc. South Africa includes political offenses among the crimes punishable by hanging. In that blighted land, what is patriotism elsewhere is criminal there.

In the U.S. South, most death sentences have been carried out against blacks. In Georgia, the proportion is about nine blacks to each two whites.

Statistically, logically, and on the basis of expressed opinion, there was no reason to expect that, if Ray were convicted, he would have been sentenced to death and then, having been sentenced, that it would have been carried out. Foreman was aware of this in his arguing with the Rays. He threatened that in this case an example would be made. He also flew into the face of all the evidence of all the ghastly racial crimes, against whites and blacks in civil-rights struggles, against white women and Catholic priests.

If Canale so much as hinted he would ask for the ultimate penalty, there is no indication in any of my extensive files and more extensive reading.

After the minitrial, Canale told two reporters—Jack Nelson and Nicholas Chriss writing for the *Los Angeles Times,* which printed the story on March 11—"he did not see how the state could have fared better than the guilty plea and sentence, noting that Tennessee had not electrocuted anyone since 1960 and no one from Shelby County (Memphis) since 1948."

I needed no persuading to convince me that, especially in Tennessee, Ray would not be electrocuted. More, any possibility that there had been a conspiracy requires, for the apprehension and conviction of co-conspirators, that Ray be kept alive—assuming public authority wants really to solve the crime and capture the others. Without reason to believe the state would take the politically unpopular course of demanding the death penalty where the majority of the electorate has a racist tradition, I was even more stunned when Foreman's dubious deal became public knowledge.

But, *had* Ray been tried, *had* he been convicted, and had he then, as without any doubt he would, appealed, his appeal would have gone to the Court of Criminal Appeals of the State of Tennessee, at Nashville.

I have been in communication with one of the judges of that court, one of the men who would have sat in judgment on that appeal. He wrote me a letter, a personal letter his secretary did not type. I doubt if anyone saw it. He added a postscript to which he then appended this handwritten note: "Not for publication as a quote from me —." I take this to mean that I may not use his name but may use his words. They are:

As you probably know, there has been no execution in Tennessee for some eight years. It is doubtful if there ever will be another. This, coupled with equally prevalent fact that there has never been a conviction (much less the infliction of capital punishment) for the murder of a civil rights leader in the South (Memphis is laughingly referred to as the "Biggest city in Mississippi" by some wags), makes some wonder if there ever was much risk of execution . . .

The dots are his. I omit nothing.

Nor need I add anything.

Nobody really expected a death sentence. The odds were against it as they were against its implementation in the remote event it had been asked and decreed. Everybody on record was unalterably opposed to it. Even the judge, as we have seen, was more concerned there would not have been a conviction.

Despite the aplomb with which the pious pretender Foreman intones his claim to have saved Ray's life, it was more appropriate when he used it to get laughs on TV. I do not believe he ever expected such a sentence. The only doubts I have are about his reasons for pulling this caper, the only real effect of which perfectly parallels that of Jack Ruby's shooting of Oswald: To prevent a trial at which there would be examination and cross-examination of evidence, in public, before an enormous press corps, where and after which every scrap of evidence presented and what was known of what was not presented could and would have been closely examined.

Foreman may have served unselfish purposes, as when, without fee, he defended the policemen accused of brutality (although this endeared him to all police, especially the brutalizers, no handicap in his career). He may have sought the favor of government for reasons that can only be conjectured. The one thing certain is that he did not serve his client's best interest. He did serve government's. As the *Washington Post*, which has not distinguished itself by its performance and record on any of the assassinations and which has religiously accepted and apologized for the unacceptable, said March 12, in an editorial written at latest the day after the minitrial, "The sentence of 99 years . . . is the most severe that could have been given short of the death penalty." Without fully realizing what it was saying, indicting itself and the rest of the press, it added, "Not much complaint is heard on this score, as capital punishment is passing from the American scene and many of those who were outraged by the slaying of Dr. Martin Luther King, Jr., would not advocate it in any case."

120

The failure of the press in this and the other assassination cases is so basic that I emphasize it here again. For example, the aging dowager of the Washington press added these tidbits to its story, again without thinking of their significance:

... the judge was a party to the arrangements in this case ...

As the Tennessee law was stated by the prosecutor, P. M. Canale, Ray will have no chance of emerging from behind bars until he is 90 years old.

And, its custom on political assassinations, it sought to cover federal nakedness:

Presumably it [the Department of Justice] will question Ray in his cell as to the meaning of his reference to conspiracy.

This would have been very wrong.

... there is not much point in jumping to the conclusion that the mystery would have been cleared up if Ray had been tried on a plea of innocence. In these circumstances he might not have taken the witness stand, and if he had done so he might not have thrown any light on the conspiracy charge.

The *Post,* representative in this instance of much of the American press, has as little faith in the processes of the American law as it has recall of their honorable tradition.

To equate the discovery of fact at a criminal trial with confession by the accused is to say there was no case. It is not by confession that the crime must be solved. It is by what there never was, despite the touted magnitude of what the FBI called its investigation. Canale boasted in court (T. 14).

Our office has examined over 5,000 printed [sic] pages of investigation work .... We have examined over 300 physical bits of evidence, physical exhibits ... traveled thousands of miles all over this country and to many cities, in foreign countries ....

What matters is not the magnitude of the investigation but what is investigated. The larger a bad investigation is, the worse it is. This one was very big and very bad.

And very public, raising the question that again parallels Dallas, whether against serious defense opposition that evidence could have been successfuly introduced in court and the added question of whether its misuse in advance of trial prejudiced the jury, so much of it having been fed to the complaisant press.

To return to the matter of Ray's stimulated fear of being killed:

No less a worry than execution for him was the possibility of being murdered. I have raised this issue before. It is not mere melodrama. Knocking off a man in jail is no trick at all. In the long campaign to poison the public mind against Ray and to make it seem that the FBI had conducted a real investigation and had the goods on him, the government regularly leaked accounts of what can and does happen in jail. These stories had Ray conducting a narcotics business inside jail, getting his dope in, selling it, and getting his loot out, all undetected. What has happened to political prisoners needs no exposition. They have been beaten seriously in jail. Murders in jail are not uncommon. They are easily arranged, by criminals as they can be by others.

Foreman did not have to tell Ray that if he was not cooperative something might happen to him. Ray knew, untold. Perhaps a few lines from Eldridge Cleaver, Black Panther leader who wrote the best-selling *Soul on Ice* while in jail, will illustrate the prisoner's thinking and awareness of this:

> If you live in a cell with nothing but bars on the front, you cannot afford to relax; someone can walk along the tier and throw a Molotov cocktail in on you before you know it, something I've seen happen in San Quentin . . . . In my present cell, with its impregnable door, I don't worry about sabotage—although if someone wanted to badly enough they could still figure something out. [Delta edition, p. 42.]

> I want to devote my time to reading and writing, with everything else secondary, but I cannot do that in prison. I have to keep my eyes open all the time or I won't make it. There is always some madness going on. [P.49.]

For those unwilling to accept the black Cleaver as an authority, there is white William Bradford Huie. In *The Klansman,* he describes two of the most heinous crimes committed, with sanction, against the innocent accused—in jail.

If, by some strange quirk, Ray, with his long history of incarceration, was not aware of the possibility of being murdered in jail, the local paper was not long in informing him of the hazard—in the jail in which he was confined. This is what Jerry Thompson wrote in the

March 12 *Nashville Tennessean:*

> In the past, inmates have been murdered by other prisoners and stabbings among prisoners are not uncommon.

Thompson cited the record proving not even guards have been secure in that prison.

Were this not intimidating enough, there was then pending a murder charge against a former city jailer. (His case was postponed by Criminal Court Judge Arthur Faquin to permit hearing the first in-court argument by Ray's post-conviction lawyers.)

Predictably, threats were made against Ray. They reached the State Commissioner of Corrections, then Harry S. Avery. Avery attributed them to "prisoners." In response to them, he kept Ray in solitary confinement after expiration of the customary period. These "prisoner" threats were received by phone. Seemingly, identifying the callers should have posed no great problem inside a jail.

Keeping Ray in maximum security reduced the chances of something happening to him. But it also kept him incommunicado, with no one available in whom he could confide anything or with whom he could take counsel, and no way of getting any uncensored message out of jail—in short, no possibility of privacy in any communication with anyone [2].

Avery did not keep his job long after disclosing that threats had been made against Ray. The disclosure may have had nothing to do with his being fired by Governor Buford Ellington, which was announced May 29, 1969. He had been under earlier criticism: For using a prison inmate as his chauffeur and for the operations of his office and the state's prisons. UPI bracketed the governor's announcement with the accusation that Avery used his position "to gather facts about James Earl Ray for a book." Avery said "he had no plans for a book about Ray 'at this time.' He added 'Some situation might arise that I would think it would be propitious for me to write an article about penology or investigative work.' "

One of Ray's new lawyers, Robert W. Hill, had charged two weeks earlier that Avery had offered to "look after" Ray if "he would write him in his own handwriting his story of the crime." Avery immediately provided partial confirmation of the complaint.

Avery said Ray had "commented at some length about" his offer—to "see that every nickel that anyone paid would be put in his trust fund"—"but I don't intend to say anything about his comments . . .

since he has attorneys trying to get him a new trial." He refused elaboration of Ray's statement "a conspiracy existed." And he repeated his belief there was a prison conspiracy to kill Ray should he be released from maximum security.

He had "talked to Ray at great length," "to get the full truth." This is the height of impropriety, regardless of motive. It is more so because Ray was denied access to unofficial people no less interested in "the full truth."

The fired official was not generous to other officials. He charged, "Any intelligent investigator who examines all the facts should know there was a conspiracy." He also believes Ray has money "stashed out that had been previously given to him." He offered to "get that also and deposit it in his trust account" at the prison.

In sum: Foreman claims as defense counsel to enforce the law against the state. This is typical of his brilliant obfuscation. It is a brazen, catchy formulation that could not be more inapplicable to his actions in the Ray case.

But it is true that defense counsel is an officer of the court, with responsibilities to the law and the court. His function is to see that justice is done, not to play legal games, not to make deals that are less favorable to his client than any probable alternative.

He is *not* part of the prosecution.

Foreman was. He did for the prosecution what it could not have done for itself. He did for the federal government, the secret prosecution, what no one else could have. He made a deal that was worse than conviction, and he prevented the presentation, testing, and airing of the so-called evidence in open court.

He got everybody unhooked.

This was probably the best of his many great performances.

The prosecution also has additional responsibilities. Canon Five of the code stipulates the function of the prosecutor is not alone to get convictions. He, too, is to seek and achieve, to be dominated by the quest for justice. Justice and the national interest required a solution that answered all questions to the degree man can in this murder. Canale saw to it that this would not happen, that, to the degree he could control it, it would never happen. He made a deal that made it impossible, instead of taking his case to court and subjecting it to the workings of that "machine for the establishing of truth," cross-examination.

And the judge, so wrongly in on the deal from the first, the indispensable part of the package, what was his concern? The presiding over and the administration of justice? Not a bit. He was worried that in court, with the open presentation and examination of evidence and with cross-examination of it, there would be no conviction, that the jury would hang or refuse to convict. So, he anointed the deal of which he had been part with the judicial holy waters (doing what Judge Herbert Walker in Los Angeles, in the Sirhan trial, would not do).

After the formalities had been tended, Judge Battle said, "I think that the Court should make a few remarks." He then launched into a self-defense, anticipating public outcry. What it boils down to is an argument that he and the state had gotten a better deal than they would have had the case really been tried. Here is the appropriate excerpt (T. 102–103):

> Why accept any plea at all? Why not try him, try to give him the electric chair? Well, I have been a Judge since 1959, and I myself have sentenced at least seven men to the electric chair, maybe a few more. My fellow Judges in this County have sentenced several others to execution. There has been no execution of any prisoners from Shelby County in this State since I took the Bench in 1959. All the trends in this country are in the direction of doing away with capital punishment altogether.

So, in other words, the self-indictment of a hanging judge!

Foreman saved Ray's life? The judge himself shot this canard down: There was no likelihood of any execution in Shelby County. There had not been one in ten years. One judge alone had sentenced at least seven men to be killed and not one of his sentences had been carried out.

So the best that can be said for Foreman's deal that "saved" Ray's life is that it guaranteed the maximum sentence possible, which is hardly a "compromise," hardly a bargain. What Foreman guaranteed is that there would be no chance for the evidence to be examined, no chance for Ray to have a chance to talk, no chance that he would ever emerge from jail alive.

What actually accomplished was a more severe penalty than any Shelby County jury would have been likely to award. This is hardly "defense." In the doing, he guaranteed there would be no official solution to the crime.

All Ray's legal "defenders," his lawyers, Hanes and Foreman, and the judge, plus the prosecutor, who has the legal and moral responsibility, served masters other than justice.

11. The Minitestimony

For all in the foregoing that cannot be excused or condoned in a society calling itself free and one of laws, not of men; for all the raping of justice by each of the three—judge, prosecutor, and defense lawyer—called her protector, there remains the possibility that, by accident, regardless of contrary motive, truth triumphed, justice was done. So, we must ask, "If only by accident, was justice nonetheless done?"

Without doubt, Ray was involved in the crime. This is not part of the question. Whether he was a conscious or unconscious partner is without judicial answer. But his involvement, in regard to the justice of the minitrial, is not the issue. The sole issue is a simple one: Is he the murderer, and the lone, unassisted murderer at that?

Denied definitive answer by the processes and servants of justice, we can still seek it in the evidence. In this case, "evidence" means those facts not suppressed by the conspiracy that prevented the normal workings of justice. With no trial, no cross-examination, what was presented in court cannot really be called or considered "evidence." However, we can examine it as Foreman did not. We can also consider what was publicly known but not presented or considered. Ours will be a literary rather than a legal cross-examination. It will be the only one to date. It will show what could have been done in court *had* the evidence been tested in the traditional, honored Anglo-Saxon way.

We shall take each of the major items said to prove Ray was the lone assassin and see if it does, "beyond reasonable doubt."

Before the jury was sworn in and after agreeing on the record to what he had helped bring about in private, for all the world as though he had not been party to it, Judge Battle asked Ray those rhetorical questions really intended to protect himself, not the accused. He described the "arrangement" (T. 3) as "a compromise and settlement on a plea of guilty to murder in the first degree on an agreed settlement of 99 years in the penitentiary" (how polite and dignified the language!). The transcript here reads (T. 4):

THE COURT: Is that the agreement?
MR. CANALE: Yes, sir.
THE COURT: All right, I will have to voir dire Mr. Ray. Mr. James Earl Ray, stand.

(Thereupon, the Defendant complied with the request of the Court.)

THE COURT: Have your lawyers explained all your rights to you and do you understand them?

MR. RAY: Yes, sir.

THE COURT: Do you know that you have a right to a trial by jury . . . ? The burden of proof is on the State of Tennessee to prove you guilty beyond a reasonable doubt and to a moral certainty, and the decision of the jury must be unanimous both as to guilt and punishment.

Had there been a real trial, the condition to be met was not only that there be no "reasonable doubt" but, in effect, that no *single* juror have any doubt, that no *single* juror be without the "moral certainty" of guilt. More, if the jury were unanimous on guilt—and any one juror could prevent this—it then had also to be unanimous on the penalty. The requirements are those stipulated by the judge.

There were no opening statements. Once the jury was sworn, the state did not explain to it what would be proven, and the defense did not outline how it would answer. That would have been a bit too much, for, as we have seen, the sole concern of that great defender had been to assure himself each juror would agree, in advance of "evidence," to jail his client until he was not less than 90 years old and that assuming his behavior warranted maximum consideration.

Instead, five witnesses were called. They were asked questions to prove that King had been murdered and that there was reason to believe Ray or property said to have been his or both were or had been at the scene of the crime. No witness said he saw Ray commit the murder.

The five witnesses were the Reverend Samuel B. Kyles, a close associate of King, with him when King was shot; Chauncey Eskridge, a Chicago lawyer who also represented King and was at the motel; Dr. Jerry Thomas Francisco, the Shelby County coroner; Memphis Police Inspector N. E. Zachary; and Robert G. Jensen, Special Agent in Charge of the FBI Memphis office, in that order.

The reader can get an idea of the extreme brevity of this presentation of "evidence" from the closing exchange (T. 59) between Assistant District Attorney Robert K. Dwyer, who questioned these five, and the court. The exchange was introduced by a nice, big, fat and entirely unwarranted plug for the FBI. Dwyer's last question of Jensen was

128

"Did the investigation made by the FBI culminate in the arrest of James Earl Ray?" To this, Jensen replied, "Yes sir, it did."

Nothing had less to do with Ray's arrest than the FBI's investigation. Dwyer did not ask if the FBI caused or was responsible for Ray's arrest. He knew better. So he asked, instead, if all of the nothingness "culminated" in Ray's arrest. The fabled FBI's "investigation" of Ray had the wrong description; placed him in Mexico when he was in Canada, in Portugal when he was in England; had him robbing banks he never saw, taking dancing lessons 2,000 miles from where he was, and myriad other arcane examples of Hoover's consummate art.

Dwyer then told the judge, "That is all the proof the State cares ["has" in Blair's transcript] to offer at this time, if the Court pleases, except some stipulations by Mr. Beasley." (In Blair's transcript, "some" is "the.") Battle asked, "Is that a lengthy stipulation?" Dwyer said, "Yes, sir." Battle rejoined, "Well, I think we have been going about an hour and 15 minutes. Maybe we had better have a short recess."

All the legal niceties, all the formalities, charging explanations, the calling, questioning, swearing of the jury, and "all the proof the State has" (or "cares") to offer—the entire questioning of all five witnesses —required but an hour and 15 minutes!

At the end of the recess (T. 60ff.), Beasley, an Assistant District Attorney who will soon be the focus of our attention, began "narrating" (his word) what he called "a stipulation of the facts and evidence that the State would prove" in addition to what was asked of the five witnesses. No one corrected him. What he should have said is, *had* there been a trial, this is what the state would have *undertaken* to *attempt* to prove. Without correction, he went into what Foreman agreed to, beginning with a mockup of the area of the murder.

And that was all over by lunch time.

We will return to Beasley's narration. Here we will examine the evidence of the witnesses.

KYLES: With regard to Dwyer's first witness, Kyles, we are fortunate in having an interview with him shortly after the murder by Matt Herron, a photographer rather than a reporter. (See the Appendix.) Herron was there photographing the story for a national magazine. The contents of that interview are so contradictory to what Dwyer contrived to lead Kyles into on the stand and what Dwyer deliberately kept out of his testimony, it makes greater our regret there were not others in the press as dedicated as this great photographer, with the guts to persevere and the perception to tape interviews with the witnesses.

Through Kyles (T. 29-37), Dwyer established that at about 6 P.M. on April 4, 1968, King had just come out of Room 306 of the Lorraine Motel, that Kyles had taken five or six steps to his right when he heard "what I now know to be a shot." He then turned to his left "and I looked over the railing. I thought it was a car backfiring . . . ."

Kyles noticed "a gaping wound," located by Dwyer rather indefinitely as "about his [King's] face." Kyles also noticed that the shot had cut his necktie, just cut it right off." Dwyer had no questions.

Kyles described his inability to get the telephone to work. Without explanation or foundation, Dwyer asked, "Did you look over towards the rooming house?" Kyles replied, "Yes, I looked over there. There were bushes and things. It wasn't clear." During the brief time he looked in that direction, he saw no movement except by the police rushing toward the motel. (They had been around it and in the adjacent firehouse.)

Kyles did *not* see King shot. He was there when it happened. Kyles in his interview with Herron explains that Reverend Andrew Young was closer to King, looking up at the victim. Young was not used by the state, for reasons we can only guess; yet the ostensible purpose in using Kyles was to establish that King was shot.

Witnesses are the creatures of their questioners. They can only respond to questions. They cannot properly answer unasked questions. Dwyer, as will immediately become clear, did not want in evidence much of what Kyles knew, so he avoided certain questions and insisted on others. The issue of whether or not there was movement in the bushes around the motel is one of these touchy areas.

Infrequently, as when Kyles volunteered that there was a dense area of underbrush between the motel and the rooming house, Dwyer adeptly asked him if he had seen any movement, careful at the same time not to have it clear that Kyles had only glanced there. Thus, the court record is made to seem that there was no movement in that dense, overgrown area, whereas Kyles in fact cannot prove this. He was occupied by other things, and all he knows is that in the brief moment he looked in that direction, he saw no movement or recalled none.

However, there are witnesses who *did* see movement *and* a man there. These include King's chauffeur, Solomon Jones, and a bystander named "Cornflakes" Carter. Consistent with his deception in questioning Kyles, Dwyer did not mention them, did not use their knowledge— which was known to him—kept it out of the record.

130

So it was that what Kyles knew was, to the degree Dwyer could accomplish it, suppressed. Dwyer wanted to establish only that Kyles had known King and was there when King was shot, to establish the corpus delicti, one of the requirements of the law.

What are the things we know from Kyles' statements to Herron at the time of the crime that Dwyer found inconvenient for his narrow purposes? This interview and much more was, of course, available to the FBI and the prosecution.

Kyles stated that a representative of the Justice Department was present in the motel. Hoover was later to say the FBI did not "protect" people, but a man identified as "Jim Lowry" (James Laue), from the Justice Department in Washington, was there and in a room near King's. He was not called as a witness. Kyles also identified a number of other witnesses from whom there is no "evidence" in any form whatsoever. The official record does not indicate their presence at the scene of the crime.

Kyles quoted the Reverend Jesse Jackson, one of these witnesses, as saying King had been hit by an exploding bullet, "said it didn't explode until it hit him." Kyles added that "in the wound I saw, all this was gone. [His gesture, of course, is not on the tape.] The necktie was gone, you know, this way, it was cut off. And then Ralph [Reverend Ralph Abernathy, King's successor and close associate] said beneath the shirt when they got to the hospital, there was—there was a larger wound under the shirt that we couldn't see."

Kyles described two wounds. What had been torn out in King's face, large as that was, was not as large as the wound hidden by the shirt ("where it *really* exploded"). He had been told by a police officer that the bullet was hollow-pointed, a manufactured dumdum, designed to mushroom and tear. The significance of all this will become plain when we examine the evidence about the shot. Here it is important to understand that Kyles possesses competent and the most significant evidence about the wounds and their number and character; that there are others who possess identically the same knowledge; and that it was not asked of him and they were not called as witnesses. This evidence was carefully suppressed.

Again, Kyles told Herron *three different ways* that the police did not go where the witnesses directed them:

Well, all of them converged *this* way, and we tried to tell them, you know, get out *there* and go *that* way . . . . Even Andy said it didn't sound like—he never heard a shot from across the street. [Emphasis added.]

In talking to Herron, Kyles was referring to a spread of pictures published in *Life* dated April 12, 1968. In the interview, the "theres" and "heres" had specific meaning, as reading the text with a copy of the magazine shows. But without benefit of the pictures, it is clear he said, and *repeatedly* said, the police went other than where directed and refused to go where the close eyewitnesses did direct them.

> And when I heard the shot I simply looked—I looked *down*.
> . . . it seemed the police came almost simultaneously with the shot, they were that close. Now, whether they heard one over *there* [where they went], you know, I can't tell. But all I heard was one that sounded like it was in *this* area.

None of this is in the court record. Nor did Dwyer call as a witness a *single* policeman on the spot. We shall have more to say later about the involvement of the police.

After reading his testimony and knowing how he was used, made to look like a black Judas, I wrote Kyles. He has not responded. Therefore, I cannot get added facts from him.

ESKRIDGE: Even with all the formalities that consume about half of it, the entire testimony of King's Chicago attorney and friend, Chauncey Eskridge (T. 38-41), is extremely brief. It takes up but a single printed page in Blair's transcript. Dwyer's purpose was to support the corpus delicti identification by Kyles, prove King was murdered. Dwyer asked, "Did you go to the hospital with Dr. King?" Eskridge answered, "I did." "And, at that time, were you informed that he was dead?" "I was." "Did you attend his funeral, Mr. Eskridge?" "I did." Cut and dried. That is all Dwyer wanted. Nothing on the wounds, no description—for the facts on this matter ruin the prosecution case.

But Dwyer could not quite avoid more. Eskridge volunteered it. It supports what Dwyer did not want from Kyles—but what a real defense counsel would so well have used in cross-examination to destroy the prosecution case. In order to lay a foundation for Eskridge's presence at the scene of the crime, Dwyer had asked him to show where he was on the mockup of the motel and the surrounding area and "were you engaging Dr. King in conversation or anything like that . . . ?"

Eskridge responded by saying he, Young, and the driver, Solomon Jones, were awaiting King.

. . . I was by the car. The driver of the car was standing in front of me. We were both on the left hand side of the car. Rev. Andrew Young was on the right hand side of the car . . . . Whereupon, the sound came from my right ear . . . Zing! And I looked to my left rear . . . .

Eskridge was looking "up at" the door to King's room. His *back* was toward the assassin. A shot past his *right* ear was from King's *left*. The bathroom window of the rooming house was far to the opposite side, to Eskridge's *left* as he faced the motel. What Eskridge's testimony really means, if we accept it, is that the shot could not have come from that bathroom window. In this, it is consistent with the other suppressed evidence. Furthermore, the "zing" of the shot past Eskridge's right ear indicates a lower trajectory. He was on the street level, not three floors up. The rooming-house window from which Ray allegedly fired was even higher than the three-stories-up victim.

When he looked back and "towards the rooming house," which Dwyer asked him if he had done, he saw no one and no movement. He was not asked if he had looked *at* or had reason to look *at* the rooming house, merely if he had turned around. He was not asked if he had looked at the thicket or if he saw movement elsewhere. The missing information not only does not support the prosecution case, as any defense attorney would have established in the cross-questioning of both witnesses; it demolishes that case.

FRANCISCO: The testimony of County Medical Examiner Francisco (T. 42–46), who performed the autopsy that night, is also amazingly brief. In Blair's transcript, it requires but two printed pages. The first half was taken up establishing his credentials and expertise in pathology and forensic pathology. This proves he has both medical competence and the knowledge of the legal aspects of medicine. Francisco knew what the prosecution wanted of him and his testimony. He delivered that and nothing else, without qualm and without protest at the character of the questions asked or the absence of those required to have been asked but which were not.

In response to two questions, he gave these two answers, the only medical descriptions of the wounds:

The examination revealed a gunshot wound to the right side of the face, passing through the body into the neck, through the spinal cord at the base of the neck, with the bullet lodging beneath the skin near the shoulder blade on the left. ["Body" in this response is "jaw" in the Blair transcript.] . . . .

The angle was from above downward, from the right to left, passing through the chin, base of the neck, spinal cord into the back, an angle of something about like this on the body [indicating].

And here we have something entirely new in medicine, geometry, physics, and evidence. A bullet that enters "the right side of the face," goes "through the body [or jaw]" and "into the neck, through the spinal cord," then lodges "beneath the skin near the shoulder blade," without deflection or fragmentation? Without mention of a broken or damaged bone! What a truly magical bullet! Here we have a bullet that goes "through the spinal cord" but does not, from the evidence, touch a single surrounding bone! Yet the spinal cord is entirely surrounded by bone. Unless, of course, there was a magical corpse to balance the magical bullet.

And magical powers to reverse the bullet's direction! For whatever indefinite point at "the left shoulder blade" it came to rest "beneath the skin" is not on a line from the right jaw to the "base of the neck."

It is not by accident there is neither question nor volunteered evidence about the bullet hitting bone. Hitting bone deforms and mutilates any bullet, the degree varying with the character and type of bullet. Soft-metal bullets deform, mutilate, and fragment more readily. In the Presidential assassination, where a military bullet with a hardened jacket was allegedly used, the FBI testimony is that had *that* bullet hit coarse cloth or leather, even these soft substances would have marked it. The medical and other scientific evidence is that bones *do* mutilate bullets. The character, speed, weight, and design of the bullet introduce other factors bearing on the positiveness with which identification can be made and the effect of impact upon both the bullet and whatever it hits. *Any* bullet with the history Francisco attributes to this one would have been battered badly. *It had to have struck bone not less than three times.* A "soft" bullet could be expected to be beyond ballistic identification.

This is reason enough for Dwyer to ask no question about the bullet striking bone or bones, for Francisco to offer no testimony of any kind about it, and for the judge and Foreman to remain mute. For otherwise there would be evidence of a conspiracy and so no deal, no frame-up.

The utterly meaningless "angle of something about like this," Francisco's words, was enough to satisfy all the legal eagles, defense attorney, prosecutor, and judge. No one asked explanation, and there is in the entire record no indication of *any* of the angles, from up to down, right to left, or through the body. (There had to be more than one angle through the body by definition, horizontal and vertical.) This made much easier the travesty of "evidence" that followed.

Francisco was shown an unidentified object. In *that* court, for *that* proceeding, it did not even require an exhibit number. He said, "This is the bullet that was removed from the body at the time of the autopsy."

So, this expert on the legal aspects of medicine identified the object as a "bullet." He *alone* did that. He would never have tried it had there been any possibility of cross-examination and had he not been carefully rehearsed. The best he could have sworn to is that he removed a piece of metal from the body.

The wounds he avoided describing—and it should be noted that the medical-forensic expert neither offered nor was asked for a description of the appearance, size, characteristics, or even specific location of the wounds—could not possibly have been made by "a bullet" emerging from this career without enormous deformity at the very least.

From his testimony, there is but a single wound, the point of alleged entry in "the right side of the face." This statement is so indefinite it is devoid of evidentiary meaning. However, we know (from the press accounts and the hospital statement) that there was at the least one other wound, the one Abernathy saw at the hospital, which may or may not be the same one that cut the tie off. The wound "in the right side of the face" could not have severed the tie if that undisturbed projectile continued into and "through the body" or "to the base of the neck" or came to rest "beneath the skin near the shoulder blade on the left," wherever that may have been on the long, wide, and very mobile bone. Without another shot, in the absence of evidence of any bone fragmentation—where a piece or pieces of bone became a secondary missile or missiles—this second wound can have been caused only by fragmentation of the bullet, at least one major part doing the damage to the victim under his shirt—suppressed by prosecutor and coroner alike. We know from other proof that fragments of the bullet were recovered.

For Francisco to identify the object he was shown as "*the bullet* that was recovered from the body" is a falsehood. No such thing as a bullet "was recovered from the body." It is willful deception and the suborning of deception, two separate crimes, one by him, the other by the prosecutor, because he and Dwyer both knew better, both intended the resultant deception. If we permit the substitution of presumptions for evidence, the most an expert like Francisco could honestly say is that he recovered *part* of what he believes was once a bullet.

Francisco's testimony ended abruptly when he was asked if, pursuant to instructions from the prosecution "did you visit the scene" and "did you make certain tests there or observations at the scene [sic] ." His answer is a redefinition of science, medicine, law, and "tests." There was *no* test, no pretense of any kind of test:

> The tests included going to the floor, going to the floor of the motel in this area and going to the room over here, from this point in the room to this location on the motel balcony, and viewing from the back of the room in this area adjacent to the motel [indicating] .

Some "test"!

The indefiniteness bothered no one, for it was all a legalized farce and no one cared about anything but getting it over with. It did not have to mean anything, but, nonetheless, it is ruinous to the case.

When Francisco refers to "the room," he does not mean King's but the room in the rooming house that even the prosecution says was *not* the source of the shot! It claims that shot was fired *not* from the room registered to Ray but from the bathroom, an entirely different part of the building. In the careless manner of the prearranged frame-up, there is here, still again, what no law-school aspirant would have overlooked. Nor was there an effort to determine whether the available evidence from the cadaver made a shot from any other point possible. There was not the slightest interest in even seeing if a shot from any other point was possible, if not more probable. The "tests" that consisted in taking a look out of and toward the wrong window were, as will become obvious, without any possible meaning as presented. The transcript is resumed without omission:

> Q. In other words, then, Doctor, you were angling from the room in the rooming house to the balcony; is that correct, sir?
>
> A. That is correct.
>
> Q. And then angling from the back of the ground of the rooming house to the balcony; is that correct?
>
> A. That is correct.
>
> Q. Which one was consistent with the angle of the wound, Dr. Francisco?
>
> A. The location of the window.
>
> Q. That is all. Thank you, Dr. Francisco. You may come down, sir. [T. 46.]

The incompetence of this put-on guised and accepted as evidence would have catapulted any lawyer but the Foreman of this case screaming to his feet. There is no such thing as *any* angle in the evidence. At a little over 200 feet, the distance nowhere asked or given in this "testimony" (assuming a shot from that bathroom), a wound "to the *right* side of the face" lodging *near* the *left* shoulder, at its flattest possible angle, would have originated in the sky if King were erect. Without knowing the position of King's body at the moment of impact, this "testimony" is fraudulent and is so designed. If the reader makes his own determination of the top and the bottom "right side" of his face, without regard to front or back (which cannot be ignored in evidence), he can, with little difficulty, find a difference of 100 per cent in the possible minimum and maximum angles.

Neither *the* nor *a* point of entry was ever established. No single question was asked about it, no single proof was offered. It is presumed, and proof is lacking—and (as will become clear) not to presume it exonerates Ray as the murderer! Aside from whether the alleged point of entry was to the front or back of the side of the face, high or low on it, the side-to-side aspect of the victim's position has to be established as consistent with the imputed angle. There is no testimony or proof of any kind on this or the other angle of his position.

For the prosecution theory (the most its fabrication can be called) to begin to warrant consideration, King at the moment of impact had to have been bent over from front to back. There now is no way of knowing how much, but he could not have been erect. If, in the absence of proof or the offer of proof, we assume that, at the very moment of being killed, he was leaning over the railing engaged in pleasant conversation with those on the street, we also assume what invalidates the imputed side-to-side angle. Of course, Francisco has already invalidated that with his straight-line from window on the right through the right side of the face, down steeply and back to the back of the neck and then laterally, or laterally and forward, to the skin somewhere near the left shoulder blade. There is no possible straight line like this. Ignore that, however, and we then must have King in a position where his body is pointed away from those to whom he is speaking while he has twisted his head toward them, both to the right and downward. To make this possible, he had to have been dancing a ballet, his left foot raised and bending from the waist. The whole thing is, of course, ridiculous, but it is the extremity required by the framing of the bird-in-hand, Ray.

So, the "tests" and "observations," which are not in any sense either, prove nothing except the total absence of any medical proof that the shot came from the alleged lair in the rooming house bathroom. The testimony is so deficient in every single requisite respect, it is an enormous fraud in itself. When it was possible and required in the autopsy for measurement to be made of everything measurable, the easiest being the locations of wounds and their angles, there is none in the evidence. Not *one* measurement of any kind! Where description is even easier, requiring no medical degree and no forensic knowledge, that also is missing, unsought and unoffered. There is no single standard of medicine or law that is met by this so-called testimony[1].

ZACHARY: The testimony of Memphis Police Inspector N. E. Zachary (T. 47–53) can be read by a *slow* reader in *two minutes!* FBI Bureau Chief Robert G. Jensen (T. 54–59) followed Zachary. Theirs is the only direct testimony seeming to connect Ray with the crime, and neither does that. Nor does either meet the requirements of "testimony" in court.

Zachary had been a Memphis policeman for 22 years. At the time of King's murder, he was at headquarters, where he is in charge of the homicide bureau. After he heard on the police radio that King had been shot, he went to the scene of the crime. At some indeterminate time after arriving there, he said "I found a package rolled up in a bedspread which consisted of a blue briefcase and a Browning pasteboard box containing a rifle [sic]." Exactly where the package was found is a matter of importance, but Zachary gave no specifics. (He also gave an incomplete listing of the contents of the package.) In the questioning, which is limited to short questions—was this in there or that?—there is no further mention of a briefcase, which is the first thing he said he "found." Zachary is questioned about what he did not testify to, "a plastic zipper bag." Four hours later, Zachary turned these things over to Jensen for FBI examination. In none of his remarks does Zachary connect any of this with Ray. He identifies objects found near the crime, a proper step in proof. But beyond identification, nothing.

If Zachary's is truthful testimony, it appears that with all those police immediately crawling all over that area not one found all of this property later associated with Ray, when it allegedly was lying right out in the middle of Main Street in front of the Canipe Amusement Company. Not until Zachary got there, some time later, going all the way from his office and going first to the motel, was it found. If this is

138

not the case, he lied under oath and was led into this lie by the prosecutor. How much time elapsed is not indicated. We know only that Zachary began some distance away and that, at the motel, he issued "certain instructions," ordered photographs to be made, things like that, detailed "men to start making an investigation"—performed the many duties of the man in charge. It may be presumed that, where the crime had been perpetrated, the chief of homicide found enough to hold him for at least a brief interval. The testimony is this:

Q. All right, Inspector, what, if anything, did you find there, please, sir?

A. I found a package rolled up in a bedspread which consisted of a blue briefcase and a Browning pasteboard box containing a rifle. It was in this doorway at about this location right here [indicating].

Assuming all that was "found" was Ray's, as could be proved but wasn't, this is either inordinate delay in "finding" it or false testimony about finding it, or both. Either is enough to cast great doubt on the dependability of any of the testimony about it.

Zachary did not "find" that package, as we shall see. (If he had, my God! What kind of police have they in Memphis when 40 of them cannot find so large a piece of evidence out in the open?*) But why was it necessary to dissemble, especially when Foreman was like a Sphinx, not saying a single word or asking a single question about any part of the testimony? And when the whole thing had been rigged in advance, when there was, by agreement, no single objection to anything the prosecutor did, why could Zachary not, even then, restrict himself to the truth and the whole truth?

JENSEN: Jensen's testimony adds to Zachary's, but not what any court would have required. He still did not connect all the "found" items to Ray and Ray alone. And, as with Zachary, even when there was no opposition, no cross-examination, he, too, unbagged a few cats.

The government has been steadfast in maintaining it has and exercises no jurisdiction in such cases, cannot and does not protect people, that there was nothing it could have done or did do in the King case in advance of his murder. We have seen, as the court record and many public statements do *not* show, that there was a Department of Justice representative with the party and physically close to King. He was not a

---

*From a suit against the government, I have obtained a picture of the package where it allegedly was found. The picture is printed later.

139

witness, naturally, nor once alluded to in the testimony. In a case like this, why bother a Department of Justice representative when he was only at the scene of the crime? It is better to suppress all reference to this and to him. Were it not for Matt Herron's interview with Kyles, we would not know of it at all.

Jensen's testimony is designedly indirect on what relates to this. After establishing his official position, Dwyer asked him:

Q. I'll ask you around 6:05 P.M. on that date, do you recall where you were, Mr. Jensen?

A. Yes, sir. I was in the office of the FBI.

Q. And did you receive a call at that time?

A. I did.

Q. And, as a result of that call, what, if anything, did you do, Mr. Jensen?

A. I called my Washington headquarters to advise them of the information which I had received, and then subsequently dispatched men to assist in the investigation.

The one question Dwyer sought the answer to is the time he sent his agents into the case. It was 6:30 P.M.

Now, if the FBI *had* no jurisdiction, how could FBI headquarters, and so very rapidly, authorize the participation of its agents in the case? Hoover pretends to be very touchy about jurisdiction, about unauthorized use of federal money. It cannot be both ways. Either the FBI did have the legal right to be in the case or it did not. Here, and expeditiously, it authorized FBI participation in the case, so promptly that, from the time the first word began to reach Jensen until the time he actually sent his derring-do boys out on the case, including the time required to reach Washington, discuss all the angles, and get a decision, less than 25 minutes elapsed.

It would seem that, with murder not a federal crime, whatever authority the FBI had *after* the murder, it had in equal measure *before* the crime. If it was right and legally proper for them to be in the King case immediately, before there was any federal aspect, it was no less right for them to have been in on it before the murder—particularly with what we now know it knew and had been so careful to suppress of the plots to kill King. More on this later.

The studied indirection of Dwyer's prepared questions is worth some attention and thought. Jensen was not asked and did not volunteer how he was called or by whom. He was not asked and did not volunteer what the message was. He was asked no more than this, "And did you receive a call at that time?" He replied only, "I did." If the Memphis police phoned him, there certainly is nothing sinister in that. Likewise there is no reason not to include it in the question or to omit it from the answer. (It is safe to assume the testimony was rehearsed, a standard practice.)

One possible explanation, and this is only conjecture, is that the call was *not* from the police. The call came less than five minutes after the crime. The fact already was on the police radio. It is no wild conjecture to wonder if the FBI is not permanently tuned to that channel, so Jensen should have known about it when Zachary did. But with Jensen's knowledge of the crime coming to him by phone or radio and apparently not from his office's watch on the police radio, there is a reasonable presumption he was not told by the police and did not hear it on their broadcast. The questioning is so indirect, this is by no means certain. It is still possible that Jensen or one of his staff heard the police broadcast. But he testified it was not until after a "call" that he called Washington. Assuming, as this testimony certainly says, that Jensen had a "call," two of the more likely and deliberately hidden possibilities are the Department of Justice representative at the motel or an FBI agent whose presence the FBI preferred to keep secret [2]. Which leads to another question: Was King murdered while the FBI *and* Department of Justice were with him? The Department was there. Was the FBI, too?

Whatever the interpretation, the inadequacies of Jensen's testimony, its built-in indirection and incompleteness, sponsor doubts and suspicions. Whether or not sinister, this hiding of basic information in a crime such as this cannot be accepted as either proper or normal police practice or proper and the usual prosecution questioning.

Jensen was asked about and testified to getting what Zachary "found" and sending it to FBI headquarters for examination. The items included, in the words of Dwyer's question (T. 55), the "green spread here, here is some pliers and a hammer, a rifle, here is some shaving articles, binoculars, beer cans, newspaper, tee shirt, shorts, there is transistor radio over there [indicating] ." (This is by no means all that was "found," not even all that had been already identified by Zachary. Jensen testified he sent them *all* to the FBI laboratory. But Zachary testified (T. 52) he gave what he "found" to the FBI "with the exception of the tee shirt and shorts." *Whose* underwear *did* the FBI trace to Ray and where did they get it?)

All Jensen testified to about these items is this:

141

The rifle "had been sent to a distributor in Birmingham, Alabama, and was subsequently sold by Aero Marine Supply Company."

The pliers and the hammer "led us to Los Angeles" where "we found a hardware store that maintained comparable items, yes, sir."

The T-shirt and shorts Zachary said he did not give the FBI had laundry marks traced to Los Angeles.

Nothing else.

It is obvious that there is no meaning at all in a Los Angeles hardware store having "comparable items" to a hammer and pliers, for there is likely to be no hardware store in the world of which this is not true. What is missing in all of this testimony is meaning. Jensen was used for window-dressing, to plant the idea that the FBI had proved all the evidence out. Of course, everyone knows the FBI is thorough, never makes a mistake, etc.

In every slight detail, Jensen's testimony is this inadequate and raises questions similar to those above. Here are the specifics:

He ordered his "men to make a canvass of the hotels and motels in Shelby County," the words of the question (with the states of Mississippi and Arkansas both adjoining Memphis!). "We found a registration card at the Rebel Motel," otherwise not identified. What a provocative name for this case! The card had the name "Eric S. Galt" on it.

Jensen was not asked and he did not say that this was all they found on their canvass. It is my unconfirmed information that Ray had been told to go to Memphis and stay at a motel flying the Confederate flag. When he came to such a place about 20 miles from Memphis, he checked in. It was the wrong one. He then checked out and registered at the Rebel.

There was no need for Jensen's testimony to suffer any deficiencies. Jensen's testimony could and should have been explicit and unequivocal. It is not. He could and should have testified that the FBI, in all its search of all the motels, found but a *single* possible relevant registration, Galt's at the Rebel. Dwyer did not ask for and Jensen did not volunteer proof that the handwriting on the registration is Ray's, an obvious requirement of the proof and any "no conspiracy" case. When people whose entire lives and careers are taken up with evidence and its requirements, people like experienced prosecutor Dwyer and the man in charge of the FBI's Memphis office so glibly avoid the minimum requirements of competent evidence, we cannot assume it is carelessness or ignorance on their part and must assume they have what

142

to them is good reason for seeming to be incompetent and for being incomplete and evasive.

The registration at the Rebel includes, as all motel registrations do, the identification of the car being driven by the person registering for a room. Here is 100 per cent of the questioning and response on that:

Q. Did you find that Eric S. Galt was driving a Mustang, white Mustang automobile?
A. Yes, sir.

Now, in a real trial, defense counsel would have protested this as a leading question (it is), predetermining the character of the answer and thereby limiting it. Properly, Dwyer would have asked a series of questions, each requiring its own answer, beginning with a general inquiry, was there a car connected with this registration. Had he done this, as the procedures require, there might have been an identification of that white Mustang to the exclusion of all others. Because Dwyer did what he knew is wrong and knew he could get away with—because it was all arranged, with no objection to come from Foreman or Battle— he succeeded in keeping any meaningful identification or description of that car out of the testimony. Not even the minimum is there— license number, year, and model. More was possible and necessary—and available, merely withheld. But the motel registration alone should have provided the tag number, state of registration, year, and model, which is positive identification, limiting the car to a single one in all the world. Here, deliberately, by avoiding the minimum requirements of evidence and testimony, by getting around them, any white Mustang ever made or any Mustang of any color repainted white could be presented as Ray's. This, as we shall see, cannot have been accidental, for *more than one white Mustang was involved.* (Indeed, here three Mustangs will interest us. Two were parked on Main Street, very near the scene of the crime, and the third is fictitious, the subject of phony broadcasts.)

The only other testimony about the Mustang given by Jensen is that it was found in Atlanta April 11. This was handled in such a way as to make it seem to say the opposite of the truth, that the FBI worked hard and found the car. It did not. It had nothing to do with the finding of the car. Its presence in Atlanta was reported to the FBI.

There is nothing else in Jensen's "testimony," save the further and concluding deception, carefully rigged by the grateful Dwyer, eager to invoke the prestige of the exalted J. Edgar Hoover and his FBI as

143

support for the prosecution case and no less eager to scratch that mighty back. Dwyer asked "did the FBI's investigation extend into" Canada, Portugal, and England? Jensen replied it did. And did this "culminate in the arrest of James Earl Ray"? "Yes, it did."

No less did it "culminate" with men landing on the moon!

Now, the FBI is prohibited by our and local laws from active investigations in foreign countries, and it did not conduct the investigation in these countries. Local authorities did. And all the rest, already noted.

It can be seen that what was presented in court, without opposition, could not stand the most primitive examination. It could no more have withstood any cross-examination than a house of cards can survive a tornado. And this, mind you, where there was no opposition, when the prosecution had no restraints upon it, when it could and did cut corners, abuse the practice and procedures of the law and courts, when it could put its best foot forward. From all the hundreds of "witnesses" available to it, there was this careful, show-piece selection, and they, even without opposition, did not prove Ray did anything.

The blacks who were witnesses were used to satisfy the legal necessity of "corpus delicti." They were not needed for this purpose. Whites could have been used and were not. They were used, meaning "abused," because they are black, to get those closest to King involved in the deal (as also was falsely done with dishonest publicity). This was done to capitalize upon them, to make it seem they were not only part of the deal but satisfied with the end, the "solution." They were exploited with such meanness and contempt that, because the other information they possessed was withheld, historically they are cast in the role of black Judases. This is but one of the crimes committed by the prosecution.

Great care was exercised in selection of the few who would be center stage. If the prosecution felt it could get by with only five witnesses, to testify to almost nothing, it could have gotten by with none, because Foreman had stipulated to the "evidence" against Ray, and the press accepts anything. Not a single thing connecting Ray with the crime came from the five witnesses. That is all in the stipulated part. These five were the showcase.

The reason for their selection also requires consideration. Why, for example, was Zachary chosen to testify falsely to "finding" what he did not find? The most obvious (but not necessarily only or even correct) answer is that he is a ranking official, less likely to wander and volunteer what is inconsistent with the framed case. And why was Jensen, who did not testify to any personal activity in the investigation (a prerequisite for a witness in a competent proceeding), chosen over, let us say, the man who was used to connect to the weapon from which it allegedly was fired the projectile causing death? Two obvious possibilities are a duplication of the Zachary situation and the unwillingness of the prosecution to focus even this slight attention on the essential evidence. (We shall examine that carefully.)

The "testimony" of Dr. Francisco is completely dubious. It is not possible to speak too harshly of a medical-forensic expert who "testifies" as he did, who was content with falsehood, distortion, misrepresentation, incompleteness—even propaganda. These did not trouble his professional, his medico-legal conscience. There is no doubt that he lied on the stand. He did *not* take a "bullet" from the corpse. That is a complete impossibility as anyone with any hunting experience knows and as the evidence proves. He failed even to describe or locate the wounds, to give their number, to specify the resultant injuries—to do *anything* required by his function and discipline. Instead, he readily gave contrived frame-up testimony.

It is not possible too thoroughly or too harshly to castigate and condemn this public raping of the law, justice, and everything decent and honorable in our society, nor to condemn sufficiently those responsible for and participating in it.

Precisely because this was a show-piece, precisely because there was to be no testing of the evidence, it was incumbent upon those who staged it fully to meet their requirements to the law and to history, to disquieted public opinion, to national unease over the proliferation of political murders (all of men leading toward peace). But, when there was *no* opposition, when they could circumvent the requirements of law, procedures and evidence, and *then* the prosecution failed to produce even a weak circumstantial case, they did not end questions. While answering none, they in fact raised more, those that had not existed previously.

So much for the "testimony."

Where the prosecution did not call witnesses to the stand and question them on the record (even the record no one was to see) and before the press, the situation is not better but worse.

145

12. The Mininarration

When the hearing resumed after the short recess, Judge Battle (T. 60)
set the tone neatly with his opening remarks: "Are you gentlemen
ready for the jury, or do you want to do some more scene-shifting
around?" The stipulation was all the "shifting around" needed. Beasley
told the judge, "No, sir. I think we are ready, yes, sir." So, the judge
ordered, with all the sense of occasion of a livestock auctioneer, "Bring
them in." In came the jury.

A stipulation is an agreement between opposing counsel. Foreman
agreed in advance by stipulating to the evidence the prosecution would
offer. He thereby authenticated it, certified its accuracy and
dependability. After the stipulated, scant bikini-like "testimony" of
these five witnesses and the recess that arduous hour and a quarter
required for the recovery of all involved, there came the jock-strap-size
presentation of the stipulation as narrated by Beasley. I am not
ridiculing him. He used these words:

> I propose at this time to narrate to you gentlemen a stipulation of
> the facts and evidence that the State would prove in addition to the
> testimony heretofore heard in the trial . . . .

He also called this a "trial."

Narrate he did—without interruption or question, with not a murmur
from the judge, jury, or that great defender, Foreman. As a matter of
fact, from the swearing of the jury, before which Foreman had satisfied
himself they would inflict the maximum penalty without question (and
had had his tense exchange with Ray), he uttered but three words in a
single phrase, at the end, when he said simply, "No, your honor."

It is precisely because Beasley knew there would be no objection,
everything having been agreed to, that we are entitled to believe he made
the best case possible, put the strongest interpretation on what, under
the rules of evidence, he might not have been permitted to mention at
all in an open trial. Stretched the truth a wee bit, too. Certainly, when
there was no objection, no cross-examination, the state *could* present
the strongest possible case.

That case does not convict Ray, does not warrant believing he was the
murderer. Exactly the opposite is true. This will become clear by
examination of what Beasley presented.

146

Although I do not say "all of what Beasley presented," what little is not considered here is merely the most irrelevant. Much of the detailed representation of what the state *said* it could prove does not connect Ray with the crime, not even by extension. To his credit, Beasley does not claim this by extension. To his discredit, he pretends it was all entirely relevant.

His presentation rose and fell like the undulations of a calm sea. Sometimes he is specific as all get-out, sometimes so indefinite what he is trying to say is not comprehensible. At times there is such carelessness with the evidence and transcript that the Pax Hotel comes out "Tact Hotel" in Blair's transcript. The farther from the crux, the more specific. The closer to the heart of the case, the more nebulous. There is the promise of abundant proof Ray used the identities "Galt" and "Sneyd." Of this, there seems little doubt. It could have been dispensed with by a simple statement, and just such a statement would have been used in a real trial, with the defense in accord. Here instead, the point is labored and belabored, with detail piled on detail, no doubt building an impressive record for the unthinking who are impressed with the mere production of detail, whether or not significant. On the other hand, on what is vital, what relates to Ray as the murderer, there is nothing and what edges toward it is outright dishonest. Little as that is, and it is very little, it is all tainted—100 per cent of it. But were it not, it still would not prove Ray was the murderer.

It is not the normal practice of writers to present their conclusions first. Standard technique calls for building suspense to a crashing crescendo, exciting the reader until he thrills to the climax. I do not follow this practice because, with no trial, it is important for the reader to be able to assess the evidence as he goes, to understand what it really does and does not say and, no less important, how government served him, truth, justice, and our once-revered traditions. It is my purpose to try to make it possible for the reader to evaluate the so-called evidence that would have been offered if there had been a trial. No single work can encompass all a writer learns in his investigation, research, and analysis. What he cannot include shapes his beliefs, helps form his writing. The reader may not agree with my interpretations and beliefs. That he may better dispute them, they are unhidden. I begin with them.

What I omit are those irrelevancies that need not be examined for other purposes. Most of these have to do with Ray as Galt or Sneyd, and with his travels after breaking jail, none of which are matters relevant to the single quintessential question: Did he kill King? If he had killed a thousand other people, robbed a thousand banks, broke 50 jails, been to a dozen countries, taken other training, yoga and karate as well as dancing and bartending, bedded with only pre-puberty and post-menopausal women, it is all irrelevant to the single charge he faced of killing King.

As a matter of fact, what the prosecution really did is assemble a credible case for the opposite, that he was part of a conspiracy, playing the role of decoy.

The reader will be able to decide for himself whether there is a case for Ray as the murderer. In my view, there is no doubt that the proof is lacking. The law requires it to be "to a moral certainty" and "beyond reasonable doubt." As he goes over the content of the Beasley narrative, I ask the reader to consider each item of promised evidence as possible proof that Ray was at the scene of the crime, was there for purposes of laying a trail leading to himself (whether or not he knew the purpose) and away from others, and that it was carefully arranged so that he would be promptly identified—that is, as promptly as the incompetence of the FBI would and did permit.

A prosecutor has, above his need to seek a conviction, the obligation to seek justice. He may not, in the discharge of his office and obligations, ignore what is inconsistent with his charge to get a conviction. It is wrong for him to withhold exculpatory evidence if he has or knows of it, wrong under the law as it is under the canons of the law.

In recent years, the adversary legal system has degenerated into a contest between opposing counsel, each eager to build his own reputation and wealth at the expense of the other and his client. As legal games replace genuine adversary law, justice suffers. When prosecutors have been caught at it, cases have been reversed.

Canale and company, unfortunately, were not caught (until now) because the judge and defense counsel were part of the game, really on Canale's side. They all ganged up on the undefended defendant.

Beasley opened (T. 60) with a mockup of the vicinity of the crime, failing to offer it in evidence. (It is the only such oversight corrected by Canale, who made the correction in the very last words of the prosecution, *after* the case was over.) Before identifying the place at which the murder occurred, Beasley pointed out the rooming house at 422½ South Main Street. Between 3 and 3:30 the afternoon of April 4, a man giving the name "John Willard" asked Mrs. Bessie Brewer, the manager, for a room. Beasley failed to note that in Canada, near where the real Sneyd, Galt, and Bridgeman (all Ray pseudonyms) live, there is also a real John Willard. One reason for not mentioning it could be not to strain further the prosecution concept that, unaided, Ray could have known of all these look-alikes, each of whom also resembles him. Mrs. Brewer showed him Room 8, on the south side. "There was some statement made with reference to not needing a refrigerator, stove, request for a single sleeping room" (T. 61), as Beasley put it, so she took him to the north side and showed him Room 5-B, which is "a single sleeping room," all in fact a single man needed.

According to Blair's transcript, Beasley said, "The defendant did rent this room for about a week." "About" does not appear in the official transcript (T. 62). We cannot know which is correct. But if Blair's is, why the uncertainty? Did Beasley not know? Did Mrs. Brewer know so little the day he rented the room, when she was interviewed within three hours of it? Had she no records? None are in evidence, again raising the question of the registration and the handwriting, which could be identified as Ray's or as other than his. The rent was $8.50, paid with a crisp, new $20 bill.

Now, what the prosecutor seeks to imply in this recitation about rooms on the south and north is that Ray knew he had to have a room on the north side for his "assassin's lair." If this were the case, how, then, could Ray have depended upon the availability of a north room? Had he planned the murder so poorly he did not know if he would be able to get a room that would afford him a shot? If he knew he could get a room, then he was not alone. Someone had to have been working with him to let him know or did he travel all those miles on the chance of finding a pad in a flophouse?

But all of Beasley's beginning has only prejudicial intent because Beasley does not allege the murder was committed from the room anyway. Believe it or not, he fails to say where it was committed, but later (T. 69) implies it was done from a non-connected bathroom, where "scuff" marks in the tub are interpreted as showing Ray stood in it, awkwardly enough, and a mark on the window sill is used to infer the rifle was there when it was fired. (We shall examine these allegations separately.)

Mrs. Brewer, like every other witness whose alleged "testimony" Beasley "narrated," would have been examined closely had there been the trial the deal frustrated. Neither the meaning given to it by Beasley nor even his representation of it would have withstood cross-

149

examination. But immediately after the murder, Mrs. Brewer was quoted in a different sense than what Beasley tailored to suit prosecution purposes. Her description is of a man clearly not Ray. Here is the beginning of the Associated Press's murder follow-up story:

> He said his name was John Willard and he spoke with a Southern drawl. He wanted a room and Mrs. Bessie Brewer, landlady of the flophouse, showed him two.

There is no implication in any statement by Mrs. Brewer indicating Ray exercised great care to get a room from which he could commit the crime—and from the prosecution's own evidence, he did not. Nor does Ray speak "with a Southern drawl," about which Mrs. Brewer was later quoted more specifically. The *Commercial-Appeal* quoted her as saying,

> I showed him Room 8, a $10-a-week kitchenette, but he said, 'I only want a sleeping room.' I showed him Room 5 and he said, 'This will be fine.' We went back to the office . . . and I wrote him out a receipt. He paid with a $20.00 bill . . . . He spoke like any other Memphian."

Ray does *not* "speak like any other Memphian." He is from the north. But that "southern drawl" description stayed in AP stories, attributed to Mrs. Brewer.

When shown by a reporter the then recent photograph of "Galt" used by the FBI for identifying "Galt" with Ray, she said, in the words of Cy Egan's April 18, 1968 dispatch to the *New York Post,* "she was uncertain whether the photograph was that of the man who checked into" the rooming house. UPI quoted her as saying " 'I just don't know. I just don't know if it's him.' She said the FBI had never shown her the photograph." (Others said this picture was not of the Ray they knew.)

Why the FBI never showed her the photograph is legitimate cause for wonderment. It cannot be because it expected her to make the necessary positive identification.

Beasley's narrative was in other respects on and at this point somewhat deficient. It is not alone Mrs. Brewer who saw the man who checked in. B. L. Reeves, the clerk, was in the office. On October 30, 1968 (shortly before Hanes was fired), when a trial seemed about to take place in less than two weeks, Charles F. Holmes, described by UPI as "press aide" for the trial, "said nine witnesses were under subpoena, but could not say whether they had been designated by the defense or the

150

prosecution." He identified them: "Bertie L. Reeves . . . Lt. R. W. Bradshaw, Memphis policeman; James N. McCraw, a taxi driver; William B. King and Charles Stone, Memphis firemen; Guy Canipe, owner of an amusement company near the rooming house; Gregory Jaynes, a reporter for the Memphis *Commercial-Appeal;* and Harvey Gipson and William E. Friedman [sic], attorneys who represented Charles Q. Stephens, believed to be a key witness in the case." (I note that this cannot have been the complete list of witnesses that were under subpoena. It does not include Stephens or Mrs. Brewer.)

The AP follow-up story cited above had quoted Reeves as saying "I saw him when she checked him in. He had his back to me . . . ." It is not reasonable to assume Beasley omitted Reeves from his uncontested narrative because Reeves completely substantiated the others.

Beasley's narration continued. Ray had checked into the rooming house between 3 and 3:30. At 4 o'clock Ray purchased binoculars at the York Arms Company, about a mile and a half north of the rooming house (T. 62). Ralph Carpenter handled the sale, which came to $41.55. These binoculars and their case were later recovered.

However, if they were essential to a crime to be committed two hours later, what odd planning it is to wait until the last moment ot seek them in a strange town. No one was produced who directed Ray to this strange company in a strange city so he could buy the binoculars for which he had no use in the crime or for any other purpose. His target-to-be was but 200 feet away (the police are quoted as measuring it at 205 feet 3 inches). If we assume what the prosecution wants assumed, Ray knew this from the outset—and therefore knew he had no need for binoculars. So he went and bought them, thereby leaving a very clear trail.

. . . between 4:30 and 4:45 P.M., Mrs. Elizabeth Copeland, who worked across the street from this area designated as Canipe Amusement Company, observed a small white automobile pull up and park in this general area, as designated by the smaller car here on the mock-up, to the north of this light pole and to the south here of Canipe Amusement Company [indicating]. Mrs. Copeland told Mrs. Peggy Hurley, "Peggy, your husband is here for you." When Mrs. Hurley came to the window and looked out, she says, "No, that is not my husband. Our car is a Falcon, white Falcon. This is a white Mustang." She did note a man sitting in the car. [T. 63.]

When Mrs. Copeland left at 5:20, the car was still there but the man wasn't.

It is right and proper to promise this kind of testimony if it is related to the murder by anything more than the thinnest innuendo. Ray's was a white Mustang. Here, however, we have no connection with Ray. Beasley give no real identification of the car. This is not because Ray's car was unknown to him. It was in government possession. There are different years and models, even of white Mustangs. They have hard and soft tops—convertibles and closed cars—with and without automatic shifts. Nowhere in any of his promised evidence does Beasley produce even this minimal identification of the car.

Now, with Ray established as at the rooming house at approximately that time, the use of evidence that was not really evidence about Ray serves only to make it seem that the case the prosecution did not have was an abundant case with many witnesses and the tiniest bits of evidence building into a strong case. This is, at best, a legal verbosity. Under cross-examination, it would have amounted to nothing. Or, worse, a liability to the prosecution.

One of the unusual aspects of this element of the case is that in the many news stories about it, I have seen no real description and no meaningful picture of the car. This is very unlike the FBI and, in itself, provokes questions about the car.

The whole of the FBI's activities in regard to the car is full of curiosities. Here a quotation from the "analyst" of the crime who had been helped by the FBI, Blair.

> The public first heard the name Eric Starvo Galt on Good Friday, April 12, the day after *Atlanta agents found the Mustang*. [Emphasis added.]

The FBI did not "find" the car, had nothing to do with finding it—in fact, failed to. It had been parked for six days on the lot of the Capitol Homes housing project in Atlanta. As Blair himself acknowledges but two pages earlier, a number of housewives, including Mrs. Mary Bridges, Mrs. Ernest Payne, Mrs. Lucy Cayton, and Mrs. John Riley, all say they noticed the strange car pull on April 5, the driver never showing up again. Little Johnny Riley heard on the news that the man wanted in the King murder had been to Mexico. He had noticed Mexican stickers on this car and told his mother. She then had several of her neighbors in for a coffee klatsch. They talked it over. Mrs. Riley consulted her minister, Reverend Ike Powell. He counseled her to notify the police. Routinely, Roy Lee Davis, of the auto-theft squad, responded. *His files*

showed nothing on the car. It was not wanted, not reported stolen.
Despite Mrs. Copeland and Mrs. Hurley and all the other reports of a
white Mustang, *the FBI had signaled no interest in it.*

What is next in Blair's paragraph sponsors even more wonder
and bewilderment:

> In Miami, apparently by mistake, the FBI office issued a statewide
> police bulletin which stated: "Reference locate and notify no warrant
> issued Eric Starvo Galt, white male, 36 years old, about 5 feet
> 11 inches and 175 pounds with blue eyes and brown hair. Last seen
> driving a white Mustang hardtop Alabama license 1-38993. If located
> notify Agent Charles Bell FBI Miami." This message meant the FBI
> wanted "Galt" spotted, not picked up. But it was withdrawn
> immediately. When newsmen monitoring police channels asked about
> "Galt," the FBI refused comment. But *newsmen ran down the
> Alabama license number and connected it to the Mustang impounded
> in Atlanta.* [Emphasis added.]

Because J. Edgar Hoover, who talks about representative society but
neither understands it nor practices its norms, refuses to make available
what I, among others, paid for and paid him to gather, I can not expand
on this inconceivable FBI action and behavior about Ray and the white
Mustang. It does not make sense, and it does no credit to the FBI.

Here I add only what the unofficial apologist, Blair, elected to omit.
It was not a "mistake" to seek the accused killer and any information
about him. This was a late hour to be giving police clues to his identity.
Ray was *not* "last seen driving" the Mustang. And the message sent by
Bell at 6:37 P.M. was canceled at 8:27 by Agent John Hanlon.

Nor does it credit Canale and his staff when they promise that they
would introduce such "evidence" were there a trial. Here they have two
witnesses, each of whom took a close look at the car and the man in it.
Even when there is no opposition, Beasley is unable to promise a
meaningful description of the man or the car. Does Mrs. Copeland know
so little about the Hurley car and Mr. Hurley, yet say "your husband is
here"? Does Mrs. Hurley also know so little of her car and mate that she
cannot be questioned about the looks of the man in the car? What made
Mrs. Copeland think this was the car? Only the color? How about
general description? Surely Mrs. Hurley took a close enough look when
she said, "No, that's not my husband" to offer at least a rudimentary
description of the man she said was not her husband. But not a word.

The absence of these minimum essentials strongly suggests that they are missing only because they are inconsistent with the prefabricated case. Were these women in a position honestly to describe a man at all like Ray, Beasley would have promised that, it seems certain. That he does not indicates they would not offer such evidence.

In turn, this focuses more attention on the strange case of FBI Bureau Chief Jensen. He testified, as quoted above, only that "we found a registration card at the Rebel Motel" in the name of Eric S. Galt and that Galt was driving a "white Mustang automobile," with no further identification, not even its license number. Neither Jensen nor anyone else is reflected as having seen or heard of any other white Mustang or any other auto possibly involved. He and the FBI and the Memphis police knew more, including Ray's tag number, Alabama 1-38993 (which Beasley is to note in his narration). Beasley, whose entire technique was to load the record with unessential details to make it seem the prosecution had scads and scads of the most intimate details of all the incriminating evidence, is entirely inconsistent in avoiding *every possible detail* about the white Mustang. His reason may soon become apparent. Here it should be enough to understand that, with what he offered, a competent cross-examiner would have had a defense-counsel's field day.

Bourbon Charley, Star Witness

Next in his representation of evidence that would have been presented in court, had there been a real trial, Beasley said (T. 64–65),

In the meantime, back upstairs at 422½ South Main, Charles Quitman Stevens, who occupied these two rooms adjacent to a bathroom here [indicating], Mr. Stevens, who earlier in the afternoon had observed Mrs. Brewer as she talked to the Defendant . . . heard movements over in the apartment 5-B rented to the Defendant . . . . At approximately 6:00 P.M., Mr. Stevens heard the [sic] shot coming apparently through this wall from the bathroom [indicating]. He then got up, went through this room out into the corridor in time to see the left profile of the Defendant as he turned down this passageway . . . .

Here, without equivocation, without any peradventure of doubt, Beasley represents that Stephens would make a positive identification of Ray as he fled the assassin's lair in the bathroom. Only the language used by the prosecutor, when carefully examined (as with his presentation of the source of the shot), does not really say this or that there had been a shot from the bathroom. Stephens "heard the shot coming apparently

154

through this wall from the bathroom"—no more.

Stephens is the *only* witness offered or promised—and Beasley does *not,* as in other cases, assure the court he would have put Stephens on the stand—to place Ray at the actual alleged point of shooting that is not quite identified as the actual point of the shooting. With Stephens the closest thing to an eyewitness—and there was not a single eyewitness to the shooting—more attention focuses on him now as it did then. With Stephens the only thing close to an eyewitness, Beasley's brevity is remarkable.

Here I recall to the reader the various official refusals to allow me to examine the public evidence introduced at the extradition hearing in London, which includes a sworn statement by Stephens. Ray's British lawyer not only refused, but said he would also "check me out" with the FBI, then fell silent. Neither the court nor the United States Embassy allowed access. Several respected British correspondents also tried for me and failed. The Department of Justice not only refused, but failed to answer any of my requests in any way. And when, as I have related, I asked for the form required to invoke the provisions of the so-called "Freedom of Information" Act, passed by the Congress for just such purposes—forms required to be executed under the law and required to be provided by the government—these repeated requests were also ignored. This, of course, nullifies the law.

Stephens, I suggest, may be the key to an explanation of the unending official violations of the law and of the suppressions, and the real reason Canale told me "none of the evidence not in the transcript will be available to anyone." For what Stephens was persuaded to swear to when it was expected there *would* be a trial, where there *would* be cross-examination, is not at all what Beasley misrepresented to the court, to the accompaniment of Foreman's silence.

As the United States Embassy's lawyer, Calcutt, presented Stephens to the English court, Stephens said merely that the profile "was very much like the man he had seen," *not* the positive and unquestioning identification represented by Beasley. Nor was Stephens positive in identifying the man he said he saw leaving as the same man he had earlier seen with Mrs. Brewer. Here are the words of his affidavit:

> Although I did not get a good look at him, I think it was the same man I saw earlier with Mrs. Brewer.

So, the firmest "identification" Stephens could be persuaded to sign is evasive and indefinite, offering only the opinion "I think," and is specific in saying Stephens "did not get a good look at him." The formulation of the affidavit, clearly not that of Stephens but the strongest he could be bamboozled into signing, is distorted to make it seem like a more positive statement than he would, in actuality, agree to.

Stephens is a former heavy-equipment operator, at the time of the murder unemployed for twelve years. He is a disabled veteran with a metal plate in the head and the recipient of a $100-a-month disability allowance. He is thin, bespectacled, middle-aged, and a heavy drinker—indeed, a well-known drunk. In the period immediately following the murder, he was twice picked up for drunkenness.

In early July, a month after the murder, he was, in the official euphemism, "taken into protective custody." A "source" asking the Associated Press for anonymity was quoted in a dispatch for the morning papers of July 6 as saying, "He wasn't as impressed at the danger as police and the district attorney general's staff were."

Who, may it be asked, was going to hurt Stephens *if there was no conspiracy?* Was not the so-called lone, unassisted assassin in jail, under maximum security, with closed-circuit TV on him 24 hours a day, deputies in the cell with him—the whole business? *If* the alleged fears of the police and Canale's office had *any* merit, then they *had* to have been persuaded there *had* been a *conspiracy* and that one of Ray's fellow conspirators would do Stephens in.

If the state was not convinced there had been a conspiracy, it then perpetrated what amounts to a fraud in court. Bill Johnson's story from Memphis July 22, on Ray's plea of innocence, made that day, includes these paragraphs:

> Also, later in the afternoon, Dist. Atty. Gen. Phil M. Canale revealed that Charles Quitman Stephens, 46, is in jail under $100,000 bond as a material witness in the case.
>
> Stephens had been in protective custody, but, Canale said, "Rather than continue voluntary protective custody, we decided to ask Judge Battle to issue a material witness warrant."

Well, it wasn't, really, quite that way at all, but with Stephens locked up, who was there to call the respected District Attorney General a liar? Especially when Stephens was "represented" by Public Defender Hugh Stanton, who more and more looks like a wholly owned subsidiary of the Canale corporation.

To grant a $100,000 bond request—or one a tenth that great (news accounts give both figures)—for an unemployed man is the same as locking him up without possibility of bond. What this really means, whatever the legal niceties, is that the judge and prosecutor got together and put Stephens on ice. No one was about to get to him—not to hurt him but to get his version of what he may have seen—as long as he was so effectively out of circulation. Three weeks later, on August 12, the Associated Press reported further. Aside from not being free and not having nipping bourbon on hand, Stephens never had it so good:

> Charles Quitman Stephens has an air-conditioned private room, three meals a day, a television, radio and telephone and plenty of newspapers, books and magazines to read.
> But the 57-year-old World War II veteran says he is unhappy.
> So unhappy, in fact, that he has fired his public defender and hired two private lawyers in an attempt to gain his release from the Shelby County penal farm.
> Stephens was not sent to the penal farm because he committed a crime. He is being held in lieu of $10,000 bond as a material witness in the slaying of Dr. Martin Luther King, Jr.

The different figures for his age are in the news accounts. The smaller figure for the bond required $1,000 cash for the bondsman.

Even the lawyers could not say a thing about the arrest of the man who had committed no crime and his indefinite jailing to "protect" him from the conspiracy the same officials also said did not exist:

> Harvey L. Gibson and Jay Fred Friedman, Stephens' new attorneys, consider themselves bound to silence under a court order issued by Judge Preston Battle . . . . But a source close to Stephens said Stephens is determined to get, if not complete freedom, "at least some of the amenities other free Americans are guaranteed by the Constitution."

Never before has bourbon been so nobly described! (He wanted at least a pint a day.)

By August 12, the official line still had not changed a bit:

> The district attorney's office said Stephens was placed in protective custody to insure his safety and to assure his presence when needed to testify.

This affair in itself is enough to cast doubt on the real purpose of Judge Battle's order silencing everyone with any knowledge of the crime.

Regardless of its intent, it served to stifle any comment, to prevent any but the official account from being published. It did not restrain officials, all of whom, from the very beginning (the U.S. Attorney General himself the day after the murder), had been speaking long, hard, and with less than a consuming devotion to unalloyed truth, and it tended to prevent knowledge of witnesses' statements other than those offered by the prosecution.

There is ample confirmation of the Associated Press story. Here are excerpts from what Carl Crawford sent the *New York Post* from Memphis the same day:

> Charles Q. Stephens has an air-conditioned private room . . . with a deputy sheriff to keep him company 24 hours a day . . . .
>
> District Attorney General Phil Canale, who is conferring almost daily now with FBI agents planning the trial, is fully aware that—if there is a conspiracy—the conspirators may well want to dispose of Stephens . . . . Helping him go on a binge and hurt himself certainly would be one way.

Is it possible that Canale and those FBI agents "planning the trial" didn't believe the Attorney General of the United States—or Canale and his staff?

Crawford quoted Stephens thus:

> "I was in there [his tiny kitchen] working on my radio. When that explosion went off, it sounded like a German 88. I went to the door and walked into the hall. I could see the man at the offset in the hall. He had something in his hand *wrapped in a newspaper* . . . ." [Emphasis added.]

That's what Stephens was telling reporters—and the next thing he knew he picked up by the police . . . . The charge was drunkenness.

Crawford then reported that when the intoxication charges against "their star witness" were dismissed,

> the FBI and the District Attorney . . . "almost went to the bottle themselves," a close source said. They promptly had Stephens picked up again and held—for his own good. That was June 16, almost two months ago.
>
> At first, officials were so unconcerned about an attempt on Stephens' life, they "simply had a deputy assigned to him as adviser and constant companion. The deputy took him on fishing trips to a resort lake . . . ."

It was not until Stephens protested his bone-dry paid vacations that Canale went to court, having developed this sudden concern for Stephens' safety. And all this so secretly Stephens had been salted away for some time before anyone knew about it.

Now, if one examines closely what Crawford reported "Stephens was telling reporters," an entirely different explanation of *why* "the next thing he knew he was picked up by the police" suggests itself rather strongly.

Stephens went into the hall immediately. By that time, this man had left his alleged assassin's lair, gone into the rented room, and gotten all that junk together. Remember Beasley's itemization? Here are the exact words selected from the Zachary testimony (T. 49-52):

> I found a package rolled up in a bedspread . . . blue brief case . . . a Browning pasteboard box . . . rifle . . . a binocular case . . . a couple of cans of beer . . . shaving kit . . . a tee-shirt . . . pair of undershorts . . . pair of binoculars . . . pasteboard box that looks like binoculars come in . . . a hair brush . . . a transistor radio . . . a pair of pliers and a hammer . . . a paper bag . . . a newspaper, *Commercial-Appeal* . . . plastic zipper bag.

Then there were all those convenient hairs and fibers we will come to. And this was not all; it is what Beasley itemized in court only.

Now, is it at all possible that the assassin got off the edge of the bathtub or out of it, ran into the other room, gathered up this odd bag of incriminating evidence, wrapped it in a newspaper securely enough to hold—and had been able to do all of this by the time Stephens took an immediate few steps into the hallway?

Quite obviously, Stephens' "star witness" story would not hold up, either. The *only* so-called eyewitness would have come apart with the first suggestion of the most incompetent cross-examination.

And this bulky, irregular-shaped, heavy package—rifle and all—was "wrapped in a newspaper"—not even tied? No newspaper could possibly have held it.

Nor did one, if we are to believe the word of the Inspector of Police in charge of the Homicide Bureau:

> A. I found a package *rolled up in a bedspread* that consisted of . . . . [Emphasis added.]

It was not for Stephens's protection that he was sequestered. It was to keep the press from destroying the entire flimsy case, to keep the only "eyewitness" from telling the truth that could confound the prosecution in court.

The real reason "the FBI and the District Attorney . . . 'almost went to the bottle themselves' " is that Stephens had already said enough to destroy his usefulness as a witness—and he is, I reemphasize, the closest thing to what the FBI and Canale do *not* have, an actual witness to the shooting. What had already been quoted in the papers, had a real defense attorney ever collected it, was more than enough to thoroughly discredit Stephens. He had to be kept from saying any more. The public record is so terribly bad only a truly desperate prosecution would have considered using Stephens at all.

Nor is the foregoing all.

Stephens was shown the FBI/"Galt" identification picture on the day the FBI issued its spurious "conspiracy" warrant charging Ray was part of a conspiracy. UPI reported Stephens said "the photograph doesn't register." Cy Egan, in the *New York Post,* quoted Stephens as saying, "Unless he was wearing a wig or had had a face lift or something, it's not the man I saw. The hair is too full and the face is too young." But he also described the fleeing man as having "long hair."

Stephens is opposed to the other witnesses. Where he finds the picture of the 40-year-old "Galt," taken of Ray less than three months earlier, is "too young," the others give the age of the man they saw as much *younger.* The women who saw the Mustang "abandoned" in Atlanta estimate the age of the man in the car at 25 or 26 or a little more. Mrs. Brewer, who had the best look at him, said he was between 26 and 32 years old.

Stephens was a great liability as a witness because he destroyed himself and contradicted other witnesses.

Yet he was, as UPI described him September 6, 1968, "billed as the prosecution's chief witness." That story reports the interview of the Haneses with him. They were so little concerned with this "chief" and "star" witness against them, they spent but ten minutes with him.

Stephens was living with Grace Walden Stevens to whom he had not been formally married. She told newspapermen he was so drunk at the time of the murder, he could not have really known anything. (A cab driver, James McCraw, whom Stephens called and who transported him regularly, found him so drunk the driver refused to accept him as a fare.)

Even using the newspaper stories about Stephens to test his credibility —and the foregoing does not exhaust those I have—jeopardized the prosecution in other ways. An AP dispatch from Memphis the day after the murder, containing eyewitness accounts of the circumstances, also reports "When he checked in, the man did not have with him the pump-action Remington rifle and telescopic sight that killed Dr. King." There was precious little time for "Galt" to have sneaked it in, between the official account of his time and Stephens's account. According to Beasley's narrative, it was as late as 3:30 P.M. when he "appeared" at the rooming house, and he went to both rooms with Mrs. Brewer before accepting the second one, after which he paid for it and moved his duffle in. He also "appeared at the York Arms Company," some distance away, "at approximately 4:00 P.M." Here he selected and purchased the binoculars and returned, parked the car, and yet, with having to make his way around a strange town, by 5 P.M., according to Stephens, had asserted a monopoly on the bathroom that was to last until the moment after the murder, when he allegedly fled it.

Is not "chief witness" Stephens one of the best reasons there was no trial—no cross-examination—why Canale says and sees to it that "none of the evidence not in the transcript will be available to anyone"?

So, Stephens fired his "defender," the public defender, the same man who immediately got Foreman off on making a deal to prevent any kind of trial—and ten days later he was sprung. Surprisingly, if the fears of the prosecution ever had any warrant, nothing happened to him.

According to Crawford, Circuit Judge William O'Hearn ruled "that the State of Tennessee had failed to prove it had justification for imprisoning Stephens . . . ." Yet, in court, Beasley told the judge Stephens had been jailed "to keep him from being disposed of—to speak plainly."

"Plainly" may not be the most apt description.

Yet the day of the substitute for the trial, the man who would have handled a trial, the man in charge of the minitrial, Assistant District Attorney General Dwyer, asked Leonard Katz, another *New York Post* reporter, "What difference would a trial have made?"

With none of this understood, none of it having been assembled by anyone and all of it having been misrepresented by the prosecution, and with the deal safely consummated, the minitrial having just ended, Katz could also report, "If Ray had stood trial Stephens was considered by the prosecution to be their most important eyewitness."

God save the mark!

That Stephens was not an "eyewitness" to the murder, and that the state had *no* eyewitness to it, is the least of it. In his story, Katz quoted Stephens, "I'm not even sure I can identify the man I saw as Ray."

But Beasley assured the court and history exactly the opposite, telling the world there was no uncertainty, no doubt at all.

"What difference would a trial have made" indeed!

Stephens would not consent to what Katz called "an in-depth interview" after the minitrial. "He said his lawyer had advised him not to talk to anyone." Smart lawyer.

Stephens was then living in "a tiny apartment in the back of an old frame house in Memphis," without molestation. If he is in any danger, it is as a consequence of what the state did to him, for if he lives, he can always destroy the entire basis of the flimsy called a "case." All that need be done is to put him under oath and question him.

There is a choice epilogue to the Stephens story and the minitrial. These quotations are from a UPI Memphis-datelined story in the *Nashville Tennessean* of April 3, 1969:

> Charles Q. Stephens, regarded as a material witness in the assassination of Dr. Martin Luther King, filed a chancery court suit yesterday seeking payment of the $50,000 reward offered in the case. [Gipson and Friedman] stated they believed that this was "the proper time to seek payment of the reward that was posted by The Commercial-Appeal, Scripps-Howard Newspapers and the State of Tennessee . . . Gipson and Friedman said Stephens' suit contends that it was information provided by Stephens that led to the arrest of James Earl Ray, who pleaded guilty to the King slaying March 10 . . . . Friedman said it was his feeling that evidence supplied by Stephens and his statements were "probably instrumental . . . in prompting Ray to plead guilty" . . .

Is it unreasonable if Stephens seems to feel he has call on the state? Was he not its "star witness"? Had it not, after twelve years off his bulldozer, given him a new career?

The Sniper, His Lair, and the Beasley Shift

If it is shocking that Beasley could so misrepresent his "star witness and what he could and would have sworn to—and to what degree he could be believed—it is something less than surprising that he managed to get the entire lie (this one, that is) off his chest in a single sentence. That is all he had for the "star witness," one sentence, with the falsehood necessary to frame history and the defendant. He got away from Stephens as abruptly as he started.

From Stephens to Canipe is like frying-pan to fire. In this next excerpt (T. 65), "mock-up" refers to the model of the area. Beasley is referring to the location of Canipe's place of business. Although he does not say it—in fact, he is so anxious to get rid of Canipe also, he doesn't even give the address—it is slightly to the left of the South Main Street entrance to the rooming house. (A map is printed later.)

Now, gentlemen, in—you can see here this mock-up, this off-set area here is in front of Canipe Amusement Company (indicating). It is reflected here on this mock-up at this point (indicating). Mr. Guy Warren Canipe, along with two customers, Bernell Finley and Julius Graham . . . when they heard a thud in the area immediately here and up in this little offset (indicating), and looking out, saw the back of a white man going away from the area in a general southern direction on down Main Street, observing momentarily thereafter a white Mustang pull from the curb, head north on Main Street with one occupant. This package was subsequently guarded and found to be the rifle, the box, the suitcase, wrapped in the green spread, etc., that has heretofore been introduced to you gentlemen through some of the witnesses.

This is all Beasley had to say about Canipe and what he might have testified to. It is both too much and not enough. Beasley's syntax (not a word he said about Canipe is omitted above) is like his fact, garbled, as though what he was saying disturbed him—as it should have. And, as do all lawyers, he knew that in the transcript, unilluminated and unexplained "heres" and "thises" mean absolutely nothing when read. He did not by accident leave a garbled record, barren as he could make it while still giving the impression that Canipe and his customers (both of them conveniently and completely forgotten) had seen the escaping Ray drop his belongings, including the rifle, then drive away in that white Mustang. If one strips away Beasley's verbiage, it is clear that Canipe never saw the face of the man he says he saw going past (Beasley's language, "going away"), never saw him drop anything, never saw him get into the car. And has not the slightest idea whether he was in the car Beasley says he said then left the curb. Beasley himself is so upset, confused, or indifferent to his responsibilities, he describes the man as "going away from that area in a general southern direction." Main Street runs north and south. The man went one way or the other, not "generally" either way.

By Beasley's own accounting, Canipe is a man of selectively fine hearing. He could hear the "thud" we are induced to believe was of the dropped package, wrapped as it was in "a green spread" and cardboard that, were it true, would have muffled any sound. But he did *not* hear the shot?

The escaping "assassin" was not running. He was merely "going away"? A new kind of assassin? Canipe saw only "the back of a white man." Beasley gave no other description of any kind, yet Canipe was going to be used as a witness, to make an identification? Of what or of whom?

Nor could Canipe have seen that Mustang pull away from the curb—if it did—if he was inside his store tending two customers (as he was and, by one of his contradictory versions, remained). There is a convenient point in Beasley's omission of Canipe's address (424 South Main). Consultation with the closest thing possible to that mock-up (and Canale will provide nothing not in the transcript, so there is no access to the mock-up), a drawing by artist John Jacobs, of the *Commercial-Appeal,* discloses the car was on the same side of the street and more than twice its length from the closest point of Canipe's store. Canipe's business is in one of the two buildings used as the rooming house, the one in which the office is. Next to Canipe's are two large outdoor signboards.

Behind these signs, extending to well past the rear of the building, is a large parking lot. From inside the store, it is not possible to distinguish between a car leaving the curb and one leaving the parking lot. If Canipe saw a car, it could have been leaving the lot. The seat of the car is approximately opposite the far end of the second signboard. And about equidistant in the opposite direction from the main entrance to the rooming house was a *second* white Mustang, the one Beasely and every other official, of whatever jurisdiction and function, entirely ignores. It was seen to leave shortly after Canipe says he saw a white Mustang leave the curb near his store. The second Mustang, however, was parked directly in front of the point from which, in the rear of the building, the murderer is alleged to have fired.

Had there been a trial, and had the prosecution dared present Canipe for the cross-examination of a reasonably competent lawyer, he would have had to answer to the discrepancies that appeared between statements in which he said he remained in the rear of his store and other statements, made a few days later, in which he is quoted as saying he went outside to the front.

Here is the account of the Minneapolis *Tribune* for April 14, ten days after the assassination:

> He [the running man] ducked into the recessed doorway of Guy Canipe's place and what Canipe did thereafter depended upon when you talked to him.
>
> The day after the killing, Canipe said he saw the man drop a rifle and a blue bag—"like a typewriter case"—in the doorway.
>
> "I didn't go out. If you had seen a man drop a rifle in your doorway, what would you have done?" Canipe asked. Then, he said, he got busy in the back of his store.
>
> But a week after the shooting, Canipe sat with his brown hat on behind a desk and, carefully spitting into a wastebasket, told how he had gone to the front of the store and had seen the man race off in a white Mustang.
>
> Canipe said he was reluctant to say so much because he was afraid he might get shot.

Other and unoffered reasons are more apparent and more credible.

With Ray first on the lam and then securely confined and no conspiracy, who was there to shoot him? A non-conspirator?

And, with the rifle inside the cardboard box, assassins always taking the extra time for such neat packages, and the box and everything else inside that spread, how did Canipe know there was a rifle in the package? But, he asks, saying in the asking that he had seen it, "If you had seen a man drop a rifle in your doorway . . . ."

In either version, moreover, it is Canipe, not Zachary, who "found" the dropped package.

This would have been the end of Canipe as a witness and another blow to the prosecution.

From him, Beasley goes into a discussion of where what police officers in the area were when (T. 66), an incomplete and carefully slanted account calculated to give the idea it would have been impossible for anyone else to have escaped the area. This will be of further interest in consideration of the evidence on conspiracy. Here I note that Beasley was unembarrassed by the fact that, if his account was true, Ray had to have taken far longer to collect and package that strange collection of personal property and rifle, whether in a newspaper or in a spread, than required for the large number of policemen almost next door, in a fire station, to swarm all over that area. Anyone who used that rifle all the way in the corner of the building farthest from the entrance, then put it in a cardboard box, then collected all that junk and added the rifle to it, then wrapped it all up in a single bundle, could not possibly have gotten to the front door and out of the rooming house, by Beasley's account and, in fact, by common sense, before policemen could and should have been there to see him. Beasley does have the police, whose number he is careful to omit, both "on Main Street" running around and on the "scene, going up into the area"— talking "with Mrs. Brewer, Mr. Anchutz, Mr. Stevens, they entered Room 5-B."

This is another and a deliberate deception, in part designed to hide police culpability. He mentions only that "various officers from attack unit [sic], which consisted of three cars, had come in at approximately five minutes before 6:00 P.M. to utilize the facilities of the Butler Fire Station . . . for a short break . . . consisted of three squad cars. . . . These officers . . . upon hearing the shot . . . ." He thus says the *only* officers in the area are those taking their break, rather magically, all three cars spontaneously selecting exactly the same moment and exactly the same place for it. In actuality, police were secretly stationed at the fire house. When the shot was fired, about 40 policemen were in it.

With no less abruptness, he declares (T. 67-68).

The testimony [had it been taken] would show, Gentlemen, that there had been a chest of drawers sitting by a window located on the south side of this apartment. This chest of drawers had been moved from the time Mrs. Brewer rented the apartment. There was a straight chair sitting at the location. You could sit in this chair and could look from the window and could see the Lorraine Motel, in a rather awkward position you would have to get into to look out through there.

"Awkward" is no exaggeration. From the Jacobs chart and from pictures, it is obvious the window of Room 5-B faces onto the narrow areaway between the two parts of the rooming house. To see any part of the motel at all is "awkward" in the least. This room is far from the back end of the building; the passageway is narrow. Sitting on the chair or not, the head would have to be outside the window. Besides, this room does *not give a view of the King room,* which casts doubt on the entire story of Ray's selecting that room so he could commit the crime he then allegedly did not commit from there anyway. But *had* this testimony been offered in a trial, it seems certain any defense questioning would have established the prosecution had already offered evidence Ray could not have done this. More time than he had is required by what was attributed to him before five o'clock. From then on, in the prosecution's own story, he allegedly was in the bathroom. But what end was served by moving the furniture, putting a chair where it served no purpose? If it did happen *before* the murder, who did it, since it could not have been Ray?

Beasley then (T. 68-69) has those unidentified policemen searching the room and finding "two leather straps." He then says,

> The proof would show, Gentlemen, that the homicide officers coming into this area of the bathroom, inspecting the bathtub here (indicating), found marks in the bottom of the tub consistent with shoe or scuff marks. The window, which is in line, as I will indicate here [sic], this is the window that's reflected here with the Lorraine Motel (indicating), was open. At the bottom, from the bottom, the screen was pushed off and was found down in this area here (indicating). The sill of this window in the bathroom was observed by Insp. Zachary to have what appeared to be a fresh indentation in it . . . the proof would show through expert testimony that the markings on this sill were consistent with the machine markings as reflected on the barrel of the 30.06 rifle . . . .

Here, not surprisingly, Beasley switches immediately to Mustangs again (T. 70), but we should not share his haste. The "machine markings" bit can await our consideration of the evidence of the firing, but not the matter of the "shoe or scuff marks in the bottom of the bathtub" that *could not be proved to be* "shoe or scuff marks" but were merely alleged to be "consistent with" this. How many other things are not? The gibberish that follows is designed to say that a murderer standing *in* the tub had an easy shot at King.

This is entirely false. At best, it was a difficult shot.

The obvious thing for the prosecution (which presumably had been expecting to go to trial four months earlier) to have done was to show the jury the pictures it had had taken. These pictures should show how easy it was to stand in that tub and have the victim in the sights. But the prosecution offered no such pictures. Particularly with the great weakness of everything else was this evidence, the evidence that would show the crime to be even possible as alleged, the most vital. If it existed and if it showed this, certainly Beasley would have offered it. Most of all would he because the angle from that window to King's position on the balcony 200 feet away is such he had to be prepared to prove the shot from the tub was possible.

167

Beasley was no less careful to avoid description of the bathtub and the window. *Paris-Match,* the French weekly picture magazine which followed this story as it did the murder of President Kennedy, helps us there. Its issue dated April 20,1968, on page 52, has a large picture of a posed assassin in that bathroom. In it, we see that both the tub and the window are as close to the north wall as possible. The tub is an old-fashioned, unenclosed one, with a steeply slanting back jammed up against the east wall, under the rather high window. *Paris-Match* could not pose the murderer *in* the tub making the shot, for the angles preclude it, as do the height of the windowsill, the walls, and the sloping, slippery back of the tub. This picture makes it apparent the last thing the assassin could have done was to use that rifle in the required trajectory and rest it on the windowsill. The posed man could not stand in the tub, the sloping back keeping him too far away from the window, so he stood on the rim in the back. This raised him too high, and the wall kept him from the end of the window, away from King. It was then almost impossible for him even to contort himself into a position which would enable him to use the rifle at all. He had to get his head almost on its right ear even to see the sights.

In the absence of the required official photographs, those that certainly should have been taken to persuade the jury it was possible to commit the crime the way the prosecution claims, the *Paris-Match* reenactment picture compels belief this, at best, was one of the more difficult and least likely ways of committing that murder and, at worst, proves it could not have been done in this manner and would not have been attempted from here and this way.

Confirmation of this will be readily available to some readers, who may still have copies of *Look* dated April 15, 1969. This is the issue in which, for generous pay, all of Ray's so-called "defenders" ganged up on him, each pledging Ray's guilt in their own self-justification. As part of Huie's writing, on page 103, there is a clear picture of this bathtub, showing its relationship to both walls and to the window, from which the sill has been removed. It is obvious the steep, sloping back of that ancient tub is far enough away from the window and the back wall to make it impossible for the shot to have been fired by a murderer standing in the tub. And unless, after the murder, when the tub should have been under police guard, it was traversed like Grand Central Station, the visible marks on it are so numerous—all over it— they cast doubt on any meaning the prosecution could have attributed to them and on the honesty of any effort to do so.

One additional thing becomes clear. The testimony of Dr. Francisco about his "tests" becomes even more dubious. If King had been standing at the railing, whether or not looking down over it, *both* angles of the bullet through his body—from top to bottom and right to left—are inconsistent with a shot from this point. The shot would have been too much at right-angles to the forward-facing victim, who would also, it seems, have had to have cocked his head and contorted his body into unnatural positions undescribed by any of those present, inconsistent with what they do describe, and serving no purpose.

So, the incoherence with which Beasley seems to be saying that this was quite a feasible shot when the available indications are to the contrary—that bit about "the window, which is in a line, as I will indicate here, this is the window that's reflected here with the Lorraine Motel," may not be plain gibberish, legal double-talk. It "reflects" the problem Beasley faced *getting around* the existing evidence. Certainly, no mock-up could prove the ease of the shot as described in the other "evidence."

Nor need it be assumed that Beasley is a bumbler, skipping around because he does not know his business. His shifts to and from the Mustang, to and from the evidence about the shooting, served to make it impossible to really consider what he was saying as he said it, made it impossible for the mind to go over and question it. It made catching his glibness and errors difficult, impossible for the uninformed.

In this case, the uninformed is everyone except the principals: virtually everyone in the world, but especially the judge, the jury, and the press.

But shift Beasley does, and in a way that should be the envy of every broken-field runner. He here (T. 69–70) abruptly returns to the Mustang, without relation to the abandoned rifle and windowsill he leaves so precipitately. This time he gives the license number. Here are his exact words:

In an effort to identify any and all white Mustangs in the area of Memphis on that night, extensive investigation was made, including to the Rebel Motel [sic], where a registration card reflected one, Eric S. Galt, had registered at approximately 7:15 P.M. on the evening of April the 3rd. He was driving a Mustang, bearing Alabama license 1-38993, with an address, 2608 South Highland, Birmingham, Alabama.

This should have been the case. If Ray were a decoy, he had to leave a record. The car license is one, his registration card is another, all the stuff dropped near the shooting is more. However, it is conspicuous that Beasley does not offer in evidence or show the jury the registration card. He also fails to say the registration card is the source of the proof Ray was driving the car with the 1-38993 license. It was well known that this was the tag number on Ray's car. It was published. Having avoided this entirely in questioning Jensen, the prosecution again sidesteps the direct statement, merely inferring the license number is on the registration, where it should be. It is impossible to avoid wondering if there is some special reason for suppressing the registration card, one of the more obvious being the handwriting. Ordinarily, a prosecutor would have offered it as proof this was Ray and not someone using his identification. The failure of both Dwyer and Beasley to do the obvious when it was called for requires suspicion.

If an effort was made "to identify any and all white Mustangs in the area of Memphis," the record is void on what the "effort" produced. There was at least one other Mustang at the same place on South Main Street. This was widely reported. We have quoted one account dated ten days after the assassination. No mention is made of it by Dwyer-Beasley. There was also a white Mustang described in a fake broadcast that led the police astray. We will examine the details later. Again no mention is made of it. From the Dwyer-Beasley record, there was but one white Mustang in "the area of Memphis" when King was killed. Why, then, given this record, was the "effort to identify any and all" made in the first place?

Rifle, Ammo, and Hidden Truth

With a verbal snakehips, Beasley is again at the rifle, no doubt confusing his auditors, including the press, even more with the reversal. In saying what he does (T. 70-72), he again leaves unsaid what must be said:

> After having traced the rifle through the manufacturer and to Birmingham, the State would show through Mr. Hugh L. Baker of Aero Marine, a sporting goods place located in Birmingham, that on Friday, March 29th, he sold a 243 caliber Winchester rifle, which is a little smaller caliber than this 30.06, to the Defendant under the name of Harvey Lowmeyer, with an address in Birmingham that was different to [sic] the 2608 South Highland, [sic] proved to be no one of that name living at that address.
>
> Capt. John DeShazo would be brought from his duty station in

170

Japan to testify as to his being present and observing the purchase of this rifle along with a Redfield Scope which was mounted on the rifle by Mr. Baker at that time.

Mr. Donald F. Woods of the Aero Marine Supply Company would be called to testify that later in the evening or afternoon of March the 29th, he received a phone call from a person identified as Harvey Lowmeyer with reference to exchanging the rifle, the 243 caliber for a 30.06 caliber. Mr. Woods gave directions with reference to bringing the gun in at 9:00 o'clock on Saturday morning, and that was done. He changed the scope from the 243 to the 30.06, and at 3:00 o'clock that afternoon delivered the 30.06, which is the same rifle which has been identified here in the courtroom to [sic] the Defendant along with—he didn't have a box with a scope on it [sic]. The regular Remington box wouldn't fit and that's the reason for the Browning automatic shotgun box being used to deliver this rifle in.

The proof would show in the investigation in the Birmingham area that the license on this vehicle, that this vehicle, the Mustang, was formerly owned by Mr. William D. Paisley . . .

Still again the bewildering switch, this time back to the Mustang. It is not because Beasley is a fool or doesn't know his business. It can only be to bewilder and befuddle, to make it impossible to follow him logically, to spot his errors and avoidances—to obfuscate—on the record as in the courtroom. Why was he so anxious to leave that rifle again, as he had been so anxious to abandon the white Mustang?

This is the rifle said to have been used in the murder. The entire case can hang on it. What better reason could there be for Beasley to offer virtually no evidence about it? The remarks I have quoted are almost all he says about the rifle and Ray's connection with it. Later, customarily out of context, he speaks of the fingerprint and related evidence. But in the little, too little, that he does say about the rifle proper, he again says too much, again says enough to cast doubt on the entire case, and again omits that which is vital to the case.

Here, with the rifle, where such information properly belongs, Beasley omits any reference to ammunition. What ammo did the murderer use? Did he buy it when he bought the rifle? If not, where did he buy it? As with Oswald, allegedly the murderer of the President, the case against Ray has no proof that he ever bought any ammunition. As with Oswald, the kind said to have been used is essential to the case—therefore, there is a total absence of proof on the type and source.

171

Beasley is silent on ammunition and empty shells, but not Huie. In his April 15, 1969 *Look* article, after the trial, Huie, having gone to Aeromarine, reports what Beasley omits, that Ray had two different kinds of ammunition, one of which was military. He says there were nine empty casings in what was abandoned near Canipe's. This is certainly a prosecution secret, for it is not in what was so painstakingly fed the press, to build public sentiment against Ray and for the prosecution.

Beasley does not disturb the equanimity of the court with mention of *any* casings or ammunition. They wouldn't add up, anyway, for according to Huie Ray bought a box of 20 of one kind alone, and nowhere is there reference to the finding of any *live* ammunition, in his possession, property, alleged property, in the rifle, or in any place he is known to have been. Aside from the narrated itemization of what was found in the Canipe lode, and where and how the rifle was bought, there had been the questioning of both Zachary and Jensen on just this. But no information about ammunition.

Every kind of ammunition is manufactured for a special purpose. Each has special characteristics. Each reacts, on firing and on striking the target, in special ways, all important in criminal investigations, all important in legal proofs.

The "evidence" on the rifle is so deficient, so entirely inadequate, Beasley gives neither its name nor model. All he says is that it was made by Remington, sold by Aeromarine on March 30, is of .30-06 caliber, and had a Redfield telescopic sight added. What he here does not allege is that he has the required proof this rifle, to the exclusion of all other rifles in the world, fired that shot. The pretended proof of this (and I do not mislead the reader, it does not exist) is handled elsewhere. The reason for the separation is to deceive on the record and, with it, the judge, jury, and press into believing in advance that Ray bought and used this rifle. For this purpose, Beasley offers only reason to believe Ray bought the rifle. And in so doing, he conveniently omits any offer of proof of the capability of the rifle and ammunition under the alleged circumstances. Rifle and ammunition cannot be separated in a murder case.

Among those who did not respond to my inquiries is the seller of the rifle. Among the questions I asked are:

Did "Lowmeyer" buy any ammunition for either rifle, the one he first got or the one he exchanged it for?

When the sight was mounted, in each case, did he order any special sighting or adjustment or did he just ask that it be mounted? Was any special effort made to see to it that the sight was in full adjustment? If so, by what means or method? Did Mr. Wood shift the sight from one weapon to another, as one public account has it, or was this done by a skilled man?

Did "Lowmeyer" seek advice on the kind of rifle he purchased? Did he appear to have a good knowledge of rifles? Ammunition?

I also said I'd appreciate any suggestion he had to make, any observations he had made or would make, the expression of any questions he had after the minitrial.

There is point to all the specific questions I asked. They should all have been addressed in the evidence. None were.

Why there should be, in the official record, no identification of the weapon alleged to have been used in the murder is a mystery to me. Here is where Beasley could safely have larded his narrative with what it so much lacks, pertinent specifics. But he didn't. I can only suggest that he was so leery of his case, he felt the less he said, the safer it would be. But how strange it is that the record does not identify the rifle, not in any way except by caliber and name of the manufacturer. From the record, the alleged murder weapon could be any one of thousands and thousands of .30-06 caliber rifles made by Remington, one of the most popular calibers by one of the largest manufacturers.

The "evidence" on the rifle is so deficient that Beasley does not even give its name or model. The weapon is a "Gamemaster" pump-action rifle, Model 760, Serial Number 461,476. The number on the sight is 17,350.

Remington's 1969 catalogue lists three different models of rifles bearing the "Gamemaster" name and 760 model number. The .30-06 caliber lists at $159.95. (The others are a carbine for 308 Winchester ammunition, listing at $139.95 and a rifle for 6-mm. Remington ammunition at the same price.) At extra charge, de luxe features, like special stocks, are available. The catalogue description of these rifles is "the fastest hand-operated big-game rifle made."

The instructions with the rifle, as readily and as publicly available as the catalogue, show bullets are fed into the rifle from a separate clip (and there is no reference to the indispensable clip in any of the testimony or narrative or in any news story I have seen). The clip holds four bullets. With the one that can be placed in the chamber by hand, this gives the rifle a five-shot capacity without reloading. Extra clips for rapid reloading are readily available.

When the rifle is used, an "action bar" under the barrel is pulled backward, then pushed forward, to eject the fired shell and load a fresh bullet.

Telescopic sights are extras. The rifle is supplied with standard, open sights. The scope is more difficult to adjust. Mounting the scope is simple and does not require an expert. But a scope not properly and precisely *adjusted* makes the rifle inaccurate. Even the simple open sights with which the rifle is equipped at the factory require careful adjustment before the rifle can be sighted accurately. The instructions are quire explicit on this. In fact, almost half the words under "instructions" in the literature supplied with the rifle are about "sight adjustment" for the open sights.

"Individual differences in eyesight or method of shooting," the instructions say, "may require sight realignment." They add that "different sight settings are required for each cartridge type, bullet type and weight, barrel length, each range and wind condition and, most likely, each individual shooter."

So, a brand-new rifle, fresh from the factory, where the simpler open sights are "targeted at 100 yards and carefully adjusted for average shooters," in the caution of the manufacturer, does not make for accurate shooting, even by an expert. There is no evidence Ray is expert. There is every reason to believe he is not. Marksmanship is a mechanical skill requiring regular, repeated practice for its maintenance. There is no evidence in the record that Ray ever fired that rifle, or tested it in any way, before allegedly firing that single, remarkably accurate fatal shot.

When "different sight settings are required for each cartridge type, bullet type and weight," the convenience for himself that Beasley built into his case by omitting all reference to the type and weight or *any* identification of the bullet used in the murder, is obvious. Also obvious is the wisdom of the law requiring, as it does, cross-examination of the evidence in open court. Standard directories list nine different standard .30-06 cartridges with bullets of five different weights (the differences are to 100 per cent) in four different styles. With home reloading of shells, possible combinations are almost infinite.

Huie wrote (in the April 15, 1969, *Look* article) that Ray bought a package of 20 Peters high velocity, 150-grain soft point cartridges, and that his entire purchase totaled $265.85. The ammunition sells for

$5.60 a box. The Redfield sight, variable from two to seven power, lists for $99.95. (There is a model of this sight with a "Lee Dot," a special type of reticle with a dot in the middle of the cross-hairs, costing $109.95.) At standard prices, Ray—given the $265.85 figure—bought nothing else and did not pay for any special sighting-in of his scope. A "collimator" (the best-known is "Site-O-Line") might have been used at no charge, for some stores do not charge for this rough equivalent of bore-sighting at the time a scope is purchased. (A pump rifle cannot be "bore"-sighted because the "action" is in the way.)

However, the scope cannot be set with the required accuracy without range-firing, using the exact bullet at the precise range. With the best luck and collimator sighting alone, an expert can expect to be from four to eight inches off target.

Here is the authoritative March 1969 account of the National Rifle Association's *The American Rifleman,* in describing the "Bushnell Collimator":

> . . . the collimator's reticle adjusts line of sight well enough so that the first sighting shots at normal sight-in range will be close to the point of aim. This avoids the need for preliminary short-range sighting-in to be able to hit the target at all . . . .
>
> A collimator can do only this. It cannot, nor is it claimed or intended to, compensate for sighting-in variations that are caused by muzzle-jump, by barrel vibrations, by the way a particular shooter holds a gun, or by different bullet weights and velocities. A skillful and knowledgeable user may be able to do so partially in some instances, however.
>
> Collimating gun sights is not a substitute for careful sighting-in.

Further, no two rifles of the same model have exactly the same characteristics. The amount of "drop" can vary at different ranges. Full familiarity with the particular rifle would, in addition, be required. If the scope were sighted for 100 yards, really accurate shooting would require repeated firing at any different range before even an expert could compensate accurately.

It is obvious that Ray, if he were the murderer, did not, at the time he bought the rifle, have the slightest idea under what conditions and at what range it would be used, if at all. Here the kind of rifle originally bought is of special interest, as is the exchange. In proper context, we examine both.

Huie says Ray lucked his one shot out, that it was easy. (Oswald again!) Confronted with a choice between Huie and the manufacturer and a number of experts I have consulted, I have little difficulty deciding who knows the facts about rifles and shooting. Huie also says that on Tuesday, April 2, while Ray was at a motel near Corinth, Mississippi, he went off on a side road and "practiced" with the rifle. "He fired several of the Peters Soft Point cartridges he had bought in Birmingham, and several Army .30-06 cartridges he had acquired somewhere else."

Here, rather than settling questions, this raises new ones, for the characteristics of the two kinds of bullets are sufficiently different so that if Ray were a real expert and could sight his own weapon in well, of which there is no evidence at all, accurate firing with the Army ammo would not be precise firing for the lighter Peters ammo, and vice versa. Also, my experts tell me it would take the average good, experienced shot about a box of shells to adjust the scope properly.

Assume with Beasley that he can prove Ray bought the rifle. This point is a proper link in his chain of proof—but is significant only if Beasley does what he failed to do. He must then prove that Ray fired the shot using that rifle to the exclusion of all others. Despite the headlines, Beasley did not try to prove this. In fact, the evidence he offered is more consistent with the belief that Ray's role in the crime was as a decoy, not an assassin. The original, official federal position is that Ray was not alone. Specifically, "Lowmeyer" is alleged to have said that he was associated with his brother, who was about to go on a hunting trip and preferred the larger caliber. It is this flimsiness and it alone that the Department of Justice, that noble upholder of the law, used as its excuse for entering the case, from which it was otherwise precluded by law. Beasley chose to ignore this part of the story, and there is no reference to any brother in his narrative.

Clay Blair's version is that "Lowmeyer" phoned Aeromarine, spoke to Donald F. Wood, said his "brother" wanted to exchange the rifle. Wood got the idea they were going deer-hunting in Wisconsin. The next morning, March 30, "Lowmeyer" appeared with the .243 rifle at 9 A.M. He got the .30-06 at 3 P.M., the Redfield sight mounted on it.

"Why had Ray exchanged rifles?" Blair asks, as Beasley should have and didn't.

Blair's own answer is ridiculous:

"He had apparently already bought at least six heavy dumdum-type bullets elsewhere. These bullets could not be fired in the Winchester without mechanically filing the rim of the firing pin so it would make

contact with the cartridge cap. It was easier to exchange rifles."
Ignoring the technical nonsense, which makes no sense at all, Blair says
Ray exchanged rifles to get one that would keep him from wasting
six bullets! Those allegedly saved bullets were worth little—less than
the cost of driving to and from the gun shop two more times. Even for
Blair, this is pretty juvenile. (He also said the total bill was but $150.00.)

Because there was no official inquiry worthy of the name, there is no
expert evidence officially available on possible reasons for exchanging
the rifle. It is not explained by what Beasley slipped in elsewhere
(T. 97), when he said what FBI firearms expert Robert A. Frazier
would have testified to, had there been a trial. The relevant part
there is:

> That his examination of the 243 caliber Winchester rifle, which
> had been purchased on March 29th and returned on March the 30th,
> was not capable of chambering or firing a slug. There were certain
> deposits on the end of the bolt which had to be chiseled away before
> the gun was capable of being fired [1].

So, the reputable store sold a new rifle that was inoperative, which
relates to nothing in the case—and is difficult to believe, but not
impossible.

There are differences between the two rifles and the ammunition
available for them and the characteristics of the ammunition. These
might provide an answer. Either rifle was suitable for the murder as
committed, if committed from that window. The differences relate to
other conditions that might have been faced by the murderer. If the
reader will assume for the moment what it seems clear to me the
evidence does show, that James Earl Ray was not the murderer and
this rifle was not used in committing it, the other differences between
the rifles and the ammunition might make sense.

The .243 ammunition is a higher-speed type, with a lighter bullet.
This combination and the design of the bullet make it more likely to
explode on impact or to mushroom as soon as it enters the skin. The
heavier, slower .30-06, unless it hit bone, could go through the fleshy
part of a man's body without much, if any, mushrooming. The
mushrooming, which the bullets are designed to do, tears horribly.
When used in hunting game or varmints, this design is desirable to
effect a kill. A hardened, jacketed bullet otherwise could go completely
through the animal without killing, thus letting it run off to die a
lingering death, but to escape the hunter.

Either bullet can be quite fatal, to man or beast.

The point is: to commit a murder in which a man out in the open is to be shot, there was no need to exchange the .243 for a .30-06.

The difference between the characteristics of the two calibers of rifles and their ammunition becomes important if the intended victim is behind something, yet visible. For example, if he is inside a closed car. In a case like this, the .243 is more likely to explode on impact with the glass, the .30-06 more likely to remain relatively undeformed and undeviated and to hit the intended victim.

Under these and similar circumstances, the .243 and some of the smaller-caliber rifles are better for *assassinations* than the .30-06. The .243 and other rifles also have desirable flatter trajectories than does the .30-06 at most ranges over which assassinations are likely to be attempted.

Now, on March 29 and March 30, when the rifles were purchased, nobody could possibly know the range of a shot at King, whose exact plans were not then known. King had left Birmingham March 28. He was scheduled to return to Memphis April 3, and anyone planning the murder would have expected him to stay at the expensive Rivermont Hotel he usually patronized, not the inexpensive Lorraine to which, in the last minute, he shifted.

If anything makes sense out of what little we have been able to learn about the weapons and the exchanges, it is that the .243 rifle was exchanged for .30-06 because the man who really did commit the murder was going to use the larger caliber, the .30-06. It was desirable for the decoy weapon left behind to be consistent with what the real murderer used and so lead investigators away from him.

Provocatively consistent with this (and unrecorded in the minitrial) is the theft of 15 weapons, immediately before the murder, from the Dowdle Sporting Goods store, at 2985 Walnut Grove Road, Memphis. Included was a Remington "Gamemaster" 760, caliber .30-06. The great advantage in using a stolen rifle is that it cannot be traced to the user by sales records and serial numbers. The great disadvantage of the "Lowmeyer" kind of sale is that it fixes itself imperishably in the minds of the sales personnel and any others present in the store, leaving a clear, solid trail. This is consistent with Ray's having been a decoy rather than the assassin, deliberately (though he himself may not have been aware of it) leaving such a trail [2].

Particularly in the absence of proof that Ray bought any ammunition for the .243 (which does not mean that he didn't—I just do not know and, typically, Beasley avoided this, too) is there a strong suggestion that the switch in rifles may have been intended to attract more attention to Ray and that more promptly. It also laid a trail that led to Alabama, which appears to have had no connection with the assassination, another false lead. (This makes one wonder about Ray's choice of an Alabama lawyer over the more famous.)

So, Ray could have been Lowmeyer and undoubtedly was, without being the murderer.

White Mustangs, the Getaway, and an Airplane Ticket

Beasley next shifts as automatically as the white Mustang he also failed to describe (T. 72–73), promising that he would have proved, at a trial, through William D. Paisley, that Ray had bought the car from him under the name Galt. Here Beasley finds it expedient to give a needless description of the sale and the conversations attendant to it. He uses this as a cover for his failure to identify the car. That Ray had bought *a* car, a white Mustang, from Paisley does not mean the Paisley car is the one abandoned at Atlanta (nor does its abandonment mean it was used by the man who murdered King). Every automobile made is unique for purposes of identification. Each has a motor and a body number. These numbers appear on the vehicle, on the title, on the registration card. They are on permanent file in the state of registration. Whether or not Paisley still has a record of this positive identification of the car he sold, the State of Alabama has. These records also show the license numbers assigned that car. But Beasley, instead of showing that Ray bought a specific car from Paisley and was driving that car, to the exclusion of all others, when he registered at the Rebel Motel and that *this* is the car abandoned in Atlanta, all easy and necessary, chatters away about the utterly meaningless. His offer to prove Ray had an Alabama *driver's* license is no substitute and in itself is culpable, as we shall see. This, too, bears on conspiracy. Thus, Beasley avoids a few other complications we need not spare *our* record, it having none of the inhibiting needs of the minitrial.

Had Beasley just given to the jury the ad to which Ray responded, put it into the evidence, he would have automatically raised a number of questions. That ad read:

Mustang. '66, V-8, auto. trans., Radio, W.W. Tires, factory warranty, individual. $1995. 592-0448.

There seems little doubt Ray bought *this* car from William D. Paisley.

He was seen in a car of this general description. Charles Stein traveled thousands of miles in it with him. (And Stein is *not* one of the witnesses Beasley said he would have called!)

Beasley's problem is simple. *This* car had an *automatic* transmission. The car with which Ray *has* been identified has a *clutch* and clutch trouble.

When the FBI could no longer avoid the "abandoned" Mustang in the private Atlanta parking lot where it did not belong, among the things found in it were some trading stamps. These were traced to a Standard Oil gas station near the Peter Cherpes' Economy Grill and Rooms, 2608 South Highland Street, Birmingham, where Ray roomed. Martin Waldron wrote in the *New York Times* of April 28, 1969, that

> At the station, two attendants remembered Galt. They said he had bought gasoline there and that they had done minor repairs on the car. The Mustang, the attendant said, also needed some work on its clutch. The white Mustang which Galt bought from Mr. Paisley did not have a clutch. It had an automatic shift. Were it not for the trading stamps, agents might have dismissed the service station attendant's statement as a case of mistaken identity.

The "agents" didn't just "dismiss" this evidence. Like Beasley, they preferred to ignore it. Otherwise, the whole case falls apart and they have irrefutable proof of a conspiracy—Ray not alone—and no official wants that when the opposite has been federally ordained.

Louis Lomax, who discovered Charles Stein and, with him, retraced Stein's travels with Ray, also reports the "clutch problem" that the Paisley Mustang could not have had because it did have an automatic transmission.

There is another pertinent paragraph in Waldron's story:

> To complicate matters further, no one who knew the California Galt or the Birmingham Galt has been able to recognize any of Ray's photographs.

Ten days earlier, Cy Egan had written this in the *New York Post:*

> An FBI photograph of Eric Starvo Galt . . . is not a picture of the man who fled a Memphis rooming house after the murder, some witnesses maintained today . . . . The mystery over whether the photograph actually depicted the killer deepened further when the man who sold the white Mustang . . .said it was not a likeness of the Eric Starvo Galt who had bought the car from him.

"It doesn't look anything like the man I sold the car to," the former owner of the Mustang, a Birmingham, Ala., resident, told the *New York Post*. "I just don't recognize him at all."

UPI quoted Paisley as saying "I couldn't recognize him from these pictures".

Non-recognition of the FBI's pictures or denial that they portrayed Galt was epidemic among virtually all the people who had seen Galt or said they had seen the fleeing man in Memphis.

Beasley says, of course, "Mr. Paisley would be called to testify." This is doubtful, essential as he may have been to any probative prosecution case. From what was available in the papers, Paisley would have ruined that case as soon as competent defense cross-examination began. Having no opposition, Beasley could talk big. And did.

But he does not talk about that second Mustang, seemingly identical, parked in the same part of the same block, on the same side of the street, and seen leaving about the same time. He could not talk of white Mustangs in any meaningful and honest way without at the same time talking about a conspiracy. This he and his boss, like all officials of all the governments involved, state and federal, had ordained never happened. So, the hell with the evidence of it.

"White 1966 Mustangs are plentiful in Memphis," the Minneapolis *Tribune* reported April 14, 1968. "In fact, a Ford dealer estimated 600 of them were sold and 400 are still on the street."

It added, "There were two white Mustangs parked on the 400 block of South Main on the evening of April 4. One drove away seconds after Dr. King was shot and the other, witnesses said, left about 14 minutes later." (Remember that immediate "effort" to identify every white Mustang in the "Memphis area" of which there is no further word in the record.)

In the drawing by John Jacobs, of the Memphis *Commercial-Appeal,* the street is almost free of parked cars. The so-called getaway Mustang was parked a short distance from the rooming house past the Canipe store, the other directly in front of the rooming house.

If the dealer estimate may be high, a very much lower one would still be significant. But the Associated Press confirms the estimate. Also on April 14, it said:

White Mustangs are almost as common as cotton in Memphis. Two of them, both 1966 models, were parked within 100 feet of the rooming house entrance at 6:01 p.m. Fifteen minutes later, both were gone. Some witnesses said the killer calmly walked down the steps to the street, turned left . . . to the Mustang bearing a red and white license plate. Red and white plates are used in both Alabama and Arkansas.

Beasley quotes two women, Mrs. Elizabeth Copeland and Mrs. Peggy Hurley, to establish the presence of *one* white Mustang in the area, right before the murder. He fails to quote *Mr.* Hurley, and not because he did not know what Mr. Hurley would have said. That appeared in the Memphis *Commercial-Appeal* of April 11.

Charles Hurley is an advertising executive. He said "last night that he saw a dirty white Mustang" parked about 20 feet south of Canipe's at 5:23 P.M. This location puts the car directly in front of the rooming house.

> "I came after my wife, who works in the area, and parked behind the Mustang, and I just glanced at the plates as I pulled away, noting they were red and white Arkansas plates" . . . Hurley said a young white man was sitting in the car at that time . . . "roughly" matched the description of the suspect.

Now, according to the basis of the prosecution case, at exactly this time, for the twenty-some minutes before it and about 35 following, Ray was locked inside the bathroom of the rooming house. Therefore, either the prosecution's information on Ray being in the bathroom, which is only conjecture, anyway, is entirely wrong and the case against him dissipates, or, if he was there or anywhere else but *not* in the car, he had an accomplice and there was a conspiracy.

Without exception, all witnesses described a "young" man as the one seen leaving the scene. He did not flee; he walked, "calmly." But it was better propaganda to pretend that he was fleeing hysterically, in desperation. Without this, how could his dropping of all that evidence right at the first place it would be found be accepted as accidental? The story is he was scared and careless, running and chickened.

This "young" man in the car is in the age group described by all witnesses. At 6:11 the Memphis police radio described the murderer as a "young white male . . . in a late model Mustang." The FBI was looking for a young man, which Ray was not, until they got his Alabama license application, when they started looking for a 37-year-old man, which he also was not. He was 41 the day of the minitrial.

Perhaps it is Hurley who was quoted by the Associated Press on

April 18. If so, he did not change his story about the plates on the car he saw:

> A businessman said last night he was certain the Mustang . . . had an Arkansas tag. "I'm clear in my own mind," he said.

So, from the evidence available to him, from the family interviewed to provide evidence, Beasley suppressed—misrepresented—the reported fact about the so-called "getaway car," that it had Arkansas tags, whereas Galt's had Alabama tags. This Arkansas-registered car could not have been Galt's, assuming it was used as the getaway car. Besides, with an almost barren street, why should Galt have parked his car farther away, giving himself more distance to travel, when there was plenty of space right outside the front door and all along the curb near it?

The same issue of the *Commercial-Appeal* that carried Hurley's statement also reported the presence of the second white Mustang near the rooming house doorway. This story gave rise to reports that, despite the earlier accounts, it, not the one tagged in Arkansas, was used for the escape. It, too, said the second departed within 15 minutes of the first.

Rereading the stories about the two Mustangs, one of which—the one with the Arkansas plates—was officially ordained non-existent to hide the evidence of a conspiracy and make it possible to frame the thoroughly intimidated accused, raises a further question that should not be ignored. All contemporaneous accounts say the alleged killer walked down the stairs and right past the main entrance. With a manager and a clerk on duty, could he have been unnoted, especially when he is supposed to have had so bulky a package and had just moved in? I raise this in connection with the officially suppressed evidence about the second white Mustang at exactly the right spot and exactly the right time because there is no reason to believe the bundle was gathered up after the shooting, every reason to believe at least part of it was prepared in advance.

Naturally, the apologists, like Blair, prefer to play Beasley and ignore this second Mustang, for it, too, destroys the entire chain of sand called a case by the prosecution. No one could have read any of the press and not been aware of it—not Blair, not Beasley—and no one could honestly tell the story and omit it—in or out of court.

In his Sunday *New York Times* article quoted above, Waldron mentioned it several times:

183

For at least two weeks there have been two separate investigations, one centered in Alabama and one centered in Alabama and Georgia. FBI agents have been investigating two Eric Starvo Galts, two rifles, two white Mustang cars, two drivers licenses and an airplane ticket .... The young white man with pointed nose who the FBI said shot Dr. King, drove away from the scene of the murder in a white Mustang. Another white Mustang parked about 200 feet further down the same Memphis street drove away about 10 minutes later.

Time magazine dated April 19 commented:

However, to make an overnight trip from Memphis to Atlanta— 382 miles—in so conspicuous a car being sought by police would be almost as bold a move as the shooting itself. Adding to the confusion was a new report that there had been two white Mustangs parked near the rooming house . . .

There were others who saw the second white Mustang and whose observations were reported in the press prior to the minitrial. Just before 4 P.M., at about 3:50, Lloyd Jowers, owner of Jim's Grill, 418 South Main Street, on the other side of the main entrance to the flophouse from Canipe's, parked bumper-to-bumper against the rear of a 1966 white Mustang to avoid being too close to a fire hydrant. He also recalls red and white tags. At that point is an open stairway to the rooming house second floor, between both buildings, offering a good possibility of going or coming unseen.

An hour later, 25-year-old David Wood stopped off at the Grill for a beer. He parked in front of a white Mustang identical to the one Jowers reported backing closely against it. As he did, he noticed it had no front tag. This car could not have been used for the trip to get the unneeded binoculars. Best estimate on Wood's parking time is about 5 P.M.

Then, at about 5:23, Charles Hurley pulled up to get his wife, and saw a young white man in a white Mustang with Arkansas plates.

The second white Mustang is firmly established as in that so-coincidental place at a time no fiction writer could improve upon.

Suppressing this from the official record is a deliberate frame-up, particularly of history, and protection of co-conspirators, for it is overt indication of their existence and presence.

Because Beasley saw fit to make no mention of an important— mentioned in the quote from the Waldron story above—airplane ticket, deciding, apparently, not to trouble the official record, history, the judge, jury, and the people with knowledge, it, too, is not in the "narrative" we are analyzing. It fits here as well as anywhere. What Waldron referred to had been reported earlier, by him and by others. A week earlier he had written:

There was an indication in Birmingham that Galt [Ray's name, of course, was still unknown, Ray having registered at the rooming house under the name of Galt] may have taken one or more airplane trips during the seven months preceding the assassination.

An employee of Delta Airlines said that FBI agents had confiscated some airline records and had asked some luggage handlers whether they recalled a certain piece of luggage being loaded on a Birmingham-to-Memphis flight on April 3, 1968.

The confiscated records were said to have included a copy of a ticket from Birmingham to Chicago for April 3. The ticket was used only as far as Memphis, a source said.

With "an employee of Delta airlines" identified as "an employee of Delta Airlines," it seems safe to assume that the second noted "source" really means "an FBI source."

"A bureau theory," Waldron also wrote, was "that more than one man may have used the name of Eric Starvo Galt . . . ."
He added to the airplane information in his April 28 article:

For several days, investigators have assumed that Dr. King's slayer had driven to Memphis in a white Mustang. Now there is some suggestion that he may have flown. An employee of Delta Airlines in Birmingham said that a man answering Galt's description flew from Birmingham to Memphis on April 3 on Delta Flight 525, a jet which goes between Birmingham and Chicago. The man bought a ticket to Chicago but left the plane at Memphis when it arrived shortly before 2 P.M. on April 3.

FBI agents spent several hours questioning luggage handlers about the April 3 flight; they wanted to know if any of them had seen a suitcase which could have had a rifle in it. A Delta official agreed last week to check the airline's manifest to see if Galt or any of his aliases were shown as a passenger that day. The official reported that the FBI had confiscated the manifest not only at the Birmingham office but also at headquarters of Delta at Atlanta.

Not too many travelers are careless or affluent enough to forget to cash in the unused part of the ticket on which a refund is immediately

185

available.

On leaving the Mustang this time, as inadequately and incompletely as he had handled it and the related offers of proof, Beasley for once had a kind of connection. Galt had told Paisley, from whom he bought the car at Birmingham, that when he went for his driver's license, "I'll take the fellow at the rooming house," meaning the owner of the rooming house, Peter Cherpes. Beasley said "Mr. Peter Cherpes would be called to testify . . . that he had rented a room to Eric Galt on August the 26th, 1967," at 2608 South Highland, "for $22.50 a week, including breakfast and supper" and that Cherpes "did accompany Galt to obtain his driver's license" (T. 73). From this point, Beasley goes into Ray's subsequent travels, including to Mexico and California, which are not disputed and do not relate to the murder, although they make impressive specification and might help persuade the jury there had been a real investigation of what is relevant.

I suggest, however, that Beasley was talking big again because he was not talking to an opponent. He would not have been happy with Cherpes as a witness. There are a number of reasons, two tending to establish the existence of a conspiracy.

Cherpes certainly saw Ray often and closely. He knew him well and would have no difficulty recognizing him. I have referred to the string of witnesses who had seen "Galt" and who, without known exception, when shown the FBI's identification pictures of Ray, said it was not "Galt" or they could not identify it as him. When Cherpes was shown these pictures, according to UPI, he said, "No, that's not him."

It seems less than likely the prosecution would have welcomed a witness, for whom it vouched and for whom it was responsible, who would have testified to this under cross-examination.

The second reason Beasley would not have been happy with Cherpes has to do with Ray's getting a duplicate driver's license in Alabama during a time when he was actually in California. Beasley does not burden the record of the minitrial with such trivialities as substantial indication Ray was part of a conspiracy. Afterward, *not* in the official record, but when questioned by a reporter on this issue, Beasley dismissed this as of no consequence because Ray could have had a "friend" phone the State Commission.

But, as Beasley well knew, it was not this simple, neither the facts nor his manner of dealing with them. What he said was not an adequate answer, and whatever the answer, it belonged in court, in the official record, not in publicity only.

Briefly, on March 1, 1968, a man identifying himself as Galt phoned for a duplicate license. Records show it was promptly mailed him at his address of record, Cherpes', and that the charge of 25 cents was as promptly received. The day of the telephoned request was the day before "Galt" graduated from bartenders' school in Los Angeles. He was, without doubt, in Los Angeles. Without doubt, also, the request was made and the license mailed to him in care of Cherpes.

Only Cherpes did not get it. Somebody did, because the enclosed bill was paid. The only explanation Cherpes could offer is that when the mail for the rooming house arrived, someone went over it and picked out the license and took it. He believed it was someone who walked in from outside. The possibility one of the other roomers did it should not be ignored. If this is what happened, it is an uninvestigated, unpunished violation of *federal* law.

But before a duplicate license is sent by mail, those requesting it must identify themselves by answering detailed personal questions about themselves and the data reflected on the application and in the files.

In the "Galt" records, every given "fact" is false. So, whoever made the phone call for Ray had to know only what was untrue about him and other things not usually exchanged in casual conversation. All the evidence is that Ray had *no* friends. Not one is suggested in all Beasley's narrative. Ray also talked very little. So, whoever phoned for him, that "friend" so glibly rolled off Beasley's tongue when there is neither evidence nor reason to believe Ray had such a friend, had to know these lies:

> That he was 37 years old, when he was three years older;
> That he had an expired 1962 Louisiana license, which he didn't;
> That he was an unemployed merchant seaman, which he was not (or he knew "Galt as *Ray* in the Chicago area, where the Seafarers' International Union has a record of one J. E. Galt as a Great Lakes member).

Plus the correct statements that might have been required, like the date of original application.

It seems entirely unlikely that Ray had a "friend"; that the "friend" would have kept going into Cherpes', undetected, until he could finally, still undetected, commit a federal offense by needlessly stealing United States mail, plus a local one, trespass; and that all of this, so strongly indicative of a partner in a conspiracy, was unworthy of vigorous investigation but was worth being withheld from the jury and the official record.

Clues within Clues

With all these witnesses Beasley said "we would call" when he knew he would not have to, he professed satisfaction. He need have no apprehension over what would befall them on cross-examination for there was none. However, when he got to Charles Stein, the man who had driven more than 5,000 miles with Ray, from Los Angeles to New Orleans and back to Los Angeles in December 1967, Beasley didn't even say the state would call him. All he said is that the state would show Stein had traveled both ways with Ray.

This brevity about Stein—brevity even for Beasley—is not accidental and not from ignorance of what Stein could have testified to. He had been interviewed often by the FBI and had retraced the trip with Louis Lomax, who had written an early, important, and sensational series of articles about that trip and what "Galt" did on it. Without going into the so-many things that should not have been ignored, and would not have been in any kind of an honest proceeding by officials at all concerned with justice and the solution of so horrendous a crime, there is the Ray contact with the wealthy New Orleans businessman. Lomax and Stein, as we saw earlier, had located the phone from which one of the calls had been made. This information had been turned over to the FBI. From that moment, learning who Ray called was child's play. Therefore, there is official silence on it, from the FBI and in the court record.

If only because there was an opportunity to disprove the widely circulated Lomax reporting, repeated by others, if only because this issue provided a perfect opportunity to lay to rest the prevalent belief there had been a conspiracy, the unbroken official silence tends to substantiate what Lomax and Stein reported, that Ray had a wealthy associate. The FBI has not been loath to make ridiculous statements in its own name, to do all sorts of wrong and unethical, if not actually illegal, things. It was leaking its head off during the entire investigation, telling the press informally what it wanted printed, regardless of reasonableness, accuracy, law, or court order and decisions. Its silence, like Beasley's in court, must be taken as affirmation of evidence of a conspiracy. (The number Ray allegedly called has been uncovered by a reporter. I will return to this later.)

Instead of going into what relates to the murder and the existence of a conspiracy, Beasley drones on (T. 74–80) with what proved nothing but was specific, what a proper defense lawyer would have stipulated because it did not relate to the charge of murder in the first degree. These items had all appeared in the papers and magazines in one form or another (which is true of virtually everything Beasley said, anyway):

Ray's room number at the Provincial Motel, New Orleans (126–but Beasley once again omits the auto registered with the room);

The days Ray was there (December 17–19);

Where he had his laundry done in Los Angeles, thus showing the laundry marks on clothing as his;

When he took dancing lessons in California (December 5, 1967 to February 12, 1968);

When he was at Thomas Reyes Lau's International School of Bartending in Los Angeles (January 19 to March 2–the day *after* the request for his duplicate driver's license was made in Birmingham);

When he had minor plastic surgery on his nose by Dr. Russell C. Hadley, of Hollywood (March 5–but Beasley conveniently ignores Ray's departure before Dr. Hadley discharged him because, we can assume, the departure is *not* consistent with Ray's total independence, *is* consistent with his acting under orders);

When he mailed a change-of-address notice from the St. Francis Hotel in Los Angeles (March 17), giving his forwarding address as General Delivery, Atlanta;

That he left Los Angeles and delivered personal packages in New Orleans for an acquaintance (but he carefully avoids the date Ray left California, for it is too close in time for a lone driver to have next appeared as, according to Beasley, Ray did, at the Flamingo Motel, in Selma, Alabama, on March 22–where the murdered man was at that very time leading those dramatic confrontations with the local and state police receiving such nationwide TV coverage).

Carefully leaving out what it suits him to omit, Beasley, with specification of detail having *no* relationship to the crime, is able to make a record impressive in detail for the unthinking and uninformed, which includes almost everybody.

Even so, it might have been nice if he had identified the person to whom Ray delivered the packages, the daughter of a Los Angeles waitress, Marie Martin. She just might have known something about Ray and whether or not he saw anyone or spoke to anyone in New Orleans, right before the murder. Or is this enough reason for Beasley's omission of identification?

So, Beasley has Ray going from the Flamingo to Jimmy Garner's Atlanta rooming house March 24, paying a second week's rent March 31, and having left by April 5, when Garner went into the room to change the linens. Garner found a note, which Beasley read as: "I have to go to Birmingham. I will be back later to pick up my, within about a week to pick up my television set and my other articles" (T. 79). (Ray left in such a hurry Beasley said he had to stop in Mississippi and purchase new toilet articles [T. 94].)

After casual mention of the finding of the car in Atlanta (T. 80) and some of what was in it, Beasley jumps to April 14, when, he said, Garner permitted the Atlanta FBI to search the room. Aside from leaning on the judge and jury with the pretense of having evidence related to the murder that he does not have, Beasley has no useful purpose in presenting this information. He does not mention what was found in that room until two pages later, and then does it incompletely.

Ray had left laundry nearby, at the Piedmont Laundry, on April 1. He picked it up the morning of April 5. In promising to call the woman from the laundry, Mrs. Annie Peters, if there had been a trial, Beasley does not say how clearly she recalled the extreme fatigue that would have had to have been so apparent in a man who had been sleepless for more than a day and night, had committed a sensational murder, escaped a police net and driven, *alone*, not less than 382 miles during the night, from Memphis to Atlanta. It would have helped Beasley's case if he had been able to say something like this. That he doesn't does not mean he could have and just didn't. This is the sort of circumstantial evidence he sorely needed. There is little doubt this is one of the avenues a competent cross-examiner would have explored. That was quite a 24-hour period for any man, more so when he could not possibly have had a minute's sleep or relaxation from the greatest tension.

Then Beasley goes into the "abandonment" of the car at the Capital Homes Apartment Project parking lot and the people who saw a man leaving it, between 8:15 and 8:30 A.M. Here, again, he would have had some trouble, for some of the reported sightings of the car were two hours earlier, and the man described is both younger (26–32 years) than Ray (who should at that moment have looked very worn and old after that exhausting, enervating, sleepless previous day and night) and "sandy"-haired, which Ray is not.

Had the ever-diligent FBI been willing for local police to help (as everyone assumed happened but the FBI was careful to prevent), had it let the people know it was seeking a white Mustang with Alabama license 1-38993, this parked car would have been reported the morning after the crime at the latest, possibly even while being parked. Meanwhile, the murderer was escaping [3].

There may have been an invisible FBI "stakeout" of the car, to apprehend anyone who might return to it. Of this, there is no indication. When, so late, the FBI was told of the car, agents "swarmed" over the area. One witness, Mrs. Cayton, said there must have been a "million" of them, they were so numerous. This immediate reaction to the "tip" is not consistent with a stakeout. It is more likely the fabled FBI still again was caught flatfooted. This was an almost inevitable consequence of departing from usual, accepted police practices by keeping the clues secret from police and the public.

By this time it may have dawned on the reader that what was broadcast as a "description" of the man sought was not a description of Ray, another perfect parallel with the Oswald case.

But, at long last, there came the search of the car and of Ray's room in Atlanta. Here is Beasley's account (T. 81–82):

Specifically, and without taking time to bring these all out, they are wrapped, we do have them here, a dark blue short sleeved shirt; there were two bed sheets in the trunk of the car; a pillowcase; a rug from the trunk was taken, along with a pillow; sweepings were made of the floor mats all through the car. There was a styrofoam case in which, the type styrofoam case in which a Polaroid 220 camera is packaged and shipped and sold. Also, the 1967 license number which had tag [sic], which was in the car. This is the same tag that had been registered to Mr. Paisley, was transferred in early September to the Defendant as Eric S. Galt, and, of course, bearing the 1968 Alabama license, 1-38993.

The officers of the Bureau there, who made the search of the room rented by Jimmy Garner, would testify with reference to a number of maps that were found, including the maps of Atlanta, maps of Texas and Oklahoma, maps of Los Angeles, map of California, maps of Louisiana, map of Arizona and New Mexico, map of Birmingham, and also a map of Mexico; that these items along with the, these maps along with the handwritten name, Eric S. Galt, was delivered over to the laboratory and will be touched upon in the testimony from that end in just a moment [4].

The word "testimony" in the last phrase is, of course, entirely incorrect. Moreover, when Beasley himself "narrated," he did not return to all these items [4]. He mentioned (T. 97–98) hairs and fibers from various sources, the camera packing-case, the sheets and pillowcases and things he did not here name. He also alluded to items not in this catalogue. Still, without careful analysis, the information he did give appears impressive for it seems specific, to point to Ray.

However, it in no way incriminates Ray as the murderer or the lone murderer. At most, it places him near the scene of the crime. This is consistent with his playing the role of decoy, not with his having been the murderer. In the light of the other evidence, it is powerful confirmation that he was and was designed and employed as the decoy.

For that "testimony" not testimony, the promised proof of the technical evidence, Beasley skips again, bewilderingly. He returns, over ten pages later, for a few words on page 94. He then does the same thing on page 98. In between, he takes Ray to Canada and around Europe. This scatter-shooting of "evidence" could not have the effect of improving comprehension of the technicalities. Even then, when he says what would be proved in a trial, had there been one, he is less than unequivocal. Of the fibers, he says (T. 98) only that they are "of the exact same type." The use of "exact" here is propaganda. What may have been true but what he carefully does *not* say is that they are *"exactly the same."* The billions of available fibers of the "same type" cannot even be estimated. Ditto with the hairs. Compared with those taken from Ray in jail (could this raise questions of law under the Fifth Amendment?), he says, deceptively, they "have the same characteristics in every respect." This is *not* saying they are identical.

Now, I happen to believe these should have been *identical* hairs and *identical* fibers. The available evidence overwhelmingly persuades it was Ray's function to leave the many clues painstakingly left so they would lead to him. But even this is equivocated in the un-challenged offer of proof.

Space prevents dealing with all of Beasley's censoring of fact, evidence, and history at this point. Let us, then, consider only two more items.

Beasley had read Ray's note to Jimmy Garner (T. 79) which said that he, Ray, would be back in about a week "to pick up" his TV "set and my other articles." But in discussing the FBI's search of the room, he refers to no TV set, no "articles." What was the note about, then? And how strange it would be if there had been no toilet articles left behind at Garner's or elsewhere, for Galt still had to stop in White Haven, Tennessee (T. 94) to get some before entering Memphis.

The TV set was of some significance because (among other reasons) it could tie the east-coast and west-coast "Galts" together as being one and the same.

Lomax wrote of it.

He established "Galt" had had two girl friends in California. To one, "Jerri," "Galt" advanced the cost of a trip to visit her parents in the upper midwest. Lomax said "Jerri" was "important to the investigation because of her close relationship to Ray while he was in Los Angeles . . . she may well have information about the various contacts Ray was known to have made in the South, particularly in New Orleans." But "Jerri" suddenly and mysteriously disappeared. She had "spent several nights, perhaps weeks, with Ray (Galt)." After she got to Milwaukee, she and her "husband" checked into a hotel from which they suddenly disappeared.

Just before leaving Los Angeles, Ray visited a different girl friend "and offered his console TV set for her portable. The girl accepted the swap. Ray loaded her portable set in his car and told the girl he was leaving town about Valentine's Day, February 14. Although they are tight-lipped about it, the FBI has found the portable TV set, probably in a Birmingham, Ala., rooming house."

There were markings that can be connected with Ray, Lomax wrote, on the back of the console TV. The portable could also be traced to the girl [5].

Beasley's avoidance of any of the evidence about the TV sets, even after he dared not avoid referring to the one in reading the note left for Garner, does not undermine confidence in Lomax's reporting or interpretation. It does focus renewed attention on the persistent and successful effort of the prosecution to edit evidence, censor history, frame the defenseless defendant. In this case, the transgression is not diminished because it leads away from what might have been proof of a conspiracy.

The second item concerns the maps. In mentioning all those maps, including the one of Atlanta, Beasley omits what the ever-leaking FBI had not, intent as it was, in violation of all honest legal practice, in

193

pinning the rap on the then-unapprehended accused. Beasley says nothing about that map of Atlanta. And with good reason. It helped frame the man he was busily framing.

Most people forget the small details of transitory events, no matter how well they are reported. This little raping of the law—for which St. Edgar himself must be held responsible, his disciples being the *only* mortals to have possession of the maps—is as subversive as anything can be in what calls itself a society of laws, not of men (with one notable, indispensable exception). The giver of the gospel on what is American and what is subversive either ordered or tolerated what, in itself, may have made a free and fair trial impossible, what could have been enough to get a conviction reversed. This little matter could not more closely parallel a similar unpardonable poisoning of the well in the Oswald case. Had it ever become part of a real trial, it would have had the same legal consequences.

With Oswald, an innocent map on which he had marked the places to which he would apply for employment was deliberately misrepresented as a blueprint of the assassination. Not by the Warren Commission— *before* it had or knew of the map. After the publicity, nothing mattered. The publicity did the job—telling a lie to incriminate Oswald.

With Ray, almost any newspaper can be consulted for what the FBI put out. It was no less venomous. It had the side benefits of tagging the suspect with a guilty label and making it appear that the FBI was close on his trail when in fact it was hopelessly lost and had not the slightest idea who or where the suspect was.

Blair's version on the maps (p. 174) is succinct and to the point:

> Agents collected items from the room, particularly the maps. There were maps of Texas, Oklahoma, Louisiana, California, Arizona, New Mexico, Birmingham, Atlanta, Mexico. On the map of Atlanta they found the four pencilled circles around Martin Luther King's home, the headquarters of SCLC, Jimmy Garner's rooming house and the Capital Homes area, where the Mustang had been left.

How truly remarkable, all those maps, yet marks on only one, Atlanta. And as for that one—has anyone ever seen such a *fine* map, with every individual house, every individual office and office building, separately indicated? Of course, it had to have been an *enormous* map to contain such exquisite detail, *individual* homes and buildings— if it did.

More, is it not at the same time inordinately strange that, with all those 19,000 miles of traveling, Ray, who seems to have felt the need to mark his Atlanta map, needed no marks on any others, not in any of the strange states or the foreign land? From all accounts, unofficial and unofficial official, he had rendezvous there. He did not speak much Spanish. *Needing* marks in Atlanta, where the ever-present phone book could always refresh failing recall, he needed *none* in Mexico. None in New Orleans, laid out as it is, like no other city, where he is known to have been and to have kept appointments. Nor in the megalopolitan sprawl of Los Angeles. Only in Atlanta. Extraordinary!

Is it not even more extraordinary, that having (according to no less authority than the greatest policeman of them all) marked those key points at which he could have murdered the man he is said to have sought to murder, he never tried? Not once! No suggestion of it. Where it was easy, where a single shot from a fast car would have done it, or a single bomb in the night could have ended it all with no ballistics or eyewitness evidence, there he did not do it and did not try to do it. Only he left marks on the map, declaring his intention? Better than a calling card. Ah! that new breed of assassin who seeks only personal glory, which is what all the "experts" tell us. The glory of the ignoble death, of the left-behind proofs.

And that mark around Jimmy Garner's. What could it possibly mean? Not that it had been marked for him and he had been directed there. Oh, no; because he was a lone assassin, was he not? No co-conspirators, confederates, or help of any kind.

Now, the only purpose of marking a map, except to leave as a calling card, is to know where to go *before* you get there. Once you get there, you *do* know. If one then needs anything, the address suffices and the phone book always replaces the lost notation.

And the Capital Homes project—that is really provocative!

Here we have a map marked before Ray left Atlanta to show him where, after all the other stops and the murder in Memphis, he was to return and abandon the white Mustang, loaded with clues. What difference did or could it make to a lone, unassisted murderer—in a case where there could not have been a conspiracy, the official line sanctified and certified by everyone from the Attorney General down as the unquestioned fact—where the devil he left his his car? Why carefully mark on a map a strange, unknown place 400 miles away and defy what had to be anticipated as the biggest police hunt in history just to leave a conspicuous, evidence-rich car in that certain place? Why not abandon it at any convenient place? Why run this great and unnecessary risk? If it was run, that is. But the map did have the location of the Capital Homes lot in Atlanta marked on it, and the car was "found" there (despite the best FBI efforts).

But this does not end the questions about the map. It was found in the room to which he did *not* return. So what help could it have been to him? Why have it marked at all?

To forget?

He *did not* need it. He got to the Capital Homes parking lot *without* it.

The question of why the map was marked and abandoned, to be found, requires answer.

Or did someone plant it? If so, was there less than a conspiracy?

It was to be more than the promised "moment," then, before Beasley "touched upon" the fingerprint evidence on the maps. First, he had to use the by-now standard Beasley shift, going to Toronto and elsewhere in Canada and then through Ray's travels in Europe. Only 13 pages later in the transcript (T. 94) did he keep his word. By then, the number of maps and the areas covered were lost in the confusion. Of *all* the maps found anywhere—of Texas, Oklahoma, Louisiana, California, Arizona, New Mexico, Birmingham, Atlanta, Mexico (Mississippi, Arkansas, Tennessee, and Memphis are missing: again remarkable—Ray had maps of *none* of the places where the crime *was* committed, none of the only states through which escape was possible)—what does Beasley say? There was but a *single* Ray fingerprint, on the map of Mexico. *No* Ray print on the *marked* map of Atlanta! (If any other was found, it is an FBI–prosecution secret.)

And to get the little evidence in the record that he did, did Beasley have to chop that fraction into three pieces, mix it up, and blend it in at three different places? This is normal, in Tennessee or in other courts and prosecutions?

So much for the maps' fingerprint evidence.

Following Beasley is to skip around. Withal, there are the things he did not go into. There are those who have facile explanations for everything government does that cannot be excused in the era of political assassinations (a facility and service not without its rewards). As Ray allegedly, like Oswald, was merely seeking to make his "mark" in the world (for which he had to be prepared to give his life, so he couldn't enjoy it), perhaps Beasley suffers only a bad memory?

In any case, the question then arises, where to include what he did not? Perhaps here, after noting the "explanation" of the apologists, that Ray was just a nutty nut who did his thing his way for his own kind of kicks, is as good a place as any to note the absence in the record of any psychiatric evidence that the alleged nut is nutty—or the offer of such evidence. Beasley was pretty good at offering what he knew he would never be asked to deliver. But this he didn't offer, didn't narrate, at any point.

There is a prison record on Ray. He was seen sufficiently often by a competent psychiatrist and by a professional warden with long experience. Dr. Henry V. Guhlman, Jr., who did study Ray at the Missouri prison, reported "no evidence of delusions, hallucinations or paranoid ideas" and that, while Ray was neurotic (what else, with a career in jail for petty crimes?), he was "not psychotic." The study had been requested by Ray, who was aware of his neurosis and sought help, entirely voluntarily, a new kind of "nut."

Before Ray was captured and the big propaganda guns turned on him, Douglas E. Kneeland, a reporter, went to that prison for the *New York Times*. His report was printed April 23. It described prison officials and inmates as "stunned" and unwilling to believe Ray was capable of the crime. Typically, also, after newspapers with "Galt" pictures and sketches circulated inside the penitentiary, "no word of recognition was heard along the prison grapevine." Warden Harold R. Swenson said of his prisoners, "Once a guy is gone they'll talk." He added, "We've got 2,000 prisoners in here and none of them recognized him."

The "prisoner who had been closest to Ray" was interviewed by Kneeland, permission being granted "because of national interest in the case." Shown the FBI's identification pictures, he said it didn't look like the man who had been his prison friend for many years. Nor did anyone on the staff recognize the pictures.

Nor had the FBI been there. Ostensibly engaged in history's greatest manhunt, it avoided the obvious and best source of proven information about their quarry, the prison from which he had escaped, where he had been studied, fingerprinted, and photographed, and where all sorts of other things handy in a manhunt were known about him. Swenson reported that no "representatives of the agency" had been there "to look at Ray's record or interview prisoners who knew him."

The warden explained his disbelief about Ray. "I was floored," he said. "This guy's penny ante. It doesn't shape up." Drawing upon 30 years' experience, mostly in the federal prison system, he said, "He's innocuous. Penny ante."

Another prison psychiatrist, who had examined Ray for five weeks in 1966, was quoted in the *New York Post* of April 22 as saying Ray was a habitual criminal, all of whose crimes were associated with money. "We didn't find anything to indicate he was a killer or had tendencies to kill."

Because of the unwarranted label of "killer" applied by the FBI, there was "growing concern," the *Post* reported, "that when Ray is tracked down he might be shot by his captors" since the FBI had labeled him "armed and extremely dangerous." Other papers questioned the "wisdom of that label." Had Ray been caught in the United States, there might, indeed, have been a shooting match in which, conceivably, he would have been killed and the embarrassment of even a minitrial averted. It has happened that way before.

There is little point in taking time for Beasley's reiteration of that brief part of what was public knowledge of Ray's Canadian adventures (T. 82–85). The judge and jury, knowing nothing of the foregoing, may have been impressed by the information, believing it all part of the official investigation rather than derived from the press. Beasley's rendition made it look like the ever-faithful, never-daunted FBI was, from the first, hot on Ray's trail until it finally got him. In turn, that made everything Beasley alleged seem credible and factual. There was no reason for the jury or others to assume the incompleteness of his narrative, though this is the painful fact.

However, if Canada is worth noting, we might add that while Ray's Canadian career and his flight and capture were with many identies, one of them, that of "Sneyd," is not mentioned in the complaint, the charge on which he was "tried." Officially, then, "Sneyd" was not one of his aliases, even if it is the name under which he was captured and first charged! Ray, Galt, and Willard he is, and Lowmeyer with two spellings —but not Sneyd or Sneya (or Bridgeman, either). This was one of the better ways of avoiding added unpleasantness: for example, how to explain three look-alike false identities in a single city. It also shows the investigators' great ignorance of the alleged criminal at the time he was charged, after that enormous manhunt.

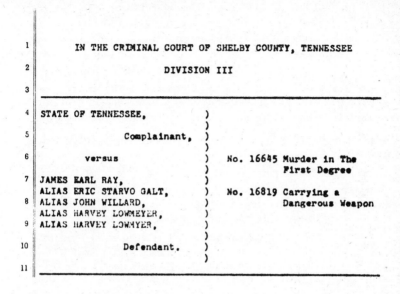

```
 1        IN THE CRIMINAL COURT OF SHELBY COUNTY, TENNESSEE

 2                         DIVISION III

 3   ─────────────────────────────────────────────────────────

 4   STATE OF TENNESSEE,            )

 5                   Complainant,   )
                                    )
 6          versus                  )     No. 16645 Murder in The
                                    )               First Degree
 7   JAMES EARL RAY,                )
     ALIAS ERIC STARVO GALT,        )     No. 16819 Carrying a
 8   ALIAS JOHN WILLARD,            )               Dangerous Weapon
     ALIAS HARVEY LOWMEYER,         )
 9   ALIAS HARVEY LOWMYER,          )
                                    )
10                   Defendant.     )
                                    )
11   ─────────────────────────────────────────────────────────
```

Whichever is the truth, Beasley has Ray leaving Lisbon for London May 17, by official Portuguese statements, but with such brilliant indefiniteness, the flight and airline are not indicated. (We have seen why—there is no record of it.) For the period of 11 days after Ray's return to London, a period during which *any* contacts he had at all would be significant and could bear on or yield proof of conspiracy, there is the unadorned, barren sentence (T. 87):

> The State's proof would show, Gentlemen of the Jury, that upon the Defendant's return to London, as Ramon George Sneyd, he lived at the Heathfield House Hotel from May the 17th to May 28th.

(In Blair's transcript, this comes out "Eckfield House.")

On the arrest, again incredible brevity and an effort to make it look as though competent, cooperative police work rather than a simple, unpredictable blunder brought it about:

> Through the cooperative efforts in law enforcement, officials of New Scotland Yard in London, England, and the Portuguese International Police, the search was started for Ramon George Sneyd .... All entry and exit points in the country were notified and a special

fugitive team was set up . . . [T. 88].

The Defendant, as Ramon George Sneyd, appeared at the Heath Row [sic] London Airport, attempting to board a flight to Brussels; that at approximately 11:30 A.M. on June the 8th, 1968, Detective Sgt. Phillip Frederick Birch, of New Scotland Yard, who was seated next to the immigration officer checking passports, when the Defendant presented the two passports, the one cancelled in the name Sneya, the current passport in the name Sneyd, which both of these passports would be introduced and shown to you gentlemen [T. 89].

This syntactical confusion is no discredit to the laboring Beasley. It is no simple matter to carry off all the many deceptions contained in this one overburdened sentence, to give the impression there had been some need for Ray to appear before the immigration officer, that the police had really tracked him down by utmost and unflagging diligence, that their work made his arrest inevitable; and withal, to have managed to give the wrong time for Ray's appearance, further to powder the red FBI face, hide its errors and the conflict between the various FBI's statements and between the FBI's statements as compared with Scotland Yard's.

The time given as that of Ray's needless appearance at the immigration stand is a new inaccuracy, preserving the consistently inaccurate record of various agencies of government which have never agreed with themselves or among themselves on this simplest and most basic element of the arrest. It was not "at approximately 11:30 A.M. on June the 8th, 1968," in Memphis, where Beasley narrated, or in London, where it happened. According to the contemporaneous accounts, it was a little after 6 A.M. London time.

So, consistent with everything else, the official record of the arrest of the accused is stripped of almost all fact, reduced to the overstated, misleading, deceptive, and outright wrong generalities without which the case could not survive. This is no inconsiderable achievement. Beasley's capabilities should not be downgraded because of his seemingly bumbling syntax. We have had Presidents of the United States whose expression was no better.

Yet there remains in this part of Beasley's narrative, despite his able efforts, still further evidence of existing proofs of conspiracy. Ray was searched (T. 90):

Also on his person were the tickets from London to Brussels and some of the ticket stubs, etc., on the London to Toronto flight along

200

with various items of correspondence which would be introduced as being relevant but not particularly for purposes of this inquiry.

Not a bad definition of the "purposes of this inquiry"!

The flight was not "London to Toronto" but the reverse. Ray had flown to London on a round-trip ticket from Toronto. Then he cashed in the London-to-Toronto ticket for a ticket to Lisbon. And how about the flights from London to Lisbon and back? How about the proof that Ray had just landed and "was in transit through Immigration on arrival from Lisbon on his way to another country" (the words of the official statement of New Scotland Yard the day of the arrest)? How about the words of British European Airways following this official statement, "We assume that he had travelled earlier that day from Lisbon to London but if he did so there is no record . . . no ticket was issued for that purpose"?

In short, Ray's–Galt's–Sneyd's–Sneya's travels remain entirely unexplained after the minitrial. So that proceeding serves merely to strengthen the suspicions more than justified by what had uncontestedly appeared in the public press. The suppression of the evidence government must have—or the acknowledgment they do not have it—either—helps establish existence of a conspiracy.

With this in mind, it is worthwhile returning to those "various items of correspondence" Beasley describes as "which would be introduced as being relevant but not particularly for purposes of this inquiry." With the overt evidence of a conspiracy, no correspondence could have been other than "relevant" unless, as seems clear by now, the "purposes of this inquiry" were to make it seem that there had been no conspiracy. Those with whom Ray had been in touch should have been questioned at length so that no question might remain about his connections, intentions, actions, or any part of his past. The matter may not rest where Beasley tries to bury it.

With these few verbal stones over the too-shallow grave, Beasley (T. 91) set forth an event that was an open illegality and abdication of British sovereignty. Scotland Yard's Chief Superintendent, Thomas Butler, after "questioning the Defendant with reference to the passports and a pistol and cautioning him with reference to his rights, . . . contacted the American authorities and subsequently turned the Defendant, was subsequently turned over to the American authorities" (sic).

From the official record as established by Beasley, then, Ray was "turned over to the American authorities" immediately, before the

201

extradition hearing, which is illegal and which did not happen officially but may have unofficially, and according to Beasley's record, there was no legal proceeding by means of which Ray was properly returned to the United States! For there is no reference to the extradition hearing in his narrative.

In this long catalogue of the trivial, what conceivable reason could there have been for suppressing reference to the legal proceeding in Britain *prerequisite* to turning Ray over to "American authorities," to extraditing him? One that suggests itself is avoidance of what was said and adduced at that hearing, avoidance of any *public* official record of it within the United States. This is consistent with the refusal of every official to make the "public" record of that proceeding available, in Britain or in the United States.

"Not available" is the phrase used to describe this "public" record by one of the friends who tried to obtain it for me. He is the most-honored British reporter of recent years. He wrote, "I cannot help you with the trial transcript, simply because it is not available."

Secret "public" evidence, denied the press.

This leads to the inevitable conclusion that what is in that official record, the basis of the legality of returning Ray, is not consistent with the alleged offering of the alleged proof that resulted in his conviction under circumstances that guaranteed he would be securely locked away for the rest of his life, inaccessible.

The one thing none of this *can* be consistent with is honesty of purpose or performance. Beasley's narrative cannot be regarded as the required clear and acceptable record of the crime. It is and must be regarded as another of the endless and unfortunately successful attempts to establish a false and fraudulent record of the crime and its "solution" and to block every effort at inquiring into it so that the truth might come out.

Immediately after his sentence about Chief Superintendent Thomas Butler, Beasley refers to some of what was in Ray's baggage. Of all that luggage (T. 91-92), what does Beasley itemize?

> A Polaroid camera which was determined to fit the styrofoam box that had been recovered from the Mustang in Atlanta.

And two suits of clothes. Not another blessed thing.)

Now, the overt purpose of this information about luggage is to establish proofs connecting the man arrested in London with the stuff abandoned at the scene of the crime or later presumed to have been connected with it. Were there none of that FBI favorite, hairs? (In their investigation of John Kennedy's murder, the FBI got pubic hairs from the then-unmurdered Oswald and compared them with those taken from a blanket uncontestedly Oswald's, made a swashbuckling display of their "science," and pretended, to the plaudits of the press, that they had proved something, that Oswald's acknowledged blanket was Oswald's blanket.) No other items of clothing? No laundry marks, another FBI favorite? No toilet articles that could be traced? No books? No notes of any kind? No receipts or records? No more maps? No references to people he wanted to see in Brussels? It is known "Sneyd" had been in touch with those who might have effectuated his entry into racist Rhodesia or South Africa. Of this and anything else at all, there is a void—nothing—raw suppression.

That the camera fit the packing case could have significance, but countless thousands of others of one of the most popular cameras ever made would also have fit exactly the case, made to fit every one. (There is no record of Ray's having bought it.) What is missing here and everywhere else, including in any of the thousands of clippings I have examined, is the slightest suggestion that Ray ever took a picture. He had this and other cameras in his possession, but not a single picture ever turned up. For what purpose, then, did he have and carry *any* camera? There are no answers, but there are questions. Among the more obvious are: who and what the pictures might have shown; to whom, if anyone, any were sent; and were any recovered. He had lady friends, but no pictures of any. He saw others, traveled extensively throughout the entire United States, its length and its breadth, repeatedly; was in Mexico and Canada on several occasions; was in Portugal and England, with a camera. But, from the record not suppressed, never took a *single* picture—even though there is existing record indicating he may have. There is the reasonable presumption he did. Why have and carry a camera if it is not used? The Polaroid gives instant pictures.

It is difficult to avoid the inference he did take pictures and that they were suppressed—and only because they might jeopardize the frame-up.

Abruptly, there is another of Beasley's out-of-context jumps connected with nothing and belonging almost anyplace else as well as at this point (T. 92). Going backward in time, "during the period of July and August of 1967," he places Ray in Montreal in "an apartment at 2589 Notre Dame . . . through August 29th of 1967." Beasley immediately (T. 93) makes still another of his abrupt shifts, even further backward, to Winnetka, Illinois, for "the period of May 3rd to June 24th." What Beasley here does is another of the endless instances of specification of precise information which make the record seem like a specific and factual one when it is not. All of this was the period *prior* to the murder. It has relevance only if *connected* with that murder. The only way it can be is in the context of a conspiracy, giving meaning to what Ray did, where he went, before the murder. This, of course, is contrary to the claim of the prosecution. This foray into Montreal, then back to Illinois (both of them during the year before the murder), save for again wrenching the mind away from the utter meaninglessness of what went before: the crucially important evidence on the arrest and extradition, can have no other, no non-conspiratorial meaning. It is the standard Beasley method, the regular interjection of the irrelevant specific deceptively to give the impression the entire case is factual and precise.

Bonebrake and Frazier: Prints and a Slug

With the minds he was addressing no doubt still reeling from the twists and turns about what relates to the crime in no manner, shape, or form, Beasley then (T. 93–96) gets into the oft-promised fingerprint evidence. George J. Bonebrake, the FBI expert, "has been working with fingerprints since 1941," enough experience to qualify him as a genuine expert.

We have already examined the fingerprint evidence on the maps. What of the rest?

Bonebrake "found a print of sufficient clarity, fingerprint of sufficient clarity on the rifle itself." Beasley stammers, is uncertain. First it is merely a "print," then a "fingerprint." Perhaps incorrectly, the press reported a palmprint, which is not as positive an identification as a fingerprint. I do not question Ray's association with that rifle. That is essential to the role of decoy. The point is, the absence of cross-examination casts doubt on everything alleged, especially when the evidence described is *not* made part of the record—is suppressed—as in this case also was done, when it was so easy and inexpensive to include it—and so desirable and necessary.

There were Ray prints on the scope and "on the aftershave bottle, which is in the little packet that was obtained or purchased from the Rexall Drug Store in White Haven, Tennessee" (again the great detail about trivia and what does not connect with the murder, to hide the total absence of anything that does).

On the binoculars bought for no apparent purpose, Bonebrake again found "a print." "He found a print on one of the Schlitz Beer cans" and "on the front page of the April 4th issue of the Memphis Commercial-Appeal."

These items—the binoculars, the after-shave lotion, the beer can, the newspaper, all contained in the package so conveniently dropped in a doorway—certainly were not necessary for taking a pot-shot at 200-foot range. But there was no one to ask the question, why would Ray have kept them in his sniper's lair. More important, why, with speed so urgent in escape, would an experienced criminal have dallied so long to gather up such unessentials and then, when not running, just drop them the first place they would be seen? The existence of Ray's prints on the newspaper, beer can, and binoculars, as on other similar items serving no purpose in the murder and not connected with it, is not proof he was the murderer. Rather, the opposite is the reasonable deduction, that he was not and that, through him, a deliberate trail to mislead the police was manufactured with them.

In the absence of cross-examination, there was no one to point this out. However, the suspicion did exist and was recorded, as was the reason to suspect it. For example, one of the reasons Attorney General Clark, barely 24 hours after the murder, gave for his immediate proclamation of "no conspiracy," in the words of the *New York Post* of April 6, is "that authorities had considerably more evidence than police 'usually get in cases like this, including a number of studies of prints that may establish identity.' " Two days later, after he flew to Memphis "to assume personal command of the search for King's killer," he was quoted by Wayne Whitt in the *Nashville Tennessean* as saying " 'substantial evidence' has been discovered" and "real progress is being made. I am confident . . . we are getting very close." He indicated an arrest could be expected momentarily. The wire services and many papers repeated these statements from the nation's top law officer. He knew someone had left too much evidence, enough to be unusual.

In court, where there was no little boy to report the evidentiary nakedness, Beasley could drone on.

There was the print from the map of Mexico. So, Bonebrake "started an extensive investigation through some fugitive files consisting of some 53,000 fingerprint cards," taking *two full weeks* to find these matched those of the Missouri escapee.

What happened to all that instant efficiency of the FBI, the propaganda about the importance of having everyone's prints so that immediate identifications could be made for non-criminal purposes—to all that taxpayer largess lavished on thousands of clerical employees, elaborate equipment, computers, filing systems, and the like? The grim fact is that, with more than enough fingerpirnts "of sufficient clarity" so Bonebrake could begin his work in Washington by "5:15 A.M. April 5," before dawn the morning after the murder, and with all the manpower added to the mechanization, *it took two weeks to identify Ray's carefully deposited prints!*

The Beasley shift again, and for the same general purposes, to hide deficiencies in police work, especially by the FBI.

First, it was not until June 24 that Bonebrake "compared the prints from these items" (rifle, map, etc.) with those he obtained from Scotland Yard—which had made them more than two weeks earlier. Then in the middle of this performance, without in any way saying why, still hiding from the jury and the official record the fact of the extradition hearing and its evidence, Beasley says, "Mr. Bonebrake went to London," as though he went to pick up the Scotland Yard prints. These five words only. No reference to the fact that Bonebrake went to England as the *only* witness in the extradition hearing. (Beasley *actually* says Bonebrake went *after* getting the prints from England [T. 95].)

Aside from prints that came to light through the public press and despite the failures of the FBI—those on a paycheck to Ray after his jailbreak and not in any way connected with the crime—there is but one other fragment of fingerprint evidence promised:

> . . . on May 6, 1968, he [Bonebrake] also examined a modern photo book store coupon [sic], bearing the name Eric S. Galt, 2608 Highland, Birmingham, Alabama, and found a thumbprint . . .

Now, this is an entrancing, a provocative item. The foregoing is an exact quotation of the transcript. It there appears as "modern photo book store coupon." What is a "modern photo book store coupon"? Clearly, the first three or four words constitute the name of a place of business, a place that could be found and its records checked. Coupons have addresses.

Where did the "coupon" turn up? Uninventoried in "Galt's" property? Then it had an address and required no sleuthing to locate. Was it reported by the company offering it, someone having recalled the order among its many? Unlikely, but again, the same would be true. There was no arduous trail to follow. The place was immediately self-located, its records instantly available. Why does Beasley hide the origin of this mysterious "modern photo book store coupon"? Where and by whom was it found? What else was found and not mentioned?

With cameras and not a single picture, there should have been even more excitement about this coupon. Especially because with a Polaroid, the only camera mentioned in the transcript, pictures require no processing. For what purpose had Ray been in touch with a photo outfit?

And for what purpose is even the city in which this business was located so carefully pruned from the record?

All we can do is conjecture. We cannot regard this as a Beasley stupidity, an accidental oversight. It is a suppression, aided by the court reporter's inadequate reflection of the proceeding, and perpetuated by the receipt being kept out of evidence and Canale's refusal to let anyone see *any* of the evidence [6].

Beasley's representation of what Bonebrake would have testified to had there not been this neat deal to prevent a trial is not at all what Bonebrake *did* testify to in England. There he swore,

> "I found one print on the rifle and one on the sight and also on the binoculars. I compared them with fingerprints of James Earl Ray in the Los Angeles police file. I found they belonged to one and the same individual."

It happens that the man in Los Angeles, as even Beasley said, was not known as "James Earl Ray" but as "Eric Starvo Galt." If there was a Los Angeles police record on Ray (as there was), Beasley troubled no one with that knowledge. On October 11, 1949, when Ray was 21 years old, he was arrested in Los Angeles on a charge of "Suspicion Burglary." As Beasley handles it here, one cannot tell if he is referring to these prints, as no doubt he was, or to non-criminal prints of "Galt."

Why Beasley is so anxious not to have this in the record can only be conjectured, which is all we can do with his editing of what Bonebrake could and would have testified to. Of course, the facts of the matter make it look as if a local police department were more on the ball than the FBI, and Hoover cannot abide such a suggestion.

In all of this promise of fingerprint proof, there is a prominent omission: fingerprints from the white Mustang abandoned in Atlanta. Did Ray drive it 400 miles, hot and sweaty from his dastardly deed, boring through the night in his daring dash, handling all its parts he had to touch, parts of the body and the controls, without leaving a *single* print?

On this, there is silence; no narrative. The driver was seen to leave the car. He was seen *not* to have gone over it with the great care necessary to remove *every single print* made in all those thousands of miles of cross-country use. Fingerprints endure. It is not possible to recall all the places they may have been deposited, inside, on, and under the body, in various corners of the trunk, on the steering wheel, the levers, the knobs, the emergency brake control, the glass—all those countless places touched in normal use of a car.

It is without question that the FBI had to go over this car with the greatest possible thoroughness, everywhere, for whatever print or prints there were. Yet there is no mention of *any* print anywhere on it.

Not only did Ray's have to be there, but Charles Stein's did, too. If there is any truth in Ray's story of "Raoul," then his prints, too, should have been somewhere on the vehicle.

But from Beasley's selective narrative, *there was no single print found anywhere on the car!*

Either prints *were* found—and the knowledge of it and the identification of each hand imparting them was learned by the FBI and suppressed—or the car was more thoroughly cleansed than Ray could have done. If prints were found and Ray's were among them, is there any doubt Beasley would have shouted it loud and clear instead of showing, by his silence, that he failed to place Ray in *that* car for his getaway?

Whose prints were on the car? Who drove it from Memphis to Atlanta if Ray's fingerprints were not there to identify him as the driver? Who left the other suppressed clues Ray could not have?

No less conspicuously missing is any promise of fingerprints lifted from the rented room or the bathroom from which the crime, allegedly, was committed. Not in the minitestimony of Zachary or Jensen, not at any point in the narrative, is there even the most distant and detached suggestion such proof exists, as it must were there to be the slightest basis for the charge that Ray committed the murder.

There is gobbledygook about furniture shifting in the room, a chest of drawers and the chair moved for no purpose at all, since the crime is not alleged to have been committed from there and could not have been, anyway, all without the use of hands. There is the use of the room, again with no prints. There is the verbal fluffery of all those unidentified "scuff" marks in that bathtub, a dishonest effort to give them a meaning they cannot sustain, the allegation Ray was in the bathroom for an hour or so, the removed sill on which he is claimed to have rested the rifle, the screen he is supposed to have pushed out to make this possible, but no word of *any* fingerprint. Ray had to be a living ghost to have accomplished all this, yet he had to have accomplished still more, like getting in and out of that bathtub with his rifle and then, merely to have rested the weapon, let alone use it, leaning so awkwardly, or to have straddled the rim of the ancient tub and contorted himself just to see down the barrel—without touching anything at all.

Many magical powers are attributed to the very ordinary Ray, but none are quite so wraith-like as his no-hands performances, 18,000 miles of driving the car, using the room and moving its accoutrements, monopolizing the bathroom, clambering all around it, pawing the walls, resting on the windowsill, handling and using the rifle, all superhuman, as the prosecution case makes him—without making a single fingerprint!

Again the companion omission, any reference to a single print *not* Ray's from either room or the furnishings of either.

The pattern is like the ages, unchanging. In all the evidence, real or narrated, where the fingerprints are required to be to connect Ray with the crime rather than the locale, there are none. Nor is there word of *any* other fingerprints on anything—the rifle, scope, maps, Mustang—anything. This is as close an approximation of impossibility as the science permits.

King was killed by a bullet. Perhaps the career of that projectile removed any trace of fingerprints from it. But the projectile was impelled on its deadly course from a brass casing charged with 150 grains of powder. That casing, the part of the entire cartridge remaining behind when the bullet is fired, is made of a material that retains fingerprints rather well. It also must be loaded into the weapon by hand, either when the single cartridge is placed in the breech or when the clip is loaded with bullets. Therefore, unless special and unusual precautions are taken, there should have been fingerprints on the empty casing recovered at the scene of the crime and on the clip [7].

Now, with the generous deposit of Ray fingerprints on everything, as officially alleged, with that abundant collection of memorabilia all bearing Ray's fingerprints, so ample it elicited special comment from the Attorney General of the United States, it cannot persuasively be argued that Ray wiped the cartridge and the clip clean, but not the rifle and scope, or that he forgot only the weapon, the most important item. Either he took precautions against leaving fingerprints or he did not. Therefore, if he loaded and used the rifle, his prints should have been on the clip and ammo. They were not.

Here Beasley is silent, all the excessive legal trash about which he is needlessly specific—and the absence of any defense, any cross-examination—making his silence and suppression of evidence possible [8].

If there was a clip in the rifle, Beasley does not mention it. If there was not a clip in it, then it could not, on this basis alone, have been the murder weapon. For without a loaded clip, the rifle could be fired but once, and no assassin, not even one who was a raving maniac, would so needlessly endanger his endeavor, depend on a single lucky shot, when he had such a difficult one, at best. (And how would he, if need be, protect and defend himself with no bullets?)

So many of the items Beasley does not avoid enumerating had to have held fingerprints of others than Ray. Therefore, there is the same cold, clammy, chilling silence, the terrifying silence of police-state justice.

On all those maps, but a single print and that Ray's? None on the unmentioned TV? The airline tickets and stubs? The suppressed correspondence? The beer cans? (Here the evidence relates to but the *single* can with a Ray print. Were other prints on any of the others?) The camera? Rifle and scope? Auto?

From the record, not a single item in this long, yet incomplete, catalogue bore any fingerprint other than Ray's, which just cannot be the case.

For the record, there is Beasley's silence, a silence his integrity, the honor of the state he represents, and justice cannot survive.

Let us pause for a moment for some comic relief to this dismal recital. Almost entirely unnoted, for it was ignored by most of the papers, Judge Battle cited Bonebrake for contempt.

Yes, sir; the FBI was in contempt of court! Imagine that! and the accompanying journalistic silence.

It was all a grim, a very bad, joke, but the newsrooms did not know it and the principals did not treat it that way. The judge was serious.

The incident is also its own kind of commentary on why the judge forbade out-of-court comment on the case—after everyone in the government, from the Attorney General down, had poisoned every private and opinion-molding mind and that of just about every potential juror.

Bonebrake is not one of those leaking what Hoover wanted believed about the case, the evidence, and him and his hearties—a never-stopping transgression against an honest and fair trial. He is the quiet laboratory type, poor Bonebrake, who sat in his office those long years looking at fingerprints, sometimes testifying in court to what he saw.

Hanes had been cited for contempt, as had others. Then Bonebrake participated in a police seminar in Wichita, Kansas. His remarks to his fellow professionals were reported in that city's September 12, 1968 *Daily Beacon.* Bonebrake had been the only technical expert in the London extradition proceeding. From the meager accounts available (what a closing of journalistic ranks behind the indispensable J. Edgar there was when his agent was cited for contempt of court!), Bonebrake discussed his role as a witness in that proceeding.

More than a month after the end of the seminar, on October 16 and 17, the Memphis *Commercial-Appeal* and *Press-Scimitar* picked up the story from the *Daily Beacon.* Hanes, the ox already gored, complained to the judge. Battle had his committee of seven local legal luminaries look into it. Their report, that Bonebrake "probably" violated the judge's order, was on the UPI wire October 24, a story and a follow-up. The second story said Bonebrake "would be asked to come here voluntarily to show cause why he should not be held in contempt." At the same time, the committee 'said it would file a petition of contempt" against him.

But, in Washington, Bonebrake was outside the court's jurisdiction.

If he did not comply voluntarily, the committee said, in a document, a copy of which was sent to the Attorney General (who placed it in his circular file), "the petition will recommend that this court issue its process at such time as the said George Bonebrake shall come into the court's jurisdiction." Translation: He had better stay out of town.

AP next reported issuance of the citation.

However, as all those lofty legal spirits seemed to have forgotten, Bonebrake, in the AP's words, was "expected to be a major prosecution witness."

To be a real witness, he had to be in town. None of that affidavit stuff. (Foreman was not in on the case yet.)

The solution was simple. When Hoover did not send his man packing down to Memphis, Battle postponed the show-cause hearing because he believed "such hearings are self-defeating."

It all died naturally, with the judge.

But the strange thing is that supposedly the extradition proceeding in England was all public, all the evidence publicly presented. How could a man who commented on the public, legal record be contemptuous in so doing?

Or did the judge know what I learned, that it was all a put-on. When there are political murders in the United States, it is a fiction to expect the norms of the law and justice to apply, to believe that "public" evidence is anything of the sort. All that can be is suppressed.

How else could Bonebrake be in "contempt"?

Unconcerned with honor, his or others', Beasley continues his presentation of promises of evidence that, in fact, prove the opposite of his representation. Next (T. 96–97) is Robert A. Frazier, "the chief, firearms identification unit at the F.B.I., with 27 years experience." Frazier is the same firearms expert whose selective recall of the evidence he chose not to ignore was used by the Warren Commission to pin the bum rap on Oswald. Called as a defense witness in New Orleans, he testified he had not made any effort to see if anyone else, anyone from any other point, might have killed the President or been part of a successful conspiracy. This is how *that* crime was "solved" [9].

So, Frazier, the man with this record, "would testify as to examination and firing of this rifle." (But he could not possibly have testified to the "firing" of the rifle during the commission of the crime, not having been there and seen it, and Beasley does not say that there had been any firing to obtain a laboratory specimen.)

Unlike Bonebrake, Frazier did examine the "hull," police slang for empty casing. Like Bonebrake, though, not a word about fingerprints:

He examined the cartridges, the hull from the chamber of this rifle, the slug removed from the body of Dr. Martin Luther King, Jr., and would testify as to his conclusions as follows:

The death slug was identical in all physical characteristics with the five loaded 30.06 Springfield cartridges found in the bag in front of Canipe's. The cartridge case had in fact been fired in this 30.06 rifle. That the death slug removed from the body contained land and groove impressions and direction of twist consistent with those that were in the barrel of this rifle.

That he also made microscopic comparison between the fresh dent in the sill of the window at the bathroom, 422½ South Main, and concluded that the microscopic evidence in this dent was consistent in all ways with the same microscopic marks as appear on the barrel of this rifle, 30.06 rifle.

That his examination of the 243 caliber Winchester rifle, which had been purchased on March the 29th and returned on March the 30th, was not capable of chambering or firing a slug. There were certain

212

deposits on the end of the bolt which had to be chiseled away before this gun was capable of being fired. That is the gun that was returned.

And this, dear reader, as Beasley and the prosecution would have it, is the end—all of Frazier—100 per cent of the ballistics "evidence." It is a repeat performance, Oswald all over again.

Even for Beasley, this is too much. We will examine the last item first. Although the offered evidence on the returned rifle—which had "certain deposits on the end of the bolt"—does not in any way relate to the murder, Beasley's narrative does reflect his honesty or understanding, and in this case, his willingness to say what is not so. If he decided, as he and the prosecution are entitled to decide, that there should be some reference to the returned rifle, the reference should have been accurate and meaningful. For the fact is that the return of the rifle was unrelated to mechanical difficulties.

In manufacture, it is not impossible for excesses of the bluing material to accumulate, particularly in extractor mechanisms by which the empty casing is removed to make room for the next shot. These extractors are part of the bolt mechanism. An accumulation of bluing of this kind can prevent proper operation of the bolt, may even prevent firing of the rifle, but cannot render the rifle "not capable of chambering" a bullet. Bullets can be chambered by hand. In such case, chambering is independent of the bolt and whether or not it functions properly (and repair is a simple matter).

In this instance, Beasley's seeming verbosity is not that. It is a distraction, a diversion, the skilled lawyer's means of directing attention the wrong way, away from what requires that attention be paid it.

We have already discussed the probable reasons for the return of the Winchester rifle. Let us now take up each item of what Frazier "would testify to as to the examination and firing of this rifle"—presumably the murder weapon.

We have seen no proof offered that this rifle was fired on that occasion. Beasley says only "the cartridge case had in fact been fired in this 30.06 rifle." This language is used to give what follows a meaning not justified by anything Beasley says.

First reference is to "the cartridges"; second, in the next paragraph, to "the five loaded 30.06 Springfield cartridges found in the bag in the front of Canipe's." Here we find an explanation for many things: the calculated vagueness of Beasley's presentation, the withholding of the available and existing evidence that should have been put into the record

213

of the minitrial, and Canale's determination not to let any of what he personally is responsible for suppressing be available to any one, at any time and under any circumstances.

The prosecution did not offer in evidence, either in its tailored account of the purchases or in copies of the records of the transaction, what ammunition "Lowmeyer" bought, if any. But Huie, who did go to Aeromarine, is specific: "20 Peters High Velocity, 150-grain, Soft Point cartridges." They come packaged in boxes of 20. One additional point about Peters needs to be understood. Remington and Peters are identical. The manufacturer says so, as do the standard literature and tables. Here is one example: "Peters cartridges are identical with Remington loads having the same basic caliber designations, hence the ballistics given will serve both brands." The companies have common ownership.

To describe the ammunition as "Springfield cartridges" is to say nothing, for *every one* of the *nine different kinds* of Remington–Peters .30-06 cartridges *is* called "Springfield." But there is no Springfield make. It is not the trade name, not a means of identification. It is, as Beasley uses it, rather the means of avoiding identification while seeming to be specific. We have already noted differences in available charges of powder, for example, of up to 100 per cent.

This omission and confusion can hardly be considered an accident, particularly not in huntin' country, which Memphis certainly is. There are special characteristics to the 150-grain soft-pointed bullets we shall not ignore, as Beasley does.

Another item. Beasley makes no reference to any clip in the rifle or any in the abandoned property, with the spare bullets. Again, this should not be regarded as accidental. There is no point in having an expensive "pump" gun without using clips. It cannot "repeat" without clips. There is reasonable certainty that any clip or clips found, in the rifle or elsewhere, did not bear Ray's prints, did bear those of others, or both. So inadequate is even the promise of what would be offered in a trial, Beasley leaves open the question of whether there was even so much as a single additional bullet in the rifle in the event the first missed. But without a clip, this is impossible. He mentions no clip. He implies, but only implies, there were other bullets in the rifle by saying "the cartridges, the hull from the chamber." But I re-emphasize, *without a clip there could have been no other cartridge in the rifle.*

Now, what was removed from the corpse is not, as the press had been told and as Dr. Francisco swore, a "bullet." It is merely a "slug."

As Beasley uses the terms, he gives the impression a "slug" is a "bullet." One definition of "slug" is bullet. Another is "an unshaped or roughly-shaped piece of metal, specifically one used as a missile." The fact is, great care was exercised at every point in the record to make it seem an intact and identifiable bullet was recovered.

This is a lie, a gross, deliberate, malevolent lie.

Describing "the death slug" (another effort to make it seem that bullets and slugs are the same, but rifles fire "bullets" which cause death, not "slugs") as "identical in all physical characteristics with the five loaded 30.06 Springfield cartridges found in the bag" is both meaningless and deliberate deception, trying to make a record that the bullet that caused the death is identical with the unfired bullets when this is anything but the case. We shall return to this, one of the most vital facts of the case and evidence, one of the most sinister deceptions. Here let us add that, aside from appearance (and the slug cannot have the appearance of the unfired bullet), there is also the physical characteristic of composition to test the identity of slug and bullet. To say that the "slug" is identical in composition without the most precise scientific comparison is to say no more than that it resembles a piece of pipe or any other leaden material.

Here still another perfect parallel with the Oswald frame-up. In that case, we know there was a spectrographic analysis—fine to parts per *million*—which would have established whether the bullet and fragments of bullet said to have been used in the crime were of identical origin. It is misrepresented in the testimony and Report. It is ruthlessly suppressed, so it cannot be consulted. In the Ray case, where there should have been such analysis or the even finer one available as a by-product of the nuclear age, neutron-activation, there is no reference to any. It is better to be silent than to be caught suppressing what can not properly be suppressed. Without such a test, there could be no competent investigation. It has to have been made [10].

"The cartridge case had in fact been fired in this 30.06 rifle." Another meaninglessness, another calculated deception. Cartridges are *not* fired." Bullets are "fired," bullets do the killing. Cases, which do *not* get aimed and do *not* fly to the target, *do not kill*. Unless it could be proven that this "slug" had been fired from that particular case, to the exclusion of all others ever manufactured, it means nothing to say the "case had in fact been fired in this 30.06 rifle"—except that Beasley was able and willing to deceive. There is no proof of where and when that case had its primer detonated and its bullet propelled by the charge

215

then set off. None is offered, the existence of none is remotely suggested, and I think the reason why is brutally clear—because the evidence does not exist or is contrary to what was being perpetrated in the name of the law and justice.

"The death slug removed from the body [the same deception: what was removed from the corpse is at best but a fragment of a bullet] contained land and groove impressions and directions of twist consistent with those that were in the barrel of this rifle." This was a pretty big mouthful, and even for this Memphis minitrial, pretty raw.

To say the "direction of twist" is only "consistent" is to raise a needless question. If there is any *identification,* there could have been no doubt. Each rifle is grooved to give the bullet a stabilizing twist. As the bullet is propelled down the barrel at great speed (this bullet has a muzzle velocity of almost 3,000 feet per second), the softer bullet is unmistakably scored by the very tough barrel. These markings are as unique and distinctive as fingerprints.

To make reference to the "direction of twist" is, really, to cheat, to take deliberate advantage of the judge, jury, press, defendant, history— everybody and everything. It means no more than to say girls wear dresses. Most girls do. Most American rifles have a right-hand or clockwise twist to the rifling.

What is lacking here is what is inevitable with *a new* rifle and a recovered "bullet." The identification of bullet with rifle—comparable to fingerprint and man—is inevitable, unquestionable, and can be stated with unqualified positiveness. A bullet fired from this rifle and recovered with even a small part of it in anything like its original shape, can be said by any kind of an expert (and Frazier *does* have the *highest* qualifications) and with no possibility of contradiction to have been fired from this rifle to the exclusion of all others of the many millions ever made.

The science is that precise. There can be no question about it.

Beasley does not say "this rifle fired this fatal bullet," although it is the requirement of the law and evidence. Instead, a careful misrepresentation was contrived to seem to say it without saying it. A comparison is with the joke about a woman being "a little bit pregnant." Either it can be proven the bullet was fired from this rifle, to the exclusion of all others, or it cannot. If it cannot, then there is and must be the presumption of innocence.

I charge that Beasley and the FBI deliberately set out to make it seem that ballistics evidence proves the bullet had been fired from this rifle and that because he purchased the rifle in the name of "Lowmeyer," Ray is the assassin.

To weave together all the things an honest prosecutor would not and an honest defense counsel could not have avoided, let us begin with the manufacturer's description of the bullet allegedly used, the bullets "Lowmeyer" bought. First, it is necessary to correct Huie. This is not a quibble; it is significant. Common reference is to a Peters soft-pointed bullet with 150 grains of powder, but there is no such bullet as he titles "Soft Point" in the Peters catalogue. There are two with 150-grain charges. One is "Bronze Point" and the other, "Pointed Soft Point Core-Lokt," the more popular one and the one apparently purchased. Remington-Peters is very proud of that particular bullet in its catalogue. It takes up the top half of the two-page color spread (Catalogue 32-3).

The headline across the top of both pages reads, " 'Core-Lokt'—the No. 1 Mushroom." This is followed by text: "Call it 'expansion' or 'mushrooming' or anything you want. Without it, big game isn't worth the powder to blow it out of the barrel. That's why so many shooters put their faith in the *corus-lockus* Remington-Peters—the deadliest mushroom . . . 'Core-Lokt' mushrooms to over twice its original caliber . . . ."

Under "Caliber Suggestions," the two 150-grain charges are recommended "for hard to reach game, antelope, mountain goat, mountain sheep."

All these bullets are designed to mushroom. This particular bullet is the apotheosis of expansion design. Without this expansion, the animal-dropping-power of the bullet is considerably reduced, as we have already discussed, for the bullet could merely perforate, leaving a non-fatal wound.

Accompanying illustrations leave no doubt of the mushrooming of the "Core-Lokt" bullets, of whichever design selected. All of the front is pushed backward and outward, onto a tiny stub of what remains of the end inserted in the casing on manufacture. On this stub, but little space remains where the markings of the barrel *can* survive—and this only with bullets that do not fragment, as they usually do, particularly when they strike bone.

So, the bullet is designed to expand into a more deadly metallic mushroom of more than twice its original diameter.

The prosecution knew this, revealing it without intending to. The March 19 *Nashville Banner* carried a lengthy article combined in its newsroom from AP and UPI dispatches. It contains these sentences:

217

Dwyer said the choice of the rifle used in the slaying was not haphazard. "Ray had familiarized himself with the caliber, ballistics and other characteristics" of possible weapons to use in an assassination attempt from long range, said the prosecutor, who added the state had witnesses to testify to this.

If the state had such witnesses, Beasley would have made a promise of that evidence. There is no reason to believe such witnesses exist. However, the prosecution had to have known about these matters because it was the responsibility of the prosecution to know it and be prepared to prove it in court, and because either the local police, the FBI, or both, without doubt, so told it.

It knew and was mute—said nothing about it—and, worse, deliberately misrepresented, with the words it carefully culled from the language to deceive and mislead and with the proof in its possession it withheld from the record—suppressed.

On several occasions I have made general reference to the fifth of the bar's "Canons of Professional Ethics." Here, as they relate to the prosecution, I deem it pertinent for the reader to have them quoted directly and in full, for here is the very heart of the case, the core of the frame-up:

> The primary duty of a lawyer engaged in public prosecution is not to convict, but to see that justice is done. The suppression of facts or the secreting of witnesses capable of establishing the innocence of the accused is highly reprehensible.

It happens it fell to Beasley to do this particular dirty work, as, under Canale's orders, it fell to Dwyer to lead the witnesses put on the stand into that particular misrepresentation of what they did know and that particular "suppression of facts" we have seen and which we will soon further see are "capable of establishing the innocence of the accused." The reader is reminded there was but a single charge against Ray in court: "Murder in the First Degree." (That of "Carrying a Dangerous Weapon" was dropped, by Canale, personally.) Every member of the prosecution staff who was silent, knowing the evidence, is equally guilty.

Nor is the press (which likes to remind us it is the bastion of our freedoms, especially when Congress considers raising the mail rates, so low they amount to a subsidy) less guilty, for these facts were known to the press. If a single newspaper or magazine, a single radio or TV station, any of the wire-services or networks, especially those earlier reporting the true facts, made a single appropriate comment on this matter after the minitrail, I have not seen it or been told of it [11].

Canale's personal knowledge that the remnant of bullet, or, I should say, the *largest* remnant, for other fragments also were recovered, could not be identified with the alleged assassination weapon was recorded after the minitrial. It is in a lengthy UPI story printed in the March 17, 1969, *Nashville Banner,* where these words appear:

> Canale admitted the slug that shattered King's spinal column was too damaged for definite ballistics tests, but he said a piece of copper and lead from the bullet about the size of the end of a man's little finger were found intact. Working with these and the empty hull found in the rifle the FBI established that the bullet was one that could have been fired by that weapon.

The size of this fragment, from Canale's description, is but a small part of the original bullet. Canale knew and failed to tell the court there were no ballistics proofs. He caused the opposite impression to be given the court and everyone else. Nor is it possible for the FBI to have "established" anything—except, if a sufficient piece had remained undeformed at the butt end of the fragment, that the size of the bullet and the size of the empty casing were the same. And this would have proved only that the bullet could have been fired from one of thousands, if not millions, of the most popular hunting rifles of countless makes that exist.

Here is where the spectrographic or neutron-activation tests could have served a useful purpose. By means of either, it could have been determined whether the recovered fraction of a bullet was of the same make as those found in the carefully abandoned duffle. From what I am told by dependable expert sources, it should have been possible to determine the manufacturer's batch from which each came. Lowmeyer bought a single box of bullets, mass-produced and automatically packaged as they came off the production line. All would test identically. The absence of FBI laboratory reports showing that the cause of death could thus be connected with the unfired bullets does not encourage belief that the FBI has this proof. Rather is the opposite credible.

These omissions, too, tend to prove a frame-up, that the alleged murder weapon was not used in the commission of the crime. When there is no proof at all that *this* bullet had been fired from *that* weapon, any proof that the bullet used was related to those found was urgently needed. If such proof exists, it would have been used. If it does not exist, the proof to the contrary does—and was suppressed.

Once again I remind the reader, in regard to the foregoing and to what will follow, the law requires, as Judge Battle put it, that the evidence *must* be "beyond reasonable doubt and to a moral certainty."

Fatal Blow

We must pause here, and momentarily leave Beasley's narrative, to consider a matter that is inseparable from the ballistics evidence in the reconstruction of this crime—the evidence about the wound. In examining this evidence, in itself enough to cast doubt upon the entire prosecution case, let us return to that expert of experts, the pathologist, Dr. Jerry Thomas Francisco. He is "County Medical Examiner for Shelby County," so he is the proper official. In addition to his license to practice medicine, he "specialized" in "the field of pathology and forensic pathology" (T. 42). This means he is qualified to have a medical opinion on the cause of death when that death is from violence and, more, that he is thoroughly grounded in the legal aspects, the requirements of the law and of proofs.

Questioned by Dwyer, here (T. 44) is his entire response to the question, "Will you tell us what your examination reflected?"

The examination revealed a gunshot wound to the right side of the face, passing through the body into the neck, through the spinal cord at the base of the neck, with the bullet lodging beneath the skin near the shoulder blade on the left.

This is a vague exposition at best. What part of the "right side of the face"? Did it strike bone, the most essential knowledge in understanding the subsequent career of the bullet, whether it fragmented at that instant and, if so, what added damage it could have caused, for fragments of bullet and bone become new missiles, causing their own injuries. What part of the neck? There are vertebrae, all neatly numbered. This knowledge is essential in plotting the trajectory, assuming it could have been plotted once the bullet struck bone, which could have deflected the bullet as well as fragmented and deformed it. Where "near the shoulder blade," which is relatively long, did it lodge? The difference of a half-inch in the body, projected backward 200 feet to the rifle, is an enormous variation. Did it strike and damage that bone? This, also, is required knowledge in forensic medicine, Francisco's overall function— in solving the crime, not to mention the basic understanding of it.

Aside from the glaringly obvious inadequacies of this response, which is all he said on the subject and all Dwyer asked of him (it can be assumed that, consistent with practice, Dwyer coached him in advance, telling him what he wanted said and what he wanted unsaid), there is, from the available record, proof of further omissions that is enough to totally disqualify his testimony and raises the gravest doubt about Francisco's integrity, professional and personal. These omissions, deceptions, and other flaws were known to the prosecution, which is responsible for them, and to the honorable judge and the eminent "defense" counsel. It is, in fact, the kind of thing instantaneous detection of which makes Percy Foreman one of the truly great trial lawyers.

Not only did all know of the fact and content of Francisco's omissions, but, because Reverend Kyles had volunteered what he had not been asked, he had made what he saw and heard about the wound part of the official record. His first description (T. 32) is of "a tremendous wound here (indicating)"—meaning somewhere in the face. The record shows Dwyer defaulted on his obligation to translate the gesture, which cannot be typed by the court reporter, into words, which can be. This volunteered evidence was not responsive to the question, which dealt with King's leaving his room. It was blurted out before Dwyer could stop him. So, Dwyer did the next best thing, ignored what Kyles testified to. But a "tremendous" wound is not made by an undeformed, nonexploding bullet on entering. Entry wounds are small and clean.

In an afterthought (T. 33), Dwyer returned to the character of the wound, again turning on Kyles' emotions. I quote only that part relating to the wound:

Q. Reverend, you noticed a gaping wound, did you say, about his face?

K. Yes, and it tore this much of his face away that I could see, and also noticed that the shot had cut his necktie, just cut it right off at that point.

Kyles did not say "gaping"; he said "tremendous." There is a difference. But neither type of wound can be the typical entry wound of a pristine, non-exploding bullet. This testimony means either that the bullet exploded or fragmented and mushroomed, or was leaving, not entering, the body at that point in the face, a point Dwyer continued to keep undescribed and unlocated.

One possible explanation of Dwyer's return to the description of the wound so inconsistent with and destructive of the prosecution case is public knowledge of the statements that the photographer, Matt Herron, had obtained and of much other immediately available eyewitness evidence that was possessed immediately after the murder by the authorities. It was known that Kyles had made an earlier statement. It can be assumed he had also been interviewed by the same authorities, who knew what he knew, what he had seen and could testify to.

Herron, a magnificent photographer but not a trained investigator, knew enough to ask Kyles the essential questions avoided by the trained prosecutor. Here is the relevant part of the interview with Kyles. Herron had asked about an "exploding bullet":

K. Now, that's what Jesse Jackson said. Jess Jackson said it was. Said it didn't explode until it hit him. I know there's a kind that would tear you apart, you know, because the wound that I saw, all this was gone. The necktie was gone, you know, this way, it was cut off. And then Ralph [Abernathy] said beneath the shirt, when they got to the hospital, there was—there was a larger wound under the shirt that we couldn't see.

Q. So there were two holes—

K. The one we saw—it must have been—it didn't go all the way down, as I seem to remember. The collar was intact, but the necktie had been blown off, so the impact here tore all this out, and then Ralph said under the shirt, about in here, there was a larger wound where it—where it really exploded, and I was asking the police officer about what kind of bullet was it.

Kyles added the police officer had explained to him the special kind of bullet that behaves this way.

So, the wound was not only other than described by Francisco, who restricted himself to the *one* wound that was not obscured by the clothing, omitting any others, but there was an additional and even "larger" wound under the shirt. Now, it is obvious one bullet could not have caused the wound in the right side of the face, then gone downward and backward, to sever the spinal column, then turn forward to tear off the necktie, come out making a "larger" hole in the front of the neck and still have lodged in the back of the body, at the left shoulder blade. There was more than one bullet or major fragmentation —an explosion—multiple wounds. Francisco testified to the presence of one and only one—and said nothing about it.

This, in turn, the suppression of the knowledge of more than the

222

single wound to which Francisco testified, while explaining Beasley's tricky use of the word "slug" to describe the single remnant he referred to, also means there had to be another major fraction of the bullet. There is no reference to it in anything I have seen. Yet the police immediately cordoned off the scene of the murder, as Kyles told Herron, even denying Kyles access to the room. Whether the police got the other fraction of the bullet or not, they knew the weight of the pristine bullet, how much got shaved off in going through the barrel, thus, approximately how much was missing. This information, too, was suppressed from the record. From Canale's description, *most* of the original bullet is not accounted for.

With prosecution connivance, Francisco called this small part of the original bullet the whole bullet. The culpability of this false testimony cannot be exaggerated, it is that important to a solution to the crime and to the perpetration of a frame-up.

There is and always was the most abundant confirmation of Kyles. Naturally, Abernathy, who saw the "larger" wound at the hospital, was not called as a witness. This wound was known to exist. It was seen and studied by the pathologist and others (all silent). In fact, the first reports were of this other wound, not the visible face wound, for those writing the stories did not see the murder or the corpse. The behavior of the bullet is also accurately described in the initial reporting. Here are some samples from my files.

The *Nashville Banner,* April 5, the day after the murder:

"The bullet exploded in his face," said Ben Branch. "It knocked him off his feet."

What better reason for Ben Branch not to have been a witness, not to have been part of Beasley's narrative?

Staff Correspondent Wayne Whitt's story in the same day's *Tennessean,* in its lead, said King "was felled by a sniper's bullet which struck him in the neck as he prepared to leave the Lorraine Motel for dinner."

Whitt, quoting both eyewitnesses and official information, also confirms what I earlier said common sense makes inevitable—and what casts doubt on Francisco's "tests" and his entirely unsubstantiated conjectures about the trajectory. "King was shot as he leaned over" the railing "and talked to aides standing below." This is repeated: After King emerged from his room, "he paused, leaned over the railing and began talking with an associate, Jesse Jackson, standing below."

223

Jackson, naturally, is not in Beasley's narrative, for this testimony would entirely ruin the fabricated "tests" that were in no sense tests, would not be consistent with a shot from that bathroom window.

At 7:30 the night of the murder, Whitt reports, there was an official statement from the hospital:

> Paul Hess, assistant administrator of the hospital, said King received "a gaping wound" at the root of his neck.

The "root of his neck" cannot describe a face wound.

Wire-service accounts say the same thing: "At 7 p.m., Dr. Martin Luther King, Jr., expired in the emergency room of a gunshot wound in the neck."

First indications all were that the bullet struck in the neck. The trouble with this evidence is that it made inevitable a lower location for the assassin. Such a location is consistent with a large number of immediate reports, but it is so inconsistent with the bathroom as the lair of the assassin that it could not be used and Ray still be called the murderer. *Time*'s first issue after the murder, dated April 12 but appearing earlier, said:

> The heavy-caliber bullet smashed through King's neck, exploded against his lower right jaw, severed his spinal cord and slammed him away from the rail, up against the wall, with hands drawn tautly toward his head.

Time was in a position to know. It not only had eyewitness interviews, but it bought the rights to and used pictures taken at the moment of the murder by Joseph Louw, there on assignment for the now-defunct Public Broadcast Laboratory. Louw, whose room was nearby, heard the shot and was immediately on the spot with a still camera.

As late as April 14, in its lengthy Sunday wrap-up story previously quoted, the Minneapolis *Tribune* reported, "One shot rang out. The bullet ripped into King's neck."

So, there is no doubt the case presented is a crooked case on the most fundamental evidence: with every official involved betraying his trust, by active participation or by the awful crime of silence making himself part of it, accessory to the frame-up of the undefended accused, of history, and directly responsible for an unsolved crime, one of the worst in history, a history so bleak it was, as *Time* reported, the twelfth recent political assassination in the United States.

There is a strange twist reported later.

range. But it is also consistent, unless interrupted or damped. This natural vibration of the barrel is part of what is taken into consideration, even if unknown, when the sights are set. Any alteration of this natural barrel vibration affects accuracy adversely. The effect of disrupting natural barrel vibration is generally more pronounced as the power of the bullet is increased. Resting that rifle on the hard sill disrupted the barrel vibrations. Under these circumstances, a sighted-in rifle cannot hit where it is aimed.

Canale was specific. He did not say the rifle was resting on the sill *prior* to the shot. His claim is the rifle was fired while it was resting on the sill, recoil making the mark.

My friend, Richard Bernabei, is a professor of classics and a gun "buff." He is an outdoorsman, loves fishing (and can tell you in which sections of the Tiber, in ancient days, the Romans caught the best-tasting pike). He is also a member of the National Rifle Association. I asked him to get me a definitive statement on this phenomenon from the NRA and from any other standard literature he had—what is readily available, without special research.

From his September 1967 *Guns and Ammo,* Bernabei sent an excellent article by Jim Corbett titled, "Know Your Nodes," subtitled, "Taming Vibration—the Key to Rifle Accuracy." There is fascinating intelligence in it, much that cannot be quoted here on trajectories as well as vibration, going back to Leonardo da Vinci, to Tartaglia, and to Lee-Metford of British Ordnance in more recent days. These few excerpts, too-brief as they are, should satisfy as to the essential importance of vibrations.

> . . . The investigations [of British Ordnance] showed that there were two distinct and different vibrations taking place each time the piece was fired [p. 77.].
>
> Heavy barrels do not vibrate as much as light barrels and because of the mass the vibrations will be more uniform from one shot to another. Due to the lesser disturbance of the barrel, the heavy one is less susceptible to small differences from one cartridge to another in the ammunition [p. 77].
>
> The higher point of impact of a bullet fired with a reduced charge . . . caused . . . by the difference in the vibrations . . . [p. 32].

On page 79, Corbett explains the muzzle is at a certain point in this natural vibration and that, if the vibration is altered, so will the position of the muzzle be at that millisecond. He then tells the reader how to perform his own tests on this phenomenon.

To illustrate this phenomenon that is so well-known (outside the FBI and Canale's office, that is), he has an exaggerated drawing on page 33. Here it is:

vibration-the key to rifle accuracy

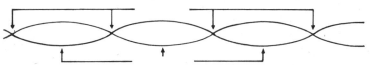

At the top is a "fundamental" vibration. The almost vertical motion that begins at the secured breech goes to the muzzle. Above is the secondary or harmonic vibrations which travel the length of the barrel causing vibration nodes.

Underneath the drawings is this explanation:

> At the top is a "fundamental" vibration. The almost vertical motion that begins at the secured breech goes to the muzzle. Above [the second drawing] is the secondary or harmonic vibrations which travel the length of the barrel causing vibration nodes.

The National Rifle Association replied to Bernabei's inquiries with several citations to the technical literature, a copy of their "Sighting In the Hunting Rifle," and the statement that in it, "under Photograph #4," there is "the desired authoritative statement." This picture shows a rifleman using a soft "bench rest" of the type commonly "available at most rifle clubs." Suitable substitutes, it says, are such things as yielding sandbags. The following comments they marked in the margin:

> Rest the firer's hand or forearm, *not the barrel,* on the support. Especially do not rest the rifle on anything hard, as it will jump away from such a support when fired and cause the bullet to strike away from the normal point of impact. [Emphasis in original].

Bernabei also had another NRA treatise, "Sighting In Rifles and Shotguns." Several brief excerpts from it relate to this entire matter:

> . . . It is equally important that the sights . . . be adjusted correctly. In fact, if the rifle does not hit where it "looks," the better one points the gun, the less chance he has of making hits.
> . . . no two persons aim precisely alike although they may be

equally expert shots.

> ... no person can sight in another's rifle perfectly ... There is no substitute for the shooter sighting in his rifle himself.
>
> ... it is necessary to sight in with the *same ammunition that will be used in the field.* ... The reason is that different types of ammunition, and especially ammunition with different weights of bullet, will generally shoot to different points of impact .... [Emphasis in original.]

The expert knowledge required by this case was readily available for a postage stamp. If one is not blessed, as I am, with a friend like Bernabei, he can write the NRA directly or use his own public library. It is that simple.

In short, the one way *not* to try to murder King is the Canale way, with the rifle resting on that windowsill.

Frazier, aside from being an excellent shot and an FBI agent, is a man with authentic credentials. As a defense witness in the New Orleans trial of Clay Shaw, the recounting of his training and experience takes up the first four transcript pages. His technical title in the FBI laboratories is "Chief of the Firearms and Tool Marks," part of the "Physics and Chemistry Section." He is college-trained in science. After graduation from the University of Idaho in 1940, he received additional FBI training lasting a year, prior to impressively extensive experience since then. He has testified "in all the States except Vermont, including Alaska and Hawaii," in each case, qualified by the courts as an expert.

Frazier, with all his extensive technical training and experience, knows the basic principles of vibration. Any number of FBI agents working on the case, any number of Memphis policemen, had to know the simple truths about which the NRA cautions. If they did not tell Beasley and others on the prosecution staff (assuming they themselves did not already know), then these officials *deliberately* framed Ray. By their silence then they are willfully part of a frame-up. Beasley certainly had to know, as did Canale, the "expert" who first thought up this "most surprising" part of the case and "evidence"!

Frazier here cannot hide behind the New Orleans explanation of the deficiencies of his work for the Warren Commission, the plea that he did only what he was told to do, even though he knew better. Anyhow, *this* was an FBI investigation, not the Warren Commission's. Frazier is and was chief of that part of the FBI. No one could properly give him such orders. He was boss. If he did not, as the expert, perform the function and assume all the responsibilities of the expert in the investigation and in the testimony he was prepared to offer, it is no one else's responsibility.

And it cannot be an accident.

It was conscious, purposeful framing, which should be a criminal offense for the federal police, too.

For Beasley, Canale, and company to withhold this information from the record and represent exactly the opposite is no less a violation of the responsibility of the prosecutor, which is to see to it that justice is done, not get a conviction by hook or crook.

For them, too, this should be regarded as a criminal offense.

Again, again, and still again, it is necessary to point out that Beasley's separation of evidence requiring association, as the medical and ballistics evidence do, is not accidental, not the result of legal incompetence, and is part of an enormous misrepresentation. It was pulled off by the prosecution and Foreman, who intimidated and threatened Ray into agreeing to plead guilty, thus preventing a real trial, where none of this would have been dared.

The evidence that was "promised" was carefully selected, in violation of the fifth canon of the bar's code of ethics. What was most opposed to the prosecution case was omitted. What was used was misrepresented. The promised evidence does not say what it is said to say. It does not mean what it is said to mean.

It does *not* prove Ray guilty of the charge of murder, the only charge against him. The most it can be claimed to do is to prove his involvement, largely by his property being near the scene of the crime. But the most reasonable interpretation of that evidence not completely suppressed is that Ray was not the man who did the shooting.

Next to the last Beasley promise (T. 97–99) is that the prosecution would have called Morris S. Clark, FBI expert on hairs and fibers. His testimony on these matters we have already examined. Where what he would have testified to is cited, it lacks positiveness. Various fibers gathered in Memphis and Atlanta and from the various items of clothing and bed-clothes are "of the exact same type," the hairs compared "have the same characteristics in every respect"—misleading descriptions that mean less than they seem to, for they are not positive identifications and the same could be said of an indeterminable number of entirely extraneous samples. (The imprecision of Clark's testimony provides still another Oswald parallel.) The only other proffer of Clark, had he testified, is less than world-shaking. It is that the Polaroid

220 camera, found with Ray when he was arrested, fit the styrofoam box (made for *all* Polaroid 220s) found in the Mustang. It proves nothing and required no FBI expert. Proving Ray and/or his property were near where the crime was committed does not prove he committed it. The pile-up of what proves Ray's presence, *in the absence of what proves he fired the shot,* helps establish that he was a decoy and is not the murderer. This is contrary to the official charge, and the pile-up of such evidence helps prove him innocent of that charge.

FBI Expert James H. Morgan is promised last (T. 99–100). He is an "examiner of questioned documents," read "handwriting expert." What he would have testified to did not have the capability of proving Ray the murderer and usually had nothing to do with anything. By handwriting comparisons, assuming he would have proved everything Beasley said he would, he would have proved Eric S. Galt is James Earl Ray; that Ray was in Los Angeles attending barkeep school; that he was in New Orleans and stayed at the Provincial Motel; that he bought the Paisley Mustang, got a driver's license, and rented a safe-deposit box in Birmingham; that he "prepared" the still undescribed "coupon" for the unidentified "Modern Book Store" (sic), undoubtedly the same as the earlier-referred-to "modern photo book store," covering that still-carefully-hidden transaction; and that he is the one "who wrote on the envelope for Jimmy Garner at the rooming house in Atlanta the name Eric S. Galt."

Ho, hum (deep yawn). So what?

This proves nothing and is designed to make it seem like there was a really detailed investigation, with all sorts of specific proofs being developed, which is true of *no* aspect of the case. The most this proves is what Ray himself said, that he is the man who used the alias Eric Starvo Galt. It was all published before the minitrial.

How appropriately Beasley ends his narrative, which he does at this point, saying, "If the Court please, that covers our stipulation."

Is there any wonder Ray almost immediately fired Foreman, and, acting as his own lawyer, asked the judge to provide him with counsel and enter an appeal? Even if he had been guilty, this over-advertised nothingness is no case against him as the murderer, the only crime charged. The prosecution insistence there had been no conspiracy exculpates him from the charge not made, accessory or co-conspirator. The conclusion of the minitrial certainly is not guilt proven "beyond reasonable doubt and to a moral certainty," the legal requirement succinctly stated by the judge.

But what is a deeper puzzle is how Percy Foreman, one of the really great trial lawyers; the man who has successfully defended so many so openly guilty, seen by witnesses in the commission of murder, did not fight this one—a relatively easy one—and, all piety and nobility, says his sole purpose was to "save" Ray's life.

13. "This Is Your FBI"

For all the talky-talk of politicians and editorial pages, in practice, the states too often abrogate their own rights, deferring to the federal government when they need not and should not. There was no proper federal jurisdiction in the King murder unless and until the government made a *serious* charge of conspiracy and proceeded with *serious* intent. The conspiracy charge against Ray was a legal shell-game. It was fictitious, a fig leaf or a fraud, depending on the point of view. It was never intended to be taken seriously, as the Attorney General himself kept saying from the first. This put the government and the Department, in particular, in the disreputable position of assuring the world there had been no conspiracy while simultaneously obtaining an indictment charging there had been. It is this spurious, made-up charge that provided the legalism without which the FBI could not have spent a cent of the taxpayers' money on the case, assigned an hour of an agent's time to it.

All those stout-hearted Tennesseans, those rugged, independent mountain, former frontier people, that doughty stock so fierce in defending the rights and sacred obligations of their state, all those editorial and headline writers, fell silent when the federals moved in and picked up their marbles. There never was any Tennessee investigation, as we have seen. (The total investigation by Hanes was by a single, part-time investigator who was on the case for four months only.)

That the local authorities never conducted any real investigation of the murder was disclosed in an announcement deceptively angled. The *Nashville Tennessean* headlined the Associated Press story in its issue of April 2, 1969, "King Murder Case Most Costly in Memphis History." This is a fair reflection of what Memphis Police Chief Henry Lux had said the day before. His figures showed a total cost of $168,776.

Now, this is not an inconsiderable sum, even if it is less than Foreman's contract might have netted him, less than Huie hoped to make from his dollar journalism. But in this case, had there been a real investigation, this figure would not begin to cover the actual costs.

Moreover, this is *not* the cost of the police *investigation*. It includes all the miscellaneous items, *which cost more than the actual investigation!*

A "guard detail . . . assigned to a key witness"—presumably Charles

Stephens—totaled 7,580 man hours and cost $31,684. Guarding Ray at the county jail came to $57,984. But the total time the homicide squad spent on the investigation cost only $16,667!

Why, this is little more than half the sum spent sporting Stephens around and watching him after he was sprung from the air-conditioned (but bourbon-proof) luxury of the penal farm!

Distressing, if not totally shocking, is this reflection of the absence of any real work on the case by local authorities. Further, it shows their total dependence upon the FBI for their "case"—yet the FBI was originally without authority to intervene in the case, although it did intervene in the first five minutes. Later, this illegality was covered by the spurious conspiracy indictment hoked up out of nothing in Birmingham.

When the President was murdered, then-existing law provided no FBI jurisdiction, no FBI right to spend a cent. Hoover spent federal money immediately—took the play away from the Secret Service, which did have proper right to investigate because of its legal Presidential-protection assignment. At the same time, States' Righter that Hoover is, agonizing over jurisdiction, he told the Warren Commission on May 14, 1964, ". . . as you are aware, there is no federal jurisdiction for such an investigation" because it then was "not a Federal crime to kill or attack the President . . ." (5H98). Before the White House found a means of getting the FBI into the case, it was in it—running it—and what a mess Hoover made of it! There is no more botched job in all of police and investigative history [1].

When the man he made his enemy, King, the man Hoover called the nation's biggest liar and a subversive besides, was gunned down in Memphis, within the first five minutes, FBI headquarters put the Memphis office in the case—illegally—and then poured the rest of its enormous resources into it, botching this job no less professionally than the Presidential-murder investigation.

So, in Tennessee, the bastion of what its orators and politicians call the stronghold of "states' rights," the state surrendered its rights—immediately. And the orators and politicians were mute. The demand for the states to exercise their rights is the political grist of the political Neanderthals. When the chips are down, when there is a viable issue of states' rights, they are all silent. They, too, abdicate to federal power and authority. When it comes to a buck, the states lose interest in their "rights."

Tennessee was content for the fabled federals to do its police

234

work. Not just because the FBI has that reputation; also because it spent federal, not Tennessee, money.

No high motive dominated anyone. The Tennesseans were mercenary, the federals looking out for themselves. Their control over the investigation was their control over their reputation and their own record. Their control over the investigation enabled them to leak what they wanted printed and believed and to suppress what they did not want known. They did both.

The author's dissatisfaction with the performance of the FBI has not been disguised. Such false pretenses befit the FBI, which lives with such pretenses, by them, and, I suspect, largely because of them. My displeasure with the FBI is not because I am opposed to such an agency. On the contrary, I regard one as essential. But it is the record and the performance that compels the dissatisfaction of any concerned citizen. While calling itself other than a police force, the FBI has made of itself a secret federal police and a political police, violating the law at will or contriving evasions that are more demeaning of the law than open contempt for it.

There is no attorney general who was ever effectively Hoover's boss. Hoover's request for authority to wiretap, for example, could not be denied without risk of serious political reprisal, especially when he invoked those now-sacred terms, "internal security" or "national security." This is the spurious ground on which he got the also-murdered Robert Kennedy to agree to tap King's wire. But as Frank Mankiewicz, Carl Rowan, Martin Agronsky, and others were to report, Hoover extended this into bugging, which is different, not restricted to the phone alone in the electronic spying it makes possible.

Because King was murdered and Hoover was in charge of the investigation of that murder, a brief recounting of the disgraceful incidents of the early summer of 1969, when the bugging of King by the FBI became publicly known, is appropriate here.

The reader will recall Hoover and Robert Kennedy had exchanged a few heated words on the matter of wiretapping and bugging King in 1966 and then both backed off.

In the early days of the Nixon administration, the decision was made to do more wiretapping. Simultaneously, it was revealed in several court actions that Hoover had been wiretapping or bugging criminals, where there was no suggestion of "internal security," and blacks, where only his own distorted view could adapt his agency's spying to this definition. He bugged union leaders and the leader of the Black Muslims, aging Elijah Muhammed. He bugged King at various places. In the course of this spying, he also eavesdropped on that dangerous bomb-thrower, the peacenik former heavyweight boxing champion of the world, Cassius Clay/Mohammed Ali, after he adopted Muslim belief.

There is reason to believe that Hoover wanted some of this impropriety and illegality to become known, hoping to get approval for his electronic intrusions into personal affairs, for as the information came out he focused on the spying he had done on those whom he alleged were members of the Mafia. Indeed, there was favorable reaction to the abuse of gangsters. Who can be for gangsters? The incident had all the earmarks of a heavy public-relations play for the sanctioning of electronic spying.

But with the disclosure of the violation of the rights of blacks by the head of the FBI, Carl Rowan, a black columnist, John Kennedy's ambassador to Finland and former head of the United States Information Agency, had what Hoover regarded as the temerity to report the facts and to suggest Hoover had earned his retirement, that he should resign.

Olympic as always, Hoover's denial of responsibility was embodied in an FBI release that claimed to be speaking for the Nixon Department of Justice (which did not contest it) but which told only part of the story:

June 6, 1969

An FBI spokesman referred reporters to the testimony of J. Edgar Hoover to the House Subcommittee on Appropriations on March 4, 1965, at which time Mr. Hoover testified as follows:

"In carrying out our investigative responsibilities, we have 44 telephone taps in operation. Each must be authorized in advance and in writing by the Attorney General. Their use is highly restricted —that is, only in matters in which the internal security of the country is involved, and in kidnapping and in extortion violations where human life is in jeopardy. All those now in operation fall in the internal security category."

A Department of Justice spokesman said Mr. Hoover's testimony was accurate in every respect.

When this didn't shake the world as he had hoped, Hoover took an unusual step, for him. He rarely grants interviews, being able to accomplish his ends without the risk they entail. He granted an exclusive interview to the Kennedy-hating, Hoover-loving Washington *Star*. On June 19, Jeremiah O'Leary's copyrighted story had a

236

front-page, black banner headline, "King Wiretap Called RFK's Idea." The also-prominent subordinate headline, aiming slander against the murdered King as well as the also-murdered Kennedy, read "Hoover Asserts Memo to FBI Cited Concern over Marxism."

Is there anyone who really believes Bobby Kennedy was "concerned" over King's non-existent "Marxism"? He is the man who stood by King when King was in jail.

Culling the files, for all the world a senior-grade Beasley, Hoover selected for his interview two memoranda. One reported a conversation with Kennedy by Courtney Evans, then Hoover's ambassador to his official boss, as "liaison man" with the Department. (Evans was also a CIA man.) The other, from Hoover, reported the feasibility of tapping King's phones.

What Hoover was saying is that it was all Kennedy's idea, exactly what the *Star* said he said. That got a tremendous international play, as did the slander of Hoover's other murdered enemy.

It is pretty obvious that, in agreeing to eavesdrop on King, Kennedy was reacting to Hoover, that the Attorney General is not the investigator of the Department of Justice and that Hoover is. Hoover put Kennedy in the position where he would be refusing to permit a check on the patriotism of his friend, the man Hoover considered Hoover's enemy. Anathematic as is this rotten espionage (there is no reason to presume Kennedy found it so in all cases), had he refused, he would have been in an untenable position. He could not refuse Hoover's challenge to King's loyalty. The record proves the guff Hoover fed Kennedy did not hold up. No such proof as Hoover alleged was ever turned up, by the wiretaps or by his other spying. Hoover did not expect it to. He merely wanted to get dirty dirt on King, as he saw it, and make Kennedy responsible. He undoubtedly thought this a smart move.

After Hoover's initial blast, astoundingly, the capons started to crow and act like fighting cocks. Rowan disclosed that, as a ranking government official, he had been sent Hoover's vilest reports of a personal nature on King and that they had been widely disseminated throughout the government. This was anything but the excuse with which Hoover had blackjacked Kennedy.

Hoover's response, dignified when compared with his behavior in this entire affair, was to call Rowan a racist. Two columnists for the Knight newspapers printed a copyrighted story in the June 25 Detroit *Free Press* in which they quote Hoover as having referred to "that racist communist Rowan." Hoover also told them, maintaining it not for the first time, "I didn't want the authority" to tap phones, so he insisted on the Attorney General's approval. It would be more precise to say he did not want the responsibility for the taps so he arranged to shift it.

Kennedy's successor as Attorney General was Nicholas Katzenbach, who had been his first assistant. As I shall disclose in other writing, he had earned Hoover's undying enmity by pulling a different plug on him. Rather than continue as a member of the cabinet and co-exist, or try to, as Hoover's "boss," Katzenbach shifted to a lower position in the State Department. Ramsey Clark was his successor. Both had preserved silence over what Hoover had done.

But at Hoover's comments on Kennedy and the King wiretap, they, too, started to cock-a-doodle-doo.

Katzenbach came right out and called Hoover a liar.

> To say or imply that this tap was the original concept of Robert Kennedy—that he was the moving force in this situation—or that he had any doubts whatsoever as to Dr. King's loyalty or integrity, is false.

The record made public shows the tap authorization ended under Katzenbach. Hoover did not respond to Katzenbach's statement.

Clark went even further, joining Rowan in the suggestion that the time had come for Hoover to retire. He declared, again without comment from Hoover, that Hoover "repeatedly requested me to authorize FBI wiretaps on Dr. King while I was Attorney General. The last of these requests, none of which was granted, came two days before the murder of Dr. King."

How strange it is, when all of Hoover's extensive and expensive spying on King disclosed only what was not his proper concern or the concern of anyone else in government, that Hoover persisted in seeking a cover for his own illicit intentions in this spying, all the while ignoring the known threats against King. Pre-eminent among these—and very much worth noting in this context—was that involving Joseph Adams Milteer, Georgia leader of the NSRP. On November 9, 1963, his reported threats against both President Kennedy and King were tape-recorded by the Miami police. They amount to blueprints of what happened. Miami authorities immediately supplied copies of the tape to both the FBI and the Secret Service, both of which withheld them from the Warren Commission. Those few inadequate reports on this that the FBI did not withhold from the Commission, the Commission suppressed. The tape was the cause of the change in plans for President Kennedy's visit to

Miami four days prior to his assassination, a change that entirely eliminated a motorcade procession through the city. (The tape may also provide the solution to the barbarous bombing of the Birmingham church in which four black children were murdered. A transcript of the Milteer tape and facsimiles of these suppressed FBI reports appear in the Appendix.) The FBI's knowledge of this plan, a concerted but until-then unsuccessful plot to murder the leader who eventually was murdered, coincided with Hoover's determination to get someone else to assume the responsibility for him of tapping *King—not* those trying to kill him [2].

Drew Pearson and Jack Anderson may have supplied the answer to the Hoover riddle—how he can get away with it and be praised for it—in the concluding three paragraphs of their June 26 column:

> Not one Attorney General in the past eight years has been able to work with Hoover. Although supposedly a part of the Justice Department, he operates entirely on his own. Months pass and he does not even speak to the Attorney General.
>
> Some Congressmen, of course, are acutely aware of the fact that Hoover's far-flung investigatory agency can, or already has, picked up some of their own private shenanigans—as when a well-known "house" was raided in Washington and the FBI picked up the "madam's" little black book listing the names of 200 Congressmen.
>
> There aren't many Congressmen with enough intestinal fortitude to probe wiretapping, but there are some and they should do it.

Let us not mince words. As with Robert Kennedy and, as we shall see, with King and other black leaders, it is blackmail.

This is an ugly word. It is ugliest when practiced by the head of the federal (secret) police. Among blacks, this blackmail also succeeded.

Just as I had written to Hanes, Huie Foreman, Aeromarine, and many of the whites involved in the Ray case and received no response—even the editors of the two Memphis papers failed to answer when I asked for copies of their papers, *what they had printed*—so I wrote to a number of black leaders and some of those involved. I also spoke to several. Apparently, terror captured black leaders after the minitrial. All those who had been close to the martyr and to whom I wrote were silent. One only had anything to say in public, and he said it long before the "deal" was made. We shall treat that in a separate chapter. A few—a very few—expressed mild disagreement about the trial, but they only parroted Ray, saying they were satisfied he had not been alone. Reverend James L. Bevel, a member of the Southern Christian Leadership Conference (King's organization) and then King's man in Philadelphia, was alone in saying he believed Ray had not fired the shot.

Toward the end of March 1969, I spoke to the New York leader of the SCLC. He expressed a great interest and said he would stop off when in Washington, at the coming observation of the first anniversary of the murder. He was driving, picking up Bevel in Philadelphia, and both would see me and my files on their return.

I never heard from him again. Not even a call to say they were not coming.

Blacks minor in the NAACP structure read the first part of this book, described it as the most shocking they had ever read, and ran up against a solid wall when they tried to elicit interest on higher levels.

Students at black Howard University, then in ferment, tried to interest the black law faculty. They failed, reporting pervading fear.

It looked so much as though black leaders of all political hues were glad King had been murdered, almost as though each felt it gave him a better chance to rise. But that could not be believed.

Even those made to appear as black Judases by the bastardization of the judicial process in Memphis preserved unbroken silence.

Not until the nasty stink about Hoover's bugging did the probable truth, the explanation I believe of most black abdications, dawn on me.

Whitney Young, head of one of the respectable and conservative black groups, the more establishment-oriented Urban League, confirmed my growing and by then fixed suspicion. I met him socially in New York on June 23, 1969. He was candid, quite straightforward. All black leaders had been and would remain silent because all feared Hoover's blackmail. All feared any open opposition to Hoover would result in his publicizing whatever it is he had spied out about King's personal life. (Young had a pretty good notion what this is.)

To report this is not to suggest that any of the silent black leaders is dominated by selfish motive. Many regarded King as the black prophet. They were anxious for this to be the continuing belief of black masses. Perhaps they were thinking also of the survivors, the wife and children.

Black militants, on the other hand, did not regard King as most of his white admirers did. They considered him an establishmentarian, a man anxious to make what to them were petty, limited deals with the white power structure, each deal, as they saw it, giving blacks much too little much too slowly, really serving restrictive white interests.

240

Time, events, the aggressiveness of the young, and pressures from their dissatisfied masses have forced conservative black leaders to voice more militant thoughts.

The silence of the blacks continues more than two years after the greatest American leader they have produced was murdered. Not one appears to be interested in solving the crime, helping to solve it, or even seeing to it that history, especially black history, is set straight. This is difficult to comprehend for one whose people experienced Auschwitz and Buchenwald, for there are no American gas chambers. It is difficult for one whose people also produced the Judenrat, those human Judas-goats of the Nazi slaughters, for this country constitutes no such environment, even if it does, in some ways, resemble the days of prelude.

The awful crime of silence is no less awful when it is black silence.

It may be worse. For, whether he was liked or not by his peers, whether they were in accord with his views and methods or not, this was their American Nobel laureate, their only leader of true international prominence, an articulate, charismatic man recognized and respected by most of the black masses, the embodiment of black American hope. He had become the public symbol of black bravery, the end to black fears of the white hood and the legal, official surrogates of the nightriders—of black emergence from four centuries of denial and terrorization and of self-liberation from fear and the fear of repression.

To permit the murder of such a man to go unsolved and to be officially obfuscated; to permit prostitution of the judicial process, so symbolic of that which for centuries had victimized the blacks, without searching for the truth, without *any* protest, *any* question, to me self-destructive.

Regardless of motive, whether it be real or fancied, it is Black Abdication.

Not one black, be he intellectual or political leader, militant or conservative, personally involved, a friend of the murdered, a disciple, or a competitor—not *one* of the so many—made a single meaningful response of the few who responded at all.

From the moment of the murder, this is the record. People flooded SCLC offices with clues and reports of which no record was made. White Matt Herron, at great personal risk, remained in Memphis, trying to investigate, trying to elicit black interest, a futility, staying until he had exhausted his resources and those available to him.

241

Bowing abjectly to Hoover's blackmail—unthinkingly, cowardly, or believing themselves politically mature and wise—black leaders became their own most successful enemies, indentured themselves in a servitude more humiliating than their past physical slavery. They guaranteed the success of the evil purposes served by the murders of their leaders. Unwittingly, they became accomplices of the murderers.

Yet the greatest futility, faced with a blackmailer, is to permit him to blackmail. He cannot succeed without the collaboration of the victim. Hoover faced only collaborators.

But he is not an honorable blackmailer, keeping his evil secret; and the black leaders, at least in this regard, have become great, black ostriches.

Hoover never intended keeping secret what to his unclean mind is dirty. Witness Rowan's knowledge of it long ago, more than enough proof that Hoover sought to retail it when and how he could, so long as it served his purposes. In effect, the blacks blackmail themselves. They just fear or say they fear greater Hoover exploitation of what they fear, never realizing that he is armed with nothing but their fear and has exhausted the possibilities of his arsenal of slanders in so-called decent outlets.

By now, everyone willing to use Hoover's disgusting filth has had ample opportunity.

It is no longer a secret—save as ostriches see things.

One of the "respectable" uses of Hoover's leaked slanders was by Drew Pearson and Jack Anderson, in the men's magazine *True* dated January 1969, written months earlier. It reports a variety of Hoover anecdotes of which the King episode is one. What immediately follows this item is also pertinent here, for it reveals Hoover's special interpretation of what "internal security" and "national security" really mean and involve and his own velvet-gloved, thoroughly Americanized variant of European secret-police acts and attitudes.

LBJ has always had a fine appreciation for a story about a leader's extracurricular love life. A typical backstairs report, passed on to the White House by Hoover, dealt with an alleged affair of a prominent civil-rights leader. The secret FBI memo quoted a confidential informant as reporting that the man "has been having an illicit love affair with (a Los Angeles woman) since 1962."

A love affair, no matter how sordid, is no business of the FBI—unless, perhaps, one of the parties happens to be a spy. There is no evidence that the leader and the lady, if the story is true at all, were plotting between tendernesses to overthrow the government. Yet J. Edgar Hoover solemnly informed the President: "(He) calls this woman every Wednesday and meets her in various cities throughout the country. The source related an incident which occurred some time ago in a New York City hotel, where (the leader) was intoxicated at a small gathering. (He) threatened to leap from the 13th-floor window of the hotel if this woman would not say she loved him."

When Washington was under siege by the Poor People's Campaign last spring, key southern legislators received copies of an FBI document which stated that another black leader had been seen in what was described delicately as an "unnatural act" with a woman. Gleefully the lawmakers showed the document to numbers of people, despite the prohibition on dissemination of FBI material.

Hoover's gumshoes sometimes have seemed overeager to chase down irrelevant facts about prominent people. The famous FBI "bug" in lobbyist Fred Black's hotel suite, for example, picked up a number of conversations about big-name lawmakers. Although no illegal activity was indicated, agents followed up the intercepted conversations for no apparent purpose other than to pry into the lawmakers' affairs.

The agents were most discreet. After overhearing Black make a breakfast date with House Democratic Leader Carl Albert and Sen. Mike Monroney to discuss the location of a new aircraft plant in their home state of Oklahoma, Hoover's men slipped up to Capitol Hill the next morning to snoop around. Their report to the director was so hush-hush that they even used a code word of "secret" and stamped the report "June."

"No surveillance was maintained in the Senate Office Building," they assured Hoover, who is touchy about spying on politicians. "However, WFO (Washington Field Office) made a discreet survey of the streets in the vicinity of the Senate Office Building for Black's car during the pertinent period with negative results . . . WFO will be alert for any information which would indicate Black did or did not keep his appointment with Sen. Mike Monroney and Rep. Carl Albert." While the G-men were checking parked Cadillacs, apparently, Black arrived by taxicab.

"June" is not a "code word for 'secret.' " It is the code name of Hoover's bugging file.

June is also the month in 1965 President Johnson authorized

243

wiretapping in "national security" cases, which may explain the sobriquet, "June file." To Hoover, anything can be stretched into the definition of "national security," including what to him is "internal security." He interpreted it to include the Nobel prizewinner, did he not?

Monroney and Albert—important, influential legislators—are now in Hoover's bugging file, if they were not earlier. It will not be easy for them to cross him, in their legislative acts and responsibilities or in other ways.

In any case, the firmament did not sunder when the "secret" about King got wide distribution. It attracted almost no attention or comment.

One of the finer examples of a disappearing journalism, the expression of traditional principle and outraged decency, is the excellent and, in context, courageous editorial article by Lawrence Stern and Richard Harwood in the June 11, 1969 *Washington Post.* The three lengthy excerpts that follow include more than what relates directly to King because these excerpts, in their own way, say what this book does:

> For several years a piece of Washington apocrypha known as "the Martin Luther King tape" was the subject of sly and ugly surmise among certain journalistic insiders. There are those who claim to have had The Tape played for them by obliging law enforcement officials. Others are said to have been given transcripts of a gathering, bugged by Government investigators, at which Dr. King and friends were present.

> It was one of those repugnant but enduring stories that cling to controversial public figures. The FBI and Justice Department steadfastly denied knowing anything specific about electronic surveillance of Dr. King. Shoulders would shrug, eyebrows would arch knowingly, fingers would point discreetly in other directions. And FBI Director J. Edgar Hoover contented himself with attacking the civil rights leader as "the most notorious liar in the country."

> Now the unseemly truth is out. It emerged in the form of sworn testimony by FBI agents in a Houston Federal courtroom in the case of former heavyweight boxing champion Cassius Clay, now Mohammad Ali. The agents acknowledged that they had snooped on Dr. King for a period of several years.

> The gist of the testimony was that a group of men—one of them a 22-year-old FBI clerk—sat in air-conditioned rooms and listened to the private conversations of this prominent American without the

faintest shred of legitimacy or sufficient cause. . . .

Why was Dr. King under surveillance? No one has said. But it may be significant that the snooping began at a time when he criticized the FBI for assigning Southern agents to protect civil rights workers in the South. It is also ironic that this seemingly gratuitous invasion of Dr. King's personal life occurred at a time when many high-ranking members of the Justice Department would have expressed nothing less than roaring outrage at the thought that his phone was being tapped by Government agents. . . .

In June, 1965, President Johnson issued an executive order prohibiting wiretapping except in "national security" investigations. In his testimony Hoover speaks of "internal security" matters.

What constitutes "internal security," this column asked of an FBI spokesman. "It has to speak for itself," he replied.

There is a spectacular ambiguity about it all.

Attorney General John N. Mitchell now intends to use the authority conferred on him by Congress last year to use wiretaps in the wide variety of cases permitted under the new Omnibus Crime Act.

When you consider the scope of the blatantly illegal wiretapping carried out by Government agents during the past few years, it boggles the mind to consider how pervasive official snooping might become once it was legitimized by local courts at the behest of local prosecutors. During the second half of 1968, for example, state officials obtained 174 wiretapping warrants, all but seven of them in New York where authorities used wiretapping for such suspected offenses as larceny and gambling.

It is chilling to contemplate the size of the electronic dragnet that might be thrown over American citizens in the name of stamping out suspected gambling violations.

Yet President Nixon and his Attorney General have embraced the new Federal eavesdropping law with resounding public enthusiasm. They may rue it when the returns start coming in.

Stern and Harwood were *not* waylaid at night. The earth did *not* open and swallow the plant of the *Post*. No one talked about King's personal life, which was entirely his own affair and of no proper official interest —not, certainly, to a "government of laws, not of men," in the land where the rights of the individual are preeminent.

The "secret" could not have been more bluntly put than in *Parade*, the Sunday supplement that appears in so many of the larger newspapers and reaches an enormous audience. Its July 27, 1969 issue reported in answer to a long question about the King bugging: "For the most part, the wiretaps revealed that King on occasion submitted to the temptations of the flesh." Yet no picket lines formed, no protests were staged, not a single voice was heard.

From the pre-Christian David to the pre-assassination Milteer, this is neither new nor disturbing, save to those anxious to be disturbed.

But it is in *The Councillor,* organ of the racist White Citizens' Council, that Hoover found his natural partner. This is a journal and an organization which understand and use words like "national security" and "internal security" with Hoover's special meanings. *The Councillor* renewed its slanders of King and praises of Hoover as soon as the flap Rowan started was in the papers. In the June 14 issue, it devoted ten column inches to promises of what was to come, under the headline, "The Truth About That Wiretap on Martin Luther King." One paragraph of this distillation of sewer overflowings should be enough:

In the next issue, The Councillor will give the never before told story of the Martin Luther King wiretap. We will report that the FBI made some tape recordings involving matters other than national security. One of these recordings involved the Reverend Doctor King's sex life with a white woman. The Councillor knew of this recording but did not print the story because of its concern with national security, and not with sexual liaisons. But the story is now intertwined with matters of security and there is a need for the public to know what happened.

If any rational interpretation can be made of such writing, the product of such minds, this means the racists had had the whole story all along and were silent because they wanted to hide Hoover's bugging, their "concern with national security."

How interesting it is that, as seems to be the case, the racist White Citizens' Council had Hoover's "secrets" about King! Any knowledge of any of this goes back to the FBI and emphasizes the futility, the incredible stupidity, of bowing to blackmail.

John Herbers touched ever so lightly on the relation between Hoover and King's enemies in the *New York Times* of June 21 when he wrote,

In 1965, white conservatives began making public statements that the bureau had secret information on Dr. King that could be damaging. The bureau would say nothing publicly about these statements.

It is conspicuous they were not denied.

In the preceding paragraph of the story quoted from *The Councillor,* the article says that King was friendly with a man it describes, without reservation or qualification, as "a Soviet agent" and a "member of a family whose corporations are responsible for millions of dollars of Madison Avenue advertising." The overtones of this kind of ellipsis are well received by *The Councillor's* audience which, among other things, hears its anti-Semitic overtones. This was a poorly disguised racist description of Corliss Lamont.

In connection with Herbers' article, the following sentence from the Soviet-spy paragraph may be of special interest:

The Councillor revealed the name of this Soviet agent in 1965.

Possible translation: *The Councillor* had the FBI's tapping and bugging of King available to it and used it in 1965.

When, in the next issue, *The Councillor* had its big "never-before-printed" espose the quarter-page story, devoted to the tedium blended with imaginings that are the political beliefs of those to whom everyone to the left of Hitler is a Communist or a "Soviet agent," added little. There really is no way of authenticating much of what they present as fact. Without authentication, it cannot be presented or accepted as fact. Some, however, is consistent with other reporting and what is known. One of the following paragraphs does suggest the truth of the quotation from the Herbers article. In this story, they number the paragraphs, possibly for the ready reference of their readership. I am unable to offer any translation of the phrase "Queen Bee" as *The Councillor* uses it.

(17) The FBI in making wiretaps is supposed to be concerned only with matters of national security and not with sexual liaisons. But the white woman involved in the King case is a "Queen Bee" with Red connections.

(18) The FBI played its wiretaps of King to a number of United States Congressmen. Information given to an agent of The Councillor indicated that the tapes dealt largely with King's sexual involvement with the "Queen Bee." This fact is generally known among Congressmen but has never appeared in print, according to our source.

(19) The Councillor did not print the information about the sex wiretaps because The Councillor is concerned with matters of national

security and the survival of the nation—not with illicit sex relationships. We did not know that the woman was a "Queen Bee."

When such "patriots" as the White Citizens' Councils and *The Councillor* have access to illegal and improper espionage against prominent Americans, the nation is indeed in safe hands, the Lord dwells in the city and the watchman need not awaken.

Eight paragraphs of the story are devoted to a mixture of red-baiting and Jew-baiting Hoover's adversary, former Attorney General Katzenbach.

Part deals with *The Councillor* having, as it euphemistically put it, "intercepted a briefcase full of papers which had belonged to King." Translation: There had been a theft.

Whether or not the allegations about King's personal life are true, they are (a) not material, (b) not secret, and (c) nobody's business, least of all, Hoover's. Most of all, they cannot justify the black abdications.

Hoover hated King and what he stood for. If Hoover did not technically violate the law in what he did pursuing his dishonorable and illegal ends, he twisted it beyond recognition. He did not spy on King just to make an unarticulated deal for suppressing such information as he obtained. He did it to use the information, in any and every way he could, against King and what he stood for. Nothing will or can change that, no submission, no silence—nothing.

All this provides a partial insight into the thinking, beliefs, capabilities, principles, and actions of the man in charge of the investigation of King's murder—and in that capacity only because of further federal trampling on the law. It says that he should have been the last man in the country to have this authority or this responsibility, the last man to be entrusted (to paraphrase the Bible) with the keeping of the vineyard of the national honor and integrity, having not kept his own.

Throughout this book, there are dozens of proofs he never did and never intended to conduct anything like a full, vigorous, and impartial investigation. He is, after all, the man who did nothing about the known threat against the victim (through Milteer) while cunningly scheming to bug the victim in a way that made his political enemy technically responsible.

There are other records of the FBI's performance or lack of performance in this investigation, not inherently part of what was said, done, and offered at the minitrial. At this point, therefore, I record a

248

few of these the better to limn the investigation and to clarify its end product—and possibly its purposes and motivations.

As with the assassination in Dallas, the FBI was in charge of a political-murder investigation although the crime was a crime under state law only.

This was a policy decision Hoover is much too shrewd to have made on his own. Even if it were his own idea, he would have required and arranged Departmental sanction. The strange anomaly of Hoover's technical right to be in the case at all on the ground of an alleged civil-rights conspiracy, the words of the charge, while the Attorney General himself was loudly maintaining exactly the opposite—that there was no conspiracy—troubled no one. But once in the case, Hoover regarded it as he regards the government, as his fiefdom.

He could not have been more authoritarian, more high-handed. When local police complain about the FBI, it is something. They did. Almost immediately. That they complained at all about the lordly FBI, with which they have to continue working after any specific case is over, is a rarity.

Within two weeks after the assassination, one unidentified Memphis police official was quoted by AP as complaining,

> They haven't given us anything but a physical description. They aren't handing out pictures of the man. They either don't have a good one or they are going it alone.

This was well after "Galt" had been identified as the owner of the white Mustang, after a composite sketch had been made.

Also quoted from the same source:

> The FBI is withholding nationwide distribution of the composite drawing of Dr. Martin Luther King, Jr.'s assassin . . .

AP commented:

> FBI officials rejected reporters' requests for a composite drawing of the man they are seeking in what perhaps is the most massive manhunt of modern times. They refuse to say whether they have prepared such a sketch.

But they had it, it did get out, and the FBI, instead of disowning it, said its release had not been authorized. When the sketch appeared in a Florida paper, it led to the arrest of an innocent man in Jacksonville because "he looks so much like the sketch."

Many as Hoover's bully-boys are in number, carefully as he trains them, they still cannot see everyone, everywhere. If they wanted citizen cooperation, the objective their TV puffery emphasizes, they had to have made a likeness widely available. Their failure—really refusal—arouses suspicions. "The most massive manhunt in history" required the largest number of eyes peeled. Without a likeness, with the indefinite and contradictory verbal descriptions, a fairly large proportion of all the men in the country could be encompassed, which could (and did) lead only to confusion and to hurting the innocent.

The Memphis police official, wise in asking that his name not be used, the FBI being of elephantine memory, also "cited" the FBI's "ban on comment about the investigation." In the political murders, with all the victims Hoover's enemies, this is FBI standard operating procedure. The prohibition of comment on the investigation is sometimes claimed to be protection for the innocent. In actuality, it serves other purposes, chiefly to protect the Bureau against its own incredible blunders. It keeps the press from catching the errors and misrepresentations. And it precludes work by other agencies[3].

On April 22, the New York *Post* reported "Police in Memphis and other cities charge that federal officials have discouraged local investigations" of King's murder. Both the *Post* and the AP story of the same day quoted Memphis Assistant Police Chief Bill Price as saying that, as a consequence, "You don't know what to look for."

Imagine that! The crime was a local, Memphis crime, and the federal FBI had confused everything so thoroughly, so completely frozen out the local police, they did not "know what to look for"!

The *Post* added that "Hoover ordered a special Mexican border alert to keep (the) fugitive from leaving the country." Thousands of notices were printed in Spanish for Mexican distribution. Dutifully, the Mexican police arrested innocent Americans. Hoover's orders here were his customary sage steps, Ray then having already escaped to Canada!

Price tried to avoid using the name of the FBI. Instead, he said, "Somebody had muddied the waters."

"Police in Atlanta, Birmingham and Los Angeles, as well as Memphis," the *Post* reported, "noticed discrepancies between the FBI's description of Ray and its earlier data on Galt." Which is one of the more effective ways of muddying the waters and keeping local police from knowing what to look for. And kidding yourself, getting nowhere. There was, in fact, almost nothing accurate about the FBI's data, and when they corrected themselves, with full access to all the prison records on Ray, they continued to have wrong such basic data as his age.

Another example: in the charge of conspiracy finally made against Ray, the FBI had said he had taken dancing lessons in New Orleans in 1964–1965. During that time, Ray was in prison!

Again: UPI reported the FBI was "in communication" with Ray's "alleged" brother. There should have been no doubt, with all those storied FBI records. When he escaped from Missouri State Prison, as Los Angeles police were quick to note, "a 'wanted' poster issued by Missouri authorities . . . said he had two brothers," both of whom were identified by name and address.

If this raises questions about the kind of records the FBI keeps, compared with its public relations about its perfection in criminal record-keeping, none were heard. It took Hoover all of 15 days to identify the fingerprints as Ray's. When he made the announcement, late as it was, his release provided an angle emphasized in the press, that his unflagging experts had compared these prints with "more than 53,000." Lost in the papers was the long delay, how much time this required.

In announcing Ray had been identified, only a few days after its announcement about Galt taking New Orleans dancing instruction when he in fact was in the Jefferson City, Missouri, jail, the FBI attributed this, as UPI phrased it, to "an error in the investigation of the background of 'Galt.' " Which is the same as saying the FBI had been after the wrong man, or was all mixed up and lost, or both. UPI also said,

Hoover did not mention the discrepancies between his statement Wednesday and his latest announcement. FBI officials handed the announcement to reporters but would answer no questions.

Who can blame them? How could this possibly be explained? Or the other questions answered?

How much more fruitful the investigation would have been had the FBI stayed out of it or just cooperated with local police can only be conjectured. The result could not possibly have been any worse. The Ray case is the epitome of lousy investigation. The New York *Post* story, in the sentence in which it reported the alert Hoover had ordered along the Mexican border—for the escapee then in Canada—also said "Memphis detectives continue working on their own theory"—that Galt was a myth carefully created by conspirators to hide the killer's real identity.

The FBI had ample reason to believe, as an AP dispatch from Atlanta published in the April 15 Nashville *Banner* says, "that the most wanted man in the nation, Eric Starvo Galt, never actually existed but was contrived months before" the murder. "It was learned that investigators have been unable to trace his existence beyond last summer, and pointed out that it is virtually impossible for a person to leave so few traces."

On information it seems to have gotten from the FBI, the wire service reported of the "occupation" given on the application for the Alabama driver's license, "unemployed merchant seaman" that "this apparently was a lie. None of the merchant seamen's unions have any record on him."

But five days later, in the same city, the *Tennessean* printed a UPI dispatch from Washington with this sentence: "Records of the Seafarer's International Union at Chicago listed a 'J. E. Ray' as a member." A Chicago report from a Washington source. FBI headquarters are in Washington. Much of Ray's life was in the part of the midwest near the Great Lakes.

The *Post* story also further reveals the totality of the FBI freeze-out of local police:

> Police in the four cities where the manhunt is concentrated have practically been shunted aside by federal agents. In Birmingham a detective lieutenant who tried to question a clerk who allegedly sold Ray a rifle was called off by the FBI when the clerk refused to talk. The FBI investigation is being handled at the highest level. Its only two press releases have been issued by Atty. Gen. Ramsey Clark and Hoover. They have given no indication why more widespread police efforts have been discouraged in a case that technically concerns a state offense, murder.

From deep south to far north, the story was the same. The FBI closed all mouths, immediately and pretty effectively.

"It seems that everywhere reporters go," the Minneapolis *Tribune* reported in its lengthy story on Sunday, April 14, "the FBI already has been there. In many cases, witnesses report the FBI has instructed them to say nothing."

The paper also reported the FBI had "taken over the registration records of two rooming houses and records of at least one gun shop."

As we now know, airline records, too.

This Memphis police official, who understands the FBI, said "they are going it alone." The FBI took over the investigation of the murder at the outset. They kept control by means of a legal fiction. They made a miserable botch of the entire thing. But because of their control and the complaisance of most of the press, they were able to avoid their just deserts. Of that part of the business, Hoover is a master. He has a survival instinct that does not depend on blackmail and intimidation alone. While he was lousing up the whole thing with unrivaled professionality, he was carefully getting exactly the opposite printed.

For example, the month after the murder, Drew Pearson told his enormous readership that, despite Hoover's hatred for King,

Having branded King "the most notorious liar in the world" . . . we have checked into the operations of the FBI in this respect and are convinced that it is conducting perhaps the most painstaking manhunt ever before undertaken . . . have checked every bar ever patronized by James Earl Ray, every flophouse he ever stopped at . . . has collected the most amazing array of evidence, all linking Ray with the murder.

It was good FBI publicity, false as it was.

Pearson's source could only have been the FBI, which until then had not found a single one of the key bars and flophouses, that awaiting their identification in publications by Huie and others. It had not found the plastic surgeon who removed the slight tip from Ray's nose—did not even know about it; had not found the restaurant in which he had worked after breaking jail; had not found the Canadian woman with whom he had had a short affair. It had not found a single one of the important clues it had been intended to find if Ray were, indeed, the decoy.

Pearson had also been fed the FBI's excuse, so far from reality, so far from any sign the FBI really knew what it was doing:

That he hasn't been found may be due, first, to the possibility that he himself was murdered by those who hired him to kill King; or second, that he might be hiding in some remote Mexican village.

At that moment "Sneyd" was in Portugal, the FBI supposedly hot on his trail.

Hoover kept planting the idea in the press that Ray had been murdered. Another FBI contrivance was fed the Birmingham *News*

253

when, on April 18th, two weeks after the murder, nothing had happened, no culprit had been located. It reported the FBI thought Ray might have made his way to Cuba. Of all places, it is the least likely, for political reasons and because of the extreme physical difficulty of getting there. But how nicely this fit Hoover's Neanderthal politics! To this possibility the "FBI informant" added insurance on the other side—"if he is still alive." This blatant falsehood, these complete inventions, persisted in the press. The *New York Times* repeated them a week later, on April 28. Their sole purpose was to hide Hoover's ineptness and failures.

To return to the sketch that somehow did get out (the FBI disowning authorization for the release only), it was seen in the *Times* by a Los Angeles commercial artist and "assassination buff," Fred Newcomb, who was immediately reminded of a series of unpublished pictures taken right after the President was murdered. The sketch bears an astounding likeness to a "tramp" in one of those pictures [4]. He sent me both. On April 23, 1968, I phoned our local FBI man and left a set of sketches and picture for him with the city editor of our local paper. It took him only two days to pick them up, possibly because his home is about ten minutes from the newspaper office, even closer than mine. That was, indeed, quite a "manhunt."

It was, indeed, as Pearson had been led to believe, one of the most thorough manhunts in history. But there is a strange omission in it, as reported to him. The FBI may have "checked every bar . . . every flophouse," but Ray seems never to have eaten, for there is nothing at all about any restaurant.

Perhaps Pearson was blinded to this lack in the evidence by what he was told:

> What the FBI has established about King's assassin was that he was a professional killer who had studied the suspense writing of Ian Fleming and Ayn Rand. His pseudonym, Eric Starvo Galt, for instance, was taken from both authors.

And, of this "student of crime," "all the evidence . . . points to the probability that Ray was hired to kill Dr. King."

Where Pearson was later to report the FBI fiction created to fit new "no conspiracy" necessities, Ray's extensive expenditures were explained away. Pearson dutifully published as fact the FBI's invention of successful bank robberies by Ray. Pearson was told, "as far as the FBI can tell, [Ray] committed no crimes following his escape." None of that smuggling in and out of Canada and Mexico? Whatever was the FBI doing—until it knew the "evidence" it needed, when it was expeditiously improvised?

How the FBI "established" Ray as a "student" of Fleming and Rand and how he "took" his aliases from both authors is disclosed in what it fed others. One newspaper had this on Ray's literary origins:

> Ernst Stavro Blofeld was the archvillain James Bond encountered in several books. In "Thunderball," Blofeld was the head of SPECTRE, a gang of highly organized espionage-for-hire criminals. Auric Goldfinger was the name used by the criminal mastermind in Ian Fleming's Bond adventure "Goldfinger." Auric is similar to the first name—Eric—used by the suspected slayer . . . Miss Rand's novel [not here identified] starts off with the words, "Who is John Galt" . . . . At least it appears the fugitive is a man who has done some reading and may be well-spoken. The FBI says the connection has already occurred to them. "We do some reading down here, too," a spokesman at the Washington office said.

A second contemporaneous newspaper story identifies the Rand book: "Ayn Rand's 1957 novel, 'Atlas Shrugged,' says 'John Galt' is 'the leader of a tiny minority people described as able, creative and ultra-conservative." Otherwise, it has the same account of "Blofeld" and Fleming's writing, but it paints Rand's "Galt" as the prototype of a man who could have committed this crime for reasons of deep belief.

Indeed, the FBI does "do some reading down here, too." It is so much easier than investigating!

All sorts of absurdities were fed the press, as with the nonsensical suggestion that Cuba would have given sanctuary to King's murderer, a "subtlety" intended to convey the idea his murder was a "Red plot." Toward the end of the Atlanta AP story, which seems to have had FBI origins, is a diversion consistent with this: "Eric Starvo, in German, can be translated 'Red Star.'"

Surprisingly, unlike Fearless Fosdick, they do not, apparently, read comic books "down here," in FBI headquarters. But just suppose they had read a horror comic book called "Eerie," dated June 15, 1968, appearing earlier, and undoubtedly prepared long in advance, as all comic strip continuities are. There, at the very time this massive manhunt was on and drawn in advance of it, if not of the murder itself, titled "Under the Skin," beginning on page 29, is a "nerve number," a "startling stunner of a story" to "chill the spine, curl the hair."

And its central character?

"Eric Starvos"!

Not as popular as Fleming, or as "literary" as Rand. But it requires no additions, translations, interpolations, or intuitions. It is the real thing, the *exact* name of a *single* character! And in a horror magazine.

Too bad the FBI did not read numbers as avidly as detective fiction, as an AP story widely printed in most papers a year too late disclosed while tactfully substituting the word "authorities" for "FBI":

> Within minutes after Dr. Martin Luther King was assassinated last April 4, authorities had in their hands a clue to the identity of James Earl Ray—but they failed to decipher it until after Ray was caught in London. The clue was on a transistor radio which was hand-etched with half-inch high numerals 00416. 00416 was the identification number of James Earl Ray in the Missouri State Penitentiary . . .

This story did not appear until morning papers of March 18, 1969, after the minitrial. The radio, conveniently, is one of the items omitted from Beasley's inventory of what had been so carefully deposited so it could be found. He told AP "the radio had been turned over to the Federal Bureau of Investigation along with other physical evidence that same night. The numerals, he said, were discovered through tests at the F.B.I. crime laboratory in Washington."

For Beasley, that was pretty good. It was part of the truth—most of it. All that was missing is *when* the FBI tests "discovered" this intelligence. The *New York Times* considered this part of AP's story not news fit to print:

> Ray bought the radio in the Missouri penitentiary canteen . . . . Prison practice is for the inmates to etch their prison numbers on the back of the case with an electric stylus to prevent theft or arguments over ownership . . . . Since secrecy surrounded the search for evidence which was being gathered there was no way for anyone at Missouri State Penitentiary to know that the radio contained Ray's inmate number . . . . Presumably had this information been made public, someone at Jefferson City would have connected the numbers with Ray. "This would not have been because of Ray, because he was an innocuous, run-of-the-mill criminal," said Fred Wilkinson, director of the Missouri Department of Corrections . . . . Warden Swenson said the FBI had not come to the prison until about a month after Ray's capture.

Then, too late, the FBI even took the electric stylus to prove it is the one Ray used.

Had the FBI gone, as almost anyone would have expected, to that prison as soon as it knew Ray had escaped from there—not "about a month after" his capture (whatever were they doing on their biggest manhunt in history?)—they would have learned much. The quoted characterization of Ray that is competent and authoritative but entirely opposed to the official fiction may have been one of the things they sought to avoid.

One of the consequences of the unseemly FBI secrecy is underlined by this incident. It makes one wonder whose side they were really on.

However, what escaped attention is a much simpler and very obvious thing. Like rifles, radios have serial numbers. Like rifles, they can be traced. It is apparent the FBI avoided this, too. The least unkind explanation is incompetence.

But wouldn't the manufacturer of that cheap radio (a Channel Master) have been delighted to cooperate! Not only would he have had fine publicity, but what an endorsement of that very inexpensive set, to have survived the rigors of the jailbreak and all of Ray's travels and adventures in all those many states and foreign countries.

The failures of the FBI in this case are so far beyond belief, its normally cool if corrupt public relations grew desperate, close to hysterical. Otherwise, they would never have used that James Bond–Ayn Rand childishness. Although they might well have grabbed credit from Scotland Yard and the Mounties for Ray's arrest anyway, as they traditionally take credit for what local United States police do, the feeling of frustration and desperation that their minor role in the capture apparently gave them seemed to add incentive.

How little they had to do with the capture—how little they *knew* about it—became disgracefully clear within a week, through their cover-up efforts.

Fred P. Graham is a lawyer on the Washington staff of the *New York Times.* He is a specialist in legal reporting and has written extensively about the assassinations. His writing is distinguished by a predisposition to agree with what the government says and to disagree with what its critics say, no matter how thoroughly proven the comments of the latter are. He once faulted my reporting of the evidence for being painstaking and overwhelming, new concepts of legal and literary criticism.

257

In a story appearing in the June 12, 1968 issue of his paper, four days after Ray's capture at Heathrow, Graham reported how late it was that the FBI learned that Ray had escaped to Canada "on April 8, and from there on May 6 to London." Graham then goes on to write: "Agents immediately began a search of airline records and about two days later they learned that Ray, using the alias Ramon George Sneyd, had flown from London to Lisbon May 7," but "Agents" here, although written in a manner to indicate the contrary, means agents of all kinds *except* FBI agents, for outside the United States, of course, the FBI can do no more than "cooperate" with local police.

On the airline records of Ray's flight or flights *out* of Lisbon there was no specially inspired "publicity."

Next, Graham reported what is of particular interest at this point in our narrative:

> The focus of the search shifted to Lisbon, and checks were being made there on June 8 when Ray was apprehended in London when he appeared at Heathrow Airport to catch a flight to Brussels.

This is contrary to one of the official FBI announcements (they had it both ways) and to the British version. But those faceless federal mouths who were priming Graham—he soon half-identifies them—had an explanation he phrased this way:

> Unknown to the Federal Bureau of Investigation and Scotland Yard, Ray left Lisbon on May 17—well ahead of his pursuers—and had doubled back to London, where he fell into the hands of investigators following his trail.
>
> The belief on the part of the FBI that Ray was in Lisbon led to the agency's mistaken announcement last Saturday [June 8] that he had been picked up at the London Airport when he disembarked from a Lisbon flight, on his way to Brussels.
>
> Spokesmen for the agency corrected this today. They confirmed reports from London that Ray returned there on May 17.

So, it is unofficially official that Ray was caught, not when he was entering England and going through customs for no good reason, but when he was trying to leave England, having been there for some weeks.

But there is also an official, this time officially official, Scotland Yard account, the one we have seen, that Ray had come off the Lisbon plane when they got him. If it is erroneous, the detective-fiction writers had better quit—before occupational unemployment is brought about by non-fiction, FBI and Scotland Yard style.

Graham's line—that Ray "fell into the hands of investigators following his trail"—is one of the smoother samples of post-Goebbels Madison Avenue. It is an imaginative way of saying that *no* "investigators," least of all the FBI, had the remotest idea where he was when he blundered "into the hands of" Scotland Yard, which was following nothing, just sitting still. No wonder they changed their name to "New Scotland Yard"!

What the omniscient *New York Times* and its no less omniscient reporter failed to note in all of this is the incredible irresponsibility of the FBI or its no less incredible willingness to do and say anything to grab a headline, anybody else's headline. Either the FBI was improvising while it went foraging for the publicity and credit not its own, or it was so hasty in its public-image lust it could not wait to get a report from Scotland Yard and made the "facts" up while it ran for the mimeograph machines and headlines.

Either way, we have a more faithful picture of the fabled FBI than the picture it paints of itself in its assassination investigations. When it is so willing to make public proclamations (designed to portray it as never failing and ever, with unfailing Hoover efficiency, on the job), can it ever be believed or trusted, in the papers or in court, without independent corroboration?

From all of this—the FBI's inconceivably consistent record of error, faulty reasoning, bad judgment, irresponsible conjecture, injudicious and improper manipulation of the press, abuse of the rights of the accused to a free trial, outright fabrications, blatant propaganda, and all-around botch of the investigation it had preempted—official displeasure would seem to follow. However, the contrary is the case. The FBI and Hoover were put out about their theoretical boss, Attorney General Clark. What had been simmering from shortly after the assassination boiled over in the Rowland Evans and Robert Novak column of April 22, headlined in the *Washington Post,* "FBI Very Unhappy with Ramsey Clark."

It is only the Indispensable Man, first in our history, who dares criticize his boss in public and by name. In almost any other country, such an action would precipitate a cabinet crisis and resignations, possibly of the entire government. But not in Hoover's fiefdom.

The reader may recall Wayne Whitt's April 6 story in the *Nashville Tennessean,* reporting Clark's announcement, on reaching Memphis from Washington, "to assume personal command of the search for King's killer." The story contains this additional quotation: "Real progress is being made . . . . We are getting very close . . . . I don't know if an arrest will be made in the next hour, in six hours or in 12 hours." The same day the *Banner* quoted him as saying "we are very close to making an arrest." Other papers headlined similar accounts.

Either Clark was making this up or he was led to believe it by his own police, the FBI. Neither possibility does honor to either the Attorney General or Hoover.

Hoover's "deep-seated unhappiness," according to Evans and Novak, "was aggravated by Clark's misleading public optimism about a quick solution to the Martin Luther King murder." What problem existed earlier that was "aggravated" by Clark's optimism, the columnists do not disclose.

One sentence in the story inspires wonder at the effect and intent of the FBI's own regular leaking of information to the press:

> . . . some agents complain that what legitimate information the attorney general did let drop risked drying up the killer's trail.

If Clark did drop "legitimate" information, it would follow that his source was not the FBI, for the Bureau then had nothing but what the considerate fugitive had supplied—and he certainly knew what he had thought out so carefully in advance—or what was simply untrue.

This is part of regular FBI public relations, digging a trench to which to retreat. It is unfailing. When the FBI does not succeed, somebody else is wrong. The Attorney General is as convenient a goat as anyone else.

There is also an explanation of Clark's conduct, labeled "justification":

> In Department of Justice conferences, Mr. Clark justified his contribution to the credibility gap on the grounds that optimistic talk about closing the case "would help morale"—that is, down [sic] Negro anger in the turbulent days immediately following the murder.

There is no lie, no abuse of public trust and confidence, for which the government does not have a ready "explanation," making each a dedication to the highest principle, an honorable thing.

The dispute simmered down. If it had not, Clark likely would have had to resign, for Hoover is the rock of ages in government. That would have caused a major government crisis, intolerable with the crime unsolved, the fugitive God knows where (the one place he never was is where the FBI indicated). A May 13 AP story out of Washington indicates that Clark is the one who cooled the dispute.

> Atty. Gen. Ramsey Clark said yesterday the FBI has not ruled
> out the possibility that the slayer of Dr. Martin Luther King,
> Jr., was hired, possibly by foreign agents.

Those "Reds" again, sop to Hoover and his politics and to the
reactionaries. But Clark added that he still believes King's slayer
"was a man acting alone." On whether Ray had been paid by
others:

> "I think it is perhaps not constructive to speculate on those
> things at this time," Clark said. "Our evidence indicates a man
> acting alone. This does not negate other theories."

There you have the perfect bureaucratic formula: All things to all
men, all contingencies anticipated. There was a conspiracy ("Red");
there was no conspiracy. Whatever the end, somebody in government
was right and *he* would be invoked and quoted. And as for Clark's
"belief," the one thing his "evidence" did not "indicate" is that this
was a crime by "one man acting alone." The one certainty about
this evidence is that it "indicated" exactly the opposite[5].

There are many ways to lie. One can tell the truth in a manner that
makes the statement false. One can tell a partial truth that is so
distorted it amounts to a lie. It is a simple matter for any police
agency to articulate nothing but literal truth in its reports of
investigations, yet utter nothing but falsehood, by the simple
expedient of selectivity—by not interviewing some witnesses or not
reporting part of what those interviewed do say.

In the J.F.K. assassination, Secret Service agents insisted, under
oath, that what FBI agents attributed to them they did not say.
Circumstances entirely corroborate the Secret Service. What the
FBI reported simply could not have been true. The complaint was
common before the Warren Commission, and it extended from
Secret Service agents through ordinary, unofficial people, to
respected officers of the Dallas police. (It appears there is substantiation
of the oath of one Dallas police officer, for Hoover disciplined the
agent involved in the incident.)

Hoover himself was proved an untruth-teller by two former
Attorneys General, both of whom specify he had told only part of
the truth about the King wiretapping (and not a word about the
unauthorized bugging) for the sole purpose of telling a falsehood.

The whole truth involved him personally in the campaign against the murdered King. It shows he persisted in his own vendetta until the very moment of the murder. Hoover failed to make as much as pro forma denial. Quite obviously, he could not. So, this self-delineated paragon of patriotic virtue, honorable man, and decider of who and what is and is not patriotic and truthful and of what is and what determines "internal security" and "national security," is called a liar by both of the last two Attorneys General of the preceding administration as well as by their predecessor, the also-murdered Robert Kennedy.

None of this means that Hoover is *only* a liar, that neither he nor the FBI *ever* tell the truth. They do corrupt records, as came out in the Cassius Clay court case. They do bug and tap phones without authorization while Hoover and every underling insist they do not. They commit what, in the author's view, are crimes against any concept of a free society, interfering in the rights of citizens in ways consistent with police-state concepts. But this does not mean that when there is disagreement with the FBI, that the FBI and Hoover are always the ones who speak other than the truth. My own view is that in matters concerning this case the FBI was mostly untruthful. I also believe that the FBI could and did have agents with King for reasons other than protecting him (remember the reason for the wiretapping and the bugging: "national security"), although he and his entourage may have misconstrued the presence of the agents as being there to provide protection.

One of the disputes in this case is whether or not the FBI had men at the scene of the crime, whether or not protecting King. The FBI says no.

John Herbers, writing from Washington in the *New York Times* of June 21, 1969, about the relationship between the Department of Justice, which had prosecuted civil rights cases, and the Southern Christian Leadership Conference, King's organization, said:

> The movement and its leaders were reportedly kept under constant surveillance by the F.B.I., both for their protection from white militants and because of the bureau's concern with Communist subversion. In his travels through the south, Dr. King had as many as six agents trailing him.

After the murder, when it was stated by King's friends and others that the FBI supposedly was protecting him at the time, Hoover's rejoinder was that it doesn't protect people, isn't supposed to. This is not currently true and, historically, Hoover has assigned agents to protective tasks, even though in regard to King he said he did not [6].

The fact that the FBI was supposedly protecting the murder victim came out in open court when Foreman asked for a delay in the trial. Here are excerpts from the UPI account:

> Percy Foreman, defense attorney for James Earl Ray, said today the FBI had a squad assigned to Dr. Martin Luther King, Jr. for the two years before his assassination to prevent the murder of the civil rights leader . . . .
>
> Word of the FBI squad assigned to King came during an exchange between Foreman and Robert K. Dwyer, assistant attorney general for Shelby County.
>
> Three times, Foreman said, he has asked FBI Director J. Edgar Hoover for the FBI's files on King and the $1.4-million murder investigation the FBI has made in the assassination.
>
> "It (the FBI file) says that for two years before April 4 there was a squad of FBI agents assigned to prevent the assassination of Martin Luther King," Foreman said.

The prosecution failed to deny this charge. It made no comment at all.

Foreman's comment revealed a change. Where the FBI file had been denied to former FBI-man Hanes, who insisted on a trial, and to Foreman when he made noises about a trial while industriously, behind the scenes, doing what he could to prevent one, when he got close to sewing up the deal, he did get access to the files as he later acknowledged. (This appears also to have been the case with Huie. While promoting the issue of *Look* in which all of Ray's "defenders" sold him out, Huie said he did not get what he called "the complete picture" until March. With the necessary time-lag in magazine production, it seems obvious that the article in the issue dated April 15, which appeared several weeks earlier, so much to FBI and other official liking, necessitated he have this "complete picture"—for which read "FBI files"—prior to the minitrial.)

Hoover and the FBI are the last people in the country to have had complete control over the investigation of King's murder. King had accused the FBI of failing to act on civil rights complaints. This antagonized those southern agents of whom it was, lamentably, only too true. The hatred some of them and Hoover nourished for King and his organization was the poorest-kept secret since building of the Brooklyn Bridge began.

Even if Hoover had conducted a good investigation, because of his intense animosity toward the victim, questions would have lingered to plague the present and the future. But when the unspeakably incompetent performance, like something from a heavy-handed parody of Gilbert and Sullivan, was the result, when Hoover froze out every local police force that had competent jurisdiction, when he regularly misinformed and his agents told lies in the guise of expert testimony— or were so quoted in court without recorded complaint—the inevitable result is and must be the deepest misgivings about the entire affair and the most worrisome apprehensions about motive.

Hoover in charge of the investigation of King's murder is like the fox guarding the chickenhouse or the cat protecting the canary.

The cited, if incomplete, record, which is possible despite all the best and rather effective official obstacles to it, compels the belief that Ray was the victim of an FBI frame-up. In my view, based on my earlier investigations, the FBI's experience with Oswald was conveniently fresh in its mind.

14. Look and You Will See

As we have studied the minitrial, so let us study from the April 15, 1969 issue of *Look* the statements made after the minitrial by Ray's three "defenders"—Huie, Hanes, and Foreman. Because each had assumed responsibility for a man's freedom and for seeing to it that justice was done, the crime solved, their purchased pronouncements of his guilt should be examined.

With such defenders as he had, James Earl Ray was plentifully supplied with enemies.

The financial arrangements his defenders made concerning the rights to Ray's story and the story of the case have been obscured because there are inconsistent statements about them and because, as will become understandable, no formal statement was ever made about them. The literary jackals who clean up after the "no-conspiracy" messes are well paid and are never called "scavengers." By the strange morals of the modern literary world, they are sought after, respected, and well publicized. But no decent, self-respecting barnyard would tolerate them.

One published account, attributed to Foreman, reports *Look* paid $85,000 for the writings of Ray's three horsemen in the magazine's April 15 issue. All accounts award Foreman a modest 60 per cent.

All three of the horsemen agree in this issue that Ray was the murderer. But none has or offers any proof, none suggests possession of secret proof, and none makes a credible argument. Foreman's contribution, which he could have dictated to his secretary in ten minutes, has no fact or pretense of fact in it. Huie and Hanes are foresighted enough to hedge on the question of conspiracy.

Even *Look* has a line to leeward at the very end. "This is the state of our knowledge up to this point. ["Knowledge" is hardly the right word.] But, more than a year after the murder of Dr. King, there still remain certain basic, nagging, unanswered questions, the result in good part of the deliberately evasive silence [sic] of James Earl Ray . . . ."

Here Ray's defenders were not limited by the rules of evidence, nor were they handicapped by confrontation with an adversary. All they had to do was satisfy *Look* it was getting its money's worth. In short, each in his individual piece is defending himself, his reputation, and his honor—is explaining the reasons behind his behavior and view of the crime.

This interest cannot readily be separated from the financial stake each had in Ray and the contracts struck with Ray. The original Huie arrangement gave him 40 per cent and Ray and Hanes each 30 per cent. In fairness to Huie, this could be interpreted as giving Ray 60 per cent, which he shared with Hanes. The lawyer *was* representing Ray against a charge that, in theory, could cost Ray his life and, in actuality, would determine what, if any, part of his life would be spent outside a jail.

Once Foreman came into the case, with his "Beggar's Opera" solution (in that work, the problem of witnesses is to be solved by nailing their lips shut—the opposite of Huie's standard operating practice of prying them open with money), the contracts were rewritten. From what was permitted to be known, the contract then became an indecency, with Foreman, as he said, getting 60 per cent up to $165,000, Huie getting 40 per cent, Hanes the $35,000 already paid him. If Foreman's share came to more than $165,000, the overage was to go to Ray and his family, provided there were "no embarrassing circumstances" in court.

In practical application, as we have seen, this meant that Ray had to be mute, could say nothing that could in any way jeopardize the deal, the real end product of which was that there would be Gay's "Beggar's Opera" solution: not a single witness in a real courtroom proceeding, including Ray. For his part, he wanted to be a witness from the first. Here I agree with his lawyers, that he should not have been, but for different reasons: It would be unnecessary. Ray may think he can prove his innocence, which is what his brother Jerry tells me. However, that is not the legal requirement. It is his guilt, not his innocence, that must be proved in court, "beyond reasonable doubt and to a moral certainty." In limiting the charge to murder in the first degree, in acceding to the political expediency of the era of political murders, that each assassination be ordained the work of a lone, alienated man—no conspiracy—the state guaranteed, on the basis of the available evidence and its own representation in court of what it would have offered in a real trial, that James Earl Ray would have been found not to be the murderer. For this purpose, he should not take the stand.

Any "embarrassing circumstances" in the courtroom endangered all

266

the deals and contracts. It is for this reason that the stipulation was included in the Foreman arrangement. Whatever did come out in court reduced the literary value of any contract with Ray by that much. A full trial erased all its value, real and potential, for there then would be nothing exclusive about anything Ray knew and could or would say. Once Ray's mouth opened, these contracts were valueless.

It is in this context that we examine the self-justifications of the lawyers (of whom Foreman regards himself as the superior of Clarence Darrow) and of Huie, who cannot be said to be in the tradition of Paine, Zola, or Steffens.

Between them, Hanes, Huie, and Foreman, there is not less than $300,000 involved. Before this issue of *Look,* Hanes had gotten not less than $35,000. He is said to be considering a book, which can have value, both as a book and through the collateral rights some books have. Foreman, soul of generosity that he says he is, restricted himself to a paltry $165,000. As of the month after the minitrial, Huie said he had spent $100,000 in his investigation. This is a rather ambiguous description, but it is all he gave. Over and above this, there was his arrangement with Dell for the now-published book and there was the anticipated movie rights.

It would not seem to be unfair to suggest that each of these stalwarts whom the accused was entitled to regard as his defenders was confronted with a serious conflict of interest. Each had a financial stake and his own reputation to weigh against Ray's interest. If Hanes had been paid off, he still had the prospect of future reward to consider. Without future literary value in Ray as a property, Huie is deeply in the hole. Foreman gets 60 per cent of Huie's take, if any, so it was to Foreman's interest to see that there remain a salable literary value in Ray.

The minitrial put an end to Ray as a source. He immediately filed suit to break these contracts. He regards Huie and Foreman as his enemies. His brother Jerry tells me that both he and James Earl regard Huie as a government agent who, in effect, corrupted Foreman. That I do not agree with this is immaterial. The belief meant an end to the Huie–Ray relationship. With Huie apparently limited to what he could buy elsewhere or reconstruct from his $100,000 shambles, of which less than half can stick to his fingers, he has problems financially which are even more important to his controlling stockholder, Foreman.

Foreman's urgency in copping a plea, the great pressure he put on the isolated Ray, his unsubstantial explanations, plus the tremendous financial stake he had in Ray's bowing to his will, can perhaps be explained by his great affection for man's worldly goods.

Huie's stake is greater even than Foreman's. The lawyer was able to pretend his was a legal victory, that he had saved a life, and that his spectacular record is intact. Huie, the man with the cash on the line, by his own accounting more than $100,000 of it, and what safely may be assumed to have been a great amount of time, for which he customarily receives one of the very highest rates of pay, lost some of his reputation. He was conned by a man he portrays as an inept petty thief. In effect, his career and future, as well as his bargaining position and reputation, were on the line with the case.

Hanes, whose career was built on racism and whose politics and personal beliefs are so extreme he found the FBI's rightist perspective inhibiting, the man in whose name vicious dogs were turned on human beings, was entirely undamaged by the debacle. He is the one who went through the motions of a fight for his client, made a show of a defense. This is separate from whether or not what he said is tenable; it is a fact that, as the law expects of lawyers, he honored his commitments.

Facing no opposition, what is the best case each could make against Ray or in justification of what each of his "defenders" and his official prosecutors did to and against Ray.

Hanes's piece is only slightly longer than Foreman's, about a page as opposed to about two-thirds of a page. For a man experienced in expressing himself and familiar with the facts, either piece is certainly less than an hour of dictation.

Huie's inadequacy is the longest, sets the tone by saying Ray was the murderer and, appropriately, this piece begins with *Look*'s apology for itself and for him, that when he wrote the first two articles, "Mr. Huie then believed that the evidence available to him pointed to a conspiracy." What follows is billed as the "answered questions," the result of "months of further investigation"—of which there is no single reflection in the article at all.

Huie

As Foreman is to end it all, so Huie begins it, by saying *not* what Ray told him, but, rather, what he believes or it suits him to *say* he believes of Ray, that he "regards himself as a political prisoner" who "fired the first shot in a social or racial conflict, a second Civil War . . . ."

Whether or not this is Ray's belief, that he is a political prisoner and that there will be a violent upheaval, he did not in any way tell Huie nor did he in any way hint he fired the shot in the material quoted by Huie from 20,000 words written for him by Ray (in the period Foreman became his lawyer). Throughout the article, lengthy quotations from Ray are set off and aside in italics. In not one selection is there anything remotely suggesting that Ray was the assassin. Only the opposite. This is tricky, dirty, treacherous writing—skilled and professional, but dishonest.

What Ray says of his position is no more than an unintended tribute to Foreman's powers of persuasion—or Foreman's means. Huie reports:

James Earl Ray wrote me he didn't have much to fear from any jury in Shelby County, Tenn., because, in his words, "70 percent of the voters in this county voted for either Wallace or Nixon." He added that certainly he didn't have to fear a death sentence because "no white man has ever been given a death sentence in a racial killing."

Huie added, "it was hard to convince James Ray that he was likely to get the electric chair," one reason being that "A deputy sheriff told him: 'That jury ain't gonna turn you loose until they've fined ya two dollars for shootin' a coon out of season.'"

"To counter such advice," Huie said, Ray was told by Foreman:

Boy, you pay attention to these half-assed jailers and you'll wind up in the chair . . . they'll - - - - in your ear about how you saved the white race . . . But jailers don't sit on juries . . . That jury will burn yore ass, and you better believe it, and let me make a deal if you want to go on living.

This is not quite the more delicate way Foreman put it in public. Huie could not have said more bluntly (for Huie) that Ray was thoroughly threatened and intimidated. He apparently did not realize what he was saying in this writing.

Ray's account to Huie of his rental of the room in the Memphis and purchase of the binoculars is consistent with what Mrs. Brewer, the landlady, and York Arms, where he bought the binoculars, said.

But he said that when the shot was fired at 6:01 p.m. he was in the Mustang, on Main Street; that the "other man" came running down the stairs, threw the rifle on the sidewalk, jumped into the back seat of the Mustang and covered himself with a sheet while he (Ray) drove away. Eight blocks from the murder scene, Ray said that the "other man" jumped out at a traffic light and he (Ray) drove on to Birmingham and Atlanta.

This is Huie's encapsulation of what Ray told him. No writer, with 20,000 words of notes prepared by a first-hand source, would be satisfied with this brevity about one of the most important parts of a crime, the getaway. Huie has a fine commercial eye. He got what he wanted, the merchandizable schmalz. He could and should have gone back to Ray for more details about the getaway part of the story, knowing all the while that Ray would be reluctant to say more because either he was the murderer or he was part of a conspiracy the living and unapprehended members of which would try to kill him if he opened his mouth too much. Huie reports neither his effort nor Ray's reticence.

This is the point at which Huie chooses to say Ray lied, therefore was the murderer:

> Month after month, I sought evidence to support this account, while I urged Ray to reveal more about the "other man." I found no supporting evidence I could believe. I had to conclude that, in all likelihood, the "other man" wasn't there, that Ray alone went to the rooming house and shot King.

More than this, he joined the Foreman campaign:

> I told both James and Jerry Ray last fall that, in my opinion, James Ray had no defense against the charge of murder. I told them further that if James Ray went to trial pleading not guilty, he would be in grave danger of the electric chair.

Accepting Huie's diversion for the moment, that "month after month" he sought "the other man," what is here lacking is any reflection of any genuine search, say, in New Orleans, or through Charles Stein, or any beginning point for that search. To find "a man" while knowing no more about him than what Huie indicates he knew is impossible. Huie, defining himself clearly as a buying investigator who pries mouths open with dollars, would have been a more successful investigator had he read newspapers. If he had read no more than the Lomax stories (I presume he did read them) and picked up where Lomax left off, he had a chance to find the man Ray allegedly phoned, his New Orleans "contact." This was not necessary to a "defense against the charge of murder," but it was a way of finding "the other man." A charge of murder, to make this point once again, is defended by proving it is not proven "beyond reasonable doubt and to a moral certainty."

270

Now, if as late as (or even after) "last fall"—when he told James and Jerry Ray that James had no defense against murder—if he had gotten that phone number from Charlie Stein, he could have learned what may not prove a thing but is oh, so very intriguing! Stein apparently had felt for some time that "Galt" (Ray) was an assumed personality. So, being with "Galt" (Ray) when Ray phoned—and, as we have seen, later was able to lead Lomax to the one phone (of all the thousands of public phones between California and New Orleans) from which Ray had made one of his calls to his "contact"—Stein made note of the number. When a reporter for the Los Angeles *Times*, Jerry Cohen, spoke to Stein, he got this number. When Cohen was in New Orleans for the Clay Shaw trial, for which the empaneling of the jury did not begin until January 21, 1969—almost a half-year after Huie began working on the case—Huie had long since written and *Look* had published his first two articles, If, instead of retracing Ray's steps when he escaped jail, which is literary tinsel only, Huie had spoken first to Stein and then phoned the number Stein would have given him, he might have had a hot lead. After the first two articles, he still had plenty of time.

Months after that, a lawyer and Washington friend of mine who had been unsatisfied with the official explanations of the assassinations, Bernard Fensterwald, Jr., former general counsel for the United States Senate committee that had investigated wiretapping—the man who had the courage to cross-examine Senator Robert Kennedy on his wiretapping activities when the Senators on the committee feared to— lunched with Cohen and got this story from him:

Cohen said he would save Fensterwald some time in his own inquiries for he, Cohen, had been fascinated by the Stein story, as Fensterwald was. He told Fensterwald he would eliminate one false lead for him. Cohen had gotten the number Ray called from Stein and, when in New Orleans, had phoned it. It turned out to be that of a Louisiana State Police barracks on Airline Highway. At this point in his story, Cohen laughed and said there was a funny thing about it.

Huie says Ray told him the man who first made contact with him was named "Raoul." So, when the number turned out to be an active one, Cohen asked for "Raoul." Lo and behold, there was a "Raoul" at that number. He answered the phone. His name is Raul Esquivel.

Cohen (whose experience with the police in the South is unlike that reported by his *Times* colleague, Jack Nelson, an excellent and courageous investigative reporter, and unlike that reflected in the indictments and convictions of police charged with civil-rights murders) felt that "Raoul," because he was a policeman, had to be a false lead.

He may have been right. Unfortunately, he assumed it without checking it out. In support of Cohen's belief, it does seem unusual that a Louisiana State Trooper could have been in Canada, when Ray was and contacted Ray at the bar, if that version by Ray of their meeting is true. On the other hand, with extremist penetration and recruiting inside police agencies (two of the more scandalous and exposed cases being those of a Klan cell in the Chicago police and one of Minutemen in the New York State police), it is not beyond possibility that there could be racist police in the South.

Cohen, like Huie, did not put himself in Ray's position, did not face a survival problem if he fingered any co-conspirators. Ray had, at one and the same time, to defend himself and not to give any conspirators more than the existing reason—that he lives and can always talk—to get him knocked off. He therefore had to improvise and dissemble. So, it is also not beyond possibility that he blended several of the characters, to give one example. It is also possible that he used the name "Raoul" because it is the wrong name.

What Cohen learned certainly is not proof that Raul Esquivel is part of the Ray saga. But he ignored what it is not safe to ignore, that he had gotten a good, live phone number from Charles Stein who had seen Ray make the call and had jotted the number down.

Not until July 1969 did I learn this story from Fensterwald. Immediately I wrote Cohen asking for confirmation and further information, including where to find Stein and the number. I had spent much time in Louisiana investigating local angles of the John Kennedy murder. I knew there is no State Police barracks *in New Orleans* on Airline Highway, but the highway is a long one. I had driven it as far as Baton Rouge on one trip and to near Jackson, just below the Mississippi state line on another. It continues to and through Mississippi [1].

Feeling better too late than never, I recounted to Cohen, whom I know, what Fensterwald had told me. I asked Stein's latest address and the phone number. His brief reply of July 28 is:

Harold,

   Wish I could help, but I'm afraid I can't on either count. I no longer have the phone number, and I have no idea where Charley Stein is. The world seems to have swallowed him up. Matter of fact, I looked for him myself when I was in New Orleans.

Troop A of the state police is at 12400 Airline Highway, Baton Rouge. Its phone number is 389-7581. Raul. V. Esquivel, Sr., lives at 4524 Persimmon Street, Metairie, Louisiana. His occupation is listed as policeman. The Louisiana Bureau of Investigation is also on Airline Highway, Baton Rouge. Its street number is 2863; the telephone number 357-8767.

Now, this story by no means proves that Esquivel was Ray's contact. But it does prove that for those "months and months" Huie was not, in any real sense, doing what he said he was, seeking evidence to support the story Ray had told him.

(I should add here that Fensterwald has come to play a prominent role in the Ray case: approximately a year after his meeting with Cohen, he became one of Ray's lawyers.)

Huie's statement that he could find no supporting evidence for Ray's story is likewise false. Again it was in the newspapers. The second white Mustang, right at the same spot, was seen and confirmed by dependable witnesses who also saw a man in it. This may not prove it was Ray sitting in the car, as he told Huie he was, but it does establish the possibility. It *is* "supporting evidence," Huie's own phrase. (Proper questioning of Ray for details may or may not have established he was in the car. For example, had he seen the arrival of Hurley? or Lloyd Jowers and his customer? Or the other white Mustang—a topic on which he might have feared speaking—and its location? Or other conditions then obtaining which might have been confirmed or disproved? A man sitting in a car and waiting does see some of the lives of others as they pass before him.)

So, Huie's own opening statement of why he believes Ray is the murderer, in Huie's own explanation, is invalid. At best, it establishes Huie as an undependable and incompetent investigator once he is outside the domain of his dollars.

Ray's motive in the slaying, according to Huie-turned-psychiatrist, was to "achieve status," a plagiarism from the Warren Report if there ever was one. In the phrase of the younger generation, this is weird. But much of the public has been flagellated into believing it. How can a secret bestow status? For Ray or Oswald to get his "status" from such spectacular murders, he had to be ready to give up his own life, which means he would be unable to enjoy the alleged status. Such a psychological disposition is perhaps possible. But if we are to believe these "explanations," we must also believe that, having achieved the "status" meaning more than life to him, Ray (and Oswald) promptly surrendered it by claiming innocence. An even weirder "status"!

This fiction, which requires that Ray be insane—and the available evidence does not support this requirement—is the *only* one Huie gives for Ray's acceptance of the Foreman deal. (Jerry Ray believes that the deal began with Huie, that Huie subverted Foreman for the FBI.) Huie also says Ray "feared that a guilty plea might cause him to lose status 'among the prison population,'" to which he adds, "I now believe he killed Dr. King to achieve such status," with secondary interest in his prison status. No simple matter, this status business.

At this point, Huie again begins defense of Huie, not Ray, hedging as much as he can. He says Ray's agreement to the deal "does not answer all questions" (a rather considerable understatement; it answers none). Huie acknowledges five (and only five) questions that "continue to trouble me."

An answer to any *one* would establish there had been a conspiracy.

These questions are: Was Ray assisted? Did he make the decision to kill? When was it made? Exactly why was it made? "What were the motives of Ray and his possible assistants?" and "Is there any connection, however remote, between the murders of John F. Kennedy and Dr. King?"

Huie believes, "I know partial answers to these questions." He seeks to justify his initial "error," that Ray was part of a conspiracy, with the explanation that "in August, September and October of 1968, as I sought these answers in Chicago, California, Canada and Mexico, I was handicapped by what I now regard as several misconceptions." What a confession! When he knew from Ray that Ray claimed a co-conspirator, a boss in New Orleans, and knew the same from Lomax's published investigation, completed and public before Huie began his work, naturally, it was *not* in New Orleans that Huie "sought these answers" but in Chicago, California, Canada and Mexico. There is no substitute for looking in the wrong places and not looking in the right one if one is diligently looking for "evidence"!

Nor is there anything quite like not asking the right questions. First and foremost of these is: What solid proof is there Ray was the murderer? Next is: Could he or any one person have been alone in this, from the evidence already available?

Having posed the wrong questions, Huie lists the "several misconceptions"—there are seven—that "must be dispelled" if "this tragedy is to be understood."

First is the "misconception" that Ray's "flight through Canada" and the many things part of it "could have been accomplished only with assistance." Huie believes Ray was unaided. Ray's account of his flight to Canada is of driving slowly and carefully from Memphis down to Atlanta (leading away from Canada) not to attract police attention; then, having gone that far in the wrong direction in the hottest car in the world, to have taken for no apparent reason a bus back in the direction from which he had just come, going to Cincinnati, then Detroit, thence to Toronto, via Windsor, by a combination of bus, cab, and train. According to Ray's story, he got the names he used from a search of old local papers. But this is palpably false. The alias he used most, that of Eric Starvo Galt, he could not have gotten that way. (Starvo, we shall see, is not Galt's middle name. See page 361.) Moreover, to believe that he was able to select three total strangers, all also unknown to each other though living in the same area, all men to whom he bore a resemblance and one having identical scars, is to believe in Mother Goose.

Ray's explanation to Huie, that he had to destroy all his Galt identification because he had been given a jaywalking ticket, is not as credible as having destroyed it because he had over-used it, leaving the broad and picked-up trail, the purpose of which seems to have been just that, to be discovered and followed away from the real culprit.

Having done some checking on the easy stuff Ray gave him because it could be checked—only things having nothing to do with the crime—Huie concludes "That is a remarkable account and, as far as I can determine, a true one."

The great investigator avoids the seeming nonsense that could not have been nonsense but had to be for a purpose, the strange route of the flight. The completely unnecessary and extremely hazardous trip to Atlanta in the hot white Mustang only to leave Atlanta as soon as he could by public transportation, having picked up none of his property and, strangest of all, having abandoned the car at a needlessly predetermined place so thoughtfully marked out on a map also carefully deposited so it would be found, are abnormal risks, not foolhardy bravado. All of this bizarre episode requires explanation and meaning. We do not get it from Huie (who also underestimates the FBI, unless they had an undetected stake-out on the car, for they did not follow the map to it, so far as any of the available data indicates). Ray could as readily and much more safely have taken any public transportation out of Memphis and left the car there. This, however, would not have left a trail. What he did do serves only a single purpose, that of leaving clues for investigators to follow in the wrong direction.

Huie's first "misconception" is itself a double one: First, without help, Ray could not have done what he said he did and in fact did do, which means there was a conspiracy. Second, Huie manages to miss the purposefulness of Ray's "flight" and its only possible meaning.

The rest of the flight story which Huie finds so persuasive also fails to hang together. Huie is something less than a diligent questioner. One example is Ray's return to England from Portugal (which the painstaking Huie, the only man with access to Ray, fails to date). Ray says he was going to Africa for only $130, which he had, but because there would be a week's delay in getting a visa "returned to England as I was getting short of money." Portugal is one of the less expensive places in that part of the world for a man running out of cash. England is by far the most expensive. This "explanation" involves the extra cost of air passage from Portugal to England (of which, as we have seen, British European Airways can find no record), which got Ray farther away from his destination. (Ray had additional fun with Huie, telling him "he held up a food store and got about $300," whereas the then public record says it was a bank.) And when Ray got to England, all he did was seek more expensive means of improvising what he had arranged at much lower cost before leaving Portugal.

It does not make sense, but Huie uses it to justify being flimflammed by a two-bit thief. Huie calls it a "true" story. Building up Ray more, Huie adds of this account, which a mature college freshman should have doubted instinctively, that "the man who wrote it requires no assistance to travel anywhere"—a fairly good-sized *non sequitur,* the question being not did Ray require assistance but did he have it and for what purpose. (It is also false, for Ray had the incredible assistance of the Memphis police. We shall go into this at the proper point.)

Withal, Huie requires an escape hatch—the emphasis is his:

> He *may* have had assistance in his escape after the murder, but he probably didn't need it, and I now don't believe he had it.

It is this kind of evasiveness to which a writer having been caught in error can later point and explain, "I emphasized 'may' " or "I said 'probably.' " Moreover, by taking separately *each* of the things in which Ray did have help of some kind, Huie avoids the greater improbability of one man having done *all* of them entirely without any collaborator.

"Misconception" two:

The second misconception is that Ray's finding the rooming house in Memphis from which he shot Dr. King, the precise timing, his "knowing where King would be at a certain time" and his escape from a murder scene crawling with police cars—that all this required assistance . . .

The typical Huie misrepresentation, the sneaky writer's tricks again. It is not that "*all* this required assistance" but that *if any single part of it had any kind of assistance, there was a conspiracy,* whoever pulled the trigger. Despite the minimum requirement, that there be *no* collaborator on any aspect of the murder, otherwise there *was* a conspiracy, Huie, knowing that there had to have been some, covers himself against future revelations in handling this misrepresented "misconception" by acknowledging the possibility Ray had help *three* times.

First:

The final decision to kill Dr. King, made by Ray or someone else, appears to have been reached on March 16 or 17.

Translated into less indirect language, there was an earlier decision to kill King and "someone else," Huie acknowledges, may have made it.

Second: On March 28, Huie says, "Ray or someone else decided he should buy a rifle." Now, if Ray were entirely alone, regardless of his function in the conspiracy, why should "someone else" have made the decision for him to buy "*a* rifle"? This belief, that someone else ordered Ray to get a rifle—and a *particular* rifle, is borne out not only by the exchange of weapons, which we have already discussed, but by the transparent falsehood of Ray's explanation to Huie. On his first mention of this point, Huie wrote, "Ray told me he decided to buy the rifle in Birmingham because 'I had I.D. in Alabama.'" But when he returns to it, Huie has to acknowledge the glaring untruth of Ray's "explanation." Despite all the many identifications he had, that of Galt being on his driver's license, his "I.D. in Alabama," Ray nonetheless "bought the rifle under an alias for which he had no identification."

Third: The last of the three escape hatches is the conclusion of this "misconception"—"Did Ray have help arranging this? He may have. But again, he could have done it without help."

What "arranging this" refers to is unclear. In a strictly literal sense, it refers only to the shooting. It could refer to finding the rooming house also. Yet it concludes passages beginning with Ray's activities the

277

previous month on the other side of the continent, in Los Angeles, and specifies a number of more convenient occasions on which a completely independent Ray, were he the lone, unconnected assassin, could have committed his murder much more conveniently and dramatically.

For example, Ray was in Los Angeles March 16 and 17. So was King, very publicly, making speeches. Why, then, did Ray have to drive all the way across the country to murder King, thereby getting so far away from the convenient Mexican border? From Los Angeles it is but a half-hour by frequent planes to San Diego, and another easy half-hour from there to Mexico by car or cab. Or, a couple of hours to the Mexican border directly by car.

Huie has Ray leaving Los Angeles March 18, stopping off in New Orleans. He does not say why Ray went to the trouble and risk of carrying Marie Martin's packages to her daughter. Carrying them was no necessity. It does not provide adequate explanation for his going to New Orleans at all. This was far from his direct route. And "then, on March 22 [notice the date], he was at the Flamingo Motel in Selma, Ala., when Dr. King was 40 miles away recruiting for the Poor People's March." Huie says no more and hastens from this. The honest analyst may not.

Including that detour to New Orleans and whatever time he spent there or elsewhere, it took Ray only a little over four days to drive across the continent, entirely alone, without a relief driver? This is quite a performance for a single, unassisted driver—a modern-day Barney Oldfield. And neither Huie, with his access to Ray, nor the FBI, nor any police of any jurisdiction, has any hint of where Ray spent a single night? There is no word of this anywhere, most of all not in the Beasley narrative.

New Orleans is the southernmost city of any size in Louisiana. Just going there, without stopping, took Ray far out of his way, aside from the consequent added delays from city traffic and the heavy traffic in and out of the city. Selma is considerably north of New Orleans. This unexplained route requires further delays because of the large bodies of water surrounding the city. Ray had to have some reason for this burdening of a difficult trip, some purpose for the detour and delay and extra cost.

As Huie tells it, Ray had no apparent reason for going to Selma, of all places. How remarkable the coincidence that put him there, however he got there and whether or not alone, precisely when King was in that area. Selma would have been one of the more dramatic places to have committed the murder, were Ray the lone murderer, because King was then very much in the news, regularly covered by TV in his dramatic confrontations, and that city played so large a part in his civil-rights struggles.

But, not having killed King in Los Angeles, where it was so convenient, this allegedly lone assassin, having set all sorts of speed records to drive across the entire country to do the job and just by accident, in this enormous land, finding himself where the victim-to-be was in an environment where accusing fingers would have pointed at King's known enemies—once again did not do it, even with all that TV coverage possible.

Ray just checked into the Flamingo Motel and let it go at that.

When King went to Atlanta the next day, Ray went to Birmingham, again for no apparent reason. Birmingham is a short trip from Selma. Driving from Selma to Atlanta would have been no sweat for this apparent speed demon, but he did not do it. He had rushed at breakneck speed across the continent only to loaf around, because he was all alone—no one telling him what to do. So for no purpose, he went to Birmingham and left, only to return to it for a real purpose—to buy the rifle—and the next day went to Atlanta. He could have bought his rifle, for example, while in Birmingham but did not.

Or, he could have rendezvoused with King and done the deed in Atlanta. He just didn't.

"On March 24–27," Huie explains, "Dr. King was in the New York area. Ray [in Atlanta] used these days to locate and observe Dr. King's home, his office at SCLC headquarters, and his church, Ebenezer Baptist. [A white man spending three days just "observing" in black neighborhoods naturally attracted no attention at all.] On a map found in Ray's Atlanta room by the FBI after the murder, all three of these locations were circled." And as though it somehow added meaning, "Ray's fingerprints were on the map." (It happens that in his representations of what he would have produced in a trial, Beasley said otherwise, that a Ray fingerprint had been found on only one map, that of Mexico.)

Ending his "first misconception," Huie had written:

> That is a remarkable account and, as far as I can determine, a true one. The man who wrote it requires no assistance to travel anywhere .... Ray has an amazingly retentive criminal mind. He can draw an accurate diagram of any place he has visited.

279

Why, then, particularly after he spent three days observing them, did Ray have to note on a map the places he was observing and then leave the map behind, to be found with seemingly incriminating evidence? For Huie's Ray, this served no purpose. And it clearly would have been safer and would have had real meaning—because to make the obvious point, maps are only general locations, do not bear specific addresses—to make notes from the public phone book or city directory.

There were in fact four places marked on the Atlanta map. Huie omits the fourth, the place the car was later to be abandoned. Omitting this makes it easier to pretend Ray was entirely alone.

Moreover, given that Ray spent three days finding and watching King's habitats, and for some reason not consistent with need, marked them on a map he was careful to leave behind to be found, what sense is there in these observations if he did not use this knowledge and kill King right there? Can it be, if Ray were the killer, that he just did all this for nothing? It would have been the easiest matter to shoot or bomb King when or after he returned home some night. Only Ray didn't, because he was the killer and because there was no conspiracy, no one telling him what to do. And, again, Huie just forgets to mention the meaningful marking of the place the car was to be abandoned on the same map, instead saying it bore Ray's prints, which it did not, according to the official evidence.

It would be a "misconception" to regard this as typical of the professional performance of the tough-minded Huie, the one-man FBI, the man whose mind and output keep so many other professions employed.

Having noted the escape hatches, let us push further into this second of the "misconceptions" that, according to Huie, "must be dispelled."

March 28, King was in Memphis, where he was shocked at the violence of the young black militants. In Birmingham, "Ray or someone else decided he should buy a rifle." This is the new literature's way of proving there was no conspiracy: someone else giving orders.

For the first three days of April, Ray and King were both in Atlanta. What better reason for not killing him then, with the "hit" so carefully cased in advance? Why, indeed, should the allegedly racist Ray not kill King in the state of the pickaxe-handle governor, Lester Maddox, or in Alabama, where the country's most prominent and influential racist politician, George Wallace, is supreme? These were, far and away, the two safest states for the murder. Therefore, it was not committed in either.

280

Instead, when "it was announced [on April 1] that Dr. King would return to Memphis on April 3, Ray left Atlanta late that afternoon and drove northwest and spent the night near Florence, Ala."

This is a matter of a couple of hours, an easy drive. Once again, it was aimless, for no purpose, again apparently because Ray was so entirely independent, unattached, and unassisted. Then, "the next day [April 2] ... Ray moved to a motel near Corinth, Miss.," an exhausting trip of about an hour or a little more, for the same non-reason. Unless, of course, he feared that the extra two hours or so from Corinth to Memphis, where he was to commit the dastardly deed, would have been too taxing. Ray could drive all the way from Memphis to Atlanta, about 400 miles, at night, after an active day climaxed by murder, and stay awake the following day with no difficulty, but for the trip half that length, he required half the time it had taken him to cross the entire continent.

For some inexplicable reason, then, Ray was deterred from the extra two hours from Corinth to Memphis. Huie offers no reason. His writing indicates this is all as natural as breathing. Perhaps the reason is that, having plotted and planned the murder for Atlanta and carefully recorded his plans on a map so thoughtfully left behind, he had no need to case the job in Memphis?

By a lucid statement of misinformation and wrong information, mixed with unwarranted assumptions to which he adds the inevitable *non sequitur,* Huie then tells how Ray was able to accomplish everything in Memphis without help. Here is the way he puts it together:

On Wednesday, April 3, Dr. King flew to Memphis on a plane that was delayed while it was searched for a bomb after a threat. He went to the Lorraine Hotel and Motel and was given Room 306. He had stayed at this place before, always in one of the new, more comfortable motel rooms fronting on Mulberry Street. Photographers took pictures of him, and on television that evening, the number 306 could be seen above Dr. King's head.

Ray came into Memphis on the morning of April 3. I assume he scouted the murder scene and could note that all the doorways of the Lorraine Motel rooms are visible from the back windows of the rooming house, which has its entrance at 422½ South Main Street. Ray got a haircut, purchased a shaving kit at a Rexall Drug Store, then registered as Eric S. Galt at the Rebel Motel inside the Memphis city limits.

Now, let us take this apart, not only because it is so carefully put together to seem to say and prove what it cannot and does not, but because, despite the seeming positiveness of the writing, it rests on "I assume," hardly a solid basis.

"I assume" will bear no evidentiary weight at all. It supports no logic —cannot even sustain itself. There is no basis for the assumption and every reason for discounting it, among the more obvious being the heavy police protection of the area. Had Ray "scouted the murder scene"—*assuming* he had *independent* knowledge of where King was to be—he and his out-of-state white Mustang would have been conspicuous and would have attracted police, if not black, attention. Because this part of the motel is so much lower than South Main Street and so thoroughly screened from it, in addition, he could not, *alone,* have "scouted the murder scene," even had he known exactly where King was, of which there is only contrary evidence.

Huie's concatenation begins with a bomb threat to the King plane. Is it just another of the endless "coincidences" that, of all King's extensive flying of that period, crisscrossing the country from east to west and west to east, then north and back and to Memphis and back, this is the *one time* there was a carefully announced and entirely fictitious bomb threat? Or was this done by one of the non-conspirators then in Atlanta? Remember, there is no apparent reason for *Ray* to have been in Atlanta.

In saying King had "stayed at this place before always in one of the new, more comfortable rooms" facing the flophouse, Huie could not have fabricated more skillful deception and, simultaneously, more seriously damaged his own case.

On the previous trip to Memphis, just a few days earlier, King did *not* stay there. He was at the more expensive Rivermont. He did not return to the better hostelry because of its greater expense, feeling the extra money could be spent better for other purposes. But anyone knowing King's recent habits in Memphis, would *not* have expected him to go to the Lorraine at all, but to the Rivermont. *But* how could Ray *alone* have known not only that King would go to the Lorraine but also that his room would be on the side toward the flophouse? (And at first, it wasn't. King had been shifted to the room in which he was registered when he was killed, having earlier been assigned a different room.) Patently, he could not have, unless someone told him, someone who had conducted the extensive investigation and made the extensive preparations that, with due deference to Huie's estimate of Ray's not inconsiderable capabilities, exceeded even this exaggerated representation of them. Or, someone on the inside. In short, Huie here argues against himself. He really says Ray had to be the creature of a conspiracy.

In the line "Photographers took pictures of him, and on television that evening, the number 306 could be seen above Dr. King's head," Huie resorts to a shabby novelist's device. He implies and leads the hasty reader to believe Ray saw the number of the room, having mysteriously already learned the name and location of the motel, and knew the unique layout—where each room was—because it was on TV. Aside from the fact that its appearance on TV does not mean Ray saw it or, having seen it, read the very small numbers above the door, if he noted them, there is a major defect in this contrivance and unlabeled added assumption: Where was Ray going to see it on TV that "evening"?

He had abandoned his own TV in Garner's rooming house in Atlanta. If it is not overly generous to assume Ray's motel room had television, there is no indication that he was in it in time to look at the news or, if he was there and used the television, that he looked at that particular newscast.

That is not the only problem. Huie "assumed" Ray "scouted the murder scene" when "Ray came into Memphis on the morning of April 3," which is well before King checked into any motel, not yet having left Atlanta. This is an impossibility.

But even if we permit Huie, the professional, this carelessness (what writer is not sometimes careless?), the rest of his presentation is still no help to him.

After "scouting" the unselected "scene," Ray, according to Huie, spent his time getting a haircut (but no barber has surfaced or been produced to say he did it), and "purchased a shaving kit at a Rexall Drug Store, then registered as Eric S. Galt at the Rebel Motel inside the Memphis city limits."

With Huie's technique calling for specific details, which makes for persuasive writing, and all the needless, unrelated minutiae with which his Ray writing is studded, is it an oversight that he says merely "a Rexall Drug Store"? Which was known. It was in the papers and in the minitrial "evidence" proffer. But there Beasley said it was at White Haven, Tennessee.

That is *not* inside the Memphis city limits. Rather, it is roughly on the Tennessee-Mississippi state boundary. Nor is it on the road Ray, from Huie's account, had used to get to Memphis (it runs to the east), but is on a road that is to the south in an area with which, presumably, Ray had no familiarity. If one wonders why the much-traveled Ray, several days after leaving on this particular trip, needed a shaving kit, is it not also to wonder why, with all the drugstores he passed on the road and in Memphis—and with him "scouting" too—he did not get one then, why he had to make this extra trip into strange territory, not near where he had to be, just to get this shaving kit? Of all his toilet articles, did he forget only his shaving kit at his previous stop?

So Huie's "second misconception"—

> Ray's finding the rooming house in Memphis . . . the precise timing, his "knowing where King would be at a certain time" and his escape from the murder scene crawling with police and police cars—that all this required assistance, that "one man just wasn't capable of doing all this by hisself (sic), he just had to have someone to help him"

is as apocryphal as his unattributed "hisself" and other quotes. Rather do all these circumstances prove the opposite, that one man could not and did not do all these things single-handedly, could not have had the required knowledge *alone*. They prove that the entire "explanation" of the murder in Memphis, if one maintains that it was Ray's idea and execution, *entirely* his, is illogical.

To this, we can add a point already made when examining Beasley's narrative. All that stuff about Ray getting a special room in the rooming house because he could see the motel from it is entirely irrelevant, because it is the official claim that he did not fire from that room anyway.

That part of the "misconception" dealing with the unassisted escape we just have to assume, on the basis of Huie's by-now-established integrity, dependability, and omniscience, for he offers not a word on it.

"The third misconception," Huie writes, is that the fatal rifle shot could have been fired only by a practiced, experienced, expert marksman.

At this point, Newcastle has no need for more coals. That has been more than adequately handled above, especially in our consideration of what Beasley said Frazier would have testified to.

But there is one phrase from the third "misconception" worth noting:

> . . . Ray killed him with one Soft Point bullet which mushroomed on contact.

What is implied is that the bullet came from Ray's rifle. But Huie knows there is no ballistics tie between the rifle and the remnant of the bullet. And on this, he is silent, the guilty silence of the guilty writer. Unless, of course, the remnant of the bullet was another "magic mushroom."

The fourth misconception is that Ray is stupid and inept.

This one is a straw "misconception," made for denial, which can be accepted. Had it been differently phrased (raising questions about Ray's initiative or capacity to plan or execute such a venture), a valid point might have been made. So, Huie phrases it this way.

The fifth misconception is that Ray could not have supported himself and his travels between April 23, 1967 [when Ray escaped from jail] and June 8, 1968 [when he was captured in England], and therefore must have had financial assistance.

Huie's conclusion on this briefly treated and fundamental "misconception" is not persuasive:

I can't prove that no one gave him money to kill Dr. King but I can prove that he could have gotten it other ways.

With this assurance, he does *not* prove it. He accounts for less than half of the $12,000 he admits Ray spent in that year, basing all of his account on Ray's word (which is all the reason he needs to disbelieve him in cases when Ray's word does not suit him). In Huie's bookkeeping, Ray got $1,450 by robbing a Montreal whorehouse (later changed to a food store), $750 for two trips across the Canadian border with narcotics, and $3,000 from "Raoul" with which to buy the Mustang and camera equipment. That is the extent of Huie's financing of Ray's travels all around the United States, Canada, Mexico, England, Portugal, and almost Brussels (paid for) enroute to Africa. There were not fewer than two transcontinental trips, two apiece to Mexico, Canada, and England, a short vacation at an expensive Canadian resort, a few girls and a little drinking, plus the bartending and dancing lessons, things like these. For this, $12,000 is not a high estimate. It was made by those who could not account for any Ray income, whose interest was in keeping his expenses low so that deficiencies in their accounting would seem smaller. It is probable Ray spent well over $12,000. No one knows how much he spent or how and where he got it[2].

Huie recalls the mysterious Raoul, of whom Ray had told him, saying that, aside from the food-store/whorehouse heist, all Ray's money came from "Raoul." He reports that Ray said he met Raoul in Canada,

Birmingham, New Orleans, and Laredo, Mexico. But, he claims, there is no reason to believe that Ray, "Raoul or anyone else ever got any money for the last big job he was supposed to pull," the King murder. His explanation is that "there were probably several Raouls, accomplices of Ray in hold-ups and other money crimes. Ray bought a large quantity of marijuana in Mexico and disposed of it in some fashion. . . . There were a number of unsolved robberies of banks, loan companies and supermarkets in the areas through which Ray moved . . . ."

With no less perception and correctness, exactly the same thing can be said of every other part of the world. There were unsolved crimes without limit. But Ray was never any good at pulling off his petty thieveries and he regularly got caught. Suddenly, he became an accomplished, professional, undetected thief, just to suit Huie and the government's needs? The fairy spirit of thieves touched him with her magic wand and made a pro of him? And thenceforth, he always got away with his robberies—leaving no clues—for the first time in his life? This of the man who could not remember to bring his razor when he checked out of a motel or needlessly blundered into British customs when there was no need for it, the man avoiding all police of all kind? The man who papered Memphis with fingerprints but left not a single one at any of these alleged robberies?

Other similar stories about Ray are common. The FBI made up a few for the same reason. Not one was proved. In not a single one of those many robberies with which Ray allegedly supported himself, his travels, and his easy life, has anyone identified a picture of him, said he is the man who pulled the job.

Some of the explanations are even less credible than Huie's. One is his alleged prison narcotics business. For this he is said to have imported the hard stuff into Missouri State Prison, maintained a stock without detection, sold it and gotten the money out, all without anyone knowing about it and without anyone later squealing. This is contrary to all official estimates of all the prison authorities who knew and studied him, but that did not discourage official retailing of the yarn, including by Memphis officials. The dope story involves a serious crime that could be traced. It involves criminal charges officials would be anxious to prosecute. There is not a scintilla of evidence behind it. It is a convenient fabrication to explain what cannot be and has not been, how Ray got all the money he had and used. Huie, with access to Ray, fares no better. He is merely less-heavy-handed, eschewing such yarns as that of Ray's alleged prison dope racket.

However, in Huie's mind this purported belief in Ray as a superb, successful criminal grew and grew to where he could say, as he did in Washington April 18, 1969, that Ray "had more mileage on him than Bonnie and Clyde as a criminal"!

After the minitrial, Chief Prosecutor Canale told reporters, as Jack Nelson and Nicholas Chriss wrote in the Los Angeles *Times* the next day, that "Ray . . . apparently lived off funds saved while in prison and obtained through robberies and smuggling."

"Apparently" is not evidence. It is not introducible in court, not acceptable. If there were a shred of evidence of any of this, that evidence could have been produced in court, and I think there is little doubt it would have been, if only to help allay the suspicions everyone expected to result from this frustration of the judicial process and of justice.

Martin Waldron reported some of the same stuff in his long interview with Canale after the conclusion of the case. He wrote that Canale "said that the state had evidence that Ray had smuggled narcotics into the United States from Canada, and jewelry either into or from Mexico," a rather indefinite reflection of "evidence."

Mr. Canale said there was no reason to assume that the money Ray spent so freely during the 14 months he was free had come from co-conspirators.

What Ray spent is a considerable sum for which to account. It *had* to come from *somewhere*. The prosecution, when it had the chance and obligation, failed to show or even to hint at *any* source; failed, even when it had a deal that silenced opposition, to offer any rational explanation or proof of any other source of Ray's funds *other* than a conspiracy.

Ray, he said, had sent a large sum of money out of the Missouri prison while he was an inmate there. There was a report that Ray had sold drugs while he was an inmate in the prison.

Canale thus claimed to have proof of other crimes, yet he did not offer it, in the face of urgent need for exactly this proof. To say there "was a report that Ray had sold drugs" is utter irresponsibility. The list of unfounded reports and those known to be wrong would make a fat book. Canale's out-of-court "explanation" is contrary to what the warden and others at that prison said and adhered to, unpopular as their views were. A fair, one-word contraction of their comment is "impossible."

As Waldron himself wrote with 24 hours of afterthought, ". . . speculation was fed by many questions either unanswered or answered only by further speculation." His only additions to the inadequacies of the press conference were all hedged, "The Memphis prosecutor said that Ray may have made some money . . ."; "Mr. Canale said that from such activities as smuggling, Ray could have made enough money . . ."; "He said he thought that Ray may have been trailing the civil rights leader"; "Mr. Canale offered two suggestions about Ray's finances. . . ." He offered even this third-hand vacuity: "a source said that the state believed that Ray sold drugs smuggled into the prison to other convicts and that the money Ray made in this fashion was smuggled from the prison and left with a relative or friend for safekeeping."

This rubbish is demeaning to public authority. Its very cheap character explains why Huie would not feed it to a responsible editor. At the same time, it is negative proof of Huie's error, for it establishes neither Memphis nor federal officials could muster the flimsiest grounds for suspicion of what they and Huie alleged.

We still do not know how Ray went on a year-long transcontinental-international vacation, by his own admissions including sojourns in Mexican and Canadian resort areas, spending money as though there could be no end to it and, entirely out of keeping for him, wasting it. It has not been and cannot be explained without accomplices. Huie could not avoid the question, so he befuddles it. He does not answer it. Accomplices mean conspiracy.

The sixth "misconception" can be stated simply (but Huie doesn't). It is that Ray wasn't a racist, had no motive. Typically obfuscating, Huie links Ray "is not a 'racist' or 'nigger-lover' " with "having been in prison so much of his life," which is no more related to his racial beliefs or prejudices than is his diet.

Canale, in his press conference, as reported in the Los Angeles *Times* by Nelson and Chriss, also said that "racial hatred was the motive."

Most of those who knew him say Ray showed no signs of special feelings against Negroes. Huie, without quoting, says that he, Huie, had "bitter anti-Negro actions or remarks by Ray" reported to him. While Ray "never evidenced this to Mr. Hanes" and, it is obvious, to Huie, still, selection of each to represent him in different ways can be taken as an indication that Ray was more anti-Negro than the average white. Hanes had been the racist mayor of Birmingham. His chief of police, Eugene "Bull" Connor, had a long and public record of racism (recorded already in the 1930s by the United States Senate committee for which I worked). Hanes accepted Connor's use of vicious dogs against black people. Hanes represented accused Klan racists charged with racial murders. Huie, for his part, was known to pay racists for their information.

Ray accepted the virulent racist, J. B. Stoner, to represent him after firing Foreman. Even though Stoner did not represent Ray, he is the only person of whom I know, other than counsel and his brothers, to see Ray in jail. (He visited Ray in September 1968, when Hanes, who was extremely displeased by the visit, still was representing Ray.) The visit required Ray's assent.

There is not doubt that Ray was part of the murder conspiracy—the evidence shows this—whether or not he pulled the trigger. There may be doubt that he knew exactly what was going to happen, but the doubt is not strong and I do not share it. This can be taken as powerful confirmation Ray was not unwilling to be part of a racist murder.

There are more cogent, more persuasive ways of suggesting Ray holds racial prejudices than Huie uses. They were known to him. This makes one wonder why he did not use them. One possible explanation is that he chose to confuse in order to divert the reader from the fact that precisely the same thing could be said about an unfortunately large number of white Americans not one of whom was in any way involved in the crime. To say that Ray is a racist is no more proof of his role as lone murderer than to say that Lester Maddox or George Wallace—or Ray's brother Jerry, who makes no effort to hide his very strong dislike of blacks and Jews—is a "nigger-hater."

So, while it may be a "misconception" to believe Ray is without racial prejudice or hatred, that does not identify him as the murderer and no more makes him a candidate than it does millions of others.

Much the same is true of the seventh "misconception," diminished to a "possible misconception" only: "that Ray is not a 'killer' and is therefore probably incapable of having killed Dr. King." Again the extraneous is woven in, for the last part of this carefully chosen formulation *is* extraneous. The world is full of those evaluated as "not a 'killer'" who *did* kill, as it abounds with those evaluated as potential killers who did not.

To seem to prove his point, Huie interviewed "the superintendent of the hospital at Fulton" (the Missouri state jail). He "is Dr. J. B. Peterson. I asked him if James Earl Ray is capable of planned killing for money." (What happened to the murder for "principle," the "racist" murder?)

The quoted part of Peterson's response—with my emphasis—is, "Certainly he is. Any man who commits armed robbery *indicates* that he *may* be *willing* to kill for gain *if necessary.*"

I have added the emphasis to underscore the scientific reservations with which the doctor felt he had to hedge his answer, the final and controlling reservation being "if necessary." In context, this seems to mean if the murder is part of the robbery. So qualified an answer is meaningless.

When Huie asked, "Is Ray capable of killing in the hope of winning distinction," the strongest agreement elicited is "perhaps."

What Huie does not trouble his readers or weaken his argument with is the fact that Dr. Peterson, in charge of the hospital in 1968, is *not* the psychiatrist who earlier studied Ray. As we have seen, that psychiatrist was Dr. Henry V. Guhlman, and his was an entirely different diagnosis and scientific appraisal. We have also seen that those in this prison who came in closest contact with Ray, knew him well, the professionals as well as the inmates, to a man considered him incapable of the crime. That the FBI avoided all these people in their "investigation," exactly what Huie does in his writing, bears repeating. The FBI did not ignore evidence supporting its frame-up.

Remember the words of the warden? "I was floored . . . . He's innocuous. Penny ante."

Huie's camouflage of the doctor who ran the hospital at the time Huie interviewed him as the psychiatrist who studied Ray (at Ray's request) is not consistent with honesty of purpose or writing. On top of this, Huie misrepresents the carefully hedged statement he got from the non-expert to pretend the "misconception" was "dispelled" by it. Huie's deliberate avoidance of the many people, experts and inmates, who knew Ray well and had contrary opinions, is unfortunately typical of his entire writing.

To this it should be added that, in his history of crimes, although Ray was armed, he never once fired a shot, never physically hurt anyone. His criminal record is all one way, entirely non-violent. Huie edits out what is inconsistent with his own prejudice: In 40 years, Ray never hurt anyone, never used a pistol on any of his victims—failed to when he was apprehended and, if Huie is right, faced electrocution as a consequence. The omission of such information is sheer dishonesty.

Huie here nears the end of his writing.

290

"When the misconceptions have been dispelled at least partially," he says, thus moderating his dose after injecting the poison, "these questions still remain." He has two, neither of which is "Did Ray really kill King?" or "Is there the legally-required proof that Ray is the murderer?" The only questions, he feels, that the foregoing permits to "remain" are " Was there a conspiracy?" and "What was Ray's real motivation? Why did he want to kill Dr. King?"

Huie's answer to the first question is no answer at all. It leaves the question still a question but adds the foresighted writer's reservations carefully hidden but retrievable for the recapture of reputation:

> Well, there are large conspiracies and little conspiracies. In large conspiracies, rich and/or powerful men are involved. Small conspiracies involve only little men.

This definition will not be found in any code of law. Conspiracy is merely a combination to do wrong. It requires but two people, large or small being immaterial. Huie says Ray "insinuated" there was a conspiracy. This is one way, the Huie way, of saying Ray said *there absolutely was a conspiracy,* for he did say this to Huie as in court. Huie only "found no confirmation." Where he looked and what he "found" are matters that he will have to live with, as is where he didn't look, what he refused to find.

Then he works in still another hedge for his reputation, which, save for the manner in which he selects the words to make them seem to say otherwise, is identical to saying he believes there was a conspiracy:

> I believe that one or two men other than James Earl Ray may have had foreknowledge of this murder, and that makes it a little conspiracy.

Consistently, he is wrong. Foreknowledge is a different crime, accessory before the fact, not conspiracy. The "one or two men" had to be part of the plot to be conspirators, not just aware of it.

So, after all those well-paid-for words seeming to say the opposite, it is Huie's considered opinion that there had been a conspiracy and, more, there was the added crime of accessory.

His answer to the only other question he says is left—Ray's motivation—is another plagiarism from the Warren Report, which we have already discussed, that to Ray this was his day of glory and he wanted it to be known that he was the murderer.

"A clue to the ultimate answer, I think, lies in the circumstances," which are Ray's purchase of a radio in jail, his taking it with him, and his abandonment of it and the other junk at the scene of the crime.

In short, he purposefully left his calling card, telling the FBI that JAMES EARL RAY WAS HERE. That was his glory. He wanted the FBI and all of us to know that James Earl Ray, that poor, contemptible little man with a price of $50 on his head [from the jailbreak] had killed one of the great Americans of this century.

Huie!

Dime novelist as psychiatrist.

But, once this sort of thing was made an acceptable line of reasoning by the federal government and was accepted as a substitute for proof and evidence, it became the official as well as the unofficial explanation of and solution to all political murders, beginning with that of the President.

It is as empty of sense as it is of fact. In the absence of any dependable psychiatric appraisal that gives this as the opinion of competent practitioners of that discipline which remains so much an art rather than a science, it cannot have any acceptance.

Can it be because "he purposefully left his calling card, telling the FBI that JAMES EARL RAY WAS HERE," because "he wanted the FBI and all of us to know that James Earl Ray" was the murderer, because "that was his glory"—that Ray denied himself this glorification, denied Huie's and all other accounts of him as murderer, while insisting there was a conspiracy?

Then this would be a new "glory," indeed. It exactly parallels the Oswald case and is no less fraudulent.

If one can almost weep over Huie's over-written description of Ray's heartless abandonment of "his companion in loneliness," the unoffending Channel Master six-transistor radio purchased in prison, one can also reason that this act is more the deliberate planting of false clues than callousness. The best evidence Huie has to offer as motive for the murder, which it is not, is excellent proof of both a conspiracy and of Ray's part in it, that of decoy.

This is Huie's last word, his defense of his reputation, his ultimate dedication to "one of the great Americans of this century," Martin Luther King, who wrote the foreword to his money-making "Three Lives for Mississippi," thus adding to its profit potential.

Hanes also was representing Hanes when he accepted *Look's* money and for it announced the guilt of the man he was well-paid to defend. Like Huie's, his writing is to defend what he did and did not do. Like all lawyers who represent themselves (Foreman is no exception), he ignored the maxim of his calling, that he who has himself for a client has a fool for a client.

Hanes's opening is as *Look* represents in the subheading, "On balance, I feel Ray was helped." But he is explicit in saying Ray "killed Dr. King." The reason? " . . . because he was directed to do it." By whom he does not say or suggest.

As for motive: Unlike Huie, examining the same evidence and more in addition (for he and his son "talked with Ray for more than one hundred hours"), Hanes "simply can't think of any motive that satisfied me in this case." On the subject of race and hatred (where it is advisable to recall Hanes's own record), he writes: "Probing for motivations, I often attempted to discuss race or politics with him. He is well informed, but his views are neither extreme nor bitterly held. I never heard him express or saw him display resentment, hatred or malice toward anyone."

Many of the nine numbered reasons he offers for believing that Ray was "helped" are proof Ray did not do the shooting. If they add little to what is known, they are nonetheless worth repeating, for they come from the lawyer who simultaneously says the man he defended is the murderer.

His son and partner "spent a week studying the rooming houses, the businesses and the people in the area of the murder." Even with advance, close personal examination, an advantage that Ray did not have,

> we can't believe that Ray could have known he would have an unobstructed line of fire at Dr. King from the room he rented, or from the bathroom the state claims the shot was fired from . . . we believe that someone must have told him which house to enter and which room to rent.

With this, and substantiated by other witnesses ignored by the prosecution, some of whose observations appear earlier in this book, he presents evidence that Ray was innocent, not that he fired the shot:

> Twenty feet below the bathroom window . . . there is a vacant lot
> . . . covered with bushes 12 to 15 feet high. Dr. King's chauffeur,
> Solomon Jones, told reporters a few minutes after the shooting
> that "just after the shot was fired, a man with a sheet over his
> head ran out of the bushes heading south." Another witness,
> "Cornbread" Carter, said that he saw "the man" fire the shot
> from the bushes and then "take off."

This is further supported:

> From a concealed position in a firehouse . . . police were
> watching the area of Dr. King's room, trying to protect him from
> what they thought was the most serious threat to him: possible
> attack by Negro militants. A Negro policeman who could recognize
> the most dangerous of these militants was at a peephole and actually
> saw Dr. King fall. Both firemen and policemen . . . heard the shot,
> and they all thought it came from the bushes, not from any
> window 20 feet above. . . .

What better reason for all of this to have been denied the jury and
judge, the press, and the record of history by the prosecution and the
federal government? Here is the possibility of evidence that could
prove Ray did not commit the crime. What more compelling reason
for its exclusion from the Beasley narrative which serves as evidence—or
for the elimination of a trial in which it and more would have come
out? Especially would this have been persuasive once all the
prosecution case fell apart, as was inevitable, before any kind of
competent cross-examination.

To this information, Hanes adds what we have already proven and
what he must have known personally, despite the contrary courtroom
presentation: "no ballistics expert could say positively that the bullet
was fired from the Remington rifle . . . ." (But, as we shall see, this
is not all that Hanes was to say on this matter.)

As we did, Hanes quotes Stephens' common-law wife as saying "that
Charlie was drunk and saw nothing" and "that she saw the man run
out of the bathroom, and he wore an Army jacket and was much
shorter and lighter than Ray, weighing no more than 125 pounds."

When this man fled the rooming house, "Ray's Mustang was parked
to his *right.* Yet, according to witnesses in the ground-floor Canipe
Amusement Co., . . . the man with the gun turned left, or south, *away*

from the Mustang, dropped the rifle, and *continued walking south.*"
(This is opposite the official version of where the "Ray" Mustang
allegedly was parked. The official account has it to the left, just
past Canipe's.)

Of the two white Mustangs, "The one that did not belong to Ray
was said to have a 'whiplash' antenna, indicating radio-broadcast
equipment," which is, as Hanes says, suggestive of the fake broadcasts
known to have been made, and which we will soon consider.

If these are unusual reasons for a lawyer to say his client was
the murderer, since they are proof that he was not and could not
have been, they are no less strange in their context than Hanes's
comments when he was engaged in public appearances promoting
Look, to which we shall turn shortly.

In the article, his brief descriptions of Ray should be trustworthy,
but he extracts no meaning from them and fails to see the most
obvious. His and his son's long hours with Ray were "a baffling
experience . . . never gave us his confidence on critical issues."
When Hanes began to ask basic questions, "he changed his attitude
and demeanor"—from courteous and respectful. ("On a human-to-
human basis we seemed to be close.") "He insisted that his accomplice,
Raoul, actually fired the fatal shot, but when I questioned him about
Raoul, he became tense and devious . . . I never met a man quite so
alone, quite so certain that he was his only keeper."

Comments from Jerry, whether or not they are correct, tend
to corroborate the fact of Ray's aloofness:

> James never did trust his two previous attorneys, as he knew
> they represented Huie instead of him, and that is the reason he
> wouldn't furnish what he believed they would turn over to Huie.

Jerry also told me James does not trust people, "that's why he
wouldn't tell Foreman or Hanes how he was going to prove his
innocence when he took the stand."

What is important is the reason for the lack of trust, which Hanes
ignores. Why did James Earl Ray change in "attitude and demeanor,"
baffle his experienced attorney, former FBI- and CIA-man, seem to
withdraw and become "so alone"?

There may be psychological reasons. Ray may be that kind of man,
with an illness. But a more likely possibility, one not anywhere
suggested and one requiring consideration, is fear—not of his lawyer
or of Huie but of still-living conspirators and the real murderer.

Ray is, as Judge Battle said, a "pretty good jail-house lawyer." He knows nothing he told his lawyer could ever be disclosed by the lawyer, hence could not be used against him in any criminal proceeding. If Hanes was to defend him, Hanes had to know what happened, to the degree Ray could tell him. Otherwise, there was great hazard he would be confounded in court, to Ray's disadvantage. If Ray confessed being the murderer, Hanes's lips were permanently sealed. (Here the reader might recall again that Huie-line officially adopted, that Ray wanted "the FBI and all of us" to know of his "glory," that "he had killed one of the great Americans.")

Unless Ray is irrational, the only rational explanation of his behavior with the lawyer presumably of his own choice is not fear of his lawyer but fear of the murderer he could identify.

With what Hanes cites that exonerates Ray (all the while proclaiming his guilt), with his high opinion of the FBI and its investigation (". . . for which I once worked as an agent, has done its usual masterful job"), we can, perhaps, understand Hanes's failure to make any effort to interpret his observations. It would be difficult to make any while insisting "Ray killed Dr. King."

Now, lacking in his *Look* writing is all that earlier stuff about an international "Red plot." Could it be that Hanes, too, thinks anything, any lie a lawyer tells in defense of his client, is justified under the adversary system?

But Hanes did not forget what he omits from *Look*. He was in New York April 1 to help sell the magazine. The news not fit to print or use in defense of the accused was fit to sell magazines.

The *New York Times* syndicated for use April 3 what is not in its own April 2 account, that Hanes "renewed his accusation that King's murder 'probably resulted from a "black power" conspiracy.' " Thus, we have a Ray who, according to Huie, is a racist and, according to Hanes, is conspiring with "black power," a new kind of Jekyll–Hyde. (Hanes's formulation suggests what Hanes made a successful career of, racism.) Further, "Ray was told to come to Alabama. He proceeded to Selma." Hanes describes Selma not as the locale of some of King's bitterest and most dangerous struggles, then at their zenith, but as "the birthplace of the Black Panther movement" (it wasn't). Hanes was loaded with such comments. He unloaded: "Hanes said that Ray's 'contact' might have been advised by one of King's assistants. 'There was a Judas in Martin Luther King's camp,' Hanes said."

Without visible or publicized embarrassment or journalistic questioning, Hanes links this presumably leftist "Black Panther" activity with that of the right, "Cuban exiles." Both *Times* stories (written by Martin Waldron), the April 2 story and the syndicated version of April 3, have the same lead. Both quote Hanes as saying

Ray went to Memphis last April 3 to try to sell rifles to Cuban exiles and that he never knew in advance that the Rev. Dr. Martin Luther King, Jr., was to be murdered. When Ray found out that Dr. King had been shot, he panicked and fled from Memphis.

Hanes's publicity-version directly opposes the paid-for version he was publicizing. He says "that Ray and a 'contact' had taken the rifle to Memphis to show to Cubans who were interested" but the contact abandoned the rifle, which had Ray's fingerprints on it, on the street, so that Ray would become a 'fall guy' in the murder" [3].

This we cannot fault *Look* for declining, if it did [4].

The *Times* also says

Mr. Hanes, a former agent of the Federal Bureau of Investigation, said that he had examined the bullet recovered from Dr. King's body and that the bullet had enough markings on it to be traced to the murder weapon.

"A six-year-old kid could have traced it," he said.

It is difficult to believe this was said by the same ex-agent, ex-mayor, and prominent lawyer who was publicizing the writing in which he said "no ballistics expert could say positively that the bullet was fired from the Remington rifle purchased by Ray."

All of which focuses attention on another and very commercial aspect of the entire *Look* production. Although the magazine is dated April 15, it was quoted directly in news stories dated April 1, indicating the usual, that it was out two weeks or so before publication date. But April 1 is only slightly more than two weeks after the minitrial, and magazines have a long lead time, especially those, like *Look*, printing in color. It is apparent this stuff was written before the minitrial and in anticipation of it.

Was *Look* once again caught with its naked Manchester showing? It paid—and also made—a fortune for and from the sickening, cloying, updated Camelot that William Manchester wrote instead of the unofficial official account of the President's murder. His book is unlike anything in literary history, presenting nothing as fact about the crime that is fact, from the sources quoted or the official records. The book faced publishing difficulties when the Kennedys filed suit against *Look* and the Harper publishing house. The Kennedy suit could have prevented the appearance of an issue of *Look* in which a fortune in advertising and the entire cost of printing were tied up. While this suit, ultimately, predictably, helped sell *Look*s and books, it is not likely Ray's last-minute attempt to withdraw from the deal— which attempt had sent Foreman scurrying back to re-persuade Ray— did less than ulcerate the *Look* offices. Had this April 15 issue appeared after Ray had withdrawn from the deal, it would have been an unparalledled editorial and legal disaster. There was no time to change the contents. It was too late, past the point of no return.

The virtual certainty that all of this was written, edited, in type, laid out, and in the magazine before the minitrial involves Foreman, then in charge of the case, the 60-percenter entirely unconcerned about such crass considerations as money, the man who cared only about "saving" Ray's life. Without Foreman's assent, this could not have been considered—and was not. He is part of it, anyway, having contributed, appropriately, a mini-article. The propriety of all of this, or the lack of it, should interest the bar associations and the courts, but undoubtedly will not, for neither are troubled so long as transgressions are always in support of the line of the executive branch, from which, theoretically, both are separate.

Before the minitrial took place, it was sold to *Look*. Each of Ray's first two lawyers is financially involved. Foreman got 60 per cent for a few minutes' work. Huie, empowered to sit on most of the 20,000 words he got from Ray, did most of the dirty work. Without prior and entirely improper advance agreement from the "impartial" judge (whose death was reported in the same papers reporting the *Look* issue), these men would not have dared. This is the judge whose defense of the deal expressed itself in terms of fear that without it Ray might have been acquitted.

Judas was a piker. And justice is blind under the ministrations of such mercenaries.

Foreman

Foreman, in his breezy manner, begins his *Look* piece saying "when a man accused of murder sends for Percy Foreman, I show him the courtesy of assuming he is guilty . . . else why should he divide his worldly goods, or hope of same, with me?"

Man's hope and his hope of "worldly goods," both are shared with defense counsel, always. Foreman's contract was for a share of Ray's "hoped"-for worldly goods. As we have seen, *with* a trial, there was nothing from which Foreman could extract it.

Next he says:

> When, last November, the brothers of James Earl Ray sought me out and handed me a letter from him, beseeching me to represent him, I didn't fly to Shelby County Jail in Memphis and run a gamut of guards to ask, "Jim, did you do it?"

Then: "I assumed Ray had sent for me not to spring him, but to try to save his life."

It just happens that precisely the day this was drafted, I had exactly an opposite version from Jerry Ray, to which I shall return.

"Why did Ray kill Dr. Martin Luther King, Jr.?" is the question Foreman says he usually ignores. Here he italicizes it. He makes an exception to answer. Ray killed for:

> credit. Top billing. Headlines. Front-page pictures. A by-line. Self-realization. A short-cut to fame. To exercise the ego. To them [by which he means Oswald, Ray, and Sirhan, "who are not assassins, but killers"—Foreman defines assassin as a secret killer for hire and says the murders committed by these men "were not assassinations, they were killings"], notoriety and fame are synonymous . . . .

Foreman should, with his record, be an expert in such matters. What one would like here, however, is an acceptable medical appraisal that the man whose prolonged travail he further prolonged (for 60 per cent) is, in fact, sick and sick this way, as certain sick people undoubtedly are. Sixty per cent and the needs of defense apparently inspired no such psychiatric evaluation. In court rather than in *Look,* if true, it could have lead to acquittal. Insanity is a recognized defense. It is a way the Foremans often "save" the lives of those they defend.

Most of Foreman's piece is actually a defense of government postures and positions. Foreman even undertakes to convince that *none* of those accused of any of the political murders is an assassin— all are merely killers. His abysmal ignorance of the simple facts of the case, undetected by *Look's* editors, can be taken as an accurate reflection of the study he made of the evidence, that evidence against which, theoretically, he had been engaged to defend the accused, as he put it, to "save him":

> . . . Ray . . . deposited on the sidewalk the murder rifle he had wrapped in *his own laundry-marked bedcover* to protect his fingerprints on the rifle from obliteration. [Foreman's emphasis.]

It is a minor objection that all indications are that a package had been made, including the boxed rifle and many other items. Foreman says only the rifle was wrapped. All those items could not be carried and ready for "deposit" unless packaged.

But there is more.

It was not *Ray*'s bedcover, which was found in the Mustang, but that of the flophouse, according to Beasley.

It did not have *his* laundry mark, or any ever used on his personal laundry, according to Beasley.

Each of the five words emphasized by this most eminent of lawyers, the "life saver," is inaccurate as a reflection of any representation of the evidence. In even his invented purpose of the package, saving the fingerprints (Ray wanted "to protect his fingerprints on the rifle from obliteration" because he "didn't want to lose credit"), Foreman is wrong, for, despite this wrapping, but a single one is claimed to have remained on the rifle.

Foreman was well aware that it was incumbent upon him to present a psychiatric evaluation of Ray to the jury. He is the man who kept asking and getting delays so he could prepare the case, remember. And he is explicit in the article: "the jury must consider the mental state of a defendant in determining his degree of guilt." But Foreman, having no such evaluation, opens the bag for the cat, saying it was not necessary because he "obtained a waiver on the death penalty for Ray." That, however, was not until March 1969, and Foreman had the case in November 1968. His explanation "explains" nothing except his intention from the first to make the deal he wound up making.

The lawyer also "must consider the mental state" to prepare the case. As with the federal government and Lee Harvey Oswald, Foreman prefers his own amateur psychiatry. That also is included in his 60 per cent.

It is his belief, he says, that "Ray believed Dr. King was a Communist; that his crusades had opened the Pandora's box of riots . . . Ray thinks war between the races is imminent and wanted to fire the first shot . . . ."

But how does Foreman, the great defender and self-contained psychiatrist, know all this? Here he is honest as only a man with his unequalled gall would dare be: "He didn't tell me any of this: it is what I believe he thinks."

For 60 per cent, plain and fancy, Foreman is also a mind-reader.

I suppose, after so profitable a career of toying with justice in the name of the law, a man like Foreman can actually believe he is Surrogate God and make up his mind, independent of fact, that what he wants to be is; that by simply not looking for evidence, he is right to make it up to suit himself; and that if this is the only means by which he can add to his own "worldly goods," there is no prohibition.

What he wrote for *Look,* which happens to be a defense of Ramsey Clark, the Department of Justice, and all the rest of the government, including the FBI, is devoid of evidence. It is only what Foreman *says* he believes Ray thinks.

What better basis for "enforcing the law against the prosecution," obtaining justice, and saving lives, to say nothing of solving the most awful crimes?

Foreman enjoys one of the more formidable reputations. He is a respected, respectable man, one of the great trial lawyers in the country, even if he says it himself. Jerry Ray enjoys one of the less attractive reputations, has an unenviable record, limited education, and no position in society at all. But, as the law in its wisdom may rule a whore is a fit mother (and so she can be and many have been), so Shakespeare put it in *All's Well That Ends Well,* Act IV:

'Tis not the many oaths that make the truth,
But the plain single vow that is vow'd true.

It is not because Foreman is a powerful, wealthy, and influential man, an agent of the court, that he must be believed; nor is it because Jerry Ray occupies a low station in society that he must be disbelieved. In regard to the discrepancy that follows I do not know which told the truth, if either did, or if both told part-truths only. The fact is I doubted Foreman's statement that, as the bar's ethics prescribe, "the brothers of James Earl Ray sought me out and handed me a letter from him" *before* he had talked to anyone about this case. The news accounts, which need not be accurate, state it was not until *after* Foreman saw Ray that such a letter was written. So, I asked Jerry, who was party to the arrangement. He did not know I would be comparing his word with Foreman's when he phoned me. (In an August 1970 affidavit, James Earl confirmed Jerry's account to me.)

Jerry assumes full responsibility for selecting and speaking to Foreman. He urged Foreman upon James when the accused was in England, before extradition. He tells me that just before the scheduled date of the trial with Hanes as counsel he, personally, phoned Foreman and asked him if he would take the case. Foreman agreed but said he would need it in writing, for Jerry to have it in writing and meet him at the Memphis airport. What Jerry says he gave Foreman instead is a copy of the Hanes–Huie contracts, and that Foreman assured him they could be broken with ease.

According to Jerry, the news accounts err in saying that all the Ray brothers and Foreman were together in the cell when the letter was written. His account is that when they reached the jail, he and John were kept behind while a Captain Smith took Foreman alone to James's cell. It was then, Jerry says, with Foreman dictating, that James wrote the letter of which Foreman said "the brothers . . . handed me a letter from him, beseeching me to represent him."

In other words, rather than "running a gamut of guards," according to Jerry, Foreman had the personal escort of a captain.

And rather than being "sent for not to spring him, but to try to save his life," Jerry says Foreman assured the brothers that he could get James off.

Jerry does not enjoy Foreman's respectability. He may be wrong in his version, although it is my disbelief of Foreman's version that prompted me to ask for an account of how Foreman became counsel. I did not cite this *Look* writing to Jerry, did not ask him questions to elicit his response. He did not know I would bracket him with Percy the Great. However, the existing public record, inconsistent with Foreman's words in *Look,* had made me wonder.

Jerry's words and inferences are not without support in the existing records in my files, of which I cite a few.

As quoted by the *Tennessean* of November 14 (several days after he took the case), Foreman claims to have spent his $200-an-hour time first arguing against his taking the case with John and Jerry Ray, then flying to Memphis and arguing against it with the defendant, all the while knowing Ray was represented by counsel with substantial reputation in precisely such cases.

"I argued against taking it for about an hour," Foreman is quoted as having told the brothers, "because I did not think I should be in the case." He need only have said "No" one time. Instead, he broke his own rules: "I have hundreds of rules which I use not to take cases. One of them is not to touch a case if the person has ever talked to another lawyer."

This was on the eve of the trial. He broke his cardinal rule and allowed himself to be talked into it? That does not fit with Foreman's personality or record. Why did he do it?

"Foreman declined to say what finally persuaded him to accept the case."

An expected $400,000 or more might be considered one persuasive factor.

The next month, on December 20, UPI carried a story out of Birmingham that began:

> Attorney Arthur Hanes accused defense lawyer Percy Foreman yesterday of using "cry-baby tactics" rather than preparing for the James Earl Ray trial in Memphis.
>
> "If Foreman would stop cry-babying to the court he would be ready to go to trial," Hanes said.
>
> "He has done nothing toward preparing a defense. . . ."
>
> "He (Foreman) chased the case for five months and now that he has it he doesn't know what to do with it."

Rather sharp words for one lawyer to use against another.

Hanes had had an experience with Foreman a month earlier, reported in another UPI Birmingham dispatch:

> Attorney Percy Foreman broke an appointment . . . he had set with Arthur Hanes. Earlier in the day, in Atlanta, Foreman said one of the purposes of the planned meeting with Hanes would be to determine "whether or not I will want to investigate further." He also said he hoped "to obtain the benefits" of the Birmingham attorney's investigation . . . .

Does it not seem strange that a few days after taking the case Foreman was quoted as saying there was uncertainty about "whether or not I will want to investigate further"? If it is possible that, in this brief time, he had conducted an exhaustive investigation, contrary to the record indicating he conducted none, how then explain his constant requests for delays in order to "prepare" the case? If Foreman lied to the judge, can anything he says be credited? Or, as seems apparent, was his lack of interest in investigating because he was planning the deal he finally pulled off?

UPI also reported why Foreman entered the case:

303

His decision to defend Ray was prompted by a series of articles in Look magazine which were not in the best interest of the defendant, Foreman said. "I felt I—at least someone—was needed."

So, at the end, Foreman also wrote for *Look.* Sixty per cent of the expected gross from the Ray property plus $1,000 cash, which Huie paid him directly, are pretty good reasons. (But if Foreman is an honorable man whose word can safely be taken against Jerry Ray's, how explain his flat declaration in *Look* that Ray killed King? Is that "in the best interest of the defendant"?)

The next month—that is, in January—Jim Squires interviewed "a source close to the James Earl Ray case." Apparently, he and his paper were satisfied the source was dependable. Foreman did not sue for libel or make recorded complaint after Squires wrote:

> The source said, "Foreman has pushed too hard to get this case to plead a man guilty."

These news items seem to corroborate the burden of what Jerry has told me, that Foreman grabbed at the case as soon as Jerry spoke to him, notwithstanding that James Earl Ray was still represented by counsel.

There also seems to have been a somewhat unusual relationship between Jerry and Foreman. One of the references to it is the April 8 article by Carl Crawford of the New York *Post.* From Memphis he wrote:

> Defense attorney Percy Foreman lent $500 to a brother of James Earl Ray "contingent upon" Ray's pleading guilty . . . the $500 was then added to Foreman's fee, $165,000, to be paid from book and magazine rights. The $500 loan was made to Jerry Ray on March 9, the day before James Earl Ray pleaded guilty and got 99 years in prison.

This information was disclosed in Ray's denied motion for a new trial.

Ray claimed his attorneys had been "more interested in money than defending him."

I remind the reader of the unconfirmed reports that Ray was about to back out on the deal in the last minute and that Foreman flew to Memphis from Houston to hold him in line. News accounts have Foreman leaving Memphis on Friday and returning on Sunday.

Foreman did write Ray two letters that Sunday. Some of the quoted language is self-serving, to make a record. In one, Foreman wrote,

> You have heretofore assigned to me all of your royalties from magazine articles, books, motion pictures or other revenue to be derived from the writings of William Bradford Huie. These are my own property, unconditionally.

This is precisely what Jerry Ray had said, that his brother gave up all his earnings to Foreman. Foreman had scoffed at the existence of this arrangement when asked about it.

Foreman then repeated what Ray knew, that in return for the state's agreeing to the 99-year sentence, the judge "would waive the death penalty." He said "it is contemplated that your case will be disposed of tomorrow," which would "shorten the trial considerably." Therefore, he would reduce his fee "in consideration of the time it would save me," with this big IF:

> If the plea is entered and the sentence accepted and no embarrassing circumstances take place in the courtroom.

More directly, when Ray was reportedly about to back out of the deal, Foreman offered to reduce his expected fee, reported at $500,000, to $150,000 (with $15,000 for expenses, the balance to go to any "bank, trust company or individual subject to your order" as a Ray trust fund, *if* Ray stuck to the deal and did nothing to jeopardize it— "no embarrassing circumstances take place in the courtroom."

What this really says is that, in return for keeping the deal he clearly opposed from the first and then had been threatened and intimidated into accepting, Ray's family would be well provided for, with a prospect of more money than any had ever dreamed of.

All of this credits Jerry's word and casts doubt on the dependability of Foreman's, for he had pretended he had not taken all Ray would ever get. It is the big finance, the six-figure carrot to go with the already applied stick of electrocution.

The petty cash was in the second letter Foreman wrote that Sunday— and how unusual it is for a lawyer to be doing this kind of business, making this kind of record, on a Sunday.

"You have asked that I advance to Jerry Ray $500" from the amount agreed to as Foreman's remaining expenses, he wrote, including the same proviso, "contingent upon the plea of guilty and sentence going through on March 10 [the next day, that of the minitrial], without any unseemly conduct on your part in court."

Between them, "no embarrassing circumstances" and "no unseemly conduct," each subject to Foreman's interpretation, came as close to clamping Ray's mouth completely during the trial as anything could.

Jerry must have been in pretty bad shape to get $500 that way. Foreman was in a good position to dictate silence as a condition and completion of the deal as a prerequisite. If Ray's brother were broke, this was an added immediate pressure on him, for until Jerry started trying to help James Earl he was regularly employed.

Foreman should be a good enough lawyer to have seen to it that this method of stifling his client was legal, or at least not illegal. But if such factors can still find consideration in the era of American political murders and fixed trials, what of the morality of it?

A comparison from my youth in the Great Depression comes to mind. It then was not uncommon for lengthy jail sentences to be inflicted on the unemployed stealing a loaf of bread (then selling for a dime or less) to feed their hungry, sometimes starving, families. Men were shot and killed in such trivial theft. But during those years, bank officials made off with vast sums. Customarily, they received slight sentences, emerging to enjoy their pillage.

I think these arrangements, in themselves, warrant assuming that Foreman's version of how he got into the case need not be considered entirely accurate, entirely complete, thoroughly dependable.

While he was talking, Jerry told me other things about James and Foreman. He also says, incidentally, that he was never allowed inside the cell with James until mid-July 1969.

James, according to Jerry, had great respect for Foreman. James reads avidly, everything he can get his hands on, including political writings of both right and left. He is well aware of Foreman's record and reputation. He told Jerry that, on any other case, he would want Foreman, but on this one he feared the friendship he said he believes exists between Foreman and Ramsey Clark. (Later, I found Foreman's confirmation of it under oath.) This, Jerry told me, is why James resisted his (Jerry's) efforts to get James to engage Foreman.

James did want to dump Hanes, Jerry confirms, but he also wanted a Memphis lawyer. The public record tends to bear that out. James did ask Judge Battle to get a lawyer for him. Before the last words in this case are written, one may wonder what difference there might have been if the judge had done this.

Society tends to look down a very long nose at the Jerry Rays and their minor offenses against it while respecting those who most wholeheartedly abuse it. I ask the reader who may wonder how a writer can confront the words of a Percy Foreman with those of a Jerry Ray to ponder the record of Percy Foreman as here set forth. Having done that, he may want to pause long enough to consider what all the other eminences did and did not do and say. A few of these are a former Attorney General of the United States; the Director of the Federal Bureau of Investigation (and so many of his agents); the judge whose expressed fear was of acquittal and, improperly, was advance party to the "deal"; the chief prosecutor who has seen to it that no one will ever see the evidence he is responsible for suppressing—and guarantees it; his several assistants, each of whom presented before a court what he knew was neither the truth nor all of it and each of whom withheld from the court that which he knew was inconsistent with what he only in part presented.

With this record of the great and respected, the nobility of the law and the dispensers of the "justice" they create, those really looked up to in our society; with the abdications of the black leaders and every "friend" of the victim; with the abandonment of its responsibilities and obligations by a complaisant press which knew the "solution" so contrived could not be accepted; with the awful silence that permeates everything, especially that of the bar, who am I to throw a stone at Jerry Ray, even if I know he hates Jews and blacks, opinions he makes no effort to hide?

With such "friends," had James Earl Ray any need for enemies [5]? Natural enemies he had in adequate supply—all of public authority and all under pressure to "solve" the crime, exactly the same pressure that existed in Dallas, November 22, 1963. Save one, all those whom Ray might have considered his friends, or at least those dedicated to helping him, which in theory meant seeking justice and establishing truth, had immense financial stake opposed to his interest. And all, compared to the lot of the average man, were generously rewarded. The most important two, Huie and Foreman, neither a Zola nor a Darrow, had six-figure interests directly contrary to Ray's.

The exception is brother Jerry. Only time will tell whether, in pressing his own prejudices and beliefs upon and speaking for his isolated brother, who had no one else he dared trust, Jerry acted in James's best interest. I think not, but the end is not yet here. It is my belief he could not have pressed worse advice, uttered more ill-chosen words, selected poorer counsel—all of which we shall now explore—for a case inevitably political as much as criminal. At least he did not profit financially from it. He gave up his livelihood to try to help. The only record of any return, the $500 of Foreman's dollars that closed his mouth for overnight, did not begin to pay his cash expenses.

15.   Between Frying Pans and Fires

Jerry Ray's racial beliefs (which may or may not be fully shared by James Earl, evidence on both sides being available) are reflected in the selection of counsel to replace Foreman, the fact of the selection a response to the failure of public authority to respond to James's request that he be provided with a court-appointed lawyer.

J. B. Stoner, chairman of the National States Right Party, took charge of the new defense team. We need no further introduction to him and the most extreme racism he represents, undoubtedly with the greatest sincerity. These intense people, so dedicated and so wrong, often do consider themselves the embodiment of Christian belief, the sole possessors of the ultimate understanding and patriotism. In this regard, they are not really unique, as so many in recent history in foreign lands so tormented and tortured by the influences of Hitler, Mussolini, Diem, Horthy, etc.—racist, super-patriot extremists all—can testify.

According to what Jerry told me, it is he who selected Richard J. Ryan as one lawyer to assist Stoner—picking him possibly in deference to James Earl's desire for a local lawyer and possibly because of his political sympathies. Ryan is little known in his area. (Jerry had had two men in mind. The other, A. J. Ryman, as he is identified in the press, was said to have been written by James Earl, to ask him to have the guilty plea set aside; but, as Jim Squires reported it March 23 in the *Tennessean:* "Efforts to locate an attorney named Ryman in Memphis were unsuccessful.")

Attorney Robert W. Hill, the second of Stoner's assistants (who has since left the case), is the president of the American Bondo Association, a minute group interested in one of the more obscure Oriental cults. Initially, he was not identified by Stoner as one of his associates.

If all of these men are a liability to any defense of Ray, Stoner is by far the worst. In the public mind, his association with Ray's defense inevitably associates Ray with racism, and of the species—of the murdering kind, as is revealed by, among other things, the Milteer tape, referred to earlier (and included in the Appendix)—that considers racism a dedication to Christianity and country. Associating Ray with these murderers tends to make credible the belief he is one of them. And like them, capable of such a crime, considering it a fine thing.

To Jerry Ray, Stoner is entirely incorruptible. There is no money, no fortune, Jerry tells me, that can persuade Stoner to abandon his principles or do what Jerry calls "sell out."

At Jerry's request, Stoner phoned me about 4:30 P.M. the afternoon of July 14, 1969 (Bastille Day), several months after he had taken Ray's case, as he was about to emplane at Baltimore to attend one of the Ray hearings. He assured me of James Earl's innocence and said he had been framed by the FBI because they wanted a conviction without the guilty being caught. And he said that, when he got into court, he would produce two former FBI informants in groups like his who, he said, had been offered $25,000 to kill King back in about 1963. Because he pledged me to secrecy on the identification of the federal bureau allegedly making this offer, I do not name it.

Jerry repeated this story to me August 3, when he also explained that Stoner had not sent me the promised copies of the public evidence he had already introduced in court because he was so busy making speeches and things like that (hardly what one would expect to be the major preoccupations of an industrious lawyer researching the law and building a defense for a client convicted of murder).

I tried to tell Jerry that, even if the alleged federal plots to kill King could be proved, which I doubted, this did not prove it is one of them that succeeded. I told him bluntly the government could prove the same thing about the NSRP. It didn't register. He did not realize the significance of his brother's being "defended" by people known to the federal government to have plotted the murders of the President and King—which gives us some insight into Jerry.

At the very time that Stoner says this federal agency was offering big money to get King killed, in 1963, a picture was taken in NSRP headquarters of King, grossly caricatured, hanging in effigy. It was published in *Candid Press* as part of a story headlined "*N.S.R.P. Answer To The Civil Rights Movement* 'HANG 'EM HIGH'!"

Jerry thinks he serves his brother's interest by these arrangements he makes with racists he trusts, in whom he finds sympathy and whose prejudices he shares.

With Stoner, the lawyer in charge if not the one doing the legal work, not having sent me the records, the following brief chronology comes from the newspapers. It should be recalled that Stoner did get to see Ray in September 1968. The visit caused so strong a reaction from Hanes, the Ku Klux lawyer, that he said he would have nothing to do with the case if Stoner were connected with it. It can be taken as a reflection of how extreme Stoner is when the man willing to defend the accused murderers of the white Mrs. Viola Liuzzo and to tolerate a police chief with "Bull" Connor's record (even *after* he turned vicious dogs against humans and after the violent international reaction against it) will have nothing to do with him or anything with which he is connected.

The first announcement that Stoner would henceforth represent Ray was made March 21, 1969. AP rewrote the story at least three times for papers of March 22.

As the story first appeared in the *Washington Post,* carrying the AP identification, it attributed the formal announcement to "the office of J. B. Stoner" and quoted "a spokesman, Edward R. Fields," without indicating that both *are* the National States Rights Party. While reporting that Stoner had been its Vice-presidential candidate and "in the past styled himself as 'imperial wizard of the Christian Knights of the Klan,'" this story contained no reference to Stoner's long anti-Semitic career, his organization of the "Stoner anti-Jewish Party," or his book "The Gospel of Jesus Christ Versus the Jews," which are mentioned in other AP accounts printed in other papers, including the *New York Times,* the *Baltimore Sun,* and the New Orleans *Times-Picayune.* It did quote Fields as saying Stoner was driving to Memphis to see Ray the next day. It also reported that "Fields said that Ray originally had contacted Stoner shortly after Ray's arrest in London and that there had been correspondence between the two since. Fields said that Stoner had visited Ray in Memphis." This, as we have already seen, is the case.

Other accounts begin with characterization of Stoner as "a lawyer long associated with anti-Jewish and anti-Negro causes" and identify him and Fields as belonging to the NSRP. They say Stoner began Klan organizing at 16, had been Klan Kleagle or chief for Tennessee, and had "urged deportation of the Jews and confiscation of their property for distribution to 'Christian Americans.'" (Shades of Adolf Hitler!)

Warden Lake Russell, of the Nashville jail, is quoted as saying they would allow Stoner to see Ray "if he can present the proper credentials . . . that he [Ray] actually hired him as his lawyer." At the same time, "in Memphis, court officials said there was nothing on file to indicate that Mr. Stoner had been designated as attorney for Ray."

Afternoon papers reported Stoner "entered the maximum security section" of the state prison at Nashville and had no difficulty seeing Ray. When he emerged, he charged "certain magazines are part of a conspiracy to libel Ray . . . . This pressured him into pleading guilty. I am representing Ray in a libel suit against some national magazines."

So it would seem, as later reports confirm, that actually, Stoner's active participation in the case was to have been restricted to civil suits. But there is no doubt in Jerry's mind he is the chief of the legal team.

Stoner was interviewed in Chattanooga the night of the 21st and "said he will be aided by a Chattanooga lawyer, Robert W. Hill." Although described as Stoner's friend, Hill has told interviewers he will not be part of the criminal case if Stoner intrudes into it, which sounds like less than a ringing affirmation of Stoner's courtroom abilities. Stoner's public record is *not* long on the law, *is* long on his special politics, and his "office" is neither a law nor a lawyer's office, but is the office of the NSRP.

Frank Ritter rewrote the AP's dispatch and added other information for the *Tennessean*. He quoted Mrs. Hill as saying her husband would accompany Stoner to Memphis.

"Mr. Stoner received a letter from Ray last Monday," he quoted Fields as saying on the 21st. "The letter said that Ray wanted to dismiss Mr. Foreman and change his plea to not guilty and move for a new trial."

He also quoted a statement by Hanes, made the 21st, "that he may also come to Nashville this week to see Ray."

Hanes "quickly" added, Ritter wrote, that

"under no circumstances will I become involved in a case with J. B. Stoner." The Alabama lawyer said he recently received a lengthy letter from Ray but declined to say what it contained. Hanes added, "If he's hired Stoner, I don't have anything to do with it. I've already told him (Ray). James Earl knows how I feel about it."

Assuming these to be facts, there is a contradiction between Ray's writing Hanes, presumably in the context of his returning to the defense, knowing full well that Hanes would in no way associate with Stoner, and Stoner's appearance as Ray's counsel. It would seem that, were he acting independently, Ray would first have spoken to Hanes, or that he had other purposes in writing Hanes, or that Stoner was being pressed upon him.

In any event, Ray and his case were again prominently in the news and in a way prejudicial to his interest with most Americans, including those from which any future jury would be selected. The public identification of Ray with the Klan and, where it was reported, the

NSRP, tended to attribute motive to Ray as being either an assassin or a co-conspirator.

The *New York Times* the next day (the 23rd) had two columns, a UPI story from Nashville and its own from Memphis. The prime evening newscasts gave it major attention, including an interview outside the jail with the smiling Stoner, smoking a cigar as though doing so were uncomfortable.

On leaving the two-hour meeting with Ray, Stoner, the *Times* reported,

> said he was not representing Ray in criminal matters but was handling several libel suits that Ray intends to file . . . [*Life* and others, according to AP.] Ray has not said who his attorney would be in such proceedings [i.e., appeals], but Arthur Hanes, Sr. . . . said he had received a letter from Ray asking assistance.

Hanes was quoted as saying he might go back to see Ray "but I've never had any intentions of getting back in the case."

Unlike Foreman, who says only that he avoided asking Ray whether or not he was guilty, Ray, the *Times* said, told his other attorneys and his relatives that he had not shot King and "If he had undergone a full trial instead of pleading guilty, Ray had wanted to try and blame 'black militants' for the murder." Illogical as this is, it made fine racist propaganda, and the *Times* harkened back to its earlier interview with Hanes and his claim "that Dr. King's murder had been paid for by 'black militants with foreign connections.'"

Simultaneously, contrary to the impression so carefully given and the deliberate language of the minitrial, Memphis Police Chief Henry Lux suddenly found it expedient to record "we are not saying flatly there was no conspiracy." This is like having the eaten cake.

When Jerry was quoted in papers of the 23rd as saying the only reason James Earl pleaded guilty is because Foreman pressured him, the Houston attorney reiterated, "I believed he would be electrocuted if he didn't." He said Ray had written him a letter asking for the deal (Foreman makes no reference to the conditions), and, "I have the letter and I showed it to the judge and the prosecuting attorney. I wouldn't leave myself open on that count." The last expression is a rather careless way of putting "I did only what my client wanted." It strongly suggests Foreman had become apprehensive over the publicity and the possibility there might yet be a trial where his role might be scrutinized.

After Stoner's two-hour visit, Jerry had spent three hours with his brother. He then announced the filing with Judge Battie of a petition for a new trial, "possibly this week," and that "a decision will be made within the next three days on exactly what the petition will say and who will file it . . . ." (It is here he introduced "Ryman" as one of the two lawyers under consideration.)

Jim Squires noted in the March 23 *Tennessean* that "Stoner was the first person to visit Ray since the prisoner was confined in State Prison here." This could be so. The court had not appointed counsel for Ray. The visit is a remarkable parallel to what happened during Ray's incarceration in Memphis. There his "biographer," Huie, could not see him but, although Ray had other counsel, Stoner, did, apparently the only person not a brother or his lawyer to do so.

Not inconsistent with one inference to be drawn from this "coincidence" is an AP picture circulated with the first of the stories quoting Foreman in his "And I'll get 60 percent" boasts. It shows a smiling Stoner in an apparently friendly conversation with a prison guard, J. W. Chilton. Stoner is whispering into the guard's ear. The same day that the picture appeared, Monday, March 24, AP quoted Stoner from Savannah as saying "his Ku Klux Klan connections would help Ray's case. They show I'm a loyal white man and the white people of Shelby County are for white supremacy . . . [King] brought about his own death with his activities across the country . . . He was a troublemaker.' "

To this, Robert B. James, chairman of the Memphis City Council, commented, "He's just making a lot of trouble that we don't need. He's certainly not welcome around here when he talks like that."

AP's dispatch from Savannah, as it appeared in the *Tennessean* of the 24th, begins,

> J. B. Stoner, James Earl Ray's new attorney, says his Ku Klux Klan background will be an asset if Ray's case is heard before a jury in Memphis where he says "people detested Martin Luther King . . ."

As though further to justify the murder he alleged his new client had not committed, Stoner added King "was in Memphis for the avowed purpose of violating a federal court injunction—he was there as a criminal." The inference is that it is proper and patriotic to kill anyone the murderer decides for himself is a "troublemaker" (such as Patrick Henry) or a "criminal" (parallels range from such unAmericans as Henry Thoreau to George Wallace).

But logic and rationality bother the extremists no more than legality, which they ordain for themselves.

Stoner refused to elaborate on his new prediction, that the civil actions "likely will include" suits for other than libel. In the ensuing months, he filed no suits of any kind. And, while saying he could not say who would represent Ray in criminal cases, he added, "there is a natural overlap between the civil and criminal functions." This "natural overlap," no doubt, derives from their being different specialties tried under different codes and in separate courts.

Stoner then described himself as vice-chairman of the NSRP executive committee and the party "as 'larger than any other white segregationist organization in the country' and 'more extreme than the Klan.'" At least the latter is no idle boast. Stoner and his "party" are more extreme than the recognized extremists of the right.

Next day's papers carried Savannah dispatches quoting Stoner as saying that, in his press statements, Fields had been "confused" (which is not unusual for Fields). Stoner, despite the considerable and unusual press he was suddenly getting would not even comment on whether a motion had been filed in Tennessee, a public action.

"I have some information on the subject but at the present time I'd rather not comment on it," he said.

And as though to eliminate any doubt that the NSRP was handling Ray's legal defenses, Fields again spoke for Stoner, in the NSRP office, saying Stoner "would not be giving any more interviews" until after the trial, then not yet obtained or officially asked for.

This promise lasted until the first TV camera pointed at Stoner. He himself alerted me to one of his television interviews on a station that is seen where I live.

What Stoner and his fellow extremists consider a good press, all that hate propaganda and racism and the allegations that King earned his own murder, continued to make the wire services, to get extensive national attention hardly conducive to the belief his new client was not the murderer. In the AP's story for newspapers of the 25th, which leads off with more of Foreman's "and I'll get 60 percent" (here containing the claims that Hanes had already gotten $35,000 and *Look* "had guaranteed another $85,000 . . . and he was entitled to 60 percent of that also"), the same boasts and racist aberrations are appended.

By the 25th, forgetting earlier assurances, Fields was again acting as public relations man. AP's story for morning papers of the 26th begins,

Edward R. Fields, chairman of the National States Rights Party, said Tuesday that James Earl Ray will try to change his plea of guilty

. . . try to plead innocent and seek a new trial. The head of the militantly segregationist NSRP said he was acting as spokesman for J. B. Stoner . . . .

This clearly says Stoner was responsible for the criminal "overlap," as Jerry asserted.

The same day's Nashville *Banner* had a story by Larry Brinton quoting James Earl as having told other prisoners he "is confident he will be granted an appeal hearing," that "I'll be going back to Memphis before long," and that "he was 'pressured' into pleading guilty." Ray preserved almost complete silence, not speaking to other prisoners unless they first spoke to him and saying nothing about his past or the case. These three paragraphs appeared under the subheading "Appeared Upset":

> The only time Ray appeared upset during his conversations with other inmates [was] when he read a newspaper story concerning his lawyer, J. B. Stoner, of Savannah, Ga.
>
> The news account related to Stoner's past association with the Ku Klux Klan.
>
> "This is what I need," Ray lamented sarcastically as he read the story. "This will really help me."

If this account is correct, it would seem to say that Ray does not really want racist lawyers to defend him, that he is not making free decisions, that he is, in fact, following a course of action dictated to him. Possibly unfairly, this also points a finger at Jerry, one of the few in a position to communicate any decisions that might be made by others to James Earl.

AP's accounts of what Stoner said are subdued compared to what UPI put on the wire to its clients. On the 24th, UPI reported, "J. B. Stoner says he will raise a 'commotion' next week when he files civil suits on behalf of James Earl Ray against 'national figures' . . . 'The suits will be of such a nature they will cause quite a commotion . . . will involve national figures but won't mention any national organization at this time.'"

These suits, rather than causing "quite a commotion," received no mention at all.

As though to emphasize the inference that public officials were giving Stoner and the NSRP special consideration, while he had no difficulty at all in seeing Ray, despite his public assurance he then had no connection with the criminal case, Ryan, who did represent Ray in the criminal actions, was turned away when he appeared at state prison the 26th. Harry S. Avery, then Commissioner of Corrections and himself engaged in improper interviews with Ray to gather material for a book, said Ryan had not been officially retained by Ray. The local papers quoted Avery as saying "Ryan would not be allowed to see the prisoner until after his prison classification is completed some time next month." He then disclosed Huie had also sought to see Ray and had been refused permission, by Avery, not Ray, who presumably was not consulted.

Avery "explained" that "prison regulations allow only the prisoner's immediate family to visit during the 'six-week classification period. As a courtesy we usually allow any attorney who has been officially retained to visit inmates at any time . . . .' "

How unlike the Foreman case this is, where the lawyer who made the deal that got public authority off the hook was given immediate access to the prisoner who had *not* "officially" hired him, and that on a Sunday, with no one except public servants present.

Regardless of intent or legalities, if any, the net effect was to deny Ray access to counsel he had sought.

By this point in the book, the author's feeling, that Ray never had counsel both competent and without possibility of the deepest conflict of interest and that he wound up with counsel of the most thorough-going incompetence who may also have had the most profound conflict, should need little pointing up. That the man accused of King's murder should have as counsel an official of the most extreme of the extremist fascists who so ardently longed for that particular murder (among many) is incredible. It is against national interest and that of the convicted defendant and his family. In and of itself, it is enough to prevent establishment of truth and cast doubt upon any court action.

One of the most bizarre mysteries of the absolutely loony legal situation that developed is that Ray wrote Judge Battle *after* the NSRP crew moved in, asking him to "appoint an attorney or the public defender," but his March 26 letter did not reach the court until after the judge died. It was recorded as "filed" by Clerk J. A. Blackwell at 2:56 P.M. April 1. This letter took more than five days and up to six and part of the seventh in transmittal. It would seem safe to assume that James Earl did not expect Stoner to be handling his criminal case, for it is doubtful he would have toyed with the judge upon whom so much he wanted depended.

What this suggests is that Stoner really was not the prisoner's preference.

Only a little less extraordinary is the fact that Ray's letter to Judge Battle constituted and was interpreted as the appeal. The legal documents subsequently filed are but an amendment of the letter. Roger Watson, Deputy Clerk, confirmed this to me April 14.

In effect, when no effort was made to provide or offer counsel after Ray notified the judge under date of March 13 that he had fired Foreman and wanted to appeal, and when his March 26 letter took so long to travel the short distance that the judge died before it could be acted upon, Ray was without counsel and was acting as his own lawyer during the crucial few days in which an appeal could be filed.

If the March 26 letter is construed as a motion for a new trial, then under Tennessee law Ray must be given one, according to Appeals Court Judge Charles Galbreath. April 7, the motion for a new trial was filed in Shelby County Criminal Court. Ray and his three new lawyers all signed it. It had the form of an amendment to his letter. It alleges Hanes and Foreman had acted not for Ray but for Huie and their own financial interests.

Two days earlier, Ryan (now allowed in the prison) discussed the move with Ray. Possibly a measure of Ryan's standing in the Tennessee legal community is this description from the *Washington Post:* "James Earl Ray's latest lawyer arrived in an old car with a wrecked front end . . . ." This is not exactly descriptive of professional success in a gray-haired lawyer.

On April 11, Hill filed suit in Nashville federal court to nullify Ray's contracts with Huie, Hanes, and Foreman to prevent further disclosure of what Ray had written for Huie.

In Memphis, on April 16, Judge Arthur Faquin, Jr., who succeeded Battle in the case, set May 26 as the date for hearing the new trial motion.

On May 22, the federal court suit was amended to claim Ray's civil rights were violated by Hanes, Foreman, and Huie. But then, when the hearing opened on May 26, the first action of the trio of lawyers was to withdraw the claim that Ray had been denied "effective counsel" and that Foreman had browbeaten him into pleading guilty. The trio declined explanations. Little, if anything, could more perfectly have suited the other side. Another Canale assistant, Clyde Mason, argued that Ray could not ask for a "new" trial because there had never been a trial, the minitrial having been only a formal hearing on a guilty plea, where the "facts" were not disputed.

Judge Faquin ruled that ". . . the plea entered was properly . . .

knowingly, intelligently and voluntarily entered," that Judge Battle had ample evidence in finding the defendant "was fully advised and has waived, intelligently and understandingly, his rights to a motion for a new trial."

He assented to the filing of an appeal.

A newspaper photo shows Stoner was smiling as he left the court. Jerry was not.

On June 16, Faquin denied another motion for a new trial but ruled his earlier decision was "interlocutory," or not finalized, and that defense lawyers had 60 days to file "a bill of exceptions." The press described the legal maneuverings as "increasingly complicated," no exaggeration. And on June 25, Chief Judge Mark A. Walker granted a petition for a review of the record leading to the conviction. The petition was denied July 15, after less than four hours of deliberation.

Meanwhile, Hill sought to get Ray released from solitary confinement and to obtain the right of personal communication with him. Conferences had been by phone, with Ray in a soundproof room. They were separated by a heavy glass partition. Ray was convinced the line was monitored. On June 19, federal court in Nashville directed Hill be allowed to be in the same room or office with Ray. Restriction to maximum security, Hill claimed, worried Ray. "He said it would be better even if he were injured . . . . It is a constitutional question as to whether or not his being held incommunicado is a violation of his rights under the 14th Amendment," Hill said. The general prison population is about half black.

The record under Stoner is hardly a successful one. Some of his meanderings and maneuverings defy comprehension, and others, like withdrawing the charge Ray had been pressured into pleading guilty, unless they have a significance not immediately apparent, served to help the other side, not Ray.

Stoner and his violent beliefs and "party" reaped a harvest of excellent publicity among the large racist population through his association on the Ray case. He spent his time capitalizing on such publicity, not on the hard work of preparing evidence, researching the law, or even filing what he first promised would be his sole activity, legal actions against the major media. It is an immense labor merely to examine the public record, analyze the minitrial, understand what happened there and its character, purposes, and effect. It cannot be done in the midst of personal and NSRP promotional appearances,

319

which, as Jerry reported to me, seem to occupy Stoner's time.

If, in his considered legal opinion, assuming such a thing to be possible, his client's interest was served by the great "commotion" Stoner was going to cause (seemingly, with accusations against the prominent, blacks, and others), after months there was no improvement in Ray's position. Only extensive personal publicity for Stoner and the NSRP and defeat after legal defeat for Ray.

Yet, it would seem that Ray's interest and that of the nation coincide. Truth must be established, to the degree it can be. From any rational understanding, no single move made on Ray's behalf seems designed for this purpose. In any event, none achieved it. The one important means of beginning it, proving what was obvious, that Ray's agreement to the guilty plea was coerced, was abandoned without explanation.

Ray, with whose interest that of the nation, truth, and justice are inextricably intertwined, chooses (if it is he who makes the choices) between frying pans and fires.

By September 4, 1969, after roughly six months of Stoner's activities, the heat grew so intense, James Earl reacted to it. He asked the warden to ban Jerry from visiting him. Jerry stayed on James Earl's mail list but could no longer visit him in person. The exclusion of Jerry (which was temporary) then restricted those that James Earl did see to his lawyers, amounting to a different and special kind of captivity.

Behind this is a preposterous grotesquery, ludicrous even for this case, ridiculous as only the rightist extremists, captive of their own bizarre concepts, cannot see. They dream up fantasies, will them into seeming reality, and are perplexed when confronted with disbelief. They do believe their fantasies, or at least some do.

Three weeks earlier to the day that his brother banished him, Jerry, on Thursday, August 14, appeared on KMOX-TV, St. Louis, a CBS station, to charge, in his brother's name, that "federal agents" killed King and "used" James Earl "as the fall guy."

The announced story behind the television appearance is that KMOX reporter Barry Serafin "accompanied" Jerry to Nashville the day before and James Earl dictated the statement Jerry read.

Here is Jerry's account to me of how the statement came to be made:

James Earl had a statement to make . . . asked me to come to Nashville and make it for him [because] Tennessee won't let him defend himself. C.B.S. was interested so they chartered a plane and

320

we flew down. I talked with James for one hour and in the process he had me write down what he wanted to say . . . C.B.S. told me it went over big and they had calls from all over the U.S. about it . . .

Jerry reports what I considered and told him to be a strange thing:

After I read his statement off to the TV camera . . . I tore the statement up as I didn't want it to get into the wrong hands.

This is a strange paranoia. The entire thing is recorded, video and audio. The statement was in Jerry's handwriting, not James Earl's. How it could in any way "get into the wrong hands," or what could be done with the holograph that could not be done with the existing and broadcast voice, escapes me. Tearing it up makes no sense at all. Unless what Jerry read was not in his own handwriting.

Jerry added, "C.B.S. asked me on camera if I knew what federal agencies he [James Earl] was referring to and I admitted he didn't say but I thought he meant the F.B.I. and C.I.A."

Of the "federal agents," not further identified, with whom it is alleged James Earl was working in the spring of 1968, the statement says:

They told me I was helping them to supply arms and guns to Cuban refugees to overthrow Castro and the Communists in Cuba . . . The reason why I've made trips to Mexico was in regard to helping the agents of the Federal government to supply arms to Cuban refugees there to overthrow Castro. The Federal agents led me to believe that I was in Memphis in April for the same purpose.

. . . I knew nothing about King being in Memphis until after King had been killed. I could not argue with the Federal agents I worked for because they would have put me back in the Missouri State Prison at Jefferson City if I failed to take orders from them. I know that the Federal agents merely used me to be the fall guy when they killed King.

The statement said Ray hopes some high government official "will expose the whole deal" so Ray will be freed.

If they don't, we have more information which we will release in the near future. I don't know what motives the Federal agents had for killing King. Ask former Attorney General Ramsey Clark. Maybe he knows.

321

This is childish nonsense. It is what Stoner had told me earlier. It inspired immediate suspicions then. I wrote Jerry, telling him that what he said just could not be believed. (Despite my distaste for Stoner and everything he symbolizes, I had been and was careful to avoid any comment on him or his legal capabilities, if any. I had, from the beginning of my relationship with Jerry, insisted to him that he was obligated to do nothing the lawyers did not want done and could give me nothing they did not approve.) I offered the opinion this statement would be hurtful to James Earl and would destroy any credibility Jerry might have if he were ever called as a witness.

His August 26 reply was blunt:

> I'll spell it out to you . . . J. B. Stoner is running my brother's case and he won't take orders or consult with any book writers before he makes any statements.

But the statement, Jerry had said, had been dictated by James Earl, not by Stoner.

Where I had cautioned him against making any statement without lawyer approval, he said, ". . . before I or any member of the family say anything concerning the case we get an okay from Mr. Stoner."

He maintains, under pressure, that Stoner authorized his statement. He goes farther, saying "before I say anything I check with Stoner first to get his okay."

Where I had told him how much his statement sounded like what Stoner had told me, he said,

> . . . the - - - - has offered $25,000 to have King murdered. I've talked in the presence of Stoner to one of the men that received the offer. Stoner has known [him] for 15 years. The other gentleman I've never had the pleasure of meeting. There is a lot more to it, but I am not at liberty to say, as it will all come out . . .

There is no way of knowing whether James Earl did ask Jerry to go to Nashville and did dictate to him the statement Jerry then made in his name. It is possible. But Jerry's destruction of the handwritten copy of the statement does not encourage belief. There is likewise no way of knowing whether, if James Earl did make the statement, it was his own idea or if he was put up to it by that government-hating legal luminary, Stoner. It is not beyond possibility that Stoner, after lionizing Jerry at racist affairs, put him up to it, telling him to attribute it to James Earl. For James Earl, three weeks later, to banish the one friendly face he saw is not consistent with his having authored the statement. It would, with normal people, be an indication of displeasure and resentment. These are not normal people, so we cannot know.

The statement itself, if we consider it seriously for a moment, is a weird hodge-podge of incredibilities. It brings in the Cuban-refugee angle from *Whitewash*, my first book, where the involvement of Oswald with these also-strange, revenge-seeking characters is brought to light. What the statement overlooks is the change in United States policy brought about by John Kennedy and since adhered to. For several years, there has been no federal support for the extremist Cuban revanchists. (And, of course, they are of the right, not "liberals." This ploy draws on the Hanes contraption already exposed. It is no less illogical and improbable coming from the mind of a Stoner than that of a Hanes.)

The nasty crack at Clark may be uninspired James Earl Ray, but there is no need to assume it is. It is entirely consistent with what Stoner told me he could and would prove. Where the innuendo falls apart, however, is in its misrepresentation of Clark's record on King. Clark refused permission for Hoover to renew electronic spying on King. He also condemned Hoover's statements about the King wiretapping, showed they were false and deceptive, as much as called Hoover a liar, and exposed Hoover's anti-King machinations as of almost the moment of the murder. This is not the record of a man involved in King's murder.

Next, what "federal agent" would risk his career and future—plus jail —to protect a prison escapee, or dare make a direct approach to any of the venomous racists, undependable blabbermouths that they are, to offer money for such a murder? Were there to be federal interest in a murder of this kind, it would have been arranged so that the murderer never knew the source of his payoff.

Most absurd of all, the product of a mind neither bright nor reasonably imaginative, is that jazz that "federal agents" had told Ray he "was helping them to supply arms and guns to Cuban refugees to help them overthrow Castro and the Communists in Cuba" [1].

Whatever the truth, whatever the origin or purpose of the statement read by Jerry, this episode is both frying pan and fire. It burned the prisoner and his brother, further reducing what little credibility any court would impart to either. It further confuses an already too-confused picture, making anything anybody says less likely to be believed. It led to an open but little-publicized split in James Earl's counsel, hardly helpful unless it brought in better attorneys. It is beneficial to the government, for the average person is sympathetic to the defamed, in this case the government.

More, whatever value seeing Jerry had to James, whatever means of communication with the outside it could have provided, it eliminated this. Only officials and that exotic trio of lawyers could speak to him. He was as isolated as though sentenced to lifetime solitary confinement.

If this phantasmagoria springs from Stoner's mind, what a fire!

If it springs from any other and he "okayed" it, what a frying pan!

16. "More Than a Whiff of Conspiracy"

In the months after the minitrial, on the few occasions when the question arose, officials and unofficial officials (those who do the dirty work of government without official tie to it) intermittently allowed as how the possibility of a conspiracy could not be entirely, 100 per cent, ruled out. Of course, all insisted, there was no proof of one—and how hard it had been sought! From the minor Memphis police official to the former Attorney General of the United States, all hewed the same line, the line of government in the new American era of political murders: No conspiracy. But now there were a few semi-hidden escape hatches.

Some spoke and wrote carefully, so they could later refer back to their *exact* words, re-interpreting them to show that the oracle had been aware of the possibility, remote as it might have seemed. Formulations varied, with the official and with the need. From the immediate one-man alone version of the Attorney General whose Department pretended it had proof of a conspiracy to get jurisdiction and then ignored all the many evidences of it; through his variation to gloss over the conflict with the FBI and to assert jurisdiction; through the Huie juvenility of a "little conspiracy" because there may have been one of "little" men; through the prosecution denial of a conspiracy and that of all the abdicating great liberals, there were countless variations on the same theme. Only some of King's former associates, who thereupon clamped their tongues, insisted there had been a conspiracy.

We have examined enough of these kinds of responses to the question of conspiracy. Before we ask ourselves the same question, there is one comment requiring special note at this point, that of the hanging judge, the man who did what he knew was wrong, what violated the legal ethic, Judge Battle. When the chips were down, when he had to be counted, he said a mouthful. It was carefully hidden, ignored. The press preferred his piety, offered in court, that "if this Defendant was a member of a conspiracy to kill the decedent, no member of such a co conspiracy can ever live in peace and security, or lie down to pleasant dreams, because in this State there is no statute of limitations in capital cases such as this . . . in the majority of cases, Hamlet was right when he said, "Murder, though it hath no tongue, will speak with the most miraculous organ.'" But what the judge *actually* said, (thus carefully obscured) is *not* that there had been no conspiracy—not even that there was *no evidence* of a conspiracy. I add emphasis to his unnoted words to make their real import clear. This is from page 103 of the transcript seen by so few and studied by none:

> It has been established by the prosecution that *at this time* they are not *in possession* of any evidence *to indict* anyone as a co-conspirator in this case. Of course, this is not conclusive evidence there was no conspiracy. It merely means that *at this time* there is not *sufficient* evidence available to make out a case of probable cause against anyone. [Emphasis added.]

Aside from being an unintended disclosure of the judge's improper intercourse with one side of the case over which he was to preside "impartially" (and of his knowledge of the state's case and beliefs), what this *really* says is that there *was* sufficient reason to believe there *had* been a conspiracy to kill—only there was not in hand evidence sufficient to make *specific* charges against specific co-conspirators. It really says there is reason to believe the evidence might yet come out, for even the statement that the prosecution did not have enough evidence to indict "at this time" is further qualified by the claim the prosecution "are not in possession of" that evidence.

It seems fair to say that the state was doing everything in its power not to find such evidence. Witness the pittance spent on the so-called "investigation." We also know the federal government was equally determined not to find this kind of proof, beginning with the determination by the Attorney General himself in advance of any investigation that there had been no conspiracy. The tragic abdications of the black leaders require no elaboration.

From whence, then, was this indictable evidence to spring? Full-born from thin air? From the mouth of the jailed Ray, whose death-warrant it could be? To seek out such evidence is the responsibility of public authority. But public authority remained, as it had been, determined to avoid it, knowing it exists while proclaiming its non-existence.

To seek such evidence is also the obligation of writers, but on this subject they find publishers ranked behind the government. The subject is taboo. There is no major magazine that will underwrite such an investigation or print the existing evidence. No major publisher would contract such a book to an investigative reporter and almost no major house would read this completed work.

As when John Kennedy was murdered and kissed off into history

326

with that dubious epitaph of a fake, inadequate investigation and the sick formality of a dishonest official "Report," the people, in their great good sense, knew better. But the people, too, have no voice.

There *was* a poll, but almost no one ever heard of it. I doubt that any poll has been less published and less publicized. It was taken by the Harris Survey. Even Louis Harris subdued it, angled it to underplay what it really discloses.

> Although a majority of Americans are convinced that James Earl Ray assassinated Martin Luther King and that Sirhan Sirhan killed Robert Kennedy, the conspiracy theory in both cases finds widespread support. A substantial 66 percent of the public is convinced that the murder of Dr. King was "a conspiracy rather than the work of one man."

As for the Ray case, "37 percent flatly say they 'disapprove of its handling' and exactly the same percent say they are satisfied." I suggest this really means that 63 per cent of the people are *not* satisfied with the handling of the case. (One of the few individuals thought worth quoting was "a black packinghouse worker in the Omaha stockyards," who said: "When they wipe out all three men that fought hardest for the blacks, you gotta believe there's something big behind it.")

It is only when the interpretations of the pollster are laid aside and those statistics he gathered are examined that the real result of the poll becomes apparent. Significant as it is that, after the Memphis "trial," 66 per cent believe there was a conspiracy, there is deeper significance. Nationwide, *after* the "trial," only 12 per cent were satisfied there had been no conspiracy. When this 12 per cent is broken down by region, in the South, only 7 per cent expressed belief there had been no conspiracy. Seventy-one per cent were convinced there had been one. We do not know the racial breakdown according to regions of those interviewed, for the numbers are not given. But it is safe to assume that most of those expressing the southern belief were not black.

So, *in the South,* the region of the crime, only 7 per cent would say they believe the murder the work of a single man.

Racial breakdown is given only "nationwide." Among blacks, only 6 per cent believe the murder was not a conspiracy, only 11 per cent express uncertainty, and a whopping 83 per cent are convinced there was a conspiracy.

After the enormous officially inspired campaign to convince the people that the murder of the great black leader was the work of a single man seeking his "day of glory," *after* the courts had acted and decided, these are incredible statistics, when only 7 per cent of southerners and only 12 per cent of the entire nation are satisfied there had not been a conspiracy.

To this must be added the common misconception of what constitutes conspiracy. Most people believe there had to be more than one killer for the murder to have been a conspiracy. In fact, the murderer need only have had any kind of associate or assistance to constitute "conspiracy."

It is the prevalent style to treat the reader as a schoolchild, carefully mustering at a single point all the evidence of a point to be made. The successful popularizers, of whom Huie is a convenient example, simplify their writing (which requires less reader thought and is considered by some better and more successful for this reason) and add the twos and twos. I do not have this contempt for the reader. I do believe he recalls what he reads, that on this subject he reads for a purpose not of entertainment, but of knowledge and understanding. Therefore, I will not here recapitulate all the foregoing evidences of a conspiracy, like the multiple Rays and white Mustangs, the utter improbability of any one man entirely alone having been able to do all that is attributed to the single Ray/Galt/Sneyd/Willard/Lowmyer/Lowmeyer, or the hiding of "star witness" Charles Stephens "to keep him from being disposed of" by the non-existing conspirators!

Throughout this book, where it has seemed appropriate, there is more than enough evidence of a conspiracy, more than is needed to show that Ray could not have been entirely alone, the legal requirement for a conspiracy. I will not demean the reader and his intelligence or lengthen an already long book with its repetition.

Nor will I rest with the over-simplified question, "was there a conspiracy?" Conspiracy is any combination to do wrong. The King murder was the end product of a conspiracy, without doubt, and in what follows I will present evidence of it not already addressed. But the question is not this simple, cannot rest with this limited expression.

As in the case with the President, with King there were certainly — unquestionably—conspiracies that did not succeed only because the successful one did, was first. At this moment, it is not possible to isolate from the many known to have existed the single one that did succeed.

It could have been the Milteer/NSRP one, incredible as that may seem when it is the NSRP that took over Ray's "defense." Or it could have been the others of which the government was well aware and against which it allegedly was and had been "protecting" the victim.

There is also the question, "was Ray the victim of a conspiracy?" The available evidence pretty clearly establishes he was framed with the murder while playing a different role in the conspiracy, that of decoy. Whether or not he was consciously part of a conspiracy he knew was intended to kill the black leader is neither unequivocally clear nor essential. It is enough that he did play a role in it. But when all the forces of society combine to pin on him what an analysis of the evidence shows is a "bum rap," when he is ordained the murderer with misrepresented and non-existent evidence while the requirement of the law is proof "beyond reasonable doubt and to a moral certainty," we have to ask if this, too, is happenstance or conscious and deliberate, a conspiracy. His own lawyer combined with the prosecution, blackjacked and then bribed him into pleading guilty and holding his tongue. Indeed, it is possible to ask if there was not still another conspiracy against the friendless convicted, a conspiracy to fleece him atop it all.

If the journalistic—the literary as opposed to the forensic—questions of this work about his lawyers, the prosecution, the judge, and the relationship between them cannot all be answered "beyond reasonable doubt and to a moral certainty," this does not relieve the writer of his responsibility to present what he knows for the reader's determination. So, new and unpublished evidence on this will follow, too.

Let us begin with the crux, evidence of conspiracy in the murder.

To Kill?

First, let us correct the erroneous formulation of Judge Battle. To prove there *had* been a conspiracy, it was *not* necessary to be "in possession of enough evidence to indict anyone as a co-conspirator." *That* is the requirement if and when co-conspirators are to be charged and brought to trial. To establish whether or not there had been a conspiracy, it was sufficient to prove whether or not one man, Ray or any other, could have done what he is said to have done entirely alone. If Ray could or did not do *everything* attributed to him *alone*, he had help. If he had help, there was a conspiracy. Unknown conspirators are included in indictments as "John Does" or as "and others unknown." This is not at all uncommon.

The judge knew better than his statement indicated. His incorrect formulation is a guilty one. Even he had to know there is evidence the King murder was a conspiracy. As we have seen, he later, *out* of court, acknowledged some of the facts proving it.

At first, before the official "line" was established, there was open disbelief of the Attorney General's denial of a conspiracy. As more and more of Ray's activities came to light, it became more and more obvious that he was not without assistance. Save among government apologists, this never changed.

To cite but two examples. A "police spokesman" in Toronto told Jay Walz, of the *New York Times*, on June 10, 1968, "He didn't come cold into the city. There was help of some kind." And *Time* magazine (March 21), as late as after the minitrial, after it had examined the record of the proceeding, had these comments: "The circumstances of King's murder carried more than a whiff of conspiracy" and ". . . not a single one of the questions that nag the public's curiosity was ever answered." Pointedly, it noted "Even Ray wanted to talk about a conspiracy at his trial, but neither the prosecution nor the defense was interested and Ray was swiftly sidetracked by Judge W. Preston Battle."

It is not because there is no evidence of a conspiracy that there is no official answer. It is only because there was official determination to avoid all the proofs of it.

Before he had his change of heart (his is a pocketbook heart), Huie was was one of the foremost conspiracy-minded writers. He did not change his position soon after his initial articles appeared in *Look,* nor had he a month after Foreman took over the case. From the public record, it is not possible to date Huie's changed position precisely. It seems to coincide with Foreman's assumption of Hanes's majority financial interest in Ray. When he was in Los Angeles in December 1968, Huie appeared on KNBC-TV. He was still committed to a conspiracy. His remarks were recorded by Dr. Stephen Pauley, a member of the San Diego Assassination Inquiry Committee but a resident of Los Angeles:

He knows of at least four people who put up the money for the King assassination. "One or two of these men were wealthy and of the extreme right. All the money, in my opinion, came from Louisiana."

There were also plots to kill President Kennedy in Louisiana. "There was Kennedy-assassination talk in New Orleans and Kennedy-assassination money being spent before he was assassinated. New Orleans is the place where the money came from to assassinate Dr. King and there is certainly that connection between the two."

He knows the names of two wealthy and prominent New Orleanians but "I can't tell their names because if the Justice Department can't arrest these people, I can't charge them with having paid the money for the murder of Martin Luther King."

He emphasized, "Our system is simply not prepared to deal with conspiracies. Knowing something can be one thing in this country and being able to prove it and provide the signed statement is something else."

If Huie was making up all of this, what dependence can be placed on anything he says? If he was not making it up, how can his later declaration that Ray was the lone murderer be credited? Here it is important to note that he and Hanes have been careful to leave the conspiracy door open, to suggest in many ways and to state openly that there had been a conspiracy, with Ray, in their later formulations, the trigger man. As late as his April 18, 1969 appearance in Washington when he was promoting the *Look* trilogy, Huie denied he had "turned full cycle in his thoughts" on the subject of conspiracy, and said he believed someone other than Ray had made the decision. Hanes also believed "someone other than Ray had made the decision."

These anchors to windward by those with the greatest access to Ray and whose expressed opinions changed with their financial interests are not without credibility and significance because their insistence on the existence of a conspiracy, even the puerile "little conspiracy" invented by Huie, is what lawyers call "declarations against interest." The men persist in their opinions when it is more to their interest to say there was no conspiracy.

Ray, who had never pulled a good, clean job by himself and who had spent most of his adult life in jails because of his incompetence as a petty crook, did not have the capacity to pull this big one and all it required entirely alone. Another writer, with established competence, addressed this point, and in doing it changed his clear and public record of having pooh-poohed the possibility of conspiracy in the Presidential assassination.

Truman Capote, whose book, *In Cold Blood*, was a best-selling study of murder, appeared on the "Today" show after the minitrial. NBC, which carries the show, and Johnny Carson, its master of ceremonies, also have strong anti-conspiracy attitudes on all the political murders. In reporting the comments of Capote, *Time* of May 10, 1969, said, "Capote's credentials make him worth listening to." These credentials include in-depth interviews with 100 murderers during the previous nine years. Capote said of Ray:

I have studied his record very carefully, and in my experience with interviewing what I call homicidal minds he's simply not a man capable of this particular kind of very calculated and cruel, exact and precise kind of crime.

Capote believes Ray's only function was to throw the FBI off the assassin's trail. "This was a setup," he declared, in ridiculing what the alleged assassin is said to have done:

> The central factor of what happens is that, after the assassination, this assassin rushes out of the rooming house and what does he do? He does a very amazing thing. He takes a suitcase and very carefully drops it up in front of a store.

"And in this," there is all the evidence, "very carefully left," including Ray's fingerprints.

Capote is not alone in finding the King murder out of character for Ray. His brothers agree. Both insist there was a conspiracy; neither believes he was the shooter. We have already seen a number of Jerry's statements. He said in them and he insists to me that, from the first time he spoke to James after his arrest, James has insisted there was a conspiracy. Before James was captured, Jerry pointed out what the record at no point and in no way disputes, that James "never was a man of violence."

His brothers raised one of the major considerations that reflects the existence of a conspiracy. "Look at all the money he came into all of a sudden," Jerry was quoted as saying the first of May 1968, a month before his brother's capture.

> Buying Mustangs, taking dancing lessons, taking trips to Mexico. You don't get that kind of money from sticking up grocery stores, and my brother wasn't the kind to stick up currency exchanges.

Jerry then feared that the people who "used him" would kill James, so he appealed publicly for him to surrender.

John Larry Ray speaks less often, for, as Jerry explains it to me, he can lose his cool easily. John immediately said to a reporter that "*if* Jimmie did it, then it was for money and that means somebody else was in on it." To this, Jerry agrees.

There remains this essential and missing evidence: How did James Earl support himself in what for him was lavish living for so long a period of time, in so many states and countries and on two different continents? As Jerry put it so well, "you don't get that kind of money from sticking up grocery stores," especially when the robberies are as inept as James Earl's, so utterly amateurish. What explanations officials offer do not make sense and cannot be believed. From the punk who cannot heist his "bread" from the breadshop, suddenly Ray—to the officials—becomes the real professional, the smoothie, able to smuggle narcotics into jail, smuggle his loot out, both without detection and, more, without any evidence of the sale or use of narcotics in the jail ever showing up.

Bernard Gavzer's AP story of March 19, 1969, reporting his investigation of this hypothesis, recounts an excellent credible investigation. It is an investigation that should have been made by officials and put into evidence—and was not. The only possible explanation of this omission in the face of the great pressing need for it is that Ray's supposed dope business dared not be alleged on the court record. Instead, Canale did it out of court, to reporters:

> After Ray pleaded guilty . . . Canale . . . said Ray had sent "a lot of money" out of the Missouri prison . . . Canale also said there was evidence Ray made money by trafficking in drugs in the penitentiary . . . Asked to detail the money Ray supposedly sent out of the prison and to whom he sent it, Canale said the figure was in the neighborhood of $7,000. He did not say to whom it was sent.

Among other things, Canale's figure of "in the neighborhood of $7,000" is far, far short of what Ray is known to have spent.

Members of Canale's staff said Ray sent these alleged funds to his sister, Carol Ann Pepper, in St. Louis. It is also alleged that they "were deposited to a Pepper Printing Co." The press could not reach Mrs. Pepper and "it was not immediately possible to find any record of a Pepper Printing Co."

Can anyone believe that, if the FBI or Canale had anything remotely within credibility on this central point, this vital deficiency in their "no conspiracy" case, that they would have failed to leak it when everything else that glossed over their deficiencies and incriminated Ray was so carefully and repeatedly fed the press? This can no more be believed than that they would have failed to present the evidence in court, where they need only have "narrated" it, not even subjecting it to cross-examination or any other kind. If it could not stand this or leaking to the press, the "evidence" does not exist.

Which is precisely what Gavzer's investigation proves.

Moreover, this claim about Ray selling narcotics involves no fewer than two additional crimes, and there has been neither charge nor prosecution for them. Narcotics violations involve the federals. Selling narcotics in jail and illegally getting out the proceeds involve others and make several state cases. They do not exist.

Prisons do keep records of money inmates send out. Ray's totaled $210. He sent $102 to Jerry and used $108 to buy merchandise, like the $9.75 transistor radio and a $4 pair of shoes, legal briefs from the West Publishing Company, and minor things from mail-order houses. The most expensive item he bought is the radio. Is it within reason that a man as loaded and successful as Canale portrays the alleged dope-magnate Ray to be would content himself with so cheap a radio, or shoes of such low quality? Or that, having escaped with all this boodle, he would have worked for eight weeks as a dishwasher, one of the most disagreeable of menial tasks? He did, at Klingeman's Indian Trail Restaurant, Winnetka, Illinois, running the risk of discovery, identification, and return to jail, a needless hazard if he had any money.

In his seven years at the Jefferson City pen, Ray had a *total* of only $909.29, of which he earned $242.03 and got $667.26 from friends and relatives. A balance of slightly over $10 was left in his account when he broke out. The most Ray ever had in his account was on June 19, 1963, when he got two $50 money orders. One was from an attorney who represented him, Phillip L. Baker, of Independence, Missouri, the other from his brother John Larry. Baker recalls that he was asked to send Ray this $50 by a brother when paid his fee. These two $50 family contributions account for the $102 that Ray sent to Jerry five days later, on June 24.

To believe the Canale fiction, we have to believe that, while Ray was dependent upon handouts from his family for the minor needs of prison life, he was simultaneously shipping his loot out to the same family.

Warden Harold Swenson was asked if Ray could have made money in prison by dealing in drugs or operating a racket.

"There is nothing to support that at all," Swenson said.

It is always possible, if you are talking about extreme possibilities, but if anyone was dealing with drugs to make that kind of money, then we'd have found out simply because we would be able to see the effects of it. If the men get whiskey, we can soon spot a drunk. If a man gets high on drugs, he can't hide it for long.

Drugs are smuggled into prisons, but usually by friends and relatives, amateurs, not professional pushers.

Missouri Department of Corrections Director Fred Wilkinson labeled the Canale story "nonsense." He said,

No one seems to have wondered where Ray would have gotten his drugs. Do you know of any supplier who would risk sending drugs into prison when the outside market has nowhere near the same dangers?

Both officials, who acknowledged the outside possibility Ray might have smuggled his alleged racketeering profits out through a corrupt prison employee, also say there is no evidence of it.

The use of that amount of narcotics, $7,000 worth, would show itself, as would the withdrawal symptoms of the users. Both responsible officials, who had every interest in knowing the truth, disprove Canale's out-of-court contrivance. The failure of any state or federal official to prosecute those who smuggled in the drugs or the money out also disproves what appears to be the desperate invention of a desperate prosecutor who had no case in court, where he got away with his "case" through a deal with the "defense," but still had to face a questioning press.

Just about the same is true of Ray's alleged smuggling between the United States and Canada and Mexico. If there were any proof of it, there would have been federal action followed by that of Canadian and Mexican officials, and there was not.

But the point is, Ray suddenly came into a sizable sum of money. Where did he get it? Aside from all this narcotics business, the officials have no answer—at least none that they can present and still maintain there was no conspiracy.

In fairness to Canale, however, it is necessary to acknowledge that his maneuver is in keeping with the federal incompetence in all other aspects of the case, the host of FBI improvisations, each designed for meeting momentary emergencies and each unembarrassedly disputed by the next.

When, on April 20, 1968, Hoover added Ray to his "Ten Most Wanted Fugitives," making him the eleventh on the list of ten, he said of the man known never to have fired a shot or to have used real force in any of his robberies, "Ray should be considered armed and extremely dangerous." This was an open invitation to shoot first and ask afterward, an invitation to a legal murder. With Ray dead, Hoover and everyone else would have been off the hook.

Hoover charged Ray conspired "to interfere with a Constitutional

Right [sic] of a United States citizen" when he had no semblance of any evidence of it, no reason to believe he would get any, and when the Attorney General himself was loud and repetitious in the contrary representation.

And of the man to whom all these special skills of the most adept criminal were imputed by Hoover, Canale, and every other official, Hoover said he "was given a General Discharge due to ineptness and lack of adaptability for military service."

Some apprenticeship for so spectacular a crime, "ineptness" in the simple soldier's life!

Less than a month later, the customary leak, this one to Drew Pearson on Ray's finances, appeared in his May 16, 1968 column this way: " . . . so far as the FBI can tell, [Ray] committed no crimes following his escape from the Missouri penitentiary." We have already seen Pearson's later contradictory FBI version, of Ray's allegedly having robbed a bank right where he escaped jail, also proven false. Well, after the minitrial and the prevalent questions and adverse editorial comment, *after* Gavzer's unequivocal and unequivocating article (March 19) had already shot down Canale's unsubstantial and unbelievable "explanation" of Ray's financing, on March 24 it appeared all over again, in Pearson's column, credited to the FBI:

> The FBI was able to trace Ray's money back to profits from smuggling narcotics into prison and to a series of holdups . . .

All without prosecution by the dauntless Hoover?

Here also Pearson had FBI information about Ray's claim to have had a "boss" he called "Raoul." "The FBI could find no evidence 'Raoul' ever existed outside Ray's imagination."

And here the extent of that largest manhunt in history became a "painstaking $3.5 million investigation."

In Louisiana, telephone calls were then still a nickel. Did they spend a nickel of this $3,500,000, while looking for "Raoul," to call 389-7581?

With all these leaks, so many to Pearson alone, how comforting it would be if any one of them had been accompanied by any evidence of any real checking-out of the available indications of precisely such a person, those leads Ray gave Huie and those Charles Stein personally observed. But no disproof was ever leaked, only the unquestionable FBI word.

The reader has a wide choice in taking the word of the FBI. It can be:

The word of the FBI that had *no* record of Ray's participation in any crime; or

The word of the FBI that had proof of crimes he committed, including smuggling across international borders and into and out of jail, and of a half-dozen robberies, according to this Pearson article, in three countries; or

The word of the FBI that had Ray in London awaiting a plane to Brussels, or the word of the FBI that had him at that moment en route to London from Lisbon; or

The word of the FBI that alleged he was part of a conspiracy so as to assert non-existent jurisdiction, or the word of the FBI convinced there had been no conspiracy; or

The word of the FBI that had him in Mexico (leading to the arrest and unpleasant detention of unidentified Americans) when he was in Canada; or

The word of the FBI that Robert Kennedy had begged it to tap King's telephone when Hoover was plaguing Kennedy and each succeeding Attorney General for "authorization"—which really meant so Hoover could later blame him—and this as late as two days before the murder, none of the previous "authorized" or unauthorized tapping or bugging having produced a scintilla of evidence that the apostle of non-violence was any kind of threat to the "national security," not even in Hoover's special definition.

There are many instances of the dependability of the word of the FBI from which the reader can make free selection in evaluating the dependability of its word that Ray had no collaborator, no help of any kind. More will follow.

All of the police are more or less in the same boat, for this inept, petty crook conned them all. It thus is less than fully persuasive when the Canadian police peremptorily dismiss "the fat man" known to have visited Ray just before he flew to London from Toronto. Their story is that Ray, supposedly just waiting to leave the country, having long since completed the arrangements and fulfilled the necessities (although according to Canadian authorities, it seems a prerequisite duplicate birth certificate was never issued), did the most natural thing in the world for a man about to go to another part of the world, separated by thousands of miles of deep Atlantic: He applied for a job. He was about to mail the application when he lost it in a telephone booth 200 feet from where he was then living, 962 Dundas Street West. The finder, this "fat man," seeing there was no return address on the unsealed envelope, found Sneyd's name and address on the inside. He recalls nothing else, not the addressee, for example. So, he walked the short distance and returned it, to a silent, frightened Ray who "didn't even say thank you."

Dick Bernabei, who, the reader will recall, has checked out several aspects of this case, has high regard for Toronto *Star* reporter Earl McRae. He says McRae "ran this story to the ground, as far as he could go with it," and is "convinced" the "fat man" could have been "an illicit contact." What the Toronto *Star* said in its copyrighted story of June 12 is that Manuel Reis, a cabdriver, drove the "fat man" and an unidentified companion away from Dundas Street—*three blocks*—to a bank. No wonder Reis described his fare as a "big fat man," using a cab for a three-block trip. Reis picked up his fare, not at 962, but across the street, at 955. Anthony Sczepura, the tenant, reported not calling the cab. This is one of four cases of cabs going to that address or very close to it to pick up fares standing on the street waiting for them, one at least said to resemble Ray.

It is not the FBI or the Canadian police alone who have established the dependability of the police work in this case. Remember Scotland Yard's assurance that Ray, already proven to have been in London, was arrested on alighting from a Lisbon plane? As we have seen, the FBI, in a single day, gave its word on this same point—both ways.

We have abundant examples of the dependability of the given police word.

What is no less interesting is the police, especially the FBI, non-word, the deafening silences about those things entirely contrary to Ray's having been either the murderer or entirely alone.

Going along with the "fat man" story is that of the "small man." Two days after Ray left for London, a "short, slight" man was looking for him. While a meager description, it is close to that given by Grace Walden Stephens, Charlie Stephens' common-law wife: much shorter than Ray and weighing no more than 125 pounds. Hanes says that, in the trunk of the Mustang, the FBI found "a man's clothing, much too small for Ray. It would fit a man who weighs 125 pounds." About the "small man," the small clothes, Grace Stephens' description of the man she saw flee the flophouse, silence.

Another very loud example is silence about the overflowing ashtray in the Mustang found in Atlanta, where it had been so carefully arranged in advance to leave it, no doubt with a non-conspirator. Ray is a non-smoker. Who, then, filled the ashtray when, from all acounts, Ray was entirely alone in his car? And what was the result of the inevitable police dusting of the car for fingerprints other than Ray's (there is no proof he drove the car to Atlanta), the testing and examination of the butts from the cigarettes Ray didn't smoke? UPI's Henry P. Leifermann prepared a lengthy story for the first Sunday after the minitrial, a journalistic cliché. It is always done. Specially interesting about this story is Leifermann's listing of a set of "unanswered questions." The first concerns "an ashtray full of cigarette butts" (also observed by countless others). The cigarette butts, along with the "non-conspirator" who got Ray his Alabama driver's license in Birmingham while Ray was in California, and "a tailored Canadian suit," Leifermann said in his lead, "are likely to become 'grassy knolls' [a reference to the unanswered questions in the Presidential assassination] of the Martin Luther King assassination."

That "tailored Canadian suit," purchased two days after Ray bought a ready-made one, is worth some police comment, but there is none. Here is Leifermann's:

> On July 21, 1967, Edward J. Feigan, owner of English and Cottonwood, Ltd., a tailor's shop in Montreal, Canada, measured Ray for a suit, the suit he wore when arrested in London June 8. Ray was living at 2589 Notre Dame St. in Montreal when he ordered the suit. But before it was made, tailor Feigan, in checking Ray's address, found orders to forward it to 2608 South Highland in Birmingham.
>
> How did Ray know he would be in Birmingham later? Why would an escaped convict return to the U.S.?

To these real questions might be added how Ray knew the exact address at which he would stay when he was a total stranger to that area—if he had no co-conspirator?

The word of the police is missing in the receipt of the "modern photo book store"/"Modern Book Store" coupon case, although Beasley used this coupon in his "narrative." This omission cannot be because the vaunted FBI could not trace out the records.

Nor is there any police word on Ray's purchase of some rather unusual camera equipment, where the word of the prosecutor is also missing. It is not because Beasley and the FBI did not know about it, for all the records were turned over to the FBI, including sales slips and Ray's letters. Here again Gavzer's reporting is first-rate, as is that of the Chicago *Sun-Times.* Both pieces are dated May 22, 1969. They tell a story strongly suggesting conspiracy and making sense in no other interpretation, which is enough to explain prosecution and FBI muteness.

The order dates to shortly after the 1967 period of the purchase of the suit in Canada. About the suit, Beasley does say, in the guise of pretending an exhaustive investigation was made, the notion there was no unturned stone in Ray's path and everything of significance was put into evidence—even to explaining the origin of his clothing—that Ray ordered the suit on July 21, 1967, and later requested it be sent to him at Birmingham. But he does it in a way that denies its meaning. However, he does not do even this wrong thing with the camera equipment. He lays great emphasis on that Polaroid camera Ray had and its shipping-box so carefully left behind, but, as we saw, somehow he forgot to mention a single Polaroid picture Ray ever took.

As with Ray's expenditures on clothing (buying a tailor-made and more expensive suit two days after buying a ready-made one), the expenditure for this camera equipment is not consistent with a man worried about keeping himself alive and going on petty thefts. Nor are the circumstances.

What Ray did, after reaching Birmingham, is to order by mail—in itself strange (not to mention the extra costs), unless one wanted a sharp record made—"at least $337.24 in camera equipment that could be used for underground surveillance" from Superior Bulk Film Co., in Chicago. He used one of their order blanks, ordered a Kodak Dual Projector M95Z, a Kodak Super 8 camera, model D38, with zoom (or variable telephoto) lens, an HPI combination 8-mm. film splicer, and a 20-foot, remote-control cable. The company received his postal money order October 3.

At the outset, it should be noted that none of this equipment ever turned up in his property, nor is there any record of his having sold any of it.

All this equipment is readily available throughout the country. Birmingham, certainly, is not a city Kodak overlooked. Yet Ray ordered the equipment by mail, leaving a traceable record, and in great urgency, saying he wanted it shipped quickly. In fact, tightwad Ray paid $17.11 in extra shipping charges because of his haste, charges entirely unnecessary because, like the rifle, he could have made the purchases locally, saving himself not only the money but also the delay in mail both ways.

Gunnar Burke, manager of Superior Bulk, said about the camera Ray

340

purchased:

It is not unusual for someone wishing to make a film from a hidden
position to use such a camera with a remote-control cable. I can see
the possibilities of a person doing surveillance work using such a
camera.

He described the camera as

highly-sophisticated equipment but not hard to operate because it is
nearly all automatic. It was the best we had at the time, much better
equipment than the average customer would buy.

When Superior Bulk filled the order, they were temporarily out of the
D38. They sent the rest of the order and included a Crestline camera, on
a loan basis, until their new D38 shipment arrived.

On October 5, Ray wrote and said he could not use and was returning
the Crestline because it "has only one speed and I wanted the Kodak M8
which has 4."

One of the features of the camera Ray ordered is its four speeds.
Unlike the more common cameras, the D38 had a "slow motion" setting
—which really means that many more frames of pictures than usual are
used in any given time span—and "fast motion" settings, which take
fewer pictures than standard speed and so permit the camera to take
pictures for a longer period of time without exhausting its film supply.
The combination, added to the telephoto lens, which brings the object
closer, and the zoom feature of the telephoto, which permits focusing
for maximum benefit over whatever distance separates the camera and
subject, make an ideal combination for surveillance. One journalistic
inference is that Ray intended using it to stalk King, from the distance
and without being seen.

Without these features, adequate home-movie cameras are readily
available for less than a fifth the D38's $160 price.

Ray was so anxious to get this equipment in a hurry and so willing to
spend money needlessly, a rarity in a tightwad, that he first phoned
Superior and then wrote them. He wrote, "As I think I told you on the
phone, I will have to leave for Mexico Saturday" and wouldn't be able
to wait. With all this need and $160 involved? An unattached man,
moving aimlessly about on his own, independent of any superior
authority or command? He did not want the camera sent to Mexico
because of the high customs rate and said he would send his address
instead and they could mail his refund.

But on October 22, 1967, politely, he wrote from Puerta Vallarte, Mexico, again requesting the refund. Superior received the Crestline camera November 2 and mailed the refund eight days later. It did not reach Ray. He wrote again from Los Angeles, giving his new addresss, 1535 North Serrano Street.

Here he used a typewriter, another object that, conveniently, has not surfaced in that $3,500,000 FBI investigation. It hardly seems that, if the FBI tried real hard, in a specific, limited neighborhood, it could not have found it. The machine was not in Ray's property, in any of the convenient deposits he left for investigators to find.

In his letter, Ray said he would be in Los Angeles "for five months."

And in the fifth month thereafter, Ray left Los Angeles, never to return!

Let us make the point again. Does this sound like the aimless wandering of a man not in any way under the control of another? He knew when he got to Los Angeles just how long he would remain there. He knew before leaving Birmingham that he would be leaving on a special date and not later.

As for the refund, do you know, by May 22, 1969 that tight-fisted Ray had not gotten it and had been content not to get it. He did not annoy Superior.

All of this story unfit for the official record, the judge and jury, is consistent only with the existence of a long-standing conspiracy in which Ray got and followed instructions and knew in advance where he would be and for how long. It is anything but the normal activity of the free and unattached wanderer, unworried about a livelihood while he was, for him, living it up. It is anything but consistent with every account of how really parsimonious Ray was.

Further, it is entirely, glaringly, inconsistent with Ray's known personal interests and needs. He carried a Polaroid, yet there is neither official nor unofficial record of the finding of a single picture of his taking. For what conceivable reason, other than the one suggested by the company, did he want a movie camera—and the best—a splicer and a projector, when he had no interest in personal pictures and took none? He had no need for photographic surveillance if he were the lone assassin and entirely independent of others. If he intended using the camera to spy on King, he would have done it in one of the places King was regularly, like his home, office, or church—in Atlanta, not the Birmingham Ray was about to leave.

One of the more reasonable inferences is that Ray was buying this equipment, in his name, with a clear record made of it (all the major items have traceable serial numbers), for another, who would use it and might leave it as clues pointing to the sucker-decoy.

If Ray was so utterly alone in this murder, why did he go to all the trouble of successfully establishing the required false identities for cover, go right down to King country, and then not tackle the job, especially if his motivation were to attain his "day of glory"? Does it make sense that he would do all this in the summer of 1967, only to remove himself for non-stop vacations, first to Mexico and then to Los Angeles? Each move was made by a predetermined date, as his move to Birmingham had been, when he had no ostensible reason for being any particular place at any particular time. Did he, alone, plan five months in advance when he would cross the entire country to kill King? Does it make sense that if this were a murder of "principle," dedication to a cause, requiring that he consider King a great hazard to his "principles" and the country—he would not have killed him immediately upon being ready, by August 1967, but instead postponed it for leisurely vacations in Mexico and California, punctuated by trips to New Orleans, also for no special reason? This does not make sense. If he were motivated by what to him was principle or that kind of sickness through which he could regard such a crime as his "day of glory," he would have done his job as soon as possible, without any delay at all.

To me, all of this is pretty clear evidence Ray was part of a conspiracy he did not control and in which he was never intended to be the murderer. It is entirely inconsistent with his being independent—or his being the murderer—or his being alone. And it is opposed to any of the attributed motives he could have had.

Not unlike this ignored evidence of a conspiracy—the strange order of special camera equipment and Ray's out-of-character conduct in it—is the officially misrepresented and inadequately investigated case of a mysterious, faked radio broadcast of the non-existent chase of the alleged escaping murderer and his white Mustang, a broadcast that led police away from the more likely escape routes and directed all attention away from them. The original broadcast was made on the citizens' band. Almost immediately, it was repeated on the police radio. The official position is that though this was a fake broadcast, it was merely the youthful prank of a couple of amateur operators. If this is the case, in addition to all the other criminal offenses involved, it is a violation of the law strictly enforced by the Federal Communications Commission.

343

If it did nothing else, the FCC could have been expected to revoke the licenses of those involved.

Typically and predictably, there was no FCC investigation.

That federal agency explains it did nothing because the FBI was investigating the hoax. Foreseeably, the FBI did nothing.

What this means is that the only agency technically equipped and with the real experts necessary to trace the hoax and punish the offender did nothing.

There were some early press comments to which we shall turn shortly. The incident could not be ignored—except, naturally, in court, in Beasley's "narrative." After the minitrial, it was explained away. As reported in the *New York Times* of March 11, 1969:

> It was a prank, said Memphis Attorney General P. M. Canale. He said that the state knew the identity of two teen-aged boys who made the broadcast, but that it does not have sufficient proof to bring them to trial.

One way not to have "sufficient proof" is not to investigate. As we have seen, there was no real investigation by the Memphis police, an expensive, futile, bumbling, and usually misdirected FBI excuse for an investigation, and here, with clear jurisdiction and responsibility, the FCC also abdicated.

There was immediate understanding of the significance of this fake broadcast, although it was little noted in the press at the time. Had Matt Herron been able to continue his investigations (he ran out of funds), it is likely he might have been able to follow some of the promising leads he had to a productive end. Because of his knowledge of a strange broadcasting episode in the Presidential murder and its inadequate examination in the investigation that followed, Herron was even more electrified by the fake broadcast in Memphis and immediately pursued it as vigorously as he could.

What happened in Dallas is that, as soon as the President was shot, one of the two police frequencies was immediately blocked, made useless. The official "answer" is only a partial one, assuming it is both correct and innocent. The claim is that just by accident the microphone switch that turns on mobile transmitters got "locked" in a police car. Thus, no other police car could use that frequency, nor could the base station be heard by any of the cars whose radios were set to that band. The Warren Report is barren on this rather remarkable coincidence.

Of course, the exact content of all Dallas police broadcasts was the most important investigative information for the Commission. Therefore, it quietly accepted a disreputable summary to begin with, getting but a fraction of what was recorded, much of that wrong. When this turned sensitive stomachs, it asked for a complete transcript, and again accepted what it received without complaint, knowing it, too, to be inadequate and wrong. Finally, it directed the FBI to make a dependable transcript for it, but only for a certain few hours. So, to this day, there is no complete, accurate, and honest transcript of all the Dallas police radio dispatches for the period beginning with the President's murder to and including that of Oswald two days later.

This record did not embarrass the President's Commission. In Memphis, the state took less chance of embarrassment by completely ignoring the fake broadcasts (not to mention the paralleling strange coincidence, if this is what it can be considered to be). Now, it happens that the Memphis police broadcasts are also recorded. They could have been offered in evidence, made part of the record, if only as a gesture by the state to show it was hiding nothing that might bear on conspiracy. Instead, the state remained mute on the subject.

However, the Memphis *Commercial-Appeal* did get a transcript and did publish it, well before the minitrial. After that proceeding, when I wrote the newspaper asking for a copy, my letter was not answered and I was not sold a copy of that issue of the paper. It certainly is unusual how the press, which claims to be the public's watchdog over government, falls in line behind the government in every murder in the era of political murders.

Although Canale told the press he knew the identities of the two teen-age boys making the single broadcast, Gavzer found one and promptly got a denial that amounts to a challenge. Again predictably, the state has been silent. Why need it comment at all after the verdict is in? So they made a little mistake, and maybe there was a conspiracy, but the case is settled, isn't it?

This young man said "I never did it" and "I can prove it." It would seem that he can because he can prove he was not near his amateur broadcasting equipment at the time of the broadcast. The equipment is in the basement of his home. He was not. He knows two respectable, substantial men who "heard it all, from beginning to end, and they know my rig and my voice. They could testify it wasn't me."

More, neither the Memphis police nor the FBI got the names of these men from him. This, no doubt, facilitated Canale's statement quoted above. Aside from delineating the character of the "investigation," this

345

raises an interesting point. There is a difference between the teen-age and mature male voices. Not one of the quotations I have seen from any public official or anyone else identifies this voice as that of a teen-ager. The police heard it. They rebroadcast it as one of their cars heard it coming in on the citizens' band receiver of a steamfitter who flagged a police car down so that the police could hear and rebroadcast it.

Had the police, not to mention the responsible federal agencies like the FBI and FCC, done what Matt Herron did, they would have had a list of people who might have been listening in at that time and might have recorded the original fake broadcasts. By not conducting an investigation, the hazard of coming up with the most irrefutable proof of a conspiracy was neatly avoided.

This *was* a false broadcast, and it *did* have the effect of leading all pursuers away from the most likely escape routes. Assuming it was a prank having no connection with the crime is assuming it was not part of a conspiracy, which was *supposedly* being investigated. But suppose it was *not* a prank? Then it was by a co-conspirator and Ray, even if he were the murderer, could not have been alone. There was still a conspiracy to track down.

Here is what happened:

A 25-year-old steamfitter was driving his red Malibu convertible, going eastward on Jackson Avenue, with the top down. He had just heard the broadcast identifying the possible getaway car as a white Mustang when, on his CB set, he heard a voice ask, "Can someone give me a land line to the police department?" The caller got an affirmative reply, to which he responded with this message, "I am chasing the white Mustang with the man in it that shot King."

Almost immediately, this steamfitter saw Police Cruiser 160 stopped at a traffic light. He shouted to it, "I have a man on the radio who says he's chasing the white Mustang with the man who shot King!" The non-driving officer got into the steamfitter's car, the two cars pulled into a parking lot, and the officer turned up the volume so the driving policeman, Lt. R. W. Bradshaw, could remain in the cruiser and hear the CB broadcast. Bradshaw radioed what he heard to the dispatcher who, in turn, broadcast it on the police frequencies.

Among the cruisers immediately in the phantom chase were 36 and 42. By this time, the unidentified voice was describing non-existent gunshots being fired from a blue Pontiac it said had joined the chase.

At least one other person is known to the police to have heard the original CB broadcast. He is a television repairman, known on the air as

"Lily White" (a bizarre and provocative touch). There is only minor disagreement between him and the steamfitter. It can, perhaps, be easily resolved. The steamfitter says he was listening to a mobile transmitter "because of the way the strength of the signal changed." Lily White, who appears to be technically better informed, says it was a constant signal, coming from a base or fixed station. If it is understood that the mobility of the steamfitter's receiver, until he parked, took it into and out of areas of greater and lesser signal strength, it can be understood that this might have caused the fading of the signal he received. His mobile receiver may also have had less capacity for pulling in the signal than Lily White's fixed receiver. The location of each is also a factor.

On the other hand, if Lily White is in error and the steamfitter is right, there is no possibility at all this high-school student could have been broadcasting from his basement and on this evidence alone the prosecution story is fraudulent.

The entire false broadcast lasted about ten minutes. They were the crucial minutes of the escape. If two receivers with movable aerials were adjusted to the point of maximum signal strength on the broadcast, it would have been a simple matter to project the resultant lines to an intersecting point which would have been the location of the broadcaster. Under the circumstances, it is reasonable to believe that the police, not knowing this was a fake designed to deceive them, felt they had no need to triangulate and get this fix, even if they had the equipment. The broadcasting voice kept giving its changing location. To a mind not married to a no-conspiracy preconception, this could have been the entire purpose of the false broadcast.

With all the many base CB units permanently installed in the Memphis area, would it not be nice to know that investigators had checked them out and really learned that none had gotten a fix on the broadcaster? Technically, even if but a single set got a fix, that line could be projected on a map and investigators could have checked the licensed CB units along that line. This would not have been an insuperable task, especially not for the FBI which spent so much time and money in such arcane pursuits as examining and tracing hairs in the course of spending $3,500,000 on their investigation. The range of CB transmitters is limited by the frequencies permitted them and by their relatively low power. Some can reach only a few miles under the best conditions.

Again, did any one listening recognize the voice? If a local voice, it certainly had been heard before.

347

If such rudimentary and obvious investigations were conducted, there is no available evidence of it, no FBI or prosecution claim of it. There is no reason to believe there was any genuine investigation. There is every reason to believe that it definitely should have been made and that, without it, none of the investigation could be credited.

Gavzer asked the student who, like the steamfitter, prefers anonymity, "Why have the police concentrated on you?"

"I don't know why," the student said. He also pointed out that in the area in which he lives, there are other known amateur operators (which are not the same as citizens' band operators, anyway).

But this student calls Canale a liar. Canale's entire "no conspiracy" case rets upon this CB broadcast being no more than a prank. He fails to accept the direct challenge to his truthfulness and credibility by the young man. This does not persuade one that Canale has confidence in his own information, not even that he really believed it when he said it.

It is not Canale alone who told this yarn, nor did its official telling await the outcome of the minitrial [1]. The press, which early learned of the spurious broadcast, had kept asking the police questions. In one of the early stories at the time of the crime, by Bill Burris in the New York *Post,* the steamfitter is confused with the student:

> Memphis police, meanwhile, have in custody two men reportedly involved in the transmission of radio messages minutes after the assassination that falsely told of a chase of the killer's getaway car. One, a 22-year-old part-time student whose identity was kept secret because of threats against him, told of relaying the messages received on a citizens' band radio in his car to a police lieutenant in a nearby patrol car.

This is a new kind of "prank," as Canale and the police too were to call it, if the innocent man who did what the "prankster" wanted is known to him or them and his life is threatened because of it. It is obvious, if the police had men in custody and did not prosecute, that they had no case at all, no proof they had the right man.

Later, at the time the trial was originally scheduled, in a November 16, 1968, UPI dispatch from Memphis, Leifermann identified the police frequencies over which the fake information was relayed as F1 and F2. He said that

> minutes after the assassination . . . it was thought the phony chase was a plot by accomplices to lure police into another part of

town. But the Memphis Police Department has leaked to several reporters hints that two teen-aged ham operators have confessed they were responsible for the phony chase broadcast and did it as a prank.

Confessions and no prosecution? No FBI or FCC action? Impossible! Then why did the police lie?

These reports—one having the men "in custody" and the other having them "confessed"—are not consistent with Canale's claim. They also are not consistent with the strong denial by the student with his offer of proof of innocence. Coupled with the lack of interest by the FBI and local police in those who heard and might identify the voice and could prove his innocence, these inconsistencies suggest that authorities were improvising and now are covering either their proof of the existence of a conspiracy or their inability to trace the fake broadcast to its source and prove that it was not part of a conspiracy. In turn, this concentrates more interest in that broadcast, what it reported and the immediate consequences.

The report of threats against those with knowledge of it, however, is indication of a conspiracy, for if this were but a prank and the pranksters were known, why threaten anybody? Threats must be taken seriously, and in this instance regarded as possibilities because of the other overwhelming evidence there had been a conspiracy. This is one of the reasons why I do not here use Matt Herron's information on this broadcast (and one of the reasons I am not able to publish all the details he early learned of those who knew in advance of its commission that the murder was planned and by whom).

Enough is available in the press. Gavzer, a "no-conspiracy" parrot in his writing about the Presidential murder, prepared an excellent article for use January 21, 1969, although most major papers ignored it. Restricting quotation to it serves the immediate purpose adequately and jeopardizes nobody.

Adequate and superior roads fan out from Memphis like spokes from a hub, in almost all directions. The fugitive fleeing the city had a variety of choices, depending upon his intent. If it were to cross the state line as fast as possible, thus getting outside the jurisdiction of the police where the crime was committed, that would have taken him across the Memphis-Arkansas Bridge to Interstate Highway 55 North, which he would have reached in less than ten minutes. Gavzer's timing, to the first town in Arkansas, West Memphis, is 6.2 miles and a greater distance than merely crossing the state line. Without violating any traffic regulations, running any red lights or doing anything else to attract police attention, this was done in 10 minutes 22 seconds. That included having to stop for four red lights and two left turns. If one begins with the official account of the time the fugitive left, he could have been in Arkansas by 6:10 P.M., certainly by 6:15 at the outside.

Memphis is on the Arkansas border, separated from it by the Mississippi River. It also borders on the state of Mississippi. If the fugitive, not without cause, considered the latter state the one least likely to be unfriendly to him or one in which he could most expeditiously find friends, the routes there were simple. The most likely better highways are US 51, 61, 78, and Interstate 55 South. If his objective were to go south or southeast, getting into Mississippi as fast as possible but also getting onto the road on which he could make best time, the probable route was Interstate 55 South. This was timed at almost exactly 19 minutes. If he found this preferable, he was in Mississippi not much after 6:20, almost certainly by 6:30.

One of the problems in analyzing the broadcast episode is knowing exactly when the police radio indicated that the getaway car might have been a white Mustang. Of the dozens of makes of cars, the phony broadcast accurately fixed on a Mustang; and of the many colors, it said white. (Of course, this fake broadcast also fixed in the police minds the idea that the actual getaway car was a white Mustang. Of this there is no proof. No one disputes the assumption, but it is no more than an assumption.)

Without connecting it with the murder, at 6:25 the police radio broadcast a report of a white Mustang going at "a high rate of speed" toward US 51 North, on Danny Thomas Boulevard. But if the getaway car was as late as 6:15 leaving Main Street, it would have passed the point described in the broadcast, by the time of the broadcast, without speeding. Two minutes later, at 6:27, a white Mustang not going north was stopped, two miles away from the area of the 6:25 broadcast. And at 6:35, still without connecting it with the murder, a broadcast described Police Car 421 chasing a white Mustang north on Danny Thomas Boulevard, away from any direct route into Arkansas or Mississippi.

If we do not know the exact moment the precisely accurate description of the alleged getaway car was aired in the phony broadcast (this determination, resting on the necessarily imprecise estimates of the steamfitter—Lily White is not quoted on this), we do know the first call from Car 160—after the steamfitter had been hearing the broadcasts, after a base station had offered the broadcaster a land line, after Lieutenant Bradshaw's partner had gotten into the steamfitter's Malibu and they had pulled into a parking lot, and after the lieutenant had heard enough from the steamfitter and the broadcaster to comprehend and call the dispatcher—was at 6:35. The dispatcher then aired this alarm:

White male, east on Sumner from Highland, in a white Mustang, responsible for this shooting. Cars 36 and 42 pull down. Subject is exceeding the speed limit west on Sumner from Highland.

This is more than five miles east of where Car 421 was chasing the white Mustang, even farther in the wrong direction. Just after this alarm, Car 421 caught the car it was chasing and told the dispatcher, at about 6:36, it "checks okay."

It is at about this point that the tape-recording made by a private citizen and excerpted by the *Commercial-Appeal* begins. In it, of course, only the dispatcher's rebroadcast paraphrasing of what Bradshaw told him can be and is included. And it is at about this point that the phony broadcaster begins describing a blue Pontiac joining the chase. There was interference on Bradshaw's broadcasts and the dispatcher repeatedly told him "you're being cut out" and asked him to repeat his messages. Then this:

A blue Pontiac north on Mendenhall from Sumner. 160 advises this car is speeding over 75 miles an hour north on Mendenhall from Sumner. There are three white males in this car, a blue Pontiac.

At 6:41 the dispatcher interpreted Bradshaw's information this way: "The subjects on the way to Raleigh, north on Jackson, north on Jackson toward Raleigh." Raleigh is a small town on State Route 14, to the northeast, about five miles away.

Then Car 36 reported it had seen a Pontiac convertible on Macon Road in the northeast suburbs. The answer to Car 36 was in the dispatcher's next paraphrasing of Bradshaw at 6:44: " . . . blue Pontiac hardtop seen northbound at Jackson and Stage, approximately 100 miles an hour."

At 6:47: "160 advising the blue Pontiac is shooting at the white Mustang following. The white Mustang has a citizens' band, following the blue Pontiac going out on Austin Peay. The subject firing at the white Mustang." Then: "160 advising that they're approaching the

Millington Road that goes into the Naval base . . . blue Pontiac is firing upon the white Mustang. The white Mustang has a citizens' band unit . . . 160 advising the white Mustang is firing at the blue Pontiac."

Another coincidence in this false broadcast episode is that it includes the report of a citizens' band radio in the fleeing white Mustang, and the second white Mustang on South Main Street—the officially non-existent one—was described as having this sort of broadcasting aerial.

By this time, Ray was certainly off and going, safely out of Memphis and out of Tennessee, however he went.

How truly remarkable it is, if this whole broadcast episode is all just another "coincidence," that the hoaxer or hoaxers picked exactly the right moment for their "prank" to describe exactly the right kind and color of car and send the police on a wild-goose chase in the wrong direction. All police attention and considerable time and effort were focused exactly opposite where they should have been, at the crucial time. And how imaginative a "prankster," selecting just the wrong directions, adding a gunbattle to the chase, and with a random, improvised selection (which is what is required of an unrehearsed, unprepared, spontaneous joke—the police position), giving so realistic a running account, complete with locations, that not until long after it was too late did the police understand they had been diverted by a false broadcast.

But even if a claim by an anonymous "Shelby County authority" is true, that there had been logged at 6:11 a police broadcast of a white Mustang that could have been connected with the crime, given the rest of the official story, Ray could still have been across the state line by then.

Failure of the fabled FBI, the police, or the prosecutors to get to the bottom of this broadcast, which could not better have suited the needs of a successful escape in a conspiracy, feeds suspicion of the involvement of public authority. There are other incidents suggesting such involvement. One is an incredible police failure that did not come to light until May 14, 1969, more than two months after the minitrial, more than a year after the murder, again as a result of Gavzer's investigation.

It had been assumed, immediately, that every usual police procedure had been put into effect forthwith. Ted Poston, for example, wrote in the New York *Post* of April 6, 1968, of Ray's escape, "There seems little doubt that he was able to flee the city, eluding city police and the Arkansas state troopers guarding bridges over the Mississippi." After the minitrial, when Judge Battle confessed his bewilderment about certain points, all bearing on conspiracy, he said he was mystified about how Ray could have passed all the police roadblocks that would have been established pursuant to an "all-points alert." "To me," he had said, "the escape seems miraculous. I don't see how he got from here to Atlanta in that white Mustang with an all-points bulletin out."

Only, *there was no all-points alert*!

Completely incredible as this may seem, the automatic police procedure was never put into effect. There never was any general alarm issued, by the Memphis or any other police, for the Mustang or any person.

And this, too, we must consider no more than another coincidence, for if it were not it is the most troubling indication that someone high in the police department wanted the murderer to escape—and that indicates a conspiracy with police involvement or participation.

This totally inconceivable fact was reported by Gavzer in an effort to *refute* the argument there had been a conspiracy. After writing that Memphis Police Chief Harry Lux "confirmed," so long after the crime, that "there was no all-points bulletin issued to stop" Ray, Gavzer said:

The widespread belief among law-enforcement officers—and consequently the public—that a bulletin had been issued and that Ray had escaped with ease despite it contributed to the suspicion that he might have been part of a conspiracy rather than a lone killer.

This "automatic alarm" was not issued at the time of the 6:11 broadcast that could have been taken by the hoaxers, if they had heard it, as proof of the involvement of a white Mustang, Lux explained, because "We did not know for sure or have proof that a white Mustang was involved."

Well, how about after 6:11? Silence.

Shelby County Sheriff William N. Morris, whose office is the automatic channel for the automatic repetition of such Memphis police alerts to the Tennessee, Arkansas, and Mississippi state police, said, "I never received any communication that night regarding a white Mustang or any request to transmit an alert to any other police agency."

"The reason we did not put out an automatic all-points is that the Memphis Police Department did not request it," the Tennessee highway patrol said.

Governor Buford Ellington's special assistant for law enforcement, Claude Armour, had "assumed" a "blockade" would have been set up.

"There is a blockade system that has been all planned out and goes into effect on a signal," he stated.

But Lux checked the records and was specific: "There was not an all-points bulletin put out on the white Mustang."

Of course, all was great confusion at the time of the murder. But the essence of the police function is to cope with confusion. It is for this contingency the police exist, are trained, and establish their "automatic" procedures.

Can it be both ways, that the "hoaxers" knew of the escape in a white Mustang and designed the misleading broadcast so admirably fashioned around this knowledge to lead the police astray while the police themselves did not know about the Mustang? And if the police did have the knowledge, how can their failure to issue the "automatic" all-points be interpreted except as indication of their involvement?

Moreover, the reason given for the failure to broadcast an all-points alarm after the police did speak to Canipe and the others who were claimed to have seen the departure of a white Mustang cannot be credited without all the accounts as later represented in the minitrial being discredited. If the minitrial stories about the white Mustang are true, then there is no possible excuse for police failure to sound the "automatic" alarm, at the very latest by 6:30 P.M. If the police did not have enough reason to transmit this alarm, the white Mustang stories as presented in court are not as initially reported to the police. Either way, this casts the heaviest, blackest shadow across Memphis public authority.

And what about the story of Bessie Brewer, the rooming house manager, immediately given to the police, or the alleged observation by the alleged "star witness," Charles Stephens, of the man later said to have been Ray, or of the observations by Canipe and others about the dropping of the rifle and additional incriminating evidence? These were immediately reported to the police, who no later than the time they spoke to Mrs. Brewer and Stephens had a description, accurate or otherwise, requiring an all-points alarm for a man.

Once again, it cannot be both ways: the reason for not sounding the alarm that there was no cause and the stories about the white Mustang and the man having been told by the witnesses, as later cited.

These are not the only apprehensions about the integrity and possible involvement of Memphis public authority.

For some strange reason, with about 40 police ostensibly "protecting" King while hidden out of sight in the adjacent fire station, none went onto South Main Street at the outset. It is difficult to explain this away by the press inferences, that they all just poured out of hiding onto the motel. The *real* reason they went to the motel has been obscured.

It is because *the police were spying on King* and those he was there to support.

Remember, there was the unheard-of occurring in Memphis, a strike by sanitation workers against the city. In the deep South, who ever heard of blacks daring to oppose public authority, in any way or form? In itself, this was regarded as "subversive." To the Memphis police, as to Hoover, King himself represented "subversion."

Yes, they were actually spying, with two black officers of the "subversive" squad among those hidden in the fire station. And along with this, there was the mysterious transfer from their assigned duty in that fire station of black firemen not conspicuously obsequious. The transfer came out first in Matt Herron's investigation. Later, it was indirectly confirmed by Hanes and Renfro Hays (Hanes's investigator on the Ray case).

On April 3, two black officers began observing the Lorraine Motel through the rear windows of Engine House No. 2. This was Wednesday, the day before the murder. Their names are Reddick and Richardson (also identified by Herron as "Richman"). They arrived around 1 P.M. One watched through the glass panel of the southernmost rear door, the other lay atop a row of lockers along the back wall while looking out a window. Sometime that night they were relieved. One of them was overheard to say, "Hell, I sure hate to go down to that temple tonight," referring to a protest meeting at the Masonic Temple. One of the two white officers who visited the black watchers briefly is a Lieutenant Papier.

On that same day, the 3rd, there were two unmarked police cruisers parked on Butler Street, east of Mulberry and in front of the motel. Police were also in the motel parking lot. About ten policemen were observed by blacks around the motel.

Among the things the black officers spying on the motel are known to have done, this being observed and overheard, is to watch who was going into what rooms.

Reddick, who was standing near the door, was heard to say to a black fireman soon transferred to another station, "Hell, they can see me as easily as I can see them." He was also heard to ask this black fireman for some newspaper with which to cover the window. The fireman gave Reddick the newspaper and masking tape with which to attach it. The policeman made two peepholes in the paper. They had a pair of binoculars, which they permitted the black fireman to use.

As the black spies wrote down the numbers of the rooms entered and, presumably, the names when known, of those entering, one was heard to say of the second room from Mulberry Street on the top deck, "That room must be headquarters. There's more of them going in and out of that room."

Reddick is said to have been checking up on a black fireman named Hall. He was heard to ask another black fireman about him.

Some of the blacks believe the black firemen were transferred from their normal assignments at Engine House No. 2 because the police were going to use that as their collection point and for spying. At first, the operation was supposed to be kept secret. Then the complaint by a policeman—"Someone told the motel people there are police in the fire station"—was overheard. The transfers followed.

The transfers were ordered in haste. One black fireman received his instructions by phone late Wednesday night (the 3rd). Based on inquiries made within the fire department, the transfers are believed to have been ordered by highest authority.

Both the police and fire services were headed by the same person, Frank Holloman, a former FBI agent.

Bearing on the transfer of black firemen the night before the murder, UPI, from Atlanta, quoted Dr. Ralph Abernathy, King's successor in the SCLC, as saying "that several black leaders in Memphis . . . reported suspicious events on the day of the murder . . . the Rev. James Lawson said Negro policemen on the beat of the Lorraine Motel . . . were removed that day after having received threatening phone calls . . . ." Further confirmation that this was common knowledge in Memphis is in the quotation from Reverend James Bevel, which follows. In the climate in the city of Memphis, such threats need not have come from conspirators!

Relevant to all this are the charges of disorderly conduct filed against Renfro Hays by Memphis attorney Russell X. Thompson, who had been associated with Hanes when Hays was his investigator. This relationship between Thompson and Hays did not begin until sometime in July, when Hanes became Ray's attorney. In the dispute, Hays claimed to be the first to learn what Herron had discovered during the first week after the murder, that a "group of firemen and policemen were 'looking through peepholes at the Lorraine Motel when the fatal shot was fired,'" in the words of the UPI account. Hays "said he told Thompson and accused Thompson of telling . . . Percy Foreman, who said in court last Friday he needed more time to . . . talk with those firemen and policemen . . . . Though Foreman did not elaborate about the 'peepholes' in his courtroom statement last Friday, Hays said a newspaper had been pasted over the window of a fire station across from the Lorraine Motel. He said policemen were looking through holes punched in the paper in order to observe those who visited King in his motel room." Hays was put out because "he has not been paid for the work he did on the case."

Now, aside from the suspicion of what the police regarded as "subversion," there is another possible explanation of police spying on King and his associates. The police claim to have feared "black militants" who regarded him as "an Uncle Tom" would attempt to harm him. Particularly if this is true is there little possibility of excusing the police failures that began with the firing of that shot, for it means they anticipated an attempt to commit the crime.

Regardless of why the police were spying on the man they were supposedly protecting, there is no doubt they were, little doubt they saw him struck and felled by the bullet, saw the position he was in when it hit him, and knew the only sources of that shot.

The position of King's body is necessary evidence in support of the prosecution claims. It is missing in any form in the minitrial. Through these police, I note parenthetically, it could have been adduced if consistent with that prosecution claim. That it was not cannot be attributed to embarrassment from it becoming known that King was being spied upon, for that, as reported above, was already known. It can only be because what the spying police saw does not support the prosecution claim.

Now, if the shot came from the direction the prosecution says it did, the police in the firehouse would have known it immediately. They therefore knew it could have come from only one of two places: the bushes along Mulberry Street or the buildings along South Main Street. But there is no evidence at all that any of the about 40 policemen went directly to South Main Street. All the evidence is that not one did. This must be taken to mean that they all believed the shot had not come from any building fronting on South Main. Otherwise, how can the failure of the police to go immediately to South Main be explained?

On the other hand, if any of them—a single one—did rush to South Main, how can there be any explanation for his not knowing at once all that was subsequently reported from there; how could he have failed to see Ray fleeing, dropping his multitudinous identifications and rifle, to see the departing white Mustang? How could he have failed to report the car leaving, and how could the police have failed to broadcast the "automatic" alarm promptly, certainly within less than five minutes of the firing of the shot?

Still again, it cannot be both ways. The Memphis police did observe the murder, did try to hide the fact, the prosecution did suppress it at the minitrial. Either they engaged immediately in at least a cover-up, or they saw what contradicts what was later claimed and are at least part of the apparent framing of Ray.

A more sinister and obvious interpretation is possible.

Reverend James Bevel had been close to King, personally and in the SCLC. At a January 19, 1969, news conference in Philadelphia, where he represented the SCLC, Bevel announced, "I have evidence that would free" Ray. "He's not guilty."

Foreman had no interest in what Bevel knew.

Abernathy supported his assistant. On January 23, he said Bevel's offer to help the man accused of murdering King is a way of moving "non-violence into a new dimension of American life." He added, speaking of Bevel, "I have absolute confidence in his judgment and integrity . . . . If a conspiracy exists, and I believe it does, it must be fully exposed."

Abernathy also said Negro leaders in Memphis believe that persons other than Ray were aware of the plan to kill Dr. King. He cited as reasons for this belief the orders to remove two Negro firemen and a Negro policeman from the immediate area of the Lorraine Motel the day of the assassination.

Nothing happened, except the minitrial, after which Bevel was interviewed by Claude Lewis, of the Philadelphia *Bulletin*. His story appeared on March 17.

Bevel said "there definitely was a conspiracy" and that the "SCLC learned of the plot" a couple of days before the murder, when, "due to an error by Memphis postal authorities . . . a letter 'addressed to a white woman was delivered to a black woman who has the same name . . . .'" The letter contained "information that Dr. King was to be assassinated while he was in Memphis . . . ." Asked why King went there despite the threats, Bevel replied,

> "We had received threats many times before and we sort of got used to them. We decided that if we were going to effect changes for the poor blacks and the poor whites, we could not do it while peeking around

corners. Dr. King often said if someone was bent on murdering him, there was little he could do about it . . . ." Mr. Bevel said the letter concerning the death plot was immediately turned over to Memphis police officials. . . .

Who took no special security precautions.

Mr. Bevel also said a tip on the plot against Dr. King had come from "a store where many Memphis policemen are known to frequent." A black policeman in Memphis who asked not to be identified agreed with Mr. Bevel that "black policemen who would ordinarily be assigned to the area of the Lorraine Motel . . . were removed from the area the day of the killing". . . . Other Memphis citizens charged that black firemen in the area were removed . . . .

Mr. Bevel pointed out that FBI agents held up Dr. King's plane . . . before his trip to Memphis to search the aircraft because they knew of a plot on his life "at least a day before the murder . . . ." A Memphis minister pleaded for a half hour not to let Dr. King enter the city because he had knowledge of the assassination plot. The minister's name was not disclosed because, Mr. Bevel said, "his life would be in immediate danger" . . . .

Bevel hoped to open up the "black community to tell what they know" and that this, in turn, might "pressure the Memphis police to release information" they had and were suppressing.

He became emotional as he spoke to Lewis, saying America is "becoming a nation of sheep who are willing to have the wool pulled over its eyes" and "America will lose confidence in itself if it cannot turn to its government for truth and justice. If a Dr. King and the Kennedys can be murdered off without adequate investigation, our government is becoming a closed shop . . . ."

Amen!

When Lewis phoned Memphis for official comment on Bevel's accusations, "Memphis police refused to comment on Mr. Bevel's charges, saying the chief of police was 'unavailable for comment.'"

Much of this closely parallels what Matt Herron learned in his investigations. Herron could not interest the FBI in it. He tried.

If all of these things that did happen but should not have, all these suspicious things involving the police, are added together, they do point an accusing finger at the police. It is not unreasonable to interpret them as substantiating what Herron learned, that the police knew *in advance*

King would be murdered when he returned to Memphis, that he "would not live to lead the march."

To think of this chills the spine—for it means, at the very least, that they allowed it to happen and, through what they did and did not do, enabled it to happen.

Not until after repeated evidences that Ray is not a racial extremist appeared in the papers did any evidence turn up that he might be one. Much of this late-to-be-adduced evidence can be interpreted as part of an assumed character and personality, a trail left to be picked up and to suggest racism. Of the many available examples—Charles Stein and his sister say Ray asked them to register for George Wallace in California in return for taking Charles to New Orleans. He succeeded in giving Stein the impression he was "some kind of politician" and that, at Wallace headquarters, "they all knew him." But Wallace's California campaign coordinator, Robert Walters, says none of them knew Ray and a thorough check of their many files showed no sign of any of the names associated with Ray. It appears that, despite his proselytizing with the Steins, even if he was for Wallace, Ray did not take time to add his own name or any alias of the many he had to Wallace petitions.

Before it was known that Ray is Galt and Galt is an assumed name, Stein, after noticing the extra pains Ray went to when using the name Galt, as when checking into motels, said he "thought he was establishing a fictitious identity."

If Ray was planting a seed, the vine grew. After the minitrial, when Canale was asked what he believed the motive was, he replied, as we saw, "There is evidence Ray was a racist." How good and persuasive this evidence is can be evaluated by its omission from the Beasley "narrative," even when there was no opposition.

In all of this there was a dead giveaway. That is in the alias "Galt," the official and unofficial explanations of how he got it, and a careless error made in it. Ray is credited with the impossible, learning about three similar-looking men who lived in the same neighborhood without knowing each other. (There is also, in that same neighborhood, a "John Willard," the name under which he registered at the flophouse.) Each resembles him, one down to similar and similarly located scars. Ray is said to have learned of these men and to have assumed their names all by himself by going over birth notices in newspaper files.

But he could not have gotten the identity of the Eric S. Galt he resembles from *any* files. Nor could he have found the name "Eric Starvo Galt" this way because the real Galt is not "Starvo." *His* middle name is "St. Vincent." In writing it, he uses the not extraordinary tiny circle for a period and his letter "v" looks like a capital letter with an extra twist. Ray was given not the name alone. He was also given the *signature*. The signature of the mature Eric St. Vincent Galt is not included in his *birth* record.

This was known before the minitrial. The information about the actual name of the real Galt was well enough known to have been on the front page of the *New York Times* of June 12, 1968. The Associated Press distributed this signature by wirephoto:

So it is safe to assume that Hoover, Canale, Beasley, Dwyer, and even Foreman, knew about it.

These are not all the strong indications, if not absolute proofs, that King was murdered as the consequence of a conspiracy of which, in some capacity, seemingly that of decoy, Ray was a part. With those evidences reported earlier, in other contexts, they seem to be more than enough to invalidate the official fictions, the shabby pretense of evidence foisted off on a complacent country by dishonest officials and their unofficial apologists as part of the framing of Ray and, with him, of history.

And the co-conspirators, their existence indicated on the basis of the evidence, including the actual murderer, are unknown, unapprehended, unsought.

This is the state of American justice and freedom, the augury for the future of American society, in the era of political murders [2].

To Frame?

To this point in our analysis of the case of James Earl Ray as the murderer of Dr. Martin Luther King, Jr., and of the evidence indicating there had been a conspiracy in this murder, we have been pretty much limited to the public record. What we have done is to compare what was leveled against the accused and then "convicted" alleged murderer with the readily available evidence, to show that essential evidence was ignored or suppressed, misrepresented and distorted, twisted into meanings it does not have, and lied about. We have seen that witnesses were said to have seen what they did not see and could not have and that witnesses who should have been used were not. This was possible only because, as in the official investigation of the murder of President Kennedy, the functioning of American law and justice once again were frustrated and by-passed.

And these things in turn were possible only because there was no trial. That there was none was due to the will of Percy Foreman, one of the great trial lawyers, who decided there would be no trial and forced his decision on the reluctant defendant. He did this by threats, by intimidation, by an unusual kind of bribery, and by misrepresentation. To lay such charges to a lawyer is a serious matter. That it can be done from the available record is another duplication of the Presidential-assassination tragedy, for these are like the malfeasances, misfeasances, and non-feasances of the Warren Commission lawyers. They also ignored what was uncongenial to their predeterminations, preconceptions, to an official position substituted for a determination of fact as required by our concepts of law and justice. And they, like the Memphis prosecutors, twisted, distorted, misrepresented, and, although they did not "narrate" evidence as Beasley did, in ways that are comparable, they, in effect, also lied about the evidence [3].

Ray had two lawyers plus a "public defender" who acted as an adjunct of the prosecution. First there was Hanes, then Foreman. Then after it was too late, he obtained the animated disaster of that venom in human form, the NSRP, which itself had plotted the crime that Ray had been charged with. But Ray's legal ruin cannot be laid to Stoner, not even against his brother Jerry, who really arranged for Stoner to be hired. The ruin came because the obligations undertaken by American lawyers when they undertake the defense in criminal cases were forgotten in this case and because of the abdications by the lawyers of the prosecution of their responsibilities, which are not primarily to obtain convictions.

As I think the reader may agree after he examines what follows, Hanes made Foreman and the deal possible, for there is credible reason to believe that, even after Ray fired him, Hanes could have prevented the deal by not acceding to the conditions that made it achievable. In considering what follows, the reader should keep in mind the public records of Ray's "defenders," for we will now be dealing with what was not public.

In his June 1969 appearance on the Dick Cavett show, Foreman boasted, "I enforce the law against the state." Asked "is there any crime too odious" for him, he drawled, "The more odious the crime, the more the skilled lawyer is required." And for this bizarre application of his skills, he said he had gotten no "bread," the slang of the question put to him. Another time, when asked how it felt to defend those accused of horrible crimes, this smiling, open-faced man who looks like the personification of goodness said, "My fee is punishment enough."

True!

But the vast sums he extracts, the rings and other jewelry and whatever else he wants from women, the warehouse full of convertible or desirable miscellany, do not prove his fee "is punishment enough" nearly as well as what he got from and did to James Earl Ray.

In telling the story to this point, we have faithfully quoted what Foreman and Hanes and their ally/agent/supplier Huie have said of their performances and their arrangements. What they have said is what it suited them to say.

What they have not said, what they have said that is not so, and what they have given other than its true meaning is what we now examine. We do this from their once-secret dealings, the contracts they extorted from Ray and each other and their once-secret letters that have the effect of contracts. I have these documents. (See the Appendix.)

Never was a prize cow milked as thoroughly and completely as the criminal, the defendant James Earl Ray. Not one spilled drop of cream or milk was to be wasted, and none was to remain with him. About their behavior I believe what properly only the courts can decide: that, in their milking, the lawyers transgressed against the law and the ethics and codes of their once-honorable calling.

It all began with a contract "entered into" when Ray could not have entered into it. While this may not be illegal, it is not factual or truthful. The contract seems to have been drafted by Hanes but to have been worked out with Huie and his lawyer in advance of Hanes's seeing Ray and getting Ray's verbal agreement to it. But, this is conjecture.

This first contract, with a blank in which the date "8" was later written in, begins: "Agreement entered into this 8 day of July" and what appears, in the indistinct typing, to be a typographical error, "1988." On July 8, 1968, James Earl Ray was not in the United States and was unable to enter into this contract because he was in a British jail, Wandsworth Prison. He did not reach the United States until July 19. Hanes had not gotten to see him until July 5. This agreement concludes, on its third page, with this language, "In witness whereof, the parties

hereto have executed this agreement as of the date first above written."
This says the agreement was executed July 8, when it was not possible
for Ray to have entered into it except through Hanes, as his agent or
representative. Under this sentence appear the three signatures over the
typed names, with Huie designated, as the contract provides, as "Author,"
Ray and Hanes as "Ray" and "Hanes."

In an apparent effort to get around this impossibility—of Ray having
signed a document on a day he could not have done so—(which to a
non-lawyer seems contrary to the contract proper), there is a separate
sheet attached. It is for the notarizing of the signatures. In each case,
the name of the signatory is typed in, but in no case is there a signature.
There is, in each case, two blanks, the first for the date, the second for
the name or function of the person administering the oath. The second
blank has the words "Notary Public" written in. The words could as well
have been typed in, unless a name or a different function were expected.
The notary is Arthur Hanes, Jr., the partner of Arthur Hanes as well as
his son, and thereby party to the contract.

Apparently because it follows the sequence of the contract proper,
the order in which the names appear is Huie, Ray, and Hanes. Unlike the
contract proper, the month is not typed in on this sheet, further
indication it was not prepared at the time the contract was. With Huie
and Hanes, the date written in is July 8. With Ray, the date is August 1.

The question, a technical one, that the August 1 date raises in my mind
is how Ray could legally enter into a contract "executed" July 8, 24
days after it was "executed."

The purpose of the contract is set forth in provision 1(d):

> Author proposes to write literary material dealing with the
> assassination of Martin Luther King, Jr., the alleged participation of
> Ray therein, and the Trial, for the purpose of establishing the truth
> with respect thereto.

Hanes is defined in 1(c) as Ray's attorney.

For some reason not without question, the fifth provision is initialed
by Huie and Hanes alone. It is the financial agreement. Under it, Huie is
to pay Hanes and Ray each "thirty per cent of the gross receipts." All
receipts are to "be paid to and collected by the Author's agent, Ned
Brown, Inc.," of Beverly Hills, California.

The more obvious interpretation of this initialing is that, because it
was necessary and because Ray was not available on July 8, Hanes acted
for him. The more obvious reason for a Hollywood rather than a New

York literary agent is that the greatest revenue was expected to be from the movies.

One other provision is initialed, 6(b), again by Hanes and Huie only. It is stricken out and the word "Excluded," in Hanes's handwriting, appears above the initials. It is the provision under which Huie could abrogate the contract if he "does not have an interview with Ray within 30 days of this Agreement or the date when Ray first enters the United States." This, among other things, leaves no doubt that, at the time the contract was drafted, it was known Ray was not in the United States and might not be on the date of execution. It also was written before it was known that Memphis authorities would not permit Huie access to Ray. Hanes had to get this provision eliminated because it gave Huie automatic right to abrogate the contract. Translation: Cut off Hanes's money. Again, except with Hanes as his agent or representative, Ray did not initial this change. Neither initialing is dated.

The other provisions seem relatively normal. They do grant Huie rather generous rights and relieve him of almost any obligation except to pay if he takes in any money. He does not have to write anything under the agreement, does not have to take in any money from which there would be the 30 per cent each for Ray and Hanes provided for by the fifth provision.

What does not seem to be normal is that this contract provides for Hanes's money not in the form of an agreement between him and Ray, nor as an agreement between him and Huie as Ray's literary representative or partner. The ordinary arrangement would have been between Hanes and Ray, with a stipulation of what Ray was to pay Hanes for his services. There was no problem if Hanes wanted to do the usual. He would have reached an understanding with Ray in England, have committed that understanding to paper, and Ray would have signed it. The usual arrangement between client and lawyer and *only* client and lawyer, would then have been observed. If Hanes had been worried about Ray's paying him, he then could have executed an additional agreement under which Ray would assign this 30 per cent share of Huie's gross to Hanes. Ray and Huie, ordinarily, would have had their own agreement, giving Huie 40 per cent of his gross take.

Aside from the matter of giving Ray nothing other than any 30 per cent that might accrue to him, and taking everything from him, there are a number of things wrong with this contract, a contract Huie and Hanes certainly never expected to be examined by others.

Huie, aside from getting a good thing, did not live up to his contractual obligations, including examining the trial and "establishing the truth" with respect to it and "the alleged participation of Ray" in the assassination. Instead, he wrote in advance of the "trial" what amounts to an additional indictment and a conviction of the man who expected him to be his literary defender.

Hanes is *two* parties to the contract, Hanes and Ray, not just one of them, Hanes. He represents himself and his own financial interest while he represents Ray and Ray's competitive, conflicting interest. This conflict will soon be amplified. Ray was *not* represented by any lawyer *not party to the contract,* one without his own selfish interests in it. Hanes's interests do not coincide with Ray's and are competitive with or opposed to them. Hanes is not without conflict of interest.

Moreover, in advance of the trial, Hanes, in return for money (provision 2) contracted to "impart" to Huie "such information with respect to the assassination of Martin Luther King, Jr., the alleged participation of Ray," and other things as he "may have or reasonably may be able to obtain." He contracted to Huie the right to use this "or any part thereof in his writing." In this and in other ways, acting as Ray's lawyer, he either permitted Ray, which is excessive politeness, or got Ray to sign away rights that include those to a fair trial.

While the requirement of the law and his client's interests were opposed to it, and when it was a seeming violation of Supreme Court decisions and the order of Judge Battle, Hanes arranged for Huie to have the legal right to publish, in advance of the trial, the "truth" about the assassination and Ray's alleged participation in it, however it is possible for humans to understand and establish that elusive, truth, under such circumstances. He then went further and, on behalf of himself and his client, Ray, gave Huie the absolute right to select what he would use and write about; the right to suppress anything he wanted to suppress, with or without reason and whether or not it was in Ray's interest, without Ray's having any chance to examine it and decide for himself whether it was or was not in his interest, assuming he could—and without Hanes himself, were he to decide it was against Ray's interest as the defendant or his as Ray's lawyer, having the right or power to do anything to prevent it.

Thus, in one fell swoop, Hanes surrendered the interest of his client (the man who hired him to protect him against just this) and his own interests and violated the ethics of the legal profession, if not the law and court decisions—for pay, very ample pay.

It is not just a writer's impassioned denunciation when I say Hanes violated the Code of Professional Ethics of the American Bar Association. It is the literal fact. The rare invocations of this code are against those who support unpopular political prisoners or share their views, not against Establishmentarians. On Hanes's arrangements with Huie, there has been abject silence from the bar association. But Hanes contracted to violate Canon 20, for a considerable sum of money and the prospect of much more. He further became involved, *personally*, in *repeated* violations—as the reader, after reading the text of this canon, will understand from what has been quoted heretofore:

20. Newspaper Discussion of Pending Litigation

Newspaper publications by a lawyer as to pending or anticipated litigation may interfere with a fair trial in the courts and otherwise prejudice the due administration of justice. Generally, they are to be condemned. If the extreme circumstances of a particular case justify a statement to the public, it is unprofessional to make it anonymously. An *ex parte* reference to the facts should not go beyond quotation from the records and papers on file in the court; but even in extreme cases it is better to avoid any *ex parte* statement.

If, aside from the personal writing and the frequent sounding off, it is "unprofessional to make" such comment "anonymously," how about all those news stories quoting "sources close to the defense" and "sources close to the prosecution"? The answer is both sides never engaged in other than "unprofessional conduct," to the accompanying and so expressive silence of the lords of the bar. Without this open violation of all decent standards of the law, the profession, and its practice, neither side could have tried the case in the papers. As the canon says, they all knew this would "interfere with a fair trial . . . and otherwise prejudice the due administration of justice." But who cared, as long as there was a pigeon for sacrifice and a cow for milking?

The language of the canon is precise. It does not say that only the defendant can suffer. Society also has its rights, and these include the apprehension and proper punishment of those really guilty and found guilty in court in a fair and open trial. Violation of this canon by either side denies the rights of the other side. Hanes thus also denied society its rights. But he did get paid, which is what seems to have interested him most of all. And he got abundant publicity, which does help the practice of law and attracts clients.

As we have seen, Hanes also went much further. In advance of the trial, he joined in the clamor *against* his client and proclaimed the guilt

367

of the man he was so abundantly rewarded for "defending."

It is against public interest for there to be the kind of pretrial publicity Hanes made possible and was part of. It was against Ray's interest, too. It was an important part of the denial of truth about the assassination. And it vested in one fallible and very commercial human, Huie, exclusive access to whatever Ray knew and said of the assassination and of his alleged participation in it. Huie is the *only* writer to have seen the 20,000 words that Ray prepared. He used only part of them, the part he wanted, the part that suited his preconception, the preconception he freely admits—even boasts about—that Ray was guilty.

If this were not enough, there is a separate letter on the letterhead "William Bradford Huie, Hartselle, Alabama," to "Dear Art," dated, in typing, "July 8, 1968." This is ample indication it was not prepared at the same time the agreement was, for on the agreement the date could not be included. The letter may or may not have been prepared July 8, but it certainly was not agreed to on that date because it has Ray's undated signature at the end of the second page, in typing and in writing. Ray was then in the British jail, not in Alabama. On the second page, Ray's absence is even acknowledged, in several places.

The first sentence is either a lie or proof that Hanes and Huie did enter into a contract on July 8 *without* Ray. It also makes clear that the agreement is between Huie and Hanes. The first clause of that first sentence reads, "This letter is meant to be part of our Agreement . . . ." Huie wrote the letter. He addressed it to Hanes. The "our," therefore, means Huie and Hanes, not Ray. The second clause is: "signed on this date." Ray could not have "signed on this date," and he didn't.

Clearly and unequivocally, this letter says that on July 8 Huie and Hanes signed an agreement, an agreement between the two of them only, "*our* Agreement."

The question immediately arises, *why was it necessary to have two separate agreements on the same date?* Or why, when Ray did not sign the original agreement until August 1, could the original agreement not have been rewritten to include the provisions of this letter, with all the signatories signing the new contract the same time Ray did.

I do not know the answer or all the possible answers to this question and its and their overtones, but one fairly obvious explanation is that the separate letter made it impossible for Ray to withdraw from or ask for changes in the provisions of the original contract. The date on which Ray affixed his signature to the letter is neither known nor indicated. But it cannot have been the date typed on the letter, July 8.

The two paragraphs preceding the last are further proof that the letter agreement was written when Ray was in the British jail. They stipulate what will be done "on Ray's return" and "after Ray's return."

The last sentence indicates that when the letter was drafted Ray was not available to sign it and that Hanes had the power and right to act for Ray in contracts and understandings (where their interests could and did conflict). It reads, "Your signature, along with that of Ray affixed by you under your Power of Attorney, will attest Agreement." This proves Hanes had gotten from Ray, in writing, the "legal" right to act for Ray when Ray's and Hanes's interests were in conflict.

Among the provisions in the letters to which, had Ray understood them, he might not have agreed, is that of the second paragraph, the "understanding" that "all advances made by publishers . . . are merely loans, returnable in full if, for any reason whatsoever, the book is not completed and accepted." The advances are described as loans from which Huie is to pay "you and Ray while I am researching and writing this book" and, "in effect, loans from me to the two of you."

This business, of course, is nonsense. Huie is no pauper. The only conceivable need to pay in advance of collection was Hanes's insistence on immediate cash. Ray had no personal need for it. (If he needed money for his legal defense, then again it is Hanes who needed it.) In fact, Huie could not have consulted him about this.

If, in retrospect, Hanes's following of Omar Khayyam's advice, "take cash," seems wise for selfish reasons, it in no way alters two facts: This provision was not in his client's interest, and the lawyer Hanes represented *both conflicting* interests.

The language "you and Ray" eliminates any further possible doubt that Huie regarded "our Agreement" as between him and the addressee, Hanes, the "you." Again I note that we shall see that the reference to Ray's getting any share, although in the contract and in this letter, is a sophistry, a fiction and a deception.

Huie then offers to make the "advances made by me to the two of you *non-returnable*" (emphasis in the original) if Hanes and Ray would agree to a schedule of payments that called for $10,000 on Huie's signing "of the first, or book, contract." "On the first day Ray has been lodged in a jail in the United States [still another proof Ray was not party to it, although his name is included, and Hanes did not sign it with his power of attorney], I will pay $5,000." Each month thereafter for the ensuing five months, an additional $5,000.

For some strange reason, these sums, $10,000 on signing of the book contract and six monthly payments of $5,000 each, which total $40,000, are in conflict with the third paragraph from the end. There this language appears:

> In short, on signing, on Ray's return, and during the first five months after his return, I am obligating myself to pay you and Ray, under the terms of our Agreement, a total of $35,000.

Not only does the earlier letter specify seven payments, the last six monthly payments rather than the five in this paragraph, but there is no provision of (again) "our Agreement" for the payment of any sum at any time, including this sum of $35,000. There is no sum mentioned at any point in "our Agreement."

This funny business with money, this bad arithmetic, this citation of non-existent provisions, this apparent hanky-panky with money, is beyond my explanation. I can suggest only that it is because Hanes was insisting on getting money that had to come from Huie's own resources, on the chance that the deal turned out to be less profitable than expected. The arithmetic is erroneous. Huie here obligates himself to pay Hanes $40,000 at the very minimum, regardless of any circumstances or conditions except these: A book contract is signed and Ray is returned to the United States. Both happened.

Clearly, none of this is of any interest to Ray, unless he were to get his 30 per cent. In the event he did (and, as we shall see, everyone involved knew he wouldn't), it made no difference to him when he got it, all of his needs being more than adequately provided by organized society.

The only other provision of the letter is that if and when the full publishing advance is paid, upon completion and acceptance of the book, any added income would be "divided and paid promptly." Huie anticipated completion of his book five months after Ray's return.

Once Hanes had Huie's signature on these papers, there was no need for him to use his power of attorney and sign for Ray. He had all the signatures his interest required with Huie's. It looked bad enough, if ever examined by an outsider, without his making his dual interest more obvious with his dual signatures. This letter agreement leaves no doubt that Hanes's part of the "action" is irrevocably his, come what may.

Each of these documents is an abnormal contract, each not the easy and proper way to accomplish its ostensible purposes. Together, they are an even stranger combination. I believe the courts and bar associations should be interested—but not only in these two.

What Hanes could anticipate did come to pass when Ray fired Hanes. After that, these contracts still guaranteed that Hanes would get his cut, whether or not he was Ray's lawyer. This made problems for everyone but Ray. He got no money, had no prospect of getting any, and had the lawyer he apparently thought he wanted. The only problem it meant for Hanes was, would there be any further loot? If there were to be, he would get his share, which is more than his public statements or these two contracts say. Huie had all the problems of the man in the middle. Foreman, however, had a very great problem, that of getting paid, an item of greater than usual importance with him. For, as we shall see from the next two documents, 100 per cent of any possible income was committed, regardless of what these two contracts show.

There is, among that part of the documentation on these matters that I have obtained, what is titled an "AMENDATORY AGREEMENT," drawn and entered after Hanes was fired. In the upper left-hand corner are the initials JJS ek 12/6/68." This would seem to indicate its preparation on December 6 by a lawyer whose initials are JJS and its being typed by someone whose initials are EK. I do not now know who these people are. It was signed by four people—Huie, Hanes, Ray, and Foreman.

This amending agreement begins with the same difficulties with dates (July dates when they should have been August, etc.), but that would appear to be not the major problem. The typing in the first sentence says it is "entered into this ___ day of December 1968" by Huie, Ray, and Hanes. Only, when it was finally consummated, the date written in is "29" and the month is changed, in hand-lettered capitals, to "January." Over and above everything else, this means that the contract, expected to be completed during the month of December, and one would presume close to the date it was prepared, was not in fact agreed to until the very end of the following month. In turn, this suggests at least one signatory was holding out.

There is no apparent reason for Huie or Ray to have held back, with their interests unchanged. This leaves only Hanes.

As soon as the original contract and letter are referred to in the "Amendatory Agreement," there is this second reference (paragraph b of the first provision):

Ray and Hanes have entered into a certain document entitled "agreement" dated July 5, 1968 [herein the "Assignment Agreement"] under which Ray assigned to Hanes a portion of his interests in any moneys accruing to Hanes under said Basic Agreement.

This is a very large mouthful.

Without examining the July 5 "assignment agreement," it is not possible to know how there could be the apparent impossibility of *Ray* having any "interest in any moneys accruing to *Hanes* under said basic agreement," which had not been executed by July 5. Furthermore, there is no such provision in the "Basic Agreement." The division of spoils there, in the fifth provision—the first initialed by Hanes and Huie but not by Ray—is specific: Hanes and Ray each get 30 per cent and there is no assignment from either to the other.

However, this formulation in the Amendatory Agreement does seem to say much about what there is no reference to in the original basic agreement or the letter supplement, that beforehand Hanes did get Ray's signature on a contract, one in which, from the foregoing, it would seem that Ray assigned his only property of any value, the literary rights to his story, to Hanes. One might conjecture that, with Ray having asked Hanes *before* Hanes got to England to engage Huie to write his story, Hanes was sufficiently foresighted to latch onto the entire property for himself. Thus, there is a purpose served by the strange subsequent agreements, cutting Huie in and seeming to cut Ray in. The pious Hanes was conniving and doing all this while he was, with proper unction, telling the press he didn't know if he would take the case.

Good man, that Hanes. He had profited from his FBI and CIA experience. It seems clear that he had *all* the "action," and he held onto it.

There is no apparent reason for Hanes to get any of the take except as his fee. In nothing that ever appeared in any form in the press is there the slightest indication that Hanes had such an "assignment agreement" or any other kind with Ray. The language of the basic agreement and the supplementary letter, if ever examined by an outsider, not only contains no reference to it, but conveys the deceptive, opposite impression.It seems safe to assume the contracts are so broken up and worded in part to make it seem that the 30 per cent allocated to Hanes is his fee for defending Ray.

In the "Amendatory Agreement," there is no description of what "portion" Ray assigned to Hanes. It is meaninglessly called only "a portion." So, that is still secret.

Paragraph (c) of the first provision says that Huie had written and was then writing "material . . . which will be published in issues of Look Magazine." As of either December 6 or January 29, this could refer only to what was written and not published or what was published in the issue dated April 15. His first two articles had already appeared. This paragraph also says that some of the "material will be published in book form by Dell Publishing Co., Inc., pursuant to a contract with Author (the working title of which book is "THEY SLEW THE DREAMER")."

How interesting this is, especially when combined. On the one hand, unless Huie wrote what *Look* would not and did not print, the agreement implies that he was writing his April 15 *Look* piece, which says Ray was the lone killer, and simultaneously he was writing a book whose title said "*THEY*," meaning more than one person, did the killing.

Ray sure was in fine, trustworthy hands! Remember, this contract was not signed until January 29.

The next paragraph says Hanes no longer represents Ray in any way and Foreman does.

Because "the parties are desirous of effecting certain releases" (the last breakdown of the first provision), "Hanes does hereby transfer and assign to Ray all Hanes' rights, title and interest in, to and under said basic agreement and the Assignment Agreement" (the first sentence of the second provision). This needs some comment. Under the basic agreement, Hanes had only a 30 per cent interest to assign to anyone, the other 30 per cent chunk being Ray's, and the remaining 40 per cent being Huie's. If Hanes did not have any further share under the assignment agreement, no purpose is served by including the reference to it here. The rest of this provision assigns any future Hanes interest and

> Hanes further agrees that he shall not hereafter write or authorize to be written any literary material relating to the murder of Martin Luther King, Jr., Ray's alleged participation in it or Ray's coming trial for such murder, or the life or activities of Ray, and that he shall not hereafter make or authorize to be made magazine, book, dramatic, motion picture, television and/or other adaptation of any kind relating to any such subjects.

Because Hanes was, at the time this contract was initiated, according to his own public statements, engaged in just such negotiations with *Life*—a sure thing, as he put it—and because he immediately violated this provision without recourse by anyone, it is

373

safe to assume that no one, least of all Foreman, objected—or objected enough to dare wash all of this out in open court.

Except for the movie, and possibly the dramatic, provisions, in writing for the April 15 issue of *Look* and in promotional appearances, Hanes also violated all the other restrictions. But the *Look* pieces involved, according to Foreman, $85,000 of which "I get 60 percent," so possibly Foreman felt sufficiently rewarded to overlook this contract violation.

Next the contract releases Huie and Ray of any obligation to Hanes and stipulates that Hanes has received everything to which he is entitled. In turn, Ray and Huie release Hanes. These releases include "oral agreements," of which there is no available record. It may, of course, be a mere precaution. Hanes also agrees to "execute and deliver to" the others "any further instruments necessary or desirable to implement or effectuate" this agreement. But it does not say for free.

In the sixth provision, Ray acknowledges "there are no moneys or other compensation of any kind" due from Huie.

Mysteriously, in provision seven, Huie replaces his agent with himself, and Foreman, as Ray's attorney, becomes the man who looks out for Ray's financial interests, replacing Hanes in this respect also, and assuming the same conflict of interest.

The other contracted arrangements are continued, and in the last provision, Huie alone is given the right to assign his interest. It will be apparent from the document to be examined next that none existed for Ray to be able to assign.

The three parties signed the agreement and, under "APPROVED AS TO FORM AND CONTENT," Foreman signed, "Percy Foreman, as Attorney for James Earl Ray."

The one thing missing from this contract is what Hanes got for giving up his hunk of Ray in perpetuity.

That "portion," as we shall see, was 100 per cent of what remained after Huie got his 40 per cent of the *gross*. With the lowest contemporaneous estimate of the value of Ray, not in perpetuity but immediately being, per Foreman's estimate, $400,000, Hanes was voluntarily giving up only a little less than a quarter of a million dollars. With good fortune, even more than the $400,000 could have been anticipated.

For nothing?

Hanes's record, especially that immediately preceding, makes this impossible to believe.

Here there is a reasonable explanation of the almost two-month delay in the signing of the agreement under which Hanes seemed to return to Ray all of his interest of any kind in any possible income. The explanation: Hanes was holding out for his price when he was bought off.

Who could buy him out? Who wanted to?

Not Ray, who had nothing and could pay nothing.

Not Huie, who by this time was holding a very bad hand, had gone deeply in the hole on the deal, and had only a minority interest, anyway.

Unless there are unseen interests, which does not seem probable, only Foreman could be the source of Hanes's payoff, whatever, if anything, it was. With what Foreman had in mind, he should not really have expected any major return from his handling of Ray. But unless he got his money from Ray, meaning from what Ray got from Huie's income, whence was it to come?

Meanwhile, if he got it from Ray, as he did in the next document we examine, he immediately assumed an additional conflict of interest. Financially interested, he has the original Hanes conflict. But now he also has the conflict between Ray's legal interest and his own financial interests, for anything that was not in Ray's legal interest but was in Foreman's financial interest is such a conflict.

Is there any doubt that making the deal under which Ray got a tougher sentence than would otherwise seem to have been likely, the deal the judge lauded in just these terms, was not in Ray's interest? And is there any doubt that, without this deal, there would be no real salable property through which Huie could recoup or from which Foreman could get anything, the return of whatever it might have cost to buy out Hanes, his own costs and fees, or profit? Once there was a trial, everything coming out in that trial would be public domain, every writer's property, without cost or payment of any kind, as was explained earlier in this book.

Even more perplexing and harder to believe is that Foreman bought out Hanes without any contract with Ray. From the documents I have, which may not be complete in this respect although they seem to be, there was no such deal with Ray until February 3, much after Foreman became his lawyer. Of course, there may have been another document under the legal table, like the Hanes-Ray contract of July 5, not referred to in any of the other documents. But I have neither record of any nor reason to believe there was any.

This means that, from the time he got the case in early November until February 3, Foreman had no certainty he would get anything. How very unlike the public record of which this same Percy Foreman boasts.

375

He is the man whose fees are "punishment enough"!

On February 3, Foreman secured an affidavit from Ray attesting,

> I . . . have signed over, given, conveyed and transferred and do, by this instrument herenow give, assign, set over and transfer to PERCY FOREMAN, of Houston, Harris County, Texas, all of my aforesaid right, title and interest in and to the proceeds that would otherwise have accrued to me [under all the earlier agreements, plus] any other right or rights that might be or have been mine because of the writing and subsequent purblication [sic] of such writing by said Author.

This means everything and forever. It even directs that payment be made directly to Foreman "in his own name and as his own property" rather than as Ray's lawyer.

A more monumental conflict is hard to conceive.

Or a more thorough and complete emptying of the "client" of everything he had or, in perpetuity, might hope to have. This is exactly what Jerry Ray said, leading to Foreman's comment that the newspapers found printable only as "bull."

The second "whereas" of this vacuuming of every cent does prove one of Foreman's points, when he pretended at first to have no concern about money and then said, humbly, that he had done no more than assume Hanes's interest. This clause proceeds to say that the July 5 agreement was an assignment by Ray of "at first a portion of his interest in any moneys accruing to Hanes under said Basic Agreement"—a basic agreement that did not exist on July 5. It adds: "and later the said Ray did assign to the said Hanes all of his interest in said moneys so accruing." This now leaves no doubt Hanes got every cent Huie didn't, exactly what Foreman wound up with. There is also no doubt that Hanes's garnering of all the money that did not go to Huie is not provided for in the July 5 agreement, unless this affidavit misrepresents it. This also is contrary to the language of the later basic agreement. It would seem there is some kind of other Ray-Hanes document or the July 5 contract is a cleaning-out of all of Ray's interest.

We have not yet fathomed the great and selfless dedication of these eminent lawyers to the defense of their clients, their totality of commitment to law and justice, unimpeded by any financial or personal considerations. Before continuing with this glorification of the legal profession, this embodiment of goodness and decency, I note a technicality.

Every cent Ray had or could hope to have was Foreman's for these

376

things: "for and in consideration of" monies Foreman had already advanced for Ray, "services heretofore rendered" in his behalf, Foreman's "agreement to represent me at the trial or trials," and nothing else. Aside from the undisclosed funds Foreman may have "advanced" for Ray, which could not be large, what do these services amount to? Merely getting the trial postponed and then preventing it—and condemning his client to guilt of a crime to which his client claims innocence. In legal work, Foreman did nothing else—not nearly enough, even at his $200-an-hour rate, to earn a quarter of a million dollars or more. His *coup de grace* for all this, was pleading Ray guilty while Ray proclaimed his own innocence of the charge of murder!

By eliminating the trial, Foreman did more than preserve any literary income he might expect. He also eliminated any real work he might be expected to do in return for this rather large income, by his own appraisal.

Huie is also a fine, decent, kind, and thoughtful man. All heart. To understand this, all one need do is read the pleasant note he wrote "Dear James Earl," dated March 7, 1969. Ray then was about to be put away for as long as he could expect to live, without recourse and without possibility of ever getting a cent from the literary property that was originally his.

First, Huie says, he is enclosing the original, three-way agreement and the letter agreement "by which I agreed to advance $35,000 in anticipation of earnings" and "Receipts from your attorneys for the $40,000 which I have advanced to date. ($30,000 to Mr. Hanes and $10,000 to Mr. Foreman.)"

He sends a copy of the "Supplementary Agreement which was signed by Mr. Foreman, Mr. Hanes, you and me." This can be interpreted to betoken Huie's understanding that Foreman was a signatory to the contracted arrangements, not just Ray's lawyer. And he asks Ray to sign "another copy so that we can have two copies bearing all four signatures."

These are all the agreements "existing between you and me," he tells Ray and, with no show of modesty, adds, "you will note that I have followed them to the letter. I will continue to do so."

This is one way of saying he "found" Ray guilty without a trial and sought the widest possible circulation for his decision, reached over the objection of the man whose interest he pretended to be serving, "to the letter."

He forecasts "additional earnings" above the $30,000 "this project has earned." How cool can you be with a man about to have the guarantee he will spend the rest of his life in jail, for which you have your responsibility, when you write him a comforting note?

Now, if by "earnings" Huie means more than gross income, means what the dictionary says the word means, the deal also got him out of the financial hole he had claimed to be in. These new "earnings" are to come from the April 15 *Look* article, "foreign magazines and from Dell Publishing Company, which will publish the book in May."

For a book to be published in May, March 7 is a late date for it not to have been completed, which pretty strongly suggests that, so far as Huie was concerned, he had completed it.

The next sentence is repetitious in an illuminating way: "LOOK Magazine will publish my next article on April 15th. The book, titled HE SLEW THE DREAMER, will be published about May 15th."

To say the "next" article is to suggest there will be others following it. If Huie expected no further *Look* articles, he would have said, "my last article." Knowing it would be published April 15, which means all the preparatory work completed and the magazine printed by April 1, also means he had written it before he wrote this letter.

May 15 is a later publication date for the book than he gave in the December broadcast recorded by Dr. Pauley. On KNBC-TV, Huie gave the old "working" title, "They Slew the Dreamer," and a publication date of March 18. So, after all of his investigation, long after he had written those first two articles and *Look* had published them, Huie was still talking of Ray's innocence of the charge—which he has also said he never believed—even before he knew anything about the case or of a conspiracy. By December, he should have written a book due for March 18 publication. Book-publishing takes time, usually much more time than that.

Yet, by March 7, he had already completed an entirely different book, one saying Ray alone "slew the dreamer"? And an important magazine article saying the same thing? Huie's change of mind about the basic facts of the case, as we noted before, seems to coincide rather snugly with Foreman's entry into it and the realization that a trial would end all the literary property for which he had paid and labored so much.

Noble soul, that Huie, even if he writes with dollars rather than the spirit of a Zola. Thoughtful, too!

"I am currently negotiating with Carlo Ponti, the film producer, over picture rights. I'll keep you informed." This is a kind touch, because Ray would not get a cent from it and everyone else would, as a result of Huie's spelling out what kind of murderer he believes Ray to be.

"We need a picture of you to use on the front cover of the book," Huie says, thus ending any doubt about the real purposes of an earlier effort to get an exclusive picture, presented as some kind of urgent constitutional right Ray was being denied. It is the usual lofty commercial right of the mercenaries.

Next to the last paragraph begins, "Jerry keeps in touch with me."

True. I asked Jerry about it. His account, which I am no less inclined to believe than anything Huie says, is not in the same tone as Huie's chatty, seemingly friendly, manner. If Jerry seems a little defensive, it may be explained by his confession to me that he is responsible for his brother's disastrous choice of Foreman.

Jerry says he met Huie but once, on November 1, 1968, that the only other times they spoke were by phone. At their November meeting:

> Huie went over the contracts with me and showed me how much money he had already paid Hanes. It amounted to thirty thousand.... Here is what convinced me [James Earl] needed another lawyer. He said he also felt that James Earl was innocent and that Hanes was a good lawyer ... felt the outcome would be the same whether James took the stand or not, but if he took the stand then he, Huie, would have no book. Huie told me that he had told Hanes that James must not take the stand.
>
> Huie then told me that if I worked with him that he would pay all of my expenses plus put me on a salary.
>
> My job was supposed to be going down and visiting James Earl every week plus telling him that Huie was doing everything for his best interest. He also told me that if worse came to worse for James Earl that he had connections in politics and that he would see to it that James would never want for anything, that no harm would come to him.
>
> After a guy told you all of that I am sure if your brother was in a fix similar to James' that you would recommend a new lawyer also.

It would be a very uncool Huie who told Jerry that were James to take the stand, he, Huie, would have no book. But the fact of it is so, he *would* have had no book, as we have seen.

Jerry says he also told Huie that

> James was unhappy because everybody was making money off of him and he was penniless. Huie replied that he could change the contract

back like it originally was . . . I replied that Hanes might not want to go along with that. Huie replied, Hanes does what I tell him. I am the one that is putting out the money.

That's when I made up my mind that James needed another lawyer.

Is Huie braggart enough to tell Jerry he controlled Hanes? Hanes is rather a big shot in that part of the country. But the fact is, Huie did not pay Hanes all the money due him under their July 8 agreement. In all, according to the letter from Huie to Ray from which I have been quoting, Huie had paid Hanes, as of March 7, 1969, a total of $30,000. But by two months earlier, he should have paid Hanes not less than $40,000—$10,000 on the signing of the book contract, about July 15-20, and $5,000 monthly for six months, beginning with Ray's return in July. So, while it may seem hard to believe, Huie apparently *did* do what Jerry quotes him as saying he would do.

And it is quite literally true that James did not get a penny. Should he have been other than "unhappy"?

At the end of it all, this man who had just ordained Ray's solitary guilt in exchange for what he hoped would amount to more than 30 pieces, promises "if it is your desire you can count on me to keep in touch with you indefinitely. I'll help you in any way I can."

Is there anything more wonderful than unending friendship, the real, genuine Alfonse and Gaston bit, the dependable, trustworthy man standing by? Ray, criminal that he is (murderer in Huie's book), must have dropped a vagrant tear when he read this touching pledge of unending "help."

Lucky Ray, to have such stalwart, selfless friends!

Naturally, my letter to Ray, addressed to him in care of Canale and offering different "help" than Huie's, never reached him. This is the word he sent me through Jerry. Isn't it strange that neither Canale nor the jail nor the United States mail returned it?

There are two other letters of importance that I have. (There may be others that I do not have.) These two are from Foreman to Ray, earlier referred to as Foreman had represented them to the press. It may be more informative to the reader if he can read what was in very few papers and was complete in none.

Both are dated March 9, 1969, and are on the letterhead of Foreman's law office. March 9 was the Sunday before the minitrial, an unusual day for the writing and hand-delivering of business letters. It happens also to be the time Ray was reportedly trying to back out on the deal that could mean so much to Foreman and, in an entirely different way, to him.

Through the great trial lawyer's elliptical use of language—and some of it is quite the opposite, brutally blunt—a little more of the financial arrangement and Foreman's milk of human kindness do come out. The errors are in the original, making one wonder if a stenographer worked that Sunday:

> You have asked that I advance to Jerry Ray five ($500) of the $5,000," referring to the first five thousand dollars paid by Wm. Bradford Huie. On January 29th, Mr. Huie advanced an additional $5,000. At that time I had spent in excess of $9,500 on your case. Since then I have spent in excess of $4,000.

Foreman, as befits a $200-an-hour man, is both a fast and a big spender. He got the case November 12, if one accepts the date of the court proceeding at which it was stated. In the next ten weeks, with no sign of an investigation, he spent $9,500? But he never let Jerry, who was jobless, have the small sum of $500.

Jerry is the one who got Foreman the case. Jerry, regardless of what one may think of him, his beliefs, and his record, also gave up regular employment to help, as he understands helping. Jerry had no apparent source of any income at all. He was doing things for James Earl, he says, and this is reasonable to believe. So, when before January 29, Ray asked the gracious, pleasant, and oh! so wealthy Foreman for a pittance from the money he had earned for the brother trying to help him, that generous defender did not give it. And by March 9 he still had not.

Not that he would not. He comes right out in this letter and says, "But I am willing to"—still as an "advance." As lawyers might be expected to do, but in a rather unlawyerly way, he attaches a condition:

> And this advance, also, is contingent upon the plea of guilty and sentence going through on March 10, 1969, without any unseemly conduct on your part in court.

In plainer English, Ray's gotta keep his yap shut and the deal goes through or his brother doesn't get helped.

Foreman says he is willing to let Jerry have this "advance" of $500— "just this one $500.00"—and add it to his take when the loot rolls in.

There are no stenographer's initials, but there is a "PF-4" code at the bottom and a P.S. In it, Foreman is less than helpful to Ray's defense against the Hays suit. (As I have noted, Hays was suing for what he alleges was due him, and he was seeking, as part of this repayment, to get possession of the rifle and the white Mustang.) Foreman, says that if there is any net return over costs, when the Hays litigation is settled, he will credit it against the $165,000 to which, with the same preconditions, he agrees to limit himself. At $200 an hour, the price at which Foreman rates his services, how much can remain of what a secondhand car and a secondhand rifle are worth?

The other letter of the same Sunday, also with no stenographer identification and with the same PF-4 code at the bottom, reminds Ray of what he will not likely ever forget, the "you have heretofore assigned to me all of your royalties . . . . These are my property unconditionally." Like J. Edgar Hoover pretending that his unsavory investigations, for which he wheedles or blackmails the Attorney General's approval, originate with the Attorney General rather than with him, Foreman smears it on, saying that Ray "authorized and requested me to negotiate a plea of guilty." Here the clever lawyer is making a false record, making it seem the idea was Ray's. Had he not desired Ray's signature on these letters, he probably would have said Ray begged him, as he said in public. It was not Ray's idea. The available record shows Ray opposed it. Foreman had begun working on the deal and on Ray to accept it soon after he had the case, within a half-hour after "Public Defender" Stanton joined him.

I asked Jerry Ray what he knew about this, if James really did ask Foreman to cop the plea. He tells me:

it is partly true, but it was Foreman's idea, not James'. James wouldn't write Foreman . . . that. James wrote Foreman a letter telling him why he wouldn't plead guilty, mainly because he was not guilty. Foreman kept bugging him about it. So, one day while Foreman was visiting him and badgering him about it, [James] wrote it down on a piece of paper . . ."

—that is, what Foreman asked him to write.

It is in this second letter that Foreman omits the specification that "you" not engage in "any unseemly conduct." There is no doubt he includes James Earl when he stipulates the reduced fee he offers is only if "no embarrassing circumstances take place in the court room." Of course, it was possible Jerry might kick up a fuss. Foreman could also interpret that as an "embarrassing circumstance." The formulation of this letter includes both Rays.

With James Earl wavering, wanting to back out on the deal, what does the wily Foreman, who has not given the needy brother the small sum asked of him of the $10,000 of James Earl's money Huie had dished up, do to hold his neat little deal together—over his client's objection? He promises to kick back his majority share of the loot over $165,000. He estimated this to total $400,000. Others anticipated more. The bait was too much for both Rays. It held them in line.

This kindness of Foreman's, reducing his expected fee by more money than James Earl had seen in his entire life, is explained:

> This will shorten the trial considerably. In consideration of the time it will save me, I am willing to make the following adjustment of my fee arrangement with you.

This is true. It did save time. It was true in the moment of crisis, when Ray was backing out. But it was also true when Foreman originally got Ray to agree to the guilty plea. The proper and appropriate time for Foreman to make this concession in his exorbitant fee was then, when Ray agreed to what would save Foreman all this time. The time of this agreement is the time Foreman should have changed his contract, but he didn't. He held onto this excessive fee, this unduly large sum he had, in effect, extorted. Not until he needed a bludgeon did he contract the kickback.

There is no doubt Percy the Great is a great trial lawyer. He has the scruple and conscience to go with it. And the cunning.

The foregoing is unstinting testimony to his skill.

Hanes is no slouch in the milking end of the law. Only he isn't as smooth as Foreman. He insisted on a trial, having gotten his $30,000. Jerry thinks this worried Huie, who feared loss of everything. And there is little doubt James did not want to go to trial in November.

I wonder what, if anything, Hanes got for selling out his 60 per cent interest in Huie's gross, for his piece of Ray.

We know what Foreman is to get and part of what he did get. It would be interesting to know what it cost him.

We know what Ramsey Clark, J. Edgar Hoover and the FBI, the rest of the federal government, and the Memphis authorities got out of it. They got a corrupt decision that seemed to buttress them. The official record is made to seem to support them. The crime is "solved."

What they did not get is the support and approval of the broad mass of the people. Only a few of those calling themselves liberals and intellectuals and those either without interest or unable to evaluate the obvious really support public authority in this case.

In the context of the hidden provisions of the secret contracts, I again draw attention to Jerry Ray's statements that amount to charges against Foreman. I asked again how Foreman got the case. Jerry's statement should be considered along with these secret records of the fleecing of his brother in the name of defending him. Jerry is explicit. I cannot prove he is right. The reader can decide whether he is or seems to be. (See the Appendix.) This is what Jerry wrote me August 2, 1969:

I was constantly after James to fire Arthur Hanes on account of I knew he was representing Huie instead of James. Without James' consent I called Percy Foreman in October of 68 and asked him if he would take the case. Percy Foreman said he would. I in return told James about it, and he said he didn't want Foreman in it as he was satisfied at the present with Arthur Hanes. I flew down to Hartsell, Ala., on the first of November to see Huie. After my visit with him, I knew for sure that James needed another lawyer, so I called Foreman again. Foreman told me to have James to write him a letter requesting him to come down. I in return told James that I had talked to Foreman and he would come down and take his case if he would write him a letter. Still, James refused to write Foreman a letter requesting his coming down. Time was running out, so just a few days before the trial, I called Percy Foreman and asked him to meet me in Memphis. He agreed to even though James hadn't requested him to come down.

My brother John and I met Percy Foreman at the airport and went straight to a motel. Percy Foreman wanted to look over the contracts that James had with Arthur Hanes and Huie. I showed him the contracts and he said they could be broken. Then we called a cab and went to the Shelby County Jail.

The reports were wrong, as John or I wasn't present when Percy Foreman talked to James. A guard by the name of Captain Smith took Foreman up to James' cell while John and I waited downstairs. About two hours later, Foreman came down with a handwritten note from James requesting that he wanted Arthur Hanes to do nothing further in his behalf and that he wished to employ Percy Foreman to represent him.

So that's how Foreman got into the case, and I feel guilty as hell, as if it wasn't for me he would never have employed Percy Foreman.

It is the height of impropriety for a lawyer to speak to another lawyer's client without advance request from the client. From this record, it seems as though Foreman did just that, which is the charge Hanes makes against him. In this case, he knew James Earl Ray did not want him, unless Jerry lies. I believe he is truthful about this.

Perhaps the scheming and manipulations of Ray's "defenders" do not constitute a conspiracy against him. However, they could not better have succeeded in the purposes of such a conspiracy had they consciously connived, for together they framed him. But their commercial interests were enough to motivate all of them, and the pursuit of the bucks they could get through using him was all they needed. No deliberate conspiracy among themselves was necessary, either for money or for some other reason. Neither Ramsey Clark nor J. Edgar Hoover nor any one else had to reach out and draw them close, whisper in their ears. Whether or not anyone did really makes no difference. The result is the same. And if there had been such a conspiracy, who is there to prosecute it, since all those who could are either involved or its beneficiaries?

What did the behavior of his "defenders" mean to Ray? If Ray is not guilty of the murder itself, who was there to defend him except those he hired at their own terms, so generous to themselves? Could he have given them more than 100 per cent? (And might it not be asked, could their lusts be sated with nothing less, not even a few pennies for him and those in his family who tried to help him?)

He had Huie, the established, respected writer who could command a wide audience, and through him and the normal commercial interests that are more successful than high principle in publicizing books and other writings, he could expect and he got a very large audience. For what? Huie's insistence on Ray's singular guilt.

Huie could not have assessed the available evidence and still concluded that it establishes Ray as the murderer or the lone murderer. It proves otherwise. It does persuade that Ray had to have been involved. It most strongly suggests his role was that of a decoy, with the purpose of leading pursuit away from the real killer. Whether or not James Earl Ray is a racist, whether or not he was conscious of his role, this is a sufficiently invidious part for him to have played in one of the more vicious crimes. And from the evidence, it would seem that he had to have known he was being set up as a decoy. It required little imagination to understand for what purpose or who would be the victim. This is a terrible thing for a man to have done, and for it he should be punished. But only in strictest conformity with the law, only for what he did, not for what he did not do or for what another did.

Writers of non-fiction assume obligations no less significant in a society calling itself free, no less sacred than those assumed by lawyers. Perhaps it is because I have spent so many years, such long and financially unrewarding years, seeking the truth about these political murders that, as a writer, I may view Huie's unfaithfulness to our calling more harshly than others. But unfaithful he has been and is. It was his self-appointed task and his contracted obligation to amass, present, and assess the evidence. This means *all* the evidence he could get. It was his trust to do more than boil the pot, stewing out more dollars that he cooked it with. He never had any intention to do more. He would buy what the accused had to say and then, with his own infallible literary Godsight, reap the dollar harvest. He began with the conviction Ray was the murderer. He looked for no other possibility, would have looked for no other, and had he done so, or had he found one, he would have faced financial disaster, for what he sold is Ray's guilt.

His "working title," THEY *Killed the Dreamer,* may have had Ray one of the murderers. His amended title, *HE Killed the Dreamer*, had Ray the *lone* murderer. Not until Foreman bamboozled Ray into pleading guilty did Huie change his title and his concept. But the concept never changed so far as Ray's guilt of murder is concerned, and Huie was, as he knew, Ray's hired defender, the man upon whom Ray depended for the presentation of whatever evidence there was contrary to the charge of murder against him. Knowing this, and knowing his own fixed belief that Ray was the murderer, it was dishonest of him to accept this responsibility. He sought and accepted it, because of his God-like concept of self and because the lure of the money he could make was too great.

By contract, Huie had available all that Hanes learned. Very early, Hanes learned enough to cast great doubt on the indictment. Adding this to what he could have picked up in the newspapers, as I did, Huie had more evidence than the minimum to satisfy himself and his potential audience that the charge of murder could not be sustained in open court.

It is, of course, possible for a man to commit a murder and for it not to be possible to prove it in open court beyond reasonable doubt and to a moral certainty. When this happens, it is the obligation of the honest writer to show it did happen, prove there is a case with evidence not admissible in court. Writers need not meet the legal requirement. This, however, Huie did not do, did not even try to do. He substituted his own judgment for fact without at any time getting into the crux of the evidence, those things we have analyzed in this book, like the medical and ballistics fact, the dependability of the witnesses, what they did and did not see. Without the most serious study of this evidence, it was not possible for an honest writer to make a judgment.

So Huie did not study and report the evidence and its meaning. Had he, he would have stood a good chance to lose his potentially profitable commercial markets, perhaps even his standing and his future ability to sell what he writes.

On the other hand, if he had sat down with Hoover and Canale and done their bidding he could not more effectively have done for them what they might have asked of him. He served the purposes of any conspiracy with government against the accused.

In this, Hanes was a perfect partner.

Hanes cannot be condemned for his willingness to defend Kluxers, for that is his duty as a lawyer. But when his willingness to undertake such a defense is bracketed with his career as segregationist mayor of Birmingham at the time of the greatest black suffering in that city, when he was responsible for a police chief with so brutal a racist record and when in his own name that chief turned vicious dogs against black humans, it is not unfair to conclude that Hanes, too, is a racist. Therefore, it is not surprising that he dreamed up a racist conclusion to the murder, that blacks had perpetrated it. This falsity, for which there is no evidence at all, no logic to support it either, achieved wide and persisting acceptance, in itself as evil a thing as anything Hanes or any other participant in this denial of justice did. Defense of his client did not require proving who committed the crime. It merely required proving that the case against him was not proven. Yet Hanes made up a fiction serving the same purposes as the murder itself and publicized it. This is a formula so crippling to the defense that, in court, Hanes may well have failed even though the prosecution case was such he should not have.

With his preconceptions, with this formula (as with his other Cuban-exile formula), Hanes was a walking, talking racist extremist adjunct of the prosecution and the federal government, especially Hoover (whom he went so far out of his way in his *Look* article to praise for the work of the FBI in this case).

Money was enough bait for Hanes, however, and with great circumspection, he proceeded, with or without connivance from Huie, to latch onto a majority interest in Ray's literary and movie values. He was willing, for money, to represent both himself and Ray in the same deal. Ray wound up with nothing—none of the case and no competent legal defense.

Whether or not Huie plotted this with Hanes—possibly he did not

387

approve, or perhaps he longed for that extra hunk for himself—he was and has been silent about this deal, in which he was the vital spark, that took everything from Ray and gave Ray nothing: no legal defense and no public, literary defense.

Once again, no consciously plotted conspiracy could have been more effective. Hanes and Huie, separately and together, served the purposes a deliberated conspiracy would have served.

Percy the Great *is* great. He is, without doubt, one of the most competent, one of the most able, imaginative, and successful of all trial lawyers. With this legal brilliance, he blends and projects an image of purity and simplicity, like that of the storied milkmaid. No sweet country girl ever squeezed and pulled a teat like Percy Foreman. He is the legal milker who drained the udder and then kicked the cow, all the while smiling a sweet, wholesome smile while calling the cow barren.

If it is possible to conclude that the real Percy Foreman, the money-grubber, the woman-taker, the warehouse-stocker, the people-fleecer, needed no other motive than money for what he did, still, that is not explanation enough. He also knew the consequences of what he did. He could not have believed he was saving Ray's life, and he could not have examined the prosecution case, as he was later to say he did—saying also that it was all public, all in the papers—and still believed there was any real prospect that, in Memphis, Ray would have been electrocuted. He had no reason to believe Ray would have been convicted, not if Foreman, in the courtroom, did as Foreman could.

When Foreman said, as he did on the Dick Cavett show, that the evidence against Ray had been published in full, he also said that the evidence against Ray is no more and no more substantial than we have just seen. That does not survive the critical examination of a lone writer. Could it possibly have withstood one of the brilliant courtroom performances of the truly great trial lawyer, this real-life Perry Mason?

It could not.

Foreman either did not know the evidence, which is criminal enough, or he did know it which is more criminal. Either way, his is a guilty course, the more so because it is so inconsistent for him and with his long and incredibly successful record, so often against greater odds and substantial evidence, substantial witnesses.

Suppose it could be proven that Foreman had met secretly in some dark backroom somewhere with Hoover, or Clark, or Canale, or anyone speaking for any of them? What could he then have done that could, in any way, have better suited their desires, more completely served the end of any conscious conspiracy?

There is nothing he could have done, nothing that better suited the only possible purpose of a conspiracy against his client (which I repeat is also a conspiracy against the law, against justice, against the national honor and any genuine, rational concept of national security).

Once Foreman hornswoggled Ray into pleading guilty, for whatever purpose, he got every public official off the hook. Hoover's unbelievable incompetence suddenly became marvelous policework. Clark's spontaneous broken-record reiteration of "no conspiracy," beginning the day after the murder and never ending, therewith became political and legal wisdom; and the no-conspiracy posture of government was, for the first time, sustained in court. That Memphis mimicry of an investigation, so scant it got less money than would be invested in the serious investigation of the murder of a skid-row derelict and was so much less than was spent on keeping Charlie Stephens as happy as he could be without bourbon, was hidden, and Memphis was justified.

Make no mistake about this, the plea of guilty was important to Memphis, to Memphis officialdom, Memphis business, to the Memphis pride and conscience.

For this there is the most competent authority, the late Judge Battle, the participant in and presider-over of the deal. At the end of the minitrial, he had a few choice comments in self- and Memphis-justification (T. 102ff):

> . . . I don't propose to keep us here much longer, but I think that the Court should make a few remarks at this place in the proceedings.
>
> The fact was recognized soon after this tragic murder took place that there was no possible conclusion to the case which would satisfy everybody. And it was decided at that time that the only thing the judge who drew the unlucky number, which was me, could do was to try this case as nearly as possible like all other cases and to scrupulously follow the law and the dictates of his own conscience. I feel I have done this [4].
>
> Memphis has been blamed for the death of Dr. King, to me, wrongfully and irrationally. Neither the decedent nor his killer lived here and their orbits merely intersected here.

There followed his justification of the deal on the grounds there would not have been an electrocution anyway and may have been an acquittal.

I cannot let this occasion pass without paying tribute to Memphis,

Southern America and Western free world justice and security which was truly a team effort involving scores and even hundreds of persons . . . the police departments of Canada, of Mexico, of Portugal, of England, of the F.B.I., the local police, the State of Tennessee, the sheriff's office . . . , Mr. Charles Holmes, the sheriff's office liaison with the news media and finally my amici curiae committee . . . and if I have overlooked anyone I want especially to thank them too.

That is nice, special thanks for those he could not recall. According to Blair's transcript, not the judge but the court reporter did "overlook" some. In the Blair version, the first thanked is the FBI, next the Department of Justice. Nothing unfair about either version, especially with this "as nearly as possible like all other cases" and so scrupulous a following of the law.

This court, nor no one else, knows what the future will bring, but I submit that up to now we have not done too badly here for a "decadent river town."

If I may be permitted a light touch to a solemn occasion I would like to paraphrase the great and eloquent Winston Churchill, who, in defiant reply to an Axis threat that they were going to wring England's neck like a chicken, said, "Some chicken, some neck."

I would like to reply to our Memphis critic, "Some river, some town."

Is there anything else?

Can there be "anything else" after such soaring, Churchillian eloquence? What could possibly follow so appropriate a peroration?

For an iconoclastic writer, one thing: Q.E.D., *quod erat demonstrandum,* what was to be demonstrated.

The role of justifier Foreman also filled—for (as no less an authority than Judge Battle listed [T. 104]) the FBI, the Department of Justice, all Memphis officialdom, and the others the judge may have overlooked, although he seems to have included everyone.

It makes little difference to Ray, if any at all, or to justice, or to the national honor and integrity, or to the murderer still free and his other accomplices unknown and also free, whether Foreman actually sat down and agreed to do what he did at the bidding and in the interest of others. The result is the same. As with Huie, as with Hanes, as with them collectively.

Although the remark does not bear on whether or not there was a talking-over of what would happen as soon as the crime was committed, which would be a conspiracy, the Churchillian judge, if that is what he was, did obliquely address this point. He did say, "And it was decided at that time that the only thing the judge who drew the unlucky number, which was me, could do . . . ." So it seems that some officials *did* get together and plan ahead, sort out what they would do and would not do, what they wanted to happen, little things like that.

Only, why did the good judge have to embroil the guiltless Mississippi River?

I would like to believe it possible something might be done about all this and the denial of justice in which it ended, a denial to the accused who by it was convicted, to the country, to those close to and followers of the martyred victim.

Unless something *is* done, the honor of the nation, already debased by everything that happened in the Presidential murder, in its official investigation, and by the official treatment of those unwilling to accept the hoked-up verdict of the eminences, will not soon recover. Can anyone, here or abroad, trust government when government plays such unseemly games with justice and history, so abuses the law and all democratic concepts?

The trial of Ray was a Shelby County trial in form only. The entire case, the investigation and the doctrine, the "solution," were federal.

More. Here we have the failure of all of society, not just of government.

The original lawyers were all the most commercial, with the interest of justice and the accused sublimated to their own uninhibited lust for money. Stoner is much worse, though he believes his fascism. He is burdened with more sinister conflicts, because his own people plotted the murder of King as they did that of the President. (But the recent entry of Fensterwald into the case—let us hope not too late—does provide hope [5].)

The press, which in some cases did seek out the fact, mostly contents itself with justice it knows is injustice, and with the piety of the pseudo-indignation of the editorial page disguises its abandonment of the responsibilities of a free press in a free society. It is silent when an honest press cannot be.

The associations of lawyers, at least some of whom must read some of the papers I read and quote, had to know of some of the shady dealings. Once again, as when the President was murdered and the accused was systematically and openly denied all of his rights, and when a Report intelligent men cannot credit was palmed off on all of us, they preserved the unseemly silence of the cowardly, preferring the security and avoidance of criticism so bought.

The blacks and their leaders, all self-blackmailing and humble. They should be afire, seeking vengeance, the murderer and his fellow conspirators; rooting out those traitors to our laws and traditions who made this frightful and frightening miscarriage possible. They assure the attempt and success of future political murders of which they and their friends will be the victims. What of their silence? Is it less dishonorable or more when they say there was a conspiracy to kill their most popular leader and yet fail from the first to produce their sons to unmask it and refuse, then and since, to help their white brothers who make the effort? Is it honorable silence when they refuse to respond to letters from those seeking the truth they fail to seek? Does it not seem thay are content with the foul murder of their own and with all it symbolizes because it makes possible the climb of other leaders? And how equally silent they are when he is defamed by his enemy who is their ancient enemy, St. Edgar the Indispensable, the man who couldn't pick up the deliberately laid trail of a petty thief, the man who is responsible for this new frame-up of them and of justice to them!

Can better be said of those who say they seek peace and are mute at the unsolved murder of their brother, as they were and are at the unsolved murder of the President who changed his course toward peace and only then was murdered?

Here in these terrible events we have fact opposite to what is legally ordained as fact; the complete abandonment of everything held dear, the prostitution of the courts, the debasement of justice, the framing of a man, and with him, of the glory of the past and the prospect of the future, jeopardy to the freedom of all—those who have it and those who seek it. And from all of society there is naught but—

The awful crime of silence!

There are few comforts for the writer of a book like this, and no pleasures. It is not in any sense a task to make him happy.

However, there is gratification in feeling he may perform useful service. And there are occasional deep satisfactions from late-coming proofs of solid work and clear analysis.

Two of these, both after this book was completed, are the unintended contribution of William Bradford Huie and a seven-page, single-spaced, typed, signed statement by James Earl Ray which he got out of jail in early August 1970. So the reader can better make his own judgment of what I shall quote from Ray, he should understand that Ray had earlier read this book and asked permission to use it in his defense. This is not to say that what Ray wrote is "feedback" nor is it to say he was not honest. While Ray deals with many matters to which there were no witnesses, I can, independently, confirm much of what he wrote. Little in this statement seems unreasonable or unlikely.

In the belated appearance of his book, Huie, without realizing (or perhaps not caring) what he was disclosing, solved the mystery of that July 5, 1968, secret agreement Hanes cadged out of Ray. In doing this, Huie also provided, certainly without the intent, what to me is a perfect self-description and a most appropriate one of Hanes.

As Huie discloses the secret provisions (pp. 155-156 of *He Slew the Dreamer*), the Haneses "were the only defense lawyers in the case and only if Ray agreed to tell and agreed to publication of his complete story after the trial." As we have seen, Huie published twice *before* any kind of legal proceeding.

What Ray assigned to Hanes on July 5, 1968, is "an undivided 40% interest in all his rights . . . in addition to any money, rights or benefits which may accrue to the said Arthur J. Hanes independently under said agreement."

Or, Hanes got his own 30 per cent cut (of which Ray then had no knowledge) and 40 per cent of Ray's. And there is more.

Huie's characterization of Hanes (p. 180) is as "a courteous and decent man." What did this man who is so "decent" in Huie's lights do to Ray? He got Ray, without Huie's knowledge [Huie says (p. 186)], to amend "the agreement between the two of them [that is, of July 5, 1968] so that, from Ray's 30 percent, Mr. Hanes would deduct not a permanent 40 percent but *only* [Huie's emphasis] 'a fee of $20,000 plus case expenses.'" By Huie's conservative estimate, which seems not to take into account what "plus case expenses" can total, "This gave Mr. Hanes the right to keep for himself every dollar I paid to him and to Ray up to perhaps $75,000." Hanes, of course, also held his own 30 per cent of the Ray package, as the contracts disclose.

Properly pious, of this Huie protests, "Had I been consulted I would not have agreed to any change in the original two-party agreement between Mr. Hanes and Ray." Talky-talk. It was a *two*-party agreement, with Huie not included. No, his "agreement" was not relevant.

Huie adds another measure of Hanes's "decency": "When Mr. Hanes realized that he might be discharged, he made sure he wouldn't owe Ray anything from what I had paid him."

Translation of "owe": Grabbed 100 per cent.

It is a fitting note that to Huie everyone is "Mister" except Ray. Huie, too, kicked his cow.

Ray's from-the-jail statement goes into his financial arrangements with Hanes:

> On July 5, 1968, Mr. Hanes did visit me in the English prison. He suggested I sign two contracts—one giving Mr. Hanes my power of attorney, the other 40% of all revenues I might receive. At this time, no mention was made of any novelist.

The reader will recall my serious misgivings about the extradition proceeding, about whether British law had been violated, and my belief that Ray had not been adequately defended and represented. What Ray says of this should be considered in the context of this deal Hanes kept secret, for if Ray had *not* been extradited, it is obvious that Hanes had neither client nor fee. This also bears on the enormity of his conflict when Hanes represented himself and his client where they had competing financial interests.

"I spoke to Mr. Hanes again before being deported but no further mention was made of contracts. [That is, nothing about *other* contracts, only this July 5 deal giving Hanes 40 per cent of Ray's interest, which Ray then had to understand to be an arrangement whereby he retained a 60 per cent interest.] Mr. Hanes did advise me to waive further extradition appeals, which I did."

Not until Hanes's second visit to the Memphis jail did Hanes tell Ray about Huie. Then, "Mr. Hanes urged me to sign the contracts to finance the suit."

Ray says his first disagreement with Hanes was over money Ray wanted for two purposes: to hire local counsel, Hanes (an Alabama lawyer) having described the permission granted him to appear in Tennessee courts "as a 'one-shot deal' "; and "Further, I wanted to hire an investigator to go to Louisiana to check some phone numbers" without Huie knowing about it. Hanes refused Ray's request.

It is interesting to note that at this point in his statement Ray decided to ink out some of it. That elimination can, in part, still be made out. Before "Louisiana," the words "New Orleans" and "Baton Rouge" are discernible. Ray makes other comments about these phone numbers without identifying them. The association of Ray, telephone numbers,

New Orleans, and Baton Rouge should be fresh in the reader's mind.

Ray confirms that he did not ask Foreman to enter the case until after Foreman appeared at the jail on November 10, 1968. Ray claims he was ready to go to trial with Hanes until that moment. His account is essentially the same as Jerry had given me, with this addition: Foreman said "that the only things Hanes and Huie was [sic] interested in was money. He said they were personal friends and if I stuck with them I would be bar-becued [sic]."

On the appointment of Stanton as co-counsel, James Earl makes several comments:

> Mr. Foreman told me in the courtroom on Dec. 18, 1968 that the court would appoint the public defender to the case. When I questioned the appointment Mr. Foreman said he, Judge Battle and Mr. Hugh Stanton, Sr., had agreed before the hearing to bring the public defender's office into the case.

The transcript of that hearing, where it was pretended that the judge was making spontaneous response to a supposedly unanticipated plea of pauperism by the millionaire Foreman, entirely confirms James Earl's account, Foreman involuntarily having blurted it out, not realizing what he was saying. I now have that transcript.

But James Earl did not want Stanton. He refused to see him when Stanton came on January 17, 1969, while Foreman was ill:

> I told Capt. Billy Smith I did not wish to see Mr. Stanton. He was permitted in the cell block anyway. I informed Mr. Stanton I didn't want to discuss anything with him and that I would write him a letter explaining why. He left the block saying he didn't have time for the case anyway. I then wrote a letter to Mr. Stanton, Sr., saying I didn't want judges and prosecuting attorneys deciding who would defend me.

If true, this bears very much on whether Ray was permitted counsel of his own choice, a minimum legal requirement. Records are kept of prisoners' mail as, presumably, Stanton also keeps files. So Ray's word is susceptible of confirmation or disproof.

The reference to Judge Battle's having decided who would defend Ray comes up again in Ray's account of his disagreements with Foreman, when Foreman was pressuring Ray to cop the plea. During one of his visits, Foreman tried to get Ray to sign releases clearing "Huie and *Look* magazine of damaging my prospects for a fair trial because of their pre-trial publishing ventures." (Ultimately, Ray did sign them.) Ray says he also protested this publicity in a certified letter to Judge Battle. In Ray's account, Foreman's "monologue was very strident that day." Foreman "insisted that I sign the papers." Ray "had to ask him several times to lower his voice" so as not to be overheard.

In addition to the fear of being electrocuted, these are the arguments Ray says Foreman used to persuade him to agree to the deal:

Ray had already been convicted by the pre-trial publicity, which the trial judge would not attempt to halt "unless it reflected on the prosecution case."

It was in Ray's financial interest to plead guilty.

The prosecution had already "fixed" a witness—presumably meaning Stephens.

The Chamber of Commerce "was pressuring the trial judge" and Canale "to get a guilty plea as a long trial would have an adverse effect on business." (Ray quotes Foreman as telling him that "The Chamber wasn't happy about Dr. King's being removed from the scene.")

"The trial judge was concerned about the effects a trial would have on the city's [Memphis] image," and the judge had even sent emissaries "to persuade some S.C.L.C. members to accept a guilty plea."

Ray says he insisted on a trial, with Foreman countering that "he could get me a pardon, after two or three years."

As the argument continued, "Mr. Foreman got the message over to me that if I forced him to trial he would destroy—deliberately—the case in the court room."

Ray's understanding of what he signed is "a guilty plea to a technical charge of homicide."

When Foreman visited him in March, just before the minitrial, Ray says, "I made a last attempt to have a jury trial. I asked Mr. Foreman to withdraw" (so Ray could get another attorney). "Mr. Foreman refused to withdraw and reminded me of Trial Judge Battle's ruling" that "it would either be him [that is, Foreman] as counsel or the public defender."

This is, indeed, what the judge had said at one of the formal hearings. In practice, it meant the defendant had no voice in his own defense. In itself, this should be sufficient grounds for reversal of the minitrial. However, when Fensterwald asked the court for access to Judge Battle's papers, he was denied it. He was also denied access to *any* of the evidence not seen by Hanes or Foreman.

Canale rides again! No one will ever see it, he wrote me.
To paraphrase His Honor: "some law; some justice."

With the minor mystery now solved the way I correctly understood it had to be, the only way, from my analysis and investigation, it could be solved, I must ask again, is there any condemnation too strong, any castigation too severe, for such mercenary wretches who, for money alone, intrude themselves into the workings of a system of laws and justice? Can *any* system work when this kind of interference is both possible and unpunished?

We hear fine speeches from the bar and its leaders; from the judges, notably Nixon's new Chief Justice, whose pre-appointment study for the bar association almost anticipated the incredible raping of justice by the judge who guarded her bower until his death that now may perhaps not be regarded as untimely, the Chief Justice who is silent on this; from the Attorney General whose expressed thoughts are so noble— as he expresses them (and to whose actions we address ourselves in the coming chapter); from even the President and his Vice President.

Is it not now past time for speeches alone?

Is it not now past time for action?

If it is not, then it is past time for justice to be expected, perhaps for justice to survive.

17. Getting the Truth

The "Freedom of Information Act" became effective July 4, 1967, a date that, in the light of subsequent history, could not have been more inappropriate. I think it useful to describe my encounters with this law—repeating some of the story already told in earlier chapters—in the course of writing this book. My experience provides one example of press "freedom" in the country today.

President Lyndon Johnson issued a special statement on signing the law on July 4, 1966. These four sentences, from three of the eight paragraphs, are most pertinent:

> This legislation springs from one of our most essential principles: a democracy works best when people have all the information that the security of the Nation permits. No one should be able to pull curtains of secrecy around decisions which can be revealed without injury to the public interest . . . I have always believed that freedom of information is so vital that only the national security, not the desire of public officials or private citizens, should determine what should be restricted . . . I sign this measure with a deep sense of pride that the United States is an open society in which the people's right to know is cherished and guarded.

Surely the *public* record of a *public* trial, the court proceeding by which the government of the United States obtained the extradition of an American citizen for a supposed public trial in the United States, does not involve "national security." And certainly it *is* "our most essential principle" in "a democracy" that the "people have all the information that the security of the Nation permits." But despite the President's assurance that, over and above all the other laws, this one prevents public officials from pulling down "curtains of secrecy," the Nixon administration was refusing me the *trial* evidence, the *public* record, after more than a half-year of effort to see it.

Attorney General Clark was no less proud of the then-new "Freedom of Information" law. The month before it became effective, he published and sent all federal agencies a memorandum on it and their obligations under it. The memo explained:

> This law was initiated by Congress and signed by the President with several key concerns:
> — that disclosure be the general rule, not the exception;
> — that all individuals have equal right of access;
> — that the burden be on the Government to justify the withholding of a document, not on the person requesting it;
> — that individuals improperly denied access to documents have a right to seek injunctive relief in the courts;
> — that there be a change in Government policy and attitude.

Throughout the memo, Clark ever so properly tells all executive agencies exactly what his own Department of Justice ignored, that the law covers all "records," whether "made or received by any agency of the United States Government in pursuance of Federal law or in connection with the transaction of public business and preserved or appropriate for preservation by that agency . . . regardless of physical form or characteristics." This certainly, in each separate aspect, covers the Ray extradition and all records of it. As though to eliminate doubt, Clark added, "It is equally clear that the definition is not limited to historical documents but includes contemporaneous documents as well" (both quotations from page 23).

On March 31, 1969, several weeks after the minitrial, I asked the Department of Justice for "a set of the evidence, including affidavits entered into evidence, in the Ray extradition hearing in London." That this letter and the subsequent reminders were *entirely* unanswered is, no doubt, due to the Nixon administration's single-minded attachment to the Freedom of Information law. The law requires not only *meaningful* response, but also promptness.

This special law required the Department of Justice to make *immediate, meaningful* response, if only not to violate the law, and to make the *public* record available to me.

Months passed and there had been not even pro forma acknowledgment of my personal repeated inquires. Such inquiries are proper for a writer —his obligation—and the right of every citizen, whether or not a writer. The official silence is, in itself, flagrant violation of the law. So, I engaged counsel. Bernard Fensterwald, Jr., who was counsel for the Senate committee from which this law came, wrote Attorney General John Mitchell for me on August 20, 1969, announcing I had retained him to represent me. He repeated the sad Department of Justice record in "protecting" American "Freedom of Information," including their persistent refusal to provide me the forms requisite for invoking the law, for which I'd asked several times. Our hope was to spare the government needless cost and embarrassment, for there is no doubt about legal requirement. What I asked for is the public record of a public trial, in open court, reported by the press of the world.

Once again weeks passed. When we were about to prepare the papers for filing the action in court, Fensterwald got an apologetic phone call from Joseph Cella, a Department of Justice lawyer. Cella asked him to delay filing the suit, suggesting that the letter he had been delegated to write might obviate the need. Because we did not want to go to court and considered it only in an effort to force the government to comply with the law and to make available to me what it cannot legally and constitutionally suppress, with or without this special law, we agreed. When the promised letter had not been received by October 4, we wrote Cella still another time, reminding him of his weeks-old call and asking for additional suppressed information. These requests were never responded to. Nor were others I addressed to Mitchell personally, in a further futile effort to get the Attorney General to observe the law he is supposed to respect and uphold.

It is almost as though J. Edgar Hoover personally was listening in when Fensterwald and I consulted. We had just decided on another date by which, if we had no response, we would file suit when Fensterwald got another, still apologetic, call from Cella. This time Cella apologized for the long delay, saying he had been "busy," an excuse specifically illegalized by the law. He said he had drafted the response, but declined to communicate it on the reasonable ground that he did not know whether it would be altered or, in fact, used at all.

This "response" was a letter from the Deputy Attorney General, Richard Kleindienst. Kleindienst's earlier claims to fame were as a leading functionary in the campaign in which Barry Goldwater made far and away the worst showing of any unsuccessful Presidential candidate and then for conducting wasteful, costly, and demeaning time-checks on Department of Justice attorneys, requiring that they account for how they spend each 12-minute segment of the day.

That Kleindienst *took 227 days* to answer at all is, in itself, an open, contemptuous law violation. It is also cute, in an immature, childish way. He wrote, ostensibly referring to my specific request, since I was required by the law to identify the records I sought:

400

I regret that I must deny your request in all particulars. No documents in the files of the Department are identifiable as being copies of the documents transmitted to British authorities through diplomatic channels at the request of the States of Tennessee and Missouri and presented to the Bow Street Court by officials of the United Kingdom.

There is another sentence, but this one needs examining. It is tricky, erroneous in a way that cannot be accidental, and is of fundamental, carefully designed dishonesty. The sentence he pretends to be quoting actually reads:

All documents filed by the United States with the Court in England in June–July, 1968, in the extradition proceeding by which James Earl Ray, convicted killer of Dr. Martin Luther King, was returned to this country.

Piece by painful piece, Kleindienst, like a child plotting a foray on the cookie jar and preparing explanations if caught, deliberately misrepresents my request so he can lie and say there are no such documents in the files of his department.

The request did not say they "were transmitted to British authorities through diplomatic channels," did not say it was "at the request of the States of Tennessee and Missouri" (although the record shows the two states provided precisely these documents), and above all did not say they were "presented to the Bow Street Magistrate's Court by officials of the *United Kingdom.*" The request is directly quoted and the reader can make his own comparison. The language of my first letter is "a set of the evidence, including affidavits entered into evidence, in the Ray extradition hearing in London." Both are specific and unequivocal. Neither bears any resemblance to Kleindienst's contrived and deliberate misquotation.

But even if there had been such errors in the request, there was but a *single* extradition of James Earl Ray, and the documents sought were, therefore, completely and adequately described, within the meaning of the law.

How cheap, however, can a Deputy Attorney General of the United States be? He is high in the administration that complains of press unfairness and makes threats against the press. Yet he deliberately lies in such a letter and childishly misquotes "filed by the United *States*" as "presented . . . by officials of the United *Kingdom*"? This is the mind, this the man entrusted with enforcement of the law, the rights and freedoms of Americans, the security of the nation, and the system of society?

Of course, as he as well as I knew, these documents were not presented by "officials of the United Kingdom." They were presented by one David Calcutt, a London lawyer hired by Kleindienst's government for precisely this purpose!

However, by this puerility that is also a debasement of his high office and function, Kleindienst sought to whistle himself past that particular graveyard by misquoting and then saying that nothing like the *misquotation* exists in his files. In this he commits another violation of the law. In court it would be a criminal act under subsection (c), where the court "may punish the responsible officers for contempt."

He then again violates the law by further indirection in his "answer," in a phrasing that does not admit the records sought are in his files. This is his next and last sentence on the subject. I have omitted nothing in quotation at this point:

> Further, such records pertaining to the extradition of James Earl Ray as may be in our possession are part of investigative files compiled for law enforcement purposes and, as such, are exempt from disclosure under the provisions of 5 U.S.C. 552(b)(7).

"As *may* be in our possession?" Can it be that the Department of Justice extradited Ray and has no records? Kleindienst, when the law requires specific answer and then, going further, prohibits "encumbering the applicant's path with procedural obstacles" (a direct quotation from Attorney General Clark's instructions to all federal agencies explaining their obligations under this law), says only that "such records . . . may be in our possession." They most certainly *are.* Each and every one was personally certified by the Attorney General, and all were collected by the Justice Department, which gave copies to the State Department for further certification, in every case by Secretary of State Dean Rusk.

But the central and incredible claim here is that the *public* record of a *public* trial of an American citizen, in which the government of the United States is the initiator and benefactor, is alleged to be "part of investigative files for law enforcement purposes" only.

Here again, and again in the finest detail, Kleindienst's words are completely false and to his knowledge so.

What I asked for is a sheaf of affidavits collected and certified by his

402

department, *to be used* and which were *actually used,* as *public evidence* in the public extradition proceeding. They are accurately described in the published accounts of their presentation in open court as of about 200 pages and an inch thick.

They are *not* "investigative files," and they were *not* "compiled for law enforcement purposes." They were compiled for use in open court. In addition, the Department of Justice has jurisdiction only in federal crimes. As already explained, the one crime alleged with deliberate falsity to cloak federal intervention in a purely state matter, murder, is that Ray was part of a conspiracy. But in open court, in London and later in Memphis, it is as specific as it can possibly be that both federal and state governments insist that there was no conspiracy and that Ray was entirely alone. This had to be made categorical in England, for its extradition provisos stipulate that a man can be extradited only on the charge for which he is to be tried. So *there was no federal law-enforcement purpose,* there being no federal jurisdiction.

Moreover, these particular affidavits for England are separate and distinct from those intended for use in Memphis. They are, in fact, a careful rephrasing of those that, with well-stretched imaginations, might be called "compiled for law enforcement purposes." They eliminate some of what is in that series of affidavits. Even if they didn't, even if they were not separate, different affidavits, their suppression is made illegal by subsection (c) of the act, once they were used in the Memphis court.

This is the government's hang-up. What they used in court in England, to get Ray extradited, *is both inconsistent with and contradictory to what was alleged in court in Memphis.* With the care with which my work is followed, the government knows I know this. Their sole intent in this open violation of the law was to deny me the official copies of the proof, which is proof that the crime remains unsolved; that Ray was inadequately represented, denied his rights, framed, and railroaded; that there was a conspiracy of which he was a part, but not the shooting part; and of Department of Justice responsibility and culpability for much of this.

The affidavits for which I asked are those produced for and used in open court in London. With only a single live "witness" produced by the United States government, FBI fingerprint expert George Bonebrake, who gave only perfunctory testimony, these affidavits are both the means by which the government avoided cross-examination of the witnesses and examination of the non-existent evidence and the basis

403

for the extradition. Chief Magistrate Milton, in handing down his decision, said that it was based "on the affidavit evidence before me." So, whether or not compiled for any other purpose—and they *were* compiled for the purpose for which they were used, court use—these affidavits are an integral part of a trial record, the basis of it—all but a tiny fragment of it.

There is no doubt and there never was any doubt that these affidavits are part of the trial record. Without them, there would have been no record, no extradition, no trial of Ray, no "solution" to the crime. Our August 20 letter to Mitchell, which was also our attempt to save the government the ignominy it insists upon, said simply, "these proceedings were public" and "should be made available to any person who desires to see them." This is the norm in the United States. Without it, there could be no real reporting of any legal proceeding.

Kleindienst, who, as Deputy Attorney General, obviously considers the law to be something to which he is as immune as he is indifferent, concluded his letter with allusion to our enunciation of the obvious:

> I have also taken note of the statements in your letter of August 20, to the effect that, in your opinion, all documents submitted on behalf of the United States [he slipped up here, not saying "by officials of the United Kingdom"] in the extradition proceedings constitute "public records" and that all the "papers" were prepared in the Department of Justice. Our refraining from making any comment respecting such statements should not be taken as acquiescence by the Department of Justice in your opinion and representation in this respect.

If the Deputy Attorney General of the United States wants to pretend that legal documents certified by the Attorney General of the United States were *not* "prepared in the Department of Justice" (which is distinct from who drafted the affidavits, to which he did not address himself), that is his affair. But to *say* they were not is to say they were forged, a serious crime, and that the Ray extradition was illegal.

And he makes it official, law or no law. We are back in the days of star-chamber trials. When the Department of Justice refuses to acknowledge that a public trial is a public trial; when it can suppress evidence produced in public trials at its whim and despite the law and long tradition, while merrily blasting the daylights out of the complacent press when it dares to lift an eyebrow in simulation of freedom—can less be said?

404

Once Kleindienst, if with uninhibited falsity, claimed that (a) the Department of Justice does not have its own affidavits and (b) they are immune to public access and process under the law, it was gratuitous abuse of and affront to the law and the entire structure of our society for him needlessly to add that a public trial is other than, his quotes, " 'public records.' "

So we answered Kleindienst's letter November 26, sick and unwilling to believe, even with the irrefutable evidence before us, that such a man is Deputy Attorney General of the United States. We corrected his deliberate misquotation and changed the wording, in the perhaps futile hope of frustrating further misquotation and deception. We used these words to describe the affidavits, "presented by Mr. David Calcutt, English barrister employed by the U.S. Government."

Knowing by now that the law is without meaning to Kleindienst (if not to his Attorney General and the entire administration) and notwithstanding its provision that he expeditiously forward the request to any other agency that might have prior, major, or collateral interest in these affidavits, we said:

If, against all tradition, the Department failed to retain a copy of the documents in this important case, can you suggest any Department or Agency, other than the Department of State, which might have retained copies in their files?

This time his reply required only three weeks.

We got a non-responsive "response" dated December 15. Here it is, in full:

Dear Mr. Fensterwald:

Reference is made to your letter of November 26, 1969, with attachment relative to the request of Mr. Harold Weisberg for disclosure of certain documents which you have stated are in the possession of the Department.

Please be advised that while we have noted and have given careful consideration to the statements in your letter we adhere to the views expressed in our prior communication.

He's quite a fun boy, that Kleindienst.

A real joker, if one can lose his concern for the law, respect of it by government, especially the government that came into power through a campaign based on observance of "law and order."

But, of course, if you are a high official of such a government, charged with just these responsibilities, law and order, if you administer the law, if you are protected by a Nixon, an Agnew, and a Mitchell, for all of whom you speak, and if you have learned your "Americanism" under so renowned an authority as Barry Goldwater, then you know the law and its observance are for the yokels, for use against dissident minorities, especially the blacks, and that under no circumstances does it apply to you or the government of which you are so important a part.

With that great respect for the law, expected of the Deputy Attorney General of the United States, Kleindienst first ignored the law's provisions and then refused to answer our direct question.

Kleindienst had claimed not to have those papers supplied by the "United Kingdom" in his first letter, the gruesome device that enabled him to lie while seeming to be truthful. Because there are no such papers, to his knowledge as to mine, he could not have them. And, of course, they are not what I asked for. Our correction of his deliberate misrepresentation? He made no reference at all to that. In saying he had "given careful consideration" to our letter, he is also saying he read that part carefully, so there is no possibility he did not know what he was—and was not—doing. Thus, we have this ignominious self-portrait by the Deputy Attorney General of the United States, a man who creates not-very-bright fictions to avoid answering proper, if embarrassing, questions and, when caught at it, says in pseudo-response only that "we adhere to the views expressed in our prior communication" —or that they do not have the non-existent papers he contrived—or that the government of the United Kingdom acts for the Justice Department of the United States.

Hear that, Barry Goldwater?

It happens the Department of State is headed by another prominent lawyer. William P. Rogers was Attorney General under President Eisenhower. So, in an effort to eliminate the possibility of more secret, fingers-crossed but nonetheless prohibited and illegal buck-passing and double-dealing by the Justice Department, we addressed the same request to him, complete with a file of the correspondence to save him time.

The Secretary of State must be a lawyer in the Kleindienst–Mitchell–Nixon–Agnew tradition. He replied under date of December 10 (a few days more quickly than Kleindienst), through J. Edward Lyerly, his Deputy Legal Adviser. State, although its primary responsibility is diplomatic, shows deep concern for the rights of Americans, adherence to the law in all its niceties. It is as expert as the other agencies in semantics. Here is State's letter:

DEPARTMENT OF STATE
Washington, D.C. 20520
December 10, 1969

Mr. Bernard Fensterwald, Jr.
Fensterwald, Bevan and Ohlhausen
927 Fifteenth Street, N.W.
Washington, D. C. 20005

Dear Mr. Fensterwald:

I have been asked to reply to your letter to the Secretary of State, dated November 26, 1969, requesting certain documents in connection with the extradition of Mr. James Earl Ray.

Affidavits submitted to a foreign court in support of a request for extradition become part of the records of that court. Mr. Ray himself, however, made a similar request some time ago, and the Department was able to have the affidavits returned to the United States by British authorities. Since the affidavits were originated by the Department of Justice, we asked that Department's views on their release to Mr. Ray. The Deputy Attorney General advised us that the affidavits were considered to be investigative files of his Department and exempt from disclosure under subsection (e)(7) of section 552 of Title 5 of the United States Code. In view of this advice, the Department of State returned the affidavits to the originating agency and so informed Mr. Ray.

Since the Department of State no longer has custody of the affidavits you have requested, we are unable to comply with that request. I regret that we cannot be of assistance in this matter.

Sincerely yours,

J. Edward Lyerly
Deputy Legal Adviser

This raises the most serious questions about the dirty-work of which governments are capable. Here are some:

If the affidavits "become part of the records" of the British court, how did the American government get them back (which, we shall see, the British court says it did)? Do not British courts *keep* their records and certify copies when necessary? And if part of an open court record, which it obviously is though this is denied by the United States government, how can they be suppressed as "investigative files"?

Did the Department of State *really*, and quite improperly, get the *original* affidavits from the British court to get copies for Ray *without* consultation with the Justice Department, without knowing the Justice Department had hoked up this Rube Goldberg Blackstone?

Getting the original affidavits away from the British court served only to make them inaccessible to Ray, his lawyers, and me when we asked for them there. It must be obvious the Department of State could have sent copies to Britain and had these copies certified by the court there. Or, standard practice, it could have had the court make and certify copies of its evidence and have *that* sent to the United States. The originals should *never* have left the court [1]. This court testimony cannot, by any stretch of even a Kleindienst–Lyerly imagination, be described as Justice's "investigative files." And State got "all copies" of that from the British court, hardly necessary when one copy only was needed. Again, this served but a single purpose in which, lamentably, British justice collaborated: suppression of the public record of a public trial. . . . ."

Lyerly also makes a liar out of Kleindienst, lily-gilding if there ever was any. Here are two Lyerly statements:

"Since the affidavits were originated by the Department of Justice . . . " and "the Department of State returned the affidavits to the originating agency . . . ."

Thus, there can be no doubt that, as the originating agency, Justice *does* have copies, and as the "originating" agency, it *now* also has the court copies—all of them!

Never was there a neater play for robbing court files and suppressing public evidence. The United States government must feel it has the most compelling reason for such underhandedness, such serious illegality, such open denial of rights, to me as a writer and citizen (for these records are required to be available to all) and to the defendant who was framed by just this evidence and just this kind of official double-dealing.

Lyerly is almost as cute as Kleindienst. He also falls short of saying the Department of State has no copies of this public evidence. There can be no doubt it used its own xeroxes for everything the Secretary certified. There is no less doubt it duplicated what it got from the British court and sent to the Department of Justice. Instead of saying "we have no copies," to which the law requires that Ray and I have access, he says, "State no longer has *custody*," which may be immaterial and certainly is not responsive or completely truthful.

Just how deliberate this overt violation of the law is former Attorney General Clark spelled out in his memorandum of "instructions" on the law sent to all agencies, not excepting his own. Here is the pertinent excerpt from page 38. He says of "the effect of the language in exemption (7)," the one on the right to restrict investigative files cited by both Kleindienst and Lyerly, that it "seems to confirm the availability to litigants of documents from investigatory files to the extent to which Congress and the courts have made them available to such litigants." The only possible avoidance he mentions is if such statements "contain information unfairly damaging to the litigant or other persons," something that cannot possibly be true in this case.

In this connection, it is worth noting that, in every alleged quotation of this law by Kleindienst and Lyerly, these concluding words are always omitted: "except to the extent available by law to a private party." So even if these affidavits (and, we shall see, "certain oral evidence" also sent) were "part of investigative files compiled for law enforcement purposes," which they are not, they are still required to be available under the always-omitted proviso of that particular section—which leaves little doubt about the reason it is invariably unsaid.

With the disclosure that all the evidence that should repose in the British court is not there and is at the Department of Justice, which lies about it and brazenly violates the law to suppress it, and with the unintended revelation that the two government departments got together on this disgraceful ploy, the question of conspiracy again comes up. Conspiracy is a combination to do wrong. State and Justice *did* combine and did do wrong in denying Ray his legal rights. Whether this is a provable conspiracy, within the meaning of the law, may be a question never to be answered in court. It is not easy to imagine Kleindienst prosecuting himself or other Justice and State officials, or Mitchell clobbering his own and the State officials who connived with him or them. (Or was it all Mitchell's doing? He is the boss.)

But conspire they did, shamefully, to deny an American the legal rights of all Americans, in a miserable device to frustrate justice and deny the normal working of the law. Tragically, it is neither new nor inconsistent. It is cast in the same Hitler–Orwell mold as the rest of the terrible, terrifying story.

England's abandonment of her own respected principles and history, her willingness knowingly to serve the base and wrong ends of the United States government, is a surprise and disappointment to me. Most Americans look to her as a bastion of freedom and individual liberties, the mother of our laws. But "Freedom of Information" enjoys no better health there than it does here when England is the mendicant of the American government, whatever party is in power there or here. As I have explained, I had representatives of two major newspapers ask for the *public* record of this *public* trial for me. They reported it simply was not available. I asked a friend to ask Ray's court-appointed lawyer, Michael Eugene, for me to have access to it. Now remember, this is the man who allegedly *defended* Ray, and all I asked was the evidence *produced in court* and *against* his client. Eugene refused, adding that, because he did not know me, he would have to "check me out" with the FBI! This is a new Anglo-Saxon concept, out-Kleindiensting the American government. Ray's "defender" would "check me out" with the FBI, part of the Department of Justice, his and Ray's adversary, before permitting me to see what they produced *in open court* and *against* his client—what they already had? With such defenders, what need had Ray for enemies and opponents?

Appeal to the court was no more productive. (Those apprehensive about the so-called "preventive detention" law may want to note that Chief Magistrate Milton, who presided over the Ray extradition, who permitted the use of evidence that could not be cross-examined, these affidavits I sought, was produced in Washington to testify before Congress about how fine it is to hold men in jail without bail pending trial.) Milton directed his chief clerk to reply to the request. Here is the pertinent part of that response:

> There is not available any complete transcript of the proceedings and the arguments at the time of Ray's appearance. Certain oral evidence was given including the making of a statement by Ray, but all copies of that were sent to the Secretary of State at the Home Office in London for transmission to the State Department at Washington, together with the papers which had been sent to this Court from Washington. As far as I know the Home Office has not retained copies of those papers.

If Wigmore, who said cross-examination is a marvelous machine for establishing truth, is not rotating in his grave, Blackstone must be.

This then, is the situation in the home of Blackstone and John Milton, author of the notable treatise on freedom of the press, "Areopagitica": There was, in England, a public trial of a man accused of one of the most heinous modern crimes. But in England, without protest or concern, "there is not available any complete transcript of the proceedings," everything having been sent to Washington, together with "the papers which had been sent to this court from Washington"— that is, exactly those Ray and I sought, the affidavits that are the basis of the action and the decision, the judgment of the court.

At the same time, Vice-president Agnew, Kleindienst, the President, others in the government, and an odd lot of assorted self-styled "defenders" of the free press, including their threatening wives in some ignoble cases, say it is not they but the press, of which I am a minor part but nonetheless part and symbol, that jeopardizes American freedom and institutions.

Orwell did not put it better than they. Government *is* rewriting history as it goes, to make history seem to support current policy and acts. But the Nixon–Agnew administration has an improvement. It is rewriting current developments, not waiting for these events to become history. If this requires suppression of *public* records, *public* trials, *public* evidence, conspiring, violation of and official contempt for the law of the land, is that too great a price to pay for having an administration that intimidates, threatens, and bludgeons the press?

But not just the Nixon administration. With the truth so unpleasant, was it not better to rescript the King assassination, to make it seem detached from life, an odd and unexpected, isolated crime by a single, unassociated man, it and he removed from connection with anyone and anything? This is what was done by the same Department of Justice under the Attorney General who then sat impotently on a panel of concerned citizens to inquire into the police murders of lesser-known blacks. Ramsey Clark is the great liberal who proclaimed publicly there was no conspiracy to assassinate King while simultaneously charging in an indictment that Ray was part of a conspiracy. He thus contrived the federal jurisdiction without which this enormous, historic debasement of the law and justice would have been impossible.

How Nixon, Agnew, Mitchell, and Kleindienst must toss sleepless at night in their great worry—about the danger to American freedoms from the American press!

Reminding the reader again that I am a symbol of that press and the reality of its freedoms, I refer to earlier letters to Attorney General Mitchell. I had been told what I was unwilling to believe, that FBI agents were telling witnesses whom I had interviewed that I am some special kind of "subversive," somehow "unAmerican." On March 12, 1969, I wrote him, "I await your assurance that I have been misinformed, that your FBI agents are engaged in nothing as entirely improper as this."

His reply of March 26 was in the name of Will Wilson, his Assistant Attorney General in charge of the Criminal Division, written by Carl W. Belcher, Chief, General Crimes Section. My file is in the Criminal Division? General Crimes?

It was less than the assurance I asked. "It should hardly be necessary to inform you," Wilson–Belcher-for-Mitchell wrote, "that such conduct would be in complete disregard of Departmental and Bureau policy. We have sent a copy of your letter to the Director of the Bureau for his consideration and such action as he may deem appropriate."

To say "such conduct would be in complete disregard" of policy is *not* to say it did not happen. To this day, although I have since solicited it, there has yet to be even a pro forma denial that this further abuse of writers, their rights and freedoms, did not happen. And under the administration of the Agnew who in Des Moines, on November 13, 1969, voiced complaints *against* the press; the Mitchell who rewrote his wife's statement that he would trade American "liberals" for Russian "Communists" to say what she did not, that these liberals are "violence prone" and the "Communists" are academic, then agreed with it wholeheartedly; and the Orwellian Kleindienst who rewrites the law they all ignore when its abuse does not satisfy their—ask them—"patriotic" purposes.

This is a bleak picture of press "freedom" under the Nixon–Agnew–Mitchell–Kleindienst administration: Othe precious freedoms may soon fit the same frame.

"Law and Order" = Official Perjury

When we got eyeball to eyeball, they blinked.

Confronted with the determination to see this thing through, the government capitulated when I pressed the suit to get the suppresed Ray material. But even that they could not carry off well, could not do cleanly, did neither honestly nor without bitterness and vindictiveness. Had I been behind every Department of Justice desk,

412

manipulating every official in an effort to make this record of complete dishonesty as clear and unequivocal as possible, no more unquestionable a record of unvarying intent to violate the letter and the spirit of the law could have resulted. No cheap trick and shabby device was missed. Not even criminality.

No more open and total departure from basic American principles of law and standards of government and its conduct comes readily to mind. But the long months of Justice's stalling provided time for negotiation and diplomacy, as State calls it, which led to Fensterwald becoming Ray's lawyer.

There is reason to believe that, more than it dares show, the government has been throughtly shaken by this simple law suit. There now is no doubt that it is being forced, if in deepest secrecy, to decide whether or not to prosecute a conspiracy case, despite all its loud and repeated denials, all carefully worded so they can later be interpreted as indicating that the government was not saying what it did say, that there was no conspiracy.

I did, ultimately and officially, get those confiscated and suppressed affidavits. They serve as little more than validation of what I had written. They are the official proof of the accuracy of this book.

Because this is the story of a frame-up by government, with the complicity of the "defense," how I finally got them is an essential part of the story.

Moreover, if I, a writer with neither resources nor connections, with the help of a volunteer lawyer to whom principle is more important than fee, could get this exculpatory evidence, is it possible that the fabled Foreman, man of influence and wealth, great lawyer that even he admits he is, could have done less well, given the will, had he had the intent of defending his client? (A Tennessee judge, after Fensterwald's first brief was presented, commented to the effect that any law school student of average intelligence could have given Ray a better defense than Foreman did.)

Kleindienst & Co. waited until the last minute of delay they got in responding to my suit, officially identified as Civil Action No. 718-70 in the Federal District Court for the District of Columbia. Then, late in the afternoon before the scheduled hearing, they telephoned Fensterwald to say they were giving me the affidavits. Thus, the government avoided a court hearing on the facts and the law and with it the attendant publicity.

413

Several days later, Fensterwald received a remarkable letter signed by Attorney General Mitchell. Behind it was a team job, involving a number of lawyers in the Civil Division—especially, I am convinced, one whose name does not appear on the Department's file copy, a man increasingly indicated as the Department's "assassination expert," Carl Eardley. In the upper left-hand corner of Justice's file copy (and not on my copy, the reader should be clear) are the initials "JNM" (those of the Attorney General); "WHR" (not those of Wm. Rogers, Sec. of State, whose middle initial is P., nor Wm. D. Ruckelshaus, head of the Civil Division); and "TEK:SJL:sgc," which seem to coincide with this notation in the upper right-hand corner: "Files Mr. Kauper Mr. Lockman Mrs. Copeland."

From the formula these pinioned legal eagles evolved, one would never know I exist, for my name is not mentioned. One would never know a suit had been filed and a court hearing impended, for none of these things is mentioned. Anyone reading this letter without knowledge of the earlier correspondence would never know Justice repeatedly denied existence of the to-be-given records. Nor that Kleindienst had firmly and finally denied both Ray and me access to these files. Instead of facing the issue Justice dares not face—whether these are "investigative files"—the letter written for Mitchell's signature is phrased in a manner calculated to present him as one of good heart and boundless generosity. That part reads:

> . . . I have determined that you shall be granted access to them. The exemptions do not require that records falling within them be withheld; they merely authorize the withholding . . . .

But big-hearted Mitchell did not say how, where, or when he would "grant access." We tried to learn by phone, after waiting a few days for any word at all from anyone in Justice. Our phone calls were not answered. So, eight days after Mitchell's letter, I went down to his cavernous office on the Constitution Avenue side of the Justice building.

Meanwhile, his legal minds were working hard. They rushed into court with two laughable motions. The government seems to be bent upon a campaign to make it appear that the Freedom of Information law also does not exist. They are following a course which suggests that, the law's provisions being so uncomfortable to those whose way of life is suppression, they will at some point go to Congress with hoked-up statistics and ask for its repeal on the ground it is not used and just clutters up the law books.

414

Both of the government's motions were variants of the same legal nonsense, that the mere promise to make available that which was sued for made my legal action moot. They asked dismissal of the suit on this self-demeaning basis, apparently in the hope that the case would be withdrawn prior to my getting the file, so they could pretend, as they did to the very end, that they were not compelled by law and court to do that which they had steadfastly refused to do.

On my motion, theirs were ignored. I also assured the court that, upon compliance, I would voluntarily withdraw the motion. More than three months later, Justice was still pretending they were not responding to the suit. In order to avoid it in the letter drafted for Mitchell, his legal brains had gone back to a three-month-old pro forma appeal he and they had, typically, ignored. As a prelude to suing, I was required to appeal Kleindienst's decision not to give me what I requested. So more than three months before Mitchell's letter, I had. The Aesopian contrivance worked out was for Mitchell to pretend to act on the one thing that *was* moot, the appeal, on which his right to act had expired and his ability to do so had been nullified by the filing of the suit.

This is the self-portrait of the legal minds that run the country and protect its freedoms!

Appropriately, Mitchell's office and those of his closer assistant and secretary are enormous emptinesses. Seeking to be proper, I knocked on the open door of his assistant's office, which turned out to be unpopulated. The door from it to Mitchell's reception room was also open. Through it his pleasant secretary, Janey Kemp, invited me in. Her office is about the size of a modestly priced two-story house. She appeared to have nothing to do until I gave her Mitchell's letter. During the time I remained, she remained unoccupied, except for personal conversation with a middle-aged black man, who seemed to be a messenger.

All around the walls were sofas and chairs, all empty. Janey Kemp escorted me to one end of one particular sofa and directed me to sit there. The reason soon became apparent. Right next to that end of the sofa was a small end table. On it was a rather large lamp, the base of which allowed space for nothing else. Teetering on the edge was a single magazine, *Newsweek* for May 11. It was carefully opened to page 47.

It was no easy matter to keep the open magazine from falling off the lamp base, but the Mitchell operation was equal to this formidable task, involving the defiance of gravity.

Two stories appeared on that page. I doubt if either Mitchell or his charming secretary was anxious for callers to read one of them, "LBJ on Assassination." That was an account of a to-be-broadcast CBS interview.

(This taped broadcast was later censored at the last minute, to eliminate Johnson's belief that there had been a conspiracy by means of which he became President. Because Johnson's belief also meant he was satisfied that the Report of his Warren Commission was wrong, it *had* to be censored. The reason given was "national security.")

The second story was of Mitchell's first and late-coming success, Senate confirmation of Andrew Blackmun to the Supreme Court. Mitchell was still licking the smarting wounds of the Senate's refusal to confirm his Carswell and Haynsworth selections.

And this stage-management of visitors' reading, too, is a measure of the minds that run the country.

When, after some time had passed and the poor woman had not been able to learn what she should do with me, I suggested there might be some significance to what was omitted from her boss's letter, that there was this Civil Action No. 718-70. Her face brightened, she made a phone call, and sent me off to another large reception room, 3143, that of William D. Ruckelshaus, Assistant Attorney General in charge of the Civil Division.

There I found three also-pleasant and also-unoccupied secretaries. Mary Lundberg, in the middle, seemed to be senior in rank.

She also did some phoning, and her phoning also seemed to do her no good because, as all three complained, Justice has a practice of omitting all initials from big-shots' outgoing letters; thus they cannot be traced back to those who did the work. Rather than make the poor girls work when they had no apparent need to, I told them what the letter did not, that their file copy contained their boss's initials and the court papers were signed by one David Anderson.

Mary Lundberg placed a call to Anderson. A long silence ensued, broken only by the feminine chatter and the small-talk between us.

It turned out, from the secretaries' knowledge, that I was the first outsider ever to walk into their reception room on serious business. If this seems hard to credit, my long wait there, during which only a messenger passed through the reception-room door, does tend to confirm it. Nuts come, I was told, once in a while. For them, Justice has a special lawyer, gifted with the remarkable quality of seeming spontaneously simpatico with the mentally disturbed. He listens patiently to them, makes them feel their imagined needs are going to be cared for, and they leave happy. His last client, to the recall of the three secretaries, had been a woman who had not heard from President Nixon after sending him her slacks with a complaint about how poorly they wore. Before her, there had been a man who wanted his fingerprints made. The sympathetic lawyer made him happy too.

Again, does one wonder that the government's legal business gets attended?

Time passed. Then, Mary Lundberg's telephone rang, after which she asked me, pleasantly enough, to go see Mr. Cella, in the Criminal Division.

I declined. I knew what she did not but what whoever telephoned her should have known. Through Fensterwald, I had tried that one earlier. Cella was out sick. Neither he nor his office had returned our 9:30 A.M. call. Nor, for that matter, had Anderson, who was not out sick.

More phoning, and I was told to go to Criminal and see a Mr. Koffsky, who is chief of what Criminal calls its legislative and special projects branch. Having been to all the pillars and posts I wanted, I again declined—unless, that is, her Mr. Anderson or one of the other lawyers took me by the hand. I did not for one minute believe, I told her, that any one of them would *think* of leading me astray—or on another wild goose chase.

Still more phoning. Then I was told a messenger would go for the papers.

Soon an unjacketed Rudolph Valentino type, Spanish-style pants and all, entered and left. On his departure, Mary told me that Anderson would take me to a conference room across the hall and watch me while I examined the file.

More small talk. The girls made no secret of the fact that "Freedom of Information" is a special kind of cuss word in those parts.

Throughout this long wait, a tall, dark-haired man wearing a pale yellow shirt passed silently from the office behind Imogene Combs to the one on the opposite side of the reception room. He never once said a word to anyone, never looked at or acknowledged me. This was Division Chief Ruckelshaus, who seemed deep in dark thoughts, as though worried about the status of the government's civil-law problems.

Yet again the telephone rang, and again Mary gave me the word: There had been "a policy decision on the highest level" to decide who

417

would show me the file.

That simple, mechanical chore had become a "high policy decision," a really big deal?

This did not flatter me. It nauseated, for it is still another view of the federal face in the era of political assassinations, another measure of the character of government and its policy- and decision-makers.

I assumed the negotiations were between Criminal and Civil, or, if that had been decided with the delivery of the file to Civil, which lawyer within Civil would play watchdog.

The commodious Ruckelshaus ante-room is expensively and comfortably furnished. Upholstery is in rich, brown leather. I sat in a deep easy chair with its back to Ruckelshaus's office, facing one lighter in shade, suggesting it had been re-upholstered. Against the hall wall, on my right, was a matching sofa (no opened *Newsweeks*). Above it was a painting in which somber greens predominated, in smeared blobs, none pleasant, with a small patch of an almost-bright yellow. On the wall I faced was more federal culture, another painting, gaudily brighter. Maybe it was supposed to represent flowers.

During the hour or so required for the decision whose "high-policy" character I doubt was to have been announced to me, I dozed several times, as I had earlier during lulls in the conversation. Sleep was closer to reality thant the never-never land of Kafka and Orwell in which I slept.

Finally, the momentous decision was made. I was led down the hall past Ruckelshaus's office, past the next door, on which were the names of Carl Eardley and Irving Jaffe, and into Room 3607, where I was introduced to a Mrs. Cavacini. She sat me at a table next to the inner entrance to the Eardley–Jaffe office, then seated herself at the diagonally opposite corner, behind a desk. It seems that even stenographic offices in Justice were built with conference purposes in mind, for hers, too, is a large one.

By this time the tiring day was wearing down toward its working end. The file was as heavy and thick as described. I knew it would not be possible to study it with care before quitting time, so I decided instead to inventory it, following hasty perusal, just on the paranoid chance there might ensue another kind of "high policy" decision.

The file was not in numerical order. Folio 11, out of a total of 194, was on top. The papers were separated into small bundles, all beribboned, with official stamps and seals in various hues attached all over. In conformity with regular practice in such cases, the documents

418

had originated with Justice, certified by Attorney General Ramsey Clark; had been transmitted to State and there certified by Secretary Dean Rusk; and all those from the various jurisdictions bore the certifications of appropriate officials on different levels, including governors and judges. Some originating in the District of Columbia were certified by Chief Judge Edward M. Curran whom in earlier years I had known when he was an assistant district attorney and I had worked for the Senate. (By happenstance, it was to be Judge Curran to whom, as the rotation of case assignments worked out, my case was sent.)

The second sheaf was labeled "Misc I." Folios 1-10 were in the middle of "Misc II," somehow placed after 127 and before 128. The fascinating affidavit of Charles Stephens, folios 184–194, was between folios 132 and 133. Otherwise, the file was in correct sequence. Bourbon Charley's affidavit has the highest numbers and should have been at the end.

There are a total of 18 affidavits, some with attachments. There are also legal petitions, the grand-jury presentment, excerpts from laws, and other customary formalities.

Included, as I had had no doubt and as the most casual glance showed, is what had been withheld in Memphis, exculpatory evidence and statements so contradictory to the official misrepresentation of them in the minitrial as to raise questions in a layman's mind about criminality and disciplinary action by the bar, an extreme improbability.

Only a few details were added to what my investigation had, I was satisfied, already proven. But this was *official* proof, *official* evidence. This fact and the content cannot be nit-picked.

Because some of the evidence was so startlingly graphic, I asked Fensterwald to accompany me the next day, when I resumed my examination, so that he could see it and so he could be there if any hitch developed in getting copies of what I wanted.

Mrs. Cavacini hoped we would not mind if we were placed elsewhere. We didn't. She led us down the long corridor, into an elevator, and up into the FBI part of the building. I mean, into the inner sanctum itself! Through doors marked "Federal Bureau of Investigation" and "Authorized Personnel Only"!

And there she left us, "authorized" FBI personnel that we were, with no watchdog to keep us from slipping papers into our pockets.

It was a bare room made, from appearances, of a wide hallway. Various dull-painted boxes, like electric and telephone junction boxes, were attached to the walls, which were othewise unadorned; but I could not help wondering about grinding cameras and hidden bugs.

There were some things in particular I wanted Fensterwald to see. These I had told him about before we got to Justice. On the chance we were less than alone in that FBI office, when we reached these documents in the file, I merely pointed to them so that only a hidden camera, not an electronic bug, might detect what interested me.

Justice had no typewriter to lend me for the preparation of a list of what I wanted xeroxed, so I made one in my illegible scrawl and copied it, as legibly as I could, to leave with the file.

As we did not look for bugs, so we did not look for "tails." Unescorted, so far as we know, we made our way out of J. Edgar Hoover's confines back to Mrs. Cavacini's office. I gave here the more legible list and asked about payment. She knew nothing about that.

Her ignorance is not exceptional, for on that day as on the one before throughout the Department, including in the office that is supposed to supply them to the public, I could not get copies of the department regulations covering the Freedom of Information law. Justice is not anxious for citizens to be able to use it.

(They *do* have the regulations. If any reader ever wants them, I recommend that he knock hard and be prepared to knock long.)

The forms that are filed under the regulation do quote (rather profitable) rates for xeroxing. However, I also wanted photographic copies of five of the bits of evidence included in the file as photographs. While we were trying to evolve a means by which I could pay in advance, which the regulations prefer, in walked Carl Eardley, whom Fensterwald and I had met—and whipped—in court on an earlier occasion. (That incident will have to await another book. It was my research and Fensterwald's court handling that had toppled Eardley.) Fensterwald later told me he had never seen so venomous a look or such hate-filled eyes as Eardley directed at me when he entered the room, while I was talking with Mrs. Cavacini.

"What's this?" Eardley asked, for all the world as though he had no inkling.

We told him. Unceremoniously, he took the list from my hand, without even a by-your-leave.

"What's this?" he asked of the first item and repeating it about the last. The first was my request for a copy of the envelope in which the file was contained, the last for a simple letter assuring me that I had, in fact, been given access to the entire file, as the court had been

420

prematurely assured and as would have been automatically provided in court.

About each of these, Eardley, suddenly forgetful and become the man in charge, muttered that he wouldn't. In each case, I responded only that I'd prefer not to fight him.

We left it that, when the copying costs were known, they would let me know, they would get a check, and I would come to pick up the papers when they were ready. Glowering, Eardley stalked into his own office without even a perfunctory goodbye. If he is by nature impolite, really rude, then he was not putting on any act.

If Justice elected not to supply the documents from their abundant existing files of them, the xeroxing required less than an hour and the printing of the pictures, from existing FBI negatives, minutes only. Therefore, two weeks elapsed before I heard another word. Wednesday, May 27, there was a telephone call from a woman who identified herself merely as in the office of H. Richards Rolapp, who is Kleindienst's deputy. The requested material was there and I could pick it up, "with two exceptions."

The first "exception" turned out to be something else: I would have to pay for it. The second was that copying the pictures would require still another three weeks. The corner drugstore performs this service, including the processing of the negatives, overnight. A photo lab can do it while you wait. But our fabled FBI, after *two* weeks, still needed *three* more—and that, as it turned out, was a very considerable underestimate.

Faced with this delay, I reduced the order for pictures to a single one, to be reproduced and discussed in a few pages.

That single picture was *never* ready. I had to go to court again to get it.

What else, having the Attorney General's sacred word?

Meanwhile, this nameless woman agreed to ascertain the cost of the picture and telephone me so I could save 100 miles of needless driving by having someone pick up the package for me. She did not, and I had to make the trip to Rolapp's office. The deputy to the deputy of the Attorney General, even then, also did not know the cost. The dilatory record and silence of the FBI on such mundane matters is a bit surprising, considering the speed with which they accomplish sensational things, like establishing that the hairs on Lee Harvey Oswald's blanket were pubic hairs and Oswald's to boot (as though whose pubic hairs were on his blanket should interest anyone other

421

than his wife). However, Rolapp was quite tractable. I suggested that I pay what the National Archives charges for an 8×10 glossy print, he agreed, and I gave him a check for the whole job.

When I asked him if he was giving me everything else I requested, he said he presumed so. I assured him I would let him know if he didn't.

He did not and I did.

Aside from the pictures, whose absence had been "explained" (if this word fits) in advance, there were but two things missing, the first and last items on my list, exactly what Eardley said he would not let me have.

Rolapp and I have had a kind of correspondence since then, on several other matters, but he never responded to my letter on the missing items. Kleindienst also got to be an unusual kind of pen-pal, but he also never responded to my polite reminders and requests. Neither they nor Eardley, nor Mitchell, nor anyone else was at all troubled by the law, the falsity of the assurances they had already given the court—or the sanctity of the Attorney General's pledge. I did not get these items and I did not get any letter or phone call about them.

After more than a reasonable time passed, I consulted my lawyer, in his office. As had happened every time we had discussed there the taking of new steps in the case, as though Hoover had a direct line, there was immediate Justice reaction.

We agreed on a new suit, for these missing items plus other claims, including the completely wasted expenses to which I had been put so needlessly by the non-stop Justice lies.

David Anderson, who had signed Justice's court papers, phoned Fensterwald to see if something could not be worked out. Sure, he was told; deliver what you are supposed to and we'll withdraw the action. He said he would call back.

Then, under date of June 26, Eardley wrote Fensterwald saying Rolapp had asked him to respond to my letter of more than three weeks earlier. Naturally, he did not write me. In this letter, in reference to the missing first item I had asked for, Eardley said:

When our attorneys inspected them [the papers] in connection with this litigation, the papers examined were contained in a plain, unmarked file folder. We are therefore unaware of what file folder Mr. Weisberg has in mind.

Blandly, Eardley concluded:

422

We assume you will take steps to have this lawsuit dismissed before the hearing set by the Court on July 7.

What *other* papers from what *other* files—for it could not be the file I had seen—"our attorneys inspected" is irrelevant, as Eardley knew. He was promptly told he knew the truth. After all, he had only held this envelope in his hands, argued about it, and then said he would suppress it. What more is needed to prove the non-existence of the file envelope? And to Eardley's *personal* knowledge! The letter informing him of these things was duly mailed. Meanwhile, we moved the court for action.

Justice crossed its own wires. Separately, I received a manila envelope with only Departmental identification on it. Inside, for all the world as though I am part of the Department, on its green "internal" routing slip, there was a handwritten note from one R. R. Richards saying, "Enclosed is copy of file identification."

Enclosed with this slip was something less than it described. There were two small scraps of paper, stuck together with Scotch tape. Never has censorship been less hidden. Someone had taken the large envelope, xeroxed it in two pieces, cut off most of each piece, and attached the remnants together. With a handwritten notation, all that remained on one scrap, the cutting was so close the tops of some of the numbers were removed. What remained is "95-100-473 Ser 3." (And I *do* hope this is not one of Hoover's closest secrets.) The other scrap bears a stamped form, inside a box, with the same numbers added. The scrap indicates the existence of still another set of the non-existing files—*not* in Criminal, *not* in Civil, but belonging to "Records Branch," to which "All material enclosed in this envelope must be returned."

I needled Kleindienst again, suggesting all of this was a bit undignified.

A desperate-sounding Anderson phoned Fensterwald and was given a truthful account of what had happened in his own Division, with the suggestion he speak to Eardley. Death, Anderson made clear, was preferable, and wouldn't Fensterwald *please* phone Eardley? Troubled at Anderson's unhidden anxiety, Fensterwald did. Eardley told him to speak to Anderson, whom Fensterwald called back. Anderson then begged that Cella be phoned. The response was a vigorous refusal.

The case was scheduled for July 7. Anderson asked that it be set for August 12, so he could take his vacation. We agreed. And waited.

Then, as what I hope was Anderson's joyous respite from Kleindienst, Rolapp, and Eardley was drawing to a close, Eardley sent another letter, this time with a xerox of still another wrong folder (how may sets of the "non-existent" files *can* they have?), and a sort of off-hand comment that, if this did not satisfy that awful Weisberg, they would see us in court August *15*—my emphasis, his date.

Because I had already filed another suit and planned more, it seemed like a practical idea to plumb the Eardley depths, so I avoided comment on this neat little trick in Fensterwald's office or over the phone, until the middle of the day before the day for which the hearing was *really* set, three days *before* the time Eardley told Fensterwald. Then I called Fensterwald with a reminder of the correct date, the next day. Not long after I used his phone and mine to disclose that we would *not* fail to appear in court the next morning, the 12th, rather than the 15th, and would *not* default by not being there, Fensterwald got still another call from Anderson, saying they were giving me the file envelope xerox and picture. Without consultation with me, Anderson was told he could do that in court.

And, once again, it did not happen—not even in court!

Once again, only a promise.

Fensterwald gave Judge Curran a short and quietly understated account of a year of effort to get what was still undelivered. The judge asked why. Anderson's response was that he had just been told by Kleindienst the previous afternoon that the picture would be given me. When Anderson was indefinite about the time required to make a print, the judge, saying that required but minutes, administered a polite chewing-out and ordered that it be accomplished within a week. (Perhaps Judge Curran recalled that he, personally, had certified those "non-existent" files?)

While we awaited the judge, Anderson told me the print would be made and showed me a xerox of the "non-existent" envelope. I asked that he give me the print he had brought to show the judge and replace that with the copy allegedly being made. Perish the thought! Impossible! That xerox looked wrong, somehow, so I compared it with the original envelope, which had magically reappeared after hiding from all those Justice lawyers, clerks, and fabulous investigators. Anderson had it with him to show the judge.

Never let it be said that the taxpayer is not supporting some of the slickest sneaks in law enforcement and investigation. That xerox was neatly doctored, which took a little doing, for the electrostatic copying process is faithful, reproducing whatever it sees. One thing was obliterated. In this, the machine alone can be innocent.

I called this defect to Anderson's attention.

"Just write it in," he told me.

"You do it," I countered—and he refused, keeping the paper.

Here I must confess my own serious error, my own (in retrospect, inexcusable) underestimation of the Department of Justice of the era of political assassinations. I never dreamed, not for a moment, they would ignore the order of a federal judge, specific and barbed as Judge Curran's had been.

They did, with contempt that was first unconcealed and then committed to paper.

Six days passed and not a word came—no letter, no phone call from a nameless female Rolapp employee, no xerox, no picture. When I got my mail on the seventh day and it also was barren, we told the judge's clerk and a hearing was set for the next morning, Wednesday, August 19, 1970.

We were there. Of all the incredibilities that are the frightening reality of the United States of the 1970s, perhaps the most incredible was the absence in that courtroom of any representative of the Department of Justice. Judge Curran issued what is called a "summary judgment" against Justice. This is a legal determination of fact on the merits of the case and, issued against the Government of the United States, is about as common as eight-day weeks.

We did not ask the judge to hold Justice in contempt. I doubt if, under opposite circumstances, Justice would not have sought this punishment against me.

When we returned to the office, I saw two things: a letter from Eardley which spelled out both the contempt and the intent to violate the order, that is, be in contempt, and an affidavit by Anderson, filed *five days* earlier, still again (consistently) seeking dismissal of my suit on no more than the promise of complete compliance. Eardley's letter, received the day *after* the maximum time permitted by the court's order, concluded with proof the order had been ignored. It said, "We have delivered the photograph which Mr. Weisburg [sic] requested to the Deputy Attorney General's office to have it reproduced. It will be forwarded to you shortly."

Where Anderson had told the judge he had been given the photograph by Kleindienst's office, on the afternoon of August 11, to have it copied, Eardley said he had given it back to Kleindienst for the same reason: to have it copied. This deliberate whipsawing, this disregard of a federal judge's order, seems more than mere contempt of court, though that it is. It had a significant timing.

Due two weeks to the day from the time we got this latest promise, there was a hearing in the effort to get a trial for Ray. It is difficult to avoid the suspicion the government was trying to stall me until after that hearing.

The Anderson affidavit, filed when he and everyone in Justice knew the department had not complied with the order, was attached to a motion signed by Ruckelshaus. The motion claimed that I had "been given access to the papers requested in this public information suit and therefore the case is moot." This was false but, not being under oath, fell short of criminality. That, however, is not true of the Anderson affidavit. It is redolent of what can be only deliberate misrepresentation and deception. Because it is under oath, if there is a false statement in it, that is perjury, if the lie is material. With the judge's order being that I be given copies of the file envelope and picture within a week, a lie about either *is* perjury, a serious crime, especially by a lawyer and most of all by a Justice Department lawyer.

I was in the unique position of getting simultaneously the perjury and the unequivocal, additional proof that it was perjury. Eardley's letter, written *after* the affidavit was filed, establishes the falsity of this, to which Anderson swore:

A copy of said file cover was delivered to plaintiff on August 12, 1970.

For stupidity as for arrogance, this has no equal. August 12 is the day the judge *ordered* that this be done. The one time in my life I had seen or spoken to Anderson was in the courtroom *before* the judge arrived. Had Anderson delivered this file cover to me, would the judge then have ordered that he do it? Of course not, nor would Anderson have been mute at the order if he had already complied with it.

Were I to commit perjury, Justice would seek to jail me for it. Perjury *is* a *serious* crime. So, while expecting nothing, I challenged the Attorney General to punish the criminal who acted as a criminal, in a criminal manner, on behalf of the Attorney General. In that letter, written August 20, 1970, I pointed out that not a single letter from Justice in a year and a half had been without a lie. The lies in Eardley's letters, of course, interested me most of all. Each of his letters proved the falsehood of all the others. Whereas Kleindienst had assured me Justice had *no* copies of what I sought, Eardley established the existence of not fewer than *three* duplicating files: the one in the envelope of which, finally, he did send a copy (as indistinct a copy as he thought he could get away with); one in "the only accordion file cover which we have been able to locate" (his letter of July 30, 1970); and one in "a plain, unmarked file folder" (his letter of June 26, 1970).

(The salamied pieces sent by R. R. Richards are probably from the court-copies file. If so, they do not represent still a fourth set of the file.)

Before leaving the temerity of Justice, one other fact should be recorded. Attached to this August 14, 1970 motion as "Exhibit 1" and described in Anderson's sworn statement as a "true copy" is Mitchell's letter of May 6, 1970. I know it is May 6, 1970, but the judge had no way of knowing, for "true copy," under oath, to the Justice Department, means with parts of it masked out in five different places! So carelessly was this done, so arrogantly, that it is visible. So stupidly that the year is censored out.

Only the judge thus had knowledge withheld from him, for I already had it. It has been described a few pages above.

Thus, we have the meaning of the word "true" as redefined by the administrators of the law and its defenders in the United States in the 1970s!

As for the picture, promised to me on May 27th, I finally got a version of it. It also had been made as indistinct as possible. This matter, too, Justice could not handle cleanly.

Soon after the summary judgment was issued, Paul Carson, an enterprising young reporter for Radio Station WWDC in Washington, phoned Eardley to ask for comment. Eardley did not either take or respond to the call. Instead, Carson later heard from the public relations office. First, the publicist ordered Carson not to record his comment for broadcast. Next, he told him, "Don't get mixed up in that bullshit of Weisberg's." The official opinion of me and my work is irrelevant. At this point, my work requires neither exposition nor defense. But what Justice was really doing was applying this designation to the finding of a federal judge, the chief judge of that court for the District of Columbia.

Rather exceptionally uncool.

Carson was told the picture had been sent me the night before. Had it been true, which seems unlikely, that would still have been after the time-limit set by the judge.

The legal eagles saw to it that the time of mailing could not be established. The franked envelope bears no cancellation. Inside was no letter, thus, no record of the date of mailing. Instead, I again joined the Departmental staff, addressed on another of those green "internal" forms. It is fig-leaf writing, but it does not hide the nakedness. In the space for "message" is typed, "Photograph enclosed per your request." "Per" my "request"? They never heard of the federal judge, his order, or my lawsuit? No signature. Rolapp's name is typed in. The date, naturally, is missing from all three blocks provided for "date."

As for the picture, it was not printed from the negative. It was rephotographed from the file with such technical skill that the folded-over preceding page hides part of it. All the smudges and fingerprints of all who had handled it, probably including me, are reproduced. The accumulated lint and dust are preserved, and other tributes to federal photographic skill may also be present, all tending to obscure the details of the picture. And there are blotches from over-hasty drying. (We shall return to the picture to discuss part of what it shows.)

I wrote Justice asking a clear copy, as ordered, from the negative, not one carefully contrived to be as indistinct as possible. I also said I would not press this further in court, leaving it to them to find, no matter how belatedly, a shred of decency with which to taint the record so devoid of it.

The response proves there is no limit to the incredible in the Justice Department. On Saturday, August 29, as he was preparing to leave for the September 2 hearing in Memphis, where he was seeking a trial for Ray, Fensterwald got a letter from Kleindienst asking him to get me to write Justice no further, pleading that my communications should be through my lawyer. The reason?

The case is still in litigation!

Thus, we have another indication of the seriousness with which Justice regards the order of a federal judge. He handed down a decision, but the case is still in litigation!

Returning to the file envelope for a moment, all this dirty work at the legal crossroads was not merely a nasty whim, not something that should be understood as no more than a misplaced sense of legal humor. (Nor was it just another effort to waste time and money for me. In driving alone, to get this material, I had wasted mileage enough to get me almost to the west coast from my east-coast home.) It had a serious, if extra-legal, purpose. All those lies about the file envelope were not for nothing.

First, that alteration on the envelope, that one thing that had been eliminated, is a rubber stamp reading "see letter of" followed by a blank, in which "12-10-69" had been written.

This is one of the items I pointed out to Fensterwald in that FBI office.

That date is long after the extradition of a year and a half earlier. It also coincides with two letters from Justice, the one from Lyerly to us and one he just happened to write to James Earl Ray the same day, after a four-month delay.

To which of the letters this notation refers is not too material, for in either case what Justice was trying to withhold from me is proof of its awareness of its denial of James Earl Ray's legal rights under the *Jencks* decision. In that case, the Supreme Court held that government can withhold from a defendant in a criminal case what is necessary for his defense *only at the cost of setting him free.*

The second item on the envelope that Justice wanted to suppress is the existence of the "Records Branch" file.

The third is quaint. It is the identification of this *public* record of a *public* trial as a "confidential" file. That stamp reads, "Please return this material to Confidential files." The type is large.

The only larger type on that envelope is "File Copy."

How the court's copy, confiscated from the compliant British court with the complicity of the British government, became the "file copy" of the Justice Department which so long and so persistently insisted that it had *no* copies I will pursue no further. But how I wish there could be a court of proper jurisdiction to do this!

So, it was not on mere whim that the existence of this envelope was denied, with the most shameless lies when all else failed.

Before we examine the file itself, however, State's letters also deserve attention. Lyerly had written us that it was because of Ray's personal request that the "Department was able to have the affidavits returned to the United States by British authorities," after which Kleindienst ruled they had to be withheld.

Never having had any direct communication with James Earl, I do not know when he requested what files, but I do know all the affidavits existed in countless files in two Departments in Washington, requiring no confiscation in Britain. I had been keeping Jerry informed of what I was trying to accomplish. I presume he informed his brother.

Without the cooperation of either Kleindienst or Lyerly, I also have a copy of Lyerly's letter to James Earl, which, by another remarkable coincidence, as I have noted, was written exactly when he wrote us. It begins, "I regret the delay in a further response to your letter of August 14, 1969." This seems to say that Ray first requested this file not before that date, hence, long after I did. The rest of the letter says what Lyerly told us about their being withheld and why.

Now, it simply is not true, as Lyerly said, that Justice and State got together in response to Ray's August 1969 request and then got the British records. Before that, I had already established that they had been filched. Earlier, I reported the unsuccessful efforts of a young woman and two British reporters to get copies for me. Aside from the message earlier sent me through this woman, John Pilger, among the most honored of British newspapermen, reported the disappearance of the files in a letter dated *June 26,* 1969. And there are other proofs that would be redundant.

In short, the existing record shows that, long before Ray's August 14, 1969 letter, the United States government was able to confiscate the only official copies of the affidavits not already in its possession, lock them in secret files, then pretend it had no copies, and later, with deceptive intent, claim that it had obtained the British copies at Ray's request.

Jencks seems much in point, and this special reason for the futility of trying to withhold the file envelope is clear. It was to try to hide the open federal illegalities that should be enough to require a full and open trial at the very least and really should mean dismissal of the charge to which Ray was persuaded to enter a guilty plea.

My word "futility" here is not an accidental choice. The great brains at Justice got no further than the envelope. That notation, there, stopped them. Had they gone further, they would have seen it was already too late, for the identical stamp appears inside the envelope, and I had copies of it, from folio 11. Some brains.

This, then, is the "law and order" record of the "law and order" government. It is a record of deliberate deceit; of lies so transparent they are below the intelligence level of an average adolescent; of contempt for the law and the courts; and of utter disregard for the rights of all Americans.

On one level, Ray was denied his. Whether he is good or bad, guilty or innocent, is entirely immaterial. The law applies equally to all. Legally, no one has any rights everyone else does not have. And no rights are denied any American without all others having theirs placed in jeopardy.

430

On another level, I was denied my rights, by law-violation and official lies, in a conscious effort to make the writing of this book more difficult, if not impossible, in a genuinely subversive attempt to prevent disclosure of official misfeasance and malfeasance, and to hide what amounts to a crime and is in violation of the bar's canon of ethics, the withholding and then the misrepresentation of exculpatory evidence.

Nitty Gritty = Official Frame-up

What the suppressed affidavit evidence shows will not be new to the reader. For me, as for the reader, it is confirmation. Its greatest significances are in its official character and as proof of purposeful misrepresentation, of suppression of exculpatory evidence, and of evidence of a conspiracy. It leaves little doubt that Ray was framed and that this framing was deliberate. The material also involves *conscious* deception.

The evidence was, of course, as such things always are in an adversary proceeding, *ex parte,* one-sided. However, there are the legal, moral, and ethical requirements that the one-sided presentation be honest and, where the evidence the prosecution holds is favorable to the other side, for it not to be withheld. Otherwise, justice also falls prey to predatory prosecution intent upon conviction at any cost.

The prosecution did have the Ray registration at the New Rebel Motel. It did not produce it in Memphis because there is handwriting other than Ray's on it. The pivotal entry on the card, that of the license number, was *not* by Ray. Several affidavits seek to explain this other handwriting. If the entry is innocent, withholding the facts from the defendant and the court cannot be.

Originally, it was planned that there would be not even the single live extradition witness—no one subject to any kind of cross-examination. The very first affidavit in the series is finger-print expert Bonebrake's. Had it been used in the Bow Street court, the single live witness would have been eliminated. With the certifications, including that of Judge Curran, this affidavit takes up ten of the pages (21–30). The last three are exceptional pictures of what are alleged to be, and undoubtedly are, Ray's fingerprints on the rifle, its scope, and the unnecessary binoculars. What is unusual is that nowhere, in this or any other file, is there any means of identifying any of the three objects, all of which bear unique serial numbers.

There is no single picture of the rifle. There is no single picture of the scope. There is none of the binoculars, either. No unrigged court could have accepted this, and there was, indeed, no need consistent with honesty of intent in the glaring omissions. Ray's prints could have been on these objects and still not in any way connect him with the crime. The second paragraph of the affidavit, intending other ends, admits Bonebrake had no personal knowledge of the origin of these three objects. The paragraph also contains their serial numbers.

The third paragraph indirectly admits that *the FBI did not identify Ray until two weeks after the crime*, and then not from its records of him as an escapee from the Missouri pen but from 1949 Los Angeles police prints.

The fourth paragraph is careful to avoid saying when the FBI connected Ray with the Missouri prints or even when the FBI got them. The latter is made clear in the seventh paragraph, which is an identification of one of the attachments to the affidavit. It was on April 4, 1960, eight years before the assassination, that the storied FBI got these Ray prints it somehow could not find when it needed them. With delicacy that is not surprising, Bonebrake's affidavit does not mention that the reverse side of this Missouri form bears the stamp, "WANTED BY BUREAU." So, the FBI not only could not find Ray's eacapee prints, it could not even find those of a man it "wanted." Among the many dates stamped on this reverse side, those that are legible include four in 1967, which does seem unusual and is unexplained.

Attention to the deficiencies of the Bonebrake affidavit and to its attempt to avoid embarrassment to the FBI should not overshadow consideration of its omissions. Adequate description of them would tax the capacity of the writers of extravagant advertising copy for Hollywood spectaculars.

Ray is alleged to have pawed his way around the flophouse bathroom and bedroom, to have moved furniture, then to have made that spectacular, all-night dash across the heart of the South in his white Mustang, later found with overflowing ashtrays (though he is a non-smoker).

Nowhere does Bonebrake allege the finding of a *single* Ray fingerprint in the car, in either of the rooms, on any of the furniture or anywhere else he is alleged to have been during, before, or fleeing the crime. It is not possible that even a prudent man would have left *none—not one*. Nor is it possible that these rooms and their furnishings, as well as the car and its contents, escaped the closest examination for fingerprints.

This means more than the absence of Ray's prints (whose absence

432

can safely be assumed, for otherwise they would have been shouted about). It also means that the identification of others, particularly in the rooms and the car—of whoever supplied all those butts—is deliberately and knowingly withheld.

The alternative possibilities are limited and simple:

There were *other* fingerprints, and the FBI is silent about them, which is culpable for the FBI and can mean conspiracy; or

There were *no* fingerprints, which means the rooms and the car were cleansed, which Ray could not have done and someone else had to have done—absolute proof of conspiracy and FBI culpability in withholding these facts.

For it is, of course, obvious that Ray could not have been in that flophouse scrubbing away at all the print-bearing surfaces while pushing that Mustang 400 miles through the night in a desperate dash to Atlanta and freedom. And it is also obvious, unless the official accounts are all false, that attention was immediately attracted to that rooming house. Hence, from the minitrial and affidavit "evidence," the cleansing of the rooms had to have been done, if at all, by leprechauns. Moreover, if credited, the government's "star witness" eliminates the possibility that Ray or anyone else remained to wipe away the prints.

"Bourbon Charley" Stephens' affidavit says there was *nobody* in the bathroom and that he *did* look. Now, Stephens may be the world's most undependable witness, "star witness" or not, but he is the *only* eyewitness. The government prepared this statement for his signature, and that is what it says. They are hooked with it, as they are with him.

The date on Stephens' affidavit persuades that it was included as the result of a delayed, difficult, and painful decision, for it is of a later date and is the last thing in the entire file (folios 184–194). It can safely be surmised that an effort was made to avoid using any statement from this lone "eyewitness" who was no eyewitness, as everyone involved had to have known. When nobody else was available to "place" the accused at the scene of the crime, the barrel was scraped.

And rather than *identifying* Ray, Stephens' affidavit, in the hands of real defense counsel, would have established two quite different things:

That Stephens did *not* make positive identification;
That it was impossible for him to make *any* identification.

Attached to the affidavit as an exhibit is a floor plan (folio 192), reprinted on the next page. It and the marks Stephens added to it are described in the paragraph numbered 9 (folio 190). So the reader can

433

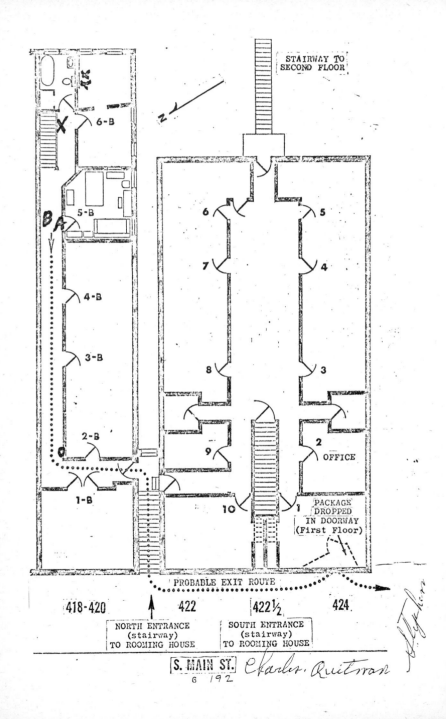

fully appreciate the possibilities for even a sober man to identify a stranger, I point out that Stephens places himself at the opposite end of a long hallway running the entire length of the flophouse. The floor plan shows no outside source of light. Stephens' own account, which really means what he would agree to swear to in the statement that was prepared for him, is that he heard the shot, heard the commotion outside, knew something was wrong, left his room, but paid no attention to a man running down that corridor! Instead, he looked in the *opposite* direction:

"First, I looked toward the bathroom and I saw that the door was open and it was empty."

To know that the bathroom was empty, Stephens had to go into it, not just look at a door open to an undescribed extent. Even if it were fully open, he still could not have known, from where he claims he was standing, whether the bathroom was empty.

Between the time he says he heard the shot and the time he claims to have seen a man running away, "a minute, not more, passed." In that "minute, not more," aside from getting out of the bathroom noiselessly, Ray had to have put the rifle into the box and made a single durable bundle out of it and that odd assortment of junk already described, even the cans of beer. This alleged bundle, found in the bedspread, Stephens said was wrapped in newspaper. Even an entire newspaper could not hold a boxed, long, and relatively heavy rifle, the bullets, beer, binoculars—all that strange collection—and stayed together while being carried at a dashing run, then hastily dropped. Nor could a single bundle have been made up and wrapped in newspaper inside the roominghouse and, by the time it got out of the rooming house, been inside the bedspread. Or there were two bundles, still another proof of conspiracy.

Alert as he was to the fact that something was seriously wrong, Stephens did not even look toward the running man until that man was at the opposite end of that long corridor. Stephens' mark on the floor plan places the man at that instant both against the left or inside wall and at the very end of the hallway, where it makes a 90-degree turn, to the left from Stephens' position. More, there is an offset in that wall, close to Stephens, at Room 5-B, the Ray room. Stephens places himself in a direct line with the wall after it passes the 5-B offset. It blocked his view. He was in a position where he could have seen almost nothing if not nothing at all.

The affidavit continues, "The man turned left toward the stairs when he reached the end of the hallway," without saying what the chart

435

shows, that it was not until this very instant that Stephens claims to have seen him. However, were everything Stephens said true, the best that can be said for it is that he had a split-second glimpse of a running stranger, whose back had been toward him, just as the man disappeared. As soon as that man got to where Stephens claims to have seen him, he was hidden by the turn in the corridor.

With all of this, the best identification the affidavit claims to make is at least uncertain. It begins with the understated obvious, "I did not get a long look at him before he turned left." Until that happened, Stephens could not see the face at all. Obviously, not a "long look." To this, Stephens could be persuaded to add only, "I *think* it was the same man I saw earlier with Mrs. Brewer." (Emphasis added.)

Were he a deacon, the epitome of respectability, stability, and dependability, Stephens' "identification" was no identification–and it is the *only* one!

The affidavit concludes with a cross-examiner's delight, the confession that after all of this, knowing something was very much wrong, after seeing "a lot of people and policemen at the Lorraine Motel," he did no more than nothing. He told no one, he called out to no one, phoned no one. He just "sat down in my bedroom."

Until his recollection was retrieved by a reporter's money, that is.

How wise Canale was to tell me that no one would ever see any of the evidence he did not use at the minitrial! How much of this could the evidence and the prosecution survive? And how wise were both Canale at the minitrial and the federal government in the extradition proceedings, not to include a statement from Stephens' common-law wife. By an unbelievable "coincidence," she was not around to be questioned by defense counsel, had either of them the intention of breaking down Stephens' story. She, however, did not enjoy an all-expense, if bourbon-free, vacation.

Prior to the filing of the suit, I was able to interest Paul Valentine, the reporter who had covered the minitrial for the *Washington Post,* in taking a new look at the case and my work. He had access to all but this final chapter. While he had had an indefinite sense of uneasiness as he sat in the courtroom listenting to the droning presentation at the minitrial, only *hearing* it did not disclose the magnitude of the frame-up.

Just before the hearing at which Judge Curran ordered Justice to give me what they were withholding, Valentine went to Tennessee to check out the strange incarceration of Grace Stephens. She was confined in a locked state mental hospital, under a questionable "diagnosis" ("chronic brain syndrome"), with the result that, after two years, she had become depressed.

Grace also had been a heavy drinker.

More mysterious than her incarceration, which John Carlisle, of Canale's staff, assured Valentine "his office was 'definitely not' behind," is the fact that she was not confined as "Stephens" but as "Walden," her name from a previous marriage far in the past. This seems less than accidental, less than innocent.

Valentine quotes her lawyer, C. M. (Pat) Murphy, in a lengthy story published Sunday, August 16, 1970, as saying Mrs. Stephens ". . . charges further that although she was a material witness and that she had informed the Memphis police . . . as to the details of her knowledge, such information was deliberately concealed . . . and she was unlawfully shuttled off . . . ."

Her confinement in this institution was highly irregular, at best. The habeas corpus action Murphy filed on her behalf elicited the ruling she is not insane and was to be provided better accommodations.

She had been put away July 31, 1968, less than two months after Ray's capture, when the state of Tennessee was keeping her Charley in what, for him, was unaccustomed luxury[2].

The picture of the bundle in the doorway, so long hidden from me, also in a way bears on the Stephens "evidence," as it does on other things. It shows the package was not wrapped in newspaper and that the wrapping could not have been mistaken for newspaper. End of Stephens as a "witness."

The copy I wanted was attached to the Canipe affidavit, for it shows other than that to which he swore. In his affidavit (folios 79–80), he attested, "When I looked up I saw a bundle lying in front of the door to my store." He then said he left the store, seeing the man *walk* away— *not* run. Of this picture, he made oath that "the attached photograph marked Exhibit III accurately portrays the front of my store and the bundle in place where I found it." His description is this: "The bundle or package appeared to include a large pasteboard box, the top of which was ajar, and from which the portion of the gun barrel was extended." Canipe certified he could read the word "Browning" on the box.

The contradiction between Canipe's swearing that *he* found the bundle and the swearing by Inspector Zachary that *he* found it needs no exposition. Only one *could* have "found it." This contradiction could have been deadly against the prosecution in a trial.

In Beasley's promise of what he would have proved had there been a trial (T. 65), he had assured the judge and jury ". . . Mr. Guy Warren Canipe, along with two customers, Bernell Finley and Julius Graham, were in the Canipe Amustment Company when they heard a thud . . . ."

Now, it happens that this picture proves Canipe, too, was wrong. The package was not "lying *in front of the door to my store*" but was *inside* the open doorway and partly blocked it. Canipe could not have walked out, as he swore he had, without walking over the bundle, unless, of course, something had happened to the bundle after that time and before the picture was taken. The wrapping is *not* open. To see what he swore he saw, he needed X-ray eyes. The cardboard box does *not* show, hence neither "the portion of the gun barrel" nor the word "Browning" was visible, as whoever prepared this affidavit for Canipe's signature *had to have known.*

The picture is reproduced on the next page.

As the reader can see, it shows the inside of the store. Guarding the bundle is a policeman, armed with a repeating shotgun, and *one* customer only is browsing, apparently undisturbed by the crime or attendant commotion. He appears to be a black man.

The three alleged witnesses are not in the picture. It is possible, of course, that one man had left, or that both had and a new customer had entered, but it is not likely. If the nature of the event did not keep them there, it was the obligation of the deputy sheriff (who Canipe says appeared first and promptly—*not* Zachary) to keep the witnesses available for identification and questioning and to arrange for their testimony.

While neither the box nor the rifle can be seen, what can be seen stretches probability. The radio is the only thing outside of the otherwise intact bundle. And although it, supposedly, just fell out when the package was tossed into the doorway, it is not on its side, not visibly cracked or broken, but is standing bolt upright, straight as can be, well inside the doorway—and not mentioned in either Canipe's affidavit or the Beasley monologue.

Nor, of course, is there any further word of Finley or Graham. They disappear from any official evidence or promise of evidence.

For the reader fully to appreciate this picture, his recollection should be refreshed.

Ray is alleged to have run out of the building a little to the left of Canipe's as the building is faced from Main Street. The get-away white Mustang is alleged to have been parked only a little past Canipe's. Naturally, it was parked in the street, near the curb, separated from the building line by a wide, paved sidewalk. A man running from either flophouse entrance to that car would have been far away from the doorway to Canipe's. A solitary man, one not part of any conspiracy, would have been even farther away than a straight-line route from the exit to the curb at that point, for he would have been running to the opposite side of the car, the driver's side.

Canipe's entrance has a deep, angular offset. It is farther away from the curb-line than is the inner edge of the pavement at that point.

If this picture shows the bundle as it was found, as Canipe first allegedly observed it, this was the weirdest getaway in history, involving a needless detour and the crazy depositing of a calling card before *three* witnesses—*entirely* off the sidewalk—on the *wrong* side, the side *away* from the car.

Assuming that it was a warm night and the door was open anyway, unless this is a picture of manufactured evidence, it means that Ray had to have run in the *wrong* direction—*away* from the car—while making his escape and, instead of dropping his bundle in panic, the officially planted "explanation," to have given it a hefty toss inside Canipe's, a fascinating detail not included in *any* version of that worthy and cooperative southern gentleman's story.

Not even a nut would have done this. Nobody, including one not in his right mind, would have taken the time to go so far out of his way to attract maximum attention to such incriminating evidence, where it would be found faster than anywhere else.

The possible explanations of this picture are limited.

It could record the planting of evidence by a decoy or as part of a decoy operation.

Or, the bundle was moved there from where it was found.

The picture and the official fairy tale are mutually contradictory. They cannot both be true.

It is, in fact, easier to credit a far-out account by Ray. In it he says "Raoul" told him to go down and wait in the car. On getting there, Ray says, he noticed a tire needed air. He claims to have gone to a gas station and had it changed, getting back to the scene of the crime after the shot was fired, finding a frantic "Raoul" looking for his missing getaway car.

However that package got there, from Ray's hands or those of others, it is not likely that it was just dropped by the fleeing assassin. Not *that* publicly, *that* far in the *wrong* direction—inside an *open* offset doorway, with people there.

It is possible the picture bears other evidence, but one cannot be certain with as indistinct a copy as I have, so what added intelligence may be in it must await the workings of the law.

But it is not possible to study even an indistinct copy of this picture, with any knowledge of the official representation of the fact of the crime, and believe this picture was so long withheld from me, even to risking a contempt citation, committing perjury, and permitting the judge to award a summary judgment by default, all by accident. This picture is that destructive of the official case. And this alone makes sense out of the official misconduct and illegality with and over it.

There is no end to the devil's advocacy possible from study of these suppressed affidavits. A book could be written in analysis of them alone. At this point, little is served by space devoted to any but two others, those of Robert Frazier (folios 31–35), the FBI firearms expert, and of

Dr. Jerry Thomas Francisco, the coroner (with attachments, folios 53–78).

The single sentence of Frazier's paragraph numbered "6" ends all ballistics evidence against Ray or any connecting the rifle with the crime. It reads:

"Because of distortion due to mutilation and insufficient marks of value, I could draw no conclusion as to whether or not the submitted bullet was fired from the submitted rifle."

Under the law, in the absence of evidence that the fatal bullet *was* fired from the alleged lethal weapon to the exclusion of all others, the presumption is that it was not.

Other things already covered about the ballistics evidence need not here be repeated. One item in the affidavit, however, cannot be ignored. It amounts to false swearing. Frazier did *not* examine what he swore to having examined, "the submitted bullet." He could not have examined it. There was no "submitted bullet." He might have described the object he studied as a piece of metal or metallic alloy, as a slug, even as a fragment of a bullet. Calling it a "bullet," which he did, borders on perjury. Frazier being an expert and an expert witness, this is consistent only with the deliberate intent to frame evidence and to frame Ray.

This false swearing to false evidence fits perfectly with the misrepresentation in Francisco's minitrial testimony, where he went so far out of his way to avoid the exacting, meaningful evidence about the fatal missile and wounds and so falsely represented just about everything else.

The death certificate (folio 61) Francisco executed says very little about the "immediate cause" of death: "Gunshot Wound to Thoracic Cord." The copy here used is neither certified nor certifiable. A note added June 10, 1968, says, "This is NOT [emphasis in original] a certified copy of the original death certificate on file in the Tennessee Department of Public Health, Nashville. It is a reproduction of a copy made in this office before the original was transmitted to the state office for filing. Legal fee $1.00 per copy." Sue Lackey, Deputy Registrar, signed it, *not* under oath.

As with the other never-questioned affidavit evidence, much time could be devoted to tearing apart Francisco's affidavit and destroying credibility and reputations. *De trop.* That is too much more than now is needed. The body charts alone proved in the most graphic manner what Francisco omitted from his testimony, what the prosecutor saw

442

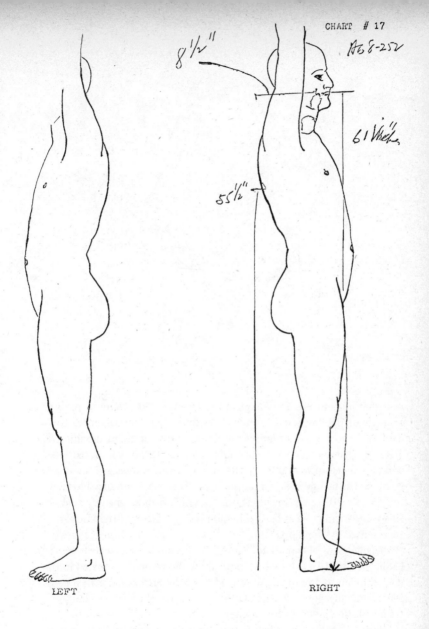

CHART # 17

AGE-252

8½"

61 inches

55½"

LEFT   RIGHT

70

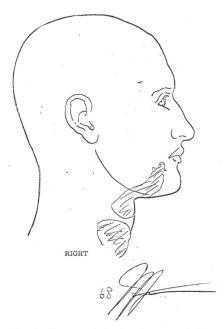

RIGHT

68

to it that he omitted. They explain the absence of the autopsy report
in the minitrial "evidence." They also explain Canale's statement to
me that nobody would ever see anything he did not use at the minitrial.

Rather than being near the shoulder, the point at which there lodged
what remained of the bullet is shown on a front-and-back body chart
(folio 67) as being far down on the back. This chart and the side-view
chart (folio 70) agree this point was 55½ inches above the left heel. The
side view orients this as below the point on the front of the body
represented by the nipple.

The side view (also marked "CHART 17") and the head view
("Special Chart 14," folio 68), both show the wound I reported in the
neck, hidden by the shirt and purged from the testimony. This means,
aside from any possible official criminality, that there had to be
fragmentation and no whole bullet.

Frazier, also, did not mention this. That omission, too, if short of
criminal, is not far from it.

These striking parallels with the autopsy said to have been performed
on President Kennedy and the testimony about it should be enough to
terrify everyone.

Reduced to its simplest, most easily understood form, the Francisco affidavit proves the murder was committed in a manner other than the one he swore it was committed in at the minitrial. It proves he there withheld evidence, with the unhidden connivance, if not at the order, of the prosecutor, to whom this autopsy report and its attachment were the most basic evidence, what lawyers call "best evidence."

These charts alone leave no doubt of the frame-up and of the deliberate intention to frame: to frame history, to frame the accused. No official can be innocent if he had any responsibility for handling this evidence and was and remains silent.

There is a popular expression, "There ought to be a law against it." I believe there is and must be a law against this kind of thing.

The problem is that those who enforce the laws are those who violated the laws. Who is going to charge and prosecute them?

Picture Canale prosecuting himself, Dwyer, or Beasley! Or Francisco!

Or Mitchell or Kleindienst prosecuting Canale or the others in Memphis or their own David Anderson in Washington! [3]

Or Jerris Leonard, chief of Justice's Civil Rights Division, charging that these men conspired to deny Ray his civil rights!

Leonard may yet charge conspiracy, but not this one.

After I examined the Lyerly letter to us, I suggested to Fensterwald that he ask Justice and all other government agencies to which Ray might have written for copies of the correspondence both ways. Ray was not equipped with a typewriter and carbon paper.

The letter to Mitchell was answered by Leonard. Leonard does not consider it a civil right for a defendant to have for his defense his own letters or those written him by officials. He rejected Fensterwald's request.

The reason?

Justice retains "prosecutive interest."

Now, of all the Assistant Attorneys General, why was this request referred to Leonard? Why did what would normally go to the Criminal Division find its way to Civil Rights? Of all the many Justice divisions, how can Civil Rights have jurisdiction?

Leonard cannot charge Ray, already sentenced. The statute of double-jeopardy precludes that.

And how does Civil Rights get jurisdiction in a murder case, with murder not a federal crime?

There is only *one* way, the one way this murder *could* be a federal crime: If it is part of a conspiracy to deny King's civil rights.

This is exactly what the government has insisted from the first is *not* the case.

This is also what I have been insisting from the first, in countless public appearances and in writing, *has* to be the fact. How closely the government watches and listens to me I have never set out to determine. Its attention is as improper as it is flattering. (We kid ourselves into believing such things happen only in societies we consider not free.) However, I have a rather thick stack of *carbon copies* of federal spying on me. And I have been nudging and needling the government on this subject. My suit for the affidavits is just such pressure. Their insane reactions cannot be considered incompetence, so it seems they are "up tight" about it and me.

Referral of this inquiry to Leonard and the Civil Rights Division means one of two things: Justice *is* considering a conspiracy charge, or it has again manufactured still another excuse to suppress what it otherwise cannot suppress.

If forced to open acknowledgment or to the filing of new charges, Justice has a prefabricated excuse: All this dishonesty was just a cover so it could continue its investigation, to the end that justice be done.

Rubbish!

The suppressed, confiscated affidavits in themselves prove otherwise, as they prove two conspiracies, one to assassinate, the other to frame. Each is equally criminal. The second is, morally, more reprehensible.

This work is a defense of James Earl Ray. If it is also the only defense he has had, it is still intended as more than a defense of one man. It was not conceived as no more than the defense of a single man accused of a crime, important as that is in a society describing and presenting itself as ours does. It is also part of a larger investigation into and analysis of a series of political assassinations, at a time in our national life that can, without exaggeration, be called the era of political assassinations.

Of the more sensational assassinations, this was neither the first nor the last. In a narrow sense, it is the most costly. It triggered an era of inchoate violence, beginning with wholesale burnings of the larger cities, where charred black skeletons of gutted structures remain as reminders of the passions kindled, of the frustrations and injustices that could find expression in no other way, and of the continuing failure of society to make meaningful effort to end these injustices and the frustrations they make inevitable.

During the period of numbing disbelief that followed the assassination

446

of John Kennedy, the organs of society assured us that this was an exceptional crime, that assassinations are typical of blighted lands, not of ours or its people. Such sanctimonious fools as Eric Hoffer were trotted before Congressional committees and the omnipresent TV cameras to pontificate that violence is foreign to us. This is worse than nonsense. It is dangerous self-deceit. Whitewash does not obliterate blood, nor can lies hide truth for long. This is a land wrenched with criminal violence and grimmest brutality from its original inhabitants whose unending mistreatment ever since is without parallel in the modern world.

Violence is as American as cherry pie.

There is no "civilized" country in which assassinations are and have been as common. We just prefer to forget them, and in this we are encouraged by all the voices of organized society.

The assassination of trade-union leaders, for example, was a commonplace during the organizational drives of the 1930s, although the assassinations did not begin at that relatively late date. I was part of the official investigation of them. In one sparsely populated coal-producing Kentucky county, Harlan, during that period, there were more homicides in a single year than in all the state of New York. Harlan County had but 50,000 inhabitants.

In Dallas, where the President was assassinated, gunshot wounds are so common nurses there are more familiar with them than doctors are elsewhere. And Dallas is not blighted Harlan. It is a modern, wealthy city. Skyscrapers and all that. One could not, in Dallas, buy an assassination, as was done in Harlan in one case of which I know, for $10. (For that price, it failed, as it deserved to, but a hotel was destroyed in the effort.)

We have not asked ourselves the necessary questions about the more spectacular recent assassinations, preferring the unction of self-deceit. But they have a unity that cannot safely be ignored.

The four best-known are those of the President, Malcolm X, King, and Robert Kennedy.

Why were these leaders assassinated *when* they were, not earlier or later in their lives? And what was the effect of each assassination and of all four together?

John Kennedy was not assassinated until he began to change national policy from one of international violence to one of domestic reconstruction and reform. (This little-known but unquestionable fact I will address in another book, titled *Tiger to Ride.*)

447

Malcolm X was not assassinated during the period of his life when he was preaching racism and the inferiority of women. It was not until he started to grow into the kind of leader who could galvanize black masses for militant action that he was shot down.

Martin Luther King, Jr., was hated throughout the South for years because he was an "uppity" black who dared confront white oppression with action, even non-violent action. But he was not assassinated until he became an open opponent of the policy of war and the war economy, until he began to radicalize, until his belief in non-violence flagged with the realization that moral suasion can be effective only against those who hold to a morality.

Robert Kennedy was not assassinated until he became the probable President and a peace candidate. He, too, had been hated and feared for years, had violence-prone enemies; but not until the moment he— by then the most prominent political leader committed for peace— became a serious threat to the national policy of war and a war-fueled economy, was his voice stilled, his leadership ended.

The better-remembered political assassinations have this in common: They removed the most influential and successful leaders who were against the national policy of war and for the belated granting, to the many so long denied them, of the basic rights of all Americans, including the rights to a decent life and self-respect.

Is it—can it be—no more than coincidence that the Barry Goldwaters, the Richard Nixons, the George Wallaces, survived? That the more conservative Whitney Youngs and Roy Wilkinses were not shot while the more militant and more activist Martin Luther King, Jr., and Malcolm X were?

Is it by accident only that only the doves were slaughtered?

Whether or not so designed by a single, calculating force, whether or not controlled by a central intelligence, all these assassinations have the effect of a *coup d'état,* an attempt to change national direction and determination, and the elimination of leadership.

In one respect, the assassination of Martin Luther King is different, and that difference is addressed in this book. His bones still rattle in the legal closet. As long as James Earl Ray lives, the whole contrived "solution" can fall apart.

Like all the others, the "solution" lacks credibility, in this case more so than in any of the others. There is no need to repeat the already-quoted statistics of the polls.

Because there was, at first, no suspect, and then a still-living suspect, although the planned publicity of the official "leaks" did jeopardize, if not prevent, a fair trial, the publicity was and had to be more restricted than the monster propaganda campaign that was a concomitant of the Warren Commission, where only prejudicial and usually false information was systematically dished out to a press that was both greedy and complacent. Fear of a courtroom disaster and an unpunished crime of this magnitude did tend to depress official propaganda. As a result, the public mind was less the captive of the opinion formers. The incredible remained largely incredible.

Evidence was manufactured in both cases, and in both cases the most essential was suppressed. The difference is that Oswald is dead and no legal actions impend.

Ray lives, and the only barrier to full exposure of the frame-up is legal technicalities, compounded by the racism and incompetence of the Stoner representation after the minitrial and of the avarice and crookedness that preceded it, all wasting most of the available legal remedies.

There is another difference. With considerable skill, the FBI, which did almost all the investigative work in both cases, was able to manipulate the Warren Commission and fasten upon it blame for the FBI's own transgressions. It remains to be seen if Memphis officialdom, in any showdown, will assume more than its own not inconsiderable responsibilities.

This time, too, the dishonesties were in a courtroom, not before an extra-legal body that no longer exists. The law can, with a live prisoner, correct error and punish wrongdoing.

Above all, this time the rascals are caught. The evidence here presented for the first time would have been overwhelming in a court of initial jurisdiction. It is the identical evidence deliberately and wrongfully withheld from that court, by those here named. There *is* a law against *that*.

The code of the bar also prohibits it. We shall yet see if the bar which so lustily assails and threatens its few members who have the courage and principle to defend the unpopular and the persecuted with all the vigor of which they are capable, will tolerate these open affronts to its standards by those who conspired to prevent justice and frustrate the workings of the law.

That is not red paint on the hands of the rascals I have caught. It is blood. It is not alone the blood of a system of law and justice, of a society that, though sick, still lives.

449

And it remains to be seen whether the system or the society can and will survive this letting of its own blood.

Unless justice is done, unless wong is undone, neither will. Or should.

Key Questions, Major Doubts

While seeking to make as full and complete a record as possible, for justice, the solution of the crime, and history—so that society might work as it should work—it is possible that I have dulled the reader's awareness both of the central questions of the King/Ray case and of those that must be addressed and answered in any appeal and trial, which procedures are the way organized society works to establish justice.

Here I emphasize again that the basic question is not, really, whether or not Ray is guilty, important as that is, but whether the oft-quoted requirement of the law, "beyond reasonable doubt and to a moral certainty," was met. Because of the *public* official posture that there was no conspiracy (now privately altered as a consequence of the work represented by this book), this means that the proof must be:

that Ray, *alone,* fired a single, fatal shot;

and that he was *not, in any way,* helped by *anybody.*

As has become the profitable, commercially acceptable custom with the recent political assassinations, further works of sycophancy are scheduled to appear. They have enormous public relations and advertising budgets behind them. Large sums are invested in their preparation. Two examples on the King/Ray case are books by Gerold Frank, who has written six best-sellers, including *The Boston Strangler,* and by George McMillan, titled *Portrait of an Assassin.* Doubleday reportedly advanced Frank $100,000 against expected royalties. McMillan's "psychological study" got what he described as a "very happy contract" from Little, Brown, with eight foreign reprint contracts signed by the time of the minitrial. Both books assume Ray's guilt. McMillan, who hired a psychiatrist to help him "understand," not the crime or the workings of society, but the second- and third-hand published pap about Ray, was forthright. He immediately said, "This guy is a loner. And I have never investigated any aspect of a conspiracy, which has left me free to work on his biography." McMillan's expressed concern was about "things like what does it do to a guy to sleep in the same bed with his parents when he is growing up." This is the Warren Commission–Oswald formula again—but with a man in the bed, too. (Understandably, McMillan's book is more than a year past

450

publication date.)

Both men had full access to Huie's material and used it, which gives further promise of their composing their own official apologia.

A well-paid-for "midwest Tobacco Road"—or two or more of them—will not help public understanding or establish what did or did not happen when the "black messiah" was assassinated at the very time he had lost confidence in non-violence and had become a real leader for peace. The enormous commercial stakes invested in them is not and never was conceived as a means of establishing truth. Especially for these reasons do I think it necessary that the reader be aware of some of the more important of these existing questions. Those that follow, not by any means all that exist, should be enough to help the reader clarify his thoughts. They relate to the evidence about the crime itself, whether or not there was a conspiracy, and about the functioning of the law and justice, meaning also the performances of prosecution, defense, and the judge.

I have grouped the questions in clusters of related issues.

Is there any proof that Ray, in person, was at the scene of the crime, particularly at the moment it was committed?

Does a single credible eyewitness place him there?

Does fingerprint evidence place him there, even at another time?

Why was the fact of the extreme drunkenness of the only claimed eyewitness suppressed from all official records, including his own sworn statement? And why was the more credible but contradictory word of his sober and lucid common-law wife suppressed? Can her mysterious sequestration, which made her unavailable to the defense, be no more than an inexplicable coincidence?

Is there *any* proof the so-called Ray rifle was used in the crime?

Even if there were, as there now is not, is there any proof Ray used it? Or that it was ever in his possession at any time after purchase?

Does the exchanging of the rifle as soon as it was bought make any sense at all, except as another means of leaving a clear and obvious trail leading to Ray?

Is there, in fact, *any* ballistics proof identifying *any* rifle or rifles used in the crime?

In the official, minitrial evidence:

Why did the prosecution and the federal government suppress and misrepresent the medical evidence, hiding the existence of another and major wound?

Why was not the eyewitness testimony of known police-spy

451

observers from the "red" squad placed in the record? And why was the *existence* of these police eyewitnesses hidden—suppressed?

Why is there no picture of the corpse as found by the police in the evidence? (If no police photographer was present, a professional photographer was and he did take pictures.)

Were any FBI agents present? If so (as seems likely), why is this also hidden?

Is there *any* established connection between the finding of Ray's property near the scene of the crime and the crime itself? If there is not, is not the finding of this Ray property at that point and at that time indicative that it was planted to be found, to link him with the crime?

Is *either* of the official and contradictory accounts of the finding of this property credible?

Is it true, as he swore, that Inspector Zachary found it?

Can Canipe's account be true?

Can a fleeing assassin—even an insane one—have detoured and tossed such incriminating clues *into the entrance of Canipe's store,* as shown in the suppressed picture I had to sue to get?

From this picture, can Canipe have seen what his affidavit says he saw? Could that bundle, not tied and with its imputed career and contents, have stayed intact after being tossed into the entrance? Could the radio, magically, have escaped it and, undamaged, just happened to stand upright, while the longer, heavier rifle did not show?

If this is not a faked picture (with the bundle itself faked), is not the evidence relating to it perjurious?

Is there any proof that Ray, personally and alone, drove that Mustang, *to* or *from* Memphis?

Why does the disappearance at Memphis of an Atlanta-to-Chicago ticketed airline passenger—and at just the right time—remain an official mystery, suppressed from the official evidence?

Is there any proof that on the way to Memphis Ray, personally, checked the car into the New Rebel Motel?

Why, whether or not innocent, was knowledge of the presence of handwriting other than Ray's on the motel registration suppressed from the evidence and thus from all publicly available records?

Why was there official suppression of the existence of other, identical white Mustangs?

When Ray is alleged to have driven that Mustang, sleepless and entirely alone, for almost 400 miles through the night, why is there no evidence of a single one of his fingerprints anywhere in or on it?

After he drove it for more than a year? Is this within possibility?

If he had been entirely alone, why was property other than his found in that car? Why is its owner not identified? Were there no other fingerprints in or on the car—*none* of *anyone*—after that spectacular dash?

Whose fingerprints are on the cigarette butts? Ray is a non-smoker.

Why would even a lunatic drive *400 miles in the wrong direction* escaping such a crime if he were entirely alone and planned flight to Canada?

Why would the entirely alone Ray have marked up that map of Atlanta and then not have committed the crime there?

How did he do it without leaving a single fingerprint on the map?

Were any *other* fingerprints on it or on any of the other maps, other property?

Why would the entirely alone Ray have ordered such specialized camera equipment, so ideally suited for spying, in a way that needlessly left so clear a record, when he could have gotten it locally in any good camera shop?

Could an entirely alone Ray, traveling aimlessly, have known as accurately and in advance when he would be where and for how long?

Could Ray, entirely alone and unassisted, have financed and planned all the traveling, including the adoption of false identities? Could he have seen the *signature* of the *adult* Eric St. Vincent Galt in the newspaper notice of the *birth* of the *infant* Eric St. Vincent Galt?

Did the government make *any real* investigation of *any* of Ray's connections, especially in New Orleans, particularly where there was credible proof of their existence?

Or, was the investigation made and its results suppressed? How can government, honorably and honestly, have sought and obtained an indictment for conspiracy in Birmingham, then claim in court in London that there was no conspiracy, and then claim again in the Memphis minitrial that there was no conspiracy?

Further, how can it now suppress evidence to which Ray is entitled under conditions which can mean only that it believes there was a conspiracy and in that preserves a "prosecutive interest"?

Were the requirements of British extradition law met?

Were they thereafter also violated?

Why did the government confiscate the only official affidavit evidence publicly accessible, with the complicity of the British government; then deny its existence and access to it?

Is there, in fact, another case in history when the public record of the public trial of an American citizen was confiscated?

Why did the Department of Justice always lie to me about this evidence and, ultimately, lie to the federal judge, under oath?

Can all this official wrongdoing be considered but the behavioral and legal norm of the "law and order" Nixon–Agnew–Mitchell administration, or was another, sinister purpose served?

With a crime of this magnitude, is it possible that no more than official carelessness caused the always automatic all-points police alert not to be issued?

Why does the prosecution refuse access to the evidence it withheld from the minitrial evidence—thereby suppressing it? And even to that part of it that is, by stipulation, part of the official record?

Why did the prosecution edit and misrepresent the evidence?

Why did Foreman agree to this?

Did the prosecution, in fact, violate the canons of legal ethics?

Was this not also true of the entire deal—and the participation in and domination of it by the judge?

Did not these things:

Deny Ray any possibility of a fair trial?

Condition his mind and thinking so that he could make no free choice?

Assure that he had to agree to the deal, "cop" the plea to a more severe penalty than any jury could have been expected to agree to?

Did Ray, within the meaning of the Constitution and the law, ever have "effective" counsel?

Did either Hanes or Foreman and Stanton ever make any *real* investigation of the merits of the case against Ray? If they did not, was any effective defense possible?

Were his lawyers ridden with conflicts of interests, where their possibilities of financial reward were opposed to Ray's and justice's legal interests and minimal needs?

Did Hanes and Foreman also not contract to violate the bar's canons of ethics?

To these questions, I would add two more, not directly related to Ray's guilt or innocence:

Can American justice survive such intrusions into and corruptions of the judicial processes and the workings of the law as these by the Huie-Hanes-Foreman "defense"?

Does an assassin or assassins roam free, set free by the official frustration of justice in the King/Ray case?

454

Notes

Chapter 1 Will the Real James Earl Ray/Ramon George Sneyd Please Stand Up?

[1]   I compare one paragraph from his book, the one quoted above, with a
by-line article in the *Washington Post* of July 5, 1968, by Karl E. Meyer, of its
London bureau:

Meyer: Ray turned up at a YWCA hostel on Warwick Way
Blair: Ray appeared at the YWCA Hostel on Warwick Way

Meyer: The hostel, despite its name, also provides rooms for men . . . .
Ray was told there was no room
Blair: The YWCA has rooms for men. But that day, they were all filled

Meyer: The woman at the desk saw Ray with a young blond man who she
thought was an American
Blair: This time also there was a man with him: a young blond who appeared
to be an American

Meyer: Ray was told there was no room at the hostel, and was referred to
the Pax Hotel, three doors down the same street
Blair: Ray was turned away. The YWCA receptionist referred Ray to another
rooming place three doors down the same street, the Pax Hotel

Meyer: When Ray turned up at the Pax Hotel he was alone
Blair: Ray appeared at the Pax alone

If we skip one paragraph in the Meyer story, we find this language from which I
have eliminated nothing and to which I have added nothing:

When he left the Pax Hotel on June 8, two paperback novels were found in
his room. One was a yellow-covered thriller, "Tangier Assignment" by Cameroun
Rougvie. It is described by its blurb: "In a time of Suez crises, the Mediterranean, from Tangier to Port Said, seethes with nationalist revolt, international
intrigue, Mafia villainy and freebooting contrabandists. Helped by the lovely
Sandra Grant, this is precisely the situation on which Robert Belacourt thrives
. . . although many interests would rather see him dead."
Written in the back flyleaf of the novel was the calculation "2.40 times 6
equals 14.40." At the time of his arrest, Ray had about 60 pounds on him.

Where Meyer begins his paragraph "When he left the Pax Hotel on June 8,"
Blair's begins with the same thought jazzed up a little, "That Saturday morning–
June 8–Ray checked out of the Pax Hotel." Here Blair has a few samples of
his character assassination, the poisonous thoughts of the sweet and charitable
lady who ran the joint, unconfirmed and unconfirmable (who but a Blair can
read thoughts, especially those of the past?). He then reports she found the place
littered, followed by this language which, word by word comparison will show
the reader, is virtually identical in the first incomplete sentence I quote and in
every respect identical in what follows, including identical elisions, to the last
clause of the last sentence, where Blair seems to have found Meyer a little unclear:

That Saturday morning–June 8–Ray checked out of the Pax Hotel early.
As he walked out of the door carrying his little travel bag, Mrs. Thomas, who
had enough, thought: "Good riddance to you." She went upstairs to clean his
room. She found a mess: the floor littered with . . . two cheap paperback
novels. One was a thriller in yellow cover, *Tangier Assignment,* by Cameroun
Rougvie, reminiscent of James Bond. The cover blurb: "In a time of Suez crises,

the Mediterranean from Tangier to Port Said seethes with international intrigue, Mafia villainy and freebooting contrabandists. Helped by the lovely Sandra Grant, this is precisely the situation on which Robert Belacourt thrives . . . although many interests would rather see him dead." Written in the back flyleaf of the novel were some figures, "2.40 times 6 equals 14.40," evidently Ray's attempt to puzzle out British currency.

There is more, but is this not enough? Here in two adjacent paragraphs in the *Washington Post* and in the later-appearing Blair, we have *exactly* the same material in *exactly* the same sequence, often in *exactly the same words* (and where this is not so, the simple substitutions are obvious), arranged to present the *identical* thoughts and meaning. Can this possibly be happenstance, another of those endless remarkable "coincidences" that become the norm in the era of political assassinations?

Astounding, is it not?

Whatever explains it, if others paid the freight for this literary fancy-pants for all those advertised thousands of miles, they might wonder in *their* boardroom what they got for their money, aside from a not-very-professional rehash of the newspapers. And those who read Blair's novel on the demise of the *Saturday Evening Post,* which he edited, entitled "The Board Room," may indeed wonder why that oldest of American magazines, tracing back to William Penn—a magazine as old as the United States—survived all those years and crises only to fail with the largest circulation it ever had.

Chapter 2   An "Ordinary Visitor"

[1]   By pleading guilty, Ray legally and technically gave up his right to a formal trial, as the judge at the Memphis minitrial told him. But the issue is larger. Ray, in agreeing to the deal that had been worked out for him—we shall be examining this in detail—relinquished other rights. These include, in the words of the judge (from Blair's transcript, p. 210), "Your motion for a new trial . . . successive appeals to the Supreme Court, to the Tennessee Court of Criminal Appeals and the Supreme Court of Tennessee . . . petition to review by the Supreme Court of the United States." There are others.

Chapter 4   Orwell, 1969

[1]   I interject here a note on one celebrated case, that of Julius and Esther Rosenberg, accused of being "atom-bomb spies" and killed for it. Their counsel agreed that some of the so-called evidence be kept secret on the altar of that new god, "national security"—as though, if they had delivered secrets to an enemy, that enemy did not have the delivered secrets. It later turned out this secret government evidence was fake evidence—long AFTER the Rosenbergs were safely dead, legally murdered by the government that faked and used the fake evidence to accomplish this.

Chapter 7   Percy Foreman: "I've Given Away $300,000 This Year"

[1]   Espionage is possible. According to Canale, Hanes was concerned about eavesdropping and the question did come up in court. Hanes filed charges that guards were listening in through microphones in Ray's cell as part of the security

precautions. In court September 25, Canale told the judge the microphones were turned off when Hanes entered the cell and that "Hanes had tests performed at his request showing to petitioner's [Hanes's] satisfaction that his conferences with Ray cannot be heard by guards in the cell." If they could not, the pictures in the papers make the cell seem smaller than it is or Ray and Hanes had to lower their voices to the weakest whispers.

Whether Hanes had known of Ray's plan for "as much as a month," from the very first, or whether the first he heard of it was when he was told at 8:20 that night, it happened. One *can* feel sorry for Hanes. There he was, at the empty altar outside the Shelby County Office Building that Sunday night, standing in the drizzle for his impromptu press conference, complaining the move came as a surprise and, "I didn't come to Memphis for the drive. I came here prepared to go to trial."

[2] The inference the government either wanted Foreman to become Ray's counsel or was anxious to facilitate it is warranted by the ease and informality with which he reached Ray. Hanes had not been able to interview him for several days. When Richard J. Ryan, one of the lawyers who succeeded Foreman, tried to see Ray in connection with a motion he was about to file for a new trial, he was turned away from the Nashville prison. The reason then given was "because he had not been officially retained as Ray's lawyer." Neither had Foreman, when he walked up to the Memphis jail Sunday night, knocked on the door, and was admitted.

Chapter 8 The Deal

[1] The leak is another exact parallel to the mishandling of the Presidential assassination investigation, where everything of any consequence was carefully leaked in advance to a complaisant press that, in accepting the information, was itself corrupted. With non-stop leaks that were not leaks but were "plants" by government, the government could never discover who was responsible for a single one, and not one could have come from any source other than government. The vaunted and vain J. Edgar Hoover, the greatest investigator of them all, could not find a single culprit. To see the one most guilty, he need only have opened his eyes when he shaved.

[2] The *Post* was not the only running dog for the government the press claims it is always trailing. UPI's Merriman Smith, soon a suicide, was then its White House correspondent. He was the first of the by-line sycophants to rush to the government's defense when the official fairy tale about the Presidential murder was under serious attack by *Whitewash* and the books that followed it. He wrote so carelessly and incompetently he could not even report where he was. He manufactured scenes he never saw and could not possibly have seen by embroidering on a wrong statement of where he was—for all of which he won that year's Pulitzer Prize for reporting!

Smith spoke about the Ray case to a good, traditional American reporter, Art Kevin, of Hollywood's KHJ radio. Art told me on March 13—three days after the minitrial—that Smith told him the deal had been made "for and with Ray because the government did not want him executed. He [Ray] had spoken some, said this guy and that guy, but never mentioned any names. They felt if they could keep him on ice, he might make up his mind to talk and give the names."

No conspiracy?

This is hardly the story of complete federal detachment that was carefully fed the press and, through it, the people. It is hardly what UPI told its vast audience.

457

The government had prepared separate stories for everyone, each suited to pacify those to whom it was directed. Had Smith been the reporter his positions and honors indicate, were he anything but a professional sycophant, he might have considered a number of other fairly obvious possibilities. One is that, safely in jail, Ray could fall victim to his own assassin, the Ruby–Oswald bit. As with Oswald, where the only purpose Ruby served was to close his mouth, Ray's mouth would thus be closed permanently and he would never name names.

Chapter 10 Would Ray Have Been Executed?

[1]   By the time that Huie's crack appeared, the afternoon of the second day following the minitrial, the Department of Justice felt it not inappropriate to don its vestments of piety. After it had, from the record, failed to interpose any objection and, in reality, had blessed the arrangement—if it did not father it—its faceless, unnamed "spokesman" pretended unhappiness. The government always winds up having the cake it eats. As the Chicago *Daily News* put it March 13, "Regrets were voiced in the Justice Department over Ray's abrupt guilty plea." The reason: A full-fledged trial might have shed light on the questions that have led to widespread suspicion that Ray was only one figure in a conspiracy. The Associated Press quoted a Department "source" as saying "the feeling there . . . 'is one of frustration.' " Translated from the officialese of propaganda intent, this was merely the Department misinforming all editors and as many others as they reached, seeking to convey the false notion that it was and had been opposed to the deal, that it regretted it but had not been able to do anything, and that it really had wanted the open examination of its evidence in open court. Remarkable how helpless the government can be at times. But had the evidence been available, the Department would have died on the spot. Knowing everything would be suppressed, and doing its own share clandestinely, it felt that, without scruple and with skill, it could further exploit the situation. So, it did. I recount in the last chapter my long-frustrated efforts to obtain the evidence that by right is in the public domain—and what it *really* says.

[2]   To cite a simple example of the tightness of the official cocoon in which Ray is encapsulated, I wrote him telling him I believed I had information that could be important to him and offering to visit him if he so desired. Months passed, and there was no response. I later mentioned this to Jerry, who discussed it with James Earl. The word is James Earl never got my letter. It was not returned, either.

Chapter 11 The Minitestimony

[1]   Here again, the perfect parallel with the incompetent autopsy on the President's corpse and the equally incompetent "testimony" about it. The difference is that, with the need for supporting a Report that had to be made, the testimony about the President's autopsy had to pretend to get closer to the standards of evidence. The result there also is perjury for sure and its subornation a probability. In both cases, the made-up medical "evidence" depends upon bullets with magical powers. In each case, the fraud presented as evidence is an indispensable part of a frame-up. But in Memphis, the deal having been packaged in advance, they were totally unconcerned. They knew there would be no other side, no questioning or cross-questioning. They may have expected the transcript never to be seen or analyzed.

What is perhaps a greater outrage than this prostitution of the entire judicial process is the abject, shameful silence of those many lawyers who have read this transcript, added without comprehension of what it says in Blair's book.

[2]   A friend of King's, who acted as a bodyguard seeking to protect King from the sudden rushes of emotional people as well as physical harm, tells me that, while he was with King, before each meeting, he was given the name and description of the FBI men who would be present and vice versa. There is no doubt in his mind that the FBI was supposed to be protecting King. With the FBI's foreknowledge, represented by its search of the plane before it departed Atlanta, its presence near him in Memphis is more likely than on other occasions.

Chapter 12   The Mini-Narration

[1]   Blair has those "deposits on the *empty* bolt," two physical impossibilities that provide a measure of his knowledge and understanding and reflect the diligence with which he checked his "facts."

[2]   Several other developments bear on this in an interesting way. First, when Birmingham witnesses who presumably had seen Ray and could identify him were shown the candid picture of him taken only a few months earlier (used by the FBI as an identification photo), like just about everyone else, they said it was not the man they had seen. Second, when Renfro Hays, who had been Hanes's investigator, sued for his fees and expenses, after the minitrial, the answer filed in court alleges that the rifle and auto were not Ray's property.

These things may not relate, may not even be entirely true. But they are, provocatively, consistent with Ray as a decoy, not alone, and not as the assassin. And, they are not in the official court record.

[3]   Everyone who dared did complain of FBI uncooperativeness. This is surprising. Local police usually preserve silence, having a future of working with the powerful federals to consider. That they here did not is significant. It indicates the acuteness of the dissatisfaction over FBI performance and policies.

[4]   Blair is delicate in his version of the verbatim transcript. He eliminates the words, "and will be touched upon in the testimony from that end in just a moment."

[5]   Lomax believed there is evidence Ray made a third trip between Los Angeles and New Orleans at this time. (Incidentally, Lomax died in a coincidental automobile accident during the summer of 1970.)

[6]   All that I can suggest on the basis of information given to me—and I cannot confirm it—is that there was a place in Chicago with a name like this. It allegedly was sort of left-wing. Ray assuredly is not of the left—not with Hanes and Stoner as counsel and brother Jerry honored by the NSRP (as he was, with a banquet where he was the guest of honor). But if my information is correct, then the coupon may be regarded as another false lead carefully planted to lead to the left for the murderers. This is the line Hanes took, in the absence of either evidence or logic. It would certainly have been the preference of murderers of the right.

A further item on Jerry and the NSRP. In the summer of 1970, Stoner ran for governor of Georgia on the NSRP ticket, with Jerry as his campaign manager. During the campaign, Jerry shot a teen-age boy from Alabama who had volunteered to help in the NSRP headquarters in Columbus, Georgia, claiming he had caught the boy stealing membership records. Jerry was later acquitted.

[7]   Again, the startling Oswald parallel. Oswald is said to have built a sniper's nest of boxes in Dallas and to have given out literature in New Orleans. But the fingerprint check in Dallas showed that many others handled the boxes it was

Oswald's *assigned job* to handle. Therefore, with typical official logic, the government said he, who handled those boxes as part of his job, made a nest of them—and those others, presumably *not* paid to handle the boxes, are not identified. The literature sample in New Orleans, given the FBI by New Orleans authorities after Oswald picketed the carrier "Wasp," had fingerprints other than his. Therefore, the unpublished files and the official record do not contain the identity of the person who left the fingerprints Oswald *alone* should have left.

[8]   Beasley's silence on these matters provides another and no less remarkable parallel with the "Oswald" rifle, as though the scenarios had been scripted by the same unimaginative mind. There is no proof Oswald ever bought a clip for that rifle as, in fact, there is no evidence he ever bought the bullets or had either given him. Further, there were no fingerprints on the three empty casings found in Dallas or on the live round in the breech or on the clip. So desperate were the Warren Commission lawyers for the answer, they asked the FBI if the act of firing the bullets could remove prints from the casings—and suppressed their apprehension in their files. They ignored, as Beasley ignores, what both knew to be consistent with a frame-up, the wiping clean of the evidence. When it was possible to prove whether the found bullet and the found fragments of a bullet or bullets were actually used in the Presidential assassination, the Commission avoided all tests and proofs, preferring to conjecture a military-type bullet was used. When the FBI found the most ample supply of ammunition for that rifle of an entirely different variety readily available in Dallas, it lost all interest in the necessary inquiry it had initiated. It conjectured one variety and hid the existence of others. The record does not disclose where—or *if*—Oswald got a clip and ammunition. Ditto with Ray.

[9]   The FBI explanation is the one discredited at Nuremberg: The agents did only what they were ordered to do. What they knew *had* to be done but was not *ordered* done, they did not do. Therefore, all they tried to do in Dallas was get into a position where they could say the shots *could* have come from this sixth-floor window. Following this, it never having been sought and having been carefully avoided, the Warren Commission could—and did—proclaim it had no evidence of shots from any other place.

[10]   The spectrographic analyses of bullet, fragments, and objects allegedly struck were withheld from the Warren Commission by the FBI, which refused me access to this seemingly public information for more than four years. I filed a suit for this evidence (Civil Action No. 2301, Federal District Court for the District of Columbia) after this book was written. If, at any point, I win a decision, the government will undoubtedly appeal. Thus the case is expected to go to the Supreme Court and may become one of the precedents governing the Freedom of Information Act (5 U.S.C. 552).

I believe that if this laboratory evidence—by its nature involving no secrets, no secret processes, no informants requiring protection—gave any comfort at all to the official stories, it would have been elaborately displayed and widely disseminated. That it is suppressed in both cases persuades that in both cases it contradicts what I regard, in Orwell's words, as the "official mythology."

[11]   Here are a few of these early accounts. A week after the murder, the *Nashville Tennessean* printed an AP dispatch, in the issue of April 12. It began,

The FBI refused to comment yesterday on whether the ballistics test matched the bullet which killed Dr. Martin Luther King, Jr., with the rifle found near the scene . . . . The *New York Post* reported yesterday that the fatal bullet was so badly deformed on impact that the FBI was having difficulty proving it was fired from the rifle . . . . An unidentified Memphis ballistics technician was

460

quoted as saying the bullet was badly damaged when it struck bones in Dr. King's neck. Another published report said the bullet may have been soft-nosed.

With Oswald already murdered and no possibility of a case in open court, the ever-faithful FBI felt no such inhibition with the ballistics evidence in that case. It sedulously leaked an entirely distorted account of its "findings," calculated to poison the public and media minds against the dead accused, an indispensable part of that frame-up. It knew there would be no defense counsel to scream at this impropriety, no one to call it to task and, above all, no cross-examination in court. But on April 11, 1968, it had to assume and did assume there would be an open trial at which it would have to answer for anything it said. Thus, it did not risk pulling the same caper in the case of the then-unapprehended accused.

On April 12, 1968, the *New York Times'* Martin Waldron wrote from Memphis:

> According to a report today, the bullet that killed Dr. King had been smashed and laboratory technicians of the Federal Bureau of Investigation had been unable to match it with the Remington 30.06 caliber rifle believed to have been the assassin's weapon . . . . The F.B.I. refused to comment on the report that the bullet could not be identified. But the report was consistent with information furnished by a source in Memphis, who said that the bullet was soft-nosed and had been squashed, apparently when it hit King's left shoulder-blade. Soft-nosed bullets are used in big-game hunting because they expand on contact and do much more damage than do the steel-jacketed bullets used by soldiers.

Precisely. This is why military conventions prohibit soft-nosed bullets in warfare, requiring them to have hard jackets.

Chapter 13 "This Is Your FBI"

[1] I refer the reader to my book *Whitewash II: The FBI-Secret Service Cover-Up.* The reference above is to the fifth volume of the hearings, p. 98.

[2] There were other disclosures in the summer of 1969 when Hoover's spying on King became known. Frank Mankiewicz and his columnist partner, Tom Braden, reported that the FBI bugged without the authorization of any lawyer in the Justice Department. There was nothing Hoover could say, because the Department had confessed this in front of the Supreme Court. In the Cassius Clay case, Clay's lawyers discovered that the FBI had altered its own records. The AP story on this commences, "The government has admitted the FBI changed— without informing the Department of Justice—a recorded log of wiretap conversations involving former heavyweight boxing champion Cassius Clay." Clay's conviction on a draft-evasion charge was the legal issue. Under the headline, "Hoffa Car Bugged," the *Washington Post* reported two FBI agents admitted the eavesdropping in Federal Court in Chicago.

The Department of Justice itself sent Solicitor General Erwin Griswold to the Supreme Court to ask it to order a new hearing for black militant Cleveland Sellers because there had been FBI electronic spying on him. And in the case of students who had protested at the 1968 Democratic convention in Chicago, the question of electronic surveillance and whether it could be justified "in the interest of" what was called "internal security" came up and decision was postponed.

More recently, there has been a new item on Hoover's bugging of King. The August 17, 1970 issue of *Time* reported that Hoover had confronted King with the details of his personal life produced by this bugging and that the FBI director demanded, as the price for his silence about it, that King end his criticism of the

FBI's poor record in civil-rights cases and become less militant. There were not fewer than three close associates of King at the meeting where these threats allegedly took place. But had Hoover done this, it would have been a crime—blackmail–committed before reputable witnesses. I do not believe Hoover did or would do that. Besides, to have done it would have been unnecessary, the same purposes being more easily accomplished by indirection. Moreover, carrying out the threat ended the Damoclean value of the spying, eliminated its continuing value in silencing black leaders. Above everything else, Hoover was using this material, to King's knowledge had been using it, and he continued to use it. I wonder if this story was leaked or fed by the FBI to *Time* (which need not have known the ultimate source) as part of its unending fight against King, even the assassinated King.

[3]   One of the more grievous cases of Bureau impropriety involves the Secret Service, which has primary obligation for the protection of the President. Within 24 hours of President Kennedy's assassination, they had pinpointed the source of the "Oswald" rifle, Klein's Sporting Goods, in Chicago. Officials there would not give the Secret Service the time of day until heavily leaned upon, whereupon they confessed the FBI had been there and warned them not to say anything to anyone. Now, at that time, the FBI had no legal authorization to do anything in the Presidential murder. It was not a violation of any federal law. The Secret Service did have jurisdiction. It wasted a precious half-day at the very outset simply because the FBI wanted to take over. This is one of the means by which it did. It was a simple matter to trace the weapon, through the importer. The FBI, having more men, could do it faster. It froze out the Secret Service. One of the unfortunate consequences is that there remains a large mystery: The rifle shipped is not the rifle Oswald, or someone using his alias if the handwriting is not his, ordered.

[4]   Ray says Foreman showed him this series of Dallas pictures, seeking information, and telling him the FBI was up-tight on the subject.

[5]   Hoover is far-sighted, experienced at the government game, with a survival instinct that is probably unique in the long history of oppressive bureaucracy. While all this was going on, he still had time to help the respected Harry and Bonaro Overstreet with their pseudo-scholarly book, *The FBI In Our Open Society.* This is the book of all books in which official sponsorship is least disguised, as abject an apology and as open a deification as man and woman are capable of. It achieved wide attention in the press, with such headlines as that in the *New Orleans Times-Picayune,* four columns wide, announcing "Critics of the FBI Get Comeuppance." The Overstreets, who earlier had staked out a successful and remunerative career as scholarly commercializers of the prevailing anti-Communist sentiment, one by one attacked Hoover's major detractors and pronounced him flawless and incorruptible, with the best of possible impartial authority: Hoover. He opened his files to them (giving them what *he* wanted), with their own fine sense of propaganda telling them what to use. Hoover, too, emerges as a little less than Christ–but only a very little. He is the defender of all liberties, the unfailing, the very pillar of society, the bastion of freedom, unerring upholder of the law—flawless and faultless.

[6]   Hoover also does what he pleases, especially when there is potential for personal benefit. In the previously quoted Pearson–Anderson article in *True* for January 1969, there are these paragraphs:

> Hoover also ingratiated himself with both Richard Nixon and Hubert Humphrey before the election. A friend of both candidates, Hoover assigned men to augment the security forces at the conventions. His men also trailed

bothersome newsmen to report on their activities. More than once, at the request of powerful politicians, the FBI has undertaken background investigations of Washington reporters whose stories rubbed sensitive skins the wrong way.

Sen. Tom Dodd, the Connecticut Democrat, who served a year as a G-man and has used the experience to his advantage both on the campaign trail and in his lucrative lectures against communism, once prevailed upon the FBI to shadow an office employee and report back on his romantic activities.

The authors have exposed their share of Washington scandals, a few of which have ended in federal convictions. More often than not, the FBI has shown more interest in who talked to us than in what was revealed. When we began exposing the chicanery in Dodd's office, FBI agents photostated all the documents in our possession, then turned the investigation around and began snooping into our news sources . . . .

Chapter 14 Look and You Will See

[1]   Recalling this triggered recollection of my investigations, perhaps of some note here, of exactly a year earlier, when I had been tracing out the swept-over leads on the anti-Castro camps near New Orleans, on the north shore of Lake Pontchartrain. There I found proof of the existence of not the one camp glossed over by the FBI and the Warren Commission but of four, three confirmed by St. Tammany Parish officials. In that investigation I learned the state police had become involved. This was after the FBI was forced to raid an ammo dump right where people live. The existence of the camps was no secret. The careless Cubans had started a fire the locals had expected to blow them all sky-high. It was not the local state police who conducted the investigation. A sergeant whose name I have was sent down from Baton Rouge. This was confirmed to me by the cooperative personnel of the St. Tammany Parish Sheriff's office, who had conducted their own quiet investigation, and by a lieutenant of the local unit of the state troopers.

[2]   Once again, the Oswald parallel. The government could account for his beginning his trip to Russia, from California, with only about $400, hardly enough. So they merely declared he had $1,500, which was contrary to their proofs. Not to do this indicated he also had a source of funds not explained—and easiest explained as from someone who had a purpose he served.

[3]   In neither the article nor any quotation from personal appearances that I have found does Hanes say what he told Fensterwald (who reported it to me), that there is a real "Raoul" and that his name is Manek. Manek is, Hanes said, a French-Canadian.

[4]   Who can believe "Cuban exiles" were interested in buying $160 hunting rifles with $100 sights? Did they not have the unused CIA generosity stashed away all around Miami and some of the islands, as well as other places (not to mention the usual access to serviceable rifles much lower in cost and no less useful), assuming, as there is no reason to, that they had the slightest prospect of using any against Castro or were still stockpiling them? One such cache was turned up at Pass Christian, Mississippi, not far from New Orleans, on the Gulf coast, after Hurricane Camille hit. While survivors of the killer storm were sought the night of August 1, 1969, three trunks full of foreign-made pistols, carbines, helmets, bullet-proof vests, and rifles were unearthed. This weaponry was in perfect condition, having been properly stored in grease and wrapped in plastic.

463

Among the wrappings were newspapers of the Bay of Pigs period.

[5]   Ray has filed civil suits against Hanes, Huie, and Foreman in regard to the *Look* articles and to void the contracts. Depositions, which are interrogations under oath but not in court, were taken in November 1969. Hanes was asked about this sentence: "But as of this moment, I simply cannot agree that James Earl Ray was not helped in murdering Dr. King. There are too many unanswered questions in my mind." He was also asked about this one: "I still believe that Ray killed Dr. King because he was directed to do it." Each thought says two things, that Ray was the murderer and that there was a conspiracy.

Hanes claimed in his deposition that he did not write this last sentence, that his original writing was edited by Huie, and insisted he never said that Ray was the murderer.

Hanes and Foreman both swore they had written for and been paid $1,000 each by Huie, the former getting a total of $31,000 from Huie, the latter $11,000.

Huie, who spoke of six-figure advances more casually than most men do of daily sports events, concurred with their testimony about what they got from him. Despite his *Look* writing, he swore that "I went along on this business of a Ray conspiracy reluctantly," because *Look* and Delacorte Press wanted it, and said that in doing so "I made a horrible mistake" (for which *Look* alone paid him $62,871.85). Huie claims to have believed from the first that Ray was the lone killer.

Huie evaded direct answer when asked, "Did you edit the articles in *Look* magazine that were written by Mr. Arthur Hanes and Mr. Percy Foreman?" His response was, "I read them, yes. I wouldn't say I edited them. I am not an editor of *Look* magazine." Asked about the following sentence from the article bearing Hanes's name, "Why did James Earl Ray murder Dr. Martin Luther King, Jr.?" Huie insisted that "*Look* magazine wrote nothing for Mr. Hanes, Mr. Hanes wrote that himself, as far as I know." He also claimed Hanes had often and widely expressed this view. In this response Huie was evasive again, for the question was and is not of writing but of editing, which involves making small changes in what was written.

Chapter 15   Between Frying Pans and Fires

[1]   If there is any sense in all of this gibberish attributed to James Earl Ray, it may be as a Stoner-type answer to the Milteer tape, the beginning of a concoction to neutralize that authenticated extremist plot as the connivings of "federal agents." The history of readily available perjury in trials of racist murderers in the South establishes the ease with which such "evidence" can be arranged. If one is familiar with the speeches and "literature" of these racists, such a plot within plots sounds like regular fare. It is the kind of fabrication they regard as brilliant, though to reasonable people it is insane.

Chapter 16   "More Than a Whiff of Conspiracy"

[1]   But by the time of Leifermann's November 17 story, he could accurately report of the police that "at the time of the assassination, it was thought the phony chase was a plot by accomplices to lure police into another part of town." In the *New York Times* of June 19, Homer Bigart wrote that "several police cars that had been stopping white Mustangs in the city raced toward the scene of the chase, which by now was reported to be at 100 miles per hour"—to which chase (among the various points to be made about it) there was no official reference.

464

This is as good a place as any to add a recent item on Leifermann. His reporting of the assassination was diligent, professional, and not congenial to the official position. It is interesting that in 1970, although he was then 28 years old, he was ordered to active duty by the Army, which was not happy about some of his other reporting, especially about Green Beret murders and military justice. Leifermann had been in the reserve since 1964 and was scheduled for discharge in November of 1970. The reason given for calling him up is his alleged missing of reserve meetings. Leifermann went to court, charged his writing was the reason for assignment to active duty, and blamed officials for disposing of the statements of doctors accounting for his absences. U.S. District Court Judge Howard F. Corcoran, in Washington, heard Leifermann's appeal on September 21 and 22, 1970.

[2]   A funny thing happened to the real Galt on the long way to the minitrial. After his name appeared in the papers as one that had been used by Ray, a truck driver pulled into the Union Carbide plant where Galt works. As Galt told Richard Bernabei, the truck driver approached Galt with what appeared to be a newspaper picture of better than usual quality. It was one of a series of pictures taken in Dallas after the assassination of John Kennedy. This one was not known to have been published and showed tramps in custody. Pointing to one of them, who was a dead-ringer for the man in the FBI sketch of the person wanted for killing King, the truck driver told Galt, "There's your pal," meaning Ray. The picture was unknown to the real Galt. The trucker's explanation is hard to credit. He said he found the picture on the seat of his truck after a stop somewhere in the United States. This means he was a rather extraordinary "truckdriver" with rather exceptional knowledge, to know of the possible significance of a picture he claims was merely left on the seat of his truck by persons and means and for reasons unknown to him.

To show the reader how bizarre this episode was, I reprint here the relevant photographs.

Sketch of man wanted for King slaying, from *New York Times* of 4/11/68 (*not* repudiated by FBI) compared with picture of man in police custody at scene of JFK assassination in Dallas, 11/22/63, shortly after that assassination. (See p. 254.)

465

[3] In the case of the Warren Commission, there was no defense counsel. There was a milk-toasty counterfeit, the sorriest pretense that the top officials of the American Bar Association would look out for the interests of the accused, then murdered, Oswald. They did this by doing nothing or, worse, acting as auxiliary to the Commission, which was the prosecution, not the equivalent of a court of justice. In the literary enormity of the Commission's Report and so-called evidence (an estimated 10,000,000 words) or in the sanctuary of hidden evidence (estimated at 300 cubic feet in volume)—which together is a fantastic total of words, unestimated and beyond estimate—there is no single instance I have seen in a diligent plumbing of this verbal immensity where a single Bar Association official on any single occasion did any one thing in the interest of the murdered accused, his reputation or his heirs. What this says is that they betrayed their nigh-to-sacred trust. They did this unfailingly, without deviation even one time.

[4] This does not follow the Blair transcript word-for-word, but the sense is identical. Perhaps the official reporter improved the judge's memorable words that proved to be his epitaph.

[5] After a year of the most delicate negotiations, all indirect, for we had never met, never exchanged letters, James Earl Ray got the idea it might be good for him to have my lawyer as his lawyer. When I had asked Fensterwald if he would take the case if I could arrange for Ray to request it, he had said, "Sure. And if you can get me to the moon, I'll go there, too." What a sickening feeling the jailed man must have had when he learned, after being milked and bled by big-name mercenaries, that there *are* lawyers who *do* take cases on principle, without selfish motivation, regardless of whether or not big retainers and abundant fees are to be had. In accomplishing Ray's ruin, Hanes and Foreman had also taken all his resources. Fensterwald took the case without fee or the prospect of the return of his costs, which he has to pay from his personal resources.

Chapter 17   Getting the Truth

[1] Lyerly carefully avoids referring to "certain oral evidence" that Chief Magistrate Milton's chief clerk said was sent to the State Department along with the affidavits. The chief clerk's letter follows in the text.

[2] This is another of the seemingly infinite, remarkable similarities to and parallels with the assassination of the President and its investigation. On July 4 of that year, I interviewed a man similarly confined in a locked mental institution in Louisiana. After he had claimed to have information about that assassination, he, too, was locked up in this new way of permanent jailing that closes mouths. His family did not authorize this; in fact, was not even consulted about it. When the contents of his pockets were returned to his family, included was a local CIA telephone number. My own investigation proved repeated evidences of Secret Service inquiry about him. That agency has since confirmed to me its interest in him, for "the security of the President." Like Canale's office, it disclaims responsibility for what amounts to lifetime incarceration without any legal process of any kind. As with Grace Stephens, the man's sequestration exactly coincided with an anticipated legal proceeding. This man was lucid when I found and interviewed him. He had sustained brain damage as a boy while playing football and had, regularly, when he felt attacks coming on, turned himself in at the closest hospital. The records of voluntary confinement that I have range from New Orleans to New York. He told me that on his last confinement, the third day

466

prior to his transfer from the institution in which he had placed himself voluntarily, his treatment was changed and his next awareness was of the still-confining bars. In his case, he is not permitted even a walk in the sun. He, too, has become frail from confinement. Authorities refused my request, made because of his pitiful plea, that I be permitted to take him for a walk. They would not handcuff him to me so he could get some air and sunshine, denied him for years, nor would they provide a guard to accompany us. He could not have escaped. He was so weak, walking was a major effort for him. If all of this sounds like the plot of a sensational novel, it is the reality in the United States in the era of political assassinations.

[3]   The seriousness with which the law-and-order Attorney General regards perjury in his behalf by a subordinate is disclosed in a September 14 letter to Fensterwald, signed by Ruckelshaus. The first two of its four sentences say it is in response to my letters of August 20 and 21 to Mitchell and Kleindienst, which it in no sense is. The third only repeats the incompetent and meaningless assurance of those without knowledge that "the entire contents of the file in question were disclosed to Mr. Weisberg." The fourth says that, to satisfy "any further complaints or demands, I can only suggest that you address yourself to the court."

Pretty clearly, whether or not Ruckelshaus or Mitchell is actually aware of it, this amounts to an invitation that I call to the attention of the judge my belief that Anderson did commit perjury, a serious crime. There is not even the most perfunctory denial of it, not even an argument about my interpretation. I think most reasonable men would assume this to be a confession of the fact and a challenge that I try to do something, based on the belief or knowledge that this is the kind of matter in which a federal judge will not take the initiative and the federal law-enforcement authority will not prosecute, itself being the criminal.

However, I did accommodate Ruckelshaus, writing the judge September 21. That date is so late in the history of this book that, even if he does act, which I do not expect, judges not being prosecutors, any result cannot be included.

Appendix

The Milteer Documents

In the final chapter of my book *Oswald in New Orleans* ("Preliminary Postscript from Miami"), I reported what was then (winter of 1966–1967) known of an intercepted threat against President Kennedy two weeks before his assassination. That threat was taped by the Miami police, who gave copies to both the FBI and the Secret Service on November 10, 1963. Stringent measures were taken to protect the President in Miami, including elimination of a planned motorcade. The files of the Warren Commission contain neither the tape nor a transcript, nor, in fact, any reference to either—which surely makes sense, considering that they were investigating his assassination and this material amounted to a blueprint of what is officially alleged to have happened. The National Archives also assured me that its files contained no reference to Joseph Adams Milteer, the Georgia functionary of the National States Rights Party who discussed the threat and the man who was planning that assassination and was doing more—attempting to kill King. The manner of King's murder—not by that man, who died before he could pull it—is exactly as set forth in the tape, which is printed here for the first time (in toto, with no changes made in the transcription, and with the addition of some necessary background material). With some effort, I did obtain at least some of the "non-existent" FBI Milteer reports. This also is the first publication of those that I could obtain.

Not only because these dedicated wrong of the extreme of the right extreme plotted the murder of the murdered King are the suppressed tape and reports relevant. The facts that NSRP chieftain Stoner alone got to see Ray, in September 1968, when others could not; that he became Ray's counsel when Judge Battle failed to appoint a lawyer, as Ray requested (and wasted many of Ray's legal possibilities); and that King hung in effigy in the NSRP headquarters, give added point to this account of NSRP ambition.

Informant: Now we are going to, you are going to have to take, Kenney, what do you call his last name?

Subject: Kenneth Adams. [Adams has had his own share of headlines and heroics. In 1956, he leaped onto a Birmingham stage to attack the late Nat "King" Cole, popular Negro musician. Five years later, he was implicated in the burning of a "Freedom Riders" bus. He was found not guilty by a directed verdict. Other charges laid to him include the shotgunning of Negro homes and churches. After deliberating 11 hours, an all-white jury, on November 21, 1966, acquitted him of a charge of receiving Army explosives. The stolen items included blocks and sticks of explosives, phosphorus bombs, hand grenades, and three boxes of .50-caliber ammunition, which is not for handguns. Because of Adams's acquittal, the judge said he would not jail the man who had already confessed the theft.]

Informant: Yeah, you are going to take him in, he is supposed to be one of the hard core of the underground, are you going to invite him into that, too? What about Brown, now, are you going to invite

Brown in? You are going to have Brown in it? [Believed to be Jack H. Brown who, like Adams, had been extremely active in the Klans. He operated a gas station in a Chattanooga suburb. He has been reported to be "contact man" for the United White Party; to have arranged for the Klan to be entered in the Chattanooga softball series; to have been an NSRP presidential elector; to believe the Klan needed a flag and to have offered to design it; to have died of a heart attack in 1965, leaving chips off the old block to continue his good works.]

Subject: Yeah.

Informant: Now, I will tell you between me and you, because we are talking, we aren't going to talk to everybody like we are talking here. Now, you know this, I like Brown, he is a good fellow, you know him, now here is something, when we was in his house, now, he knows me and you, but he didn't know Lee McCloud, well I think he done too much talking in front of a man he didn't know. Brown trusts a lot of people, he figures everybody is good.

Subject: Yeah.

Informant: And you know when he was telling her [or him, not legible] about blowing up all those churches and, you know, I don't think he should have said all that in front of McCloud.

Subject: That is exactly the way I feel about it, too. And I didn't talk about it any more after we left there.

Informant: No, I see you didn't, you see, these things come to my mind, I don't know McCloud well, and Brown never seen him before in his life, that I know of, now you seen this boy, Jackie, didn't open his mouth, he just sit there and listened. Jack Caulk [phonetic] he is a very quiet boy, Brown it just seems, well, he, I guess he has gotten by with so much he just don't care. He come out with all that about going over to Atlanta carrying that stuff, and showing them how to operate, I didn't want to say anything to him, but I don't think it is a good idea for people to discuss things like that in front of strangers. What do you think about it?

Subject: No, I—He should operate that, the same as he does the rest of it.

Informant: That's right, damn right that is right. Now you take like the Birmingham . . . [Subject breaks in]

Subject: Any conclusion they come up with, that's them, not him.

Informant: That is true.

Subject: He didn't give them anything.

Informant: Well, he didn't give them nothing.

Subject: Just like me at home there folks want to know, "Joe, where do you get all of your information?" "Well, I get it, that is all you are interested in," and that is as far as it goes, see. And the same guy will turn around and give me some information, but he doesn't

469

know where I am getting my information. The same guy who asks me where I get my information, will turn around and give me information.

Informant: Well, sure, of course, I realize that.

Subject: That is the way you have got to operate.

Informant: Well, that is what I say, if you are going to take Brown in, and Brown is going to be one of the head men, the man behind you, then you have got to talk to Brown a little bit, and tell him, you know, "You have got to be a little more conscientious, especially on these bombings, and killings," after all he comes right out with it.

Subject: We have got to let him understand, that, that is his operation, and not ours.

Informant: Yeah, that is true. We don't care, if he wants to go to Birmingham and blow up a church, let him.

Subject: If he wants to blow up the National Capital, that is alright with me. I will go with him, but not as a party though, as an individual.

Informant: Well, if you want to go with him and help him blow it up, that is not the party, it is an individual, you are going to have to make him understand that.

Subject: There is a party movement, and there is also an individual movement.

Informant: Yeah, that is right.

Subject: And they are distinct and separate.

Informant: Well, you are going to have to make him understand that, right there, he didn't exactly admit it, but Jesus Christ, he intimated, he indicated right there, he backed the bombings of killing the negroes in Birmingham, well, you know damn well we don't want anybody talking like that.

Subject: Can't afford it.

Informant: Well, you know damn well that is bad talk especially to somebody he don't know. He could have said that to me, and you would have been alright, it would have been between you and me then.

Subject: That is true.

Informant: But to go ahead and say it in front of Lee McCloud, what that hell [Subject breaks in]

Subject: Well, I think he thought that he would [not] have been with us, if he had not have been alright. But that is still not enough.

Informant: No, hell no, that is no good, at least before he made all those statements, he should have called you outside, or consulted about this man a little bit.

Subject: You have to have reservations, you know.

Informant: That is right. Hell, he didn't say these things in any way to try to get us in trouble, because the only one who could be in trouble would be him, he was confessing on his damn self, he wasn't

470

confessing on us, because we hadn't done a damn thing.

Subject: You and I would not get up there on the stand and say that he told us a cotton picking thing either.

Informant: Well, he knows that, but how about the other man.

Subject: Well, that is what I say.

Informant: Yeah, hell yes. I tell you something, you take Kenneth Adams over there, he is a mean damn man, like Brown was saying, the guy he was sending him to, well Kenneth is real mean, and the way Brown indicated they [not legible] the negroes, well, we don't care anything about that. I would rather he wouldn't tell us those stories.

Subject: You sure can't repeat them.

Informant: Yeah. That is the set-up we are in now, I mean, we have to work with them, but let them operate their grollings [phonetic], like you say, if you want to go with them, that is your opinion, you go with him up to Washington and blow with him, if you want to go [Subject breaks in].

Subject: I have a man who is the head of his underground of his own up there in Delaware, and since I worked on the Supreme Court, he wanted me to give him the lay-out there so they could go over there and do some things there, you know. But he called it off, I don't know why, I didn't even ask him why. That was his affair, but he called it off. But I was ready to go with him. I gave him the damn information he wanted.

Informant: You worked on the Supreme Court.

Subject: Yeah, three and a half years.

Informant: Well, that is why he wanted you to go, then, well, them things have got to be done, but outside the Party, we have got to be mighty careful who the hell we let know anything. Now, here is one thing you have got to realize, transporting dynamite across the state line is a federal offense, well you better let them know that.

Subject: Well, there is a way to beat that, you know. All you have to do is pull up to the state line, unload it there, slide it across the line, get in the car and load it again, and they can't accuse you of transporting it then, because you didn't do it. I have done the same thing with a woman. I had one, then I had a woman frame me on it. I got to the state line, and I said, "Listen, Toots, this is the state line, get out, and I will meet you over there," she got out, walked across the line, got in my car in the other state, I didn't transport her, there wasn't a fucking thing she could do about it, I had her ass for a long time.

Informant: I was talking to a boy yesterday, and he was in Athens, Georgia, and he told me, that they had two colored people working in that drug store, and that them, uh, they went into the basement, and tapped them small pipes, I guess that they are copper together, and let that thing accumulate, and blowed that drug store up. He told me that yesterday, do you think that is right?

Subject: It could have happened that way.

Informant: Well, that is what he told me, and he is in town right now.

Subject: Does he know who did it? Do they think these negroes did it?

Informant: Oh, no, they killed the negroes, because they had two negroes working in the place, that is what he told me. He is in town now, he is from Chattanooga. He knows Brown, he knows all of them, his uncle is in the Klan there. He is a young boy, he has been in the Marines, and he really knows his business. He went there, he went down and looked, and he told me that is what happened. So he has been involved in quite a little bit of stuff, according to his story about Nashville, Chattanooga, and Georgia. I have no reason not to believe him, because he told me too much about Brown's operation, that is the reason I [not legible].

Subject: Yeah. You take this boy, Connor McGintis [phonetic] [reference is probably to an old-time northern racist, Conde McGinley], boy up there in Union, N.J., of course he doesn't go to anything like that, but he is on our side, he is the one that puts out that *Common Sense*. He is an ex-Marine. He is all man, too.

Informant: Now, you see, we will talk to these other people, you have made up your mind that you are going to use the Constitutional Party as a front.

Subject: Yeah, Constitutional Party States Rights.

Informant: Yeah, and it will strictly secret, and nobody will be exposed except you.

Subject: Yeah.

Informant: Because when we talk to them today, you want to know exactly what to tell them, how it operates.

Subject: Yeah, and we have got to set up a little fund there to get it operating.

Informant: Oh, yeah, sure.

Subject: And I am going to devote my time to it, I don't have any idea of getting elected to that City Commission, but I am just making it cost them bastards, it cost them as it is, it cost them between $1,500 and $2,000 to beat me before, so I want to make it cost them another couple of thousand dollars. If they want to get rid of me, they can buy my fucking property, and I will get out of the damn town. In other words, they will save money. I am going to put that out in one of the damn bulletins there, see. We put, the way I operate, put out these little bulletins, like a typewriter page, eight and a half by eleven, and brother don't you think they ain't waiting for them, when I don't put them out, "Joe, where is the bulletin?" Bill, that could go all over the country the same way. That was just a trial proposition, if it will work in a little stinking town like that, it will work anywhere.

Informant: I don't know, I think Kennedy is coming here on the 18th, or something like that to make some kind of speech, I don't know what it is, but I imagine it will be on the TV, and you can be on the look for that, I think it is the 18th that he is suppose to be here. I don't know what it is suppose to be about.

Subject: You can bet your bottom dollar he is going to have a lot to say about the Cubans, there are so many of them here.

Informant: Yeah, well he will have a thousand bodyguards, don't worry about that.

Subject: The more bodyguards he has, the easier it is to get him.

Informant: What?

Subject: The more bodyguards he has the more easier it is to get him.

Informant: Well how in the hell do you figure would be the best way to get him?

Subject: From an office building with a high powered rifle, how many people [room noise—tape not legible] does he have going around who look just like him? Do you know about that?

Informant: No, I never heard that he had anybody.

Subject: He has got them.

Informant: He has?

Subject: He has about fifteen. Whenever he goes any place they [not legible] he knows he is a marked man.

Informant: You think he knows he is a marked man?

Subject: Sure he does.

Informant: They are really going to try to kill him?

Subject: Oh, yeah, it is in the working. Brown himself, Brown is just as likely to get him as anybody. He hasn't said so, but he tried to get Martin Luther King.

Informant: He did.

Subject: Oh yes, he followed him for miles and miles, and couldn't get close enough to him.

Informant: You know exactly where it is in Atlanta don't you?

Subject: Martin Luther King, yeah.

Informant: Bustus Street [phonetic].

Subject: Yeah 530.

Informant: Oh Brown tried to get him huh?

Subject: Yeah.

Informant: Well, he will damn sure do it, I will tell you that. Well, that is why, look, you see, well, that is why we have to be so careful, you know that Brown is operating strong.

Subject: He ain't going for play you know.

Informant: That is right.

Subject: He is going for broke.

Informant: I never asked Brown about his business or anything, you know just what he told me, told us, you know. But after the conversation, and the way he talked to us, there is no question in my mind about who knocked the church off in Birmingham, you can believe that, that is the way I figured it.

Subject: That is right, it is about the only way you can figure it.

Informant: That is right.

Subject: Not being there, not knowing anything.

Informant: But just from his conversation, as you and me know him, but if they did, it is their business, like you say [Subject breaks in].

Subject: It is up to the individual.

Informant: That is right. They are individual operators, we don't want that within the party. Hitting this Kennedy is going to be a, a hard proposition, I tell you, I believe, you may have figured out a way to get him, you may have figured out the office building, and all that. I don't know how them Secret Service agents cover all them office buildings, or anywhere he is going, do you know whether they do that or not?

Subject: Well, if they have any suspicion they do that of course. But without suspicion chances are that they wouldn't. You take there in Washington, of course it is the wrong time of the year, but you take pleasant weather, he comes out on the veranda, and somebody could be in a hotel room across the way there, and pick him off just like [fades out].

Informant: Is that right?

Subject: Sure, disassemble a gun, you don't have to take a gun up there, you can take it up in pieces, all those guns come knock down, you can take them apart.

Informant: They have got a damn, this boy was telling me yesterday about, they have got an explosive that you get out of the army, it is suppose to be like putty or something, you stick it up, and use a small fuse, you just stick it like that, he told me, and I think that is what happened in the church in Birmingham, they stuck this stuff, somebody stuck it under the steps with a short fuse, and went on home.

Informant: This boy is pretty smart, demolition is that what you call it?

Subject: Demolition, that is right.

Informant: I am going to talk with him some more.

Subject: Yeah I would.

Informant: I am going to talk with him some more, and find out a lot more about his operation, because he knows a hell of a lot.

Subject: You need a guy like that around, too. Where we can put our finger on him, when we want him.

Informant: Yeah. Well, you have got somebody up there in that country now, if you need him.

Subject: Well, we are going to have to get nasty first [not legible].

Informant: Yeah, get nasty.

Subject: We have got to be ready, we have got to be sitting on go, too.

Informant: Yeah, that is right.

Subject: There ain't any count down to it, we have just got to be sitting on go. Count down they can move in on you, and on go they can't. Count down is alright for a slow prepared operation, but in an emergency operation, you have got to be sitting on go.

Informant: Boy, if that Kennedy gets shot, we have got to know where we are at. Because you know that will be a real shake, if they do that.

Subject: They wouldn't leave any stone unturned there no way. They will pick up somebody within hours afterwards, if anything like that would happen just to throw the public off.

Informant: Oh, somebody is going to have to go to jail, if he gets killed.

Subject: Just like that Bruno Hauptman in the Lindberg case you know. [Dials telephone.]

Informant: "Hello, is Jim there?" "Has he gone to the office?" "Uh, huh, well, is he coming back home?" "Alright, I will do that, thank you." He has gone out to one of his apartment houses, and he will be back later. We will go see *whatamacallit,* he closes at 1:00 o'clock. We will go up and see Andrew, and we will double back to Jim's [room noise].

Subject: Actually the only man we are interested in up at that place [room noise—not legible—door closes].

MM 89-35
FPG:ggr/ds
1

Re: Threat to Kill President
KENNEDY by J. A. MILTEER,
Miami, Florida
November 9, 1963

On November 10, 1963, a source who has furnished
reliable information in the past and in addition has furnished some information that could not be verified or
corroborated, advised SA LEONARD C. PETERSON that J. A.
MILTEER on November 9, 1963, at Miami, Florida, made a
statement that plans were in the making to kill President
JOHN F. KENNEDY at some future date; that MILTEER suggested
one JACK BROWN of Chattanooga, Tennessee, as the man who
could do the job and that he (MILTEER) would be willing to
help. MILTEER reportedly said that he was familiar with
Washington and that the job could be done from an office
or hotel in the vicinity of the White House using a
high-powered rifle.

U. S. Secret Service was advised of the foregoing
information.

The FBI's titling of this report, page 119 of Warren Commission File (CD) 1347,
is unequivocal. It is a *serious* "Threat to Kill President KENNEDY," by one
Joseph Adams Milteer, of the NSRP. These reports exactly coincide with the
Miami tape, here also reproduced, and with the cancellation of the scheduled
motorcade when the President addressed the Inter-American Press Association, in
Miami. The "source who has furnished reliable information in the past" may be
the informant or the Miami police, which gave dubs of the tape to both the FBI
and the Secret Service. (The man had also been an FBI informant.)

Re: THREAT TO KILL PRESIDENT KENNEDY
BY J. A. MILTEER, MIAMI, FLORIDA,
NOVEMBER 9, 1963

On November 26, 1963, a source who has furnished
reliable information in the past and in addition has
furnished some information that could not be verified or
corroborated, advised SA PETERSON as follows:

On November 23, 1963, J. A. MILTEER was in the
Union Train Station, Jacksonville, Florida, and at about
4:25 p.m. on that date stated he was very jubilant over
the death of President KENNEDY. MILTEER stated, "Everything
ran true to form. I guess you thought I was kidding you
when I said he would be killed from a window with a high-
powered rifle." When questioned as to whether he was
guessing when he originally made the threat regarding
President KENNEDY, MILTEER is quoted as saying, "I don't
do any guessing."

On the evening of November 23, 1963, MILTEER
departed Jacksonville, Florida, by automobile en route to
Columbia, South Carolina. During this trip, MILTEER
stated that he had been in Houston, Ft. Worth, and Dallas,
Texas, as well as New Orleans, Louisiana, Biloxi and
Jackson, Mississippi, and Tuscaloosa, Alabama. MILTEER
said he was acquainted with one R. E. DAVIS of Dallas,
Texas, whom he described as a "good man," but did not indicate
he was personally acquainted with DAVIS. MILTEER did not
indicate on what dates he was in the above cities, except
for Tuscaloosa, Alabama.

MILTEER related that he was in Tuscaloosa,
Alabama, and contacted ROBERT SHELTON of the United
Klans of America, Inc., Knights of the Ku Klux Klan
(United Klans), on the evening prior to the bombing of the

Having blueprinted the JFK assassination in advance, NSRPer Milteer here took
credit for it. What better reason for total suppression—*after* Oswald was officially
ordained assassin? R. E. Davis also figures in an also-suppressed Secret Service
investigation (the copies of which I have) of a suspected Minuteman involvement.
Neither investigative agency made this correlation for the Commission.

The Federal Bureau of Investigation has requested that certain pages of this document not be disclosed. This request was incorporated in a letter of August 13, 1965, to Dr. Wayne C. Grover, Archivist of the United States from Norbert A. Schlei, Assistant Attorney General, Office of Legal Counsel, Department of Justice.

Commission Document Number: *1347*

Pages Withheld: *121*

From the file index (the FBI slipped up, not editing their indexes to hide what they were suppressing), it is apparent that what is suppressed here deals (like the Miami tape, pp. 468-475) with the November, 15, 1963 bombing of a Birmingham, Alabama, church in which innocent black children were murdered. (Names mentioned on the suppressed page are: "Association of South Carolina Klans; Baptist Church, Birmingham, Alabama; Bolen, A.O.; Hendricks, Jack; Kennedy, Robert; King, Martin Luther; Knights of Ku Klux Klan [United Klans] ; Mims, Belton; Ulmer, Will; United Klans of America, Inc.; Wade Hampton Hotel, Columbia, S.C.") This National Archives form proves the FBI is directly responsible for the suppressions—not, as Hoover pretends, the Department of Justice. (In almost every case that I have been able to check—by getting what was suppressed by the FBI— what is withheld deals with the extreme of the radical right or is designed to prevent embarrassment to the government. *Defamatory* material *should* be withheld, but I have found *no single case* where defamations of those even slightly liberal or anti-war were withheld.)

MM 89-35
3.

A characterization of the Association of South
Carolina Klans follows. Sources therein have furnished
reliable information in the past.

After their arrival, MILTEER stated that there
was no point in discussing President KENNEDY, and again
stated, "We must now concentrate on the Jews." MILTEER
advised that he was preparing a pamphlet which he wanted
to disseminate throughout the country. Prior to concluding
their discussion, information was received that JACK RUBY
had killed LEE HARVEY OSWALD. In view of this, MILTEER said
he would have to alter the information he was setting out in
his pamphlet.

The source advised that based on his contact with
MILTEER, he could not definitely state whether MILTEER was
acquainted with either RUBY or OSWALD.

122

The handwritten note was made by the Archives staff. It may help the reader's
understanding to know that, passionately as the NSRPers hate blacks, they hate
Jews even more.

MM 89-35 Other FPG:ggr investigations
FPG:ggr Involved or Interviewed
1

Re: Threat ~~to Kill~~ President KENNEDY
~~by~~ J. A. MILTEER, Miami, Florida,
November 9, 1963

J. A. MILTEER is also known as JOSEPH ADAMS MILTEER. He was born February 26, 1902, at Quitman, Georgia, and lives at Quitman and Valdosta, Georgia. He reportedly is a wealthy bachelor who inherited an estimated $200,000 from his father. He is reported to have no family, no employment and to spend a great deal of time traveling throughout the Southeastern United States. He has been unsuccessful in city politics in Quitman and publishes a weekly pamphlet critizing the operation of the Quitman City Government. MILTEER has associated himself with the Constitution Party of the United States and attended a convention of this party held at Indianapolis, Indiana, during October, 1963. He was reprimanded by this party for describing himself as being the party regional chairman for the Southeastern states. MILTEER reportedly became disillusioned with the Constitution Party of the United States and has attempted to form a party known as the Constitutional American Parties of the United States. MILTEER allegedly intends to use the Constitutional American Parties of the United States as a front to form a hard core underground for possible violence in combatting integration.

123

CR 1347

CD 1347

1

DL 89-43
PEW/ds

The interview of JOSEPH ADAMS MILTEER, as well as additional information regarding him, is contained on pages 24-26 of the report of Special Agent CHARLES S. HARDING, Atlanta, Georgia, dated December 1, 1963, in the case entitled "LEE HARVEY OSWALD; INTERNAL SECURITY - RUSSIA".

124

P.125 and 126 are withheld from research.

What a filing system, what FBI logic: reports on a murderous native fascist (p. 124)

FEDERAL BUREAU OF INVESTIGATION

Date ___December 1, 1963___

1

       JOSEPH ADAMS MILTEER, Quitman, Georgia, was interviewed November 27, 1963, at which time he advised that during April, 1963, he attended a national meeting of the Congress of Freedom, New Orleans, Louisiana. He described this organization as one that believed in Americanism and he attended this meeting as the result of an invitation by a Mr. THOMAS, Chairman of the organization, Omaha, Nebraska. He stated during this meeting neither he nor anyone in his presence discussed the assassination of President KENNEDY.

       MILTEER stated further that in June, 1963, he went to Dallas, Texas, to attempt to persuade DAN SMOOT, author of the "Dan Smoot Report" to run as Vice-President on the Constitution Party ticket in the election in November, 1964. He stated he had no other business in Dallas.

       MILTEER further stated that on October 18-20, 1963, he traveled to Indianapolis, Indiana, with BILL SOMERSETT of Miami, Florida, and LEE McCLOUD of Atlanta, Georgia. They attended the National Convention of the Constitution Party. He stated he attended this meeting as the result of an invitation by CURTIS B. DALL, former son-in-law of the late President FRANKLIN D. ROOSEVELT.

       MILTEER described himself as a non-dues-paying member of the White Citizens Council of Atlanta, Georgia, the Congress of Freedom and the Constitution Party.

       MILTEER emphatically denies ever making threats to assassinate President KENNEDY or participating in any such assassination. He stated he has never heard anyone make such threats. He also denied making threats against anyone subsequent to the assassination of President KENNEDY. He stated he does not know, nor has he ever been in the presence of LEE HARVEY OSWALD or JACK RUBY to his knowledge.

       MILTEER denied any knowledge of the bombing of the Sixteenth Street Baptist Church in Birmingham, Alabama, on November 15, 1963.

- 24 -

On ___11/27/63___ at ___Quitman, Georgia___ File # ___Atlanta 105-3193___

       SAs KENNETH A. WILLIAMS and
by ___DONALD A. ADAMS   :cb___ Date dictated ___12/1/63___

With Milteer's voice on tape blueprinting the assassination for which he later took credit, the FBI here reports his denial dead-pan, and keeps secret the fact that it had a dub of precisely these threats in Milteer's own voice! The last sentence of this page pretty clearly relates to the suppressed page of the FBI report printed on p. 468ff.

The Kyles Tape

Matt Herron, a truly great photographer, was covering the King assassination for a national magazine, saw no real investigation was being made, and, although not an investigator, made an excellent one. Within less than a week, when there was no official interest and seemed to be some hazard, he located me at 2 A.M. one morning, when I was conducting my own investigations in the J.F.K. assassination case in New Orleans. Matt piped his tapes of interviews into the telephone of his Memphis motel room and I recorded them in a phone booth of the very noisy waterfront French Quarter Bar, thus making a back-up record should anything happen to him or his tapes. With one exception, disclosing the contents of these tapes could endanger all the witnesses, who overheard advance and accurate predictions of King's murder. In one case, two people overheard a public official say a man who was going to kill King when King returned to Memphis had been in that official's home the night before. In another case, a braggart, citing a police-department source, said that King would be shot when he returned to Memphis. Matt told me he had reported his information to the FBI. He also quoted the FBI agent to whom he spoke as being perplexed by the Attorney General's statement there was no conspiracy. The one interview I feel can be used without jeopardy to the person interviewed is that of King's friend and associate, the Rev. Samuel B. Kyles, who was misused in the minitrial. Kyles's contemporaneous account is a warm and moving one as it relates to King as an individual. It also contains evidence that is essential to an understanding of the crime, disclosing what government suppressed, as the text shows.

The tape was transcribed by my wife. She and I are without personal knowledge of some of those named. We may have misspelled some names. Short parts of the tape are indistinguishable. The phone rings constantly, throughout the taping, with the voice of the man answering sometimes over and obliterating Kyles's. These omissions are indicated by dots.

Q. I have Reverend Kyles describing what happened.

K. —and I turned and came back. So when I turned, all I saw was this much of the body because he was behind the wall here. I couldn't see. And I came to about where Andy was and looked at the wound. I don't remember if Ralph was there then or not. But I looked at the wound and it was just—you know, all this was gone, this here.

Q. . . .

K. And then I went in and picked up the phone.

Q. . . .

K. The way I am now.

Q. Yes. That must be after you called, though.

K. Yes. But I couldn't get the darned phone. So I came out and hollered. I came out the hall. The police were coming from everywhere, you know, in a matter of seconds. I said, "Call an ambulance. I can't get the phone." And then an ambulance came—I guess in about five minutes.

Q. You guess it was about five minutes.

K. This was a guy from the *New York Times* calling.

Q. Reverend Kyles is looking at *Life* magazine's spread as he tells the story.

K.   Then an ambulance came about—I guess it was about five minutes. This was a guy from the *New York Times* calling.

Q.   Who is this man up here, do you have any idea? The one in that upper window there?

K.   He's, uh—he was with a band, from Chicago. That's the Breadbasket Band. And they had been playing up here where the . . . I was up there singing with them. So—I think it was a minister, a Lutheran minister—

Q.   Looks like he has a collar on.

K.   Yes. He was beating the drum. This was part of the band. This was about eight or ten minutes after it—eight or nine minutes after it happened.

Q.   The picture at the bottom of page 76.

K.   Now, this is right—much earlier, because we hadn't put the cover on him. I took two spreads off the bed and covered him.

Q.   How—how soon would you say that picture was?

K.   This?

Q.   Yes.

K.   Maybe two minutes, three minutes, here.

Q.   The picture at the top of page 76.

K.   And this one was about eight to ten minutes, here.

Q.   Here they are getting the body down the stairs.

K.   Now, this is a fellow here. He's from Jeffer—or from Community Relations, Justice Department, down here.

Q.   Do you know his name?

K.   Yes—

Q.   It looks like Jim Lowry [James Laue] to me. Yes, that's him.

K.   Yes.

Q.   Jim Lowry, from the Justice Department?

K.   He came out of his room.

Q.   Where does he work out of—Washington?

Voice.   New York, I believe.

Q.   . . .

K.   Yes. Now, I say—

Q.   We're on page 78.

K.   —for the . . . to see anybody from the street, he'd have to look through the entrance which is down here. He couldn't see that he was standing. And he was standing—well, the car—this is the car he was going to—no, next to it, maybe. The car was in this area. You can't see it here.

Q.   The car that Dr. Stevens—that is it, isn't it? Four-door?

K.   Anyway, it's like this. So, in falling he was someplace in here, which means that if he did see it he would have had to see it through the drive here.

Q. Is this a policeman down here?

K. Yes. They came after us. "What happened and where'd the shot come from?" Now, see they're back here, and this is the fire station. And this is how the buildings run into the fire station. They were in all this area here.

Q. Page 78.

K. They were in that area.

Q. Now, the police came out of the bushes here, above the wall?

K. Yes; they were jumping down the wall here.

Q. Jumping down the wall.

K. It may have been a car passing about that time. I don't know, because if I'm not mistaken, the police did call the ambulance, 'cause I hollered back, "Get an ambulance."

Q. Well, those bushes are very heavy in there. They must have really had to work their way in because I couldn't walk through that area.

K. This way, mainly, and from across the street.

Q. You think there were some up in those bushes and jumped down.

K. Yes, that's my thought. But it sounded just like the shot came from—you know, it sounded like an explosion in here.

Q. . . .

K. I only heard one shot.

Q. —exploding bullet.

K. Now, that's what Jesse Jackson said. Jesse Jackson said it was. Said it didn't explode until it hit him. I know there's a kind that would tear you apart, you know, because the wound that I saw, all this was gone. The necktie was gone, you know, this way, it was cut off. And then Ralph said beneath the shirt, when they got to the hospital, there was—there was a larger wound under the shirt that we couldn't see.

Q. So there were two holes—

K. The one we saw—it must have been—it didn't go all the way down, as I seem to remember. The collar was intact, but the necktie had been blown off, so the impact here tore all this out, and then Ralph said under the shirt, about in here, there was a larger wound where it—where it really exploded, and I was asking the police officer about what kind of bullet was it.

Q. The self-same kind of bullet that they got Kennedy's head with.

K. Called hollow—hollow—

Q. Hollow—

K. Yes, called hollow-head, or something.

Q. A dumdum explodes from the impact. There are also bullets

484

that have a charge—that carry a charge, that explode from a natural powder charge.

K. When I saw the wound, it was just terrible. It's something I'll never forget.

Q. He was dead instantly, don't you think?

K. I would think so. His eyes, uh—were not closed, and they did move within—it seemed to me, you know, that he was looking up at—they moved; I know, I saw them move.

Q. Quickly, like this?

K. No, not quickly. Just slowly

Q. Slowly.

K. Real slowly. Like as if he was controlling them at that point. I don't know—you know, he looked this way and he looked that way. Well, Ralph was there—I don't know—I can't remember whether Ralph got—

Q. . . . wound . . . ?

K. Yes. We couldn't see.

Q. But the shirt wasn't like torn open or anything like here?

K. No. The thing went in but—

Q. It sounds like an internal explosion and then coming out.

Voice. They must have performed an autopsy, . . . but there's no—you can't see that . . .

Q. Well, we've got to go talk to the doctors in the hospital.

K. Well, these people were—were telling the police. They were answering them. They just ke—kept asking, "Where did it come from?" "Who was it?" and all that kind of stuff. And they were pointing, the shot came from across the street. Well, all them converging this way, and we tried to tell them, you know, get out there and go that way. That's what they were saying, because it just sounded to me like it was right in here. Even Andy said it didn't sound like—he never heard a shot from across the street.

Q. Um-hm.

K. Now, here, this scene. This was maybe four or five minutes, because we covered him—no, it isn't. We covered him a while before they got here. So right away we put—Hosea came out of his room. Now here, they had been—they had been in conference most of the day down here, room 2-0-—one of these rooms—over here. I don't know what—what time Hosea came back to his room. But they had been in conference downstairs. I went in the room about 5:30 or 5:35, and we had just a very pleasant conversation. Talked about normal things; talked about his father in a real beautiful sort of way—tender, about dad. Then we talked about soul food. He teased me about he didn't want to go to my house like he went to another preacher's house. He went out to his house and didn't have any—had ham—a big ham, but there was no meat on the bone and the Koolaid wasn't sweet. Said, "Don't do us like that, are you?" And he teased about—he and Ralph teased about whether my wife could cook soul food or not. Then he talked about—he asked me what I thought made the people of Memphis come together so much on—you know, backing the garbage workers. He was real enthused over the way the community had come together supporting them. This was the kind of conversation we made. He was in just a real good mood. And by the time we came out, I said, "All right, we are getting late." He said, "No, we are on time."

I had told them 5 because I knew how slow he and Ralph were and —and when I had called the house for him and Gwen had said 6, I told Gwen 6 but I told them 5. But he said, "Oh, no; we have plenty of time." And they were—they got ready. He put a shirt on that was too small; too tight to button up. And he said, "Oh, ..." I said, "You're getting fat." He said, "Oh, I got to take this shirt off." Ralph said, "You mean you're not going to wear that shirt after I washed it? That's the shirt I washed for you." He said, "Yes, but I can't wear it." And he—he dressed. Ralph was dressed at the time. We talked about who was going to run his revival. Ralph talked about his revival. Ralph talked about he had taken an after offering in his church Sunday of $300 and some odd dollars. Something had come up. I think to help somebody or something.

Q.   . . .

K.   And this was the kind of conversation we had, you know. He stepped out and we stood here about three minutes, you know, talking to different people. I didn't see Chauncey, but "Hi, Chaunce, I haven't seen you." And I talked to some people and he talked to some people. Uh—and we must have been out there a good three or four minutes. And he said, "All right, load up; we're getting ready to go." And at that point I turned and walked down this way.

Q.   . . .

K.   Much—no, I hadn't. I know I hadn't gotten here.

Q.   You hadn't gotten to the stairway.

K.   No, I hadn't gotten to the stairway. I was still on the same level. And when I heard the shot, I simply looked—I looked down. I didn't think for sure I had heard an explosion and—and when I—I heard—and when I looked down, I heard somebody say, "Oh, they've got Martin!" Then I turned—I don't know if I turned left or right, but I turned and came back and this is as much as—when I turned I couldn't—this is all I could see.

Q.   You couldn't see his head because it was behind the corner.

K.   No. No. That's right.

Q.   Is there—

K.   But I came and looked. I looked at the wound. I went immediately in to call the ambulance. I tried to call the ambulance but couldn't get the operator.

Q.   Then you came out—

K.   I came out here.

Q.   —would you say it was a minute, 60 seconds, 30 seconds—

K.   It wouldn't be more than a minute. It wouldn't be a minute. It wouldn't have been a minute. Because I turned immediately and came back. Went in the room—it seemed the police came almost simultaneously with the shot, they were that close. Now, whether they heard one over there, you know, I can't tell. But all I heard was one that sounded like it was in this area. And then uh, when I couldn't raise anybody on the phone, uh, I came back out and hollered for the police to get an ambulance on their radio and what's taking them so long? I don't know if an ambulance is stationed at that fire station . . . .

Q.   . . . I believe it's down on Front Street.

K.   And I kept hollering, "Get the ambulance!" At that point, uh, this fellow came up with a towel and, uh—

Q.   . . .

K.   Ralph was there, you know. Ralph took him and patted his face and said, "Martin, this is Ralph. Can you hear me?" But he never made a sign.

Q.   First reports said that he walked into the hospital holding his heart. This was the report we got in New Orleans. We thought he might make it.

K.   Oh, no. It was, uh—

Q.   Yes.

K.   There was a report that both of his shoes were knocked off, but that wasn't true, because both of them were on there.

Q.   . . .

K.   He was in just a real good mood. We must have talked 20 minutes or half an hour. And . . . leaning over this rail and—

Q.   . . . was that?

K.   No, the shot didn't make me. The noise made me look over here to see what it was. You know, it might have been a car back-firing or a firecracker. You know; I just didn't associate it with being a shot, even though I was apprehensive, too.

Q.   The police got there immediately

K.   Oh, yes. They came—they were coming there, I guess, but appar—I turned immediately and went back to the room and picked up the phone but couldn't raise anybody. I left the phone off the hook, I think. I don't know. But I went out and hollered, "Somebody get an ambulance!" And I said, "Call an ambulance on the radio." I could see them myself coming from this point.

487

Q. . . .

K. They were coming from a place—you can't see that area.

Q. Pretty much from the direction of the firehouse.

K. Yes. Pret—yes. Like—I don't know whether they were steps over there or not. But they were coming from that direction, and they were in there within minutes—within seconds, really. Because it wasn't four minutes that we had—

Q. . . .

K. No, I don't.

Q. . . .

K. I don't know who was in charge there. I had spoken to some guys the day before. They were plainclothes men. They were sheriff's deputies. No, this is a sheriff's deputy here, and city policemen. City policemen and sheriff's deputies. Oh, they were mixed. But as they put him in the ambulance, his color had changed already. I looked at him as they passed him in.

Q. Well, they sure—

K. And they stationed two guys here after they moved the body. I was trying to come down to this room for something, and they kept shouting at me, "Get out of here; you can't disturb the scene," or something. I just looked at them and kept walking.

Q. Umhm. Did they bring the squad in right away to look at the—at the scene and take evidence—

K. No. I was on the phone from that time on . . . .

Q. There's some talk about a bullet lodged in the wall, but obviously it was an exploding bullet. You couldn't tell anything about trajectory.

K. I think it was later that evening that—they got involved by that time, that they looked. They looked. I don't know what they were looking for, but they looked.

Q. . . .

K. Oh.

AGREEMENT

AGREEMENT entered into this ___6___ day of July, 1968, by and between William Bradford Huie (herein "Author"), James Earl Ray (herein "Ray") and Arthur J. Hanes (herein "Hanes").

1. This Agreement is entered into with reference to the following:

(a) Author is and has been for many years a writer of international reputation and has had numerous books and articles published and serialized throughout the world.

(b) Ray has been charged with the murder of Martin Luther King, Jr.; and it is anticipated that a trial (herein "the Trial") of Ray for such murder will be held in the State of Tennessee in the near future.

(c) Hanes is an attorney at law licensed to practice as such in the State of Alabama; Ray and Hanes and each of them represent that Ray has engaged Hanes to act as his attorney in the Trial, that Hanes has accepted such engagement and that he will so act.

(d) Author proposes to write literary material dealing with the assassination of Martin Luther King, Jr., the alleged participation of Ray therein, and the Trial, for the purpose of establishing the truth with respect thereto.

(e) Ray and Hanes are desirous of assisting Author in such writing by furnishing to him such material relative to the subject matter of such writing which Author might not otherwise be able to obtain.

2. Ray and Hanes and each of them agree that they will use their best efforts to arrange as many personal interviews between Author and Ray and on the earliest occasions which may be permitted by the authority having jurisdiction over the institution in which Ray is then confined; and that they and each of them on such occasions and otherwise, through Hanes or other persons, will impart to Author such information (herein the "Private Material") with respect to the assassination of Martin Luther King, Jr., the alleged participation of Ray therein, and the life and activities of Ray, as they or either of them may have or reasonably may be able to obtain; and that Author shall have the right to use the Private Material or any part thereof in his writing of said literary material.

3. The literary material which Author proposes to write as aforesaid, including such of the Private Material as Author in his sole discretion elects to use, is hereinafter referred to as "said work". Author shall have, and if and to the extent that they or either of them have any rights, titles, or interests therein, Ray and Hanes, and each of them, give, sell, assign and transfer to Author, forever, the following absolute, exclusive and unqualified rights: the right to write said work and to use the same, in whole or in part, in whatever manner Author in his sole discretion may elect, including but not limited to the right to make and/or cause to be made magazine, book, dramatic, motion picture, television and/or other

adaptations of every kind, of said work or any part thereof, and for the purpose of making any of said adaptations Author or his designees may change, interpolate in, add to or subtract from or make foreign language versions of, said work, to such extent as Author in his sole discretion may elect; the sole and exclusive right to make motion pictures and television pictures of all kinds based in whole or in part on said work and/or containing characters of said work (including remakes of and/or sequels to any such pictures), with the right to sell, lease, license and generally deal in the same throughout the world, forever; the right to use the name, voice and/or likeness of Ray and Hanes, or either of them, in or as the title of said work; the right to obtain copyright in the name of Author or otherwise in all countries throughout the world, in and to said work and/or any of said adaptations; the sole and exclusive right to negotiate for, execute and deliver, in the name of Author alone or in the names of Author, Ray, and Hanes, or any of them (but without consulting with or obtaining the approval or consent of Ray or Hanes thereto), such licenses, grants, agreements, and contracts with respect to said work, any of said adaptations, and/or any of the rights herein-above set forth, as Author in his sole discretion may elect; for this purpose (but without limiting the generality of the foregoing) Ray and Hanes and each of them hereby irrevocably appoint Author the true and lawful attorney of them and each of them to negotiate for, execute and deliver, in the names of Author, Ray and Hanes, or any of them, as Author may elect, any and all such licenses, grants, agreements and contracts.

4. Without in any manner limiting the generality of the foregoing, Ray and Hanes and each of them agree, upon demand, to execute and deliver to Author or his designees any and all such instruments, including but not limited to assign-ments, consents, approvals, and releases, which in the judgment of Author may be necessary or desirable to implement, effectuate or protect the rights of, or rights, titles and interests herein given or agreed to be given to, Author with respect to said work and/or any of said adaptations.

5. In full consideration for all rights, titles and interests given or agreed to be given by Ray and Hanes to Author hereunder and for all agreements and acts of Ray and Hanes hereunder or pursuant hereto, Author agrees to pay to Ray and Hanes each, thirty per cent of the gross receipts from said work. All receipts shall be paid to and collected by the Author's agent, Ned Brown, Inc., 315 South Beverly Drive, Beverly Hills, Calif., and said Author's agent shall make payments to Ray and Hanes each, or their respective designees or assignees, within ten days after receipt. The Author's agent shall also, at quarterly intervals, furnish statements reflecting all transactions in reasonable detail. The Author's agent shall also, within ten days after their completion, furnish to Ray and Hanes copies of any and all contracts entered into by the Author.

6. **Notwithstanding** anything elsewhere herein contained, the parties expressly understand and agree as follows:

(a) Author has no obligation of any kind to Ray, Hanes or others to write or make or cause to be written or made said work or any of said adaptations, or to use any of the Private Material in said work or said adaptations. Author has not represented, warranted or agreed and does not represent, warrant or agree that if he does write or make or cause to be written or made said work or any of said adaptations he will in fact enter into any license, grant, agreement or contract relative thereto, or that in any event there will be any Author's net profits from said work in any particular amount or at all.

(b) ~~In the event Author does not have an interview with Ray within 30 days after the date of this Agreement or the date when Ray first enters the United States hereafter, whichever is the later date, Author shall have the right and option, by written notice to Ray and Hanes, to terminate this Agreement and all of the respective rights and obligations of the parties hereunder. In the event any such notice is given, notice to Ray shall be deemed to have been sufficiently given, if mailed or delivered to the warden or other person in charge of the institution in which Ray may be confined at the time of the giving of such notice.~~

(c) Author shall receive credit for the writing for said work and/or said adaptations in such manner as Author may elect.

7. **This** Agreement shall be binding upon and inure to the benefit of the parties hereto and their respective personal representatives, executors, administrators, heirs, legatees, and assigns. Author may transfer or assign this Agreement, all or any part of the rights, titles and interests herein given or agreed to be given to Author hereunder, and/or all or any part of any rights herein referred to, to any persons, firms and/or corporations.

IN WITNESS WHEREOF, the parties hereto have executed this Agreement as of the date first above written.

William Bradford Huie
William Bradford Huie
                                        Author

James Earl Ray
James Earl Ray
                                        Ray

Arthur J. Hanes
Arthur J. Hanes
                                        Hanes

On _July 8_ ,1968 before me, the undersigned _Notary Public_ personally appeared WILLIAM BRADFORD HUIE known to me to be the person whose name is subscribed to the within instrument and acknowledged that he executed the same.

WITNESSETH my hand and official seal.

Arthur J Hanes Jr

On _Aug 1_ 1968 before me, the undersigned _Notary Public_ personally appeared JAMES EARL RAY known to me to be the person whose name is subscribed to the within instrument and acknowledged that he executed the same.

WITNESSETH my hand and official seal.

Arthur J Hanes Jr

On _July 8_ 1968 before me, the undersigned _Notary Public_ personally appeared ARTHUR J. HANES known to me to be the person whose name is subscribed to the within instrument and acknowledged that he executed the same.

WITNESSETH my hand and official seal.

Arthur J Hanes Jr

AMENDATORY AGREEMENT

January/ AMENDATORY AGREEMENT entered into this 2 9 day of ~~December~~/ 1968, by and between WILLIAM BRADFORD HUIE (herein "Author"), JAMES EARL RAY (herein "Ray") and ARTHUR J. HANES (herein "Hanes").

(1) This Amendatory Agreement is entered into with reference to the following:

(a) The parties hereto have entered into a certain Agreement and letter agreement supplementary thereto, both dated July 8, 1968 (herein "said Basic Agreement"), relating to the writing of certain literary material by Author and the grant of certain rights to Author by Ray and Hanes.

(b) Ray and Hanes have entered into a certain document entitled "Agreement" dated July 5, 1968 (herein the "Assignment Agreement") under which Ray assigned to Hanes a portion of his interest in any moneys accruing to Hanes under said Basic Agreement.

(c) Under and pursuant to said Basic Agreement Author has in fact written and is presently writing certain literary material with respect to the murder of Martin Luther King, Jr., Ray's alleged participation in and Ray's coming trial for such murder, and the life and activities of Ray, some of which material has been and other of which will be published in issues of Look Magazine by Cowles Communications, Inc. pursuant to a contract with Author, and other of which material will be published in book form by Dell Publishing Co., Inc. pursuant to a contract with Author (the working title of which book is "THEY SLEW THE DREAMER").

(d) At the time of the execution of said Basic
Agreement and for some period thereafter, Hanes was engaged
to act and did act as attorney for Ray in connection with
Ray's coming trial, but such engagement has been terminated,
Hanes no longer represents Ray as his attorney in any capacity, and Percy Foreman, an attorney at law, has been substituted to act and now acts as attorney for Ray.

(e) The parties are desirous of effecting certain
releases and other acts with respect to said Basic Agreement
as hereinafter provided.

(2) Hanes does hereby transfer and assign to Ray all of
Hanes' right, title and interest in, to and under said Basic
Agreement and the Assignment Agreement, including but not being
limited to any and all moneys and other compensation of any kind
to which Hanes may now or hereafter be entitled thereunder.
Hanes further agrees that he shall not hereafter write or authorize to be written any literary material relating to the murder
of Martin Luther King, Jr., Ray's alleged participation in or
Ray's coming trial for such murder, or the life or activities of
Ray, and that he shall not hereafter make or authorize to be made
magazine, book, dramatic, motion picture, television and/or other
adaptation of any kind relating to any such subjects.

(3) Hanes hereby forever releases and discharges Ray and
Author and each of them from any and all claims, demands, actions
and causes of action which Hanes, but for this release, might now
have or hereafter might have against them or either of them under
or pursuant to said Basic Agreement, the Assignment Agreement or
any other agreements or contracts, written or oral, of any kind
or nature whatsoever heretofore entered into between said parties
or any of them with respect to the subject matter of said Basic
Agreement. Without limiting the foregoing, Hanes does hereby
acknowledge that he has received from Author and Ray any and all

moneys and other compensation which Hanes heretofore may have
been entitled to receive from Author or Ray under said Basic
Agreement, the Assignment Agreement or otherwise.

(4) Author and Ray, and each of them, do hereby forever
release and discharge Hanes from any and all claims, demands,
actions and causes of action which they or either of them, but
for this release, might now have or hereafter might have against
Hanes under or pursuant to said Basic Agreement, the Assignment
Agreement or any other agreements or contracts, written or oral,
heretofore entered into between said parties or any of them with
respect to the subject matter of said Basic Agreement.

(5) The parties hereby agree that for any and all purposes
Hanes shall no longer be or be considered as a party to said Basic
Agreement, and shall have no further right, title or interest of
any kind or nature whatsoever thereunder or under the Assignment
Agreement or any other agreements or contracts, written or oral,
heretofore entered into between the parties or any of them, with
respect to the subject matter of said Basic Agreement. Hanes
hereby agrees to execute and deliver to Author and/or Ray upon
demand any further instruments necessary or desirable to implement
or effectuate this Amendatory Agreement.

(6) Ray does hereby acknowledge and confirm that as of
the date hereof there are no moneys or other compensation of any
kind now due or payable to Ray from Author under or pursuant to
said Basic Agreement, the Assignment Agreement, or otherwise.

(7) Author and Ray hereby agrees that paragraph 5. of
said Basic Agreement shall be and the same hereby is amended to
provide that all acts therein specified to be done by Author's
agent shall be done, instead, by Author, and to provide further
that all payments to be made and all statements, notices and other
documents to be furnished or given to Ray shall be made, furnished

or given to Ray in care of Ray's Attorney, Percy Foreman, Esq.,
at 1116 Capitol Avenue, Huston, Texas, 77002.

(8) The parties do hereby confirm and agree that except
as hereinabove expressly set forth said Basic Agreement is in
full force and effect and has not been and is not hereby altered,
amended or modified in any manner or particular whatsoever, that
Author has and shall continue to have all of the rights, titles
and interests given or granted, or agreed to be given or granted,
to him by Ray and/or Hanes under said Basic Agreement, and that
the writing by Author and the publication by Cowles Communications, Inc. in Look Magazine and by Dell Publishing Co., Inc. of
certain literary materials, hereinabove referred to, has been
and is authorized under said Basic Agreement and such rights,
titles and interests.

(9) This Amendatory Agreement shall be binding upon and
inure to the benefit of the parties hereto and their respective
personal representatives, executors, administrators, heirs,
legatees and assigns. Author may transfer or assign this Amendatory Agreement, and/or all or any part of the rights, titles
and interests herein referred to, to any person, firm or corporation.

IN WITNESS WHEREOF the parties hereto have executed this
Amendatory Agreement as of the date first above written.

William Bradford Huie
William Bradford Huie, "Author".

James Earl Ray
James Earl Ray, "Ray".

APPROVED AS TO FORM
AND CONTENT:

Percy Foreman
Percy Foreman, as Attorney
for James Earl Ray

Arthur J. Hanes
Arthur J. Hanes, "Hanes".

HARTSELLE, ALABAMA
July 8, 1968

Mr. Arthur J. Hanes
Attorney at Law
617 Frank Nelson Building
Birmingham, Alabama 35203

Dear Art:

This letter is meant to be part of our Agreement, signed on this date, and is an extension and clarification of Article 5 of said Agreement.

It is known and understood by you, Ray, and me that all advances made by publishers to an Author on a book contract are merely loans, returnable in full if, for any reason whatever, the book is not completed and accepted; and these advances or loans become income to the Author only after completion of the book and after its acceptance by the publisher.

Therefore, any monies paid by me to you and Ray while I am researching and writing this book are, in effect, loans from me to the two of you. However, under the circumstances, I am willing to consider these monies or advances made by me to the two of you non-returnable, if you and Ray will agree that these payments or advances shall not exceed the following schedule of payments:

1. On the signing of the first, or book, contract, I will pay you the sum of $10,000.00. It is assumed that this will be on or about July 15th, not later than July 20th.

2. On the first day after Ray has been lodged in a jail in the United States, I will pay $5000. It is assumed that this will be about August 1st.

3. One month after Ray has been lodged in the United States, I will pay $5000.

4. Similarly, a month later, another $5000.

5. Similarly, a month later, another $5000.

6. Similarly, a month later, another $5000.

7. Similarly, a month later, another $5000.

In short, on signing, on Ray's return, and during the first
five months after his return, I am obligating myself to pay
you and Ray, under terms of our Agreement, to pay you and
Ray a total of $35,000. All payments, as per our Agreement,
will be made to you by my agent, Ned Brown, and these payments
in equal amounts, will be charged against whatever may become
due to you and Ray under the Agreement.

Five months after Ray's return, assuming that I receive all
the cooperation from you and Ray guaranteed by the Agreement,
I expect to have completed the book, or to have obtained legal
extentions from the publisher, you and Ray. Normally a publisher has 30 days in which to accept or reject the book. Onc
the book has been accepted, the entire publishing advance will
be paid; and thereafter, all payments made to me, from any and
all sources, will be income, not loans; and this income will b
divided and paid promptly as provided under the Agreement.

Your signature, along with that of Ray affixed by you under
your Power of Attorney, will attest Agreement.

William Bradford Huie

Arthur J. Hanes

James Earl Ray

STATE OF TENNESSEE |
COUNTY OF SHELBY |

WHEREAS, William Bradford Huie ("Author"), JAMES EARL
RA Y (Ray") and ARTHUR J. HANES ("Hanes"), did, on or about
July 8th, 1968, enter into what has been called a "Basic
Agreement" relating to the writing of certain literary material
by Author and the grant of certain rights to Author by Ray and
Hanes; and

WHEREAS, ON and after July 5th, 1968, by assignment agreements, Ray assigned to Hanes at first a portion of his interest
in any moneys accruing to Hanes under said Basic Agreement, and
later the said Ray assigned to the said Hanes all of his interest in said moneys so accruing under any agreement or agreements
with said Author; and

WHEREAS, by an instrument designated "Amendatory Agreement"
on the 29th day of January, A. D., 1968, also entered into by and
between the said Author and the said Ray and Hanes, the said
Hanes did by said Amendatory Agreement transfer and assign to
Ray all of his (Hanes') right, title and interest in, to and under said Basic Agreement and the Assignment Agreements, including
but not limited to any and all moneys and other compensation of
any kind to which the said Hanes may now or hereafter be entitled thereunder; and

WHEREAS, Percy Foreman, a duly licensed and practicing attorney at law of H ouston, Texas, has been admitted by the trial
judge at Memphis, Tennessee, to its bar for the purpose of representing the said James Earl Ray in the trials of cases pending before said judge, said admission having been at the request
in open court on November 12, 1968 made by the said James Earl
Ray, and the said Ray desires to secure the fees of the said attorney for his said defense, and desires to assign to the said
Percy Foreman all of the rights, title and interest he may have
or heretofore at any time may have had under any contract or contracts with the said Author and or as assignee of any rights at

any time held by the said Hanes, and any and all rights of whatsoever kind or character he may have as a result of the writings of said author and of their subsequent publication, including the right to receive, accept and retain the proceeds derived from said rights in his own name absolutely, now, therefore,-

KNOW ALL MEN BY THESE PRESENTS:

THAT I, JAMES EARL RAY, presently in Memphis, Shelby County Tennessee, for and in consideration of monies heretofore advanced by him in my behalf, and, further, in consideration of his services heretofore rendered in my behalf and his agreement to represent me at the trial or trials of any cases presently pending against me in Shelby County, Tennessee, have signed over, given, conveyed and transferred, and do, by this instrument herenow give, assign, set over and transfer to PERCY FOREMAN, of Houston, Harris County, Texas, a ll of my aforesaid right, title and interest in a nd to the proceeds that would otherwise have accrued to me pursuant to said Basic Agreement andto said Amendatory Agreement, and to all of my rights thereunder as well as to any other right or rights that might be or have been mine because of the writing and subsequent purblication of such writing by said Author, whether included in said assignment by the said Hanes to me under the Amendatory Agreement of January 29th, 1969, or otherwise, said assignment and transfer herein to the said Percy Foreman being a bsolute and irrevocable, and I here now authorize and direct any person , firm or corporation having funds due and owing me by virtue of said Basic Agreement or any subsequent as - signments, including said Amendatory Agreement, or otherwise owing me because of the writings of said Author, to pay the same to the said Percy Foreman, at his office in Houston, Harris Co., Texas, in his own name and as his own property.

IN WITNESS Whereof, I have signed this conveyance, assignment and contract at Memphis, Shelby Co., Tennessee, this the

JER to PP - 2 - 3 - 69.

3rd day of February, A. D., 1969.

James Earl Ray
JAMES EARL RAY

THE STATE OF TENNESSEE |
COUNTY OF SHELBY |

BEFORE ME, the undersigned Notary Public in and for Shelby
County, Tennessee, on this day personally appeared JAMES EARL
RAY, known to me to be the person whose name is signed to the
foregoing instrument, and he acknowledged to me that the executed the same for the purpose and consideration therein expressed.

GIVEN under my hand and seal of office at Memphis, Tennessee,
this 3rd day of February, A. ., 1969.

Roy C. Nixon
Notary Public in and for Shelby Co.,
Tennessee.

My commission expires April 23, 1969.

March 7, 1969

Dear James Ray....

Enclosed you will find:

1. The original agreement signed by you, Mr. Hanes, and me.

2. The letter attached to that agreement by which I agreed to advance $35,000 in anticipation of earnings from this project.

3. Receipts from your attorneys for the $40,000 which I have advanced to date. ($30,000 to Mr. Hanes and $10,000 to Mr. Foreman.)

I am also having sent to you, from my attorneys, the Supplementary Agreement which was signed by Mr. Foreman, Mr. Hanes, you and me. I suggest that you sign another copy of this for Mr. Foreman, so that we can have two copies bearing all four original signatures.

This gives you copies of all agreements existing between you and me; and you will note that I have followed them to the letter. I will continue to do so.

To this date this project has earned $30,000. Additional earnings will shortly be received from LOOK magazine, from foreign magazines, and from Dell Publishing Company, which will publish the book in May.

LOOK Magazine will publish my next article on April 15th. The book, titled HE SLEW THE DREAMER, will be published about May 15th.

I am currently negotiating with Carlo Ponti, the film producer, over picture rights. I'll keep you informed of developments.

As soon as you are moved to Nashville, I will attempt to see you....or rather we will attempt to get permission for you to see me. We need a picture of you to use on the front cover of the book.

Jerry keeps in touch with me; and if it is your desire you can count on me to keep in touch with you indefinitely. I'll help you in any way I can.

And of course I will keep both you and Mr. Foreman informed as to earnings.

Best wishes, Bill Huie

LAW OFFICES OF

PERCY FOREMAN
804 SOUTH COAST BUILDING
HOUSTON, TEXAS 77002

MAIN AT RUSK

CA 4-9321

March 9, 1969

Mr. James Earl Ray,
Shelby County Jail,
Memphis, Texas.

Dear James Earl:

You have asked that I advance to Jerry Ray five ($500.00) of the "$5,000.00", referring to the first five thousand dollars paid by Wm. Bradford Huie. On January 29th, Mr. Huie advanced an additional $5,000.00. At that time I had spent in excess of $9,500.00 on your case. Since then, I have spent in excess of $4,000.00 additional.

But I am willing to advance Jerry $500.00 and add it to the $165,000.00 mentioned in my other letter to you today. In other words, I would receive the first $165,500.00. But I would not make any other advances - just this one $500.00.

And this advance, also, is contingent upon the plea of guilty and sentence going through on March 10, 1969, without any unseemly conduct on your part in court.

Yours truly,

Percy Foreman

PF-4

P.S.   The rifle and the white mustang are tied up in the suit filed by Renfro Hays. Court costs and attorneys fees will be necessary, perhaps, to get them released. I will credit the $165,500.00 with whatever they bring over the cost of obtaining them, if any.

Percy Foreman
Percy Foreman

James Earl Ray

March 9th, '69

Mr. James Earl Ray,
Shelby County Jail,
Memphis, Tennessee.

Dear James Earl:

      You have heretofore assigned to me all of your
royalties from magazine articles, book, motion picture or
other revenue to be derived from the writings of Wm. Bradford Huie. These are my own property unconditionally.

      However, you have heretofore authorized and re-
quested me to negotiate a plea of guilty if the State of
Tennessee through its District Attorney General and with
the approval of the trial judge would waive the death penalty. You agreed to accept a sentence of 99 years.

      It is contemplated that your case will be dis-
posed of tomorrow, March 10, by the above plea and sentence.
This will shorten the trial considerably. In consideration
of the time it will save me, I am willing to make the following adjustment of my fee arrangement with you:

      If the plea is entered and the sentence accepted
and no embarassing circumstances take place in the court
room, I am willing to assign to any bank, trust company or
individual selected by you all my receipts under the above
assignment in excess of $165,000.00. These funds over and
above the first $165,000.00 will be held by such bank, trust
company or individual subject to your order.

      I have either spent or obligated myself to spend
in excess of $14,000.00, and I think these expenses should
be paid in addition to a $150,000.00 fee. I am sure the ex-
penses will exceed $15,000.00 but I am willing to rest on
that figure.

                        Yours truly,

                         Percy Foreman

PF-4   *James Earl Ray*

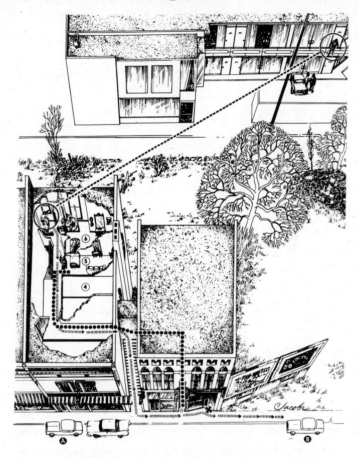

"A report of a second Mustang (B) added a new angle yesterday to investigation of the slaying of Dr. Martin Luther King, Jr. Earlier theories had indicated that a man being sought in the murder entered a flight of stairs at 422½ South Main, went to the second floor where he rented a room (line of black dots) and crossed a passageway to 418½ South Main to Room 5. Sometime before 6 pm the night of the murder, it is believed that he went to the bathroom of the rooming house and from the window of that room shot Dr. King as he stood on the second floor balcony of the Lorraine Motel in front of Room 306. He then went out the hallway (broken line) and down steps between the two buildings. Reports indicate the same man dropped a rifle and a suitcase in front of the Canipe Amusement Co. at 424 South Main (cross). The second Mustang reportedly bearing Arkansas license plates, was seen leaving shortly after 6:01 pm. Customers in Jim's Grill at 418 South Main said the other Mustang (A) was seen leaving the area about 6:15 pm."

The drawing (by John Jacobs) is from *The Commercial-Appeal* (Memphis, Tennessee), Thursday, April 11, 1968. The explanatory material appeared under the picture.

6. Because of distortion due to mutilation and insufficient marks of value, I could draw no conclusion as to whether or not the submitted bullet was fired from the submitted rifle.

Robert A. Frazier

ROBERT A. FRAZIER

This excerpt from FBI firearms expert Robert A. Frazier's affidavit, used in the Ray extradition, then confiscated and suppressed, says what is false, that a *bullet* was recovered, and admits there is no proof it came from the "Ray" rifle (see pp. 225ff).

9. Right after the shot, I heard through a broken pane in my kitchen window a lot of voices yelling and hollering across the street from my building near the Lorraine Motel. I looked out my window toward the noise and I saw a lot of people milling around near the motel. Then I went to my door and opened it. I would say that about a minute, not more, passed between my hearing the shot and when I opened the door. First, I looked toward the bathroom and I saw that the door was open and it was empty. Then I went to the banister and looked the other way. When I did, I saw a man running near the end of the hallway. I have put an "O" mark on the floor plan, Exhibit I, to show about where he was when I saw him. He was carrying a bundle in his right hand. From what I could see, the bundle was at least three or four feet long and six or eight inches thick. The bundle appeared to be wrapped in what looked like newspaper. The man turned left toward the stairs when he reached the end of the hallway. Although I did not get a long look at him before he turned left, I think it was the same man I saw earlier with Mrs. Brewer looking at Room 5-B. The man running down the hall had on a dark suit, the same as the man I saw earlier.

Charles Quitman Stephens

CHARLES QUITMAN STEPHENS

Charles Quitman ("Bourbon Charley") Stephens' affidavit, used to get Ray extradited, fails to make positive identification, says other than represented in the minitrial, is actually proof he saw and could have seen nothing of the alleged

CERTIFICATE OF DEATH
TENNESSEE DEPARTMENT OF PUBLIC HEALTH
DIVISION OF VITAL STATISTICS

MEMPHIS AND SHELBY COUNTY HEALTH DEPARTMENT :: 814 JEFFERSON AVENUE, MEMPHIS, TENNESSEE 38105

Martin Luther King, Jr. — Male — Age 39 — Negro — Memphis, Shelby, Tennessee

Married — Alberta Williams — Coretta — Minister & Civil Rights Leader — Atlanta, Fulton, Georgia

Martin L. King, Sr.

Gunshot Wound to Thoracic Cord — Homicide — 4-4-68 — 406 Mulberry — Hotel

J. T. Francisco, M.D. — 4-5-68

Removal — P. S. Lewis Funeral Home, 374 Vance Avenue

For court purposes, what was used could not qualify for court purposes. (See p. 442.)

REGISTRATION CARD

NOTICE TO GUESTS: — This property is privately owned and management reserves right to refuse service to anyone, and will not be responsible for accidents or injury to guests or for loss of money, jewelry or valuables of any kind.

RENTAL PAYABLE IN ADVANCE

NAME Eric S. Galt
STREET 2608 Highland ave
CITY Birmingham STATE Alabama

REPRESENTING
American Hotel Register Co., 226-232 W. Ontario St., Chicago 10, Ill.

ROOM 34 RATE 6.24 CAR LICENSE 38993 STATE Ala
ARR. DATE 4-3-68 DEPT. DATE NO. IN PARTY 1 CLERK MAKE OF CAR Mustang
REMARKS

THIS IS YOUR RECEIPT   THANK YOU

Jim Loyd's New Rebel MOTOR HOTEL
3466 LAMAR AVE.
MEMPHIS, TENN.
PHONE FA 3-7641

44-38861 JK
FBI LABORATORY

Suppressed New Rebel Motel registration card, with handwriting other than Ray's. Pivotal evidence, license number not in his handwriting. (See

After this book was written, I was able to obtain transcripts of some of the legal proceedings preliminary to the minitrial. They disclose that what the reader may have taken as harshness on my part was actually rather generous to the principals, particularly Foreman, Stanton, and the late Judge Battle. The excerpts that follow are retyped because of the excessive waste space that is in the court reporter's stock-in-trade, transcript being sold by the page and the pages being mostly blank.

The hearing of December 18, 1968, addresses itself with a marvelous lucidity to a number of the more important points bearing on whether or not Ray had minimum legal rights; whether or not Foreman committed fraud, including on the court; whether or not a preliminary deal had been cooked up behind the scenes; the effects of commercial intrusion in the legal process; and other relevant things.

Foreman began it with a long speech (cited accurately by Ray in his August 1970 affidavit), saying he had rejected publication offers because

> I am not willing at this late period of my life to prostitute principles that I hold dear in defense of a thorough case to a pandering press . . . they did not induce me to come into this case and they will not keep me in the case. I intend to stay in this case as long as your Honor will permit me to do so and without compensation . . . [T. 2–3.]
>
> I am prepared [sic] and paying at my own expense interrogatories to be mailed to each [potential witness]. [T. 4.]
>
> I have put every minute into this case both day and night, a great deal of money, money is no problem to me as an individual but I don't think it is my responsibility, I think that is the responsibility of the State of Tennessee to assist my fee indigent [sic] . . . . If the Court would make available to the defense or to me as defense counsel, whatever rights the defendant has at the bar in the State of Tennessee as an indigent defendant . . . [T. 5–6.]

And, he protested, the court was pressing for trial before the defense could be adequately prepared.

Canale's assistant, Dwyer, argued that Foreman had had plenty of time and the case should not be delayed. He reminded the judge of Foreman's promise of a month earlier (T. 10) to arrange Tennessee counsel, which Foreman had not done, that Foreman "got a valuable asset of some kind in the eyes of the news media," that "Mr. Haynes [sic] seems to have made, or gotten his fee out of this case . . . ." (T. 11.)

Undoubtedly not so intending, Dwyer confirmed that the investigation of the Tennessee crime had not been by Tennessee authorities (T. 11):

> We made an investigation into the investigation that had been made

by different law enforcement agencies involved.

He ridiculed Foreman's posture, which he represented this way:

"I am counsel and I am his last hope, but I got problems, all kinds of problems and because of my problems justice should be stalled." [T. 12.]

Canale, who was to write me that nobody would ever see what had not been presented at the minitrial and who refused to let Fensterwald, when he became Ray's counsel, see anything Hanes had not seen, entered the argument (T. 14) to disclose what seems to be inconsistent with this position. While seeming to be addressing himself to whether or not there should be a delay in the trial, he admitted:

The law requires the State to furnish the defense or show the defense any physical evidence that the State might have in its possession . . .

The wily Foreman (T. 16), in the guise of praising Canale, described Dwyer's remarks as "impassioned and oratorical," which set Dwyer off, as Foreman seemed to want. Dwyer began,

I don't know why he has to put personalities into everything he says to the Court about me, your Honor . . .

To which the judge commented that Dwyer and Foreman are "more or less abrasive to each other."

Foreman resumed with a recounting of efforts to get the FBI files covering "$1,400,000 of investigation . . . the works of over 400 agents assigned solely to that investigation." He then disclosed that when Ray was in jail "there was a squad of FBI agents assigned to prevent the assassination of Martin Luther King," so

I am working on the assumption that someone other than James Earl Ray was concerned with a desire to assassinate the deceased . . . [T. 17–18.]

Foreman specified having "communicated with J. Edgar Hoover three times," and having been in touch with others, including the Assistant Attorney General in charge of the Civil Rights Division. (Elsewhere, he said he had been seeking the FBI file on its bugging of King.)

As he continued with his argument, he denounced as worthless the Renfro Hays investigation for Hanes (T. 21) and denounced Hanes for saying he had been ready to go to trial when he wasn't:

. . . he was about to go to trial, your Honor, not because this case was ready for trial but to meet a publication date and I stepped in because it was my responsibility to do it, and I'm not claiming any glory . . . . [T. 22.]

507

Still not claiming any glory, he made reference (T. 23) to "the school that I was raised in for the sense of responsibility to his profession and to the public":

If I were willing to sell this man's life for some royalties on a picture and on a book, magazine articles, it would be logical for money but I don't practice law for money now.

Following this quaint representation of 60 per cent of an estimated half-million dollars and a few comments by Dwyer, the judge took over, beginning with an exposition of why

This is a most unusual case. It was so from the beginning. As it goes on, it gets more and more unusual. [T. 25.]

He interpreted Ray's firing of Hanes to mean "the funds were cut off." His interpretation of what in the text I referred to as Foreman's "big heart" is unequivocal:

Now, Mr. Foreman has volunteered and donated his services to Mr. Ray and informs the court that there is no money coming forth. I don't think that because Mr. Foreman has donated his services to Mr. Ray that he has also undertaken to finance the entire cost to properly investigate the case or the expenses and so forth. He informs me that Mr. Ray is indigent . . . that puts an onus on the Court to determine that indigency and if he is indigent I think the requirements for a proper investigation of this case would necessitate that somehow we provide the necessary manpower to ready this case for trial. [T. 26.]

At several points, the judge did emphasize this purpose, "to ready this case for trial." After Ray swore that he had neither funds nor property, the judge ruled Ray an indigent, even denying Dwyer "the right to ask him any questions about his indigency" (T. 27). The judge then launched into the highest praise for Stanton's office, which he described as "one of the finest Public Defender's Offices as I know anything about . . . they don't put up a token defense."

Then, for all the world as though it were an unexpected, pleasant surprise (T. 28),

. . . I see Mr. Stanton here, Mr. Hugh Stanton. Draw an order, please, Sir, I want to appoint the Public Defender in this case. Mr. Stanton, I want you and your office to ready this case for trial under the directions of Mr. Foreman. I want you to find as many assistants as necessary to that end . . . . I want the Public Defender's office to give you the necessary help to ready this case for trial. [T. 28.]

Blabbermouth Foreman began showing his appreciation, as though none of this had been arranged in private, with unembarrassed praise for Stanton's office as one of the "three outstanding Public Defender's

Offices in this country" (T. 29).

Foreman's blabbing destroyed the judge's, his own, and Stanton's innocence. At the end of the hearing, after Battle said "I want them to enter an order here and I want them to sign the jacket" (meaning Stanton and his office were to be co-counsel with Foreman), Foreman disclosed, without so intending, that it had all been prearranged, not just something that developed in court, saying,

> I talked with Mr. Stanton a few minutes before Court and he has some reservations, your Honor, about the investigative feature of the case but I understand the Court's order to include both investigation and representation. [T. 33–34.]

Battle said this was his intent. He then adjourned the court.

Aside from having worked out this charade in secret, which would seem to be less than proper, the more so given the courtroom effort to make it seem to have been spontaneous, it is worth noting that Stanton's concept of "preparing the case for trial," of not just putting up "a token defense," was to get cracking on the deal—as soon as he had official status.

Other records indicate it was months before even a "token" investigation was begun.

Does Ray's refusal to accept or even see Stanton seem paranoid in the light of this hitherto unpublished evidence?

In Ray's affidavit, he also said the judge had ruled he would permit no further changes in counsel. At the November 12, 1968, hearing (T. 4), Dwyer had anticipated that Ray might want to fire Foreman, too, thus further delaying trial:

> . . . . what assurance or what guarantees does the Court have that at the last moment, he might not come in here again and say to the Court, "Well, I don't like this gentleman here," Mr. Foreman . . . "I want an opportunity to hire counsel."

In his opposition to Dwyer (T. 6), Foreman began his poor-mouthing ("I would be much better off physically and financially" if not accepted as Ray's counsel). For several pages thereafter he cited precedents.

Battle gave a lengthy ruling (T. 9ff.), beginning with "I think the defendant in a criminal case has the right at any time to dispose of counsel. He has an absolute right to if he wants to." Gradually, however, Battle worked his way around to exactly the interpretation Ray put on his remarks, which Ray interpreted and claims Foreman interpreted as the judge's threat that he would never let Ray get another lawyer:

> The right to select his own counsel can not be insisted upon in a

509

manner that will obstruct an orderly procedure in Courts of justice and deprive such Courts of their inherent powers to control same. See Lee against the United States, 35 Federal (2nd), 219 . . . . The right to select his own counsel can not be insisted upon in a manner that will obstruct an orderly procedure in the Courts of justice and deprive such Courts of the exercise of their inherent powers to control same. The case must be tried on the next setting . . . . You have been granted extraordinary relief at a great cost and this Court will certainly examine most critically any further attempts to change counsel.

After this, there could have been no doubt in Ray's mind that he was forever married to Foreman. He no longer had the capacity to make a voluntary decision, the requirement of the law, in his own defense.

At this juncture (T. 14), there is a further legal aberration, where again the question of violation of British extradition law comes up. That law, as we have seen, requires that extradition can be only for the charge on which there will be a trial. Here Canale volunteered:

> Your Honor, I would like the record to show . . . and we still assume that the charge of carrying a dangerous weapon will be held in abeyance . . . the dangerous weapon charge was not to be taken up for consideration today . . .

As late as after the end of the minitrial, as we have seen, this charge remained against Ray, even though Battle said, "As this Court has already ruled, that can never be tried."

Another of the issues involved in whether or not Ray was able to make a voluntary decision to cop the plea, relating to whether or not Foreman was ready for trial or could have been at the time set, is in this same transcript (T. 18), where Foreman argues for time. He claimed that, with the State having announced it would call witnesses from a list of 360, he had to interview all 360 before trial and before arranging for and interviewing defense witnesses. His calculations are modest:

> Therefore, taking the figures as presented by the District Attorney himself, 360 witnesses, and taking two hours per witness, and taking eight hours a day, or at least taking eight hours a day into 360 witnesses, . . . you come up with 90 days of interviews.

Assuming that no witness would require more than two hours of questioning, Foreman might have included the time required to reach them, scattered as they were all around this country, Europe, and Canada, if not also Mexico.

He then set forth his legal obligations (T. 19):

> . . . it is not only the right of defense counsel to interview all of the

witnesses of the prosecution but that it is his duty to do that or at least to attempt to do that . . . . I assure your Honor I intend to do my best to talk to everyone of the 360 who will talk with me. [T. 20–21.]

As it was to turn out, this is either a fraud upon the court or a remarkable self-indictment by Foreman and ample proof that Ray did not have effective counsel.

Foreman never ceased protesting he was getting nothing for his work. In the February 7, 1969 hearing, for example (T. 20–21),

. . . I want it said at the conclusion of this trial that I did not receive anything for my part in this case . . .

He had then gotten $5,000 and was soon to get another $5,000. As late as the February 14, 1969 hearing (T. 2–3), Foreman, as the judge put it, was still

seeking that material that was heard in London in the extradition by two means there and you are asking it from Mr. Eugene who handled Ray's extradition defense in London and you are also seeking it from Mr. Hanes, is that correct?

Foreman's response was, "We have given up any hopes of getting it from Mr. Hanes." Nobody considered asking the government?

In this hearing, the younger Stanton disclosed that what is called the "investigation" had just begun—on *February 14, 1969*—less than four weeks before the minitrial. He estimated that just the investigation, on which, with the full resources of the State of Tennessee at his disposal, he had but two investigators working (T. 4), "would probably take 90 days at the rate we are now proceeding" (T. 5).

It would seem that again the Court was imposed upon or there was never any adequate preparation of the Ray defense. With the investigation in charge of the man who began working on a deal rather that preparing for trial; with what preparation there was not even commenced until very late, then with an inadequate staff assigned to it, the fact of the clandestine arranging of the state-paid Public Defender's Office to be co-counsel in the case (and to remain that over Ray's expressed objections) and the official pretense that this came about spontaneously, in open court, when the judge for the first time learned Ray was indigent and Foreman's big heart was bleeding dollars, lends itself to conspiratorial interpretation. It certainly should not have been another shabby and shaded deal, consummated behind closed doors. Above all, Stanton's beginning to make the ultimate deal a half-hour after being assigned for the sole purpose of preparing the case for trial, something entirely different, has to be regarded as

511

a very questionable thing.

While these transcripts can be interpreted as a kind of defense of the judge, this can be done only if Foreman's statement in his November 11, 1969, deposition in Ray's civil suits is perjurious. There he swore that throughout this period he had six to eight private meetings with the judge. He was asked,

> ... In regard to James Earl Ray's criminal case, you made an agreement with the State of Tennessee, subject to the approval of Judge Battle, to enter a plea of guilty, is that correct? [T. 15.]

Foreman's response was,

> No, sir, that is not correct. I never made an agreement with the State of Tennessee subject to the approval of Judge Battle. All the agreements I made with the State of Tennessee were made with Judge Battle. I didn't talk with the prosecution about a plea, Judge Battle was running this lawsuit. [T. 16.]

This is not the same as saying the prosecution was not consulted or was not party to the deal for, as we have seen, Foreman had approved Stanton's working on the deal within a half-hour of Stanton's December 18, 1968, assignment to the defense. If it is true, it means only that Foreman *personally* had no negotiations or agreement with the State, not that the defense did not.

Asked when "did Judge Battle and you get together on entering a plea of guilty," Foreman evaded precise answer, finally said "it was within a day or two after I got back to Memphis from being ill," sometime in January.

The first time he was asked this question (T. 16), he avoided answer entirely:

> It wasn't a matter of getting together. I simply told Judge Battle what I decided was proper and what I would like to do and what I thought my client would like to do and I was attempting to find out whether or not he would do what the Judge did in the Sirhan case, queer the deal, in case I was able to negotiate with the District Attorney. I wasn't going through the District Attorney and a lot of work there and then come to see the Judge because the Judge, in California, had already indicated that he would not approve such a disposition of the Sirhan case. [T. 16.]

Aside from the falsehood of this sworn testimony (which certainly seems like perjury, negotiations with the State having begun in December, as we have already seen), and aside from the utter impropriety of this kind of plea-bargaining, especially with the judge

512

personally involved (which may be unconstitutional and is certainly against national interest in such a case), there is hidden in this statement further proof that Ray had no possibility of voluntary action or of making his own decisions. He was, as a matter of fact, foreclosed from his own defense. I repeat Foreman's words, with emphasis added:

> . . . what *I* decided was proper . . . what *I* would like to do . . . what *I* thought my client would like to do . . .

Not only does Foreman not indicate what he could not say without perjuring himself, that Ray had asked him to negotiate a deal or had even sanctioned it, he goes much farther and says *he* made the decision for Ray ("what I *thought* my client would like to do"). If there is one thing and only one thing clear in the Ray record, it is that he never wanted any kind of plea-bargaining and, more, insisted upon being a witness, even when it was not in his interest to subject himself to cross-examination.

Whether or not those wrong things that the judge did can be pardoned, it is possible to make a kind of defense of him and what caused him to make such wrong decisions, be party to such wrongful actions.

It is without doubt that he had been told, in paraphrase and no less inaccurately than it was done in the minitrial, what the evidence allegedly showed. With the kind of misrepresentation already documented, it is not illogical to assume the judge believed what he was told, that there was an overwhelming case against Ray. When Foreman, with his big reputation, started making the same pitch, it would have been an exceptional judge indeed who would not have been sold on the fact of Ray's guilt. Believing this, Battle's transgressions against propriety and history could have come easier.

Indeed, with the investigation of the crime preempted from the State by the FBI, the same kind of plea can be made to a lesser degree for the prosecution, where responsibilities were divided among a number of lawyers. If there is no justifying the misrepresentation of the ballistics and "eyewitness" evidence or the total suppression of the autopsy report and the total distortion of the medical evidence—and these things could be regarded as criminal misbehavior—it can, nonetheless, be argued that, persuaded by what it had been told and shown by the FBI, it also was persuaded that Ray alone was guilty.

Nor, with this record here cited for the first time, is the press without legitimate defense for not picking up these things as they transpired in the various court proceedings. Foreman did have this big reputation as a diligent defense lawyer. The details and complexities are enormous for one devoting himself entirely to the evidence, so, especially with the vast difference between hearing the perishable spoken words in court and being able to read them critically afterwards, busy reporters, for whom this case was but one of many assignments, can be excused—to an extent—for not catching what was going on while it was going on.

Postscript by James Earl Ray

From the time of our first contact, Jerry Ray had an invitation to visit me and read the manuscript of this book. He never took advantage of this offer, but he said James Earl would undoubtedly want to read it. I have *never* had any direct contact with James Earl. However, in early 1970, I was able to get him a copy of the book in the version called *Coup d'Etat*, complete to that time but without appendix. The first of March I received a message from him to the effect that he found it interesting and hoped its contents could be used in his defense.

When he received the book he also got my request that he annotate it, if he felt he could without jeopardy. That copy has never been returned to me. Unknown to me, James Earl gave it to J. B. Stoner, who returned it to him late in the year. If Stoner expressed any opinion, it has not reached me. Nor have I any way of knowing the extent to which, if any, Stoner may have commented on the book to James Earl.

Then there came the message that James Earl would volunteer a postscript, with a single stipulation: that it be explicitedly stated he did this without any compensation of any kind. This, of course, I welcomed.

Fensterwald immediately mailed his personal portable typewriter to James Earl. As we might have expected but didn't, with the attention our mail seems to have been receiving, the machine was broken when it reached the Tennessee State Prison at Petros. (On once occasion during this approximate period, letters I wrote and mailed to the publisher on several different days all reached him in a *single* delivery. Ordinarily they should have been delivered overnight.)

With Ray's comments were the first sign of a sense of humor we had seen in him: "Tell Weisberg 'thanks.' We Irish have to hang together."

I draw the reader's attention to one issue in the letter. Of "the contention of the prosecution" that he had "left laundry on April 1 [1968] at the Piedmont Cleaners, in Atlanta, " Ray writes that he left no laundry" on that day and was then in Alabama, not Georgia. The next night, that of April 2, he says he spent "at the Desoto Motel in Desoto County, Mississippi." He claims to have left Atlanta March 28, noting that it was not known that King was returning to Memphis until four days later. In what seems like a clear indication of conspiracy, Ray says he was asked to go to Memphis March 30, two days after he claims he left Georgia and the day before knowledge of King's decision to return. Somewhat elliptically and ambiguously, Ray adds that this "might indicate that close associates or, more probable, the professional

buggers who were tapping his [King's] phone, were the only ones aware
he would return to Memphis."

I take the first reference to be King's rather than Ray's associates and
the second to be the FBI.

It is not by accident or from reluctance that I avoid my own estimate
of these or any other of Ray's statements and opinions (his comments
on the media, for example). Rather it is because Ray, not yet having
had his day *in* it, is entitled to this brief day *out* of court.

The reader should keep in mind that if, as I believe the weight of the
evidence shows, Ray did not fire the shot that killed Martin Luther
King, then anything he might say bearing on the crime could have more
serious consequences for him than a lifetime in jail.

Ray's letter was typed all in capital letters. Caps and lower case have
been used here. Aside from the correcting of a few typographical
errors, the statement is printed here exactly as Ray wrote it.

Dear Mr. Weisberg,

I have recently read with interest your book titled "Coup d'Etat." It
was recommended reading to me for defense purposes due to its
detailed references.

I would not want to comment as to the author's conclusions as I
believe—apparently unlike defense adversaries—that any statements by
the adversaries of a possible imputative nature should be made in the
court room under the cross examination system—at least while the suit
is in subjudice in state courts. (To dispel any pretension of piousness I
also believe the above mentioned path is in the defendant's best interest.)

Conjunctively, while there does seem to be a tendency by most
prosecutors and a few defense attorneys to use the media to assist with
law suits—and probably a few judges to justify their decisions—I came
to the conclusion shortly after the instant charge was filed, what should
be the obvious, that the national media in essence represents but two
spheres of society, the hippie type and the Chamber of Commerce kind.
I suppose they are the only sort that can, or will affect the media—
beyond their usual pitch—where it's intolerable, [in] their pocketbooks.
Though naturally not in the same manner. Therefore the defendant was
never under the illusion that he could try the law suit in the press even
if he had been so disposed: which he wasn't.

Turning to the book's contents, I note the author dedicated considerable
space to the celebrated Texas attorney, Mr. Percy Foreman. Specifically
to Attorney Foreman's attempt to convict his client via the media. I
wouldn't here attempt to refute Mr. Foreman's assortment of post-trial

stories. (I believe this book does that quite well.) It's evident that Mr. Foreman began chasing the boob tube minutes after the plea in Memphis to try to justify his game. However, I don't think any normal person of western mental background could follow his here-to-fore meandering soliliquy to a rational conclusion. I suggest poet Ginsburg (no affront to the guru) would qualify as the essence of logic in comparison. But since Attorney Foreman has made numerous statements to the media concerning the case in toto, the defendant anticipates he will have no objections to testifying "under oath" at the forthcoming post-conviction proceedings, as the defense, and possibly even the prosecution, may have some questions for the counselor.

The only one, of many, controvertible issues in this book between defense and prosecution which I believe should be mentioned at this time—since it has already been made part of the court record by the prosecution—is the contention of the prosecution that the defendant left laundry on April 1, 1968 at the Piedmont Cleaners in Atlanta, Georgia (which is mentioned on page 357 [in the original typescript] of this book). The fact is that the defendant left no laundry at the above mentioned cleaners on April 1st, nor was he even in Atlanta, Georgia on that date, rather in Alabama. Further, Defendant spent the night of April 2nd at the DeSoto Motel in DeSoto County Mississippi. The defense is sure the F.B.I. knows this along with the rest of the prosecution. I mention this one incident because all those associated with the prosecution has for some reason zealously insisted that I admitted to being in Atlanta until April 1st, rather than the correct date of March 28th, 1968.

(Note.) Since Dr. King didn't decide 'publicly' to return to Memphis until April 1st, 1968, and the defendant was asked to go to Memphis March 30th, it might indicate that close associates or, more probable, the professonial buggers who were tapping his phone were the only ones aware he would return to Memphis period. Possibly that is one of the purposes of the adversary trial system, to resolve questions such as the aforementioned.

In concluding, this is the first and probably the last statement the defendant will make ot those associated with the media while the suit is pending in state courts. I've no knowledge of any defendant in a law suit winning legal relief by complaining to the media: except of course the professional complainers. Moreover, I believe while there

517

may be considerable merit to any given account of a law suit, the accumulative effects of multiple written articles combine to confuse much and resolve nothing.

Sincerely,
James E. Ray
State Prison
Petros, Tennessee

Index

523